STRATEGIES AND GAMES

STRATEGIES AND GAMES

THEORY AND PRACTICE

PRAJIT K. DUTTA

THE MIT PRESS

CAMBRIDGE, MASSACHUSETTS · LONDON, ENGLAND

This book was set in Melior and MetaPlus by Windfall Software using ZzTEX and was printed and bound in the United States of America.

Library of Congress Cataloging-in-Publication Data

Dutta, Prajit K.
    Strategies and games : theory and practice / Prajit K.
  Dutta.
    p.   cm.
  Includes bibliographical references and index.
  ISBN-13   978-0-262-04169-0
  ISBN-10   0-262-04169-3
  1. Game theory.   2. Equilibrium (Economics).   I. Title.
  HB144.D88   1999
  330'.01'5193—dc21   98-42937
                                                    CIP

10 9 8

MA AAR BABA KE

Brief Contents

Contents

Preface

This book evolved out of lecture notes for an undergraduate course in game theory that I have taught at Columbia University for the past six years. On the first two occasions I took the straight road, teaching out of available texts. But the road turned out to be somewhat bumpy; for a variety of reasons I was not satisfied with the many texts that I considered. So the third time around I built myself a small bypass; I wrote a set of sketchy lecture notes from which I taught while I assigned a more complete text to the students. Although this compromise involved minimal costs to me, it turned out to be even worse for my students, since we were now traveling on different roads. And then I (foolishly) decided to build my own highway; buoyed by a number of favorable referee reports, I decided to turn my notes into a book. I say foolishly because I had no idea how much hard work is involved in building a road. I only hope I built a smooth one.

THE BOOK'S PURPOSE AND ITS INTENDED AUDIENCE

The objective of this book is to provide a rigorous yet accessible introduction to game theory and its applications, primarily in economics and business, but also in political science, the law, and everyday life. The material is intended principally for two audiences: first, an undergraduate audience that would take this course as an elective for an economics major. (My experience has been, however, that my classes are also heavily attended by undergraduate majors in engineering and the sciences who take this course to fulfill their economics requirement.) The many applications and case studies in the book should make it attractive to its second audience, MBA students in business schools. In addition, I have tried to make the material useful to graduate students in economics and related disciplines—Ph.D. students in political science, Ph.D. students in economics not specializing in economic theory, etc.—who would like to have a source from which they can get a self-contained, albeit basic, treatment of game theory.

Pedagogically I have had one overriding objective: to write a textbook that would take the middle road between the anecdotal and the theorem-driven treatments of the subject. On the one hand is the approach that teaches purely by examples and anecdotes. In my experience that leaves the students, especially the brighter ones, hungering for more. On the other hand, there is the more advanced approach emphasizing a rigorous treatment, but again, in my experience, if there are too few examples and applications it is difficult to keep even the brighter students interested.

I have tried to combine the best elements of both approaches. Every result is precisely stated (albeit with minimal notation), all assumptions are detailed, and at least a sketch of a proof is provided. The text also contains nine chapter-length applications and twelve fairly detailed case studies.

DISTINCTIVE FEATURES OF THE BOOK

I believe this book improves on available undergraduate texts in the following ways.

- **Content** a full description of utility theory and a detailed analysis of dynamic game theory

  The book provides a thorough discussion of the single-agent decision theory that forms the underpinning of game theory. (That exercise takes up three chapters in Part Five.) More importantly perhaps, this is the first text that provides a detailed analysis of dynamic strategic interaction (in Part Three). The theory of repeated games is studied over two and a half chapters, including discussions of finitely and infinitely repeated games as well as games with varying stage payoffs. I follow the theory with two chapter-length applications: market-making on the NASDAQ financial market and the price history of OPEC. A discussion of dynamic games (in which the game environment evolves according to players' previous choices) follows along with an application to the dynamic commons problem. I believe many of the interesting applications of game theory are dynamic—student interest seems always to heighten when I get to this part of the course—and I have found that every other text pays only cursory attention to many dynamic issues.

- **Style** emphasis on a parallel development of theory and examples

  Almost every chapter that introduces a new concept opens with numerical examples, some of which are well known and many of which are not. Sometimes I have a leading example and at other times a set of (small) examples. After explaining the examples, I go to the concept and discuss it with reasonable rigor. At this point I return to the examples and analyze the just introduced concept within the context of the examples. At the end of a section—a set of chapters on related ideas—I devote a whole chapter, and sometimes two, to economic applications of those ideas.

- **Length and Organization** bite-sized chapters and a static to dynamic progression

  I decided to organize the material within each chapter in such a fashion that the essential elements of a whole chapter can be taught in one class (or a class and a half, depending on level). In my experience it has been a lot easier to keep the students engaged with this structure than with texts that have individual chapters that are, for example, over fifty pages long. The topics evolve in a natural sequence: static complete information to dynamic complete information to static incomplete information. I decided to skip much of dynamic incomplete information (other than signaling) because the questions in this part of the subject are a lot easier than the answers (and my students seemed to have little stomach for equilibrium refinements, for example). There are a few advanced topics as well; different instructors will have the freedom to decide which subset of the advanced topics they would like to teach in their course. Sections that are more difficult are marked with the symbol $\triangle$. Depending on level, some instructors will want to skip these sections at first presentation, while others may wish to take extra time in discussing the material.

- **Exercises**

    At the end of each chapter there are about twenty-five to thirty problems (in the Exercises section). In addition, within the text itself, each chapter has a number of questions (or concept checks) in which the student is asked to complete a part of an argument, to compute a remaining case in an example, to check the computation for an assertion, and so on. The point of these questions is to make sure that the reader is really following the chapter's argument; I strongly encourage my students to answer these questions and often include some of them in the problem sets.

- **Case Studies and Applications**

    At the end of virtually every theoretical chapter there is a case study drawn from real life to illustrate the concept just discussed. For example, after the chapter on Nash equilibrium, there is a discussion of its usage in understanding animal conflicts. After a chapter on backward induction (and the power of commitment), there is a discussion of poison pills and other take-over deterrents. Similarly, at the end of each cluster of similar topics there is a whole chapter-length application. These range from the tragedy of the commons to bankruptcy law to incomplete information Cournot competition.

AN OVERVIEW AND TWO POSSIBLE SYLLABI

The book is divided into five parts. The two chapters of Part One constitute an *Introduction*. Part Two (Chapters 3 through 10) covers *Strategic Form Games: Theory and Practice*, while Part Three (Chapters 11 through 18) concentrates on *Extensive Form Games: Theory and Practice*. In Part Four (Chapters 19 through 24) I discuss *Asymmetric Information Games: Theory and Practice*. Finally, Part Five (Chapters 25 through 28) consists of chapters on *Foundations*.

I can suggest two possible syllabi for a one-semester course in game theory and applications. The first stresses the applications end while the second covers all the theoretical topics. In terms of mathematical requirements, the second is, naturally, more demanding and presumes that the students are at a higher level. I have consequently included twenty chapters in the second syllabus and only eighteen in the first. (Note that the numbers are chapter numbers.)

Syllabus 1 (Applications Emphasis)

1. A First Look at the Applications

3. Strategic Form Games and Dominant Strategies

Syllabus 2 (Theory Emphasis)

PREREQUISITES

I have tried to write the book in a manner such that very little is presumed of a reader's mathematics or economics background. This is not to say that one semester each of calculus and statistics and a semester of intermediate microeconomics will not help. However, students who do not already have this background but are willing to put in extra work should be able to educate themselves sufficiently.

Toward that end, I have included a chapter on calculus and optimization, and one on probability and expectation. Readers can afford *not* to read the two chapters if they already have the following knowledge. In calculus, I presume knowledge of the slope of a function and a familiarity with slopes of the linear, quadratic, log, and the square-root functions. In optimization theory, I use the first-order characterization of an interior optimum, that the slope of a maximand is zero at a maximum. As for probability, it helps to know how to take an expectation. As for economic knowledge, I have attempted to explain all relevant terms and have not presumed, for example, any knowledge of Pareto optimality, perfect competition, and monopoly.

ACKNOWLEDGMENTS

This book has benefited from the comments and criticisms of many colleagues and friends. Tom Gresik at Penn State, Giorgidi Giorgio at La Sapienza in Rome, Sanjeev Goyal at Erasmus, Matt Kahn at Columbia, Amanda Bayer at Swarthmore, Rob Porter at Northwestern, and Charles Wilson at NYU were foolhardy enough to have taught from preliminary versions of the text, and I thank them for their courage and comments. In addition, the following reviewers provided very helpful comments:

Amanda Bayer, Swarthmore College

James Dearden, Lehigh University

Tom Gresik, Penn State

Ehud Kalai, Northwestern University

David Levine, UCLA

Michael Meurer, SUNY Buffalo

Yaw Nyarko, NYU

Robert Rosenthal, Boston University

Roberto Serrano, Brown University

Rangarajan Sundaram, NYU

A second group of ten referees provided extremely useful, but anonymous, comments.

My graduate students Satyajit Bose, Tack-Seung Jun, and Tsz-Cheong Lai very carefully read the entire manuscript. Without their hawk-eyed intervention, the book would have many more errors. They are also responsible for the *Solutions Manual,* which accompanies this text. My colleagues in the community, Venky Bala, Terri Devine, Ananth

Madhavan, Mukul Majumdar, Alon Orlitsky, Roy Radner, John Rust, Paulo Siconolfi, and Raghu Sundaram, provided support, sometimes simply by questioning my sanity in undertaking this project. My brother, Prajjal Dutta, often provided a noneconomist's reality check. Finally, I cannot sufficiently thank my wife, Susan Sobelewski, who provided critical intellectual and emotional support during the writing of this book.

A Reader's Guide

Game theory studies strategic situations. Suppose that you are a contestant on the quiz show "Jeopardy!" At the end of the half hour contest (during Final Jeopardy) you have to make a wager on being able to answer correctly a final question (that you have not yet been asked). If you answer correctly, your wager will be added to your winnings up to that point; otherwise, the wager will be subtracted from your total. The two other contestants also make wagers and their final totals are computed in an identical fashion. The catch is that there will be only one winner: the contestant with the maximum amount at the very end will take home his or her winnings while the other two will get (essentially) nothing.

Question: How much should you wager? The easy part of the answer is that the more confident you are in your knowledge, the more you should bet. The difficult part is, how much is enough to beat out your rivals? That clearly depends on how much they wager, that is, what their strategies are. It also depends on how knowledgeable you think they are (after all, like you, they will bet more if they are more knowledgeable, and they are also more likely to add to their total in that case). The right wager may also depend on how much money you have already won—and how much they have won.

For instance, suppose you currently have $10,000 and they have $7,500 each. Then a $5,001 wager—and a correct answer—guarantees you victory. But that wager also guarantees you a loss—if you answer incorrectly—against an opponent who wagers only $2,500. You could have bet nothing and guaranteed victory against the $2,500 opponent (since the rules of "Jeopardy!" allow all contestants to keep their winnings in the event of a tie). Of course, the zero bet would have been out of luck against an opponent who bet everything and answered correctly. And then there is a third possibility for you: betting everything . . .

As you can see the problem appears to be quite complicated. (And keep in mind that I did not even mention additional relevant factors: estimates that you have about answering correctly or about the other contestants answering correctly, that the others may have less than $5,000, that you may have more than $15,000, and so forth.) However, game theory has the answer to this seemingly complicated problem! (And you will read about it in Chapter 20.) The theory provides us with a systematic way to analyze questions such as: What are the options available for each contestant? What are the consequences of various choices? How can we model a contestant's estimate of the others' knowledge? What is a rational wager for a contestant?

In Chapter 1 you will encounter a variety of other examples—from real life, from economics, from politics, from law, and from business—where game theory gives us the tools and the techniques to analyze the strategic issues.

In terms of prerequisites for this book, I have attempted to write a self-contained text. If you have taken one semester each of calculus, statistics, and intermediate micro-economics, you will find life easier. If you do not have the mathematics background, it is essential that you acquire it. You should start with the two chapters in Part Five, one on calculus and optimization, the other on probability and expectation. Read them carefully and do as many of the exercises as possible. If the chapter on utility theory, also in Part Five, is not going to be covered in class, you should read that carefully as well. As for economic knowledge, if you have not taken an intermediate microeconomics class, it would help for you to pick up one of the many textbooks for that course and read the chapters on perfect competition and monopoly.

I have tried to write each chapter—and each part of the book—in a way that the level of difficulty rises as you read through it. This approach facilitates jumping from topic to topic. If you are reading this book on your own—and not as part of a class—then a good way to proceed is to read the foundational chapters (25 through 27) first and then to read sequentially through each part. At a first reading you may wish to skip the last two chapters within each part, which present more difficult material. Likewise you may wish to skip the last conceptual section or so within each chapter (but don't skip the case studies!). Sections that are more difficult are marked with the symbol $^{\triangle}$; you may wish to skip those sections as well at first reading (or to read them at a more deliberate pace).

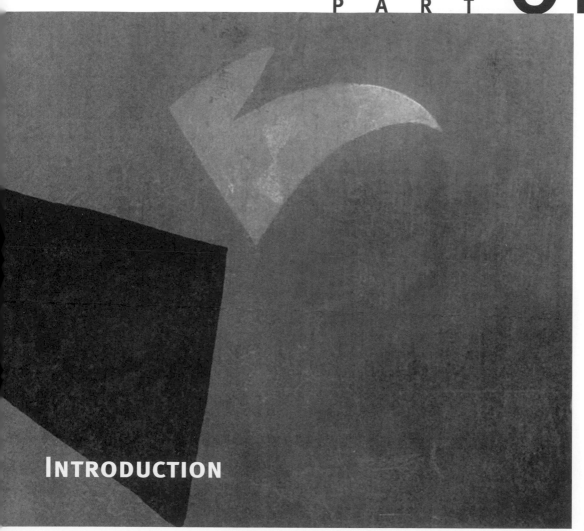

PART ONE

INTRODUCTION

CHAPTER 1

A FIRST LOOK AT THE APPLICATIONS

This chapter is organized in three sections. Section 1.1 will introduce you to some applications of game theory while section 1.2 will provide a background to its history and principal subject matter. Finally, in section 1.3, we will discuss in detail three specific games.

1.1   GAMES THAT WE PLAY

If game theory were a company, its corporate slogan would be *No man is an island.* This is because the focus of game theory is *interdependence*, situations in which an entire group of people is affected by the choices made by every individual within that group. In such an interlinked situation, the interesting questions include

- What will each individual guess about the others' choices?

- What action will each person take? (This question is especially intriguing when the best action depends on what the others do.)

- What is the outcome of these actions? Is this outcome good for the group as a whole?

- Does it make any difference if the group interacts more than once?

- How do the answers change if each individual is unsure about the characteristics of others in the group?

The content of game theory is a study of these and related questions. A more formal definition of game theory follows; but consider first some examples of interdependence drawn from economics, politics, finance, law, and even our daily lives.

- *Art auctions* (such as the ones at Christie's or Sotheby's where works of art from Braque to Veronese are sold) and *Treasury auctions* (at which the United States Treasury Department sells U.S. government bonds to finance federal budget expenditures): Chapters 3, 14, and 23, respectively

- *Voting at the United Nations* (for instance, to select a new Secretary General for the organization): Chapter 4

- *Animal conflicts* (over a prized breeding ground, scarce fertile females of the species, etc.): Chapter 5

- *Sustainable use of natural resources* (the pattern of extraction of an exhaustible resource such as oil or a renewable resource such as forestry): Chapters 7 and 18

- *Random drug testing at sports meets and the workplace* (the practice of selecting a few athletes or workers to take a test that identifies the use of banned substances): Chapter 8

- *Bankruptcy law* (which specifies when and how much creditors can collect from a company that has gone bankrupt): Chapter 9

- *Poison pill provisions* (that give management certain latitude in fending off unwelcome suitors looking to take over or merge with their company): Chapter 11

- *R&D expenditures* (for example, by pharmaceutical firms): Chapter 12

- *Trench warfare in World War I* (when armies faced each other for months on end, dug into rival trench-lines on the borders between Germany and France): Chapter 13

- *OPEC* (the oil cartel that controls half of the world's oil production and, hence, has an important say in determining the price that you pay at the pump): Chapter 17

- *A group project* (such as preparing a case study for your game theory class)

Game theory
A formal way to analyze *interaction* among a *group* of *rational* agents who behave *strategically.*

Game theory is a formal way to consider each of the following items:

group   In any game there is more than one decision-maker; each decision-maker is referred to as a "player."

interaction   What any one individual player does directly affects at least one other player in the group.

strategic   An individual player accounts for this interdependence in deciding what action to take.

rational   While accounting for this interdependence, each player chooses her best action.

Let me now illustrate these four concepts—group, interaction, strategic, and rational—by discussing in detail some of the examples given above.

Examples from Everyday Life

- Working on a group project, a case study for the game theory class: The *group* comprises the students jointly working on the case. Their *interaction* arises from the fact that a certain amount of work needs to get done in order to write a paper; hence, if one student slacks off, somebody else has to put in extra hours the night before the paper is due. *Strategic* play involves estimating the likelihood of freeloaders in the group, and *rational* play requires a careful comparison of the benefits to a better grade against the costs of the extra work.

- Random drug testing (at the Olympics): The *group* is made up of competitive athletes and the International Olympic Committee (IOC). The *interaction* is both between the athletes—who make decisions on training regimens as well as on whether or not to use drugs—and with the IOC, which needs to preserve the reputation of the sport. *Rational strategic* play requires the athletes to make decisions based on their chances of winning and, if they dope, their chances of getting caught. Similarly, it requires the IOC to determine drug testing procedures and punishments on the basis of testing costs and the value of a clean-whistle reputation.

Examples from Economics and Finance

- R&D efforts by pharmaceutical companies: Some estimates suggest that research and development (R&D) expenditures constitute as much as 20% of annual sales of U.S. pharmaceutical companies and that, on average, the development cost of a new drug is about $350 million dollars. Companies are naturally concerned about issues such as which product lines to invest research dollars in, how high to price a new drug, how to reduce the risk associated with a new drug's development, and the like. In this example, the *group* is the set of drug companies. The *interaction* arises because the first developer of a drug makes the most profits (thanks to the associated patent). R&D expenditures are *strategic* and *rational* if they are chosen to maximize the profits from developing a new drug, given inferences about the competition's commitment to this line of drugs.

- Treasury *auctions:* On a regular basis, the United States Treasury auctions off U.S. government securities.[1] The principal bidders are investment banks such as Lehman Brothers or Merrill Lynch (who in turn sell the securities off to their clients). The *group* is therefore the set of investment banks. (The bidders, in fact, rarely change from auction to auction.) They *interact* because the other bids determine whether a bidder is allocated any securities and possibly also the price that the bidder pays. Bidding is *rational* and *strategic* if bids are based on the likely competition and achieve the right balance between paying too much and the risk of not getting any securities.

Examples from Biology and Law

- Animal behavior: One of the more fascinating applications of game theory in the last twenty-five years has been to biology and, in particular, to the analyses of animal conflicts and competition. Animals in the wild typically have to compete for scarce resources (such as fertile females or the carcasses of dead animals); it pays, therefore, to discover such a resource—or to snatch it away from the discoverer. The problem is that doing so can lead to a costly fight. Here the *group* of "players" is all the animals that have an eye on the same prize(s). They *interact* because resources are limited. Their choices are *strategic* if they account for the behavior of competitors, and are *rational* if they satisfy short-term goals such as satisfying hunger or long-term goals such as the perpetuation of the species.

- Bankruptcy law: In the United States once a company declares bankruptcy its assets can no longer be attached by individual creditors but instead are held in safekeeping until such time as the company and its creditors reach some understanding. However, creditors can move the courts to collect payments before the bankruptcy declaration (although by doing so a creditor may force the company into bankruptcy). Here the *interaction* among the *group* of creditors arises from the fact that any money that an individual creditor can successfully seize is money that becomes unavailable to everyone else. *Strategic* play requires an estimation of how patient other creditors are going to be and a *rational* choice involves a trade-off between collecting early and forcing an unnecessary bankruptcy.

At this point, you may well ask what, then, is not a game? A situation can fail to be a game in either of two cases—the *one* or the *infinity* case. By the one case, I mean contexts where your decisions affect no one but yourself. Examples include your choice about whether or not to go jogging, how many movies to see this week, and where to eat dinner. By the infinity case, I mean situations where your decisions do affect others, but there are so many people involved that it is neither feasible nor sensible to keep track of what each one does. For example, if you were to buy some stock in AT&T it is best to imagine that your purchase has left the large body of shareholders in AT&T entirely unaffected. Likewise, if you are the owner of Columbia Bagels in New York City, your decision on the price of onion bagels is unlikely to affect the citywide—not to speak of the nationwide—onion bagel price.

[1] *These securities are Treasury Bonds and Bills, financial instruments that are held by the public (or its representatives, such as mutual funds or pension funds). These securities promise to pay a sum of money after a fixed period of time, say three months, a year, or five years. Additionally, they may also promise to pay a fixed sum of money periodically over the lifetime of the security.*

Although many situations can be formalized as a game, this book will not provide you with a menu of answers. It will introduce you to the *methodology* of games and illustrate that methodology with a variety of examples. However, when faced with a particular strategic setting, you will have to incorporate its unique (informational and other) features in order to come up with the right answer. What this book *will* teach you is a systematic way to incorporate those features and it will give you a coherent way to analyze the consequent game. Everyone of us acts strategically, whether we know it or not. This book is designed to help you become a better strategist.

1.2 BACKGROUND

The earliest predecessors of game theory are economic analyses of imperfectly competitive markets. The pioneering analyses were those of the French economist Augustin Cournot (in the year 1838)[2] and the English economist Francis Edgeworth (1881)[3] (with subsequent advances due to Bertrand and Stackelberg). Cournot analyzed an oligopoly problem—which now goes by the name of the Cournot model—and employed a method of analysis which is a special case of the most widely used solution concept found in modern game theory. We will study the Cournot model in some detail in Chapter 6.

An early breakthrough in more modern times was the study of the game of chess by E. Zermelo in 1913. Zermelo showed that the game of chess always has a solution, in the sense that from any position on the board one of the two players has a winning strategy.[4] More importantly, he pioneered a technique for solving a certain class of games that is today called backwards induction. We will study this procedure in detail in Chapters 11 and 12.

The seminal works in modern times is a paper by John von Neumann that was published in 1928 and, more importantly, the subsequent book by him and Oskar Morgenstern titled *Theory of Games & Economic Behavior* (1944). Von Neumann was a multi-faceted man who made seminal contributions to a number of subjects including computer science, statistics, abstract topology, and linear programming. His 1928 paper resolved a long-standing puzzle in game theory.[5] Von Neumann got interested in economic problems in part because of the economist Oskar Morgenstern. Their collaboration dates to 1938 when Morgenstern came to Princeton University, where Von Neumann had been a professor at the Institute of Advanced Study since 1933. Von Neumann and Morgenstern started by working on a paper about the connection between economics and game theory and ended with the crown jewel—the *Theory of Games & Economic Behavior.*

In their book Von Neumann and Morgenstern made three major contributions, in addition to formalizing the concept of a game. First, they gave an axiom-based foundation to utility theory, a theory that explains just what it is that players get from playing a game. (We will discuss this work in Chapter 27.) Second, they thoroughly characterized the optimal solutions to what are called *zero-sum games,* two-player games in which

[2] *See Cournot's* Researches Into the Mathematical Principles of the Theory of Wealth *(especially Chapter 7).*

[3] *See* Mathematical Psychics: An Essay on the Application of Mathematics to the Moral Sciences.

[4] *That, of course, is not the same thing as saying that the player can easily figure what this winning strategy is! (It is also possible that neither player has a winning strategy but rather that the game will end in a stalemate.)*

[5] *The puzzle was whether or not a class of games called zero-sum games—which are defined in the next paragraph—always have a solution. A famous French mathematician, Emile Borel, had conjectured in 1913 that they need not; Von Neumann proved that they must always have a solution.*

one player wins if and only if the other loses. Third, they introduced a version of game theory called *cooperative games*. Although neither of these constructions are used very much in modern game theory, they both played an important role in the development of game theory that followed the publication of their book.[6]

The next great advance is due to John Nash who, in 1950, introduced the equilibrium (or solution) concept which is the one most widely used in modern game theory. This solution concept—called, of course, Nash equilibrium—has been extremely influential; in this book we will meet it for the first time in Chapter 5. Nash's approach advanced game theory from zero-sum to *nonzero-sum* games (i.e., situations in which both players could win or lose). As mentioned above, Nash's solution concept built on the earlier work of Cournot on oligopolistic markets.[7] For all this he was awarded the Nobel Prize for Economics in 1994.

Which brings us to John Harsanyi and Reinhard Selten who shared the Nobel Prize with John Nash. In two papers dating back to 1965 and 1975, Reinhard Selten generalized the idea of Nash equilibrium to *dynamic games*, settings where play unfolds sequentially through time.[8] In such contexts it is extremely important to consider the future consequences of one's present actions. Of course there can be many possible future consequences and Selten offered a methodology to select among them a "reasonable" forecast for future play. We will study Selten's fundamental idea in Chapter 13 and its applications in Chapters 14 through 18.[9]

In 1967–1968, Harsanyi generalized Nash's ideas to settings in which players have *incomplete information* about each others' choices or preferences. Since many economic problems are in fact characterized by such incompleteness of information, Harsanyi's generalization was an important step to take. Incomplete information games will be discussed in Chapter 20 and their applications can be found in Chapters 21 through 24.[10]

At this point you might be wondering why this subject—which promises to study such weighty matters as the arms race, oligopoly markets, and natural resource usage—goes by the name of something quite as fun-loving as game theory. Part of the reason for this is historical: Game theory is called game theory because parlor games—poker, bridge, chess, backgammon, and so on—were a convenient starting point to think about the deeper conceptual issues regarding interaction, strategy, and rationality, which form the core of the subject. Even as the terminology is not meant to suggest that the issues addressed are light or trivial in any way, it is also hoped that the terminology will turn out to be somewhat appropriate and that you will have fun learning the subject.[11]

1.3   EXAMPLES

To fix ideas, let us now work though three games in some detail.

1.   Nim and Marienbad. These are two parlor games that work as follows. There are two piles of matches and two players. The game starts with player 1 and thereafter the

[6] *In this book we will study zero-sum games in some detail in Chapter 10. We will not, however, look at cooperative game theory.*

[7] *John Nash wrote four papers on game theory, two on Nash equilibrium and two more on bargaining theory (and he co-authored three others). Each of the four papers has greatly influenced the further development of the discipline. (If you wish, perhaps at a later point in the course, to read the paper on Nash equilibrium, look for "Equilibrium Points of N-person Games," 1950,* Proceedings of the National Academy of Sciences.*) Unfortunately, health problems cut short what would have been a longer and even more spectacular research career.*

[8] *The Selten papers are "Spieltheoretische Behandlung eines Oligopolmodells mit Nachfrage-tragheit" (1965),* Zietschrift für die gesamte Statswissenschaft, *and "Reexamination of the Perfectness Concept for Equilibrium Points in Extensive Games" (1975),* International Journal of Game Theory.

[9] *Many interesting applications of game theory have a sequential, or dynamic, character to them. Put differently, there are few game situations where you are never going to encounter any of the other players ever again; as the good game theorist James Bond would say, "Never say never again." We will discuss, in Chapters 15 and 16, games where you think (there is some chance) that you will encounter the same players again, and in an identical context. In Chapters 17 and 18, we will discuss games where you think you will encounter the same players again but possibly in a differerent context.*

players take turns. When it is a player's turn, he can remove any number of matches from either pile. Each player is required to remove some number of matches if either pile has matches remaining, and he can only remove matches from one pile at a time.

In Nim, whichever player removes the last match wins the game. In Marienbad, the player who removes the last match loses the game.

The interesting question for either of these games is whether or not there is a winning strategy, that is, is there a strategy such that if you used it whenever it is your turn to move, you can guarantee that you will win regardless of how play unfolds from that point on?

Analysis of Nim. Call the two piles *balanced* if there is an equal number of matches in each pile; and call them *unbalanced* otherwise. It turns out that if the piles are balanced, player 2 has a winning strategy. Conversely, if the piles are unbalanced, player 1 has a winning strategy.

Let us consider the case where there is exactly one match in each pile; denote this (1,1). It is easy to see that player 2 wins this game. It is not difficult either to see that player 2 also wins if we start with (2,2). For example, if player 1 removes two matches from the first pile, thus moving the game to (0,2), then all player 2 has to do is remove the remaining two matches. On the other hand, if player 1 removes only one match and moves the game, say, to (1,2), then player 2 can counter that by removing a match from the other pile. At that point the game will be at (1,1) and now we know player 2 is going to win.

More generally, suppose that we start with n matches in each pile, $n > 2$. Notice that player 1 will never want to remove the last match from either pile, that is, he would want to make sure that both piles have matches in them.[12] However, in that case, player 2 can ensure that after every one of his plays, there is an equal number of matches in each pile. (How?)[13] This means that sooner or later there will ultimately be one match in each pile.

If we start with unbalanced piles, player 1 can balance the piles on his first play. Hence, by the above logic, he has a winning strategy. The reason for that is clear: once the piles are balanced, it is as if we are starting afresh with balanced piles but with player 2 going first. However, we know that the first to play loses when the piles are balanced.

CONCEPT CHECK

Are there any other winning strategies in this game? What do you think might happen if there are more than two piles? Do all such games, in which players take turns making plays, have winning strategies? (Think of tic-tac-toe.)[14]

Similar logic can be applied to the analysis of Nim's cousin, Marienbad. Remember, though, in working through the claims below that in Marienbad the last player to remove matches loses the game.

[10] *The original 1967–1968 Harsanyi papers are "Games with Incomplete Information Played by Bayesian Players," Management Science. Do not—as David Letterman would say after a Stupid Human Tricks segment—try them at home, just yet!*

[11] *There are several books that I hope you will graduate to once you are finished reading this one. Two that I have found very useful for their theoretical treatments are* Game Theory *by Drew Fudenberg and Jean Tirole (MIT Press) and* An Introduction to Game Theory *by Martin Osborne and Ariel Rubinstein (MIT Press). If you want a more advanced treatment of any topic in this book, you could do worse than pick up either of these two texts. A book that is more applications oriented is* Thinking Strategically *by Barry Nalebuff and Avinash Dixit (W. W. Norton).*

[12] *Else, player 2 can force a win by removing all the matches from the pile which has matches remaining.*

[13] *Think of what happens if player 2 simply mimics everything that player 1 does, except with the other pile.*

[14] *These three questions have been broken down into further bite-sized pieces in the Exercises section.*

CONCEPT CHECK
ANALYSIS OF MARIENBAD

We claim that: If the two piles are balanced with one match in each pile, player 1 has a winning strategy. On the other hand, if the two piles are balanced, with at least two matches in each pile, player 2 has a winning strategy. Finally, if the two piles are unbalanced, player 1 has a winning strategy. Try proving these claims.[15]

Note, incidentally, that in both of these games the first player to move (referred to in my discussion as player 1) has an advantage if the piles are unbalanced, but not otherwise.

2. Voting. This example is an idealized version of committee voting. It is meant to illustrate the advantages of strategic voting, in other words, a manner of voting in which a voter thinks through what the other voters are likely to do rather than voting simply according to his preferences.[16]

Suppose that there are two competing bills, designated here as A and B, and three legislators, voters 1, 2 and 3, who vote on the passage of these bills. Either of two outcomes are possible: either A or B gets passed, or the legislators choose to pass neither bill (and stay with the status quo law instead). The voting proceeds as follows: first, bill A is pitted against bill B; the winner of that contest is then pitted against the status quo which, for simplicity, we will call "neither"(or N). In each of the two rounds of voting, the bill that the majority of voters cast their vote for, wins. The three legislators have the following preferences among the available options.

voter 1: $A \succ N \succ B$
voter 2: $B \succ A \succ N$
voter 3: $N \succ A \succ B$

(where $A \succ B$ should be read as, "Bill A is preferred to bill B.")

Analysis. Note that if the voters voted according to their preferences (i.e., truthfully) then A would win against B and then, in round two, would also win against N. However, voter 3 would be very unhappy with this state of affairs; she most prefers N and can in fact enforce that outcome by simply switching her first round vote to B, which would then lose to N. Is that the outcome? Well, since we got started we might wish to then note that, acknowledging this possibility, voter 2 can also switch her vote and get A elected (which is preferable to N for this voter).

There is a way to proceed more systematically with the strategic analysis. To begin with, notice that in the second round each voter might as well vote truthfully. This is because by voting for a less preferred option, a legislator might get that passed. That would be clearly worse than blocking its passage. Therefore, if A wins in the first round, the eventual outcome will be A, whereas if B wins, the eventual outcome will be N. Every

[15] *Again you may prefer to work step by step through these questions in the Exercises section.*

[16] *This example may also be found in* Fun and Games *by Ken Binmore (D. C. Heath).*

rational legislator realizes this. So, in voting between A and B in the first round, they are actually voting between A and N. Hence, voters 1 and 2 will vote for A in the first round and A will get elected.

CONCEPT CHECK
TRUTHFUL VOTING

In what way is the analysis of strategic voting different from that of truthful voting? Is the conclusion different? Are the votes different?

3. **Prisoners' Dilemma.** This is the granddaddy of simple games. It was first analyzed in 1953 at the Rand Corporation—a fertile ground for much of the early work in game theory—by Melvin Dresher and Al Tucker.

The story underlying the Prisoners' Dilemma goes as follows. Two prisoners, Calvin and Klein, are hauled in for a suspected crime. The DA speaks to each prisoner separately, and tells them that she more or less has the evidence to convict them but they could make her work a little easier (and help themselves) if they confess to the crime. She offers each of them the following deal: "*Confess* to the crime, turn a witness for the State, and implicate the other guy—you will do no time. Of course, your confession will be worth a lot less if the other guy confesses as well. In that case, you both go in for five years. If you *do not confess,* however, be aware that we will nail you with the other guy's confession, and then you will do fifteen years. In the event that I cannot get a confession from either of you, I have enough evidence to put you both away for a year."

Here is a representation of this situation:

Calvin \ Klein	*Confess*	*Not Confess*
Confess	5, 5	0, 15
Not Confess	15, 0	1, 1

Notice that the entries in the above table are the prison terms. Thus, the entry that corresponds to (*Confess, Not Confess*)—the entry in the first row, second column—is the length of sentence to Calvin (0) and Klein (15), respectively, when Calvin confesses but Klein does not. Note that since these are prison terms, a smaller number (of years) is preferred to a bigger number.

Analysis. From the pair's point of view, the best outcome is (*Not Confess, Not Confess*). The problem is that if Calvin thinks that Klein is not going to confess, he can walk free by ratting on Klein. Indeed, even if he thinks that Klein is going to confess— the rat—Calvin had better confess to save his skin. Surely the same logic runs through Klein's mind. Consequently, they both end up confessing.

Two remarks on the Prisoners' Dilemma are worth making. First, this game is not zero-sum. There are outcomes in which both players can gain, such as (*Not Confess, Not*

Confess). Second, this game has been used in many applications. Here are two: (a) Two countries are in an arms race. They would both rather spend little money on arms buildup (and more on education), but realize that if they outspend the other country they will have a tactical superiority. If they spend the same (large) amount, though, they will be deadlocked—much the same way that they would be deadlocked if they both spent the same, but smaller, amount. (b) Two parties to a dispute (a divorce, labor settlement, etc.) each have the option of either bringing in a lawyer or not. If they settle (50–50) without lawyers, none of their money goes to lawyers. If, however, only one party hires a lawyer, then that party gets better counsel and can get more than 50% of the joint property (sufficiently more to compensate for the lawyer's fees). If they both hire lawyers, they are back to equal shares, but now equal shares of a smaller estate.

Summary

1. Game theory is a study of interdependence. It studies *interaction* among a *group* of players who make *rational* choices based on a *strategic* analysis of what others in the group might do.

2. Game theory can be used to study problems as widely varying as the use of natural resources, the election of a United Nations Secretary General, animal behavior, and production strategies of OPEC.

3. The foundations of game theory go back 150 years. The main development of the subject is more recent, however, spanning approximately the last fifty years, making game theory one of the youngest disciplines within economics and mathematics.

4. Strategic analysis of games such as Nim and the Prisoners' Dilemma can expose the outcomes that will be reached by rational players. These outcomes are not always desirable for the whole group of players.

Exercises

SECTION 1.1

1.1
Give three examples of game-like situations from your everyday life. Be sure in each

case to identify the players, the nature of the interaction, the strategies available, and the objectives that each player is trying to achieve.

1.2

Give three examples of economic problems that are not games. Explain why they are not.

1.3

Now give three examples of economic problems that are games. Explain why these situations qualify as games.

1.4

Consider the purchase of a house. By carefully examining each of the four components of a game situation—group, interaction, rationality, and strategy—discuss whether this qualifies as a game.

1.5

Repeat the last question for a trial by jury. Be sure to outline carefully what each player's objectives might be.

Consider the following scenario: The market for bagels in the Morningside Heights neighborhood of New York City. In this example, the *dramatis personae* are the two bagel stores in the Columbia University neighborhood, Columbia Bagels (CB) and University Food Market (UFM); and the interaction among them arises from the fact that Columbia Bagels' sales depend on the price posted by University Food Market.

1.6

By considering a few sample prices, say, 40, 45, and 50 cents—and likely bagel sales at these prices—can you quantify how CB's sales revenue might depend on UFM's price? And vice versa?

1.7

For your numbers what would be a rational strategic price for CB if, say, UFM's bagels were priced at 45 cents? What if UFM raised its price to 50 cents?

Consider yet another scenario: Presidential primaries. The principal group of players are the candidates themselves. Only one of them is going to win his party's nomination; hence, the interaction among them.

1.8

What are the strategic choices available to a candidate? (Hint: Think of political issues that a candidate can highlight, how much time he can spend in any given state, etc.)

1.9

What is the objective against which we can measure the rationality of a candidate's choice? Should the objective only be the likelihood of winning?[17]

[17] *Bear in mind the hope once articulated by a young politician from Massachusetts, John F. Kennedy, that his margin of victory would be narrow; Kennedy explained that his father "hated to overspend!"*

SECTION 1.3

1.10

Show in detail that player 2 has a winning strategy in Nim if the two piles of matches are balanced. [Your answer should follow the formalism introduced in the text; in particular, every configuration of matches should be written as (m, n) and removing matches should be represented as a reduction in either m or n.]

1.11

Show that player 2 has exactly one winning strategy. In other words, show that if the winning strategy of question 1.10 is not followed, then player 1 can at some point in the game turn the tables on player 2.

1.12

Verbally analyze the game of tic-tac-toe. Show that there is not a winning strategy in this game.

The next four questions have to do with a three pile version of Nim. The rules of the game are identical to the case when there are two piles. In particular, each player can only choose from a single pile at a time and can remove any number of the matches remaining in a pile. The last player to remove matches wins.

1.13

Show that if the piles have an equal number of matches, then player 1 has a winning strategy. [You may wish to try out the configurations $(1, 1, 1)$ and $(2, 2, 2)$ to get a feeling for this argument.]

1.14

Show that the same result is true if two of the piles have an equal number of matches; that is, show that player 1 has a winning strategy in this case. [This time you might first try out the configurations $(1, 1, p)$ and $(2, 2, p)$ where p is a number different from 1 and 2, respectively.]

1.15

Show that if the initial configuration of matches is $(3, 2, 1)$—or any permutation of that configuration—then player 2 has a winning strategy. As in the previous questions, carefully demonstrate what this winning strategy is.

1.16

Use your answer in the previous questions to show that if the initial configuration is $(3, 2, p)$—or $(3, 1, p)$ or $(1, 2, p)$—where p is any number greater than 3, then player 1 has a winning strategy.

The next three questions have to do with the game of Marienbad played by two players.

1.17

Show that if the configuration is (1, 1) then player 1 has a winning strategy.

1.18

On the other hand, if the two piles are balanced, with at least two matches in each pile, player 2 has a winning strategy. Prove in detail that this must be the case.

1.19

Finally, show that if the two piles are unbalanced, player 1 has a winning strategy.

1.20

Consider the voting model of the second example of section 1.3 (pg. 10). Prove that in the second round, each voter can do no better than vote truthfully according to her preferences.

1.21

Suppose voter 3's preferences were $N \succ B \succ A$ (instead of $N \succ A \succ B$ as in the text). What would be the outcome of truthful voting in this case? What about strategic voting?

1.22

Write down a payoff matrix that corresponds to the legal scenario discussed at the end of the chapter (p. 12). Give two alternative specifications of payoffs, the first in which this does correspond to a Prisoners' Dilemma and the second in which it does not.

Suppose the Prisoners' Dilemma were modified by allowing a third choice for each player—*Partly Confess.* Suppose further that the prison sentences (in years) in this modified game are as follows.

Calvin \ Klein	*Confess*	*Not*	*Partly*
Confess	2, 2	0, 5	1, 3
Not	5, 0	$\frac{1}{2}, \frac{1}{2}$	4, $\frac{1}{4}$
Partly	3, 1	$\frac{1}{4}, 4$	1, 1

  (As always, keep in mind that shorter prison terms are preferred by each player to longer prison terms.)

1.23

Is it true that Calvin is better off confessing to the crime no matter what Klein does? Explain.

1.24

Is there any other outcome in this game—other than both players confessing—which is sensible? Your answer should informally explain why you find any other outcome sensible (if you do).

A First Look at the Theory

This chapter will provide an introduction to game theory's toolkit; the formal structures within which we can study strategic interdependence. Section 2.1 gives some necessary background. Sections 2.2 and 2.3 detail the two principal ways in which a game can be written, the *Extensive Form* and the *Strategic Form* of a game. Section 2.4 contains a discussion of *utility*—or *payoff*—functions, and Section 2.5 concludes with a revisit to some of the examples discussed in the previous chapter.

2.1   RULES OF THE GAME: BACKGROUND

Every game is played by a set of rules which have to specify four things.

1.   **who** is playing—the group of players that strategically interacts

2.   **what** they are playing with—the alternative actions or choices, the strategies, that each player has available

3.   **when** each player gets to play (in what order)

4.   **how much** they stand to gain (or lose) from the choices made in the game

In each of the examples discussed in Chapter 1, these four components were described verbally. A verbal description can be very imprecise and tedious and so it is desirable to find a more compact description of the rules. The two principal representations of (the rules of) a game are called, respectively, the *normal* (or *strategic*) *form* of a game and the *extensive form*; these terms will be discussed later in this chapter.

Common knowledge about the rules
Every player knows the rules of a game and that fact is commonly known.

Extensive form
A pictorial representation of the rules. The main pictorial form is called the *game tree*, which is made up of a root and branches arranged in order.

[1] *It may seem completely mysterious to you why we cannot simply stop with the assertion "everybody knows the rules." The reason is that, knowing the rules, there might be certain behaviors that a player will normally not undertake. However, if a player is unsure about whether or not the others know that he knows the rules, he will consequently be unsure about whether the others realize that he will not undertake those behaviors. This sort of doubt in players' minds can have a dramatic—and unreasonable—impact on what they end up doing, hence the need to assume every level of knowledge.*

[2] *This tree could represent, for example, transportation choices in New York City; a player can either take the bus, a cab, or the subway to his destination. Note that driving one's own car is not one of the options—these are choices in New York City after all!*

There is, however, a preliminary question to ask before we get to the rules: what is the rule about knowing the rules? Put differently, how much are the players in a game supposed to know about the rules? In game theory it is standard to assume **common knowledge about the rules.**

That everybody has *knowledge about the rules* means that if you asked any two players in the game a question about who, what, when, or how much, they would give you the same answer. This does not mean that all players are equally well informed or equally influential; it simply means that they know the same rules. To understand this better, think of the rules of the game as being like a constitution (of a country or a club—or, for that matter, a country club.) The constitution spells out the rules for admitting new members, electing a President, acquiring new property, and so forth. Every member of this club is supposed to have a copy of the constitution; in that sense they all have knowledge of the rules. This does not mean that they all get to make the same choices or that they all have the same information when they make their choices. For instance, perhaps it is only the Executive Committee members who decide whether the club should build a new tennis court. In making this decision, they may furthermore have access to reports about the financial health of the club that are not made available to all members. The point is that both of these rules—the Executive Committee's decision-making power and access to confidential reports—are in the club's constitution and hence are known to everyone.

This established, the next question is: does everyone know that everyone knows? *Common knowledge* of the rules goes even a few steps further: first, it says yes, everybody knows that the constitution is available to all. Second, it says that everybody knows that everybody knows that the constitution is widely available. And third, that everybody knows that everybody knows that everybody knows, *ad infinitum*.[1] In a two-player game, common knowledge of the rules says not only that player 1 knows the rules, but that she also knows that player 2 knows the rules, knows that 2 knows that 1 knows the rules, knows that 2 knows that 1 knows that 2 knows the rules, and so on.

In the next two sections we will discuss the two alternative representations of the three rules *who, what,* and *when.* The final rule, *how much,* will be discussed in section 2.4.

2.2   WHO, WHAT, WHEN: THE EXTENSIVE FORM

The **extensive form** is a pictorial representation of the rules. Its main pictorial form is called the *game tree.* Much like an ordinary tree, a game tree starts from a *root*; at this starting point, or root, one of the players has to make a choice. The various choices available to this player are represented as *branches* emanating from the root. For example, in the game tree given by Figure 2.1, below, the root is denoted α; there are three branches emerging from the root which correspond to the three choices *b(us), c(ab),* and *s(ubway).*[2]

At the end of each one of the branches that emerge from the root, either of two things can happen. The tree might itself end with that branch; this signifies an end to the

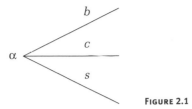

FIGURE 2.1

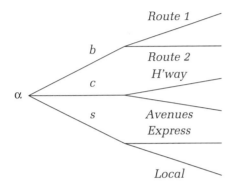

FIGURE 2.2

game. Alternatively, it might split into further branches. In Figure 2.1, for instance, the tree ends after each of the three branches *b*, *c*, and *s*. On the other hand, in Figure 2.2 each branch further divides in two. The branch splits into *E*(*xpress*) and *L*(*ocal*); the implication is that *after* the initial choice *s* is made, the player gets to choose again between the two options *E* and *L* (whether to stay on the *Local* train or to switch to an *Express*). The end of branch *s*, where the subsequent decision between *E* and *L* is made, is called a *decision node* of the tree. Figure 2.2 is therefore a two-stage decision problem with a single player.

Of greater interest is a situation where a different player gets to make the second choice. For instance suppose that two players are on their way to see a Broadway musical that is in great demand, such as *Rent*. The demand is so great that there is exactly one ticket left; whoever arrives first will get that ticket. Hence, we have a game. The first player (player 1) leaves home a little earlier than player 2; in that sense he makes his choice at the root of the game tree and subsequently the other player makes her transportation choice. The extensive form of this game is represented in Figure 2.3.

From these building blocks we can draw more complicated game trees, trees that allow more than two players to interact, allow many choices at each decision node, and allow each player to choose any number of times. The extensive form answers the question *who*—any individual who has a decision node in the game tree is a player in the game. It also answers the question *what*; the branches that come out of a decision node represent the different choices available at that point. Finally, it answers the question

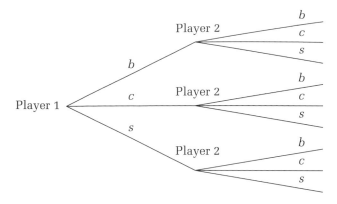

FIGURE 2.3

when; for example, a node that is four branches removed from the root is reached only after these first four choices have been made.

2.2.1 INFORMATION SETS AND STRATEGIES

The extensive forms discussed above permit only one player to move at a time; the next question is how to represent *simultaneous moves* within the extensive form. The key idea here is that a player will act in the same way in either of two circumstances; first, if he literally chooses at the same time as his opponent and second, if he actually chooses *after* his opponent but is unaware of his opponent's choice. Consequently, a simultaneous move in the Prisoners' Dilemma can be represented by Figure 2.4. In this figure, the "first" choice is player 1's while the "second" choice is that of player 2. Notice that there is an oval that encircles the two (second-stage) decision nodes of player 2. By collecting the two decision nodes into one oval we are signifying that player 2 is unable to distinguish between the two nodes, that is, he cannot tell whether the first decision of player 1 was c or n.

The oval here is called an **information set**.[3]

Finally, every player needs a **strategy** to play a game! A strategy is a blueprint for action; for every decision node it tells the player how to choose. More precisely, since a player cannot distinguish between the nodes within any one information set, a strategy specifies what to do at each set.

For example, in the theater game above (Figure 2.3), player 1 has a single decision node, the root. Thus, he has three possible strategies to choose from: b, c, or s. Player 2 has three decision nodes; what to do if player 1 took the *bus*, what to do if he took a *cab* instead, and, finally, what choice to make if player 1 hopped on the *subway*. Hence every strategy of player 2 must have three components, one for each of her decision nodes. A possible strategy for player 2 is (s, s, b); the first entry specifies her choice if player 1 takes the bus (and this choice is s); the second component specifies player 2's choice if 1 takes a cab (and this choice is also s); and the third entry is player 2's choice conditional

Information set
A collection of decision nodes that a player cannot distinguish between.

Strategy
A strategy for a player specifies what to do at every information set at which the player has to make a choice.

[3] *Information sets will play an important role in a class of games called games of asymmetric information that we will study in Chapters 19 through 24. At that point we will discuss, in greater detail, properties that information sets must satisfy.*

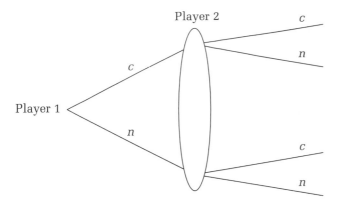

Figure 2.4

on having seen player 1 take the subway (and in this strategy that conditional choice is b).

CONCEPT CHECK
HOW MANY STRATEGIES ARE THERE?

Can you show that player 2 has 3^3, that is, 27 strategies? Can you enumerate some of them?

A pair of strategies, one for player 1 and the other for player 2, determines the way in which the game actually gets played. For example, suppose that player 1 chooses the strategy c while player 2 chooses (s, s, b). Since the strategy for player 2, conditional on player 1 taking a cab, is to pick s, the pair of strategies yields as outcome: 1 takes a cab and 2 follows by subway. In any game, a collection of strategies, one for each player, will determine which branch of the game tree will actually get played out.

2.3 WHO, WHAT, WHEN: THE NORMAL (OR STRATEGIC) FORM

An alternative way to represent the rules of a game is called the **normal** or **strategic form.**
For example, the strategic form of the theater game can be represented in a table in which the three rows correspond to the strategies of player 1 and the 3^3 columns correspond to the strategies of player 2. In each cell of the table we write the *how much* rule, in other words, the payoffs associated with that pair of strategies. Since we have yet

Strategic form
A complete list of who the players are, what strategies are available to each of them, and how much each gets.

TABLE 2.1

Player 1 \ Player 2	sss	ssb	ssc	bbs	. . .	ccb	ccs	ccc
b	N, T	N, T	N, T	T, N		N, T	N, T	N, T
c	T, N	T, N	T, N	T, N		T, N	T, N	T, N
s	T, N	T, N	N, T	T, N		T, N	T, N	N, T

to discuss payoff functions, for now we will simply write the outcome—rather than the payoffs—in each cell. Suppose that player 1—the first person to start for the theater—gets the ticket regardless of player 2's mode of transport as long as he takes a *cab.* He also gets the ticket if he travels by *subway* provided that 2 has not taken a *cab,* and likewise gets the ticket after catching the *bus* if 2 catches a *bus* as well. Writing *T* for *Ticket* and *N* for *Nuttin'* the outcomes are presented in Table 2.1. (Note that in each cell the outcome for player 1 is the first of the listed pair of outcomes.)

Whenever we have a two-player game, we can represent the strategic form as a table. The rows will stand for the strategies of player 1, the columns for the strategies of player 2, and the entry in a cell for the payoffs of the two players from the associated pair of strategies.

You might be wondering about the *when* question: in a strategic form, who moves when? The simplest context for the strategic form is a one-time simultaneous move game such as the Prisoners' Dilemma. In this case, each player makes only one choice and, hence, every strategy has a single element. But we can also study sequential move games in strategic form; strategies then are more complicated, and they answer the question of who moves when. A useful interpretation of the strategic form in such cases is that the players choose their strategies simultaneously although the game itself is played sequentially.

For instance, in the theater game, suppose player 1 chooses *s* while simultaneously player 2 chooses (*c, s, c*)—*c* if player 1 picks *b, s* if he picks *c,* and *c* if he travels by *s.* These strategies are chosen simultaneously in that neither player knows the opponent's strategy at the time of their choice. However, the actual play of the game is sequential. By the choice of strategies player 1 leaves first by subway; player 2 observes that and then follows by cab.

In summary, the extensive and strategic forms are two ways to represent a game.[4] For the purpose of clarity, this text uses the strategic form to study games that are played simultaneously. This is the content of Part II (Chapters 3 through 10). Conversely, we will employ the extensive form to study sequential game situations; these will be studied in Part III (Chapters 11 through 18). At the beginning of each part there will be a more detailed description of the two game forms; Chapter 3 does this for the strategic form while Chapter 11 details the extensive form. Part IV, Chapters 19 through 24, will use both representations.

[4] *Later in this book you will see that the two representations are interchangeable; every extensive form game can be written in strategic form and, likewise, every game in strategic form can be represented in extensive form.*

2.4   HOW MUCH: VON NEUMANN–MORGENSTERN UTILITY FUNCTION

The last rule specifies *how much:* how much does each player stand to gain or lose by playing the game (in the way that she does)? Put differently, what is the *payoff*— or *utility*—function of a player, a function that would specify the payoff to a player for every possible strategy combination that she—and the others—might pick? When the outcome of a game is monetary, each player pays out or receives money; the amount of the winnings is a candidate for the payoff. But what of games in which the outcome is not monetary—games such as the theater game, the Prisoners' Dilemma, Nim, or the voting game?

   To start with, note that a player will typically have opinions about which strategy combinations are preferable. For instance, in the Prisoners' Dilemma each prisoner is able to rank the four possible strategy outcomes: Most preferred is the lenient sentence of a canary (who implicates the nonconfessing partner). Next in preference is the outcome in which neither confesses. Further down is the outcome of both confessing, and the worst outcome is to be done in by the other guy. This suggests that we could simply attach numbers that correspond to the ranks—say, 4, 3, 2, and 1—and call those numbers the payoffs. A higher payoff would signify a preferred alternative.

   This argument can be made more generally. The various outcomes in a game can be thought of as different options from among which a player has to choose. If the player's preferences between these options satisfy certain consistency requirements, then she can systematically rank the various outcomes. Any numbering that corresponds to the ranking—a higher number for a higher rank—can then be viewed as a payoff or utility function.[5]

   In the extensive form these utility numbers would get written at each one of the nodes where the game terminates. For instance, in the theater game there are two possible outcomes: either player 1 gets the ticket or player 2 does. Presumably, each player would rather have the ticket than not; hence, any pair of numbers, $\pi(T)$ and $\pi(N)$, with $\pi(T) > \pi(N)$, would serve as a payoff function in this game for player 1. (Likewise for player 2, any two numbers $\phi(T)$ and $\phi(N)$, with $\phi(T) > \phi(N)$, would serve as a payoff function.) Filling in the payoffs, the extensive form of this game is depicted in Figure 2.5.

   In the strategic form, the payoff numbers would get written in the cells of the strategic matrix. The theater game's strategic form would therefore look like Table 2.2. (Only some of the cells have been filled in; by referring to Table 2.1 you should fill in some of the remaining ones.)

   Matters are a little more complicated if the game's outcome is not known for sure. This can happen for a variety of reasons. A player may choose her strategy in a probabilistic fashion by, for example, letting a coin toss determine which of two possible strategies she will go with. It is also possible that there may be some inherent uncertainty in the play of the game; for instance, if several firms are competing for the market share of a new product, then nobody knows for sure how the market will view that product.

[5] *A more detailed discussion of this subject can be found in Chapter 27. You should especially read the section titled* Decision-Making Under Certainty.

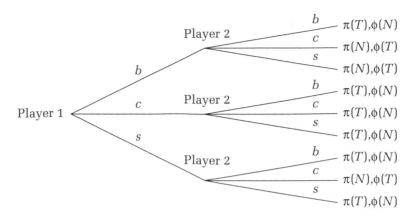

FIGURE 2.5

TABLE 2.2

1 \ 2	sss	ssb	ssc	bbs	...	ccb	ccs	ccc
b		$\pi(N), \phi(T)$						
c		$\pi(T), \phi(N)$						
s				$\pi(T), \phi(N)$				

When there is uncertainty a simple ranking of the outcomes will no longer suffice. In their book Von Neumann and Morgenstern asked the following question: Under what conditions can we treat the payoff to an uncertain outcome as the average of the payoffs to the underlying certain outcomes? More concretely, suppose that player 2 picks the strategy *sss* (she always travels by subway) while player 1 tosses a coin—taking a bus if the coin comes up heads or a cab if it comes up tails. In this case, there is a 50% chance that player 1 will get the remaining ticket and a 50% chance that he will not. Under what properties of player 1's preferences is this uncertain outcome worth a payoff halfway between the certain outcomes, $\pi_1(T)$ and $\pi_1(N)$? In other words, under what conditions is it worth the payoff $\frac{1}{2}\pi_1(T) + \frac{1}{2}\pi_1(N)$?

You can—and should!—read more about Von Neumann and Morgenstern's answer in Chapter 27; they offer conditions under which preferences satisfy the **expected utility** hypothesis. In this book, we will presume that each player's preferences do satisfy these required conditions. When there is no uncertainty in the underlying game, or in the way players choose to play the game, you may continue to think of the payoffs as simply a ranking.

Expected utility
Preferences satisfy expected utility when the payoff to an uncertain outcome is precisely the average payoff of the underlying certain outcomes.

2.5 REPRESENTATION OF THE EXAMPLES

In this section we will examine the extensive and strategic forms of the three examples that were discussed in detail at the end of Chapter 1.

Example 1: Nim

Suppose, to begin with, there are two matches in one pile and a single match in the other pile. Let us write this configuration as (2,1). Winning is preferred to losing and, hence, the payoff number associated with winning must be higher than the one that corresponds to losing; suppose that these numbers are, respectively, 1 and -1. Figure 2.6 represents the extensive form of this game.[6]

The strategic form representation is as follows:

$1 \setminus 2$	$l\,L$	$l\,R$	$r\,L$	$r\,R$
u	$1, -1$	$1, -1$	$1, -1$	$1, -1$
m	$-1, 1$	$-1, 1$	$-1, 1$	$-1, 1$
d	$1, -1$	$-1, 1$	$1, -1$	$-1, 1$

If there are more matches in either pile at the beginning of the game, then the game tree would simply be bigger. For instance, if the configuration is (2,2), then branches that come out of the root would lead to any one of the following configurations: (2,1), (1,2), (2,0), and (0,2). From (2,1) onwards, the game tree would look exactly like the tree in Figure 2.6; similarly, from (1,2) onwards, except in this case everything would be switched around since it is the first pile, rather than the second, that has the single match. From (2,0) and (0,2) onwards the tree would look like the part of the tree in Figure 2.6 starting from those configurations. The full extensive form of this scenario is depicted in Figure 2.7.

[6] *For compactness, I have written u, m, and d to be the three actions of player 1 that take the game to (1,1), (0,1), and (2,0), respectively. Similarly, l and r correspond to player 2 taking the game from (1,1) to (1,0) and (0,1), respectively, while L and R have him take the game from (2,0) to (1,0) and (0,0).*

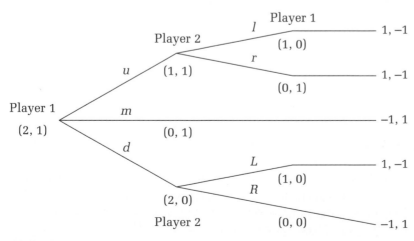

FIGURE 2.6

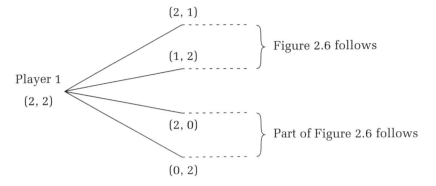

FIGURE 2.7

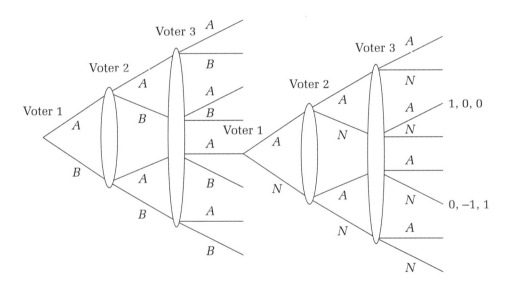

FIGURE 2.8

Example 2: Voting Game

Suppose that a voter gets a utility payoff of 1 if her favorite bill is passed, 0 if her second choice is passed, and −1 if her least favorite choice is passed. The extensive form representation of this game with two representative payoffs is shown in Figure 2.8.

The strategic form of the voting game is somewhat complicated to represent and so we will suspend that discussion until the next chapter.

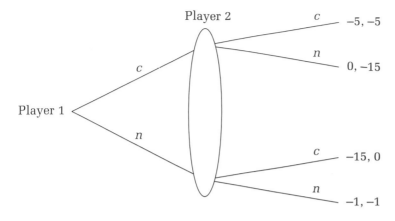

FIGURE 2.9

Example 3: Prisoners' Dilemma

Suppose we write a prison term of 5 years as a utility payoff of -5, and so on. The extensive form of this game is shown in Figure 2.9.

(Note that simultaneous moves have been represented using an information set.) The strategic form is as follows:

1 \ 2	c	n
c	$-5,-5$	$0,-15$
n	$-15,0$	$-1,-1$

SUMMARY

1. The rules of a game have to specify who the players are, what choices are available to each player, and how much each player gets from a set of choices made by the group of players.

2. There are two principal representations of the rules of a game, the extensive form and the strategic form.

3. The extensive form is a pictorial representation of the game. It specifies the order in which players make choices, how many times each player gets to choose (and what choices are available to her each time), and the eventual payoffs to each player for any sequence of choices.

4.   The strategic form is a representation in which the each player's choices (strategies) and the payoffs for a set of choices are specified. You can think of this as the right game form when players make once for all choices.

5.   The payoffs in a game should be thought of as Von Neumann-Morgenstern utilities. For an uncertain situation, payoffs should be computed by taking an expectation over the possible resolutions of the uncertainty.

EXERCISES

SECTION 2.2

2.1

Consider the following decision situation. You have a choice to make about which two courses to take and you have available four courses, A, B, C and D. Depict this problem in a tree form.

2.2

Suppose that after deciding which two courses to take you have a further decision to make: which course you will concentrate your efforts on. To keep matters simple, suppose that—if you take courses B and C, for instance—you can either choose to *Work Hard for B* or *Work Hard for C*. Depict this full decision problem.

2.3

Draw the game tree for Nim with initial configuration $(3, 2)$. Assume that the payoff for winning is 1 while that for losing is 0.

2.4

Do the same for Marienbad with initial configuration $(3, 3)$.

2.5

Consider the following game of "divide the dollar." There is a dollar to be split between two players. Player 1 can make any offer to player 2 in increments of 25 cents; that is, player 1 can make offers of 0 cents, 25 cents, 50 cents, 75 cents, and \$1. An offer is the amount of the original dollar that player 1 would like player 2 to have. After player 2 gets an offer, she has the option of either accepting or rejecting the offer. If she accepts, she gets the offered amount and player 1 keeps the remainder. If she rejects, neither player gets anything. Draw the game tree.

2.6

Write down the modified version of the "divide the dollar" game in which player 2 can make a counteroffer if she does not accept player 1's offer. After player 2 makes her counteroffer—if she does—player 1 can accept or reject the counteroffer. As before, if there is no agreement after the two rounds of offers, neither player gets anything. If there is an agreement in either round then each player gets the amount agreed to.

2.7

Consider the following variant of the "divide the dollar" game. Players 1 and 2 move simultaneously; 1 makes an offer to 2 and 2 specifies what would be an acceptable offer. For instance, player 1 might make an offer of 50 cents and player 2 might simultaneously set 25 cents as an acceptable offer. If player 1's offer is at least as large as what is acceptable to player 2, then we will say that there is an agreement and player 1 will pay player 2 the amount of his offer. Alternatively, if player 1's offer is smaller than what player 2 specifies as acceptable, there is no agreement, in which case neither player gets anything. Draw the game tree for this game.

SECTION 2.3

2.8

Write down the strategies of player 1 in the "divide the dollar" game of question 2.5. Then do the same for player 2.

2.9

Use your answer to the previous question to write down the strategic form of the "divide the dollar" game. (You do not have to list every strategy for player 2.)

2.10

Write down the strategic form of the simultaneous move "divide the dollar" game of question 2.7.

2.11

Write down the strategic form of Nim when the initial configuration is (2,1). (You do not have to fill in the payoffs of all the cells, but do fill in some.)

2.12

Consider the Morningside Heights Bagel Market example that is described in the previous chapter. Assume that prices are simultaneously chosen by University Food Market and Columbia Bagels and that they can be 40, 45, or 50 cents. Assume that the cost of production is 25 cents a bagel. Assume further that the market is of fixed size; 1000 bagels sell every day in this neighborhood and whichever store has the cheaper price gets all of the business. If the prices are the same, then the market is shared equally. Write down the strategic form of this game, with payoffs being each store's profits.

2.13

Redo the previous question with the total number of bagels sold being, respectively, 1500, 1000, and 500 bagels at the three possible prices of 40, 45, and 50 cents. (Assume that all other factors remain unchanged.)

2.14

Redo question 2.12 such that the store with the cheaper price gets 75% of the business. (Assume that everything else remains unchanged.)

2.15

Redo question 2.12 yet again, presuming that Columbia Bagels has, inherently, the tastier bagel and, therefore, when the prices are the same Columbia Bagels gets 75% of the business. (Assume that everything else remains unchanged.)

SECTION 2.4

2.16

Let us return to the course-work problem (question 2.2). Suppose that working hard produces a grade of A while not working hard produces a grade of B. Fill in the payoffs to that decision problem.

2.17

Redo the extensive form of the theater game from this chapter to allow for the possibility that the first person to get to the theater has a further choice to make between a good seat costing $60 and a not-so-good (but, nevertheless, expensive) seat costing $40. (The later arrival then gets the remaining ticket.)

2.18

Discuss briefly how you might redo the original extensive form of the theater game if there is a 50% chance that the show's star might be replaced by an understudy for that evening's performance.

2.19

How would you compute the payoffs to the game of question 2.18?

Consider the following group project example. Three students—Andrew, Dice, and Clay—simultaneously work together on a problem set for their game theory class. The instructor has asked them, in fact, to submit a joint problem set. Each student can choose to *work hard (H)* or *goof off (G)*. If all three students work hard, their assignment will get an A; if at least two students work hard, the assignment will get a B; if only one student works hard, the assignment will get a C; and, finally, if nobody works hard the assignment will get an F. Denote the payoff function π; this payoff depends on the grade and the amount of work. For example, the payoff to H and a grade of B is denoted $\pi(H, B)$.[7]

[7] *A natural assumption is that a better grade is preferred to a worse grade, but goofing off is preferred to working hard. For instance, $\pi(G, B) > \pi(H, B) > \pi(H, C)$.*

2.20

Write out the extensive form.

2.21

The strategic form is easiest to read if it is written in two parts. First, consider the case where Clay is expected to be a hard worker. Andrew and Dice can choose either H or G. Write down the strategic form.

2.22

There is also a second possibility, namely that Clay chooses to goof off. Show that in this case, the strategic matrix becomes

Andrew \ Dice	H	G
H	$\pi(H,B), \pi(H,B)\pi(G,B)$	$\pi(H,C), \pi(G,C), \pi(G,C)$
G	$\pi(G,C), \pi(H,C), \pi(G,C)$	$\pi(G,F), \pi(G,F), \pi(G,F)$

PART TWO

STRATEGIC FORM GAMES:
THEORY AND PRACTICE

CHAPTER 3

STRATEGIC FORM GAMES AND DOMINANT STRATEGIES

In this chapter we will discuss two concepts: in section 3.1, we will examine in greater detail the *strategic form* representation of a game. Then, in section 3.3, we will look at the first of several solution concepts that are applied to strategic form games, the *dominant strategy solution*. Sections 3.2 and 3.4 will serve as practical illustrations for the two concepts. While section 3.2 will discuss the strategic form of an art auction, section 3.4 will hunt for the dominant strategy solution in such an auction.

3.1   STRATEGIC FORM GAMES

The strategic form of a game is specified by three objects.

1.   the list of *players* in the game

2.   the set of *strategies* available to each player

3.   the *payoffs* associated with any strategy combination (one strategy per player)

The payoffs should be thought of as Von Neumann-Morgenstern utilities. The simplest kind of game is one in which there are two players—label them player 1 and player 2—and each player has exactly two strategies. As an illustration, consider a game in which player 1's two strategies are labelled *High* and *Low* and player 2's strategies are called *North* and *South*. The four possible strategy combinations in this game are (*High, North*), (*High, South*), (*Low, North*), and (*Low, South*). The payoffs are specified for each player for every one of the four strategy combinations. A more compact representation of this strategic form is by way of a 2 × 2 matrix.

Player 1 \ Player 2	*North*	*South*
High	$\pi_1(H, N), \pi_2(H, N)$	$\pi_1(H, S), \pi_2(H, S)$
Low	$\pi_1(L, N), \pi_2(L, N)$	$\pi_1(L, S), \pi_2(L, S)$

Here, for example, $\pi_1(H, N)$, $\pi_2(H, N)$ are the payoffs to the two players if the strategy combination (*High*, *North*) is played.

When there are more than two players, and each player has more than two strategies, it helps to have a symbolic representation because the matrix representation can become very cumbersome very quickly. Throughout the book, we will use the following symbols for the three components of the strategic form: players will be labelled $1, 2, \ldots N$. A representative player will be denoted the *i-th* player, that is, the index i will run from 1 through N. Player $i's$ strategies will be denoted in general as s_i and sometimes a specific strategy will be marked s_i^* or $s_i^\#$ and so on. A strategy choice of all players other than player i will be denoted s_{-i}. Finally, π_i will denote player $i's$ payoff (or Von Neumann-Morgenstern utility) function. For a combination of strategies, $s_1^*, s_2^*, \ldots s_N^*$, one strategy for each player, player $i's$ payoff will be denoted $\pi_i(s_1^*, s_2^*, \ldots s_N^*)$.

3.1.1 EXAMPLES

Let us develop intuition for the strategic form through a series of examples. We start with two player-two strategy games.

Example 1: Prisoners' Dilemma (*c* = confess, *nc* = not confess)

This is the first example that we met in Chapter 1—the tale of Calvin and Klein.[1]

Calvin \ Klein	*c*	*nc*
c	0, 0	7, −2
nc	−2, 7	5, 5

Example 2: Battle of the Sexes (*F* = football, *O* = opera)

The (somewhat sexist) story for the Battle of the Sexes game goes as follows. A husband and wife are trying to determine whether to go to the opera or to a football game. They each, respectively, prefer the football game and the opera. At the same time, each of them would rather go with the spouse than go alone.

[1] *The entries in each cell are now in utility units, unlike in Chapter 1 where they represented lengths of prison terms. Hence, a bigger number here is better than a smaller one.*

Husband \ Wife	*F*	*O*
F	3, 1	0, 0
O	0, 0	1, 3

Example 3: Matching Pennies (*h* = heads, *t* = tails)

Two players write down either *heads* or *tails* on a piece of paper. If they have written down the same thing, player 2 gives player 1 a dollar—or, strictly speaking, 1 utility unit. If they have written down different things then player 1 pays 2 instead.

Player 1 \ Player 2	*h*	*t*
h	1, −1	−1, 1
t	−1, 1	1, −1

Example 4: Hawk-Dove (or Chicken) (*t* = tough, *c* = concede)

Two (young) players are engaged in a conflict situation. For instance, they may be racing their cars towards each other on Main Street, while being egged on by their many friends. If player 1 hangs *tough* and stays in the center of the road while the other player *concedes*—chickens out—by moving out of the way, then all glory is his and the other player eats humble pie. If they both hang tough they end up with broken bones, while if they both concede they have their bodies—but not their pride—intact.

Player 1 \ Player 2	*t*	*c*
t	−1, −1	10, 0
c	0, 10	5, 5

The matrix form can be used to compactly represent the strategic form when there are two players even if each player has more than two strategies to choose from.

Example 5: Colonel Blotto (individual locations are 1, 2, 3, 4; pairs of locations are 1, 2; 1, 3; 1, 4; 2, 3; 2, 4; 3, 4)

In this war game, Colonel Blotto has two infantry units that he can send to any pair of locations (1, 4, for example, means the units go to locations 1 and 4), while Colonel Tlobbo has one unit that he can send to any one of four locations. A unit wins a location if it arrives uncontested, and a unit fights to a standstill if an enemy unit also comes to the same location. A win counts as one unit of utility; a standstill yields zero utility.

Tlobbo \ Blotto	*1, 2*	*1, 3*	*1, 4*	*2, 3*	*2, 4*	*3, 4*
1	0, 1	0, 1	0, 1	1, 2	1, 2	1, 2
2	0, 1	1, 2	1, 2	0, 1	0, 1	1, 2
3	1, 2	0, 1	1, 2	0, 1	1, 2	0, 1
4	1, 2	1, 2	0, 1	1, 2	0, 1	0, 1

We can also generalize in the other direction, that is, we can depict with matrices a strategic form game with more than two players.

Example 6: Coordination Game

Three players are trying to coordinate at some ideal location—for example, they would like to be together at a New York Knicks game at game time, *7:30* P.M. It does them no good if two—or all three—of them show up at *10:30* P.M. nor does it do them any good if two of them show up at game time and the other shows up at *10:30.*

Player 1 \ Player 2	*7:30*	*10:30*
7:30	1, 1, 1	0, 0, 0
10:30	0, 0, 0	0, 0, 0

Player 3 plays *7:30*

Player 1 \ Player 2	*7:30*	*10:30*
7:30	0, 0, 0	0, 0, 0
10:30	0, 0, 0	0, 0, 0

Player 3 plays *10:30*

Note that the first matrix represents the payoffs if players 1 and 2 choose any one of the four possible strategy combinations—*7:30,7:30; 7:30,10:30; 10:30,7:30;* and *10:30,10:30*—while player 3 arrives at *7:30.* The second matrix represents the payoffs if players 1 and 2 choose any one of those four strategy combinations and player 3 chooses to arrive at *10:30.* In every cell, the first payoff is that of player 1, the second is that of player 2, and the third is that of player 3. If each player had three strategies, there would be three 3 × 3 matrices representing the strategic form, and so on.

Here is an example of a non-matrix representation of the strategic form.

Example 7: Voting

Consider the following variant to the voting game that we studied in Chapter 1. The three voters who vote in round I are only told what the outcome of the election at that stage was. They then have to decide what to vote for in round II. No voter is told, in particular, the exact votes of the other voters in round I. So for every voter a strategy in this game has three parts: how to vote in the first round and the second-round vote, which itself has two components. The first component is how a voter would vote in round II if bill *A* passed the first stage, and the second component is how she would vote if, instead, bill *B* passed. In particular, each voter has the following eight strategies to choose from.[2]

AAN; *AAB*; *ANB*; *ANN*

BAN; *BAB*; *BNB*; *BNN*

For example, *BAB* is a first round vote for *B*; in the second round, vote for *A* if *A* passes the first round; otherwise vote for *B*. By contrast, *ANB* is a strategy in which the first round vote is *A*. In the second round, this strategy votes for *N* if *A* were the first stage winner but votes for *B* if *B* was the first stage winner instead.

Given any triple of strategies, one for each of the voters, we can then figure out what the outcome to voting will be. For instance, suppose that voter 1's strategy choice is *AAN*, voter 2's is *BAN*, and voter 3's is *ANB*. In this case, in the first round, *A* is passed (by virtue of the votes cast by voters 1 and 3) and then gets passed again at round II (by

[2] *A voter does, of course, know how she herself voted in round I. In principle, her strategy could be based on this information as well. We will ignore this complication for the moment, since all it would do is increase the number of parts in every strategy to five—instead of three. (Why?)*

virtue of the votes cast by voters 1 and 2). In this fashion, we can specify the outcomes to every one of the 8^3 strategy triples that are possible in this game.

3.1.2   EQUIVALENCE WITH THE EXTENSIVE FORM

In Chapter 2 we had also looked at an alternative representation for a game, the extensive form. These two ways of representing a game are equivalent in the sense that every extensive form game can be written in strategic form and vice versa. That every extensive form game can be written in strategic form is easy enough to see. All we need to do is write down the set of strategies for each player—in the extensive form—and then write down the associated outcomes and payoffs for every vector of strategies. We have then the strategic form.[3]

In order to do the converse, that is, to write in the extensive form a game that is already in the strategic form, all we have to remember is that a strategy is best thought of as a conditional plan of action. Any strategy specifies what is to be done in every contingency. Consequently, once a particular strategy is decided upon, its actual implementation can be left to a machine. Given this interpretation, a strategy vector— one strategy for each player—can be viewed as a simultaneous and one-time choice by the group of players. For example, if there are three players, and each player has available two strategies—say, a, b, for player 1; A, B for 2; and α, β for player 3—the extensive form of this game can be written as in Figure 3.1(a).

Of course, there are at least as many extensive form representations of a strategic form game as the number of players. (Why?) For instance, an alternative extensive form representation for the same game is given in Figure 3.1(b).

[3] This was, after all, exactly what we did with the voting game in the previous paragraph.

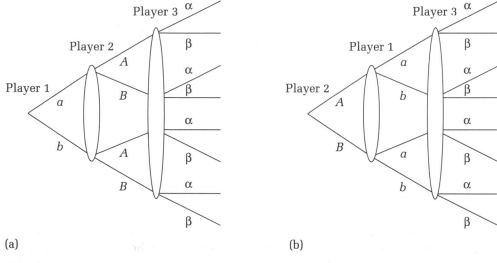

(a)   (b)

FIGURE 3.1

3.2 CASE STUDY: THE STRATEGIC FORM OF ART AUCTIONS

In this section we will look at a real-world situation that can be—and indeed should be!—modelled as a game.

3.2.1 ART AUCTIONS: A DESCRIPTION

Suppose that we are transported into one of the large auction rooms of Sotheby's Parke-Bernet at Rockefeller Center in New York City. The auctioneer stands on a podium in the front of the room. At her side are a couple of attendants who hold up on the viewing stand the object that is being auctioned. Let us imagine that the objects being auctioned are a set of drawings by Renoir; you would love to own the lovely cafe scene that has been labelled "Lot #264." Here is how you need to proceed.[4]

- *Registration:* If you intend to bid, you have to register at the entrance to the salesroom, at which point you are handed a numbered bidding paddle. (In order to register, you will, I am afraid, need a major credit card.)

- *Bidding procedure:* Once lot #264 comes up, "all you have to do to bid is to raise your paddle and wait for the auctioneer to acknowledge you. You don't have to call out the amount of your bid—higher bids are automatically set by the auctioneer, generally in increments of 10%. Don't feel you have to sit on your hands; scratching your nose or pulling on your ear will not be counted as a bid (unless you have made a prior arrangement with the auctioneer). If nobody tops your bid, that is, there are no other paddles up, then the auctioneer brings the hammer down to close the sale."[5]

Let us now translate this auction into a strategic form game.

3.2.2 ART AUCTIONS: THE STRATEGIC FORM

- *Players:* Those who register—and only those individuals—can "play." Thus, the list of players is the list of individuals who carry paddles.[6]

- *Strategies:* An easy way to think of a player's strategy is to think of the maximum amount to which a player will raise his paddle. In other words, a player's strategy can be thought of as the highest bid he is willing to make.[7] So player i's strategy s_i is simply a dollar figure.

- *Outcomes:* The bidder with the last remaining standing paddle wins the Renoir (and the nose-scratchers and ear-pullers do not). It should be easy to see that another way of saying the same thing is, the bidder who sets up the highest bid (in his own mind) will take home the drawing.

[4] *This information is drawn from Sotheby's Information catalog on the World Wide Web (at sothebys.com). The quotations are from the section "Auctions: FAQ (Frequently Asked Questions)."*

[5] *In practice, the highest bid also has to be higher than the so-called reserve price, the minimum price set by the seller and Sotheby's below which they would rather withdraw the item than sell it.*

[6] *Sotheby's also allows something called an* absentee bid. *A bidder may register ahead of time and not attend the auction itself but simply leave with the auctioneer a maximum bid amount. They will be counted as a bidder until such time as the going bid exceeds this maximum amount. If the bidding stops before the maximum amount, the absentee bidder will be given the object at the last announced bid.*

[7] *In this sense, a bidder who is present at the auction is very much like the absentee bidder referred to in the previous footnote. Note that, in principle, you could bid in more complicated ways. For instance, you could decide that you don't want the drawing if you get it for less than $1,000 or you could decide on your maximum bid after you see how many other people are bidding. For expositional ease, we will ignore these complicated strategies for now.*

- *Payoffs:* How much will the winner pay? Suppose, for example, that you win the Renoir for which you were willing to pay up to $2,000. Would you end up paying $2,000? Typically not. After all, the fact that you are the last remaining bidder means that the auctioneer brought down her gavel when your last competitor dropped out—at some amount less than $2,000. Indeed, the winning bid is the *amount that your last competitor was willing to pay*.

How much is the Renoir worth to you? Well, hopefully more than what you pay for it! For example, suppose its dollar-equivalent utility is $3,000 and you get it at $1,800; you have come out ahead by $1,200. On the other hand, if you do not win the bidding war your payoff is the utility of the status quo—$0.

3.3 DOMINANT STRATEGY SOLUTION

Consider the Prisoners' Dilemma (p. 36). The strategy *confess* has the property that it gives Calvin a higher payoff than *not confess*—7 rather than 5—if Klein *does not* confess. It also gives him a higher payoff—0 rather than −2—if Klein *does* confess. Hence, no matter what Klein does, Calvin is always better off confessing. Similar logic applies for Klein. In this game it is therefore reasonable to predict that both players will end up confessing.

These ideas can be made more precise.

Definition. Strategy s_i' strongly dominates all other strategies of player i if the payoff to s_i' is strictly greater than the payoff to any other strategy, regardless of which strategy is chosen by the other player(s). In other words,

$$\pi_i(s_i', s_{-i}) > \pi_i(s_i, s_{-i}), \quad \text{for all } s_i \text{ and all } s_{-i} \tag{3.1}$$

where s_{-i} is a strategy vector choice of players other than i.

To interpret equation 3.1 in words, let us see what the condition tells us for the two-player (1 and 2), two-strategy (a and b) case. Let us consider player 1. We say that strategy b for this player—denoted s_1^b—dominates the other strategy—s_1^a—if it does better against *both* strategies of player 2; thus,

$$\pi_1(s_1^b, s_2^a) > \pi_1(s_1^a, s_2^a)$$
$$\pi_1(s_1^b, s_2^b) > \pi_1(s_1^a, s_2^b) \tag{3.2}$$

The first inequality says that s_1^b yields a higher payoff than s_1^a if player 2 plays her first strategy; the second says that the same is true even if 2 plays her second strategy.[8]

A slightly weaker domination concept emerges if s_i' is found to be better than every other strategy but not always strictly better:

Definition. A strategy s_i' (weakly) dominates another strategy, say $s_i^\#$, if it does at least as well as $s_i^\#$ against every strategy of the other players, and against some it does strictly

[8] *If player 2 had ten strategies there would be ten such conditions in order for s_1^b to dominate s_1^a. Furthermore, if the player herself had ten strategies, there would be 90 such inequalities; there would be ten each for s_1^b to dominate each one of the remaining nine strategies. Finally, if there are three players, each with ten strategies, we would have 900 such inequalities! All of this is compactly denoted by equation 3.1.*

better, i.e.,

$$\pi_i(s_i', s_{-i}) \geq \pi_i(s_i^\#, s_{-i}), \quad \text{for all } s_{-i}$$

$$\pi_i(s_i', \widehat{s}_{-i}) > \pi_i(s_i^\#, \widehat{s}_{-i}), \quad \text{for some } \widehat{s}_{-i}$$

(3.3)

In this case we say that $s_i^\#$ is a *dominated strategy*. If s_i' *weakly dominates* every other candidate strategy s_i, then s_i' is said to be a *weakly dominant strategy*.[9]

Let us build intuition by determining which strategies are not dominant. Every strategy that is dominated is clearly not a dominant strategy. So *n* in the Prisoners' Dilemma is not a dominant strategy. In the Battle of the Sexes, *f* (*football*) is not a dominant strategy because it does not always yield a higher payoff than *o* (*opera*)—it does better if the other player chooses *f* as well but does worse if the other player's choice is *o*.

CONCEPT CHECK

Show that there are no dominant strategies in the games of matching pennies and Colonel Blotto.

CHECK AGAIN

Each player can only have a single dominant strategy. Can you show that fact for strong domination? What if a strategy is weakly dominant? Can there be another one?

Let us see an example of a strategy that is weakly but not strongly dominant. Consider a two player-two strategy game in which the payoffs of player 1 alone are as follows.

	Left	Right
Top	7	5
Bottom	7	3

In this case the first strategy, *Top*, weakly—but not strongly—dominates the second strategy, *Bottom*. From now on, in order to avoid confusion, any strategy termed a dominant strategy will refer to a weakly dominant strategy.

When every player has a dominant strategy, the game has a **dominant strategy solution**.

For example, in the Prisoners' Dilemma (*confess, confess*) constitutes a dominant strategy solution. As a second example, consider the following game.

	Left	Right
Top	7, 3	5, 3
Bottom	7, 0	3, −1

Dominant strategy solution
A combination of strategies is said to be a dominant strategy solution if each player's strategy is a dominant strategy.

[9] *The same definitions apply for strong domination. A strategy s_i' strongly dominates strategy $s_i^\#$, if equation 3.1 applies for $s_i = s_i^\#$. The strategy $s_i^\#$ is then said to be strongly dominated.*

In this case, (*Top,Left*) is the dominant strategy solution. The argument for predicting that players will play dominant strategies, when such strategies exist, is quite persuasive. After all, such a strategy is better than the alternatives regardless of what other players do. So a player can ignore strategic complications brought on by thoughts such as "What will the others do?" and "How will that affect my payoffs?"

The problem with the dominant strategy solution concept is that in many games it does not yield a solution. In particular, even if a single player is without a dominant strategy, there will be no dominant strategy solution to a game. Consider, for example, the Battle of the Sexes, the matching pennies, or the Colonel Blotto games. In each of these games, players do not have a dominant strategy, so the solution concept fails to give a prediction about play. In the next chapter we will see that there is a slightly weaker concept that also uses the idea of domination and which may yet work for some of these games.

3.4 CASE STUDY AGAIN: A DOMINANT STRATEGY AT THE AUCTION

In this section we will see that the following startling statement is true: in the art auction game of section 3.2, the strategy in which a bidder *sets the maximum bid at her true valuation* for the Renoir is a dominant strategy. To see why this is startling consider what it says: no matter how the other bidders bid you cannot do any better than bid what the drawing is worth to you. Put differently again, if the drawing is worth $3,000 to you, you can do no better than shut your eyes and keep your paddle up until such time as you hear the auctioneer announce a bid above $3,000 (or when you hear the auctioneer say, "Going, going, gone—the lady to my right has the Renoir" while pointing in your direction).

To see why this is a dominant strategy let us compare it with a couple of alternatives. Suppose you decide to "shave your bid" and set your paddle down at $2,500. Well, there are two possible scenarios. First, somebody else has a maximum bid above $3,000 anyway, so it makes no difference whether your maximum bid is $2,500 or $3,000. Second, the highest bid—the bid that wins the Renoir—is $2,700. Now you feel like a fool! You let a drawing that you valued at $3,000 slip by, a drawing you could have purchased for (a little above) $2,700. Hence, a maximum bid of $3,000 never does worse—and sometimes does strictly better—than a maximum bid of $2,500.

CONCEPT CHECK
OTHER LOWBALL BIDS

Check that the same argument works for any maximum bid below $3,000, in other words, that a bid of $3,000 dominates every bid less than $3,000.

What if you overextended yourself and (carried away by the giddy excitement of the auction) bid all the way up to $3,500? Again, there are two possible scenarios. First, somebody else rescues you by bidding above $3,500. In that case it makes no difference whether you bid $3,000 or $3,500. However, what if the next highest bidder drops out at $3,200? You feel like a fool again, this time because you are carrying home a drawing which (although nice) you paid more for than what you think it is worth.

CONCEPT CHECK
OTHER HIGHBALL BIDS

Show that a bid of $3,000 dominates any bid higher than $3,000.

One thing that is especially nice about the above argument is that it is valid irrespective of whether you know how much the Renoir is worth to the other bidders or (as is more likely) you do not have a clue. Either way you can do no better than "bid the truth."

SUMMARY

1. A strategic form game is described by the list of players, the strategies available to each player, and the payoffs to any strategy combination, one strategy for each player.

2. The strategic form can be conveniently represented as a matrix of payoffs whenever there are two players in a game. With more players, a symbolic representation is more convenient.

3. Every extensive form game can be represented in strategic form. Every strategic form game has at least one extensive form representation.

4. A dominant strategy gives higher payoffs than every other strategy regardless of what the other players do.

5. A dominant strategy solution to a game exists when every player has a dominant strategy.

6. An art auction can be modelled as a strategic form game. Bidding truthfully is a dominant strategy solution in that game.

EXERCISES

SECTION 3.1

3.1
Consider the game of Battle of the Sexes. How would you modify the payoffs to (f,o) and (o,f) to reflect the following: the husband is unhappiest when he is at the opera by himself, he is a little happier if he is at the football game by himself, he is happier still if he is with his wife at the opera, and he is the happiest if they are both at the football game? (Likewise, the wife is unhappiest when she is at the football game by herself, she is a little happier if she is alone at the opera, happier still if she is with her husband at the football game, and the happiest if they are both at the opera.)

3.2
Provide yet another set of payoffs such that both players would rather be alone at their favorite activity—the husband at the game and the wife at the opera—than be with their spouse at the undesirable activity.

3.3
Consider the game of Colonel Blotto. Suppose that Blotto is allowed to send both of his units to the same location, such that (3,3) is a feasible deployment [as are (1,1), (2,2), and (4,4)]. In addition, he can send units to different locations. Clearly outline the consequent strategic form. Detail additional assumptions that you need to make.

3.4
How would the strategic form change if locations 1 and 2 are more valuable than locations 3 and 4 (for instance, if winning the first two locations gives twice as much utility as winning the last two)?

3.5
Consider the voting game. Suppose that each voter conditioned her second stage vote on how he voted the first time around. Explain why every strategy has five components in this case.

3.6
Suppose that at the end of the first round, the votes are publicly announced, i.e., each voter is told how the others voted. Write down the nature of the strategies that are now available to voter 1.

3.7
Explain why there are at least as many extensive form representations of a strategic form as the number of players.

SECTION 3.2

3.8

Consider an art auction with two bidders in which the auction procedure is that described in the text. Suppose that the auctioneer raises bids by multiples of one thousand dollars starting at the buyer's reservation price of $2,000 and stopping when there is only one bidder left. The Renoir is worth $6,000 to bidder 1 and $7,000 to bidder 2. Each bidder's strategy specifies the maximum that he is willing to bid for the drawing. List all of the strategies available to the two bidders.

Suppose that, if the two bidders bid an equal amount, bidder 1 is given the drawing.[10] If the bids are unequal, the higher bidder pays the lower bid. Furthermore, the payoffs are as follows: if bidder 1 wins the drawing and pays p dollars for it, then his utility is $6,000 - p$, while if bidder 2 wins, his utility is $7,000 - p$. Utility to a bidder is zero if he does not win the object.

3.9

Write down the strategic form of this auction.

3.10

What would be the strategic form if a coin toss decides the winner when the bids are equal (and a 50% chance of winning implies an expected utility equal to $\frac{1}{2} \times$ utility of winning)?

SECTION 3.3

Consider the following model of price competition. Two firms set prices in a market whose demand curve is given by the equation

$$Q = 6 - p$$

where p is the lower of the two prices. If firm 1 is the lower priced firm, then it is firm 1 that meets all of the demand; conversely, the same applies to firm 2 if it is the lower priced outfit. For example, if firms 1 and 2 post prices equal to 2 and 4 dollars, respectively, then firm 1—as the lower priced firm—meets all of the market demand and, hence, sells 4 units. If the two firms post the same price p, then they each get half the market, that is, they each get $\frac{6-p}{2}$. Suppose that prices can only be quoted in dollar units, such as 0, 1, 2, 3, 4, 5, or 6 dollars. Suppose, furthermore, that costs of production are zero for both firms.

[10] *Specifically, if the auctioneer finds both bidders are in the auction at a bid of $3,000, but neither bids at $4,000, then she awards the Renoir to bidder 1 at a price of $3,000.*

3.11

Write down the strategic form of this game assuming that each firm cares only about its own profits.

3.12

Show that the strategy of posting a price of $5 (weakly) dominates the strategy of posting a price of $6. Does it strongly dominate as well?

3.13

Are there any other (weakly) dominated strategies for firm 1? Explain.

3.14

Is there a dominant strategy for firm 1? Explain.

3.15

Rework questions 3.11 through 3.14 above, under the following alternative assumption: if the two firms post the same price, then firm 1 sells the market demand (and firm 2 does not sell any quantity).

3.16

Give an example of a three player game in which two of the players have dominant strategies but not the third. Modify the example so that only one of the players has a dominant strategy.

In this game, each of two players can volunteer some of their spare time planting and cleaning up the community garden. They both like a nicer garden and the garden is nicer if they volunteer more time to work on it. However, each would rather that the other person do the volunteering. Suppose that each player can volunteer 0, 1, 2, 3, or 4 hours. If player 1 volunteers x hours and 2 volunteers y hours, then the resultant garden gives each of them a utility payoff equal to $\sqrt{x+y}$. Each player also gets disutility from the work involved in gardening. Suppose that player 1 gets a disutility equal to x (and player 2 likewise gets a disutility equal to y). Hence, the total utility of player 1 is $\sqrt{x+y} - x$, and that of player 2 is $\sqrt{x+y} - y$.

3.17

Write down the strategic form of this game.

3.18

Show that the strategy of volunteering for 1 hour (weakly) dominates the strategy of volunteering for 2 hours. Does it strongly dominate as well?

3.19

Are there any other (weakly) dominated strategies for player 1? Explain.

3.20

Is there a dominant strategy for player 1? Explain.

3.21

Rework questions 3.17 through 3.20 above, under the following alternative assumption: player 1's utility function is $2\sqrt{x+y} - x$.

SECTION 3.4

Consider again the art auction problem that you saw in questions 3.8 and 3.9.

3.22

Show that for player 1 the strategy with a maximum bid of $6,000 dominates a strategy with a maximum bid of $5,000. Repeat with an alternative maximum bid of $7,000. Do all this under the first tie-breaking rule in which player 1 gets the drawing when the maximum bids are identical.

3.23

Repeat the previous question, using a tie-breaking rule in which a coin toss decides the winner.

3.24

Explain why your arguments in the previous two questions would still be valid even if player 1 had no idea about how much the drawing is worth to player 2.

DOMINANCE SOLVABILITY

In this chapter we look at a second solution concept for strategic form games, *dominance solvability* or *iterated elimination of dominated strategies.* The concept is informally introduced and discussed using examples in section 4.1. Section 4.2 contains a Case Study: Electing the United Nations Secretary General, while section 4.3 contains a more formal definition. Section 4.4 concludes with a discussion of this concept's strengths and weaknesses.

4.1   THE IDEA

4.1.1   DOMINATED AND UNDOMINATED STRATEGIES

Here is a rewording of the dominance definition from the previous chapter.

Definition.   A strategy $s_i^{\#}$ is dominated by another strategy s_i', if the latter does at least as well as $s_i^{\#}$ against every strategy of the other players, and against some it does strictly better, such that[1]

$$\pi_i(s_i', s_{-i}) \geq \pi_i(s_i^{\#}, s_{-i}), \quad \text{for all } s_{-i}$$

$$\pi_i(s_i', \widehat{s}_{-i}) > \pi_i(s_i^{\#}, \widehat{s}_{-i}), \quad \text{for some } \widehat{s}_{-i}$$

(4.1)

If a strategy is not dominated by any other, it is called an **undominated strategy**. It is useful to think of a dominated strategy as a "bad" strategy and an undominated strategy as a "good" one. Of course, a *dominant* strategy is a special kind of undominated strategy, namely one that itself dominates every other strategy. Put differently, it is the "best" strategy.

Consider the *High-Low, North-South (HLNS)* game from Chapter 3.

Undominated strategy
A strategy that is not dominated by any other strategy.

[1] *Note that throughout we will use the concept of weak, rather than strong, domination. Do see section 4.4, however, where some disadvantages (and advantages) to using weak domination in the definition of dominance solvability are discussed.*

Player 1 \ Player 2	*North*	*South*
High	$\pi_1(H, N), \pi_2(H, N)$	$\pi_1(H, S), \pi_2(H, S)$
Low	$\pi_1(L, N), \pi_2(L, N)$	$\pi_1(L, S), \pi_2(L, S)$

In this strategic form *Low* is dominated by *High* if

$$\pi_1(H, N) \geq \pi_1(L, N) \quad \text{and} \quad \pi_1(H, S) \geq \pi_1(L, S)$$

with at least one of those inequalities being strict.

Low is not dominated by *High* (and vice versa) if it does better against, say, *South*, but does worse against *North*.[2]

$$\pi_1(H, N) > \pi_1(L, N) \quad \text{but} \quad \pi_1(H, S) < \pi_1(L, S)$$

Let us consider the situation a little more generally. Consider a game in which player *i* has many strategies. Either of two things have to be true. First, there may be a dominant strategy. All of the remaining strategies are then dominated. Alternatively, there may not be a dominant strategy, in other words, there may not be any best strategy. There has to be, however, at least one undominated—or good—strategy. (Why?)

CONCEPT CHECK

Consider the *HLNS* game. Show that each player has at least one undominated strategy. Under what conditions are both strategies undominated? Can you generalize your argument to any game?

Consider the examples that we have seen so far.

CHECK AGAIN

Show that in the Battle of the Sexes, as well as in matching pennies and Colonel Blotto, all strategies are undominated but that in the voting game, of the four possible ways to vote in round II, three are dominated by truthful voting.

---

[2] *Or,* Low *is undominated if it does better against* North *but worse against* South. *For completeness, we will also say that* High *does not dominate* Low *if they are just as good as each other all the time, i.e., if*

$\pi_1(H, N) = \pi_1(L, N)$ *and* $\pi_1(H, S) = \pi_1(L, S)$

The problem with the dominant strategy solution—as the examples show—is that in many games a player need not have a dominant or best strategy. What we will now pursue is a more modest objective: instead of searching for the best strategy why not at least eliminate any dominated—or bad—strategies?

4.1.2 ITERATED ELIMINATION OF DOMINATED STRATEGIES

Consider the following game.

Player 1 \ Player 2	Left	Right
Up	1, 1	0, 1
Middle	0, 2	1, 0
Down	0, −1	0, 0

For Player 1—the row player—neither of the first two strategies dominate each other, but they both dominate *Down*. For the same reason that it is irrational for a player to play anything but a dominant strategy (should there be any), it is also irrational to play a dominated strategy. The reason is that by playing any strategy that dominates (this dominated strategy) she can guarantee herself a payoff which is at least as high, no matter what the other players do. Hence, the row player should never play *Down* but should rather play either *Up* or *Middle*.

What is interesting is that this logic could then set in motion a chain reaction. In any game once it is known that player 1 will not play her bad strategies, the other players might find that certain of their strategies are in fact dominated. This is because player 2, for instance, no longer has to worry about how his strategies would perform against player 1's dominated strategies. So some of player 2's strategies, which are only good against player 1's dominated strategies, might in fact turn out to be bad strategies themselves. Hence, player 2 will not play these strategies. This might lead to a third round of discovery of bad strategies by some of the other players, and so on.

To illustrate these ideas, note that if it was known to player 2—the column player—that 1 will never play *Down,* then *Right* looks dominated to him. (Why?) Therefore, a rational column player would never play *Right*. But then, the row player should not worry about player 2 playing *Right*. Hence she would choose the very first of her strategies, *Up*.

The strategy choice (*Up, Left*) is said to be reached by *iterated elimination of dominated strategies* (IEDS); the game itself is said to be *dominance solvable*. Indeed, in any game, if we are able to reach a unique strategy vector by following this procedure, we call the outcome the solution to IEDS and call the game dominance solvable.

4.1.3 MORE EXAMPLES

Example 1: Bertrand (Price) Competition

Suppose that either of two firms in a duopoly market can charge any one of three prices—*high, medium,* or *low*.[3] Suppose further that whichever firm charges the lower price gets the entire market. If the two firms charge the same price, they share the market equally.[4] These assumptions—and any pair of prices—translate into profit levels for the two firms. For example, firm 1 only makes a profit if its price is no higher than that of firm 2. Suppose that the profits are given by the following payoff matrix.

[3] *Price competition in duopoly markets was first studied by the French economist Bertrand in 1883. He presented his analysis as an alternative to the Cournot model (in which firms decide how much to produce); we will study Cournot's model in Chapter 6.*

[4] *The analysis is easy to extend to the case where a firm can charge more than three prices. The other two assumptions make sense if you imagine that this is a market with no brand loyalty (because the products are identical) and all customers go to the vendor who charges the lower price. Think of two grocery stores or two discount electronic outlets.*

Firm 1 \ Firm 2	high	medium	low
high	6, 6	0, 10	0, 8
medium	10, 0	5, 5	0, 8
low	8, 0	8, 0	4, 4

Bertrand game

Let us now apply the concept of dominance solvability to this game. Notice first that the strategy *high* (price) is dominated by the strategy *medium* (and indeed this is true for both the firms). Hence, we can eliminate *high* as an irrational strategy for both firms (it either leads to no sales or a 50% share of a small market). Having eliminated *high* we are left with the following payoff matrix.

Firm 1 \ Firm 2	medium	low
medium	5, 5	0, 8
low	8, 0	4, 4

We can now see that *low* dominates the *medium* price. Hence, the outcome to IEDS is (*low, low*). Notice that *medium* is a useful strategy only if you believe that your opponent is going to price *high;* hence, once you are convinced that he will never do so, you have no reason to price *medium* either.

Example 2: The Odd Couple

Felix and Oscar share an apartment. They have decidedly different views on cleanliness and, hence, on whether or not they would be willing to put in the hours of work necessary to clean the apartment.[5] Suppose that it takes at least twelve hours of work (per week) to keep the apartment clean, nine hours to make it livable, and anything less than nine hours leaves the apartment filthy. Suppose that each person can devote either three, six, or nine hours to cleaning.

Felix and Oscar agree that a livable apartment is worth 2 on the utility index. They disagree on the value of a clean apartment—Felix thinks it is worth 10 utility units, while Oscar thinks it is only worth 5. They also disagree on the unpleasantness of a filthy apartment—Felix thinks it is worth -10 utility units, while Oscar thinks it is only worth -5. Each person's payoff is the utility from the apartment minus the number of hours worked; for example, a clean apartment on which he has worked six hours gives Felix a payoff of 4, while it gives Oscar a payoff of -1. Hence, the strategic form is as follows.

[5] *Any similarity to situations that you may have seen on the TV sitcom* The Odd Couple *is entirely intentional. On the other hand, I am sure that you have also personally encountered the roommate who you think is a slob—or, perhaps the one that you think is a fusssy neatnik!*

Felix \ Oscar	3 hours	6 hours	9 hours
3 hours	$-13, -8$	$-1, -4$	$7, -4$
6 hours	$-4, -1$	$4, -1$	$4, -4$
9 hours	$1, 2$	$1, -1$	$1, -4$

Note first that Oscar—the slob—views *9 hours* as crazy; this strategy is dominated by *6 hours*. But that implies that the relevant game is

Felix \ Oscar	3 hours	6 hours
3 hours	−13, −8	−1, −4
6 hours	−4, −1	4, −1
9 hours	1, 2	1, −1

However, *3 hours* is now a dominated strategy for Felix, the neatnik; he so values cleanliness that he would rather work at least *6 hours*. Hence, the relevant game is

Felix \ Oscar	3 hours	6 hours
6 hours	−4, −1	4, −1
9 hours	1, 2	1, −1

In turn, that implies *6 hours* is dominated for Oscar (because Felix is going to work hard enough anyway), which in turn implies that *6 hours* is also dominated for Felix. Therefore, the outcome to IEDS is that Felix works the maximum *9 hours* and Oscar works the minimum *3 hours*.[6]

Example 3: Voting Game

Recall the voting game of Chapter 1: by majority rule, three voters select either of two bills, *A* or *B*. The bill that passes the first round then faces a runoff against the status quo *N* (*"Neither"*). The true preferences of the three voters are as follows.

voter 1 : A ≻ N ≻ B
voter 2 : B ≻ A ≻ N
voter 3 : N ≻ A ≻ B

Every strategy has three components. The strategy *A* (followed by) *AN* says, "Vote for *A* against *B*, and then in the second round vote for *A* (against *N*), but vote for *N* (against *B*)." For payoffs, let us use the convention that a voter gets payoff 1 if his most preferred bill is passed, 0 for the second best, and −1 if the third best (i.e., least preferred) option passes. For example, voter 1's payoffs are 1 if *A* is eventually passed, 0 if *N* passes, and −1 if *B* passes.

Now recall from the previous section that voting truthfully in the second round dominates voting untruthfully; thus, for voter 1, *AAN* dominates *ANN, ANB,* and *AAB*. Similarly, *BAN* dominates *BNN, BNB,* and *BAB*. By the same logic, for voter 2, *AB* as the second round voting strategy dominates *NB, NN,* and *AN*; for voter 3, a second round voting strategy of *NN* dominates the alternatives. Note that if the voters vote truthfully in round II, then at that stage *A* defeats *N* but *B* loses to *N*.

After eliminating the (second round untruthful) dominated strategies, the remainder of the strategic form can be written as shown below.[7]

---

[6] *In the sitcom this outcome corresponded to Felix keeping the entire apartment clean, except for Oscar's room; Oscar had the responsibility of keeping his room clean—and did so after a fashion.*

[7] *Note that the first payoff in every cell is player 1's, the second is player 2's and the third player 3's.*

Voter 1 \ Voter 2	AAB	BAB
AAN	1, 0, 0	1, 0, 0
BAN	1, 0, 0	0, −1, 1

Voter 3 plays ANN

Voter 1 \ Voter 2	AAB	BAB
AAN	1, 0, 0	0, −1, 1
BAN	0, −1, 1	0, −1, 1

Voter 3 plays BNN

Now note that AAN dominates BAN for voter 1, AAB dominates BAB for voter 2, and BNN dominates ANN for voter 3. Hence, we are left with the IEDS outcome AAN for voter 1, AAB for voter 2, and BNN for voter 3; A wins the first round (with two votes) and goes on to defeat N in the runoff.

4.2 CASE STUDY: ELECTING THE UNITED NATIONS SECRETARY GENERAL

The United Nations elected a Secretary General for the 1997–2001 five-year term in December 1996. One of the candidates was Boutros Boutros-Ghali, from Egypt, who had been the Secretary General from 1992 to 1996. He was seeking re-election but faced the daunting prospect of early and strong opposition from the United States government.[8] Rumor had it that the U.S. was in favor of a woman as Secretary General; one of the women mentioned as a possibility was Glo Harlem Brundtland, the Norwegian Prime Minister.[9] However, the African member countries of the UN wanted to have a second term from an African Secretary General.[10] The name of another African—and a United Nations veteran—Kofi Annan, of Ghana, surfaced late in the campaign.

Let us use a simple game model to analyze this election. Consider an election with two voters—say, the United States and Africa. Voter 1—U.S.—votes first and gets to veto one of three candidates A(nnan), B(outros-Ghali), or H(arlem Brundtland). Then voter 2—Africa—vetoes one of the two remaining candidates. Suppose the United States' and Africa's preferences over the three candidates are as follows.

U.S.: $H \succ A \succ B$
Africa: $B \succ A \succ H$

In other words, the U.S. most prefers H(arlem Brundtland) but, failing that, prefers A(nnan) over B(outros-Ghali). Africa, on the other hand, is perfectly happy with B(outros-Ghali) but would rather have a second African than H(arlem Brundtland). Suppose the payoff is 1 if the voter's best candidate is elected, 0 if the second best is elected, and −1 if only the third best is elected.[11]

The United States has exactly three strategies to choose from: A or B or H; that is, the U.S. can veto Annan or Boutros-Ghali or Harlem Brundtland. Africa has three components in its strategy; whom to veto if, respectively, A, B, or H has already been vetoed. There are clearly two choices that Africa has for each of its three components; hence, it has eight strategies in all to choose from. A representative strategy for Africa is

[8] *In the late summer of 1996, the U.S. administration announced that it was going to oppose Boutros-Ghali who (they said) had not done enough to eliminate waste and mismanagement within the U.N. Some political observers speculated that the decision had as much to do with U.S. Presidential politics; President Clinton wanted to take the wind out of his Republican opponents who viewed Boutros-Ghali with disfavor and the Presidential elections were coming up in November 1996.*
[9] *She even resigned her position as Prime Minister in early November, supposedly in order to campaign more effectively for the Secretary Generalship.*

[10] *Traditionally, each Secretary General has served two terms in office and so the point was that if Boutros-Ghali, an African, could not serve a second term his replacement, at least, should be another African.*

[11] *In Example 3 above, and in this case study, the exact numbers in the payoffs are unimportant. What matters is that the election of the most preferred candidate gives a voter the highest payoff and the election of the least preferred candidate gives him the lowest payoff.*

BAA; in this case, it follows a veto of *A* by the U.S. by vetoing *B*, while it follows a veto of either *B* or *H* by vetoing candidate *A*. The strategic form of the game is shown here.

U.S. \ Africa	*HAA*	*HHA*	*HAB*	*HHB*	*BAA*	*BHA*	*BAB*	*BHB*
A	$-1, 1$	$-1, 1$	$-1, 1$	$-1, 1$	$1, -1$	$1, -1$	$1, -1$	$1, -1$
B	$1, -1$	$0, 0$	$1, -1$	$0, 0$	$1, -1$	$0, 0$	$1, -1$	$0, 0$
H	$-1, 1$	$-1, 1$	$0, 0$	$0, 0$	$-1, 1$	$-1, 1$	$0, 0$	$0, 0$

Start with Africa. Note that between *B* and *H*, it prefers *B*; between *A* and *H*, it prefers *A*; and between *A* and *B*, it prefers *B*. Hence, the strategy *HHA* dominates every other strategy. Put differently, if Boutros-Ghali were available Africa would veto the alternative and get him elected; in the event that he had already been vetoed Africa would veto *H*. Hence, after this one round of elimination, the effective game becomes:

U.S. \ Africa	*HHA*
A	$-1, 1$
B	$0, 0$
H	$-1, 1$

It follows that *A* and *H* are dominated; the best thing that the U.S. can do is veto *B*. (Put differently, by vetoing either Annan or Harlem Brundtland, the United States opens the door for Boutros-Ghali; hence it is best to veto Boutros-Ghali instead.) The IEDS outcome therefore is the U.S. starts off by vetoing Boutros-Ghali, and Africa follows by vetoing Harlem Brundtland; the compromise candidate Annan is elected Secretary General.[12]

4.3   A MORE FORMAL DEFINITION ⚠

The symbol ⚠ signifies more challenging material.

Let us look at a somewhat more formal treatment of dominance solvability. Consider a strategic form game with N players; player $i's$ strategies are denoted s_i; let the set of strategies of player i be denoted S^i. At round I, denote the set of dominated strategies of player i, $D^i(I)$. In other words,

$$D^i(I) = \{s_i \text{ in } S^i : s_i \text{ is a dominated strategy}\}$$

Rational players will not play strategies that are dominated, that is, strategies that lie in $D^i(I)$. And this is true for $i = 1, 2, \ldots N$.

Now in round II, player i can do a further determination among the strategies that are left over for him, $S^i - D^i(I)$, to see if any of them have now become dominated. A strategy $s_i^{\#}$ has now become dominated if there is an alternative strategy s_i' in $S^i - D^i(I)$ which does at least as well all the time and sometimes does strictly better, provided every

[12] *The United States stuck to its announced intention of opposing Boutros-Ghali even after the November presidential elections. The Africans insisted on a second African term thereupon. On December 17, 1996, Kofi Annan, United Nations Under Secretary General for Peacekeeping Operations, was elected Secretary General for 1997–2001.*

other player also eliminates strategies that are dominated in round I. Thus,

$$\pi_i(s_i', s_{-i}) \geq \pi_i(s_i^{\#}, s_{-i}), \quad \text{for all } s_{-i} \text{ in } S^{-i} - D^{-i}(I)$$

$$\pi_i(s_i', \widehat{s}_{-i}) > \pi_i(s_i^{\#}, \widehat{s}_{-i}), \quad \text{for some } \widehat{s}_{-i} \text{ in } S^{-i} - D^{-i}(I)$$

where $S^{-i} - D^{-i}(I)$ is the set of undominated strategy combinations of all players other than i.[13] Denote the sum total of all strategies of player i that are dominated, either in round I or round II, $D^i(II)$. Repeat the procedure to weed out any further strategies that are now dominated, once it is known that no player will play a strategy that belongs to $D^i(II)$. By doing this, construct the set of strategies that have been dominated in the first three rounds; call this set $D^i(III)$. And so on.

Suppose we arrive finally at a situation in which there is a single strategy left over for each player, i.e., suppose that after T rounds of elimination, the left over set, $S^i - D^i(T)$, contains exactly one strategy and this is true for $i = 1, 2, \ldots N$. In that case, this vector of strategies is said to be the outcome to *iterated elimination of dominated strategies* (IEDS) and the game is said to be *dominance solvable*. If this does not happen—if at some round, and for some player, there are no more strategies that can be eliminated although there are multiple strategies still outstanding—the game is said to have no IEDS solution.

In the Bertrand Price Competition example, there were two rounds of elimination. In the first, *high* price is eliminated as dominated, and in the second round, *medium* price is then found to be dominated and eliminated. The IEDS outcome is *low* price for each firm.

In the Odd Couple example, there were four rounds of elimination. In the first Oscar eliminates *9 hours,* which leads Felix to eliminate *3 hours.* In the third round, Oscar eliminates *6 hours,* whereupon Felix eliminates *6 hours* as well. The IEDS outcome has Felix work *9 hours* while Oscar only works for 3.

Finally, in the voting game of example 3 there were two rounds of elimination. In the first, each voter eliminates all the strategies that involve untruthful stage two voting and in the second, each voter eliminates one of the remaining two strategies.

Notice the chain of logic that was employed in the definition (and in each of the examples).

- Player 1 is rational in that she never plays a dominated strategy, and this is known to player 2.

- Hence, in round II, player 2 has a dominated strategy and will never play it, and player 1 knows that.

- Player 1 only considers payoffs in the event that 2 plays a remaining undominated strategy. Consequently, she has a dominated strategy which she never plays.[14] And so on. . . .

[13] *Specifically, $S^{-i} - D^{-i}(I)$ contains strategy vectors $(s_1, \ldots s_{i-1}, s_{i+1}, \ldots s_N)$ in which every strategy s_j is undominated.*

[14] *There is a symmetric and simultaneous chain of logic starting with player 2: player 2 will never play a dominated strategy; 1 knows that and hence will not play a now dominated strategy; 2 knows that and may further eliminate a strategy. This logic is similar to common knowledge about the rules (recall Chapter 3).*

4.4 A DISCUSSION

The solution concept—Iterated Elimination of Dominated Strategies—is widely used in game theory and its applications. The *advantage* of this solution concept is inherent in the simplicity of the dominance concept. If a player is convinced that one of his strategies always does worse than some alternative strategy, then he will never use it. It is also clear that other players should realize this and take this into account in determining what they should do. (Later in this book you will see that dominance solvability has a link with a solution concept used in the extensive form called backwards induction.)

The *disadvantages* of this solution concept are the following.

• **Layers of rationality.** That no player will play a dominated strategy is a reasonable assumption. That no player will play a strategy that is dominated once the others' dominated strategies are eliminated also appears reasonable. That no player will play a strategy that becomes dominated only after fifteen rounds of elimination of dominated strategies seems less reasonable. This is because it presumes that everybody agrees that every body else is reasonable in this form over succeeding (fourteen) higher orders. This is especially problematic if a "mistake" about the other player's rationality can be costly. Consider the following game.

1 \ 2	Left	Center	Right
Top	4, 5	1, 6	5, 6
Middle	3, 5	2, 5	5, 4
Bottom	2, 5	2, 0	7, 0

CONCEPT CHECK

Show that the outcome to IEDS is (*Middle, Center*) with payoffs of (2,5).

However, player 2 could have guaranteed a payoff of 5 by playing *Left.* Indeed by playing *Center,* she runs the risk of getting 0 should player 1 not be as rational as she thinks he is and instead plays *Bottom. Left* ceases to be a good strategy only if she is sure that player 1 will *never* play *Bottom*, but she can be sure of that only if she is, in turn, sure that he is convinced that she will never play *Right* herself. As you can see, the logic begins to look a little shaky even with as little as four rounds of elimination and would only look worse after 30 or 300 rounds of such elimination.

• **Order of elimination matters** (and *nonunique outcomes*). When strategies are dominated but not strongly, the order of elimination matters. Consider the game below.

1 \ 2	Left	Right
Top	0, 0	0, 1
Bottom	1, 0	0, 0

If we eliminate dominated strategies for both players simultaneously, as we are asked to do in the definition of IEDS, then we have a unique outcome (*Bottom,Right*). We may ask, however, if the elimination procedure could have been defined sequentially, eliminating dominated strategies for one player at a time. In other words, we eliminate all dominated strategies for player 1, then eliminate dominated strategies for player 2, return to eliminate newly dominated strategies for player 1, and so forth.

In the game above, if we start with player 1, we can eliminate *Top*. Then we can go no further since player 2 is indifferent between *Left* and *Right*. If we start with player 2, we can eliminate *Left*. Again we can go no further, since player 1 is indifferent between *Top* and *Bottom*. Iterated elimination of dominated strategies—following this sequential elimination procedure—does not lead us to a unique outcome. This makes us wary about the robustness of the solution concept because it gives us different answers when we follow, seemingly, similar procedures.

It turns out that this problem is not a problem if we use strong domination in our definition of IEDS. I will discuss this a bit more after the next point.

- **Nonexistence.** Not all games are dominance solvable. For example, in the Battle of the Sexes as well as in matching pennies and Colonel Blotto there are no dominated strategies and, hence, there is no outcome to IEDS. In the game below, each player has one dominated strategy—*Bad*—but after eliminating that strategy we are left with a 2 × 2 game with undominated strategies.

1 \ 2	Left	Middle	Bad
Top	1, −1	−1, 1	0, −2
Middle	−1, 1	1, −1	0, −2
Bad	−2, 0	−2, 0	−2, −2

There is an alternative definition for IEDS in which the concept of domination that is used throughout is that of *strong domination*. This concept is identical in every way to the one that I have discussed except that a strategy is eliminated if and only if it is *strongly dominated* by some other strategy. We can call this concept *strong IEDS*.

For example, in the Pricing game, *high* is strongly dominated by *low*; once, that strategy is eliminated, *medium* becomes strongly dominated by *low*. In other words, the strong IEDS outcome is also (*low, low*). In the voting games of example 3 and the Case Study, however, the strategies that are eliminated are weakly (but not strongly) dominated. Hence, if we used the strong dominance criterion, there would be no strong IEDS solution, although, as we have seen, there is an IEDS solution in each case.[15]

[15] *There is a more general point behind these two examples. Games whose strategic forms are derived from an extensive form game tree will have dominated but not strongly dominated strategies. When we get to the extensive form—and the related solution concept called backwards induction in the extensive form— this point will become clearer.*

The strong IEDS solution has the attractive feature that the order of elimination does not matter; if simultaneous elimination of strongly dominated strategies yields a solution so does sequential elimination (and the solutions coincide). The disadvantage of the concept is that there are many games that are dominance solvable where strong IEDS yields no solution.

SUMMARY

1. No rational player will play a dominated strategy but would rather play one of his undominated strategies. A rational player would not expect his opponents to play a dominated strategy either.

2. Elimination of dominated strategies can lead to a chain reaction that successively narrows down how a group of rational players will act. If there is eventually a unique prediction, it is called the IEDS solution.

3. When there are many rounds of elimination involved in an IEDS solution, there is reason to be concerned about the reasonableness of its prediction.

EXERCISES

SECTION 4.1

4.1
Explain why we can determine whether or not strategy s_i' dominates strategy $s_i^{\#}$ based solely on player i's payoffs.

4.2
Prove that in every game and for every player there must be at least one undominated strategy, as long as each player has a finite number of strategies.

4.3
Can you give a simple example of a game with an infinite number of strategies in which a player has no undominated strategies?

4.4
In the voting game, explain carefully why the strategy of honest voting in the second round dominates every other way of voting in that stage.

4.5

Consider voter 1. There are two strategies that involve voting truthfully in the second round: *AAN* and *BAN*. Does *AAN* dominate *BAN,* or vice versa?

4.6

Return to the game in section 4.1.2 and carefully work through every step of the IEDS procedure. Be sure to show all of the comparisons that make a strategy dominated.

Bertrand price competition: Suppose that we have two (duopoly) firms that set prices in a market whose demand curve is given by

$$Q = 6 - p$$

where p is the lower of the two prices. If there is a lower priced firm, then it meets all of the demand. If the two firms post the same price p, then they each get half the market, that is, they each get $\frac{6-p}{2}$. Suppose that prices can only be quoted in dollar units (0, 1, 2, 3, 4, 5, or 6 dollars) and that costs of production are zero.

4.7

Show that posting a price of 0 dollars and posting a price of 6 dollars are both dominated strategies. What about the strategy of posting a price of $4? $5?

4.8

Suppose for a moment that this market had only one firm. Show that the price at which this monopoly firm maximizes profits is $3.

4.9

Based on your answer to the previous two questions, can you give a reason why—in any price competition model—a duopoly firm would never want to price above the monopoly price? (Hint: When can a duopoly firm that prices above the monopoly price make positive profits? What would happen to those profits if the firm charged a monopoly price instead?)

4.10

Show that when we restrict attention to the prices 1, 2, and 3 dollars, the (monopoly) price of 3 dollars is a dominated strategy.

4.11

Argue that the unique outcome to IEDS in this model is for both firms to price at 1 dollar.

There is a more general result about price competition that we have established in the course of the previous five questions.

In any model of duopoly price competition with zero costs the IEDS outcome is the lowest price at which each firm makes a positive profit, that is, a price equal to a dollar.

Let us investigate why price competition appears to be so beneficial for the customer! Suppose that our earlier model is modified so that the demand curve is written more generally as

$$Q = D(p)$$

where $D(p)$ is a downward sloping function, i.e., the quantity demanded at price $(p - 1)$, $D(p - 1)$, is larger than the quantity demanded at price p, $D(p)$. Denote the monopoly price p_m and suppose, without loss of generality, that it is 2 dollars or greater.

4.12

Show, by using similar logic to that of question 4.9, that charging a price above the monopoly price p_m is a dominated strategy.

4.13

Now show that, as a consequence, charging price $p_m - 1$ dominates the monopoly price. [Hint: You need to show that $\frac{1}{2}D(p_m)p_m \leq D(p_m - 1)(p_m - 1)$. What can you assert about $\frac{1}{2}p_m$ versus $p_m - 1$? What about the quantities $D(p_m)$ versus $D(p_m - 1)$?]

4.14

Generalize the above argument to show the following: if it is known that no price greater than p will be charged by either firm, then p is dominated by the strategy of undercutting to a price of $p - 1$, provided $p \geq 2$.

4.15

Conclude from the above arguments that the IEDS price must be, again, 1 dollar for each firm.

4.16

Suppose, finally, that costs are not zero. Can you sketch an argument to show that all of the previous results hold as long as undercutting to price $p - 1$ (and serving the entire market as a consequence) are higher than the profits from sharing the market at price p?

SECTION 4.2

4.17

Consider the veto game of section 4.2. Show that Africa has a dominant strategy. What is it?

4.18

Prove the following general proposition.

> *Whenever $N - 1$ players in a game have dominant strategies, there must be an IEDS solution to the game.*

4.19

Suppose now that the preferences of the U.S. and Africa are slightly different than those in the text.

U.S.: $H \succ A \succ B$

Africa: $B \succ H \succ A$

What is the dominant strategy for Africa? What is the IEDS solution?

SECTION 4.4

4.20

Show that if strategies were eliminated only if they are strongly dominated, then the outcome to IEDS is independent of the order in which we eliminate strategies. It suffices to answer the question for a two-player, three-strategy game.

4.21

Give another example (in addition to the one in the text) to show that the order of elimination matters if we eliminate strategies that are dominated but not strongly.

4.22

Give an example of a game that has an outcome to IEDS although no player has a dominant strategy. Do this for strong as well as weak domination.

4.23

Give an example of a game that has an outcome to IEDS although the strategies picked out by this procedure did not, initially, dominate any other strategy. Again, do this for strong as well as weak domination.

CHAPTER 5

NASH EQUILIBRIUM

In this chapter we will look at the third—and by far the most popular—solution concept for strategic form games: *Nash equilibrium.* Section 5.1 will present the intuition of Nash equilibrium and give a precise definition. Section 5.2 will work through a cluster of examples, and section 5.3 will be a case study of Nash equilibrium among animals. By that point you will have seen three different solutions to a game: dominant strategy solution, IEDS, and Nash equilibrium. In order to keep you from being fully confused, section 5.4 will outline the relation between these concepts.

5.1 THE CONCEPT

5.1.1 INTUITION AND DEFINITION

Suppose that you have a strategy b that is dominated by another strategy, say a. We have seen that it is never a good idea to play b because no matter what the other player does, you can always do better with a. Now suppose you actually have some idea about the other player's intentions. In that case, you would choose a provided it does better than *b given what the other player is going to do.* You don't, in other words, need to know that a performs better than b against all strategies of the other player; you simply need to know that it performs better against the specific strategy of your opponent. Indeed, a is called a *best response* against the other player's known strategy if it does better than any of your other strategies against this known strategy.

Typically you will not know exactly what the other player intends to do; at best you will have a guess about his strategy choice. The same logic applies, however; what you really care about is how a performs vis-à-vis b—or any other strategy for that matter—when played against your *guess* about your opponent's strategy. It only pays to play a best response against that strategy which you believe your opponent is about to play.

Of course, your guess might be wrong! And then you would be unhappy—and you would want to change what you did. But suppose you and your opponent guessed correctly, and you each played best responses to your guesses. In that case, you would have no reason to do anything else if you had to do it all over again. In that case, you would be in a Nash equilibrium!

Definition.   A strategy s_i^* is a best response to a strategy vector s_{-i}^* of the other players if[1]

$$\pi_i(s_i^*, s_{-i}^*) \geq \pi_i(s_i, s_{-i}^*), \quad \text{for all } s_i$$

In other words, s_i^* is a "dominant strategy" in the very weak sense that it is a best strategy to play provided the other players do in fact play the strategy combination s_{-i}^*. We need a condition to ensure that player i is correct in his conjecture that the other players are going to play s_{-i}^*. And, likewise, the other players are correct in their conjectures. This analysis gives us the following definition:

Definition.   The strategy vector $s^* = s_1^*, s_2^*, \ldots, s_N^*$ is a Nash equilibrium if

$$\pi_i(s_i^*, s_{-i}^*) \geq \pi_i(s_i, s_{-i}^*), \quad \text{for all } s_i \text{ and all } i \tag{5.1}$$

Equation 5.1 says that each player i, in playing s_i^*, is playing a best response to the others' strategy choice. This one condition includes the two requirements of Nash equilibrium that were intuitively discussed earlier:

- Each player must be playing a best response against a conjecture.

- The conjectures must be correct.

It includes the first requirement because s_i^* is a best response against the conjecture s_{-i}^* for every player i. It includes the second because no player has an incentive to change his strategy (from s_i^*). Hence, s_i^* is stable—and each player's conjecture is correct.

Consider the case of two players, 1 and 2, each with two strategies, a^1 and a^2 for player 1, b^1 and b^2 for player 2. Here (a^2, b^1), for example, is a Nash equilibrium if and only if

$$\pi_1(a^2, b^1) \geq \pi_1(a^1, b^1)$$
$$\pi_2(a^2, b^1) \geq \pi_2(a^2, b^2)$$

5.1.2   NASH PARABLES

There are various other ways in which the Nash equilibrium concept has been motivated within game theory. These motivations are parables in the sense that we will only offer a verbal description of each one. Some of these motivations have been precisely worked out in mathematical models; some others have turned out to be simple and intuitive verbally but virtually impossible to analyze formally. In either case, the parables are

[1] As always, s_{-i}^* refers to a strategy choice by all players other than player i, while s_i^* is a strategy of player i. In other words, s_{-i}^* is a list of strategy choices; $s_{-i}^* = s_1^*, s_2^*, \ldots, s_{i-1}^*, s_{i+1}^*, \ldots, s_N^*$, where, for example, s_2^* is a strategy choice of player 2.

worth telling because Nash equilibrium will be the most widely used solution concept in this (and every other) game theory text. Hopefully, these parables will convince you even more about the reasonableness of this solution concept.

Play Prescription

One can think of a Nash Equilibrium s^* as a *prescription* for play. If this strategy vector is proposed to the players, then it is a stable prescription in the sense that no one has an incentive to play otherwise. By playing an alternative strategy, a player would simply lower her payoffs, if she thinks the others are going to follow their part of the prescription.

Preplay Communication

How would the players in a game find their way to a Nash equilibrium? One answer that has been proposed is that they could coordinate on a Nash equilibrium by way of *preplay communication*; that is, they could coordinate by meeting before the game is actually played and discussing their options. It is not credible for the players to agree on anything that is not a Nash equilibrium because at least one player would cheat against such an agreement.[2]

Rational Introspection

A related motivation is *rational introspection*: each player could ask himself what he expects will be the outcome to a game. Some candidate outcomes will appear unreasonable in that there are players who could do better than they are doing; that is, there will be players not playing a best response. The only time no player appears to be making a mistake is when each is playing a best response, that is, when we are at a Nash equilibrium.

Focal Point

Another motivation is the idea that a Nash equilibrium forms a *focal point* for the players in a game. The intuitive idea of a focal point was first advanced by Thomas Schelling in 1960 in his book *The Strategy of Conflict*. It refers to a strategy vector that stands out from the other strategy vectors because of some distinguishing characteristics.[3] A Nash equilibrium strategy vector is a focal point because it has the distinguishing characteristic that each player plays a best response under that strategy vector.

Trial and Error

If players started by playing a strategy vector that is not a Nash equilibrium, somebody would discover that she could do better. If she changes her strategy choice, and we are still not in a Nash equilibrium, somebody else might want to change his strategy. This process of trial and error would go on till such time as we reach a Nash equilibrium—and then nobody has the incentive to change her strategy choice. This reasoning is persuasive but not entirely correct because there is no guarantee that this process would ever lead to a stable situation. Moreover, it is easy to construct examples in which this process could

[2] *The problem with this story, though, is that for it to be internally consistent, the preplay communication stage should itself be modeled as part of the game.*

[3] *As an example, consider the following coordination games: (a) two players have to write down either heads or tails. They are paid only if their choices match. (b) Two players have to meet in New York City and have to choose a time for their meeting. Again they are paid only if their chosen times coincide. (c) Same as game b except that the players also have to choose a place to meet. In experiments that he conducted with his students, Schelling found that in a disproportionate number of cases, students chose heads in a, twelve noon in b, and twelve noon, Grand Central Station in c.*

leave us trapped in cycles in which players keep changing their strategies in search of higher payoffs but nowhere is everyone satisfied simultaneously.

Two questions about Nash equilibrium arise:

- **Existence.** (When) Do we know that every game has a Nash equilibrium?

  Recall that one problem with the dominance-based solution concepts, such as Dominant Strategy solution or Iterated Elimination of Dominated Strategies, was that these concepts yield no solution in many games. In Chapter 28 we discuss conditions under which Nash equilibria are known always to exist.

- **Uniqueness.** (When) Do we know that a given game will have exactly one Nash equilibrium?

  The answer to this question is a lot less satisfactory; in many games we have an embarrassment of riches in that there are many Nash equilibria. And then the (third) question becomes, Which one of them is the most reasonable?

5.2   EXAMPLES

Let us now examine the Nash equilibrium concept in several examples.

Example 1: Battle of the Sexes

Husband \ Wife	Football (F)	Opera (O)
Football (F)	3, 1	0, 0
Opera (O)	0, 0	1, 3

Here a best response of player 1 (the husband), to a play of F by 2 (the wife) is to play F; denote this choice as $b^1(F) = F$. Likewise, $b^1(O) = O$. For player 2, the best response can be written as $b^2(F) = F$ and $b^2(O) = O$. Note that an alternative definition of a Nash equilibrium in a two-player game is that it is a pair of strategies in which each strategy is a best response to the other one in that pair. In the Battle of the Sexes, (F, F) is a Nash equilibrium because

$$F = b^1(F)$$
$$F = b^2(F)$$

CONCEPT CHECK
ANOTHER NASH

Show that there is another Nash equilibrium, (O, O).

Example 2: Prisoners' Dilemma

1 \ 2	*Confess*	*Not Confess*
Confess	0, 0	7, −2
Not Confess	−2, 7	5, 5

In the Prisoners' Dilemma, we know that *confess* is a dominant strategy. In the notation being used here that is the same thing as saying that the best response to either strategy of the other player is *confess*. Hence, the only Nash equilibrium of the Prisoners' Dilemma game is (*confess, confess*). This is, of course, also the dominant strategy solution.

Example 3: Bertrand Pricing

Firm 1 \ Firm 2	*High* (H)	*Medium* (M)	*Low* (L)
High (H)	6, 6	0, 10	0, 8
Medium (M)	10, 0	5, 5	0, 8
Low (L)	8, 0	8, 0	4, 4

In this game, $b^1(H) = M$, $b^1(M) = L$, and $b^1(L) = L$. Likewise for firm 2 one can derive the best response function—and note that it is identical to that for firm 1. The only Nash equilibrium in this game is therefore (L,L). This is also the IEDS solution, as you may recall from the previous chapter.

Example 4: The Odd Couple

Felix \ Oscar	*3 hours*	*6 hours*	*9 hours*
3 hours	−13, −8	−1, −4	7, −4
6 hours	−4, −1	4, −1	4, −4
9 hours	1, 2	1, −1	1, −4

CONCEPT CHECK
NASH EQUILIBRIA

Show that there are three equilibria: (1) Felix works *9 hours* and Oscar works *3*. (2) They both work *6 hours*. (3) Felix works *3 hours* and Oscar works *9*.

The first Nash equilibrium is also the IEDS solution—as you may recall from the previous chapter.

Example 5: Two-Player Coordination Game

1 \ 2	7:30	10:30
7:30	1, 1	0, 0
10:30	0, 0	0, 0

CONCEPT CHECK
BEST RESPONSES

Show that $b^1(7:30) = 7:30$, $b^1(10:30) = 7:30$ or $10:30$ (symmetrically for the other player). What are the Nash equilibria in this game?

---

[4] *The Maynard Smith and Price paper was "The Logic of Animal Conflict,"* Nature, *246, pp. 15–18. For a good survey of subsequent work, see "Game Theory and Evolutionary Biology" by Peter Hammerstein and Reinhard Selten in* Handbook of Game Theory, *vol. 2, ed. R. J. Aumann and S. Hart (North-Holland). Most of that chapter will be too technical for you, but see section 8 for the many fascinating stories it contains about strategic animal behavior.*

[5] *Here is another story—this time about the common toad. The male-to-female ratio is really high (and you men were complaining about your school!), making it very difficult for a male toad to find a fertile female. During mating season, the females come to one area (to be mated) and the males strike preemptively. If a male toad sees a female headed for the mating area, he climbs onto her back in order to assert property rights. For another male to wrest control he has to also get onto the back of this female toad and try to push the incumbent off. When a fight breaks out, biologists report seeing as many as five to six male toads on the back of one poor female. (Budweiser should make a commercial based on this!)*

5.3   CASE STUDY: NASH EQUILIBRIUM IN THE ANIMAL KINGDOM

One of the more fascinating applications of game theory in the last 25 years has been to biology, in particular, to the analysis of animal conflicts and competition and, consequently, to the evolution of whole species. The seminal work in this area was done by the English biologist John Maynard Smith in 1973 (along with G. R. Price).[4]

Animals in the wild typically have to compete for such scarce resources as fertile females, safe places for females to lay eggs, or carcasses of dead animals. Having a mate, a safe haven, or more food will likely lengthen an animal's lifetime or perpetuate the species. Given the scarcity of resources, it pays to discover such a resource—or snatch it away from a competitor. The problem is that the competitor is unlikely to give up without a fight, and fighting is costly. An animal may lose an arm and a leg—or even worse.

Consider the story of the desert spider *Agelenopsis aperta*, found in New Mexico. The female lays its eggs within a web. Webs are scarce because they are difficult to build. Biologists have noticed that female spiders often fight—or almost fight—over an existing web; two females line up in front of a web and make threatening gestures such as violently shaking the web (although they rarely have actual physical contact). The conflict is settled when one spider retreats leaving the other in sole possession of the web.[5]

Biologists have tried to explain two stylized facts about animal competition:

1.   Most conflicts are settled without fighting. Furthermore, the winner of the conflict is often "differently endowed" from the loser in certain vital characteristics.

2.   When the stakes are higher, fighting is more likely.

Let us see if we can explain these facts with the game theory that you have learned so far. Recall the Hawk-Dove game from Chapter 3:[6]

Spider 1 \ Spider 2	*Concede* (*c*)	*Fight* (*f*)
Concede (*c*)	5, 5	0, 10
Fight (*f*)	10, 0	x, x

Suppose the value—or utility—of having the web is 10.[7] If one spider fights, and the other concedes, she has the web. If neither fights there is a 50–50 chance that either of them will have the web. Finally, if they both fight, then, again, there is a 50–50 chance that either of them will have the web, but there is also a likelihood that they will be physically harmed by the fighting. If the physical costs are higher than the expected value of the web, then the payoff x will be less than 0; otherwise, it will be bigger than 0.

What is the Nash equilibrium of this game? Suppose, to begin with, that $x < 0$; that is, the physical harm is large or, put differently, the stakes to winning the web are not high enough. It should be easy to see that there are two Nash equilibria—spider 1 *fights* and the other *concedes*, and vice versa. On the other hand, if $x > 0$, then the only Nash equilibrium is for both spiders to *fight*; higher stakes engender more fights.

How are we to predict which of the two spiders will win the web in the case when there is no fighting? The authors of the study found that two things mattered—incumbency and weight. If the spiders were more or less equal in weight, then the incumbent kept the web. If, however, the challenger was considerably heavier, she would win.[8] To see this last fact explained, suppose that the payoffs to (*f*, *f*) are (*x*, *y*) with $x < 0 < y$; the second spider—because she is heavier—suffers less from a fight than the first one. Now the only Nash equilibrium is for the first spider to *concede* because the second one is going to *fight*. The two stylized facts have been explained in terms of our simple Hawk-Dove game.[9]

5.4 RELATION BETWEEN THE SOLUTION CONCEPTS ⚠

The general relation between the two solution concepts—*IEDS and Nash equilibrium*—can be summarized by the following result:

Proposition. Consider any game in which there is an outcome to IEDS. It must be the case that this outcome is a Nash equilibrium. However, not every Nash equilibrium can be obtained as the outcome to IEDS.

We have seen this proposition illustrated in examples 3 though 5. For example, in the Bertrand pricing game, the IEDS solution (*low, low*) is the only Nash equilibrium of the game. In the Odd Couple game, the IEDS solution (*9 hours, 3 hours*) is a Nash

[6] We have written the payoff to both spiders fighting as *x*, *x* rather than −1, −1, as earlier.

[7] You may wonder what it means to assign payoffs or utilities to spiders. The authors of the spider study, P. Hammerstein and S. Riechert, have a very precise answer. They measured the value of having a web by calculating how many more eggs survive inside a web than outside it. They calculated the costs of fighting—broken limbs— by how many fewer eggs the female could lay or shepherd to birth as a consequence of injuries suffered while fighting.

[8] You may wonder how the spiders know which of them is heavier. Well, that, apparently, is the point of shaking the web violently (before engaging in any combat). From the intensity of the shaking the spiders are able to figure out which of them is heavier.

[9] Apparently the toads fight more. Indeed so many of them sometimes clamber onto the female's back that she drowns—and there goes any chance of mating. One explanation is that the physical harm in this case is more likely to fall on the female rather than the male combatants; that is, that the payoff to fighting, *x*, is likely to be bigger than the payoff to conceding, 0.

equilibrium. There are also two other Nash equilibria (that were eliminated in the IEDS procedure).

We will not prove the proposition in full generality. What we will do is give you the idea of proof in a simple special case—a two-player three-strategy game. The players' strategies are a^1, a^2, a^3 for player 1 and b^1, b^2, b^3 for player 2. Suppose that the pair of strategies (a^2, b^3) is the IEDS solution. In order to establish that this pair is also a Nash equilibrium we need to show that a^2 has a higher payoff than a^1 or a^3 when played against b^3. Likewise, b^3 has a higher payoff than b^2 or b^1 against player 1's strategy a^2.

Suppose that a^1 is the strategy of player 1 that is eliminated in the last round of elimination, and likewise b^1 is a last-round elimination. We can then proceed by way of the following three-step proof (and be sure to fill out the details):

- **Step 1.** Regardless of whether player 2 plays b^3 or b^1, a^2 has a payoff as high as a^1. In particular, against b^3, a^2 is at least as good a response as a^1.

- **Step 2.** Similarly, b^3 is as good a response for player 2 as b^1 against a^2.

How do a^2's payoffs compare with those of a^3? Since a^3 got eliminated in the very first round, it must have been dominated by either a^2 or a^1. If it is dominated by a^2 we are done. (Why?) If it is dominated by a^1, then we know that it does worse than a^1 against player 2's strategy of b^3. But in turn, a^1 has no higher a payoff than a^2 against that same strategy, b^3. We have therefore concluded:

- **Step 3.** For player 1, a^2 is a best response against b^3. Likewise, b^3 is a best response for player 2 against a^2. ◇

The reverse implication is not necessarily true; there may be Nash equilibria that are not the solution to IEDS. This point is easy to see in any game, such as Battle of the Sexes, in which there is a Nash equilibrium but the game is not dominance solvable. Another situation where Nash does not imply IEDS can arise when there are multiple Nash equilibria; some of these Nash equilibria would be eliminated by iterated elimination of dominated strategies. We saw this illustrated in examples 4 and 5.

As regards the relation between dominant strategy solution and Nash equilibrium, exactly the same result holds. First, note that every dominant strategy solution is an IEDS outcome; if there is a dominant strategy every other strategy is immediately eliminated. But we have just learned that every IEDS outcome is a Nash equilibrium. It follows therefore that every dominant strategy solution is a Nash equilibrium. The converse (again) need not hold. The coordination game had a dominant strategy solution (7:30, 7:30). However, (10:30, 10:30) is also a Nash equilibrium.

SUMMARY

1. A strategy choice of player i is a best response to his opponents' strategy choice if it yields him the highest payoff possible against that choice.

2. A strategy combination is a Nash equilibrium if each player's strategy choice is a best response against her opponents' choices in that combination.

3. Nash equilibrium is the most popular solution concept in all of game theory. It can be motivated in a variety of ways.

4. Nash equilibrium has been used to explain observable behavior patterns among animals living in the wild.

5. Any IEDS solution has to be a Nash equilibrium. However, there may be Nash equilibria that are not IEDS solutions.

6. The same thing is true of a dominant strategy solution; it must be a Nash equilibrium, but the reverse implication need not hold.

EXERCISES

SECTION 5.1

5.1
Give examples of games with (a) one Nash equilibrium, (b) two Nash equilibria, and (c) three Nash equilibria.

5.2
Find Nash equilibria in the game of Colonel Blotto (example 5 in Chapter 3).

5.3
Do likewise for the voting game (example 7 in Chapter 3).

Recall the voluntarism question from Chapter 3. Each of two players can volunteer 0, 1, 2, 3, or 4 hours. If player 1 volunteers x hours and player 2 volunteers y hours, then the resultant garden gives each of them a utility payoff equal to $\sqrt{x+y}$. Each player also gets disutility equal to the number of hours spent working in the garden. Hence, the total utility of player 1 is $\sqrt{x+y} - x$ (and that of player 2 is $\sqrt{x+y} - y$).

5.4
Write down the best response of a player to every strategy of the other player.

5.5
Determine the Nash equilibria of the game.

5.6
Suppose that an outside observer asked the following question: How much total time should be volunteered in order to make the sum of their utilities the highest? How would you answer this observer?

SECTION 5.2

And now, yet again (!) we return to the duopoly price competition game. Recall that the demand curve is given by

$$Q = 6 - p$$

where p is the lower of the two prices (and prices are quoted in dollar amounts). The lower-priced firm meets all of the market's demand. If the two firms post the same price p, then each gets half the market; that is, each gets $\frac{6-p}{2}$. Suppose that costs of production are zero.

5.7
Show that the best response to your rival posting a price of 6 dollars is to post the monopoly price of 3 dollars. What is the best response against a rival's price of 5 dollars? 4 dollars?

5.8
Can you show that the best response to 3 dollars is to price at 2 dollars instead?

5.9
Show that the Nash equilibrium of this price competition model is for each firm to price at 1 dollar.

There is a more general result about price competition that can be established. The result is the following:

In any model of duopoly price competition with zero costs there is a single Nash equilibrium; each firm charges the lowest price at which it makes a positive profit, that is, one dollar.

Suppose that the demand curve is written as

$$Q = D(p)$$

where $D(p)$ is a downward-sloping function. Denote the monopoly price p_m and suppose that it is 2 dollars or greater.

5.10
Show that if the rival firm charges a price above the monopoly price p_m, then the best response is to charge the monopoly price.

5.11
Show further that if the rival firm charges a price p (> 1) at or below the monopoly price, then the best response is to charge a price below p. (Hint: Can you show that charging a price $p - 1$, for example, is more profitable than charging p or above?)

5.12
Conclude from the preceding arguments that the unique Nash equilibrium price must be, again, 1 dollar for each firm.

5.13
How would your answers to exercises 5.7–5.9 change if there were 3 firms in this market? More generally, if there were N firms? Explain.

Suppose in the same three questions we assume instead that firm 1 has unit costs of production; that is, for every output level Q, its costs are Q dollars.

5.14
What is firm 1's best response to a price of 1 dollar (posted by firm 2)? Can you show that firm 1 posting a price of 2 dollars and firm 2 posting a price of 1 dollar is a Nash equilibrium?

5.15
Are the following prices a Nash equilibrium—firm 1 posts a price of 3 dollars, while firm 2 prices at 1 dollar? What about 3 and 2, respectively? Can you demonstrate that there cannot be a Nash equilibrium in which the firms post different prices unless it happens to be 2 and 1 dollars, respectively (for firms 1 and 2)?

5.16
Argue that there cannot be a Nash equilibrium in which each firm posts a price of 2 dollars? Indeed show that there cannot be a Nash equilibrium in which the firms post the same prices and these are above the minimum price of a dollar?

5.17
Show that there is a Nash equilibrium in which each firm posts a price of a dollar.

SECTION 5.3

Consider again the Hawk-Dove game.

5.18

Suppose that the payoff to winning the web is higher (than 10). Clearly explain how the payoff to (f, f) might change as well. What difference, if any, would that make to the analysis?

5.19

Show that what determines whether or not the spiders fight is the difference between the payoffs to fighting and conceding when the other spider chooses to fight.

5.20

Argue that both spiders conceding can never be a Nash equilibrium of this game. For what payoffs would this be the socially desirable outcome?

SECTION 5.4

5.21

Argue that if we arrive at an IEDS outcome by eliminating strongly dominated strategies alone, then (a) the strong IEDS outcome is a Nash equilibrium, and (b) there cannot be any other Nash equilibria.

5.22

Give an example—other than the coordination game—where there is a dominant strategy solution and multiple Nash equilibria.

5.23

Prove that the situation in the previous question can arise only if the dominant strategies are weakly dominant. In other words, show that if there is a dominant strategy solution in which the strategies are strongly dominant, then there cannot be any other Nash equilibrium.

CHAPTER 6

AN APPLICATION: COURNOT DUOPOLY

In this chapter an application of the Nash equilibrium concept to a model of a duopolistic market, the Cournot model, will be discussed.[1] Section 6.1 offers appropriate background for the problem, and section 6.2 outlines the basic model. (Cournot) Nash equilibrium is computed in section 6.3, and then in section 6.4 we study the cartel solution. Section 6.5 is devoted to a case study of today's OPEC. Finally, sections 6.6 through 6.8 explore various extensions of the basic model.

6.1   BACKGROUND

Historically, economists have expended the greatest amount of time and energy studying two extreme forms of markets: a *monopoly,* where there is a single firm, and a *perfectly competitive market,* where there are (infinitely) many firms. A reason for this focus is that one does not have to worry about strategic interaction in either of these cases; in a monopoly by definition, and in perfect competition because it is unreasonable for one firm to track the actions of all of its very many competitors. However, in real-world markets, the most prevalent scenario is one where there are a few firms in any given market.

For instance, in automobile manufacturing there are three domestic and, roughly, ten major foreign manufacturers in the United States. In the aircraft manufacturing industry, there is only one domestic manufacturer of large passenger aircraft and one foreign manufacturer.[2] In the world oil market, about ten manufacturing nations account for more than 80 percent of production, and one group, the Organization of Petroleum Exporting Countries (OPEC), accounts for three-quarters of that output. On a smaller scale, the two large grocery stores in your town, or the two bagel stores in your neighborhood, are examples of "local duopolies"—duopolies in your town or in your neighborhood.

[1] *It is entirely appropriate that we discuss the Cournot model as our first application of Nash equilibrium. This model, first published in 1838 by Antoine Augustin Cournot, is the earliest predecessor of modern game theory. Cournot also proposed a solution for the model that has many features similar to a Nash equilibrium.*

[2] *These are, respectively, Boeing and the Airbus consortium of Europe.*

When there are only a few firms in its market, a firm will analyze the likely effect of its actions on its competitors, and it will try to anticipate what the competition might do. For example, senior management in a major airline is very likely to ponder the following questions before a price increase: Will the competition match the change? Will they raise prices too, or will we lose customers? Will the competition offer discounts? If they do, what will we do then? And so on.[3] In a similar fashion, when OPEC's oil ministers meet to consider future production plans, they clearly worry about the response from non-OPEC oil-producing nations. Will their attempt to maintain a high world crude oil price be frustrated by increased production from those nations?

Game theory, of course, is precisely the tool designed to formalize these questions.

6.2   THE BASIC MODEL

In the model proposed by Cournot, two firms compete in a market for a *homogeneous product*. In other words, the two firms' products are virtually indistinguishable from the consumers' standpoint.[4] Therefore, the two firms are faced with a single demand curve in the market; suppose that the demand curve is given by

$$Q = \alpha - \beta P$$

where $\alpha > 0$, $\beta > 0$, and $Q = Q_1 + Q_2$, is the aggregate quantity produced by firms 1 and 2. An alternative way of reading the demand curve is that if $Q = Q_1 + Q_2$ is the amount that the duopolists produce between themselves, then the price that results is

$$P = \frac{\alpha}{\beta} - \frac{Q}{\beta}$$

Let us simplify the expression for this (inverse) demand curve by writing $a = \frac{\alpha}{\beta}$ and $b = \frac{1}{\beta}$; that is, the inverse demand curve that we will use from this point on is

$$P = a - bQ$$

Indeed, as illustration, we will refer occasionally to the special case where $a = 10$ and $b = 1$, that is, to the inverse demand curve $P = 10 - Q$. Of course the picture for this demand curve is given by Figure 6.1.

Suppose now that the cost function is the same for each firm and that the cost per unit does not vary with the number of units produced. More formally, each firm has a constant marginal cost function; the cost of producing quantity Q_i is cQ_i, where $c > 0$ is the constant marginal cost and $i = 1, 2$.

How much would each firm produce? To make that decision, each firm has to take two steps:

[3] *Indeed, the dangers of not doing this analysis carefully or getting the answers wrong can be quite serious. Recall, for example, the summer of 1992 when American Airlines decided to make pricing, "rational." They raised business fares, eliminated multiple fares, reduced the number of discount price categories, and so on. The competition responded by cutting prices and left the fare structure in terms of categories virtually unchanged. American had to backtrack, a fare war of sorts started, and, some insiders claim, the airline industry suffered huge losses consequently.*

[4] *The particular product that Cournot used as an example was mineral spring water. Of course, this was in the old days when there weren't supposedly distinctive mineral waters such as Perrier and Evian (which, somebody pointed out to me, is naive spelled backward).*

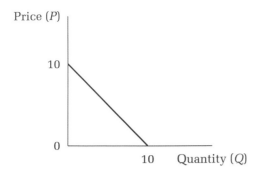

Price (P)

10

0

10   Quantity (Q)

FIGURE 6.1

1. *Make a conjecture about the other firm's production.* This step will give the firm an idea about the likely market price; for instance, if it thinks the rival is going to produce a lot, then the price will be low no matter how much it produces.

2. *Determine the quantity to produce.* To make this determination the firm has to weigh the benefits from increasing production—that is, that it will sell more units—against the costs of doing so—that is, that these extra units will sell at a lower price (and will need to be produced at a higher total cost). An industry-wide —or Nash—equilibrium will obtain when both firms satisfactorily resolve these two issues.

6.3   COURNOT NASH EQUILIBRIUM

Let us first analyze the two questions from the perspective of firm 1. If it was the only firm in the market, firm 1's production decision would determine the market price. It could then compute the profits from selling different quantity levels and pick the quantity that maximizes profits. This is no longer true; the market price will depend on both its own production Q_1 and the other firm's production. As a start, what firm 1 can do is ask, *if firm 2 were going to produce* $\overline{Q}_2$, what quantity should I produce in order to maximize profits?

Note that the market price when the total production is $Q_1 + \overline{Q}_2$ is $a - b(Q_1 + \overline{Q}_2)$. The revenues of firm 1 are therefore $[a - b(Q_1 + \overline{Q}_2)]Q_1$. Since costs are cQ_1, the total profits are given by $[a - b(Q_1 + \overline{Q}_2)]Q_1 - cQ_1$. Hence, the quantity that maximizes profits can be determined from the following exercise:

$\text{Max}_{Q_1}\ [a - b(Q_1 + \overline{Q}_2) - c]Q_1$

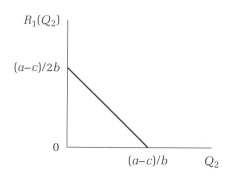

$R_1(Q_2)$

$(a-c)/2b$

0

$(a-c)/b$ Q_2

FIGURE 6.2

The expression for profits is a quadratic function. There is a maximum profit quantity, denoted Q_1^*, which we can compute by the first-order condition to the problem[5]

$$a - c - b\overline{Q}_2 = 2bQ_1^*$$

or $Q_1^* = \frac{a-c-b\overline{Q}_2}{2b}$.[6] What we have just computed is the *best response* of firm 1 to a quantity choice $\overline{Q}_2$ of firm 2. For example, if $P = 10 - Q$, $c = 1$, and $\overline{Q}_2 = 5$, then $\frac{a-c-b\overline{Q}_2}{2b} = 2$; that is, the optimal quantity for firm 1 to produce is 2. Indeed, this formula gives us the best response of firm 1 for any quantity that it conjectures firm 2 might produce. Let us denote this best response function R_1. So we have shown that

$$R_1(Q_2) = \begin{cases} \dfrac{a - c - bQ_2}{2b}, & \text{if } Q_2 \le \dfrac{a - c}{b} \\ 0, & \text{if } Q_2 > \dfrac{a - c}{b} \end{cases}$$

Let us observe the graph that goes along with this best response function, Figure 6.2. By symmetric reasoning the best response function of firm 2 is given by

$$R_2(Q_1) = \begin{cases} \dfrac{a - c - bQ_1}{2b}, & \text{if } Q_1 \le \dfrac{a - c}{b} \\ 0, & \text{if } Q_1 > \dfrac{a - c}{b} \end{cases}$$

Figure 6.3 incorporates both best-response functions—also called *reaction functions* in the Cournot model. Notice that there is a unique pair of quantities, Q_1^*, Q_2^*, at which the reaction functions cross. Hence this is a pair of quantities for which

$$R_2(Q_1^*) = Q_2^*$$
$$R_1(Q_2^*) = Q_1^*$$

In other words, this pair is a Cournot Nash equilibrium of this game. Explicit computation now yields the following equilibrium quantities, price, and profits:

[5] By the first-order condition we refer to the fact that at the profit-maximizing quantity, the slope, or derivative, of the profit function must be zero. The profit function is $(a - b\overline{Q}_2 - c)Q_1 - bQ_1^2$; its derivative is therefore $(a - b\overline{Q}_2 - c) - 2bQ_1$. Also note that the profit maximization is done subject to the constraint that the quantity chosen has to be zero or positive. For a further discussion of first-order conditions, see Chapter 25.

[6] If $\overline{Q}_2 > \frac{a-c}{b}$, then this formula yields a negative value for Q_1^*; put differently, the quantity that maximizes firm 1's profits in that instance is $Q_1^* = 0$.

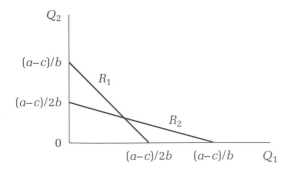

FIGURE 6.3

Per-Firm Quantity	Price	Per-Firm Profit
$\dfrac{a-c}{3b}$	$\dfrac{1}{3}a + \dfrac{2}{3}c$	$\dfrac{(a-c)^2}{9b}$

Example

Consider the case where $P = 10 - Q$ and $c = 1$. Show that we reach the following conclusions in the example:

Per-Firm Quantity	Price	Per-Firm Profit
3	4	9

6.4 CARTEL SOLUTION

As a contrast let us compute the quantities that would be produced if the two firms operate as a cartel, that is, if they coordinate their production decisions. If firms operate as a cartel, it is reasonable to suppose that they set production targets in such a way as to maximize their joint—or total—profits. Call the production "quotas" Q_1 and Q_2; these are selected so as to maximize the total profits:

$$\text{Max}_{Q_1, Q_2} \; [a - b(Q_1 + Q_2) - c][Q_1 + Q_2]$$

The difference between the cartel problem and the best response problem is that here the two firms acknowledge explicitly that their profits are determined by their *total* production. In the best response problem, however, each firm computes profits on the basis of its own output alone (and assumes that the other firm would hold rigidly to some quantity level).

Again, the profit-maximizing aggregate quantity is characterized by the first-order conditions; writing $\widehat{Q}_1$ and $\widehat{Q}_2$ for the cartel-mandated quantities, the first-order condition can be written as

$$a - c - 2b\widehat{Q}_2 = 2b\widehat{Q}_1$$
$$a - c - 2b\widehat{Q}_2 = 2b\widehat{Q}_1$$

The two equations are easily seen to solve for the cartel quantities, price, and profits:[7]

Per-Firm Quantity   Price   Per-Firm Profit

$\dfrac{a-c}{4b}$ $\dfrac{a+c}{2}$ $\dfrac{(a-c)^2}{8b}$

Notice that if the firms operate as a cartel they produce a smaller quantity than in the Nash equilibrium; the cartel output is 75 percent of the Cournot Nash equilibrium output level. Both firms make lower profits in Nash equilibrium than if they operate as a cartel (because in equilibrium they overproduce).

Example

Again consider the case in which $P = 10 - Q$ and $c = 1$. Ascertain the following values:

Per-Firm Quantity   Price   Per-Firm Profit

2.25   5.5   10.125

(whereas, they are, respectively, 3, 4, and 9 in Cournot Nash equilibrium).[8]

A natural question to ask is, Given that there are higher profits to be made in this market, why don't the two firms increase profits (by cutting back production)? The answer to this seeming puzzle, as with the Prisoners' Dilemma, is that what is good for the group is not necessarily good for the individual. If the firms tried to produce as a cartel, there would be incentives for each firm to cheat and increase its own profit at the expense of the other firm.[9]

Indeed if firm 2 produced $\frac{a-c}{4b}$, the cartel quantity, it follows from firm 1's reaction function that its profit-maximizing production level would be $\frac{3(a-c)}{8b}$; firm 1 would increase its own profits by producing more than the cartel output level. When Q_1 increases but Q_2 does not, firm 2 is unambiguously worse off. After all, the market price goes down, but firm 2 sells exactly the same amount.

The cartel weighs the profit loss of firm 2 against the profit gain of firm 1 and chooses not to recommend a higher production quota than $\frac{a-c}{4b}$. Firm 1, in deciding whether or not to cheat against this quota, simply notes that it can increase profits by expanding output to $\frac{3(a-c)}{8b}$. In particular, it ignores the effects of its cheating on firm 2's profit levels.[10]

CONCEPT CHECK

Show that, by cheating on the cartel, a firm increases its own profits, but it necessarily lowers its rival's profits by an even larger amount.

[7] We looked for a solution in which $\widehat{Q}_1 = \widehat{Q}_2$. In general, the two equations can be solved only for $\widehat{Q}_1 + \overline{Q}_2$.

[8] These differences in profits may seem small to you, but note that the quantity unit could be 200 million (as in the case of barrels of crude oil produced daily by OPEC); then, the profit difference needs to be multiplied by 200 million.

[9] The duopoly problem is different from the Prisoners' Dilemma in one important respect—there is no dominant strategy. An easy way to see this point is to note that the reaction function is a downward-sloping line; that is, the more the other firm produces, the less a firm should produce in best response. (What would the reaction functions look like if there were a dominant strategy?)

[10] In the real world, firms do not completely ignore the effect of their production on the profits of their competitors. For instance, they worry about possible retaliation by competitors in the future. These future considerations will be analyzed in Part III when we turn to dynamic games.

6.5   CASE STUDY: TODAY'S OPEC

The Organization of Petroleum Exporting Countries (OPEC) is a consortium of major oil-producing countries.[11] OPEC was formed in 1961 and has tried since then to keep world oil prices high by restricting production levels (through production quotas on its members). It has had varying degrees of success with this policy; the early 1970s was a period of spectacular success, but the recent history has been mixed.[12]

Here are some facts about recent performance. First, by keeping prices high, OPEC quotas have made it worthwhile for non-OPEC oil-producing nations to invest in new oil fields and increase production levels.[13] Second, this response has put pressure on OPEC itself. Some members have left—such as Ecuador in 1992. Others have been known to cheat on their quotas. Yet the core of OPEC is holding steady; the larger producers show no signs of dissolving OPEC anytime in the near future.

Let us analyze the first two facts by way of a simple Cournot model. I simplify the number of real-world players down to two: OPEC and the non-OPEC producing nations. We will assume that the costs of production are $5 a barrel for OPEC and $10 a barrel for the non-OPEC producers.[14] Finally, We will assume the following demand curve for the world oil market:

$$P = 65 - \frac{Q_O + Q_N}{3},$$

where Q_O is OPEC's production and Q_N is non-OPEC production (in each case, in million units of barrels per day, mbd).[15]

CONCEPT CHECK
BEST RESPONSES

Show that the reaction functions for OPEC and non-OPEC producers are[16]

$$R_O(Q_N) = \frac{180 - Q_N}{2}, \quad \text{if } Q_N \leq 180$$

$$R_N(Q_O) = \frac{165 - Q_O}{2}, \quad \text{if } Q_O \leq 165$$

Direct computation yields oil market equilibrium, as follows:

OPEC Quantity	Price	OPEC Profit
65	$\frac{80}{3}$	$\frac{4{,}225}{3}$

Non-OPEC Quantity	Price	Non-OPEC Profit
50	$\frac{80}{3}$	$\frac{2{,}500}{3}$

[11] OPEC includes most of the Middle Eastern producers, such as Saudi Arabia, Kuwait, Iran, Iraq, and the United Arab Emirates; most of the African producers, such as Libya, Nigeria, and Gabon; and many of the Latin American producers, such as Venezuela. It does not include the European producers, such as Norway, the Netherlands, Britain, and the former Soviet Union, nor does it include the United States.

[12] For a detailed history of OPEC and world oil prices, see Chapter 17.

[13] For example, more than 60 percent of the total increase in production since 1990 has come from non-OPEC producers. Non-OPEC oil production has grown from 27.2 million barrels per day (mbd) in 1974 to 39.7 mbd in 1994. (Scenarios for Non OPEC Oil Production through the Year 2010, by Herman T. Franssen, International Energy Association, mimeo, October 28, 1995).

[14] The Franssen mimeo cited in note 12 reports the costs of production of OPEC oil to be $4 a barrel; we round this off to $5 to simplify the computations. The same report quotes a variety of cost estimates for various non-OPEC producers ranging from $7 for U.S. producers to $18 for North Sea oil from Britain.

[15] Put differently, the demand curve is $P = 65 - \frac{\text{Total Quantity}}{3{,}000{,}000}$, if total quantity is expressed as barrels per day.

[16] Note that the costs of production are different for the two "firms" in this example. Hence, the two reaction functions are a little different from each other.

What would happen if non-OPEC producers joined OPEC? We can compute quantities and profits from the cartel formula obtained in the previous section. Note though that costs of production are lower in OPEC's fields ($5 versus $10 in non-OPEC fields). Hence, if this giant cartel wants to hold down costs, all production should come out of OPEC fields. (Why?) Applying the general formula we can now infer the following global oil cartel solution:

Total Quantity	Price	OPEC Profit
90	35	2,700

Again, total profits are higher than in Nash equilibrium (because production is lower). Even if OPEC paid the non-OPEC producers their profits in the Nash equilibrium—that is, even if they paid $\frac{2,500}{3}$ to the non-OPEC producers—OPEC would still have $\frac{5,600}{3}$ left over. In other words, OPEC would make $\frac{1,375}{3}$ or approximately $458 million more per day in this arrangement. The problem for OPEC is that there is no obvious arrangement whereby it can pay cost-inefficient non-OPEC producers not to produce. And what is worse is that ex-OPEC members like Ecuador have found that it is more profitable to benefit from OPEC quotas by being outside OPEC; they are no longer subject to the quotas and yet they benefit from the consequent higher prices.[17]

6.6   VARIANTS ON THE MAIN THEME I: A GRAPHICAL ANALYSIS ⚠

Let us look briefly at a graphical analysis of the Cournot model. (As a side benefit, we will also be able to infer its IEDS solution.) The starting point is the concept of an *isoprofit curve:*

Definition.   Firm 1's *isoprofit curve,* at a profit level $\overline{\pi}$, is given by all combinations of Q_1 and Q_2 that yield a profit of $\overline{\pi}$.

These combinations of Q_1 and Q_2 can be expressed as

$$[a - b(Q_1 + Q_2) - c]Q_1 = \overline{\pi}$$

For different profit levels—that is, for different $\overline{\pi}$, there are different isoprofit curves. The family of such curves is shown in Figure 6.4.

[17] *The third fact about OPEC— its surprising longevity—will be examined in great detail from a dynamic game theoretic perspective in Chapter 17.*

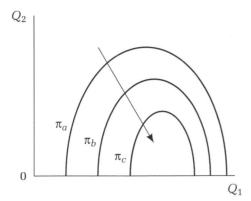

FIGURE 6.4

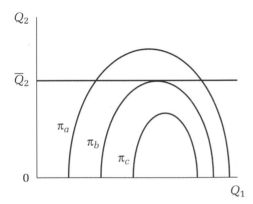

FIGURE 6.5

CONCEPT CHECK

In Figure 6.4, show that profit levels increase in the direction of the arrow, that is, that $\pi_c > \pi_b > \pi_a$.

We can use the isoprofit curves to graph the best response of firm 1 to an output level, say $\overline{Q}_2$. In the figure, that response corresponds to the following problem: Get to the highest isoprofit curve for firm 1, while remaining on the horizontal line that represents $Q_2 = \overline{Q}_2$. The solution to this problem, shown in Figure 6.5, is profit level π_b.

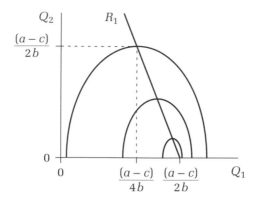

FIGURE 6.6

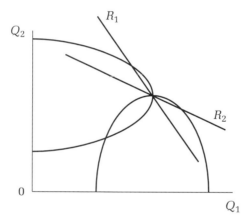

FIGURE 6.7

As we vary firm 2's quantity, we map firm 1's reaction function, as in Figure 6.6. We can do a similar exercise—complete with isoprofit curves—for firm 2 as well. The two representative isoprofit curves and the reaction functions are pictured in Figure 6.7. The intersection of the two reaction functions is the Nash equilibrium (Q^*, Q^*).

6.6.1 THE IEDS SOLUTION TO THE COURNOT MODEL
The isoprofit curves and the reaction functions can be used to prove the following result:

Proposition. There is an IEDS solution in the Cournot model, and it is precisely the Cournot Nash equilibrium.

We will sketch a proof of the proposition by analyzing firm 1. Symmetric arguments apply for firm 2. Suppose we compare two quantity levels, say, $Q_1^\#$ and Q_1'. Quantity $Q_1^\#$ dominates Q_1' if for every possible production level of firm 2, Q_2, the isoprofit curve passing through $(Q_1^\#, Q_2)$ lies below the isoprofit curve passing through (Q_1', Q_2).

- **Step 1.** *Every quantity level in excess of $\frac{a-c}{2b}$ is dominated by $\frac{a-c}{2b}$.*

  Take a quantity level $Q_1 > \frac{a-c}{2b}$. For any Q_2, Figure 6.6 shows that the isoprofit curve passing through Q_1, Q_2 is below that passing through $\frac{a-c}{2b}, Q_2$. Hence, Q_1 is dominated.

  Note that the best response to $\frac{a-c}{2b}$ is $\frac{a-c}{4b}$ and that firm 1 produces quantities less than $\frac{a-c}{4b}$ only if firm 2 produces quantities in excess of $\frac{a-c}{2b}$. Since, by step 1, it is known that firm 2 will actually never produce above $\frac{a-c}{2b}$, it turns out that firm 1 has no reason to produce amounts below $\frac{a-c}{4b}$ either.

- **Step 2.** *Every quantity level less than $\frac{a-c}{4b}$ is dominated by $\frac{a-c}{4b}$.*

  Take $Q_1 < \frac{a-c}{4b}$. By step 1, we only have to consider $Q_2 \leq \frac{a-c}{2b}$; it should not be difficult to see from Figure 6.6 that the isoprofit curve passing through Q_1, Q_2 is below that passing through $\frac{a-c}{4b}, Q_2$. Hence, Q_1 is dominated.

  Now note that the best response to $\frac{a-c}{4b}$ is $\frac{3(a-c)}{8b}$; firm 1 produces quantities in excess of $\frac{3(a-c)}{8b}$ only if firm 2 produces quantities less than $\frac{a-c}{4b}$. Since, by step 2, it is known that firm 2 will never produce such small quantities, it turns out that firm 1 has no reason to produce amounts greater than $\frac{3(a-c)}{8b}$ either.

- **Step 3.** *Show that quantities between $\frac{3(a-c)}{8b}$ and $\frac{a-c}{2b}$ are dominated by $\frac{3(a-c)}{8b}$.*

  This procedure of iteratively eliminating dominated strategies is essentially eliminating portions of the two reaction functions. Some thought (and exercises at the end of the chapter) should convince you that this process of elimination can only stop at the intersection of the reaction functions, that is, at the Nash equilibrium.

6.7 VARIANTS ON THE MAIN THEME II: STACKELBERG MODEL

In the Cournot analysis discussed up to this point, we presumed that the two firms would pick quantities simultaneously. In his 1934 criticism of Cournot, the German economist Heinrich von Stackelberg pointed out that the conclusions would be quite different if the two firms chose quantities sequentially.

Suppose that firm 1 decides on its quantity choice before firm 2. How much should each of the two profit-maximizing firms produce? Note that firm 2's decision is made when it already knows how much firm 1 is committed to producing. It follows from our reaction function analysis that, if firm 1 is producing $\overline{Q}_1$, then firm 2 can do no better than produce its best response quantity $R_2(\overline{Q}_1)$. Hence, in turn, firm 1 should choose the value $\overline{Q}_1$ realizing that $R_2(\overline{Q}_1)$ is going to be firm 2's subsequent production choice. In other words, firm 1 should solve the following problem:

$$\text{Max}_{Q_1}\{a - b[Q_1 + R_2(Q_1)] - c\}Q_1$$

Substituting for $R_2(Q_1) = \frac{a-c-bQ_1}{2b}$, we get

$$\text{Max}_{Q_1} \frac{1}{2}(a - bQ_1 - c)Q_1$$

It follows from the first-order condition that the optimal choice is $\tilde{Q}_1 = \frac{a-c}{2b}$. We can therefore conclude, from firm 2's reaction function that $\tilde{Q}_2 = \frac{a-c}{4b}$.

CONCEPT CHECK
STACKELBERG PROFITS

Check that firm 1's profits are higher in the Stackelberg solution than in the Nash equilibrium but firm 2's are smaller.

The reason why firm 1 is able to make a higher profit is straightforward. By committing to produce more than it would in the Nash equilibrium, firm 1 forces firm 2 to cut back on its own production. This commitment keeps the price relatively high—although lower than in the cartel solution—but more importantly yields firm 1 two-thirds of the market—as opposed to the market share of half that it gets in the Nash equilibrium.

6.8 VARIANTS ON THE MAIN THEME III: GENERALIZATION

The Cournot model can be generalized in two directions. First, it is easy to generalize the analysis to an oligopolistic market. If there are N firms in the market producing identical products, the inverse demand function can be written, as before, as $P = a - bQ$, the only difference being that the aggregate quantity $Q = Q_1 + Q_2 + \cdots + Q_N$. If firm 1 conjectures that each of the other firms is going to produce an amount $\overline{Q}_i$, then its profit-maximizing quantity can be shown to be

$$R_1(\overline{Q}_i) = \frac{a - c - (N - 1)b\overline{Q}_i}{2b}$$

Why? In a Cournot-Nash equilibrium, the best responses have to be to correct conjectures, so it must be the case that $R_1(\overline{Q}_i) = \overline{Q}_i$. (Why?) This equation, therefore, yields the following Nash equilibrium quantity:[18]

$$Q_i^* = \frac{a - c}{(N + 1)b}$$

Total quantity produced in the market is therefore $\frac{N(a-c)}{(N+1)b}$, and hence the price is $\frac{a}{N+1} + \frac{Nc}{N+1}$. Note that as the number of firms becomes very large—that is, as N approaches infinity—the price approaches the (marginal) cost of production c.[19] In other words, an oligopoly with many firms looks a lot like a perfectly competitive industry (in which competition drives price to marginal cost).

We could also work out the cartel and Stackelberg solutions by following exactly the same reasoning as in a duopoly.

A second generalization involves examining demand functions that are non-linear and cost functions for which marginal cost rises with output. Under appropriate restrictions on the demand and cost function, we can show that there is a Nash equilibrium, that production is higher in this equilibrium than in a cartel solution, and that the leading firm in a Stackelberg solution does better than in the Nash equilibrium.[20]

SUMMARY

1. Many real-world markets are oligopolistic. In the analysis of such markets, the study of strategic interaction is of utmost importance.

2. The Cournot model studies quantity competition among duopolistic firms facing linear demand and with constant marginal cost. It predicts play of a Nash equilibrium in quantities.

3. In the Cournot Nash equilibrium, each firm produces a greater quantity than it would produce as part of a cartel. This result occurs because each firm ignores the adverse effect its overproduction has on the other firm's profits.

4. OPEC's role in the world oil market can be analyzed by use of a Cournot model. Such a model explains how non-OPEC oil producers can be the biggest beneficiaries of OPEC's policies.

5. There is an IEDS solution to the Cournot model, and it coincides with the Cournot Nash equilibrium.

6. If firm 1 can make an early commitment to a production level, it can make more profits (in this Stackelberg solution) than in the Cournot Nash equilibrium.

[18] *In the preceding analysis, we restricted ourselves to Nash equilibria in which all firms produce the same quantities. Could there be any other equilibria, that is, equilibria in which each firm might produce a different quantity? How would you go about finding these asymmetric equilibria?*

[19] *This is because $\frac{1}{N+1}$ approaches 0 and $\frac{N}{N+1}$ approaches 1 as N approaches infinity.*

[20] *The restrictions include the following: the demand function is decreasing and concave, and the cost function is increasing and convex. (See Chapter 25 for greater detail on these concepts.)*

$$\boxed{\textbf{EXERCISES}}$$

SECTION 6.3

In the next few questions, we will walk you through the Cournot version of the Bertrand (price) competition model that you have previously analyzed. Recall that we have a duopoly with inverse market demand:[21]

$$p = 6 - Q$$

Assume that each firm can only choose one of the quantity levels 0, 1, 2, 3, . . . , 6 and that costs of production are zero.

6.1
Write down the strategic form of this game.

6.2
What is the best response for firm 1 if it thinks that firm 2 will produce 4 units of output? What if it thinks firm 2 will produce 2 units of output?

6.3
Show that the market price in Nash equilibrium is 2 dollars. Contrast your answer with that under Bertrand competition.

6.4
What is the Stackelberg solution to this model? Detail any additional assumption that you need to make to answer this question.

Suppose now that the two firms produce slightly different products; suppose, as a consequence, the first firm's price is more sensitive to its own product than that of firm 2. In particular, letting the outputs be denoted by q_1 and q_2, ($q_i = 0, 1, \ldots, 7$), suppose the two demand curves are[22]

$$p_1 = 7 - \frac{3}{2}q_1 - \frac{1}{2}q_2$$
$$p_2 = 7 - \frac{3}{2}q_2 - \frac{1}{2}q_1$$

6.5
Write down the strategic form of this game. Argue that neither firm will produce an output greater than 4 units.

6.6
What is firm 1's best response if it thinks that firm 2 is going to produce 2 units?

---

[21] Whenever $Q > 6$, $p = 0$.

[22] Again, $p_i = 0$ if $\frac{3}{2}q_i + \frac{1}{2}q_j > 7$.

6.7

Find a Cournot Nash equilibrium for this duopoly model.

SECTION 6.4

(Calculus problem) The model analyzed in exercises 6.5 through 6.7 is called a differentiated goods duopoly model. Let us now derive some general properties of this model. Suppose the demand curves are

$$p_1 = a - bq_1 - dq_2$$
$$p_2 = a - bq_2 - dq_1$$

where $b > 0$ and $d > 0$ (and any quantity, including fractions, can be produced). Suppose also that the costs of producing a unit of output is the same for both firms and is equal to c dollars where $a > c$.

6.8

Set up the best response problem for firm 1. Show that the best response function is given by

$$R_1(Q_2) = \begin{cases} \dfrac{a - c - dq_2}{2b}, & \text{if } q_2 \leq \dfrac{a - c}{d} \\ 0, & \text{if } q_2 > \dfrac{a - c}{d} \end{cases}$$

6.9

Compute the Cournot Nash equilibrium of this model.

6.10

Compute the cartel quantities.

6.11

Show that even in this model, the cartel produces less than what gets produced in the Cournot Nash equilibrium. Explain this answer.

6.12

Show that the ratio of cartel output to Nash equilibrium output is greater than the corresponding ratio in the homogeneous-good case ($\frac{3}{4}$) if and only if $b > d$. Explain this answer as well.

6.13

Suppose instead that the effect of the other firm's production is positively felt; that is, $d < 0$. What does this tell you about the nature of the two goods?

6.14

Redo your computations in questions 6.9 and 6.10 for this specification.[23]

[23] *You will need to make the further assumption that $b + d > 0$.*

6.15

How does the Nash equilibrium output compare with the cartel output? Explain your answer.

SECTION 6.6

The next few questions will work through the details of the IEDS analysis of the Cournot model.

6.16

Show, using isoprofit curves, that every quantity level in excess of $\frac{a-c}{2b}$ is dominated by the quantity level $\frac{a-c}{2b}$.

6.17

Show that amounts below $\frac{a-c}{4b}$ are dominated by the amount $\frac{a-c}{4b}$. Argue that this is equivalent to removing quantities between 0 and $\frac{a-c}{4b}$ from the reaction function. Use isoprofit curves again.

6.18

What is the best response to $\frac{3(a-c)}{8b}$? Call this q'. Argue that quantities in between $\frac{a-c}{4b}$ and q' are dominated. Carefully mark the corresponding elimination on the reaction functions.

6.19

Explain in detail why this procedure of eliminating dominated strategies will eventually lead to the Cournot Nash equilibrium.

SECTION 6.8

6.20

(Calculus problem) Solve the Cournot model—that is, find the Cournot Nash equilibrium—when the demand curve is given by

$$Q = 10 - p$$

and there are N firms. For this problem continue to assume that costs of production are zero and, for ease of calculus-based computation, that any quantity, including fractions, can be produced.

6.21

Compute the cartel solution in this problem. Contrast your answer to that in the previous question.

CHAPTER 7

AN APPLICATION: THE COMMONS PROBLEM

In this chapter we will discuss yet another application of Nash equilibrium, the usage of a commonly owned resource (such as deep-sea fisheries or the environment). One conclusion that we will draw from our study is that such resources are often overused. On account of this overuse, the phenomenon goes by the name of the *tragedy of the commons*.

Section 7.1 will provide a background to the commons problem. In section 7.2 we will introduce a simple model and characterize its Nash equilibrium. Section 7.3 will contrast the equilibrium overuse with the socially desirable outcome, and the subsequent section will show that this contrast is even more stark in a large population. Section 7.5 will discuss several case studies: buffalo, global warming, and the Internet. Possible resolutions to the tragedy will be the topic of section 7.6.

7.1 BACKGROUND: WHAT IS THE COMMONS?

The terminology—and background—to this problem can be traced to 16th-century England. Villages were designed in such a fashion that in the center of a village there would be a piece of green land that everybody could use. In addition to its serving as a site for village celebrations, this land—the *commons*—was also used by villagers as pastureland for their cattle.[1] There was, of course, pastureland that was privately owned—and in those cases only the owner had access to that land. However, everybody had access to the commons.

Indeed a common property resource is more than just a historical curiosity. In today's world, international waters (and the fish in them) form a common. The waters on the high seas, outside national boundaries, are commonly owned by all nations of the world, and so each one of these nations—or strictly speaking, fishing companies in

[1] *Indeed, even towns in the United States that were settled early—and presumably by Englishmen—have village commons. For instance, Morristown, New Jersey, has one. Only these days it is surrounded by Macy's and Wendy's with no cattle in sight!*

these nations—can fish freely in these waters. Perhaps the most important example of a common natural resource is the environment. Every one of us "owns" the environment (jointly) with everyone else. Usage of this common resource, by individuals or firms, adds pollution and greenhouse gases. For example, the burning of fossil fuels such as coal, oil, and natural gas adds carbon dioxide to the earth's atmosphere.

There are other examples that are not as immediate but that have the feature that everybody has access to the resource or commodity in question. Library books are commonly owned by all the students at any one college. Another (New York City) example is fire hydrants. Although these are meant to be used only by the fire department and only in an emergency, anybody who has spent a summer afternoon in the city knows that such an image is merely a myth perpetuated by the fire department. In actual fact, anybody can use the hydrants for some impromptu cooling off!

As the preceding discussion suggests, there are two critical characteristics of a commons:

- **Access to (nearly) everyone.** It is infeasible (think of the environment) or undesirable (think of National Parks) to restrict access.

- **Resource depletability.** The more people use the resource—or the more intensively each person uses the resource—the less there is of the resource in the future.

The second characteristic is worth a comment. The reason why we worry about commonly owned resources is precisely because they can be used over a long, long period of time—and by generations of our descendents—provided they are used in such a manner that they regenerate from time to time. The more fish are in the waters today, the more there will be a year from now. Conversely, the smaller is the buildup of carbon dioxide in the earth's atmosphere today, the less there will be 50 years from now. In other words, the result of our usage today bears a stamp well into the future. Of course this is not to say that the resource should not be used today at all; rather, the question is how much constitutes the "best" usage. And that brings us to the tragic part.

On account of the commonality of access, there are two sources of *externality* in the usage of such a common property resource or commodity: (1) a *current externality*—one person's usage may decrease the benefits to usage for other people—if you borrow a library book then I cannot use it today; and (2) a *future externality*—the condition in which you return the book determines how long the library will be able to keep it in circulation. Indeed, in many interesting problems—such as the environmental ones—the important externality is really the future externality. In this sense, this problem is different from the duopoly application of the previous chapter. In that application, overproduction by one firm generates an immediate externality for the other because it reduces the market price. However, this externality does not carry over into future market interactions.

The consequence of the fact that the resource is commonly owned is that it might get overused. This conjecture—or phenomenon, if indeed it is a correct conjecture—is

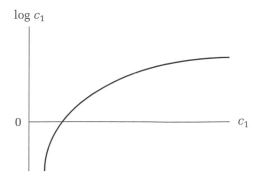

FIGURE 7.1

called the *tragedy of the commons*. The intuition for this conjecture is straightforward. Consider pollution. If your firm produces a chemical pollutant that it releases into the local river rather than treating it to remove the pollutant, you save yourself the costs of treatment. You—and everybody else in town—pay a cost for the polluted river, but this cost is shared among everyone. Hence, unless checked by regulation or your exemplary conscience, you have every incentive to dump that pollutant into the river waters. What is worse is that every other firm in town has exactly the same incentive to pollute. If you all ended up dumping your wastes in the river, the townspeople would have a very polluted river. They would have a tragedy of the commons.

7.2 A SIMPLE MODEL

Suppose that we have a common property resource of size $y > 0$. Each of two players can withdraw a nonnegative amount—c_1 or c_2—for consumption, provided of course that $c_1 + c_2 \leq y$. In the event that they attempt to consume in excess of what is available, suppose that the total amount is simply split between them; that is, each player ends up consuming $\frac{y}{2}$. When total consumption is less than y, then the leftover amount, $y - (c_1 + c_2)$, forms the future resource base, out of which comes future consumption. To keep matters simple, let us collapse the future into just one more period of consumption; that is, there are two time periods in this model.

In period 2, each player has to decide how much to consume out of the available quantity $y - (c_1 + c_2)$. Since there are no more periods left, there is no reason to save any fraction of the amount that is available in period 2. Each player would therefore like to consume as much as possible. Hence, in period 2, the total amount is divided among them—each gets $\frac{y-(c_1+c_2)}{2}$.

Now let us turn to period one. If player 1 were to consume an amount c_1, his utility from doing so will be taken to be $\log c_1$; that is, his utility of consumption looks like Figure 7.1.[2]

[2] *We assume that the Von Neumann–Morgenstern utility function is of this logarithmic form for computational simplicity alone. Much of what follows is true for any concave utility function.*

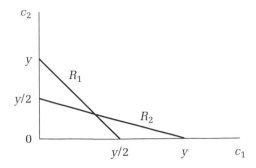

FIGURE 7.2

Player 1 has to determine how much he would like to consume out of the available stock of the resource. His utility depends on the amount that player 2 chooses to consume because the latter (partly) determines the size of the resource base that will be left over. As always, player 1 has a conjecture about player 2's consumption and determines his consumption level on that basis. In other words, Player 1's best response problem is

$$\text{Max}_{c_1} \ \log c_1 + \log \frac{y - (c_1 + \overline{c}_2)}{2}$$

where $\overline{c}_2$ is the amount that player 1 conjectures player 2 is going to consume in the first period. From the first-order conditions, player 1's best response consumption is[3]

$$\frac{1}{c_1} = \frac{1}{y - (c_1 + \overline{c}_2)}$$

or

$$c_1 = y - (c_1 + \overline{c}_2)$$

$$R_1(c_2) = \frac{y - c_2}{2}$$

CONCEPT CHECK

By similar logic, carefully derive the best response function of player 2 and show it to be

$$R_2(c_1) = \frac{y - c_1}{2}$$

The two reaction functions are pictured in Figure 7.2. The Nash equilibrium is therefore given by consumption levels c_1^* and c_2^* such that $R_1(c_2^*) = c_2^*$ and $R_2(c_1^*) = c_1^*$. Substituting into the reaction functions, we can compute the Nash equilibrium to be

[3] *The derivative of* $\log x$ *is* $\frac{1}{x}$*. The derivative of* $\log (ax + b)$ *is* $\frac{a}{ax+b}$*. (See Chapter 25.)*

$$c_1^* = c_2^* = \frac{y}{3}$$

In the first period, each player consumes $\frac{y}{3}$, leaving a total of $\frac{y}{3}$ for the second period, which is then split in half to yield a consumption of $\frac{y}{6}$ each in the second period. Each player's utility from this consumption pattern is $\log \frac{y}{3} + \log \frac{y}{6}$.

7.3 SOCIAL OPTIMALITY

In order to determine whether or not this equilibrium pattern constitutes a tragedy, let us see what pattern of resource use would constitute socially optimal usage. Let us define social optimality as follows: suppose that these two players constituted society and got together to decide how much they should each consume for the "common good." The common good is equivalent to making sure that the aggregate utility is maximized:

Definition. A pattern of consumption, $\widehat{c}_1, \widehat{c}_2$, is socially optimal if it maximizes the sum of the two players' utility, that is, if it solves the following problem:

$$\text{Max}_{c_1,c_2} \ \log c_1 + \log c_2 + 2 \log \frac{y - (c_1 + c_2)}{2}$$

This procedure leads to a socially optimal solution of

$$\widehat{c}_1 = \widehat{c}_2 = \frac{y}{4} \qquad\qquad\qquad\qquad \textbf{(7.1)}$$

CONCEPT CHECK

Write down the first-order conditions, one for $\widehat{c}_1$ and another for $\widehat{c}_2$, of the social optimality problem. Solve those conditions to derive the socially optimal levels of consumption, equation 7.1.

Note that in this case, exactly half of the resource is used in the first period—in contrast to the Nash equilibrium where as much as two-thirds of the resource is used up in the first period.[4] In this sense we have an overextraction of the resource in the Nash equilibrium; that is, we have a tragedy of the commons.

The reason for this overextraction is precisely the externalities discussed previously. Notice that if player 1 were to cut back his consumption in the first period by one unit, he makes this one unit available for consumption by both players in the second period. He is, however, able to recover only half of this unit as additional consumption in the second period, because the other half accrues to player 2. Consequently, player 1—and by extension both players—tends to overconsume. This phenomenon does not arise in the socially optimal solution, however, because in that solution we

[4] *It should be clear that in the socially optimal solution, each player then consumes a quarter of the resource in the second period as well.*

care about the utilities of both players. A unit of consumption set aside for tomorrow—by either player—continues to be a unit of consumption for society as a whole in the second period. Hence, there is no externality that distorts first-period consumption.

7.4 THE PROBLEM WORSENS IN A LARGE POPULATION

To fix these ideas even more firmly, let us see what happens in this example as the number of players increases. The intuition would be that this increase makes the tragedy even more acute. The reason is that if player 1 forgoes a unit of consumption in the first period, he is able to retrieve only $\frac{1}{N}$ of that unit as consumption in the next period (where N is the number of players). That should make player 1 even less willing to set aside any resource for the future.

If player 1 conjectures that the others will consume an amount $\overline{c}$ in the first period, then his utility-maximizing consumption is determined from the following optimization problem:

$$\text{Max } \log c_1 + \log \frac{y - [c_1 + (N-1)\overline{c}]}{N} \tag{7.2}$$

From the first-order conditions, player 1's best response consumption is

$$\frac{1}{c_1} = \frac{1}{y - [c_1 + (N-1)\overline{c}]} \tag{7.3}$$

In the Nash equilibrium in which each player consumes the same amount, that is, $c_1 = \overline{c}$, it follows from equation 7.3 that the equilibrium consumption level is

$$c_1 = c_2 = \cdots = \frac{y}{N+1} \tag{7.4}$$

CONCEPT CHECK

Derive equations 7.2, 7.3, and 7.4.

The total consumption in a Nash equilibrium is therefore $\frac{N}{N+1}y$. Consequently, the amount that remains after the first period is $\frac{y}{N+1}$. As N becomes large, a vanishingly small amount of the resource reaches the second period. *The tragedy of the commons is exacerbated in large populations.*

CONCEPT CHECK
SOCIAL OPTIMALITY

Show that in order to maximize the total utility of all players, consumption should be

$$c_1 = c_2 = \cdots = \frac{y}{2N}$$

In other words, society would always like half the resource to be saved for the future, no matter how many members there are in society. This result should also be intuitive. A unit of consumption withheld from social consumption today is always available as a unit of consumption in the future, regardless of how many members there are in society. So the conclusion that half of the total resource should be withheld for social consumption in the future is a result that is independent of the number of players.

7.5   CASE STUDIES: BUFFALO, GLOBAL WARMING, AND THE INTERNET

A very popular historical example of the tragedy of the commons is that of the *buffalo in the American West*. Till the middle of the 19th century great herds of American buffalo roamed the Great Plains. They were a commons in that any hunter could hunt them down if he so desired. Starting in the middle of the century, the hunting grew increasingly widespread and effective, and the buffalo herds had a more and more difficult time regenerating. By the end of the century many of these sprawling herds had disappeared. Here is a commentary on their usage:

> The Plains Indians very eagerly accepted modern technology in the form of horses, guns and steel tools. . . . By 1840 the Indian had driven the buffalo from portions of the Great Plains area and there is evidence of concern about this problem. . . . Given multiple tribes and the fact of no real cooperation, the Indians were incapable of managing the buffalo as a common pool resource. . . . The benefits from harvesting one more buffalo accrue to the individual hunter, while the costs of depletion of the herd are spread among all hunters. The true costs of hunting are not borne by the hunter and overuse is predictable. (American Indians: A Test of the Conservation Ethic, *by John Baden, Rick Stroup and Walter Thurman).*[5]

[5] *As quoted in* Costs of Innovation in the Commons, *September 1996, by Douglas Noonan, mimeo, Foundation for Research on the Economics and the Environment.*

Here is a more recent example, *global warming*. Much of the energy that is produced to heat our homes, drive our cars, or produce our economy's goods and services comes from carbon sources. It comes from burning coal, oil, or natural gas. This combustion releases carbon dioxide into the earth's atmosphere and (although some of it is broken down by plant photosynthesis) much of it remains in the atmosphere. Carbon dioxide (and certain other "greenhouse gases") traps heat, in much the same way that a greenhouse does. Imagine then the total amount of carbon dioxide in the atmosphere as a common pool, since it is this total that determines temperatures all over the world. Each individual or firm—or simply, each nation—adds to this stock of carbon dioxide by its energy consumption. Whereas the benefits to this energy consumption—a higher national output, or a better standard of living—are entirely experienced by the energy user, the costs—hotter temperatures and consequent climatic and economic dislocation—are shared by everyone. Scientists say that average surface temperatures have risen between 1 and 2°F in the last 200 years and, more alarmingly, can arise another 4 to 8°F in the next 100 years if present trends of carbon dioxide buildup continue.[6]

Here is another recent example; let us call it the *Internet jam*. Starting in the summer of 1996, a number of online companies started offering a fixed-monthly-rate service; you pay a fixed rate, say $19.99, for the month, and you can gain access to the Internet as many times and for as long as you want that month. Under the pricing practice that existed before, consumers were charged an hourly rate for Internet access.[7] Note that since customers use phone lines to access the Internet, the resources of the phone system—the switches, the lines, and so on—can be thought of as a commons for all Internet users.[8] Once the monthly fee has been paid, it is a sunk cost; that is, it is as if Internet access is a free good. It is not of course free for society, since there is a fixed capacity for the phone lines. Unsurprisingly, phone systems were completely overloaded, systems broke down several times, and some customers complained of having to wait up to an hour before they could get through to the Internet.[9]

7.6   AVERTING A TRAGEDY

The question that many economists and other social scientists grapple with is how to balance the private desire for utility or profits against the social imperative of sustainable resource use. Many (incomplete) solutions have been proposed to deal with the tragedy of the commons. Some economists favor a privatization of the resource ownership. Privatization is clearly a solution that has been employed, up to a point, for land. There is no longer a common pasture in villages, nor are there common town centers in suburban developments.[10] Privatization would certainly remove the externality inherent in the common ownership of the resource. (Why?) The problem with privatization is that it simultaneously takes away the common access to usage that may be desirable for a variety of other reasons. Furthermore, for some resources—such as the environment—it is not even a practical solution.

Other economists have proposed a tax or fee for usage. This is the solution that is most widely used when dealing with pollution. It is also the solution that is used in

[6] More details on global warming can be found in an authoritative report of the Inter-Governmental Panel on Climate Change, Climate Change 95: The IPCC Scientific Assessment New York: Cambridge University Press, 1995.

[7] The most significant switch came when the biggest access provider, America Online, started offering the new service in October 1996. Details on this story can be found in the New York Times, December 17, 1996.

[8] In the United States, some estimates put the number of people accessing the Internet at 50 million—and growing.

[9] In a development that only makes the tragedy of the commons worse, there is now software that will keep redialing for you and, once you get access, will keep you logged on while you sleep, go to class, or attend to the other duties of your daily life! (See the Times article referenced in note 7 for further details.)

[10] There is, of course, the ubiquitous shopping mall.

National Parks. The problem here is that assessing fees is an inefficient solution whenever the marginal cost of production is near zero. In other words, if the cost of allowing one more person into the park is virtually zero, then that person should not be charged a high fee. Put differently, a fee of $5 would simply discourage from coming to the park a person who is only able to pay $2 (or who only derives a utility of $2 from using the park). This approach would be inefficient if the actual extra cost of cleanup is 10 cents. A desirable fee would be one that varies with the number of users, charging more as the park becomes more and more crowded. A proxy to this scheme is one that charges different fees for different times of the year (or even different times of day). The problem with these schemes is that they are more complicated to implement.

A third solution that has been proposed is to simply put a ceiling on the number of users of the resource. The size of the ceiling could be designed in such a manner that the resource is able to regenerate itself. For instance, park rangers close off Yosemite National Park in the middle of the afternoon if they determine that too many people have already entered the park that day. The same inefficiency problem discussed in the previous paragraph also plagues this solution. Yet from a long-term standpoint either of these last two solutions can be better than an unregulated tragedy of the commons.

It should be noted that the model analyzed in this chapter can be generalized in a variety of ways without changing the qualitative flavor of the result. First, we only analyzed an *exhaustible resource* problem; the amount of the resource that remains at the end of the first period, say, x, is precisely the amount available for consumption in the second period. However, the analysis carries over to a *renewable resource* model, that is, a model in which the amount x becomes something larger, say, $f(x) > x$, by the start of the second period. It is still true that there is a future externality because sacrificing a unit of consumption yields a player only half of the consequent increase in second-period resource stock. Hence, she overconsumes in the first period.

A second direction in which the model can be generalized is to allow several future periods or more general utility functions. Again the basic externality is unchanged and so therefore is the tragedy. Indeed in Chapter 18 you will see just such a generalization.

SUMMARY

1. A common (resource or commodity) has two characteristics: it is accessible to everyone, and its amount depletes upon usage.

2. In the Nash equilibrium of a commons game, each player overuses the resource because he gets all of the immediate benefits from usage and bears only a fraction of the future costs of depletion.

3. In a socially optimal solution, there is enough of the resource set aside for desirable regeneration.

4. The tragedy of the commons is exacerbated in large populations.

5. There are many real-world illustrations of the tragedy of the commons; the historical extinction of the American buffalo and the current possibility of global warming are two such examples.

6. Various solutions have been proposed to avert a tragedy. They include privatization, taxes or user fees, and limits to accessibility.

EXERCISES

SECTION 7.1

7.1
Give an example of a resource, natural or otherwise, to which there is not common access, that is, a resource that only selected people can use.

7.2
Give an example of a resource, natural or otherwise, that is not depletable, that is, a resource that does not deplete in quantity (for all practical purposes) when more people use the resource.

7.3
Is there a tragedy of the commons in either of your examples? Does a resource have to be commonly accessible and depletable for it to be overused?

7.4
Are the resources devoted to public education an example of a common property resource? Explain.

7.5
From your daily life can you think of a tragedy of the commons phenomenon? Explain your answer.

SECTION 7.2

(Calculus problem)   The resource that we analyzed in the text is an exhaustible resource. To see that the phenomenon of the tragedy of the commons can also arise if the resource is *renewable*, consider the following variant of the model in the text. Each player extracts an amount c_i in the first period, $i = 1, 2$. Whatever is not extracted, that is, the amount $y - c_1 - c_2$, regenerates and becomes an amount equal to $\sqrt{y - c_1 - c_2}$ in period 2.[11] The rest of the model will be identical to that in the text; in particular, the utility function will be log c, and the allocation rule (if the total desired is more than what is available) will be to give half to each player.

7.6

Write down the best response problem for player 1.

7.7

Show that the best response function is given by[12]

$$R_1(c_2) = \frac{2(y - c_2)}{3}$$

7.8

Compute the Nash equilibrium.

(Calculus problem)   In the next few questions, we will walk you through a *private property* version of the common property model that is analyzed in the chapter. Suppose that we have two (duopoly) firms and they each own a homogeneous resource, such as a forest or a fishing pool, of size 25. Each of them can withdraw any nonnegative amount, c or d, in the first period, provided of course that $c \leq 25$, $d \leq 25$. There are two periods, and whatever is not extracted in the first period is extracted in the second. Finally, the extracted amounts are sold in a (common) market whose demand curve is given by

$$p = 100 - Q$$

where Q is the total amount extracted in any period. Assume that each firm is a profit maximizer and that costs of production are zero.

7.9

Write down the strategic form of this game.

7.10

What is the best response for firm 1 if it thinks that firm 2 will produce 7.5 units of output? What is the best response function of firm 1? (In answering this question, you will need to use the facts that profits are maximized when the slope of the profit function is zero and that the slope of a quadratic function $a + bx - cx^2$ is $b - 2cx$).

7.11

What is the Nash equilibrium extraction levels in period 1? period 2? What about market price?

[11] *In order that the resource is seen to grow, that is, in order for $\sqrt{y - c_1 - c_2}$ to be greater than $y - c_1 - c_2$, we will make the assumption that $y \leq 1$. This is simply an accounting convention; if the actual maximum amount is 100 we would simply consider a regeneration function like $\sqrt{100} \times \sqrt{y - c_1 - c_2}$.*

[12] *Use the fact that $\log \sqrt{x}$ is the same as $\frac{1}{2} \log x$.*

SECTION 7.3

7.12

Set up and solve the social optimality problem in the renewable resource problem. Show that the socially optimal extraction is $\frac{V}{3}$ for each player.

7.13

Explain why exercise 7.12 differs from the exhaustible resource model in which the socially optimal extraction is $\frac{V}{4}$ for each player.

7.14

In the private property model, how would your answers change if the firms operated as a cartel? Explain your answer carefully.

SECTION 7.4

7.15

Analyze the renewable resource problem for N players. Is it true that all of the resource is extracted in the first period if N approaches infinity?

7.16

Analyze the private property resource problem for N players. Is it true that the price of the resource is driven to zero as the number of firms increases without bound? Explain very carefully any assumptions that you make in order to do your analysis.

SECTION 7.6

7.17

Explain why privatizing the common resource would solve the overextraction problem.

7.18

Consider the *Internet jam* problem. Suggest a solution that would avert a tragedy in that case. Is the solution you propose in the interests of the online companies to implement? If so, speculate on why they have not done something similar already.

CHAPTER 8

MIXED STRATEGIES

This chapter will present a more general class of strategies, called *mixed strategies,* that players can profitably employ. We will define these strategies precisely in section 8.1.1 and present a few examples in section 8.1.2. In section 8.2 we will discuss an important implication of using mixed strategies. Sections 8.3, 8.4, and 8.5 will give three different answers to the question, Why would players in a game ever want to use mixed strategies? Finally, in section 8.6, we will see a *case study of random drug testing* that involves mixed strategies.

8.1   DEFINITION AND EXAMPLES

8.1.1   WHAT IS A MIXED STRATEGY?

Suppose that you are playing the game Battle of the Sexes. Seemingly, you have only one of two choices to make—go to the football game or the opera. Actually, those are *not* the only choices you have. For instance, you can toss a coin. If it comes up heads you can go to the football game, whereas if it comes up tails you can go to the opera instead. Hence, you have at least *three* strategies to choose from: (a) football, (b) opera, and (c) a coin toss, that is, a strategy with an equal likelihood of going to football or opera.

Notice that *after* the coin has been tossed, you will end up doing one or the other—football or opera. In that sense, the coin toss has not enlarged the set of eventual actions available to you. However, it has clearly enlarged the set of initial choices; strategy c is evidently distinct from a or b. *Before* the coin lands, you are not sure—and neither is your spouse—whether you will be at the game or at the opera house.

Strategies a and b—as well as every other strategy that we have discussed so far—are called *pure strategies*. A strategy such as c is called a *mixed strategy*. Indeed, strategy c is just one of many mixed strategies. For every distinct likelihood of football versus opera, there is a corresponding mixed strategy. For instance, there is a mixed strategy in which football is twice as likely an eventual choice as the opera; this corresponds to a strategy in which the probability of playing the pure strategy football is $\frac{2}{3}$ while the probability of playing opera is $\frac{1}{3}$.[1]

Definition. Suppose a player has M pure strategies, $s^1, s^2, \ldots, s^M$. A mixed strategy for this player is a probability distribution over his pure strategies; that is, it is a probability vector $(p^1, p^2, \ldots, p^M)$, with $p^k \geq 0$, $k = 1, \ldots, M$, and $\sum_{k=1}^{M} p^k = 1$.

A particularly simple mixed strategy is one in which each pure strategy is equally likely, that is, $p^k = \frac{1}{M}$. This would correspond to writing down the numbers $1, \ldots, M$ on separate (equal-sized!) pieces of paper, folding up the pieces, and getting your roommate to pick one for you. It is not necessary that each pure strategy have a positive probability in a mixed strategy. For example, you can write down the numbers $1, \ldots, M - 1$ and repeat the procedure. The corresponding mixed strategy is, $p^k = \frac{1}{M-1}$, $k = 1, \ldots, M - 1$ and $p^M = 0$. Similarly it is not necessary that the pure strategies that are assigned positive probabilities are all picked with equal probability. For instance, you could have written the number 1 on two of the original M scraps and omitted, say, the number 2. Then you would have constructed a mixed strategy for which $p^1 = \frac{2}{M}$, $p^2 = 0$, and $p^k = \frac{1}{M}$, $k = 3, \ldots, M$.

Every pure strategy is—in a trivial sense—also a mixed strategy. For instance, the pure strategy s^1 is equivalent to the mixed strategy in which $p^1 = 1$ and $p^k = 0$ for all other pure strategies.

The next question is, How should a mixed strategy's payoffs be evaluated? Recall that the payoffs in a game are Von Neumann–Morgenstern utilities. Hence, from the expected utility theorem of Chapter 27 it follows that the right way to evaluate the uncertainty inherent in a mixed strategy is to take its *expected payoff.* Expected payoffs are computed in two steps:

- **Step 1.** Weight the payoff to each pure strategy by the probability with which that strategy is played.

- **Step 2.** Add up the weighted payoffs.

Consider the following strategy pair in the Battle of the Sexes: the husband goes to the opera with probability $\frac{1}{3}$, while his wife plays the pure strategy football. The payoff matrix of the game is

[1] *For a discussion of probabilities and expectation, see Chapter 26. Before reading any further, you should make sure that you have a good understanding of that chapter.*

Husband \ Wife	F	O
F	3, 1	0, 0
O	0, 0	1, 3

For this pair of strategies, the likelihood that both spouses go to the football game is $\frac{2}{3}$, while the probability of the husband going by himself to the opera is $\frac{1}{3}$. These two probabilities should be multiplied by the corresponding payoffs, respectively, 3 and 0, and then added. Hence, the husband's expected payoff is

$$\text{Expected payoff} = \left[\frac{2}{3} \times 3\right] + \left[\frac{1}{3} \times 0\right] = 2$$

On the other hand, if the wife plays the pure strategy opera, then the husband's expected payoff is

$$\text{Expected payoff} = \left[\frac{2}{3} \times 0\right] + \left[\frac{1}{3} \times 1\right] = \frac{1}{3}$$

Note that the expected payoff is different for the husband in the second case; this computation illustrates the somewhat obvious point that a mixed strategy's payoff depends on the strategies chosen by the other players.

Finally, suppose the wife also plays a mixed strategy; she is equally likely to go to the football game or the opera. Since the probability of any pair of pure strategies being chosen is the product of the probability of each strategy, the probability that husband and wife both end up at the football game is $\frac{2}{3} \times \frac{1}{2}$. The expected payoff to the husband is therefore

$$\text{Expected payoff} = \left[\frac{1}{3} \times 3\right] + \left[\frac{1}{6} \times 0\right] + \left[\frac{1}{3} \times 0\right] + \left[\frac{1}{6} \times 1\right]$$
$$= \frac{7}{6}$$

Definition. Suppose that player i plays a mixed strategy $(p^1, p^2, \ldots, p^M)$. Suppose that the other players play the pure strategy $s_{-i}^{\#}$. Then the expected payoff to player i is equal to

$$p^1 \times \pi_i(s^1, s_{-i}^{\#}) + p^2 \times \pi_i(s^2, s_{-i}^{\#}) + \cdots + p^M \times \pi_i(s^M, s_{-i}^{\#})$$

Definition. Now suppose that the other players play a mixed strategy themselves; say, the strategy $s_{-i}^{\#}$ is played with probability q while s_{-i}^{*} is played with probability $1 - q$. Then the expected payoff to player i is equal to

$$\left[p^1 q \times \pi_i(s^1, s_{-i}^{\#}) + \cdots + p^M q \times \pi_i(s^M, s_{-i}^{\#})\right]$$
$$+ \left[p^1(1 - q) \times \pi_i(s^1, s_{-i}^{*}) + \cdots + p^M(1 - q) \times \pi_i(s^M, s_{-i}^{*})\right]$$
(8.1)

In equation 8.1 we have used the fact that the likelihood that the pair of pure strategies $(s^1, s_{-i}^{\#})$ gets played is given by $p^1 q$ and likewise the probability that the pair $(s^M, s_{-i}^{\#})$ gets played is given by $p^M q$, and so on. By collecting the common terms, equation 8.1 can be written more compactly as

$$\left[p^1 \times \pi_i(s^1, s^{\#}_{-i}) + \cdots + p^M \times \pi_i(s^M, s^{\#}_{-i}) \right] q$$
$$+ \left[p^1 \times \pi_i(s^1, s^*_{-i}) + \cdots + p^M \times \pi_i(s^M, s^*_{-i}) \right] (1 - q)$$

(8.2)

8.1.2 YET MORE EXAMPLES

In each example we will focus on player 1 and write out in detail his mixed strategies and their expected payoffs. Symmetric computations can be done for the other player(s), and you should be sure to do them as practice.

Example 1: Matching Pennies (h = heads, t = tails)

Player 1 \ Player 2 h t

h 1, −1   −1, 1

t −1, 1   1, −1

Consider the mixed strategy in which player 1 plays h with probability $\frac{2}{3}$ while player 2 plays t for sure. Then, player 1's expected payoff is $\frac{2}{3} \times (-1) + \frac{1}{3} \times 1 = -\frac{1}{3}$. More generally, suppose that player 1 plays h with probability p while player 2 plays t for sure. Then, player 1's expected payoff is $p \times (-1) + (1 - p) \times 1 = 1 - 2p$.

COMPUTATION CHECK

Show that if player 1 plays h with probability p while 2 plays h for sure, then player 1's expected payoff is $2p - 1$. What are player 2's expected payoffs?

Example 2: Hawk-Dove (or Chicken) (t = tough, c = concede)

Player 1 \ Player 2 t c

t −1, −1   10, 0

c 0, 10   5, 5

Consider the mixed strategy in which player 1 plays t with probability $\frac{9}{11}$ while player 2 plays t for sure. Then, player 1's expected payoff is $\frac{9}{11} \times (-1) + \frac{2}{11} \times 0 = -\frac{9}{11}$. On the other hand, suppose that player 1 continues to play t with probability $\frac{9}{11}$ but player 2 plays c for sure. Then, player 1's expected payoff is $\frac{9}{11} \times 10 + \frac{2}{11} \times 5 = \frac{100}{11}$.

ANOTHER COMPUTATION CHECK

Show that if player 1 plays t with probability $\frac{9}{11}$ while player 2 plays t with probability $\frac{3}{5}$, then player 1's expected payoff is $\frac{173}{55}$. What are player 2's expected payoffs in this case?

Example 3: No-Name

Player 1 \ Player 2	L	M_1	M_2	R
U	1, 0	4, 2	2, 4	3, 1
M	2, 4	2, 0	2, 2	2, 1
D	4, 2	1, 4	2, 0	3, 1

THIRD COMPUTATION CHECK

Suppose that player 1 plays U, M, D with probabilities .2, .3, and .5, respectively, while player 2 plays L and M_2 with probabilities .4 and .6. Show that player 1's expected payoffs equal 2.32. What about player 2's expected payoffs?

Finally, suppose that player 1 plays U, M, D with probabilities p^1, p^2, and p^3, respectively,[2] while player 2 plays L and M_2 with probabilities q and $1 - q$. Player 1's expected payoffs are then given as

$$\text{Expected payoff} = q\left(p^1 \times 1 + p^2 \times 2 + p^3 \times 4\right) + (1 - q)\left(p^1 \times 2 + p^2 \times 2 + p^3 \times 2\right)$$

$$= q\left(p^1 \times 1 + p^2 \times 2 + p^3 \times 4\right) + 2(1 - q)$$

8.2 AN IMPLICATION

In this section, we will discuss an implication of using mixed rather than pure strategies. In order to do so, we will need one more definition.

Definition. Consider a mixed strategy given by the probability vector $(p^1, p^2, \ldots, p^M)$. The support of this mixed strategy is given by all those pure strategies that have a positive probability of getting played (in this strategy).

For example, if $p^1 > 0$ and $p^3 > 0$ but $p^k = 0$ for all other k, then the support of this mixed strategy is made up of the pure strategies 1 and 3.

The expected payoff to a mixed strategy is simply an average of the component pure-strategy payoffs in the support of this mixed strategy. If the payoffs to each of the pure strategies in the support are not the same, then deleting all but the pure strategies that have the maximum payoff must increase the average, that is, must increase the expected payoff. In other words, if strategies s^1 and s^3 yield the highest payoff against, say, $s^\#_{-i}$, then a mixed strategy that only involves these two pure strategies will yield a higher expected payoff than one that also involves strategies $s^2, s^4, \ldots, s^M$.

[2] *Of course, p^3 must equal $1 - p^1 - p^2$. (Why?)*

Implication.   (a) A mixed strategy $(p^1, p^2, \ldots, p^M)$ is a *best response* to $s^{\#}_{-i}$ if and only if each of the pure strategies in its support is itself a best response to $s^{\#}_{-i}$. (b) In that case, *any* mixed strategy over this support will be a best response.

Regarding part b of the implication, note that if each of the remaining strategies in the support is a best response, then each yields the same payoff. Hence any average of these strategies will also yield exactly the same payoff; that is, any mixture of these strategies must also be a best response.

Consider the No-Name game of example 3:

Player 1 \ Player 2	L	M_1	M_2	R
U	1, 0	4, 2	2, 4	3, 1
M	2, 4	2, 0	2, 2	2, 1
D	4, 2	1, 4	2, 0	3, 1

Take the column player's strategy to be R. The implication simply says that a mixed strategy involving U and M is worse than U alone. It further says that *any* mixed strategy that has U and D as its support is a best response.

Why would a player in any game use a mixed strategy? In the next three sections we will give three related reasons. The common observation in all three situations is that by doing so, a player may "do better" than she would do by playing *some* of the pure strategies that she has available to her, and sometimes she may even "do better" than all of her pure strategies.

8.3   MIXED STRATEGIES CAN DOMINATE SOME PURE STRATEGIES

Let us start with the most unambiguous notion of doing better—a strategy does better than an alternative if it *dominates* the latter. We will now see an example in which there is a mixed strategy that dominates a pure strategy, say $\widehat{s}$, even though no other pure strategy is able to dominate $\widehat{s}$. The example is in fact the No-Name game.

It is clear that no pure strategy dominates any other pure strategy in the No-Name game. Consider now the mixed strategy in which player 1 plays U and D with equal probabilities of $\frac{1}{2}$. By playing this strategy, player 1 can *guarantee* herself an expected payoff of at least 2 and possibly more. Note that if player 2 plays either L or M_1, then the mixed strategy yields an expected payoff of 2.5, whereas if 2 plays R then the mixed strategy's payoff is 3. The only time that the mixed strategy yields an expected payoff exactly equal to 2 is when player 2 plays M_2. On the other hand, by playing the pure strategy M, player 1 always gets a payoff equal to 2. We can conclude, therefore, that the mixed strategy dominates the pure strategy M.[3]

[3] *Since we are considering mixed strategies, the definition of dominance needs to be carefully specified. We say that a mixed strategy p dominates another mixed strategy p' if $\pi_i(p, s_{-i}) \geq \pi_i(p', s_{-i})$, for all s_{-i}, and $\pi_i(p, \widehat{s}_{-i}) > \pi_i(p', \widehat{s}_{-i})$, for some $\widehat{s}_{-i}$, where $\pi_i(p, \widehat{s}_{-i})$ denotes the expected payoff $p^1 \times \pi_i(s^1, \widehat{s}_{-i}) + p^2 \times \pi_i(s^2, \widehat{s}_{-i}) + \cdots + p^M \times \pi_i(s^M, \widehat{s}_{-i})$ [with a similar definition for $\pi_i(p', \widehat{s}_{-i})$].*

CONCEPT CHECK
OTHERS?

Are there any other mixed strategies for player 1 that also dominate M? Make sure you detail them!

The intuition for the preceding conclusion is quite straightforward. Notice that player 1 does very well by playing U whenever player 2 plays M_1 but does rather poorly if player 2 plays L. Strategy D is exactly the opposite: it does very well against L but poorly against M_1. Playing U and D with equal probabilities allows player 1 to "insure" herself: no matter what player 2 does, player 1 is equally likely to do well or poorly; that is, she guarantees herself a superior outcome to that under M.

CONCEPT CHECK
OTHER PLAYER

Show that for player 2, the mixed strategy L, M_1, M_2 with equal probabilities dominates the pure strategy R.

So this is the first of our three reasons for playing a mixed strategy rather than *some* of the available pure strategies:

Reason 1. A mixed strategy may dominate some pure strategies (that are themselves undominated by other pure strategies).

8.3.1 IMPLICATIONS FOR DOMINANT STRATEGY SOLUTION AND IEDS

Adding mixed strategies changes absolutely nothing with regard to the dominant strategy solution. If there is a pure strategy that dominates every other pure strategy, then it must also dominate every other mixed strategy. (Why?) However, if there is no dominant strategy in pure strategies, there cannot be one in mixed strategies either. (Why?)

Mixed strategies do make a difference, however, for the IEDS solution concept. They do make a difference in the sense that a game that ostensibly has no IEDS solution when only pure strategies are considered can have an IEDS solution in mixed strategies. Consider the No-Name game. We have already seen that the strategies M for player 1 and R for player 2 are dominated (by mixed strategies). Ruling them out, we are left with the following payoff matrix:

Player 1 \ Player 2	L	M_1	M_2
U	1, 0	4, 2	2, 4
D	4, 2	1, 4	2, 0

In turn L is now dominated (by M_1), and removing L leads to D becoming dominated for player 1. That in turn leads player 2 to eliminate M_1; the IEDS solution is therefore (U, M_2). Had we not examined mixed strategies we would not have found this IEDS solution.[4]

However, whenever a game has an IEDS solution in pure strategies, that solution will also be the mixed strategy IEDS.

8.4   MIXED STRATEGIES ARE GOOD FOR BLUFFING

We turn now to a second reason why a player may want to use a mixed strategy. The idea can be explained quite simply by employing a sports analogy: an unpredictable player is better able to keep his opponent off balance.

Imagine that you are playing the effete East Coast game of squash. In the middle of a rally you have to decide whether to position your next shot (softly) in the *front* of the court or hit it (hard) to the *back*. Your opponent likewise has to move in anticipation of your shot; he could start moving *forward* or *backward*. Of course, if he does move forward, he is likely to finish off the rally if you dropped your shot in front, but you are likely to win if you did in fact hit the hard shot behind him. If he moves backward, converse reasoning applies. In the following table are displayed your chances of winning the rally in the four possible cases:

	Forward (F)	Backward (B)
Front (f)	.2	.8
Back (b)	.7	.3

[4] *You might wonder why it is that we only eliminated pure—and not mixed—strategies while finding the IEDS outcome. Actually we did implicitly eliminate mixed strategies as well. For example consider step 2; we eliminated the pure strategy L because it is dominated at that point by M_1. However, any mixed strategy containing L and M_1 is also dominated by M_1. Hence those mixed strategies can also be eliminated. By similar reasoning one can show that all mixed strategies are eliminated in the process of reaching the IEDS outcome (U, M_2).*

Suppose that you picked the strategy *front* (hereafter f). If your opponent correctly guessed that you were going to make this choice—alternatively, if in every rally you play f—then he will move *forward* (F) and he will win 80 percent of the rallies. By the same logic, if you *always* picked b, or if this choice was correctly guessed, you would only win 30 percent of the rallies. What happens, though, if you occasionally bluff— half the time you go f (and the other half b)? If your opponent goes forward, you win 45 percent (the average of 20% and 70%) of the rallies, while if he goes *backward,* you win 55 percent of the rallies. In other words, even though your opponent is correctly guessing (that you go f with probability $\frac{1}{2}$), you nevertheless win at least 45 percent of your rallies. This outcome is in contrast with either of the pure strategies where your opponent could hold you down to either 20 percent or 30 percent wins.

The intuition is also straightforward; if you are predictable, your opponent can pick the move that will kill you (and win the game). If you are unpredictable—that is, if you use a mixed strategy—he has no one move that is a sure winner. If he goes F, he gives up on your shots to the back, and if he goes B he conversely loses when you hit to the front. You could conceivably do even better than a 50–50 mix. In Chapter 10 we will examine the following question: In what proportions should you mix between f and b so that you have the highest guaranteed probability of winning?

That mixed strategies are good for bluffing is true more generally. Consider the No-Name game again (and from the perspective of player 2). If she plays the pure strategy L, then her lowest possible payoff is 0 (which happens when player 1 picks U against her). Similarly, the lowest payoff from the pure strategies M_1 and M_2 is also 0, while that from playing R is 1. Now consider instead the mixed strategy that places probabilities $\frac{1}{3}$ each on L, M_1, and M_2. In the previous section, we saw that the expected payoff of this mixed strategy is 2, regardless of what player 1 does. In other words, mixing *guarantees* a higher payoff than not mixing; its worst-case outcome is better than the worst-case outcome of any of the pure strategies.

Again the intuition is that if player 2 plays a pure strategy—no matter whether it is L or M_1 or M_2 or R—there is something that player 1 can do that would be terrible for player 2's payoffs. By mixing, player 2 can avoid a disaster; no matter what player 1 does, $\frac{1}{3}$ of the time player 2 is very happy, $\frac{1}{3}$ of the time she is fairly happy, and only $\frac{1}{3}$ of the time is she faced with a disastrous payoff of 0.

So this is the second of our three reasons.

Reason 2. The worst-case payoff of a mixed strategy may be better than the worst-case payoff of every pure strategy.

8.5 MIXED STRATEGIES AND NASH EQUILIBRIUM

Without mixed strategies, Nash equilibria need not always exist. Recall the game of matching pennies:

	H	T
H	$1, -1$	$-1, 1$
T	$-1, 1$	$1, -1$

Note that $b^1(H) = H$ and $b^1(T) = T$, but $b^2(H) = T$ and $b^2(T) = H$. So in this game (it appears as if) there is no Nash equilibrium.

Suppose now that player 1 plays a mixed strategy: (H, p); that is, with probability p he plays H (and with remaining probability $1 - p$ he plays T). Player 2's expected payoff from playing a pure strategy H is[5]

$$E\pi(H) = p(-1) + (1-p)1 = 1 - 2p$$

[5] Note that $E\pi(H)$ denotes the expected payoff to the strategy H.

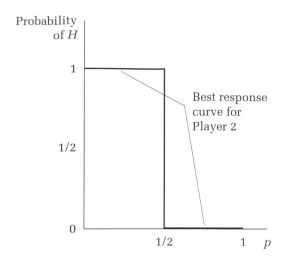

Probability
of H

1

1/2

0

1/2   1 p

Best response
curve for
Player 2

FIGURE 8.1

Likewise the payoff to playing T is

$$E\pi(T) = p(1) + (1-p)(-1) = 2p - 1$$

Evidently, H has a higher expected payoff than T if and only if $p < \frac{1}{2}$. At $p = \frac{1}{2}$ both pure strategies yield the same expected payoff, and hence by the implication of section 8.2, the best response of player 2 is any mixed strategy. The best response can therefore be represented in Figure 8.1.

Hence, if player 2 were to play the strategy $(H, \frac{1}{2})$ herself, she would be playing a best response to the strategy $(H, \frac{1}{2})$. In other words, this pair of mixed strategies constitute a Nash equilibrium.

The intuition for the preceding analysis is straightforward as well. In matching pennies no matter what pure strategy combination we examine, one of the players always has an incentive to change his strategy; player 1 is always trying to match, while player 2 is always trying to mismatch. However, a mixed strategy can help. If player 1 mixes between heads and tails (with equal probabilities), then player 2 can do no better by switching from H to T (or vice versa). Half the time she inevitably matches in either case. A similar logic applies to player 1's choices if player 2 mixes between H and T with equal probabilities.

This reasoning brings us to the final imperative for considering mixed strategies.

Reason 3. If we restrict ourselves to pure strategies, we may not be able to find a Nash equilibrium to a game.

In Chapter 28, "Existence of Nash Equilibria" we will see a general result that says that in strategic form games there is always a Nash equilibrium in mixed strategies.

Despite all these arguments in favor of the use of mixed strategies, I should point out that many economists and game theorists remain skeptical about their usefulness. Part of the skepticism stems from a belief that people do not actually toss coins or use other forms of randomization in their day-to-day lives to make decisions. (Do you?) Another reason to view Nash equilibria in mixed strategies with some skepticism is that although individual players may in fact use mixed strategies, it seems heroic to assume that their opponents are able to correctly conjecture the exact probabilities that are being used by those players. The Nash equilibrium logic requires opponents to do just that.

There is an alternative interpretation of a mixed-strategy Nash equilibrium that was first pointed out by the Nobel laureate John Harsanyi in 1973.[6] Imagine the following scenario: Each player is unsure about exactly whom he is playing against. For instance, in a two-player game, player 1 may be unsure about player 2's payoffs; these payoffs might be either $\pi_2 - b$ or $\pi_2 + b$. Suppose a high-payoff player 2 is expected to play a (pure) strategy s that is different from the (pure) strategy that a low-payoff player 2 is expected to play—say s'. If high and low payoffs are equally likely, it is *as if* player 1 is facing a mixed strategy with equal probabilities on s and s'. Although each player actually plays a pure strategy, to the opponents—and an outside observer—it appears as if mixed strategies are being played.

8.5.1 MIXED-STRATEGY NASH EQUILIBRIA IN AN EXAMPLE

Consider the Battle of the Sexes. We have already seen that there are two asymmetric pure strategy Nash equilibria in this game: (F, O) and (O, F) yielding payoffs of, respectively, $(3, 1)$ and $(1, 3)$. There is also a symmetric Nash equilibrium in which both players play the same mixed strategy.

Suppose the wife plays F with probability q (and O with probability $1 - q$).

COMPUTATION CHECK

Show that the husband's expected payoffs from playing F is $3q + 0(1 - q) = 3q$. And the expected payoff from playing O is $1(1 - q) + 0q = 1 - q$.

These two payoffs are equal if $3q = 1 - q$, that is, $q = \frac{1}{4}$. By the implication of section 8.2, the husband will mix only if $q = \frac{1}{4}$, and at that point it is a best response for him to play *any* mix of F and O.

CHECK AGAIN

Similarly show that the wife is only willing to mix if her husband plays O with probability $\frac{1}{4}$.

[6] *Harsanyi's article, "Games with Randomly Disturbed Payoffs: A New Rationale for Mixed Strategy Equilibrium Points," appeared in the* International Journal of Game Theory, *vol. 2, pp. 1–23.*

In other words, a mixed-strategy Nash equilibrium is one in which each spouse plays his or her undesirable action—O for the husband and F for the wife—with probability $\frac{1}{4}$.

8.6   CASE STUDY: RANDOM DRUG TESTING

Random drug testing is a fact of corporate and sports life in many places. For example, in the United States, 81 percent of firms in 1996 had workplace drug testing. Among manufacturing firms, about 89 percent test their employees, although less than 25 percent are required by law to do so.[7] These tests seek to identify employees who have been using illegal drugs and whose on-the-job performance could therefore be affected. Sports organizations such as the NCAA, the U.S. Olympic Committee (USOC), and the International Olympic Committee (IOC) also routinely test athletes. Typically athletes are selected at random at their meets and subjected to a test that looks for the usage of performance-enhancing drugs, especially steroids.[8] In this case, the objective is to weed out athletes who give themselves an unfair advantage and hurt the credibility of the sport and its organizing body.

The outstanding feature of all these testing procedures is that they are random; a worker or athlete does not know whether she is going to be tested, or when; the testing protocol is designed to maintain randomness and an element of surprise.[9] In other words, the firm or the sports body uses a mixed strategy—not every athlete is selected, and the ones who are, are notified only at the time of testing. The question is, Why a mixed strategy?

To answer that question let us look at a very simple example of testing at a sports meet. Two swimmers—Evans and Smith—are to participate in a runoff. Each athlete has the option of using a performance-enhancing steroid (s) or not using it (n) before the meet. The two swimmers are equally good, and each has a 50 percent chance of winning, everything else being equal, that is, if neither uses steroids or they both do. If only one swimmer uses steroids, then she will win. Without any IOC intervention, therefore, the payoff matrix is as follows (we denote the payoff to winning as 1 and the payoff to losing as -1):

Evans \ Smith	s	n
s	0, 0	1, -1
n	-1, 1	0, 0

where the expected payoff when the swimmers both do the same thing is computed as $\frac{1}{2} \times 1 + \frac{1}{2} \times (-1) = 0$. Note that s is a dominant strategy, and hence, without IOC intervention, both swimmers would use steroids. Neither swimmer will be better off, and the IOC will acquire a disreputable stench once word comes out about the rampant drug use among its athletes. So the IOC needs to intervene.

[7] These numbers are from a survey of 961 companies conducted by the American Management Association. For further details, consult Workplace Drug Testing and Drug Abuse Policies, *AMA Research* mimeo, accessible at their website: amanet.org/ama/survey.

[8] For details on drug testing within the NCAA and the USOC consult ADR: Athletic Drug Reference, an instructional report issued by a company called Helix and available at their web site, helix.com. Sports bodies typically use a combination of random testing and testing by position of finish. For example, in the 1996 Summer Olympics swimming events, two of the top four finishers were tested as well as some of the also-rans.

[9] The ADR guideline relates that upon (random) selection, an athlete has 60 minutes within which he or she has to report to the drug-testing station. Throughout this time, an official stays with the athlete. The test is conducted on a urine specimen, and dehydration is no excuse for delaying the test; the rules require that the athlete remain at the testing station and be pumped full of fluids till the job is done!

To begin with, suppose that the IOC can test only one swimmer. So the choices are (a) test Evans, (b) test Smith, or (c) use a mixed strategy and test Evans with probability p (and Smith with probability $1 - p$). In fact, let us keep the third option simple and symmetric: take $p = \frac{1}{2}$. Let us keep the IOC's payoffs simple as well; if the tests uncover drug use, the IOC looks vigilant (and improves its reputation), and if the tests turn up negative, then the IOC's reputation remains unchanged. The former will be given a payoff of 1 and the latter a payoff of 0. Finally, if a swimmer tests positive she faces a penalty, and this penalty is typically worse than simply losing; let this payoff be denoted $-(1 + b)$, where $b > 0$. Also the race is awarded to the other swimmer. All of this gives us the following payoff matrices for the three players—Evans, Smith, and the IOC:

Evans \ Smith	s	n		Evans \ Smith	s	n
s	$-1 - b, 1, 1$	$-1 - b, 1, 1$		s	$1, -1 - b, 1$	$1, -1, 0$
n	$-1, 1, 0$	$0, 0, 0$		n	$1, -1 - b, 1$	$0, 0, 0$

IOC Tests Evans   IOC Tests Smith

Let us start with the two (pure) strategies of the IOC. If they test Evans for sure, then we are in the first matrix. It is easy to see that Evans has a dominant strategy—n—and so does Smith—s. Exactly the opposite is true if Smith is tested for sure. So the outcome is that the swimmer who knows she will be tested stays away from drugs, but the other swimmer uses steroids. Over time the IOC's reputation suffers.

Consider instead the mixed strategy. We claim that now n is a dominant strategy for both players.

CONCEPT CHECK
TO DOPE OR NOT TO DOPE

(a) Show that Evans' expected payoffs from playing n are 0, regardless of whether Smith plays s or n. (b) On the other hand, Evans' expected payoffs from playing s are $-\frac{1}{2}b$, regardless of what Smith plays.

So (n, n) for the two swimmers and random testing for the IOC is a Nash equilibrium.[10] This outcome is better for the IOC than testing both swimmers because it achieves the same desired objective (no doping) and costs less.

SUMMARY

1. A mixed strategy is a probability distribution over a player's pure strategies; not every pure strategy need be included in every mixed strategy.

[10] *Make sure you understand why random testing is a best response for the IOC.*

2. The payoff to a mixed strategy is computed as the expected payoff to its component pure strategies.

3. A mixed strategy is a best response if and only if every one of the pure strategies in its support is itself a best response.

4. A mixed strategy can dominate a pure strategy even if the latter is undominated by every other pure strategy.

5. The worst-case payoff to a mixed strategy can be better than the worst-case payoff to every pure strategy.

6. There are games with no Nash equilibrium in pure strategies, but there will always be such an equilibrium in mixed strategies.

7. Random drug testing is a cost-effective way to ensure a desirable no-doping outcome on the part of employees and athletes.

EXERCISES

SECTION 8.1

8.1

Consider a game in which player 1 has three pure strategies s', $s^{\#}$, and s^{*}.

a. Write down the three mixed strategies that correspond to these pure strategies.

b. Write down the mixed strategy that corresponds to the case in which s' is twice as likely as either $s^{\#}$ or s^{*}.

c. Write down the mixed strategy that corresponds to the case in which s' is three times as likely as $s^{\#}$, which in turn is twice as likely to be played as s^{*}.

     Consider the following game:

1 \ 2	L	R
s'	$-1, 3$	$6, 2$
$s^{\#}$	$5, 0$	$-2, 5$
s^{*}	$0, 9$	$4, 9$

8.2

Suppose that player 2 plays L for sure.

a. Compute the expected payoff of player 1 from the mixed strategy in part b of exercise 8.1.

b. Repeat the exercise for part c of exercise 8.1.

8.3

Suppose that player 2 is equally likely to play L as she is to play R.

a. Repeat parts a and b of exercise 8.2.

b. In exactly the same circumstances, compute the expected payoffs of player 2.

8.4

Suppose instead that player 2 plays L with probability p and R with probability $1 - p$.

a. Repeat exercise 8.3 for this case.

b. Can you give the general formula for the expected payoffs of the two players when, additionally, player 1 plays s', $s^{\#}$, and s^* with probabilities q, r, and $1 - q - r$ respectively?

And now, yet again (!) we return to the price competition game, this time from the standpoint of mixed strategies. Recall that we have two (duopoly) firms that set prices in a market whose demand curve is

$$Q = 6 - p$$

where p is the lower of the two prices. If firm 1 is the lower priced firm, then it meets all of the demand; the converse applies if firm 2 is the one that posts the lower price. If the two firms post the same price p, they each get half the market $\frac{6-p}{2}$. Suppose that prices can only be quoted in dollar units and that costs of production are zero for both firms.

8.5

Write down the mixed strategies that correspond to the following randomizing procedures for firm 1:

a. Roll a die and post as price the number that shows up on the die roll.

b. Roll a die twice and post the average of the two numbers provided it is a round dollar figure; otherwise, post the nearest round dollar figure above the average.

c. Roll a die twice and post the higher of the two numbers that show up on the two rolls.

8.6

a. What is firm 1's expected profit in the three preceding mixed strategies if firm 2's price equals 3?

b. What is firm 2's expected profit in the three cases?

8.7

What are the two firms' expected profits if

a. Firm 1 plays the mixed strategy of exercise 8.5a, while firm 2 plays the mixed strategy given by exercise 8.5b?

b. Firm 1 plays the mixed strategy of exercise 8.5c, while firm 2 plays the mixed strategy given by exercise 8.5b?

SECTION 8.2

8.8

Illustrate the implication from section 8.2 by using exercises 8.2 and 8.6. In each case, what is player 1's best response strategy?

8.9

Give a complete proof of the implication.

SECTION 8.3

Let us return to the pricing game. Suppose that we want to iteratively eliminate dominated strategies in this game but we look at mixed as well as pure strategies.

8.10

Show that if a mixed strategy q yields an expected payoff that is at least as high as that from another mixed strategy p, against every pure strategy of the other player, then it must also yield as high a payoff against every mixed strategy of the other player. Conclude that we only need to check how each strategy does against the pure strategy prices 0 through 6.

8.11

Use exercise 8.10 to show that any mixed strategy that places positive probability on a price of six dollars—that is, a mixed strategy p in which the probability $p^6 > 0$—is dominated. Explain carefully the strategy that dominates p.

8.12

Can you show that, as a consequence, any mixed strategy that places positive probability on a price of five dollars—that is, a mixed strategy p in which $p^5 > 0$—is dominated as well.

8.13

What is the outcome to IEDS in this game? Explain your answer carefully.

8.14

Show that if there is a pure strategy that dominates every other pure strategy, then it must also dominate every other mixed strategy.

8.15

Show that if there is no dominant pure strategy, then there cannot be a dominant mixed strategy either. (You may want to use some game examples to illustrate your answer to this question.)

SECTION 8.4

Consider the game of squash:

	Forward (F)	Backward (B)
Front (f)	.2	.8
Back (b)	.7	.3

8.16

a. What percentage of the rallies do you expect to win if you are twice as likely to pick f as you are to pick b and your opponent goes *forward*?

b. What if he goes *backward*?

c. What is the minimum percentage that you will win from playing this mixed strategy?

8.17

Repeat exercise 8.16 for the case that in four out of ten rallies you pick f.

SECTION 8.5

8.18

Find mixed-strategy Nash equilibria in the game of Chicken (example 2, p. 106).

8.19

Are there any mixed-strategy Nash equilibria in the No-Name game of Example 3? Explain.

Consider the following three-player game:

1 \ 2	s	n
s	1, 1, 1	−1, −2, −1
n	−2, −1, −1	1, 1, −1

3 Plays s

1 \ 2	s	n
s	−1, −1, −2	1, −1, 0
n	1, −1, 1	0, 0, 0

3 Plays n

8.20

a. Is there an equilibrium in which only one of the three players plays a mixed strategy (and the other two play pure strategies)? Explain your answer.

b. Repeat part a for the case in which exactly two of the three players play mixed strategies.

8.21

Compute a Nash equilibrium in which no player plays a pure strategy and they all play identical strategies.

CHAPTER 9

TWO APPLICATIONS: NATURAL MONOPOLY AND BANKRUPTCY LAW

This chapter will present two applications of mixed-strategy Nash equilibrium. Both have at their core the game of Chicken (aka Hawk-Dove) that you have seen in previous chapters. In section 9.1, we will review that game and find a "plausible" *symmetric* equilibrium that requires mixed strategies. In section 9.2 we will provide economic background for the problem of a *natural monopoly* and then use two extensions of Chicken to analyze that problem. In section 9.3 we turn to *bankruptcy law* and give legal background for something called *voidable preference law*. Then we will present a game-theoretic analysis of this law, first by way of a numerical example and then via a general model.

9.1 CHICKEN, SYMMETRIC GAMES, AND SYMMETRIC EQUILIBRIA

9.1.1 CHICKEN

Recall the game of Chicken, introduced in Chapter 3 with an example of two daredevil drivers and retold in Chapter 5 with the two fighting spiders. Let us now write the payoffs using symbols rather than actual numbers.

Chicken (*t*=tough, *c*=concede) [1]

Player 1 \ Player 2	t	c
t	a, a	$d, 0$
c	$0, d$	b, b

[1] *This chapter will refer to this game as Chicken rather than Hawk-Dove.*

where $d > b > 0 > a$. In other words, as a group, the players are better off if both concede rather than if both act tough ($b > a$). However, if the other player is going to concede, then a player has an incentive to be tough ($d > b$)—and, conversely, against a tough opponent conceding is better than fighting ($0 > a$).[2] The *numerical version* used in previous chapters was $d = 10 > b = 5 > 0 > -1 = a$.

This discussion should convince you that there are exactly *two pure-strategy equilibria* in this game; one of the players concedes, while the other acts tough.[3] Their payoffs are respectively 0 and d.

There is also a *mixed-strategy equilibrium* in this game, and let us now compute it. Suppose that player 2 plays t with probability p (and c with probability $1 - p$). Then the expected payoffs of player 1 from playing t are $ap + d(1 - p)$ and from playing c are $b(1 - p)$. By the implication of Chapter 8, it follows that in a mixed-strategy best response of player 1, the two pure strategies must give him the same expected payoffs. Hence, the probability p must satisfy

$$ap + d(1 - p) = b(1 - p)$$

After collecting terms, we get $\frac{p}{1-p} = \frac{d-b}{-a}$ and hence $p = \frac{d-b}{d-b-a}$. Furthermore, by the same implication, if player 2 plays t with probability $\frac{d-b}{d-b-a}$, then *any* mixed strategy is a best response for player 1; in particular, the mixed strategy in which player 1 plays t with exactly the same probability is a best response. Hence, we have the following:

Mixed-Strategy Nash Equilibrium. There is a mixed-strategy equilibrium in which the two players play identical strategies; each plays t with probability $\frac{d-b}{d-b-a}$.

The expected payoffs are the same for the two players and equal $\frac{-ab}{d-b-a}$, a number between the two pure-strategy payoffs of 0 and d.

In the numerical version, each plays t with probability $\frac{5}{6}$ and c with probability $\frac{1}{6}$, and the expected payoff is $\frac{5}{6}$ for each player (while in the pure-strategy equilibria, the tough player gets 10 and the weakling gets 0).

9.1.2   SYMMETRIC GAMES AND SYMMETRIC EQUILIBRIA

A game such as Chicken is called a **symmetric game**. Roughly speaking, a symmetric game is one in which each player is equal to every other player: each has the same opportunities, and the same actions yield the same payoffs. Equivalently, you can think of a symmetric game as one in which the players' names are irrelevant and only their actions are relevant.

By identical payoff functions we mean that, if player i plays s_i^* while the others play $s_{-i}^\#$, then i's payoff $\pi(s_i^*, s_{-i}^\#)$ does *not* depend on who she is, that is, does not depend on whether $i = 1$ or 3 or N. The definition is a bit abstract. To better understand it, let us try it for two players.

Symmetric game
A game is symmetric if each player has exactly the same strategy set and the payoff functions are identical.

[2] *Strictly speaking, therefore, the relationships that need to be satisfied are $d > b$ and both b and 0 are bigger than a. For simplicity, we also assume that $b > 0$.*

[3] *These are the equilibria that were discussed for the fighting spiders in Chapter 5.*

Definition. A two-player game is symmetric if the strategy set is the same for each player, say $(a, b, \ldots, m)$. Furthermore, if player 1 picks b and player 2 picks e—that is, if the strategy pair (b, e) is picked—then player 1's payoff is the same as player 2's would be under the pair (e, b).

An implication of the definition is that if they pick the same strategy, say, (m, m), then their payoffs are identical. (Why?) As you can readily verify, Chicken is a symmetric game and so is the Prisoners' Dilemma. On the other hand, the Battle of the Sexes is not a symmetric game, nor is Colonel Blotto.[4]

CONCEPT CHECK
SYMMETRY AND NO SYMMETRY

(a) Show that the Coordination game and the Bertrand game are symmetric. (b) Show that neither the Odd Couple game nor the Veto Voting game of Chapter 4 are symmetric.

The fact that each player in a symmetric game is identical to every other player motivates the definition of a **symmetric equilibrium**, a Nash equilibrium in which every player has the same strategy.

Some game theorists argue that in a symmetric game, a symmetric Nash equilibrium is more compelling than an asymmetric one. After all, if players are identical in every respect, why would they play in different ways? Think of some of the motivating parables for Nash equilibrium. If there is preplay communication between the players, it is likely that the player(s) who have low payoffs in an asymmetric equilibrium will push instead for the symmetric mixed-strategy equilibrium that equalizes payoffs. If Nash equilibrium play arises from rational introspection, then again it is likely that a player will expect his opponent—the twin—to play as he plans to play. And, finally, a symmetric equilibrium is more likely to be a focal point of a game.[5]

It should be clear that the mixed-strategy equilibrium in Chicken is a symmetric equilibrium but the pure-strategy equilibria are not. And that difference makes the mixed-strategy equilibrium more plausible.

9.2   NATURAL MONOPOLY

9.2.1   THE ECONOMIC BACKGROUND

A natural monopoly is an industry in which technological or demand conditions are such that it is "natural" that there be only one firm in the market. One *technological* reason for a natural monopoly to arise is seen when the costs per unit of production decline with the size of output. This phenomenon might occur if there are increasing returns to scale in production[6] or if there are large unavoidable costs[7] of doing business.[8] A

Symmetric equilibrium
A Nash equilibrium in a symmetric game, whether pure or mixed, is said to be symmetric if identical strategies are chosen by the players. Payoffs are identical for all players in such an equilibrium.

[4] *Colonel Blotto has different strategy sets for the two players. Battle of the Sexes has the same strategy sets, but the payoff functions are not symmetric.*

[5] *After all, if there is one asymmetric equilibrium in a symmetric game, then there are at least as many qualitatively identical asymmetric equilibria as there are players. (Why?) Consequently no single one of these equilibria can be the focal point in players' minds.*

[6] *Increasing returns means that twice as much output can be produced with less than twice as much input. Consequently, total costs do not double when total output is doubled.*

[7] *For instance, there may be a minimum size at which some inputs can be purchased; it may not be possible to rent production space of size less than 10,000 square feet. Again, output can be doubled without doubling input costs.*

[8] *The aircraft manufacturing industry is a technological natural monopoly because of the large unavoidable costs associated with manufacturing planes (and possibly, because of increasing returns as well). Perhaps unsurprisingly, there is now a single domestic manufacturer of large airplanes in the United States (Boeing having taken over McDonnell Douglas).*

natural monopoly can also arise when *demand* is low (and consequently the only way to make any money is to keep the price relatively high). Recall that duopoly competition—whether Cournot or Bertrand—drives down the price.

The question that economists are most interested in is, How will a natural monopoly become an actual monopoly? If we start off in an industry with two or more firms, which firms will drop out? In many cases there are obvious candidates; firms with higher costs will be the first ones to leave. If a firm has "deep pockets," then a rival will throw in the towel earlier. If the products are differentiated, then the firm with greater demand is more likely to remain. And so on.

The question that remains is, How will a natural monopoly become an actual monopoly when, to begin with, there are two (or more) essentially identical firms in the market?[9]

9.2.2 A SIMPLE EXAMPLE

Consider a duopoly that will last two more years, in which each firm is currently suffering losses of c dollars per period. If one of the firms were to drop out, then the remaining firm would make a monopoly profit of π dollars per period for the remainder of the two years. Each firm can choose when to drop out: today (date 0) or a year from now (date 1), or it can stay till the end (date 2). Furthermore, each firm only cares about profits.[10] The payoff matrix is therefore

Firm 1 \ Firm 2	*date 0*	*date 1*	*date 2*
date 0	$0, 0$	$0, \pi$	$0, 2\pi$
date 1	$\pi, 0$	$-c, -c$	$-c, \pi - c$
date 2	$2\pi, 0$	$\pi - c, -c$	$-2c, -2c$

Let us first look for *pure-strategy Nash equilibria* of this game. Note that $b^1(date\ 0) = date\ 2$, $b^1(date\ 1) = date\ 2$, and $b^1(date\ 2) = date\ 0$.[11] Firm 2 has an identical best response function.[12] Consequently, there are two asymmetric pure-strategy Nash equilibria in this game: one of the two firms drops out (i.e., *concedes*) at *date 0*, and the other then remains in the market for the two years.

The problem is that there is no reason that firm 1 should think that firm 2—an identical firm—is going to concede, especially since by conceding firm 2 would lose out on 2π dollars worth of profits.[13]

What of a symmetric *mixed equilibrium*? Let us turn now to that computation. Suppose that firm 2 plays *date 0* with probability p, *date 1* with probability q, and *date 2* with probability $1 - p - q$. Firm 1's expected profits from its three pure strategies are

Expected profits (*date 0*) $= 0$

Expected profits (*date 1*) $= \pi p - c(1 - p)$

Expected profits (*date 2*) $= 2\pi p + (\pi - c)q - 2c(1 - p - q)$

If there is to be a mixed-strategy best response for firm 1 that involves all three dates, it must be the case that each strategy yields the same expected payoff. This fact leads to the following exercise:

CONCEPT CHECK
EQUAL PROFITS

Show that firm 1 is indifferent about its date of exit only if (a) $p = \frac{c}{\pi+c}$ and (b) $q = 0$.

Hence, in particular, playing *date 0* with probability $\frac{c}{\pi+c}$ and *date 2* with remaining probability $\frac{\pi}{\pi+c}$ is a best response for firm 1 as well. This then is the symmetric mixed-strategy Nash equilibrium: $p = \frac{c}{\pi+c}$, $q = 0$, and $1 - p - q = \frac{\pi}{\pi+c}$.

CONCEPT CHECK
OTHER EQUILIBRIA?

Convince yourself—by doing the necessary computations!—that there are no other mixed-strategy Nash equilibria; for example, none involving only *dates 0* and *1*.

Consider a numerical example; suppose $\pi = 10$ and $c = 2$. Then in the symmetric equilibrium, each firm drops out with probability $\frac{1}{6}$ at *date 0* itself. If a firm does not drop out at *date 0*, it remains till *date 2*. Hence, with probability $\frac{1}{6} \times \frac{1}{6}$ or $\frac{1}{36}$ both firms exit the market at *date 0*, with probability $\frac{25}{36}$ they both stay the course, and with the remaining probability $\frac{10}{36}$ one or the other leaves at *date 0*.

Note that the first two outcomes—both leaving and both staying—are collectively unprofitable; in the first case a market that would be profitable for a monopoly is abandoned, while in the second case a market that is only profitable for a monopoly remains a duopoly.[14]

9.2.3 WAR OF ATTRITION AND A GENERAL ANALYSIS

In this subsection we show that the previous conclusion—a firm will only consider the extreme options of leaving immediately and leaving at the end—continues to hold in a more general version of Chicken called the War of Attrition.[15] Suppose that instead of three dates, there are $N + 1$ dates; a generic date will be denoted t. As before, a monopolist makes profits of π dollars per period, while a duopolist suffers losses of c dollars per period. The payoff matrix is

[14] *One interpretation of a mixed strategy is that it is based on events outside a firm's control. For instance, a firm might believe that its rival will leave the market immediately if the Fed's projection for GDP growth is less than 2 percent. If the firm further believes that there is a likelihood p of such a projection, then it is as if it plays against a mixed strategy with probability p on date 0. Alternatively, a firm may not know some relevant characteristic about its rival, such as costs. If it believes that high-cost rivals will exit at date 0 but not low-cost ones and that the likelihood of high costs is p, then again it is as if it faces a mixed strategy with probability p on date 0.*

[15] *War of Attrition was introduced by the biologist Maynard Smith, who used it to analyze the length of animal conflicts.*

1 \ 2	date 0	date 1	...	date t	...	date N
date 0	0, 0	0, π		0, $t\pi$		0, $N\pi$
date 1	π, 0	$-c, -c$		$-c, (t-1)\pi - c$		$-c, (N-1)\pi - c$
$\vdots$						
date t	$t\pi$, 0	$(t-1)\pi - c, -c$		$-tc, -tc$		$-tc, (N-t)\pi - tc$
$\vdots$						
date N	$N\pi$, 0	$(N-1)\pi - c, -c$		$(N-t)\pi - tc, -tc$		$-Nc, -Nc$

Notice that the War of Attrition retains the essential features of Chicken; both players conceding immediately is better collectively than both conceding simultaneously but later. If the rival concedes at *date t*, and a firm is still in the market at that date, then it is best to go all the way to *date N*.

Let us first look at the pure-strategy Nash equilibria. Start with the best response function of firm 1. Suppose that firm 2 is going to drop out at *date t*.

CONCEPT CHECK

BEST RESPONSE: STEP 1

Show that the best response to *date t* must be either *date 0* or *date N*. The former strategy yields a payoff of 0, while the latter yields a payoff of $(N - t)\pi - tc$. Hence,

BEST RESPONSE: STEP 2

Show that the best response function of firm 1 is

$$b^1(t) = \begin{cases} 0 & \text{if } t \geq \frac{N\pi}{\pi+c} \\ N & \text{if } t \leq \frac{N\pi}{\pi+c} \end{cases}$$

The two best-response functions are pictured in Figure 9.1, where $t' = \frac{N\pi}{\pi+c}$. It follows that even in this more general game there are exactly the same two pure-strategy equilibria; one of the two firms drops out at *date 0*, but the other stays till *date N*.

What of symmetric mixed-strategy equilibria? In principle, a firm can exit the market at any date between 0 and N with positive probability. We will show, however, that a firm will never choose an intermediate date at which to exit; either it will leave at *date 0*, or it will stay till *date N*. This conclusion will seem intuitive given what we just saw about the best response functions. We have to be a little careful, however; the rival can now play a mixed strategy, and the best response function that we have so far analyzed was only computed against a pure strategy of the rival.

We will now prove the following:

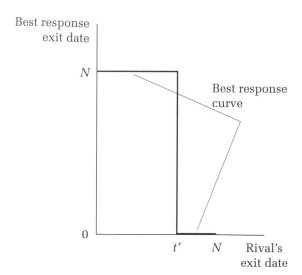

Best response
exit date

N

Best response
curve

0

t' N Rival's
exit date

FIGURE 9.1

Dominance Proposition.   Every pure strategy other than *date 0* and *date N* is dominated by some mixed strategy that has *date 0* and *date N* in its support.

Proof

Consider the pure strategy *date t* and compare it to the mixed strategy in which a firm plays *date N* with probability $\frac{t}{N}$ and *date 0* with the remaining probability. Suppose that its *rival* plays the pure strategy *date τ*. There are two cases to consider:

Case 1 $\tau < t$: In this case the pure strategy *date t* yields a payoff equal to $(t - \tau)\pi - \tau c$, while the mixed strategy yields $\frac{t}{N}[(N - \tau)\pi - \tau c]$. The mixed-strategy payoff is greater if $t(N - \tau)\pi - t\tau c \geq N(t - \tau)\pi - N\tau c$. Collecting and eliminating common terms, that is equivalent to $\tau(\pi + c) \geq 0$, which is true.

Case 2 $\tau \geq t$: Here the pure strategy *date t* yields a payoff equal to $-tc$, while the mixed strategy again yields $\frac{t}{N}[(N - \tau)\pi - \tau c]$. The mixed-strategy payoff is greater if $t(N - \tau)\pi - t\tau c \geq -Ntc$. Collecting common terms, that is equivalent to $(N - \tau)(\pi + c)$, which is clearly true.[16] The proof is complete.   ◇

Since the mixed strategy dominates the pure strategy, the latter will never be used in a best response even if the rival firm plays a mixed strategy. (Why?) Hence, in order to compute the mixed-strategy equilibrium we can concentrate on *date 0* and *date N* alone. Put differently, qualitatively the same symmetric mixed-strategy equilibrium that we computed in the previous subsection is the symmetric mixed-strategy equilibrium of this general model as well.[17]

[16] *Note the inequalities are strict of $N > \tau > 0$.*

[17] *We have assumed so far that a firm makes a once-for-all decision about its exit date. In practice, if a firm finds itself as a monopoly, it should abandon any earlier commitment to drop out by date t and instead should stay till date N. We can generalize the analysis to incorporate this possibility (see Exercises). In this general analysis it is possible that a firm might stay till intermediate dates such as $1, 2, \ldots, N - 1$.*

9.3   BANKRUPTCY LAW △

9.3.1   THE LEGAL BACKGROUND

In the United States, once a company declares bankruptcy[18] its assets can no longer be attached by *individual* creditors. Instead they are held in safekeeping till such time as the company and the *group* of creditors reach some understanding; the assets might get liquidated and creditors paid out of the proceeds, or the creditors might refinance the failing company. The reason for this protection is to prevent creditors from going into a reclamation frenzy that might dismember the remaining assets.[19]

Bankruptcy law actually goes even further. After all, if assets were only safeguarded *after* a company declares bankruptcy, then individual creditors might have an incentive to attach assets just *prior to* that declaration. Hence, in many instances, a firm is allowed to recapture any transfers it makes to creditors within a 90-day period prior to bankruptcy (as long as it can show that it was insolvent during that period). These recapturable transfers are called *voidable preferences*. The traditional legal view of voidable preferences is that they strengthen bankruptcy law's protection of creditor assets.

As you might have begun to see already, this issue has elements of the tragedy of the commons problem. Voidable preference law appears to be an attractive way to avert a tragedy, that is, the dismemberment of the company's assets (which are jointly the property of all of its creditors). In this section, we will analyze the question, Is it really?

9.3.2   A NUMERICAL EXAMPLE

Suppose that a company has assets valued at 15 (million) dollars. There are three creditors; for simplicity suppose that each creditor has lent 10 dollars to the company. The company's assets are therefore less than its liabilities. If the company declares bankruptcy, then its assets are liquidated (and each creditor gets 5 dollars back). Since recovery of loans from this bankrupt company is partial, each creditor has an incentive to try to recover his own loan. He can do so by conducting a fire sale that will yield 12 dollars (i.e., 3 dollars worth of assets will be dismembered).

Suppose that each creditor has to decide today whether or not to try to recover his loan. If two (or three) creditors make such an attempt, then the company goes into immediate bankruptcy, voidable preference law kicks in, and the proceeds of the fire sale are split between the three creditors; each receives 4 dollars. If only one creditor tries to preemptively attach the company's assets, she is successful; in this case, the company declares bankruptcy at some later date and distributes the proceeds of the remaining assets, 2 dollars, among the other two creditors. Similarly if no creditor preempts, then again the insolvent company is sold at a later date and the proceeds distributed among the creditors, except now each creditor gets a third of the original assets; that is, each gets 5 dollars.

[18] *A company declares bankruptcy (becomes insolvent) if its assets are less than its liabilities (to its creditors).*

[19] *The discussion in this section is based on "A Reexamination of Near-Bankruptcy Investment Incentives" by Barry Adler, 1995, University of Chicago Law Review, vol. 62, pp. 575–606. I thank my colleague Chris Sanchirico for drawing my attention to this paper.*

The payoffs to an individual creditor can therefore be written as

Number of other creditors grabbing	0	1	2
grab	10	4	4
refrain	5	1	4

It is easy to see that *refrain,* which is collectively the best thing to do, is dominated by *grab.* Hence there will be a mad dash by creditors to collect their share of the company's assets, the assets will be dismembered, and each creditor will end up with only 4 dollars. Voidable preference law in this case has *no* deterrent effect whatsoever. (After all, there are *no* rewards to refraining; either it leaves a creditor with a stripped company [if one other creditor grabs], or it yields only a third rather than two-thirds of the company [if nobody else grabs].)

You might think that there must be some benefits to being the nice guy if recovering assets is costly. (After all, creditors have to pursue the company to pay them back; they may have to move the courts to get payment; etc.) It would appear that in this case *refrain* may sometimes be a smart strategy.

Suppose that it costs a creditor 1 dollar to institute recovery proceedings, regardless of whether recovery is successful or not. The payoff matrix is now

Number of other creditors grabbing	0	1	2
grab	9	3	3
refrain	5	1	4

Note that the payoff to *grab* has been reduced by 1 dollar across the board. Now *grab* is no longer a dominant strategy. In fact we now have a generalized version of Chicken.[20] Everybody *grabbing* (i.e., acting tough) is worse than everybody *refraining* (i.e., conceding), since the former yields a payoff of 3 each while the latter yields 5 each. However, if at least one of the other players concedes, then it is better to be tough than to concede; conversely, if the other two creditors are tough it is better to concede.

Pure-Strategy Equilibria

There are three Chicken-like pure-strategy equilibria; exactly two creditors *grab* and dismember the company's assets, voidable preference kicks in, and they have to return the seized assets. Each creditor ends up with a third of the reduced asset base. Interestingly, the creditor who sits out the fight ends up with a higher net payoff because he avoids the costly recovery process.[21]

Mixed-Strategy Equilibrium

As always, in this symmetric game a more plausible equilibrium is the symmetric mixed-strategy equilibrium. Suppose that each of the other creditors *refrains* with a probability p (and *grabs* with probability $1 - p$).[22] Then the expected payoff to *grab* is

[20] Note that in the natural monopoly problem we looked at a generalization of Chicken in which each player has more than two strategies. Now we are looking at a generalization in which there are more than two players.

[21] Another way of saying the same thing is that the asymmetric equilibria in Chicken can have the weakling do better than the tough players when there are more than two players. This outcome can occur because the tough guys fight each other and expend resources in doing so.

[22] Since we are looking for a symmetric equilibrium, we can restrict attention to the case in which the other two creditors use the same mixed strategy.

$$(1-p)^2 \times 3 + 2p(1-p) \times 3 + p^2 \times 9 \tag{9.1}$$

In equation 9.1 we have used the fact that the probability that neither of the other two creditors *refrains* is $(1-p)^2$, the probability that exactly one of the other two creditors *refrains* is $2p(1-p)$, and, finally, the probability that they both *refrain* is p^2. Equation 9.1 can be rewritten as $3 + 6p^2$. On the other hand, the expected payoff to *refrain* is

$$(1-p)^2 \times 4 + 2p(1-p) \times 1 + p^2 \times 5 \tag{9.2}$$

Equation 9.2 can be simplified to $4 - 6p + 7p^2$. Equating the two expected payoffs, we can see that p is the solution to the following quadratic equation:

$$p^2 - 6p + 1 = 0 \tag{9.3}$$

By standard techniques[23] p is found to equal $3 - 2\sqrt{2}$; that is, p is approximately equal to $0.\dot{2}$. Put another way, there is an 80 percent chance that each creditor will *grab* and hence only a 0.2^3 (or less than 1%) chance that everybody will *refrain*. Voidable preference law is therefore spectacularly unsuccessful in achieving its stated purposes, since 99 percent of the time the company's assets are dismembered.

9.3.3 A GENERAL ANALYSIS

In this subsection we will present a general analysis of voidable preference law. To keep the game symmetric we will retain the assumption that there are three creditors who have identical debts outstanding and identical costs of collecting. We will also retain the assumption that an attempt by two or more creditors to collect sends the company into immediate bankruptcy.

Suppose that each creditor is owed d dollars, and the value of the firm's assets is V dollars. The firm is insolvent in that $3d > V$. If one or more creditors attempt to collect, they reduce the firm's assets to v dollars; that is, the size of the dismemberment is $V - v$. Finally, the costs of collection are c dollars. The payoff matrix is therefore

Number of other creditors grabbing	0	1	2
grab	$d - c$	$\frac{v}{3} - c$	$\frac{v}{3} - c$
refrain	$\frac{V}{3}$	$\frac{v-d}{2}$	$\frac{v}{3}$

Again this is a Chicken game; it is collectively better for all three creditors to *refrain* than for all three to *grab* ($V > v - 3c$). If two other creditors are going to *grab*, then it is better not to ($\frac{v}{3} > \frac{v}{3} - c$). Finally, assume that it is better to *grab* if nobody else does[24] ($d - c > \frac{V}{3}$).

Pure-Strategy Equilibria

There are two possibilities for pure-strategy equilibria. If the best response to one other creditor grabbing is to grab as well, then the equilibria are *exactly two creditors grab*. If, however, the best response is to refrain, then the equilibria are *exactly one creditor grabs*. Notice that in either case the company's assets are dismembered.

[23] *For the quadratic function $ax^2 + bx + c$ the two values at which the quadratic function equals zero can be found from the formula $x = \frac{-b \pm \sqrt{b^2 - 4ac}}{2a}$.*

[24] *If the opposite is true, that is, if the costs of collection c are so high that it is better to refrain even if the others are refraining, then a pure-strategy Nash equilibrium is for everyone to refrain. In this case the firm does not need the protection of bankruptcy law because its creditors have no incentive to strip the company's assets.*

CONCEPT CHECK
PURE EXERCISE

Show that these are indeed the only two possibilities and, in particular, that there is no symmetric pure strategy equilibrium.

Mixed-Strategy Equilibrium

Suppose that each of the other two creditors *refrains* with probability p. The expected payoff to *grab* is then

$$p^2(d - c) + (1 - p^2)\left(\frac{V}{3} - c\right) \tag{9.4}$$

Equation 9.4 can be simplified and written as $p^2(d - \frac{V}{3}) + (\frac{V}{3} - c)$. The expected payoff to *refrain* is

$$p^2\frac{V}{3} + 2p(1-p)\frac{v-d}{2} + (1-p)^2\frac{V}{3} \tag{9.5}$$

Equation 9.5 can also be simplified and written as $p^2(d + \frac{V-2v}{3}) - p(d - \frac{V}{3}) + \frac{V}{3}$. An individual creditor will play a mixed-strategy best response if *grab* and *refrain* are equally profitable, that is, if the expressions in equations 9.4 and 9.5 match. Equating them and simplifying we get a quadratic equation in p:

$$\frac{V - v}{3}p^2 - \left(d - \frac{V}{3}\right)p + c = 0 \tag{9.6}$$

Equation 9.6 is worth spending a few moments on.

Relevant Parameters. Three intuitive parameter combinations decide the size of p: (1) the per-creditor size of *dismemberment* $\frac{V-v}{3}$ (denote this D), (2) the size of *insolvency* $d - \frac{V}{3}$ (call this I),[25] and (3) the *collection costs* c.

In terms of our new and simpler notation, equation 9.6 can be rewritten as[26]

$$Dp^2 - Ip + c = 0 \tag{9.7}$$

This quadratic equation can be solved to yield the equilibrium probability p^*:

$$p^* = \frac{I - \sqrt{I^2 - 4Dc}}{2D}$$

It is straightforward now to figure out how p^* might change if any one of the three determinants—dismemberment D, insolvency I, or collection costs c—changes.

[25] *Recall that the firm's liability toward each creditor is d. A dismembered firm will return $\frac{v}{3}$ dollars to each creditor. Hence, the per-creditor size of insolvency is $d - \frac{v}{3}$.*

[26] *Be sure to check the general formula of equation 9.5 against the numerical version of the previous subsection. In that case, what was the value of D? I? c? (How) Does equation 9.6 generalize equation 9.3?*

CONCEPT CHECK
MIXED EXERCISE (CALCULUS)

Show that if the size of dismemberment D or collection costs c are *higher*, then *refraining* is *more likely;* that is, p^* is larger. Similarly, if the size of insolvency I is *smaller*, then again *refraining* is *more likely*.

The result should be intuitive. If a creditor figures that her costs are small, or that she will not destroy too much of the assets, or that her loans are very large relative to the firm's assets, she will be more aggressive in trying to recover her loans. Note that bankruptcy (and voidable preference) law becomes more successful as a deterrent as the value of p^* becomes larger. Put differently, the law only works if collection or dismemberment costs are very high and the size of insolvency is very small.

SUMMARY

1. A symmetric game is one in which all players are identical in their choices and payoff functions. A symmetric equilibrium is one in which all players take identical actions.

2. The game of Chicken is a symmetric game. Its symmetric equilibrium is in mixed strategies.

3. Natural monopoly is a market in which economic reasons suggest that there should be only one firm. For instance, it may be unprofitable for two or more firms to operate at the same time.

4. A generalized version of Chicken can be used to analyze the behavior of firms in a natural monopoly. In a symmetric equilibrium, a firm will choose probabilistically between its extreme options—leave immediately or never.

5. Bankruptcy law, via voidable preferences, seeks to protect an insolvent company's assets against predatory creditors.

6. A generalized version of Chicken can be used to analyze the behavior of creditors in the presence of such a law. The law is successful only if the cost of collection or asset dismemberment is high and less successful if insolvency costs are high instead.

EXERCISES

SECTION 9.1

9.1

Consider the following symmetric game:

Player 1 \ Player 2	t	c
t	$-5, -5$	$d, 0$
c	$0, d$	$10, 10$

Find the symmetric equilibrium of this game. Be careful to spell out any assumptions that you make about the value of d.

9.2

Consider the payoff matrix of any 2×2 game, that is, any game with two players and two pure strategies:

Player 1 \ Player 2	t	c
t	a, a	d, e
c	e, d	b, b

a. Write down parameter restrictions so that (t, t) is a symmetric Nash equilibrium.

b. Under what restrictions, can (c, c) be a symmetric Nash equilibrium? Are the restrictions in parts a and b compatible with each other; that is, can such a game have multiple pure-strategy symmetric Nash equilibria?

9.3

Keep the parameters d and e fixed; that is, consider the same payoff matrix with two free parameters a and b that can take on any values.

a. Suppose that $a > e$ and $d > b$. What is the symmetric Nash equilibrium in this case?

b. Repeat the question when $a > e$ but $d < b$. Be sure to check for more than one symmetric Nash equilibirum in this case.

c. In this fashion map out the entire set of symmetric equilibria in this game. Can you draw a figure, with the parameters a and b on the two axes, that shows the symmetric equilibria for each parameter combination?

9.4

Write down modifications of Battle of the Sexes, Colonel Blotto, and the Odd Couple games that would turn them into symmetric games. Be careful to spell out in detail all the changes that you make.

9.5

Consider the definition of a two-player symmetric game. Using the definition, prove the following statement in a semirigorous fashion: *If the two players play identical actions, they get exactly the same payoff.*

9.6

Consider a symmetric game. Prove the following statement in a semirigorous fashion: *If there are any asymmetric equilibria in the game, then there have to be at least as many asymmetric equilibria as the number of players.*

SECTION 9.2

9.7

Consider the following numerical version of the natural monopoly problem:

Firm 1 \ Firm 2	*date 0*	*date 1*	*date 2*
date 0	0, 0	0, 15	0, 30
date 1	15, 0	−5, −5	−5, 10
date 2	30, 0	10, −5	−10, −10

a. Compute the symmetric equilibrium.

b. What is the expected payoff of each firm in equilibrium?

c. What is the probability that exactly one of the firms will drop out of the market at date 0 in the symmetric equilibrium?

9.8

a. Redo parts a and b of exercise 9.7 but with an increase in the costs of staying from 5 dollars to 10 dollars, so that the payoff matrix becomes

Firm 1 \ Firm 2	*date 0*	*date 1*	*date 2*
date 0	0, 0	0, 15	0, 30
date 1	15, 0	−10, −10	−10, 5
date 2	30, 0	5, −10	−20, −20

b. How does this cost increase affect the probability that exactly one firm exists on the market at date 0? Explain.

9.9

Consider instead the general model studied in the text:

Firm 1 \ Firm 2	date 0	date 1	date 2
date 0	$0,0$	$0,\pi$	$0,2\pi$
date 1	$\pi,0$	$-c,-c$	$-c,\pi-c$
date 2	$2\pi,0$	$\pi-c,-c$	$-2c,-2c$

a. In the symmetric mixed-strategy equilibrium of this game, can you tell whether dropping out at *date 0* is more likely if costs c increase? Explain your answer.

b. How is the probability that exactly one firm drops out at *date 0* affected if c increases? What about the probability that at least one firm drops out?

c. Does an increase in c make a monopoly more likely? Explain.

9.10

a. Redo exercise 9.9 for the case where c is unchanged but the profits π increase.

b. Is there a sense in which an increase in costs and a decrease in profits have *exactly* the same effect on market outcomes, that is, exactly the same effect on the symmetric equilibria of the game? Explain your answer.

The next few questions will explore the interpretation that *date t* really is the following strategy: "If my opponent has not dropped out by *date t* − 1, then I will drop out at *t*; otherwise I will continue till the end."

9.11

a. Argue that the consequent payoff matrix when there are three exit dates becomes

Firm 1 \ Firm 2	date 0	date 1	date 2
date 0	$0,0$	$0,2\pi$	$0,2\pi$
date 1	$2\pi,0$	$-c,-c$	$-c,\pi-c$
date 2	$2\pi,0$	$\pi-c,-c$	$-2c,-2c$

b. What are the pure-strategy Nash equilibria of the game?

9.12

Compute the symmetric mixed-strategy equilibrium of this game.

9.13

a. How do the expected payoffs in this symmetric equilibrium compare with the one that follows from exercise 9.9?

b. What about the probability that at least one of the firms drops out at *date 0*?

SECTION 9.3

9.14

Consider the bankruptcy model. Show that *grab* always dominates *refrain* as long as collection is costless; this statement is true no matter what size the outstanding debt is, what the company's assets are, and how much is dismembered in the attachment process.

9.15

(How) Would your answer change if the company's assets are so low that the attempt by even one creditor to attach his loan drives the company into immediate bankruptcy? What if up to two creditors can recover their loans before the company has to file for bankruptcy? Explain your answers carefully.

9.16

Consider the following bankruptcy model (with collection costs of two dollars):

Number of other creditors grabbing	0	1	2
grab	8	2	2
refrain	5	1	4

a. Compute the symmetric mixed-strategy equilibrium.

b. Compare the probability that each creditor *refrains* with the probability that was derived in the text. Explain your answer.

c. How successful is voidable preference law as a deterrent in this case?

9.17

a. Redo exercise 9.16 for collection costs of four dollars.

b. How high would the costs need to be for all three creditors to *refrain* from stripping the insolvent company's assets?

Now consider the general bankruptcy model:

Number of other creditors grabbing	0	1	2
grab	$d - c$	$\frac{V}{3} - c$	$\frac{V}{3} - c$
refrain	$\frac{V}{3}$	$\frac{V-d}{2}$	$\frac{V}{3}$

9.18

a. Write down a parameter configuration in which all creditors refraining is a symmetric Nash equilibrium.

b. Similarly find parameter restrictions so that only one creditor grabbing is a Nash equilibrium.

c. Are the restrictions in parts a and b compatible; that is, can there be a model in which there are two symmetric Nash equilibria?

9.19

Can you think of any changes in the law that would make creditors less likely to strip the assets of an insolvent company? Explain.

ZERO-SUM GAMES

In this chapter we will discuss two-person *zero-sum* or strictly competitive games. Section 10.1 will formally define this category of games and present several examples. Section 10.2 will discuss a conservative approach to playing such a game and define a related concept called a *security strategy*. Section 10.3 will revert to the by now more familiar best-response approach and show that a player can do better with this approach than the conservative one. Finally, in section 10.4, you will see that when both players play a best response—that is, when we are in a Nash equilibrium—then, surprisingly, the two approaches to playing a zero-sum game turn out to be equivalent.

10.1 DEFINITION AND EXAMPLES

In a (two-player) **zero-sum game** the payoffs of player 2 are just the negative of the payoffs of player 1.[1] Consequently, the incentives of the two players are diametrically opposed—one player wins if and only if the other player loses. Most games that are actual sporting contests—such as card games, chess, one-on-one basketball—are, therefore, zero-sum games. Two economic applications that are zero-sum games are (1) the transaction between a buyer and a seller, say, on a house or a used car, and (2) the battle for market share by two firms in a market of fixed size.[2]

Many economic applications are, on the other hand, not zero-sum games; the Cournot duopoly model, the commons problem, and the natural monopoly problem, for instance, are not zero-sum games. In the Cournot problem, collective profits are highest if total production is at monopoly level, but these profits are a lot lower if each firm overproduces. In the natural monopoly problem, if both firms remain in the market, they lose money, but it is profitable for only one of them to remain.

Zero-sum game
A zero-sum game is one in which the payoffs of the two players always add up to zero, no matter what strategy vector is played; that is, for all strategies s_1 and s_2, $\pi_1(s_1, s_2) + \pi_2(s_1, s_2) = 0$.

[1] Zero-sum games are studied only in the case where there are two players. Hence, we will say "zero-sum game" rather than "two-player zero-sum game" whenever we refer to this category of games.

[2] Assume for the first example that the payoff to a buyer is his valuation of the car minus the price while the payoff to the seller is the price minus the seller's valuation. For the second example, assume that, since the market is of fixed size, so also is the total profit (of the two firms). Under these assumptions, the payoffs of the two players always add up to a constant number. We will see in a short while that such a situation can be effectively reduced to a zero-sum game.

Zero-sum games are more important, perhaps, because of the historical role they have played in the development of the subject; that, by itself, is a reason to discuss them. A second reason is that several concepts that were first introduced for zero-sum games have turned out to be very useful for non-zero-sum games as well. In the course of this chapter (and the exercises that follow) we will try to point out which of the results and concepts of zero-sum game theory are valid even outside its confines.

Here are two examples of zero-sum games, one that you have already seen and another that you have not:

Example 1: Matching Pennies

1 \ 2	H	T
H	1, −1	−1, 1
T	−1, 1	1, −1

Example 2

1 \ 2	L	C	R
U	5, −5	8, −8	4, −4
M	−7, 7	9, −9	0, 0
D	9, −9	1, −1	−2, 2

One example that we will use extensively is the squash game of Chapter 8:[3]

Example 3: Squash

1 \ 2	Forward (F)	Backward (B)
Front (f)	20, 80	70, 30
Back (b)	90, 10	30, 70

where in each cell, the entries are, respectively, the winning percentages of players 1 and 2. Example 3 is an example of a related class of games that look, smell, and talk much like zero-sum games. These are called **constant-sum games**. In these games, the two payoffs always add to a constant.

In the game of squash, that constant is 100. Note that if we subtract the constant out of the payoffs, the game would become zero-sum. Furthermore, the players would play this zero-sum transformation exactly the same way that they would play the original constant-sum game.

To see all this, subtract the constant b from every payoff of player 1. In other words, suppose the new payoffs are $\tilde{\pi}_1(s_1, s_2) = \pi_1(s_1, s_2) - b$ for all pairs (s_1, s_2). Evidently this new game is zero-sum because $\tilde{\pi}_1 + \pi_2 = 0$.

Would player 1 behave any differently if her payoffs are $\tilde{\pi}_1$ instead of π_1? The answer is no because $\tilde{\pi}_1$ and π_1 represent exactly the same set of preferences: if a strategy s is preferred to s' under π_1, then it is also preferred under $\tilde{\pi}_1$. Indeed that statement is

Constant-sum game
A constant-sum game is one in which the payoffs of the two players always add up to a constant, say b, no matter what strategy vector is played; that is, for all strategies s_1 and s_2, $\pi_1(s_1, s_2) + \pi_2(s_1, s_2) = b$

[3] For variety's sake we have changed the payoffs just a little bit.

true for mixed strategies as well. Consider a pair (p^1, p^2), p^1 being a mixed strategy of player 1 and p^2 that of player 2:

CONCEPT CHECK
JUST SUBTRACT A CONSTANT

Show that the expected payoffs under $\tilde{\pi}_1$ are nothing but the expected payoffs under π_1 less the constant b, that is,

$$\sum_{s_1} \sum_{s_2} \left[p^1(s_1) \times p^2(s_2) \right] \tilde{\pi}_1(s_1, s_2) = \sum_{s_1} \sum_{s_2} \left[p^1(s_1) \times p^2(s_2) \right] \pi_1(s_1, s_2) - b$$

Hence, if p^1 is preferred to $p^{1'}$ under $\tilde{\pi}_1$, then so must it be preferred under π_1. (Why?) Another way of thinking about it is to interpret the payoff $\tilde{\pi}_1$ as π_1 with an additional penalty $-b$; this is a penalty that player 1 pays regardless of what she does. Such an indiscriminate penalty therefore does not influence her decision making in any way.

From this point on the discussion will apply to zero-sum and constant-sum games; to avoid clutter we will refer to both as zero-sum games. Furthermore, we will only write player 1's payoff, since player 2's payoff is simply the negative of player 1's. Accordingly we will drop the player subscript in the payoff function; for any strategy pair (s_1, s_2) we will write player 1's payoff as $\pi(s_1, s_2)$.

Hence the squash game's payoffs will be written:

Example 3: Squash (again)

1 \ 2	*Forward* (F)	*Backward* (B)
Front (f)	20	70
Back (b)	90	30

10.2 PLAYING SAFE: MAXMIN

10.2.1 THE CONCEPT

In a zero-sum game player 2 does well if and only if player 1 does badly. For any strategy s_1, there is a strategy $b(s_1)$ that player 2 can select that makes his payoff the highest possible and simultaneously makes player 1's the lowest. The strategy $b(s_1)$ is formally defined as

$$\pi[s_1, b(s_1)] = \min_{s_2} \pi(s_1, s_2) \tag{10.1}$$

In the *conservative approach,* player 1 presumes that no matter which strategy she plays, player 2 will correctly anticipate it and play the worst-case or payoff-minimizing strategy $b(s_1)$. Hence, in order to play it safe, player 1 should play that strategy s_1 whose worst-case payoff is better than the worst-case payoff to every other strategy.[4]

It is important that, in choosing her best worst payoff, player 1 consider mixed strategies as well. After all, recall that when we studied the game of squash we found that a player is better off bluffing a little bit; the percentage of times she wins is higher if she mixes her shots between *front* and *back.*

We now come to the formal definition of the guaranteed payoff (or best worst-case payoff). This payoff is called the *maxmin* payoff and denoted m_1:

$$m_1 = \max_p \min_{s_2} \pi(p, s_2)$$

where $\pi(p, s_2)$ is player 1's expected payoff when she plays a mixed strategy p and player 2 plays a pure strategy s_2.[5]

A strategy p^* is a **security strategy** for player 1 if $\pi[p^*, b(p^*)] = m_1$. Two remarks about the safe—or maxmin—approach are worth making.

Remark 1: Since the strategy $b(p)$ minimizes player 1's payoff, it is a *best-response* for player 2 against p (and hence the notation). Consequently, the safe approach is one in which a player expects her opponent to play a best-response strategy and wants to guard against any consequent adverse outcomes.

Remark 2: The safe approach gives player 1 a unilateral way to play the game. She knows that she can do no worse than m_1 if she plays her security strategy p^*. If her opponent in fact does not play a best response, then her payoffs can only be higher. This is unlike best-response behavior, which requires player 1 to think through the question: what is it that I am best responding to? Of course such unilateralism may come at a price; safe play may not be as profitable as best response play. That possibility will be the subject of Section 10.3.

10.2.2 EXAMPLES

Example 1: Matching Pennies

To begin with, let us compute the maxmin payoff if player 1 only uses pure strategies. This pure strategy maxmin payoff is defined as

$$\max_{s_1} \min_{s_2} \pi(s_1, s_2)$$

In matching pennies, regardless of whether player 1 plays H or T, her payoffs are at a minimum if player 2 mismatches; in each case player 1's payoff is -1, and so her *pure-strategy maxmin* payoff is -1.

However, suppose that player 1 does use mixed strategies. Let p denote the probability with which she plays H. If player 2 plays H for sure, player 1's expected payoffs

Security strategy
The strategy that guarantees player 1 her maxmin payoff is called her security strategy.

[4] *This is exactly the same concept that was called the Stackelberg solution when we discussed the Cournot model.*

[5] *The expected payoff $\pi(p, s_2)$ is equal to $\sum_{s_1} p(s_1) \times \pi(s_1, s_2)$, where s_1 is a pure strategy for player 1. Note that in the definition of a maxmin payoff, we only consider pure strategies for player 2 (while considering mixed strategies for player 1). The reason is that player 2 gets no higher a payoff from playing mixed strategies; that is, $\min_{s_2} \pi(p, s_2) = \min_q \pi(p, q)$, where q is a mixed strategy for 2. (Hint: think of the implication of Chapter 8.)*

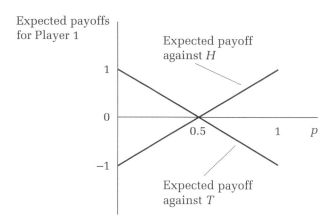

Expected payoffs for Player 1

Expected payoff against H

Expected payoff against T

FIGURE 10.1

are $2p - 1$, while if player 2 plays T for sure, then player 1's expected payoffs are $1 - 2p$. (Why?)

The two sets of expected payoffs are graphed in Figure 10.1. The minimum payoff for any player F is the smaller of the two payoffs; that is, it is the lower envelope of the two expected payoff lines in the figure. It is clear that the highest minimum payoff is realized where the two expected payoff lines intersect, at $p^* = \frac{1}{2}$. Furthermore, the maxmin payoff is 0. Note that this *mixed-strategy maxmin* payoff is higher than the pure-strategy maxmin payoff computed earlier. This is another instance where a mixed strategy guarantees a player a higher worst-case payoff than the pure strategies.

Example 3: Squash
Pure-Strategy Maxmin. Show that the pure-strategy maxmin payoff is 30.

On the other hand, suppose that player 1 plays f with probability p.

Mixed Strategy's Payoffs. Show that the expected payoffs for player 1 when player 2 plays F and B for sure are, respectively, $20p + 90(1 - p)$ and $70p + 30(1 - p)$.

Figure 10.2 displays these two expected payoff lines. As before, the lower envelope represents the minimum expected payoff for each p. It is clear that the highest such minimum payoff is achieved at the intersection of the two expected payoff lines:

Maxmin. Show that the maxmin payoff is achieved at $p^* = \frac{6}{11}$ (with associated payoffs of $\frac{570}{11}$).

(Notice that, yet again, the mixed-strategy maxmin payoff is higher than the pure-strategy maxmin payoff.)

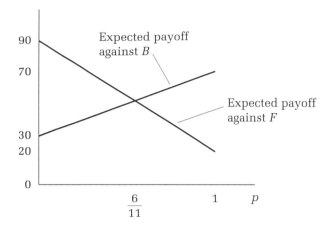

FIGURE 10.2

So far we have concentrated on maxmin payoffs—and the security strategy—of player 1. Analogous arguments however hold for player 2. Player 2's maxmin payoff is denoted m_2 and is defined as

$$m_2 = \max_q \min_{s_1} -\pi(s_1, q)$$

Notice that we have used the fact that player 2's payoffs are given by $-\pi$. Let q^* denote the security strategy of player 2; m_2 is the highest payoff that player 2 can guarantee himself (and he can do that by playing q^*).

10.3   PLAYING SOUND: MINMAX

In the previous section we reached the following conclusion: player 1's payoffs must be *at least as high as* her maxmin payoffs, m_1, and she can guarantee these payoffs by playing safely, that is, by playing her security strategy p^*. In this section we will see that there is an alternative (sound!) way for player 1 to play the game.

10.3.1   THE CONCEPT AND EXAMPLES

Instead of playing to guard against worst-case outcomes, player 1 could play "more aggressively" by playing best responses against player 2's strategies. One could think of this as the more optimistic approach; try to predict the opponent's play and do the best against it. The associated concept is called the *minmax* payoff; it is the worst of the best (response) payoffs for player 1 (and is denoted M_1):

$$M_1 = \min_q \max_{s_1} \pi(s_1, q)$$

where, again, $\pi(s_1, q)$ is the expected payoff to player 1 when she plays the pure strategy s_1 and her opponent plays the mixed strategy q.[6]

[6] *In the minmax definition we restrict attention to pure strategies for player 1 (while considering mixed strategies for player 2). This is because player 1 can do no better by using mixed strategies, that is, $\max_{s_1} \pi(s_1, q) = \max_p \pi(p, q)$. (Why?) If player 2 is also restricted to pure strategies, then the pure-strategy minmax payoff of player 1 is defined as $\min_{s_2} \max_{s_1} \pi(s_1, s_2)$.*

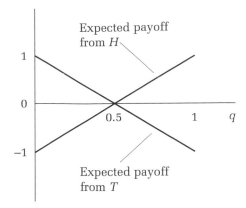

FIGURE 10.3

Let us examine the minmax payoff in examples 1 and 3.

Example 1: Matching Pennies
Pure-Strategy MinMax. Show that the pure-strategy minmax payoff of player 1 is 1.

If, instead, player 2 plays a mixed strategy, say, plays H with probability q, then player 1's payoffs from playing H and T are, respectively, $2q - 1$ and $1 - 2q$.

As before, these expected payoffs can be graphed as in Figure 10.3. The maximum of these expected payoffs is the upper envelope of these two lines. The minmax payoff is then the lowest value of these maximum expected payoffs; that is, the *mixed-strategy minmax* is 0. Note that these payoffs are realized when $q = \frac{1}{2}$; that is, they are realized when player 2 plays his security strategy.

Example 3: Squash
Pure Strategy Minmax. Show that the pure strategy minmax payoff is 70.

Now suppose player 2 plays a mixed strategy, putting probability q on the strategy F.

Mixed MinMax.
- **Step 1.** Show that the two pure strategies for player 1, f and b, give player 1 expected payoffs of, respectively, $20q + 70(1 - q)$ and $90q + 30(1 - q)$. See Figure 10.4.

- **Step 2.** Show that the minmax payoff is $\frac{570}{11}$ and that the strategy of player 2 against which this payoff is realized is $q^* = \frac{4}{11}$. Verify that this is the security strategy of player 2.

Let us collect the computations:

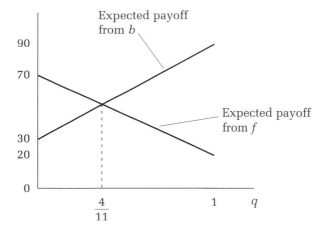

FIGURE 10.4

Example	Pure Maxmin	Mixed Maxmin	Pure Minmax	Mixed Minmax
1	-1	0	1	0
3	30	$\frac{570}{11}$	70	$\frac{570}{11}$

Player 1 realizes her maxmin payoff by playing her security strategy; she gets her minmax payoff when her opponent, player 2, plays his security strategy.

10.3.2 TWO RESULTS ⚠

The examples illustrate two very general results. The first is that by playing the best-response approach, a player can do no worse than by playing safely. The second is that one person's safe approach is another player's best-response approach. After stating the two results, we will prove them in reverse order.

Proposition 1 (Minmax Is Better Than Maxmin). The minmax payoff of player 1 is at least as high as her maxmin payoff, that is, $M_1 \geq m_1$. This statement is true regardless of whether we consider pure or mixed strategies.

Note that the same result also holds for player 2's minmax and maxmin payoffs; that is, his minmax payoff is at least as much as his maxmin payoff. The second result is as follows:

Proposition 2 (One's Minmax Is the Other's Maxmin). The minmax payoff of player 1 is precisely (the negative of) the maxmin payoff of player 2, that is,

$$M_1 = -m_2 = \pi[b(q^*), q^*]$$

(Conversely, the minmax payoff of player 2 is the negative of the maxmin of player 1.)

Proof of Proposition 2

When player 2 plays his security strategy q^*, his payoffs are at least m_2. Put differently, when 2 plays q^*, player 1's payoff is at most $-m_2$. (Why?) In fact it is her best response $b(q^*)$ that gets player 1 a payoff of exactly $-m_2$, that is, $-m_2 = \pi[b(q^*), q^*]$.

If player 2 plays any other strategy q, his worst-case payoffs are less than m_2 by definition; hence, player 1's best payoffs are more than $-m_2$ in this case, that is, $-m_2 \leq \pi[b(q), q]$. (Why?)

The inequality and the equality taken together say that $-m_2$ is in fact player 1's minmax payoff M_1. (Why?) Put differently, player 2's safe approach—playing q^*—when coincident with player 1's sound approach—playing $b(q^*)$—generates the latter's minmax and the former's maxmin payoff. $\diamond$

Proof of Proposition 1

Suppose that player 2 plays his security strategy q^*; by definition, it is better for player 1 to play her best response $b(q^*)$ than to play her security strategy p^*. In other words, $\pi[b(q^*), q^*] \geq \pi(p^*, q^*)$.

In turn, $\pi(p^*, q^*)$ is a payoff higher than what player 1 would get if 2 switched to his best response against p^*, that is, $\pi(p^*, q^*) \geq \pi[p^*, b(p^*)]$. (Why?)

In the preceding proof, we saw that $\pi[b(q^*), q^*] = M_1$. Furthermore, $\pi[p^*, b(p^*)] = m_1$. Hence, Proposition 1 has been proved.[7] $\diamond$

Here is a summary:

- **Safe Strategy.** Player 1 can guarantee herself a payoff of at least m_1 by playing her security strategy p^*; she gets exactly m_1 when her opponent plays his best response to p^*.

- **Sound Strategy.** Player 1 cannot get payoffs any higher than her minmax payoff M_1 if player 2, in turn, plays his security strategy q^*. She gets exactly M_1 by playing a best response to q^*.

10.4 PLAYING NASH: PLAYING BOTH SAFE AND SOUND ⚠

What if both players played best responses; that is, what if we have a Nash equilibrium? Well, somewhat remarkably, that situation turns out to be the same thing as both players playing safe! That conclusion is the main result of this section.

First, note that Nash equilibria in zero-sum games have an interesting characterization:

Definition. A pair of mixed strategies $(\tilde{p}, \tilde{q})$ constitute a Nash Equilibrium of a zero-sum game if for all pure strategies s_1 and s_2,

[7] *The result that a player's minmax payoff is at least as high as his maxmin payoff holds in all games, whether they be zero-sum or non-zero-sum, and whether they be two-player or many-player games.*

$$\pi(\widetilde{p}, s_2) \geq \pi(\widetilde{p}, \widetilde{q}) \geq \pi(s_1, \widetilde{q}) \tag{10.2}$$

Note that the second inequality in equation 10.2 simply says that $\widetilde{p}$ is a best response against $\widetilde{q}$. On the other hand, the first inequality in equation 10.2 says that player 1's payoffs are minimized, among all possible strategies of player 2, by the choice of $\widetilde{q}$. That statement, of course, is the same thing as saying that $\widetilde{q}$ is a best response for player 2 against $\widetilde{p}$.

We will now show that any pair of strategies that constitute a Nash equilibrium of a zero-sum game also constitutes a pair of security strategies for the two players—and vice versa; that is, the security strategies form a Nash equilibrium, provided the maxmin and minmax payoffs are equal to each other.

Proposition 3 (Playing Safe and Sound). Let $(\widetilde{p}, \widetilde{q})$ constitute a Nash equilibrium of a zero-sum game. Then $\widetilde{p}$ and $\widetilde{q}$ are security strategies and the maxmin (and minmax) payoffs are equal to each other and to $\pi(\widetilde{p}, \widetilde{q})$. Conversely, suppose that the minmax and maxmin payoffs are equal. Then the security strategies constitute a Nash equilibrium of the game.

Proof
If $(\widetilde{p}, \widetilde{q})$ constitutes a Nash equilibrium of the game, then

$$m_1 \geq \min_{s_2} \pi(\widetilde{p}, s_2) = \pi(\widetilde{p}, \widetilde{q}) = \max_{s_1} \pi(s_1, \widetilde{q}) \geq M_1 \tag{10.3}$$

The outer inequalities in equation 10.3 follow from the definition of maxmin and minmax payoffs, and the inner ones follow from the definition of a Nash equilibrium, equation 10.2. However, by virtue of Proposition 1 we already know that $m_1 \leq M_1$. Hence, it must be the case that $m_1 = M_1$, that is, that the maxmin and minmax payoffs are equal to each other and to $\pi(\widetilde{p}, \widetilde{q})$.

Since $m_1 = \min_{s_2} \pi(\widetilde{p}, s_2)$ it follows that $\widetilde{p}$ is a security strategy for player 1. (Why?) Proposition 2 and the fact that $\max_{s_1} \pi(s_1, \widetilde{q}) = M_1$ imply that $\widetilde{q}$ is a security strategy of player 2. (Why?)

In order to see the reverse implication, suppose that the maxmin and minmax payoffs are equal. In particular, then, for the security strategies p^* and q^* we have

$$m_1 = \min_{s_2} \pi(p^*, q) = \max_{s_1} \pi(p, q^*) = M_1 \tag{10.4}$$

Since, by definition, $\min_{s_2} \pi(p^*, s_2) \leq \pi(p^*, q^*) \leq \max_{s_1} \pi(s_1, q^*)$ it follows that it actually must be the case that $\min_{s_2} \pi(p^*, s_2) = \pi(p^*, q^*) = \max_{s_1} \pi(s_1, q^*)$. Equation 10.2 then tells us that p^*, q^* must be a Nash equilibrium. ◇

An implication of the above result is seen in the following problem.

CONCEPT CHECK
ALL EQUILIBRIUM PAYOFFS ARE EQUAL

Show that if there are many Nash equilibria in a zero-sum game, then they must all have exactly the same payoffs for both players.

SUMMARY

1. A zero-sum game is one in which the payoff of player 2 is the negative of player 1's payoff; hence player 1's worst possibility is also player 2's best.

2. A safe approach for player 1 is to play a strategy whose worst-case payoff is better than the worst-case payoff of any other strategy. Such a strategy is called a security strategy, and its worst-case payoff is called the maxmin payoff.

3. The maxmin payoff is typically greater when player 1 plays a mixed rather than a pure strategy.

4. A "sound" approach for player 1 is to play a best response against her opponent's conjectured strategy. The lowest best-response payoff is called the maxmin payoff.

5. Player 1's minmax payoff is at least as high as her maxmin payoff. Player 1's minmax payoff is exactly the negative of player 2's maxmin payoff.

6. In a Nash equilibrium, both players play security strategies; that is, the safe and sound approaches coincide. Conversely, when the maxmin and minmax payoffs are equal, the pair of security strategies constitute a Nash equilibrium.

EXERCISES

SECTION 10.1

10.1
Give two real-world examples of game situations between two players in which player 1 gains if and only if player 2 loses. Are your examples zero-sum (or constant-sum) games? Explain.

10.2

Take the duopoly pricing game that we have studied extensively so far.

a. Show that it becomes a constant-sum game if the two firms care only about market share (rather than profits).

b. Write down the zero-sum version of the same game.

c. Would we have a zero-sum game if the two firms were interested in sales (rather than profits)? Explain.

10.3

Consider the two economic examples of constant-sum games that were discussed at the beginning of this chapter: a buyer-seller transaction and two firms competing in a market of fixed size.

a. Write down the strategic form of each of these examples. (Be sure to carefully spell out any assumptions that you need to make in order for these examples to be constant-sum games.)

b. Now write down the zero-sum version of each example.

10.4

Consider a zero-sum game. Suppose that the players play mixed strategies, p and q, respectively. Show that the expected payoffs of the two players—from the strategy pair p, q—add up to zero.

SECTION 10.2

In the questions that follow we will sometimes ask you to compute the *pure-strategy* maxmin or minmax payoff. When there is no such qualification mentioned it means that we have in mind the usual mixed-strategy maxmin or minmax.

10.5

Consider example 2 from the text:

1 \ 2	L	C	R
U	5	8	4
M	−7	9	0
D	9	1	−2

a. Compute the pure-strategy maxmin payoff of player 1.

b. What is the minimum expected payoff if she mixes between the strategies U and M playing the former with probability $\frac{1}{2}$ and the latter with probability $\frac{1}{2}$ as well?

c. What is the minimum expected payoff if she mixes between all three strategies playing U, M, and D with equal probabilities of $\frac{1}{3}$ each?

d. Show that no matter what mixed strategy p player 1 employs, player 2 can hold her expected payoffs from p at or below 4.

e. What can you conclude about the maxmin payoff of player 1 in this example?

10.6

a. Repeat parts a–c of exercise 10.5 for the following variant of the payoff matrix:

1 \ 2	L	C	R
U	5	8	−4
M	−7	9	0
D	9	1	−2

b. Compute the maxmin payoff and the security strategy.

10.7

Consider the following two-firm pricing game in which the two firms—Columbia Bagels and H&H Bagels—can choose either of two prices—high and low—and care only about their market share:

Columbia \ H&H	High	Low
High	60, 40	30, 70
Low	80, 20	50, 50

a. Turn this into a zero-sum game.

b. Compute the security strategy for each firm as well as the maxmin payoff.

10.8

a. Based on your answer to the previous question, what can you conclude about the security strategy and the maxmin payoff if each of the two players has a dominant strategy in the game?

b. What if only one of them has a dominant strategy? (Use game examples if you need to in order to make your point.)

c. What can you conclude about the minmax payoff in either of the two preceding situations?

10.9

Consider the following two-firm advertising game in which the two firms—Columbia Bagels and H&H Bagels—can choose either of two levels of advertising expenditures— high and low—and each firm only cares about long-run market share.

Columbia \ H&H	*High*	*Low*
High	0, 100	70, 30
Low	40, 60	30, 70

a. Turn this into a zero-sum game.

b. Compute the maxmin payoffs and the security strategy for Columbia Bagels. Do this computation first for pure strategies alone and then for mixed strategies.

c. What are the maxmin payoffs for H&H Bagels?

10.10

Consider the following variant of the advertising game in which H&H Bagels has a third strategy of spending modest amounts on advertising. The payoffs—for Columbia Bagels—in this case are represented as follows:

Columbia \ H&H	*High*	*Modest*	*Low*
High	0	10	70
Low	40	36	30

a. Compute the pure-strategy maxmin payoffs and the security strategy for Columbia Bagels. Then repeat the exercise for mixed strategies.

b. What are the maxmin payoffs for H&H Bagels?

SECTION 10.3

10.11

Consider the zero-sum game of exercise 10.5.

a. Compute the minmax payoff of player 1 if player 2 only uses pure strategies.

b. Redo the exercise for mixed strategies; that is, compute the minmax payoff of player 1.

10.12

Consider instead the zero-sum game of exercise 10.6.

a. Compute the minmax payoff of player 1 if player 2 only uses pure strategies.

b. Redo the exercise for mixed strategies; that is, compute the minmax payoff of player 1.

c. Is the pure-strategy minmax equal to the pure-strategy maxmin? What about for mixed strategies?

10.13

Write down the minmax payoff of player 1 in each of the three exercises, 10.7, 10.9, and 10.10. Do the same for the minmax payoff of player 2.

10.14

Give a complete argument for two results that we keep seeing in each of the examples:

a. The pure-strategy maxmin payoff is less than or equal to the maxmin payoff.

b. The pure-strategy minmax payoff is greater than or equal to the minmax payoff.

10.15

Write out fully a proof of the statement: *the minmax payoff for player 2 is precisely the negative of the maxmin payoff for player 1.*

10.16

Sketch an argument to show that Proposition 1 holds for non-zero-sum games as well, that is, that the minmax payoff is at least as high as the maxmin.

SECTION 10.4

10.17

Verify that the security strategies in examples 1 and 3 of the text do in fact constitute Nash equilibria.

10.18

Do a similar verification for the zero-sum games of exercises 10.5 and 10.6.

10.19

Give an example of a zero-sum game that has more than one Nash equilibrium. Be sure to compute all Nash equilibria including those in mixed strategies.

10.20

Consider a further modification of the bagel store model. Suppose that Columbia Bagels can spend modestly on advertising (as well as H&H Bagels). In fact, suppose the payoff matrix is as follows:

Columbia \ H&H	*High*	*Modest*	*Low*
High	0	10	70
Modest	15	50	60
Low	40	36	30

a. Compute the pure-strategy maxmin payoff and minmax payoff for Columbia Bagels.

b. Now compute the (regular) maxmin and minmax payoffs.

c. What are the Nash equilibria of this game?

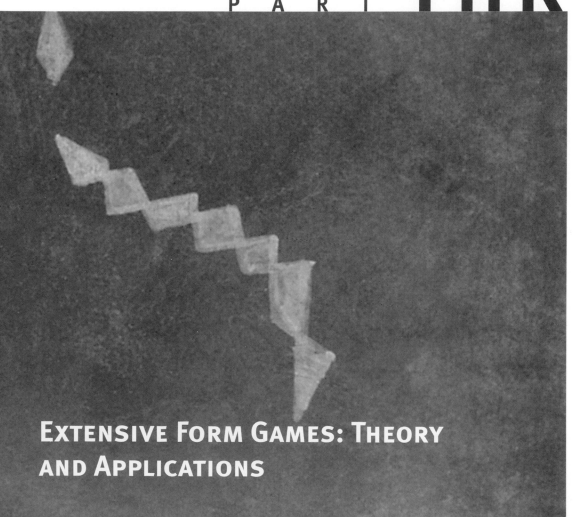

EXTENSIVE FORM GAMES: THEORY AND APPLICATIONS

CHAPTER 11

EXTENSIVE FORM GAMES AND BACKWARD INDUCTION

This chapter is the first stop in the extensive form magical mystery tour. In section 11.1 we will formally discuss the *extensive form* of a game, a representation informally introduced in Chapter 2. In section 11.2 we will discuss a special class of extensive form games called *games of perfect information*. Within this class, we will discuss a solution concept called *backward induction* and illustrate it with several examples in section 11.3. In section 11.4 we will show that backward induction is the same thing as Iterated Elimination of Dominated Strategies in the associated strategic form of the same game. Finally, in section 11.5, we will turn to a case study of poison pills and other takeover deterrents.

11.1 THE EXTENSIVE FORM

Let us recall the basic concepts and terminology of the extensive form. This form is pictured by way of a *game tree* that starts from a unique node called the *root*. Out of the root come several *branches* and at the end of each branch is a *decision node*. In turn, branches emanate from each of these decision nodes and end in yet another set of nodes. A decision node is a point in the game where one player—and only one player—has to make a decision. Each branch of the tree emanating from that node corresponds to one of his choices. If a node has no branches emerging from it then it is called a *terminal node* (and the game ends at that point).

A representative extensive form is the *theater game* that was first discussed in Chapter 2.[1] For convenience, we reproduce the extensive form of that game in Figure 11.1. By following a sequence of branches we get a play of the game. In the theater game, if player 1 picks *c* while player 2, upon seeing this choice, chooses *b*, then the play of the game takes us along the middle branch (*c*) emerging from the root followed by the top

[1] *Two theater-goers have to decide which form of transportation— b(us), c(ab), or s(ubway)—they should take to the Nederlander Theater to see the hit musical* Rent. *There is exactly one ticket left, and whoever gets to the Nederlander first will get it. Player 1 leaves before player 2. A cab is faster than the subway, which, in turn, is faster than the bus. Player 2 gets a ticket under three circumstances: she takes a cab and player 1 takes a bus or the subway, and she takes the subway while player 1 takes a bus.*

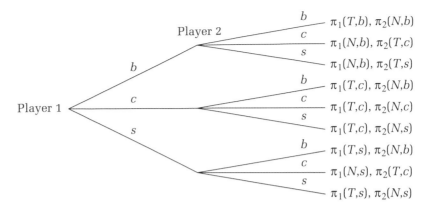

FIGURE 11.1

branch (b) thereafter. For each play of the game, there is a *payoff* to every player. For the play just described, player 1 gets the last ticket. Hence, player 1's payoff is $\pi_1(T, c)$, while that of player 2 is $\pi_2(N, b)$.[2]

We also introduced *information sets* in Chapter 2 to represent simultaneous moves. An information set is made up of nodes that are indistinguishable from the decision maker's standpoint. Suppose for instance that our two theater-goers actually leave simultaneously. Each makes a transportation choice, and if they happen to be the same choice, then there is a 50 percent chance that player 1 will get the ticket (and a 50% chance that 2 will instead).[3] Hence, for example, $\frac{1}{2}\pi_1(T, c) + \frac{1}{2}\pi_1(N, c)$ is the expected payoff to player 1 if both players choose a cab.

The extensive form can be written as in Figure 11.2. Note that the difference between Figure 11.1 and Figure 11.2 is that in the latter case player 2 cannot make her transportation choice conditional on player 1's choice. This is signified by the fact that all three of her decision nodes belong to one information set.

11.1.1   A MORE FORMAL TREATMENT ⚠

In order for a tree to represent a game, the nodes and the branches need to satisfy three consistency requirements:

1. *Single Starting Point.*   It is important to know where a game starts, and so there must be one, and only one, starting point. Hence, a situation as in Figure 11.3 is inadmissible.

2. *No Cycles.*   It is important that we not hit an impasse while playing the game; it must not be possible for the branches of a tree to double back and create a *cycle*.

3. *One Way to Proceed.*   It is important that there be no ambiguity about how a game proceeds, and so there must not be two or more branches leading to a node. Figure 11.4 is inadmissible.

[2] *We have now made the payoffs dependent on ticket availability as well as the mode of transportation. After all, getting a ticket and spending $10 on a cab ride is not quite the same thing as getting it after a $1.50 subway ride.*

[3] *If they make different transportation choices, then suppose, as before, that a cab arrives before the subway and a subway in turn arrives before a bus.*

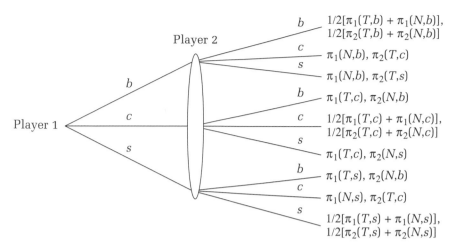

FIGURE 11.2

FIGURE 11.3

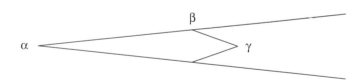

FIGURE 11.4

In order to state the three consistency requirements more precisely, let us introduce one more concept, the **predecessor** of the node. For instance, in the theater game of Figure 11.1, for every one of player 2's decision nodes there is a single (common) predecessor: the root node. Each terminal node, on the other hand, has two predecessor nodes; the root and a decision node of player 2. The root of a tree is the only node that has no predecessors.

To guarantee the three consistency requirements, the following restrictions are imposed on predecessor nodes:

Predecessor

The predecessors of a node, say α, are those nodes from which you can go (through a sequence of branches) to α.

1. *A node cannot be a predecessor of itself*.

2. *A predecessor's predecessor is also a predecessor*: if a node β is a predecessor of α, and a node γ is, in turn, a predecessor of β, then γ is a predecessor of α as well.

3. *Predecessors can be ranked*: if β and γ are both predecessors of α, it must be the case that either β is a predecessor of γ or vice versa.

4. *There must be a common predecessor*: Consider any two nodes, α and β, neither of which precedes the other. Then there must be a node γ that is a predecessor of both α and β.

Restriction 4, by itself, implies that there cannot be two or more roots in a tree. If there are two roots, then there are two nodes neither of which precedes the other. But then there must be yet a third node that precedes them both, and that is a logical contradiction.

Restrictions 1 and 2 together imply that there cannot be a cycle. Suppose it were the case that β is a predecessor of α, γ is a predecessor of β, and so on until we reach a node λ for which α is a predecessor. (This, after all, is what we mean by a cycle.) But then, by restriction 2, α is a predecessor of α. And that result violates the first restriction.

Finally, restriction 3 implies that there cannot be two or more branches leading to α. If there were, then there would be two associated nodes, say, β and γ, that are predecessors of α. However, it must then be the case that either β is a predecessor of γ or vice versa. Put differently, the road from, say, γ, has to come through β.

CONCEPT CHECK
SINGLE PLAY

Show that an implication of restrictions 1–3 is that starting from any node we can find a way—and only one way—back to the root of the tree.

11.1.2 STRATEGIES, MIXED STRATEGIES, AND CHANCE NODES

In our discussion of the extensive form thus far there has been no role for uncertainty. You might wonder how mixed strategies fit into the extensive form. Let us now turn to that and other uncertainties.

Strategies

Recall from Chapter 2 that a player's strategy is a *complete, conditional* plan of action. It is *conditional* in that it tells a player which branch to follow out of a decision node *if* the game arrives at that node. It is *complete* in that it tells him what to choose at *every* relevant decision node.

In the sequential theater game of Figure 11.1, for example, player 1 makes only one choice—at the root. Hence he has three strategies to pick from—take b, take c, or take s. Player 2 is faced with three possible conditionalities: what to do if player 1 takes the bus, what if he took a cab, and, finally, what if player 1 hopped the subway. Hence, each strategy of player 2 has three components, one component for every conditionality. A representative strategy is cbs; take a cab if player 1 takes the bus, bus if player 1 takes a cab, and subway if player 1 hops a subway as well. Since there are three possible ways to choose in every conditionality, player 2 has $3 \times 3 \times 3$, that is, 3^3 such strategies.

CONCEPT CHECK
SIMULTANEOUS THEATER GAME (OF FIGURE 11.2).

Show that the strategy sets of the two players are identical and contain the three strategies, b, c, and s.

Once the strategies have been determined, we can write down the strategic form of an extensive form game by enumerating the list of players, their respective strategies, and the payoff associated with every strategy vector. In the sequential theater game, for example, the strategic form is as follows:

1 \ 2	bbb	cbb	...	ssb	sss
b	$\pi_1(T, b), \pi_2(N, b)$	$\pi_1(N, b), \pi_2(T, c)$		$\pi_1(N, b), \pi_2(T, s)$	$\pi_1(N, b), \pi_2(T, s)$
c	$\pi_1(T, c), \pi_2(N, b)$	$\pi_1(T, c), \pi_2(N, b)$		$\pi_1(T, c), \pi_2(N, s)$	$\pi_1(T, c), \pi_2(N, s)$
s	$\pi_1(T, s), \pi_2(N, b)$	$\pi_1(T, s), \pi_2(N, b)$		$\pi_1(T, s), \pi_2(N, b)$	$\pi_1(T, s), \pi_2(N, s)$

(There are 3^3 columns, one for each one of player 2's strategies.)

Mixed Strategies

A mixed strategy is defined in exactly the same way as in the strategic form; it is simply a probability distribution over the pure strategies. So in the sequential theater game a mixed strategy for player 1 is given by two numbers p and q, which are, respectively, the probabilities with which b and c are chosen (and $1 - p - q$ is the probability with which s is picked). A mixed strategy for player 2 is given by $3^3 - 1$ numbers, one for the probability attached to every pure strategy.

Chance Nodes

We can also build uncertainty that is inherent to the game (as opposed to uncertainty that the players introduce via mixed strategies) into the extensive form. For instance, the amount of time it takes on the subway might depend on whether or not there is a rush-hour delay in the subway system. One way to model that possibility is to allow for a

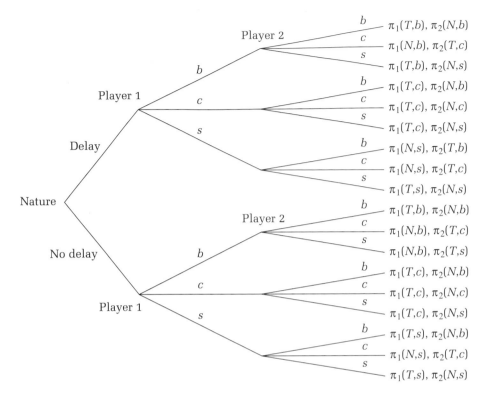

FIGURE 11.5

third kind of node, called a *chance node*; this is a node whose branches represent several random possibilities.

For example, suppose that there are two possible subway outcomes—delay or no delay. This uncertainty needs to be incorporated into the extensive form. Exactly how it will be incorporated will depend on when this uncertainty is resolved: do the players know whether or not there is a delay before they make their choices, and so on. For the simplest possibility, suppose that when our theater-goers make their transportation choice they do know whether there is a delay or not (perhaps because it is reported on the radio).[4] In that case, the extensive form of the sequential theater game becomes Figure 11.5, where the chance node is the root of the tree.

Game of perfect information
An extensive form game with the property that there is exactly one node in every information set.

[4] *Note that the payoffs are specified to reflect the fact that if there is a delay, then even the bus is faster than the subway.*

11.2   PERFECT INFORMATION GAMES: DEFINITION AND EXAMPLES

A **game of perfect information** is one in which there is no information set (with multiple nodes). If an information set has three nodes, then a player cannot tell which of the three immediately preceding nodes is the one that was actually played, although she knows

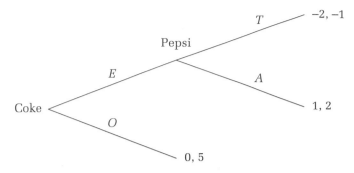

FIGURE 11.6

that one of them must have been played. If, on the other hand, an information set has a single node then there is no such ambiguity; any time a player has to move she knows exactly the *entire* history of choices that were made by all previous players. (Why?)[5]

CONCEPT CHECK
NO SIMULTANEOUS MOVES

Show that a game of perfect information cannot have any simultaneous moves.

Example 1: Entry I

Consider the following economic model. A firm—say, Coke—is debating whether or not to enter a new market—say, the Former Soviet Union (FSU)—where the market is dominated by its rival, Pepsi. Coke's decision is guided by the potential profitability of this new market, and that depends principally on how Pepsi is going to react to Coke coming into its market. If Pepsi mounts a big advertising campaign, spends a lot of money upgrading facilities, ties up retailers with exclusive contracts—in other words, acts "tough"—then Coke will lose money. On the other hand, if Pepsi were not to mount such a tough counterattack—which after all is costly—Coke would make money.[6] In Figure 11.6, *E* (for enter) and *O* (for stay out) stand for Coke's alternatives, whereas *T* (for tough) and *A* (for accommodate) refer to Pepsi's two choices on how to counter Coke's entry. Note that the first entry in each pair of payoffs is Coke's payoff.

Example 2: Entry II

For a (slightly) more complex setting let us consider the following variant. Suppose that after Pepsi's decision, Coke has a further decision to make; it has to decide whether or not it will itself mount an aggressive advertising campaign and spend a lot of money on facilities, and the like. In other words, suppose that after observing Pepsi's response, Coke will itself have to act "tough" or "accommodate" (Figure 11.7).

[5] *The very first time the concept of the extensive form appeared was in John Von Neumann's 1928 article "Zur Theorie der Gesselschaftsspiele,"* Mathematische Annalen, *vol. 100, pp. 295–320. In this article, Von Neumann only considered the two extreme assumptions: (1) when a player knows everything, that is, a game of perfect information, and (2) when a player knows nothing, that is, a game of simultaneous moves.*

[6] *Under Communist rule the only American soft-drink manufacturer with a presence in the Soviet Union was Pepsi. Indeed this was true of all the countries in the Soviet bloc. After the demise of communism, Coke had to make a decision about whether or not to enter these markets. Stay tuned till the next section to find out what happened!*

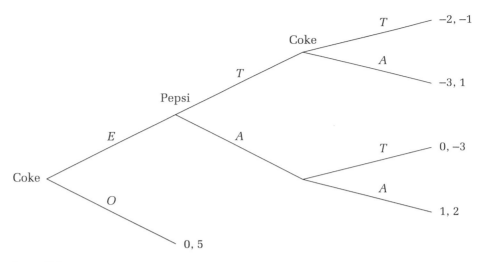

FIGURE 11.7

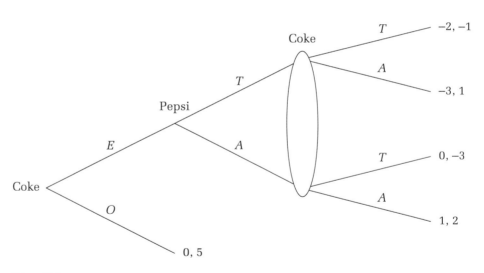

FIGURE 11.8

Example 3 (Not): Entry III

Suppose that, should Coke enter the FSU market, both Coke and Pepsi will make a decision about how much to invest in this market, that is, whether to act tough or accommodate. However, unlike Example 2, suppose these decisions are taken *simultaneously* (and that fact makes this *not* a game of perfect information) (Figure 11.8).

11.3   BACKWARD INDUCTION: EXAMPLES

The question we are interested in is, What is a reasonable prediction about play in examples 1 and 2? It will turn out that this is really a question about *sequential rationality*. It will involve rationality because a player will pick the best action available to him at a decision node, given what he thinks is going to be the future play of the game. It will involve sequentiality because a player will infer what this future is going to be knowing that, in the future, players will reason in the same way. In particular, the decision maker at a subsequent node will pick the best available action given what he, in turn, believes about the remaining future of the game.

Example 1

To illustrate these ideas, let us start with example 1. A first natural step to take in order to predict play is to find the Nash equilibria. Those are actually easier to see in the strategic form of the game.

Coke \ Pepsi	Tough	Accommodate
Enter	$-2, -1$	$1, 2$
Out	$0, 5$	$0, 5$

Note that there are two Nash equilibria of this game: (*enter*, *accommodate*) and (*out*, *tough*). The Nash equilibrium (*out*, *tough*) is, however, unreasonable: Pepsi undertakes to fight Coke if Coke were to enter the market. But if Coke *were* to enter the market, Pepsi would be better off accommodating. Indeed Pepsi's strategy, *tough*, is a best response—to *out*—only because that strategy is actually never used, since, anticipating a tough response, Coke chooses to stay out of the market. However, Coke might not find a tough stand by Pepsi credible precisely for this reason; if its bluff were called, Pepsi would accommodate. By this line of logic, the only reasonable equilibrium behavior is for Pepsi to accommodate; hence, (*enter*, *accommodate*) is the only reasonable Nash equilibrium.[7]

Example 2

The logic employed can be further understood in the more complicated example 2. Again let us start with the strategic form of this game. Note that every strategy of Coke's must have three components. The first component tells Coke whether or not to enter the market, the second tells it whether or not to act "tough" if Pepsi acts "tough," and the third specifies behavior if Pepsi accommodates. For example, *EAT* means (1) enter, (2) against a tough Pepsi, accommodate, and (3) against an accommodating Pepsi, act tough. Pepsi, however, has exactly two strategies—either to act tough or to accommodate Coke.

[7] *Are there any mixed-strategy Nash equilibria in this game? Explain.*

Coke \ Pepsi	T	A
ETT	$-2, -1$	$0, -3$
ETA	$-2, -1$	$1, 2$
EAT	$-3, 1$	$0, -3$
EAA	$-3, 1$	$1, 2$
OTT	$0, 5$	$0, 5$
OTA	$0, 5$	$0, 5$
OAT	$0, 5$	$0, 5$
OAA	$0, 5$	$0, 5$

where the outcome to the strategy pair EAT and T is: Coke enters, Pepsi acts tough, and consequently, Coke accommodates.

There are essentially three pure-strategy Nash equilibria of the strategic form:

1. Nash equilibria in which Pepsi plays T and Coke plays any one of the (four) strategies in which it stays out—OTT, OTA, OAT, or OAA.

2. (ETA, A)—with outcome that Coke enters and both firms accommodate.

3. (EAA, A)—with the same outcome as in the second equilibrium.

Consider Pepsi's decision. What should Pepsi's action be? The answer will depend on whether Coke will subsequently act tough or accommodate. For example, it is more profitable for Pepsi to accommodate if it thinks Coke will accommodate as well, but it is better for Pepsi to fight if it thinks Coke will act tough. In order to determine which of these options will be chosen by Coke—and therefore what Pepsi should do—we can apply the logic of sequential rationality twice.

Suppose that Pepsi accommodates. At this point it is more profitable for Coke to accommodate than to fight. Hence, the only credible choice for Coke is to accommodate. On the other hand, if Pepsi acts tough, Coke will find it more profitable to fight (and so this is the only credible thing for Coke to do). Knowing Coke's responses, Pepsi now has to compare the profits from (T, T) against (A, A), that is, the two profit levels of -1 and 2. Pepsi will therefore accommodate.

One can, finally, back this logic out to Coke's initial decision. Coke can either enter—and then it expects Pepsi to accommodate and expects to do the same thing itself. Or it can stay out. The profit level in the first case is 1, while it is 0 for the second option; Coke enters.

In conclusion, the only sequentially rational strategy for Coke is ETA, while for Pepsi it is to play A; the only one of the three types of Nash equilibria in the strategic form that is sequentially rational is the second one.[8]

[8] *After the demise of communism, "Things have gone better with Coke"; Coke is now the market leader in all of the former Soviet bloc countries, except Rumania and Bulgaria. For an interesting economic account that underlies the model studied in this chapter, see the* New York Times, *March 15, 1995.*

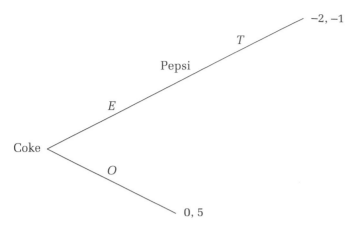

FIGURE 11.9

11.3.1 THE POWER OF COMMITMENT

In life, having fewer choices is typically worse than having more choices. You might think that this should be true for games as well. However extensive form games, and in particular games of perfect information, provide examples where less (choices) can mean more (equilibrium payoffs). This statement may sound paradoxical at first, but the intuition is actually straightforward. If a player has more options later, she may behave very differently in the future than she would if she had fewer options. In turn, this behavior will affect current play by her as well as by the other players. This change can, in principle, be beneficial or harmful to the player with enlarged options.

Let us make matters more concrete by going to our two examples but with a twist.

Example 1′: Only Tough Pepsi

Consider example 1. Suppose that we simplify this (already simple!) example in the following way: after Coke enters the FSU market, Pepsi has no choice but to play *tough* (i.e., let us reduce Pepsi's options by eliminating the choice *accommodate*).[9]

The extensive form is therefore as seen in Figure 11.9. Since Pepsi has only one option, it will necessarily exercise that option and fight Coke's entry. So Coke suffers a loss if it enters this market. Hence, Coke will prefer to stay out. By having fewer options— or, alternatively, by committing to one option in the future—Pepsi is able to increase its (backward induction) equilibrium payoffs.

Example 2′: Only Tough Coke

Consider example 2. Suppose that we modify the example in the following way: after Coke enters the FSU market, Coke has no choice but to play *tough* (i.e., suppose Coke has one option less; it cannot *accommodate*).

The extensive form is therefore as seen in Figure 11.10. Let us apply sequential rationality to this tree. At Coke's second stage "decision nodes" there is only one choice

[9] *This may happen if Pepsi's local management is told by headquarters that they will lose their jobs if Coke gets a toehold in the market. Or management may have already signed contracts with advertising agencies, newspapers, and such to trigger an advertising blitz if Coke comes into the market.*

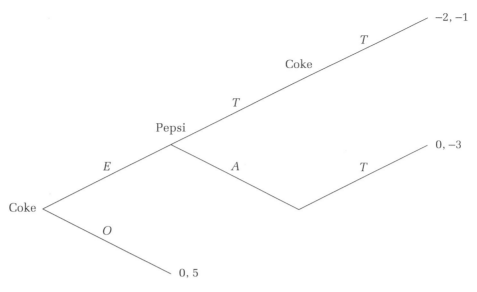

FIGURE 11.10

available—*tough*. This fact implies that while making its choice Pepsi knows that it will surely face a tough opponent in the future. Pepsi's best response is therefore also to play *tough*. Consequently, at the entry stage Coke is better off deciding to stay out, since coming in will entail a loss of 2. Here fewer options for Coke benefits Pepsi because it renders Pepsi's threat to be tough credible.

11.4 BACKWARD INDUCTION: A GENERAL RESULT ⚠

The solution concept employed in the two examples can be generalized; the generalization goes by the name *backward induction*. The logic is the following: suppose the game is at a *final decision node;* any decision by the player who chooses at that node terminates the game. The only reasonable prediction for play is that this player will pick that action which maximizes her payoffs. For instance, in example 2, Coke as the final decision maker gets a higher profit from playing tough if Pepsi is being tough; hence, a rational Coke must pick *tough*. In the other final decision node, that which follows Pepsi accommodating, Coke must pick *accommodate* because it gets a higher profit by doing so.

Consider now a *penultimate decision node*—for instance, Pepsi's decision node in example 2. At any such node, the decision maker knows the *exact* consequence of each of his choices because he knows the subsequent decision that will be taken at the final decision node. For example, Pepsi's tough stance will be reciprocated; so will an accommodating stance. Hence a decision maker at the penultimate decision node can compute the exact payoff to each of his choices, and he must make the best available choice.

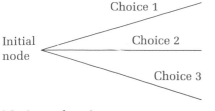

Maximum length $n = 1$ **FIGURE 11.11**

By similar logic, at decision nodes three steps removed from a terminal node, the decision maker knows the exact consequence of her choices. This is the case because she knows the choice that will be made by any player in a penultimate decision node as well as the choice that will be made at the consequent final decision node. Hence such a three-step removed decision maker has a best choice. And so on.[10]

In other words, we fold the game tree back one step at a time till we reach the beginning. The fact that we start at the end of the tree is the *backward* part of the terminology. The fact that we work one step at a time in doing the tree folding is why it is called an *induction* procedure. Note that this procedure works as long as there is a last node to start from.

The above arguments yield the result called *Kuhn's theorem*. A special case of this result was proved in 1913 by E. Zermelo, who showed that the game of chess must always have a winning strategy.[11]

Kuhn's (and Zermelo's) Theorem. Every game of perfect information with a finite number of nodes has a solution to backward induction. Indeed, if for every player it is the case that no two payoffs are the same, then there is a unique solution to backward induction.

Sketch of the Proof

The logical structure of the proof goes by the name of *proof by induction*. The idea is the following: consider any problem that comes in n steps, where n is some positive number. In order to show that an n-step problem is solvable, no matter what the value of n is, it suffices to show that (a) the problem has a solution whenever n equals 1 and (b) if a problem in $n - 1$ steps has a solution, then so must a problem in n steps.[12]

Consider any game of perfect information. Let n refer to the maximum number of steps you need to take in starting from a terminal node and working your way back to the root.[13] Since there are only a finite number of nodes, the maximum number of steps is in turn finite.

For example if $n = 1$, we have a picture like the one seen in Figure 11.11. Clearly there is an outcome to backward induction in this case; pick that action which yields the highest payoff. So we know the theorem is true for $n = 1$. What about a game with $n > 1$ steps? Suppose that any game with $n - 1$ as the maximum number of steps has a backward induction solution.

[10] *In the preceding discussion we implicitly assumed that every choice at a decision node is the same number of steps removed from a terminal node. In general, this need not be the case, but the procedure works anyway. If the maximum number of steps to a terminal node is n, then we can solve the decision problem at that node after n steps of backward induction.*

[11] *But try finding it! This argument suggests, however, the reason why an IBM computer (Big Blue) was able to match up well against the world champion Gary Kasparov in their six-game encounter in Philadelphia in February 1996. By brute force—also called parallel processing!—the computer can do backward induction better than any human being. The computer cannot do backward induction perfectly, since the problem is too big, that is, there are too many branches in the game tree of chess. But one day it will. The world champion then will be a computer!*

[12] *Suppose we know that we can solve the problem whenever n equals 1. By b, we then also know that a problem with n = 2 is solvable. But then, again by b, we know that a problem with n = 3 is solvable. And so on for any finite n.*

[13] *For instance, in example 1, the maximum number is 2, whereas in example 2 it is 3—terminal node to Coke's accommodate/tough decision to Pepsi's accommodate/tough decision to Coke's initial node.*

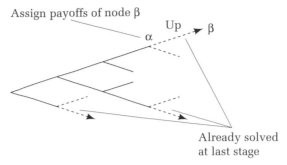

Assign payoffs of node β

Up β

α

Already solved
at last stage

FIGURE 11.12

Take the game with n steps and turn this into an artificial game with $n-1$ steps by folding the tree once; at every final decision node, find the payoff-maximizing—or best-response—action for the player at that node. (For example, suppose that at node α, player 1 has to move and his best move is Up.) Now imagine that the original game "ends" at each of its final decision nodes with payoffs equal to the payoffs that would be realized had the original game proceeded along the best-response branches emanating from these nodes. (For instance, the payoff assigned to "terminal" node α is precisely the payoffs that correspond to the terminal node that comes after playing Up at the node α.) This procedure is illustrated in Figure 11.12.

The modified game has, by construction, a maximum number of steps equal to $n-1$. Hence, by the induction hypothesis, it has a solution to backward induction. Attach this solution to the best response choices at each final decision node of the original game. It is not difficult to show that now we have a backward induction solution to the complete original game.

If no two payoffs are equal—that is, if there are no ties in the payoffs—then the best response is unique at each one of the final decision nodes. But this logic is also true at the first $n-1$ decisions. Put differently, there is a unique solution to backward induction. ◇

11.5 CONNECTION WITH IEDS IN THE STRATEGIC FORM

Backward induction in the extensive form of a game turns out to be exactly the same as solving the game by iterated elimination of dominated strategies (IEDS) in the strategic form. To see this point, let us return to the two examples that were discussed previously.

In example 1 the backward induction outcome was for Coke to enter and for Pepsi to accommodate. For ease of discussion, we reproduce the strategic form of the game here:

Coke \ Pepsi	Tough	Accommodate
Enter	−2, −1	1, 2
Out	0, 5	0, 5

Note that *tough* is a dominated strategy for Pepsi. Hence, the IEDS outcome is indeed (*enter*, *accommodate*).

Consider instead example 2. Again for ease of discussion let us reproduce the strategic form of this game:

Coke \ Pepsi	T	A
ETT	−2, −1	0, −3
ETA	−2, −1	1, 2
EAT	−3, 1	0, −3
EAA	−3, 1	1, 2
OTT	0, 5	0, 5
OTA	0, 5	0, 5
OAT	0, 5	0, 5
OAA	0, 5	0, 5

Note that the first, third, and fourth strategies of Coke are dominated by *ETA*. Eliminating those strategies, we have the following payoff matrix:

Coke \ Pepsi	T	A
ETA	−2, −1	1, 2
OTT	0, 5	0, 5
OTA	0, 5	0, 5
OAT	0, 5	0, 5
OAA	0, 5	0, 5

For Pepsi, *T* is now dominated by *A*. Hence the IEDS outcome is in fact (*ETA*, *A*) exactly as we saw by way of backward induction in the extensive form.

From the two examples you may begin to see why backward induction in the extensive form is equivalent to IEDS in the strategic form. Take a final decision node in the extensive form with, say, two choices at that node. Consider the two strategies that are identical everywhere else except at this decision node:

CONCEPT CHECK
DOMINANCE

Show that, in the strategic form, the strategy that contains the better decision at this node dominates the alternative strategy.

By extension, the strategy that contains the right—or best—decision at each final decision node dominates all other strategies. Hence all other such strategies will be eliminated in the very first stage of the IEDS procedure. In Example 2, the strategy in which Coke reciprocates at both of its final decision nodes—T against T but A against A—dominates the three other ways of deciding at this pair of decision nodes; ETA dominates EAA, EAT, and ETT.

But now take a penultimate decision node in the extensive form. There is a best decision at this node, given what we know is going to be the choice at the subsequent, final, decision nodes. Consider any two strategies that are identical everywhere except at this penultimate node.

CONCEPT CHECK
DOMINANCE, STEP 2

Show that, in the strategic form, the strategy that contains the better decision at this penultimate node must dominate the other strategy.

Indeed all strategies, except those that take the best action at the penultimate node, are thereby eliminated. This procedure, of course, is analogous to folding the tree a second step. (In example 2, A is therefore a better response for Pepsi than T.)

And then we can go to decision nodes three steps from the end. And so on.

11.6   CASE STUDY: POISON PILLS AND OTHER TAKEOVER DETERRENTS

A fact of corporate life is the merger of two companies or the takeover of one company by another.[14] Sometimes the merger is friendly in that the boards of the two companies agree to the terms and necessity of the merger. At other times, the attempted takeover is decidedly unfriendly; the management and board of the target company "fight" the takeover, and the aggressor firm too may take steps to force the transaction.[15]

A target company can fight potential aggressors by building in various legal or economic defenses that make it an unattractive prize. These defenses include, (a) requiring a company that takes over to make costly buyout payments to the management; (b) allowing the board to dilute the company's shares by issuing new shares in the event of an offer by a rival; (c) prohibiting the board from considering any offer that is "not in the long-term interest of shareholders"; and (d) prohibiting management from entertaining certain competitors' offers. These various statutes are sometimes given the common moniker of a "poison pill."[16]

[14] In any given month between 1980 and 1991, the proportion of companies listed on the New York Stock Exchange that received merger or takeover offers varied between 0.25 percent and 2.5 percent. During the height of the takeover mania, between the middle of 1987 and 1988, there was just one month when less than 1 percent of the companies received such offers. (See the article by Robert Comment and G. William Schwert, "Poison or Placebo: Evidence on the Deterrence and Wealth Effects of Modern Antitakeover Measures," 1995, Journal of Financial Economics, vol. 39, pp. 3–43.)

[15] A recent friendly acquisition was Boeing's takeover of McDonnell Douglas. An unfriendly takeover war was the one recently fought over Conrail, the freight carrier with a virtual monopoly in the northeastern United States; Conrail and CSX Corporation together fought Norfolk Southern.

[16] The Comment and Schwert article referred to above reports that 87 percent of all exchange-listed firms now have some form of poison pill statutes built in.

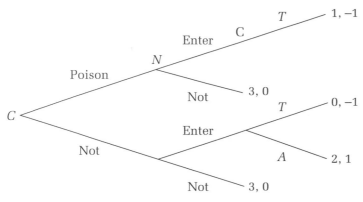

C = CSX/Conrail
N = Norfolk Southern

FIGURE 11.13

In this section we will analyze the working of poison pills. The game-theoretic idea that will be relevant is the power of commitment, the idea that poison pills act as commitment devices.[17]

Let us consider two different ways in which a poison pill may work: they may either discourage aggressors from trying or they may change the terms of the eventual takeover agreements. The first game is a variant on examples 1 and 1′.

Legal Poison Pill 1

Suppose that *without* a poison pill provision the game is that of example 1—Norfolk Southern has to decide whether or not to fight the CSX-Conrail combine. On one hand, if they do decide to fight (and make a share offer), CSX-Conrail can either play *tough* by refusing to negotiate, by upping their own terms, and the like, or they may *accommodate* and reach some trilateral settlement. On the other hand, suppose that *with* a poison pill provision the game is that of Example 1′: CSX-Conrail is committed to fight.

Additionally, now suppose that there is an initial choice that CSX-Conrail has to make, and that is to decide whether or not to arm themselves with the poison pill. The extensive form is therefore as seen in Figure 11.13 (note that the first entry in the pair of payoffs is that of the first mover, i.e., CSX-Conrail).

Without the poison pill, CSX-Conrail will accommodate and hence Norfolk Southern will enter; the former's profits are therefore 2. With the poison pill, Norfolk Southern will choose to stay away from the takeover, and hence CSX-Conrail will make profits of 3. Clearly, CSX-Conrail prefers to adopt the poison pill, and this commitment nets them an extra dollar (billion dollars) of profits.

[17] *A story to keep in mind for illustrative purposes is the freight-rail flap. On October 15, 1996, CSX Corporation and Conrail announced a $8.6 billion dollar friendly merger that would make the merged company the largest freight railroad on the East Coast and give it a monopoly in much of the Northeast. CSX's main rival on the Atlantic Coast, Norfolk Southern, announced on October 22 an unfriendly takeover bid for Conrail that topped the CSX terms. In the meantime, Conrail's board adopted a provision that prohibited it from discussing a merger agreement with any other company until 1999 without CSX's approval. They also invoked certain Pennsylvania statutes that allow management of a company to ignore offers that it considers not to be in a company's long-term interest. Subsequently, the National Transportation Safety Board (NTSB) got involved, the offers were revised upward, and so on. At the end of the section, you will see the denouement to this plot.*

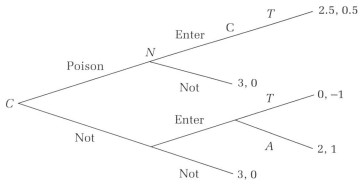

C = CSX/Conrail
N = Norfolk Southern

FIGURE 11.14

Legal Poison Pill 2

All this is fine you think, but didn't Norfolk Southern actually *make* a takeover offer? Well, perhaps then the payoffs—in the extensive form—are slightly different. Consider Figure 11.14. As before, without the poison pill, CSX-Conrails's payoff is 2. Now, though, despite the poison pill, Norfolk Southern finds it profitable to enter (since they make profits of 0.5). However, CSX-Conrail makes a profit of 2.5, which is still better than the 2 they would make by not adopting the poison pill.

So the backward induction outcome is that CSX-Conrail prefers to adopt the poison pill provisions, Norfolk Southern prefers to make a share offer (mount a takeover of Conrail), and CSX-Conrail fights that offer. This example mirrors what actually happened in the freight-rail flap.[18]

SUMMARY

1. The extensive form representation specifies who moves at different points in a game, what their choices are at such moves, and what the eventual consequences are for all players.

2. Restrictions are placed on the precedence between decision nodes to ensure that there is a well-defined play for every choice of strategies.

3. A game of perfect information is one in which every information set has a single element.

4. Backward induction is a general solution concept for games of perfect information. Every finite game of perfect information has a backward induction solution.

5. Backward induction in the extensive form of a game of perfect information is identical to Iterated Elimination of Dominated Strategies in the associated strategic form.

6. In a perfect information game, being able to commit to having fewer choices in the future may be beneficial for a player.

7. Poison pills are commitment devices that restrict management's options in the event of an unfriendly takeover. Consequently, they may increase the payoffs of a target firm.

EXERCISES

SECTION 11.1

11.1
Draw an extensive form game with two players and three decision nodes. Is there more than one game tree for this description of players and decision nodes? Explain.

11.2
Redo the *theater game* of Figure 11.1 to allow for the possibility that a cab can get caught in a traffic jam (and in that case is slower than the subway, although it is faster than the bus). Suppose that traffic conditions are known to both players before they make their transportation choices. Be sure to explain carefully the payoffs that you assign.

11.3
Redo exercise 11.2 to allow for the possibility that traffic conditions become known only after the theater-goers make their choices. Suppose also that there is a 25 percent chance that a cab can get caught in a traffic jam. Be sure to explain the payoffs carefully.

SECTION 11.2

11.4
Represent the game of Marienbad (see Chapter 1)—with a starting configuration of 3 matches in each pile, that is, (3, 3)—in extensive form. Is this a game of perfect information? Explain.

11.5

Use backward induction to solve the game from a configuration of $(1, 0)$. What about $(2, 0)$ and $(3, 0)$?

11.6

Similarly, use backward induction to solve the game from a configuration of $(1, 1)$. What about $(2, 1)$ and $(3, 1)$?

11.7

Now use backward induction to solve the game from a configuration of $(2, 2)$. What about $(3, 2)$? Finally, what about the starting configuration $(3, 3)$?

11.8

How does the solution that you uncovered in exercises 11.5–11.7 compare with what we called the "winning strategy" in our discussion of Marienbad in Chapter 1? Explain your answer.

11.9

Repeat the analysis of exercises 11.5–11.7 for Nim; that is, uncover the backward induction solution to Nim if the initial configuration of matches in the two piles is $(3, 3)$.

11.10

Consider example 2. Recall that there are four strategies—*OTT*, *OTA*, *OAT*, and *OAA*—in all of which Coke makes an initial decision not to enter the FSU market.

a. Explain carefully how, from each of these four strategies, we can find answers to the counterfactual question "What would Coke do *if* it entered the market?"

b. Explain carefully why, in order to check for sequential rationality, we need to be able to find answers to the same counterfactual question.

11.11

Consider example 2 again. Show that there are no (fully) mixed-strategy Nash equilibria in that game of entry, that is, there are no Nash equilibria in which both players play mixed strategies. (Hint: Show that if Pepsi mixes between T and A, then Coke will never play any of the strategies *ETT*, *EAT*, and *EAA*—since these are all dominated by *ETA*.)

11.12

Based upon your answer to exercise 11.11, what can you say about the existence of mixed-strategy Nash equilibria in games of perfect information? In particular, is it true that the backward induction procedure picks out the only sequentially rational solution among the full set of pure as well as mixed strategies? Explain.

11.13

Suppose that Coke's decision on the FSU market is reversible in the following sense: after it has entered and after Pepsi has chosen T or A, Coke has any one of three options to choose from: T, A, and $O(ut)$. Suppose that exiting at that point nets Coke a payoff of -1 and Pepsi a payoff of 3 if it had been *Tough* and 4 had it *accommodated*. Write down the extensive form of this game.

11.14

Solve the game of exercise 11.13 by backward induction. Explain any connection to the power of commitment that you unearth in your solution.

SECTION 11.4

11.15

Show an example of a game of perfect information in which the maximum number of steps you need to take, n, starting from a terminal node and working back to the initial node, is 3. Give an example where $n = 6$.

11.16

In the game tree of Marienbad that you drew in exercise 11.4, do a one-step induction. In other words, solve the game at every one of the final decision points, and create a game with $n - 1$ maximum number of steps.

11.17

Show that if we attach a backward induction solution to the $n - 1$ step problem to the best choices at the final decision nodes, we get a backward induction solution to the n step problem.

SECTION 11.5

11.18

Write down the strategic form of the game of exercise 11.13.

11.19

Solve the game by IEDS.

11.20

Explain carefully how each of your steps of iterated elimination corresponds to steps in which you fold the game tree while doing backward induction.

CHAPTER 12

AN APPLICATION: RESEARCH AND DEVELOPMENT

This chapter will present an application of the backward induction solution proposed in the previous chapter. The economic problem is that of *research and development (R&D),* and the setting for this particular application is that of a *patent race.* The R&D problem will be discussed in section 12.1, and a model of a patent race will be presented in section 12.2. In section 12.3 we will derive the backward induction solution of that model. Section 12.4 will conclude with a discussion of possible generalizations of the model.

12.1   BACKGROUND: R&D, PATENTS, AND OLIGOPOLIES

The engine of growth for modern economies is technological progress; indeed, this has been the engine for some 250 years, ever since the early years of the Industrial Revolution.[1] Some economists have estimated that by far the majority of the growth that has taken place in the United States economy in the 20th century has been driven by technological advancement.[2] Even today, many of the sectors that are experiencing the highest rates of growth—such as computers, telecommunications, pharmaceuticals, and biotechnology—are, in fact, the sectors where the growth rates of technology are the highest. It is therefore extremely important to answer such questions as, What drives the growth of new technologies, and how can government R&D policy further stimulate this growth?

A central aspect of an innovation is that it is a *public good*; a new idea can be exploited by whoever has access to it—and the next person who gets access to it will not have any less of the idea to work with. For example, if a new gene is sequenced, and the result is announced in a scientific journal, then the same code will be available to

[1] *A spate of technological breakthroughs launched the Industrial Revolution in England in the middle of the 18th century. Important innovations of the 18th and 19th centuries included the steam engine and the spinning jenny in the textile industry, and the Bessemer process in the iron and steel industry.*

[2] *For instance, in a famous study published in 1957, Robert Solow of MIT estimated that 87.5 percent of the growth in United States GNP between 1909 and 1949 could be attributed to technological growth (see Technical Change and the Aggregate Production Function, Review of Economics and Statistics, vol. 3: pp. 312–320).*

every person who reads the scientific paper. Furthermore, using this information, a new drug could be developed by any pharmaceutical company that has the requisite drug development infrastructure.

This brings up the question, If the original gene sequencing was a costly enterprise, why would any drug company do this spadework? They would all rather have some other company's laboratory do the initial sequencing, acquire the information from the scientific journal, and then only spend money to actually develop the consequent drug.[3] However, if all drug companies thought along these lines, nobody would do the initial, but critical, work.

That is precisely where patents come in; they are a way of rewarding the company that did the original sequencing. A patent on a sequence gives a company the exclusive right to develop any drugs that emerge from that initial research breakthrough. Patents can be awarded with different degrees of comprehensiveness: some cover all developments that emerge from the first innovation, whereas others only cover developments that arise directly from it. The important point is that patents give private companies an incentive to do R&D[4] and they have a "winner-take-all" element to them.[5]

In most major modern economies, R&D is conducted by private firms in oligopolistic industries. For instance, the U.S. pharmaceutical industry, which spends $15.8 billion annually on R&D, is an industry with a few major firms and another cluster of smaller players. Hence there is intense competition among these companies in the development of new drugs.

In an oligopoly, since there are only a few rivals and doing R&D is a costly business, its conduct is a strategic variable. In choosing how much R&D to do, how many new projects to fund, when to fund them, when to pull the plug on an R&D project that is not proceeding satisfactorily, and the like, an oligopolistic firm takes into account decisions on similar matters that its rivals make. That factor brings game theory into this important issue and brings us to the analysis of this chapter.

12.1.1   A PATENT RACE IN PROGRESS: HIGH-DEFINITION TELEVISION

High-definition television (HDTV) is thought by many to be the next frontier in home entertainment. HDTV, by using a digital technology, will provide a much higher picture quality than conventional (analog) television images. In particular, picture quality will not depreciate even on very large screens, and the color quality will be several times better. On Christmas Eve, 1996, the Federal Communications Commission finally approved the industry-wide standard for this technology. The FCC is also encouraging broadcasters to switch to the new technology by granting them the necessary increase in the broadcasting spectrum.[6]

The history of HDTV is interesting especially for the insights it gives about the R&D process. The first steps toward its development were taken in Japan, where at the urging of the Japanese Broadcasting Corporation a consortium of Japanese television manufacturers started research on digital television technology in 1964.[7] In the early 1980s they carried out the first experimental transmission of HDTV signals, and at an

[3] This statement is especially true given the costs of developing a new drug from start to finish. One study estimated that the average cost of doing so is about $359 million (see "Pharmaceutical R&D: Costs, Risks, and Rewards," 1993, U.S. Congress, Office of Technology Assessment). This study is based on drugs that were developed in the 1980s, and it may actually underestimate the costs of developing new drugs today, because the length of time that drugs undergo clinical trials has now increased to an average of 15 years.

[4] Edward Mansfield of the University of Pennsylvania estimated the percentage of commercially introduced innovations that would not have been developed without patent protection (see Intellectual Property Rights and Capital Formation in the Next Decades, University Press of America, 1988). The numbers range from 60 percent for pharmaceuticals and 38 percent for chemicals through 17 percent for machinery and 1 percent for primary metals.

[5] A company that holds a patent can license the technology to other companies or can enter into joint development agreements with others. The point remains, though, that a patent is a way of making a research breakthrough less freely available to those who did not make the breakthrough.

[6] Since HDTV signals carry more information, they need wider bandwidths for transmission than does conventional television technology. Incidentally, much of the information in this subsection comes from the article "The Next Generation of Television" by Dale Cripps, featured in the HDTV Newsletter and available at the web site teletron.com/hdtv/

international meeting in Algiers in 1981, they presented the first set of standards for the new technology. About this time, the American Electronics Association decided that HDTV was indeed going to be the technology of the future and urged the American administration to take steps to help catch up with the Japanese. A consortium of largely American companies that goes by the (sinister sounding) name of the Grand Alliance[8] was formed. The American consortium has made rapid progress since its inception and is now acknowledged to be the technological leader. But the race is still on. . . .

12.2   A MODEL OF R&D

The setting for our model is a duopolistic industry—say, consumer electronics—in which each firm is working toward a technological breakthrough—say, HDTV. To the winner go the spoils; the winner gets a patent for the new innovation. The questions of interest are these: How much should each firm spend on R&D, and how often? When should it get into a race, and at what point should it opt out of such a race? What factors determine the likely winner: is it an advantage to be in a related manufacturing area, is it more important to have a superior R&D department, and so on?[9]

Suppose there are two firms in an industry, RCA and Sony—hereafter firm R and firm S—each of which is conducting R&D to produce HDTV.[10] There are several stages that need to be completed successfully before HDTV can be brought to the market. To make the analysis tractable, we will make several simplifying assumptions:

1.   The distance from the eventual goal can be measured; we can say, for example, that firm S is n steps from completing the project.

2.   Either firm can move 1, 2, or 3 steps closer to the end in any one period.

3.   It costs $2 (million) to move one step forward, $7 to move two steps forward, and $15 to move three steps forward.[11]

4.   Whichever firm completes all the steps first gets the patent; the patent is worth $20.

Discussion of the Assumptions

The first assumption says, in essence, that there is a one-dimensional index by which the technology can be measured. For instance, the number of technological problems that need to be resolved before a company can apply for a patent may be the number of steps from completion of the project.

The second assumption asserts that infinite progress cannot be made in one period. You can think of a period in this game to be, say, anything from one to three months. The assumption says that if the project is at an early stage, we cannot expect to complete it

[7] The consortium included such household names in consumer electronics as Sony, Panasonic, Toshiba, Hitachi, Mitsubishi, and JVC.

[8] The Grand Alliance is made up of David Sarnoff Research Laboratories (David Sarnoff as head of RCA was the pioneer in color television), General Instrument, Zenith, AT&T, Philips, MIT, and Thomson.

[9] The model in this chapter is drawn from Christopher Harris and John Vickers' "Patent Competition in a Model of Race," Review of Economic Studies, 1986, vol. 52, pp. 193–209. They do not, however, suggest the application to HDTV and should not therefore be held responsible for any awkwardness in the fit between their model and the facts of the HDTV world.

[10] Alternatively, there are two consortia conducting R&D. We use the terminology "two firms" rather than "two consortia" simply because the latter term is a little unwieldy.

[11] A firm can also decide not to make any progress at all, that is, move 0 steps. The cost is $0.

over the next three-month period. As the project nears completion—that is, when it is already within three steps of completion—it can indeed be finished in one period.[12]

The third assumption says there is no free lunch. If the project is to move faster, its managers have to hire more personnel or invest in greater infrastructure, and so on, all of which costs more money. The actual numbers have been chosen to reflect an underlying decreasing returns to scale in R&D; costs go up faster when a firm tries to complete 3 rather than 2 steps than they do in going from 1 to 2 steps.

Finally, the fourth assumption is the definition of a patent; it gives the winner a positive reward (whereas the loser gets zero). This reward can be thought of as the increased profits from selling a product with an exclusive technology, a technology that no other competitor possesses. Hence, the total profit to the patent winner is the value of the patent less the cost incurred in winning it. For the other firm, the total loss is the R&D cost.

The numbers that we use are for illustrative purposes. In the Exercises section you will redo the analysis with other sets of numbers. Also, at the end of this chapter we will suggest some further generalizations of the assumptions.

Before getting to the game-theoretic analysis, however, let us first ask what would happen in this simple model if the two firms were able to coordinate their R&D activities and operate as a *cartel* (and hence pick the R&D expenditures to maximize joint profits).

CONCEPT CHECK
CARTEL, STEP 1

Verify the following statement: *Since only one of the two firms is going to get the patent, it only pays to have one of them do R&D.*

CARTEL, STEP 2

Verify the following statement: *Whichever firm does R&D does so by spending the smallest possible amount and moving forward a step at a time. Furthermore, the firm chosen will be the one that is closer to finishing.*

(Hint: For the first part of the statement remember that there are decreasing returns to doing R&D.)

The two steps would be true in a modified form if there is uncertainty and impatience.[13]

To summarize, a cartel would minimize R&D competition. It would let the technologically more advanced member firm advance toward the patent in minimal cost increments.

[12] *This assumption can be a consequence of technological constraints as well. If, for example, five technological problems need resolution and the project team can start on the fourth problem only after the first three have been satisfactorily resolved, then it is very likely that they will not get to it within the next period.*

[13] *The argument of step 1 would be less true if there were uncertainty in the R&D process. In that case, the cartel might wish to have both firms do R&D because there is a greater probability that at least one of the two will finish the project quickly. The second step would need to be modified if the cartel had reason to want to bring the new product to the market as quickly as possible. We will discuss these generalizations in the last section.*

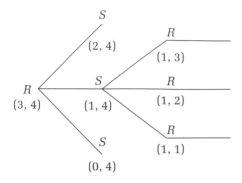

FIGURE 12.1

12.3 BACKWARD INDUCTION: ANALYSIS OF THE MODEL

What would be the duopoly outcome (with the two firms competing in their pursuit of the patent)? Somewhat surprisingly, it turns out that we get a sharp answer to that question if we make one last assumption:

5. The two firms take turns deciding how much to spend on R&D; if RCA makes an R&D decision this period, it waits to make any further decisions till it learns of Sony's next R&D commitment. Furthermore, Sony makes its announcement in the period following RCA's announcement.

One way to think about this assumption is that each firm's management makes periodic reviews of the project. These reviews are conducted every few months, and at each such review a decision is taken about R&D spending until the next review. The decision might be to step up spending levels, to hold them at the current level, or to cut back. Firms alternate in their decisions if the review dates are different, although the length of the review period is the same for the two firms.

Assumption 5 turns the patent race into a game of perfect information; let us look at its extensive form. In Figure 12.1, RCA has the first R&D decision, and RCA and Sony are, respectively, 3 and 4 steps from completing the project.

A somewhat more transparent depiction of this same situation can be given in a *location space* picture. By that we mean a picture in which the "coordinates" of the two firms—that is, how far they are from finishing—are graphed. In this location space picture, the northeast point refers to the joint finish line for both firms; that is, successful completion of R&D by both firms. The finish line for *S* is the vertical terminal line, whereas the finish line for *R* is the horizontal terminal line; see Figure 12.2.

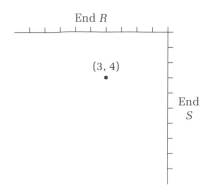

FIGURE 12.2

The following notation will be useful for the location space. If R is r steps from completion while S is s steps away, we will denote their location as (r, s). The game will be solved by backward induction on the location space. In other words, we will show that when either firm is near completion there is a best way for them to make their R&D choice. In turn, these eventual decisions will affect the choices the firms make at more formative stages of R&D.

To illustrate these ideas, we will proceed in a stepwise fashion:

• **Step 1.** Suppose that the game is at $(1,s)$, and it is firm R's turn to move. Its optimal decision evidently is to finish the game in one move. That will yield a patent of value $20 (million) and will cost $2 (million). Similarly, if the location is $(r, 1)$ and it is firm S's turn to move, S will complete the project in one step.[14]

• **Step 2.** Now suppose that the two firms are at either $(2, 1)$ or at $(3, 1)$, and it is firm R's turn to move. It can complete in one move, and if it does R makes a positive profit at both locations: $20 − $7 in the first case and $20 − $15 if it is 3 steps from finishing. Indeed, if R does *not* finish the game in one move, it knows that S will do so at the very next opportunity (why?), and hence R will either make nothing from that point on or suffer a loss. For example, if R chooses to make no progress, which is costless, it will find that S will win the patent in the next period. If it makes incomplete progress—1 step starting from $(2, 1)$ or 2 steps or less from $(3, 1)$—it will incur a cost but will not win the patent.

Hence, it is best for R to complete in one step if it has a move at $(2, 1)$ or at $(3, 1)$. Of course, the same result holds if the firms are at $(1, 2)$ or at $(1, 3)$ and it is firm S's turn to move; S will complete in one step.

In turn this result has the following implication:

• **Step 3.** (a) Use the previous analysis to show that if the game is at $(2, 2)$, whichever firm has the first move should invest for two steps and finish the game. (b) Can you then

[14] *Note that we made no mention of how much either firm may already have spent. Regardless of how much has already been spent, a firm one step from finishing stands to make a net profit of $18 by completing the project. We will come back to this idea—the irrelevance of sunk costs—at the end of this chapter.*

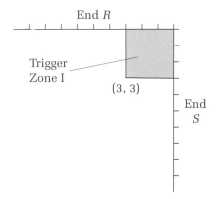

FIGURE 12.3

show that if the game is at $(3, 2)$ and it is firm R's turn to move, it should finish in one step. What if the game is at $(2, 3)$ and S has the first move?[15]

In fact what we have shown via steps 1 through 3 is the following:

Proposition (TI).   If the game is at any location (r, s), $r \leq 3$ and $s \leq 3$, whichever firm has the first move at that point will trigger a completion, that is, will end the project in one step.

Call this set of locations *Trigger Zone I,* as seen in Figure 12.3. Let us use the information about Trigger Zone I to analyze what happens at other locations. What we are really going to do is fold the location space back; that is, we will do backward induction on it. Since we know what is going to happen at the "end" of the space, we can now ask what will happen at a penultimate zone of that same space.

• **Step 4.**   For instance, what can we conclude about a location such as $(4, 3)$ when it is firm R's turn to move? Note that R cannot finish the game in one step. The most that it can do is move its project forward by three steps to $(1, 3)$. Or it can move two steps to $(2, 3)$ or one step to $(3, 3)$. Or it can remain where it is by stopping R&D. In the first three of these cases, R knows that S will, in fact, finish the game at the next step. (Why?) So the best response for R is to pick the fourth option, make no progress. This is equivalent to dropping out of the race.

If firm R finds it in its best interest to drop out of the patent race at $(4, 3)$, what should firm S do subsequently? Well, firm S, as the sole survivor, will get the patent eventually. Since rapid R&D is more costly than slow R&D, the best approach for S is to move in the least costly fashion, one step at a time, toward the patent.

• **Step 5.**   Show that the same conclusion, R should drop out of the race and S should then advance slowly, is true also for locations $(4, 2)$ and $(4, 1)$. What about locations $(5, 3)$, $(5, 2)$, and $(5, 1)$?

[15] *In all of these cases, ask yourself what would happen if the first mover did not complete the project in one step. What, in particular, would its rival do in the next period?*

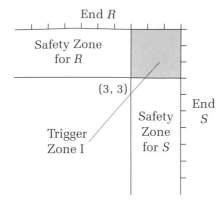

FIGURE 12.4

Iterating, we can, in fact, conclude the following:

Proposition 2. For all locations (r, s), whenever $r > 3$ and $s \leq 3$, the best thing that firm R as a first mover can do is drop out. After this, firm S can take a step forward at a time.

This set of locations is therefore called *Safety Zone I* for S; in these locations, S can coast and R will drop out. Since the game is symmetric, we can also conclude that all locations (r, s), $r \leq 3$ and $s > 3$, is Safety Zone I for firm R. The two safety zones are pictured in Figure 12.4.

Let us continue with the backward induction argument. We know that in Trigger Zone I there will be a preemptive move while in Safety Zone I, the "war" is over. The next question to ask is, Is there an incentive for either firm to try and get into its own safety zone even if doing so means doing rapid R&D?

• **Step 6.** Consider a location such as (4,4). Suppose it is firm R's turn to move. Firm R can, in fact, take the game into its Safety Zone I in one step—at a cost of 2. Thereafter it knows that S will drop out, and hence it can move a step at a time toward eventual completion; those three steps will cost a further $6. The total costs then will be $8, and that is less than the value of the patent.

More is true; as long as R has a way to get into its safety zone—and thereafter move a step at a time—while incurring costs that are no more than $20, the value of the patent, it is worth R's while to do so. The argument applies symmetrically, of course, to firm S.

• **Step 7.** Show that from locations (r, s), if $r, s = 4, 5$, the first mover will find it profitable to take the game in to its Safety Zone I. Show that if R has to move at $(5, 4)$, its consequent net profit is $7.

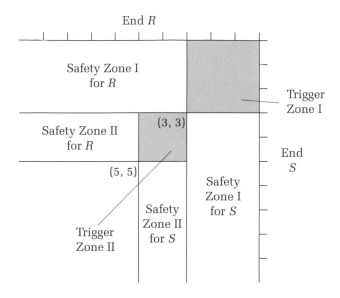

FIGURE 12.5

However, it is not worth firm R's while to move into its safety zone if it is at $(6, 5)$. That would cost \$21 in total (why?), which exceeds the value of the patent. Of course, this result implies that, from that location, the best response for R, if it is the first mover, is to drop out of the race. (Why?)

These arguments give us the following:

Proposition 3.   There is a second Trigger Zone between $(3, 3)$ and $(5, 5)$; the first mover in this zone should move the game into its own Safety Zone I. There is also a second set of safety zones. The one for R is $3 \leq r \leq 5$ and $s > 5$ (and symmetrically for S). In Firm R's Safety Zone II, S should immediately drop out. See Figure 12.5.

Continuing in this fashion, we get the picture shown in Figure 12.6 for the solution in location space.

To summarize, the associated strategies are the following: If S is in R's safety zone—whatever the zone number—the best thing it can do is drop out of the race. Firm S in its own safety zone spends the minimum amount on R&D, moves a step at a time, and coasts to win the patent. In Trigger Zone n, each firm spends what it needs to—profitably—to get an invincible advantage for itself and move the game into safety zone $n - 1$.[16]

For these numbers on costs and patent value, there are six trigger zones and five corresponding safety zones. Different numbers on the cost and patent value variables will change the size and number of these zones, but will not change the qualitative feature of the solution. Indeed, you will establish the truth of this assertion in the Exercises.

[16] *Note that except for the trigger zones, the outcome looks a lot like the cartel solution. In other words, the duopolists fight—or spend money—to establish initial advantage, but once that advantage has been established there is only a single firm that continues to do R&D.*

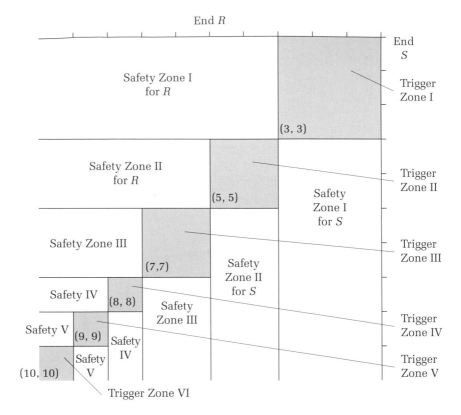

End R

Safety Zone I
for R

End
S

Trigger
Zone I

(3, 3)

Safety Zone II
for R

Trigger
Zone II

(5, 5)

Safety
Zone I
for S

Safety Zone III

Trigger
Zone III

(7,7)

Safety
Zone II
for S

Safety IV

(8, 8)

Safety
Zone III

Safety V

(9, 9)

Safety
IV

Trigger
Zone IV

(10, 10)

Safety
V

Trigger
Zone V

Trigger Zone VI

FIGURE 12.6

12.4 SOME REMARKS

First, our solution teaches us the importance of "sunk costs." Even if firm S has already spent a large sum up until some point, it will be ready to spend up to $20 additionally in order to secure the patent. It will be willing to do so because its net profit from that point on is the patent value minus additional costs, and this net profit is positive as long as the additional costs are less than $20. Hence the way that the game gets played from any location (r, s) is completely independent of how the game got to that point, that is, is independent of the investments that have been sunk by the two firms in getting to that location.

Second, the symmetry assumptions that we made—each firm's costs of doing R&D are identical, and so is the value of the patent—are completely inessential. The entire analysis can be repeated for the case of dissimilar costs or patent valuations. All that changes is that the sizes of the trigger and safety zones become firm-specific. If a firm has lower costs, its zones are going to be bigger, for example. It still remains true, however, that from any location we will see a one-step movement to a safety zone or an immediate dropout by the first mover.[17]

[17] *Again, you will work through some exercises to better understand this point.*

Third, the larger the value of the patent, the larger are the trigger zones. For instance, if the value of the patent is $30, then the size of Trigger Zone II would be the "square" between (3,3) and (6,6), and that of Trigger Zone III would be between (7,7) and (9,9). Put differently, the patent race would be much more of a race; a firm would drop out only if it was more than three steps behind its rival but would remain in the race if it was any closer. The higher the value of the patent—or the lower the costs of doing R&D—the more likely it is that we have a horse race.

Fourth, if there is uncertainty about the outcome to R&D, then that might induce a firm to stay in the race longer, because there is some chance that would looks like an insurmountable lead now will not remain so forever.

Fifth, if a firm has a preference for quick profits—rather than profits that accrue further off in the future—it may choose to do R&D more rapidly even when there is no competitive threat. For example, consider the cartel doing R&D. If a cartel member is three steps from finishing the cartel, how much should the cartel spend in the current period? If the patent is only useful when acquired immediately, the cartel will clearly choose to complete all three steps in the current period (and pay the higher cost of $15). More generally, if the future is discounted, the analysis applies except the size of the trigger and safety zones and the behavior within a safety zone depend on how heavily the future is discounted.[18]

Sixth, public policy toward R&D is extremely important in this setting because it pays to be ahead even if it is by a small amount. In the case where the other firm is a foreign competitor, for example, it will pay the domestic government to subsidize the R&D efforts of the domestic firm so as to give the latter the necessary small advantage. Furthermore, since all that is required is a small advantage, public policy is also very cost-effective in this context.[19]

Finally, what have we learned about HDTV from our model? We know that neither consortium has dropped out. This fact suggests that profits are expected to be high (or R&D costs are low). Both these inferences sound reasonable; clearly both consortia (and their administration backers) view HDTV as the technology of the future—and hence expect large eventual profits. (Further, each government has defense or other motivations that make the nonmonetary payoffs also loom large.) Doing R&D through the consortia has lowered the riskiness as well as the capital costs of doing R&D. Finally, if the firms are in their (large) trigger zones, they should be doing R&D as rapidly as possible. There is certainly evidence to suggest that they are.

[18] See Chapter 15 for a discussion of discounting.

[19] Of course, if both governments are subsidizing their respective R&D efforts, public policy may not be quite as effective. In particular, relative positions may be completely unchanged if the two governments spend the same—or similar—amounts on subsidizing R&D. This may be a better description of Japanese and U.S. public policy toward R&D in HDTV. Both governments are active—the Japanese through the Japanese Broadcasting Corporation's Science and Technology Center and the Americans through the Advanced Television Center; their efforts might therefore be a wash.

SUMMARY

1. A technological breakthrough can be profitably utilized by more than one company, and hence each company has an incentive to let somebody else make a costly breakthrough. Patents are a way of solving this incentive problem.

2. In many industries, firms battle furiously to win patents on new technologies; high-definition television (HDTV) is an example of an ongoing patent race.

3. A two-firm patent race in which the competitors take turns making R&D investments can be modeled as a game of perfect information. Furthermore, this game can be solved using backward induction on location space.

4. The backward induction solution has the feature that two firms that are similar distances from project completion invest heavily to get an R&D advantage. A firm that falls sufficiently behind is better off dropping out of the patent race.

5. Dropping out is less likely the higher the value of the patent and the lower the costs of doing R&D. These characteristics describe the current HDTV race.

EXERCISES

SECTION 12.1

12.1

Give an example of a research breakthrough that was patented by the company that made the breakthrough (you might wish to explore the pharmaceutical industry for this example).

12.2

Give an example of a research breakthrough that was privately developed but not patented. Explain whether it was nevertheless profitable for the company in question to make the breakthrough.

12.3

Give an example of a research breakthrough that was achieved in the public domain either at a university or at a government research laboratory.

SECTION 12.3

Let us redo the analysis of the chapter with somewhat different patent values and costs to doing R&D.

12.4

Suppose that the patent is worth $25. Everything else is unchanged. Solve the R&D game by backward induction.

12.5

What is the difference between your conclusion and that reached in the text? Explain your answer. What general conclusion can you draw about the effect of patent valuation? Explain carefully.

12.6

Suppose instead that the costs of moving 1, 2, and 3 steps are $4, $10, and $15, respectively (but the patent value remains at $20). Solve the R&D game by backward induction.

12.7

What is the difference between the conclusion that you arrived at in exercise 12.6 and that reached in the text? Explain your answer. What general conclusions can you draw about the effect of costs? Explain carefully.

The next few questions explore a game in which two firms—firms A and B—have different costs and benefits from doing R&D. Let us start with different benefits. Suppose that all of the data of the chapter remain unchanged except for the fact that the patent is worth only $12 to firm B (whereas it is worth $20 to firm A). Let a (respectively, b) denote the distance that firm A (respectively, firm B) is from completing its R&D project.

12.8

Show that Trigger Zone I is made up of all locations in which firm A is within 3 steps and firm B is within 2 steps, that is, is made up of all locations (a, b) such that $a \leq 3$ and $b \leq 2$.

12.9

Show then that Safety Zone I, for firm A, is made up of all locations in which firm A is within 3 steps and firm B is more than 2 steps from finishing, that is, is made up of all locations (a, b) such that $a \leq 3$ and $b > 2$. Similarly, show that Safety Zone I, for B, is made up of all locations in which firm B is within 2 steps and firm A is more than 3 steps from finishing, that is, is made up of all locations (a, b) such that $a > 3$ and $b \leq 2$.

12.10

Show that Trigger Zone II is made up of all locations in which firm A is between 3 and 5 steps from finishing and firm B is between 2 and 4 steps, that is, is made up of all locations (a, b) such that $3 < a \leq 5$ and $2 < b \leq 4$.

12.11

Based upon your answer to the previous question, what do you conclude about Safety Zone II. Explain.

12.12

Explain how you would go about finding the next level of a trigger zone and how that procedure would pin down the next level of safety zones. What is the size of Trigger Zone III and Safety Zone III? Explain.

12.13

Find the backward induction solution to this game.

12.14

How would your answers to exercises 12.8–12.13 differ if the firms had different costs—in particular, if firm B is only able to take 1 or 2 steps at a time? Explain in detail.

SECTION 12.4

12.15

Explain how the principle of sunk costs plays a role in all of your arguments. Briefly describe how these arguments change if one of the firms is operating with a budget for the entire R&D project.

12.16

Suppose that public policy toward R&D gives one of the two firms—say, firm A, the "domestic" firm—an initial advantage. Does it necessarily mean that firm A will win the patent? Under what conditions will this outcome be predicted? Explain.

12.17

Redo the analysis of the chapter when public policy subsidizes firm R's R&D by 50 percent; that is, it costs Firm A, 1, 3.5, and 7.5 dollars to make, respectively, 1, 2, and 3 steps of progress.

CHAPTER 13

SUBGAME PERFECT EQUILIBRIUM

This chapter will present a generalization of backward induction called *subgame perfect (Nash) equilibrium* that applies to any game in extensive form (and not just to games of perfect information). We will first motivate the equilibrium concept by way of an example, in section 13.1. Then, in section 13.2, we will informally define something called a *subgame* (of a larger game). In section 13.3 we will discuss the equilibrium concept itself and apply it to the example with which we began the chapter. To illustrate the idea further, in section 13.4, we will then discuss subgame perfect equilibria in two more examples. Some remarks about this equilibrium concept follow in section 13.5. Finally, in section 13.6, we will analyze a case study: Peace in the World War I Trenches.

13.1 A MOTIVATING EXAMPLE

A game in extensive form that is not a game of perfect information is called a game of *imperfect information*—and those are the games that we will study in this chapter. The question that motivates subgame perfection in imperfect information games is the same as the one that motivated backward induction in perfect information games: What future behaviors are "credible"? When should a player believe an opponent's threat to "do *x* in the future unless you do *y* today"? What promises, likewise, are "credible"? Consequently, which equilibrium is "reasonable"?

To motivate the concept of subgame perfect equilibrium, consider the second variation of the entry game that was unveiled as example 3 in Chapter 11:

Example 1: Entry III
Recall that Coke is debating whether or not to enter a previously untapped East European market, this time in Transylvania. Pepsi is the current provider in that market and will

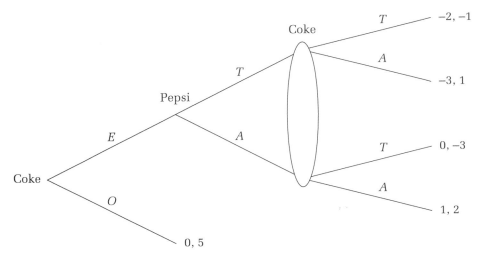

FIGURE 13.1

certainly respond to Coke's entry either by being *tough (T)* or by *accommodating (A)*. Coke can make a similar set of choices—*T* or *A*. Suppose, finally, that these postentry choices by Coke and Pepsi are made *simultaneously*. (Hence this is a game of imperfect information.) The payoffs to the *postentry* competition phase are as follows:

Coke \ Pepsi	T	A
T	−2, −1	0, −3
A	−3, 1	1, 2

If Coke stays out of this market, Pepsi continues to make profits of 5. Hence, the full extensive form is as seen in Figure 13.1.

What would we predict about the play of this game? For starters, let us ask, What are the Nash equilibria of the game? Those are easier to spot in the strategic form of the game:

Coke \ Pepsi	T	A
ET	−2, −1	0, −3
EA	−3, 1	1, 2
OT	0, 5	0, 5
OA	0, 5	0, 5

There are exactly three pure-strategy Nash equilibria in this game:

1. Coke plays (*enter, accommodate*)—that is, *EA*—while Pepsi plays *A*.

2.   Coke plays (*out*, *accommodate*)—that is, *OA*—while Pepsi plays *T*.

3.   Coke plays *OT* while Pepsi plays *T*.

The question is, are all these equilibria "reasonable"; that is, is each player's future action "credible"? In this simple example there is only one future date, namely, the postentry competition phase, and so the question can be rephrased as, Is each firm's anticipated behavior in the postentry market "credible?"

At this point we have to be precise about what we mean by "reasonable" and "credible." The idea motivating credibility is very similar to that underlying backward induction; an anticipated choice in the postentry phase is credible if, after Coke has entered the market, a player would have the payoff incentives to follow through and make precisely that choice. In particular, it has to be the case that she cannot do any better by reneging and playing some other action; that is, her anticipated choice must be a best response. For the pair of players therefore, the *two choices must be a Nash equilibrium in the postentry market.*

Let us examine the three Nash equilibria of the whole game. Consider the second one; the pair of strategies, *OA* and *T*. This equilibrium requires Coke to play *A* in the postentry game against Pepsi's strategy—which is to play *T*. However, if Coke does enter the Transylvanian market, then *A* is not a best response for Coke (nor indeed is *T* a best response for Pepsi). Against a tough Pepsi, Coke would stanch its losses by being tough as well, while Pepsi would make greater profits by reciprocating against an accommodating Coke (rather than by being tough). Put differently, the pair (*A*, *T*) is *not a Nash equilibrium within the postentry game.*

Another way of thinking about credibility is that the postentry game is a game in and of itself; once Coke has entered the Transylvanian market, both firms have to take that entry as a fact of their (corporate) life and maximize whatever profits they can make at that point. Equivalently, at that point it should be irrelevant what Coke's prior—or preentry—beliefs might have been about Pepsi's intentions—and vice versa. To summarize, however the two firms plan on playing the entire game, it must be the case that once they find themselves in the postentry part of the game, their actions must constitute a Nash equilibrium of the postentry game. Otherwise, at this stage, one or both firms would not stick to their strategy (or strategies).

CONCEPT CHECK
CREDIBLE POSTENTRY BEHAVIOR

Show, using the preceding logic, that the postentry behavior of the first and third Nash equilibria—respectively, (*A*, *A*) and (*T*, *T*)—are, in fact, credible. Is there any other credible behavior within the postentry phase? (Hint: think mixed-strategy Nash equilibrium.)

Anticipating, (A, A), *entry* is a best-response choice for Coke preentry, and so the pair of strategies (*entry*, A) and A is a reasonable Nash equilibrium for the entire game. Likewise, since staying out is better if there is going to be a drag-down all-out fight upon entry, (*out*, T) and T is also a reasonable Nash equilibrium for the whole game.[1]

An implication of this approach is worth pointing out: whether or not Coke *actually* enters the Transylvanian market is irrelevant to the credibility argument. The reasonableness of a Nash equilibrium in the whole game is to be judged by the counterfactual: *if* Coke chose to enter—or, even, by mistake ended up entering—is its subsequent behavior—and that of Pepsi—credible?[2]

This idea—that reasonableness of an equilibrium can be judged by the reasonableness of what may *not* get played—is similar to what we saw under backward induction. In that case, only one branch of the tree is actually played, but in order to determine which branch it is, we folded back the entire tree; that is, we checked credibility everywhere. There is one key difference between a game of imperfect information and one of perfect information. In the latter, at any node, only one player is called upon to make a decision. Credibility of a strategy can therefore be judged by simply asking if that player would find it in her best interest to make that decision at that particular node.[3] In a game of imperfect information, two or more players make simultaneous decisions. So it is the credibility of the *group's* decisions that we have to judge, and one way to do so is to check whether or not the group plays a Nash equilibrium in that component of the larger game.

The credibility arguments of example 1 can be generalized. To do so, however, we need a few more concepts.

13.2 SUBGAMES AND STRATEGIES WITHIN SUBGAMES

Some parts of a game look very much like a game by themselves. For example, the postentry phase in the entry game is a game by itself. When we have such a feature we call that part of the original game a *subgame*.

Definition. A subgame is a part of the extensive form; it is a collection of nodes and branches that satisfies three properties: (1) It starts at a single decision node. (2) It contains every successor to this node. (A successor to node x is all of those nodes that can be reached by following some sequence of branches originating from x.) (3) If it contains any part of an information set, then it contains all the nodes in that information set.

The idea of a subgame is internal containment. So the second and third restrictions simply say that you cannot stray out of the subgame once you are in it and that you will have, within the subgame, all the information that you need to make decisions. The first restriction is similar to the requirement that the root of a tree be well defined; it says that we have a unique starting point for the subgame. It is also customary to call the entire game a subgame (of itself).

[1] *The mixed-strategy Nash equilibrium of the postentry part of the game also begets a reasonable equilibrium;* out *coupled with that mixed-strategy equilibrium pair. If Coke anticipates this mixed-strategy play, with its associated losses of 1, then it is better off staying out.*

[2] *For example, in the pair of strategies* (O, T) *for Coke and* T *for Pepsi, the postentry game is never actually played. Yet* (T, T) *would get played if somehow the players found themselves in the postentry game. Knowing that* (T, T) *is a credible continuation, it makes sense for Coke to stay out of the market (and away from that part of the game).*

[3] *For instance, in example 2 in Chapter 11, Coke makes its* T *or* A *decision* after *it knows whether Pepsi is going to play* T *or* A. *Hence, reasonableness can be judged by asking, If Pepsi plays* T, *what is the best response for Coke? If Pepsi plays* A, *what is the best response for Coke?*

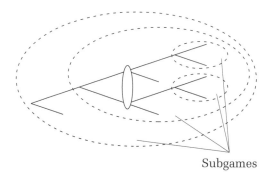

Subgames

FIGURE 13.2

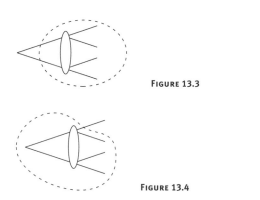

FIGURE 13.3

FIGURE 13.4

Examples of subgames are those parts of the extensive forms—in the graph shown in Figure 13.2—that have been enclosed in a dot-dash-dot surrounding.

However, the parts of the extensive form shown in Figures 13.3 and 13.4 are not subgames. The first is not a subgame because it does not start from a single node. The second is not a subgame because it does not contain all successor nodes.

Finally, since a strategy specifies what a player should do in all contingencies, it tells, in particular, what to do in any subgame. For example, in the subgame that starts after Coke enters the Transylvanian market, its strategy tells Coke whether or not to play T. Likewise, Pepsi's strategy tells it whether or not to play T in that subgame. If player i's strategy for the entire game is denoted s_i, then it will be useful to denote the strategy in a subgame, say g, as $s_i(g)$.

13.3 SUBGAME PERFECT EQUILIBRIUM ⚠

To paraphrase the definition, s_1 and s_2 constitute a **subgame perfect (Nash) equilibrium** if for every subgame g, $s_1(g)$ and $s_2(g)$ constitute a Nash equilibrium within the subgame.[4]

We will determine subgame perfect equilibria in games of imperfect information (that have an end) by a backward induction procedure. We will start with a final

Subgame perfect (Nash) equilibrium
A pair of strategies is a subgame perfect (Nash) equilibrium if the strategies, when confined to any subgame of the original game, have the players playing a Nash equilibrium within that subgame.

[4] *For N-player games, the definition extends in the natural way; $s_1, s_2, \ldots, s_N$ constitute a subgame perfect (Nash) equilibrium if the vector of subgame strategies, $s_1(g), s_2(g), \ldots, s_N(g)$, form a Nash equilibrium in every subgame g. This equilibrium concept was introduced by Reinhard Selten (and it got him the Nobel Prize in 1993).*

subgame—that is, with a subgame that ends only in terminal nodes—and determine Nash equilibria within that subgame. We will do the same with all final subgames. We will then back out to a subgame that precedes final subgames and restrict attention to Nash equilibria within this penultimate subgame that only involve the play of Nash equilibria in final subgames. And so on.

Let us briefly revisit the game of entry.

CONCEPT CHECK
EQUILIBRIA

Show that there are three subgame perfect (Nash) equilibria to the whole game: (1) (*enter*, *A*) and *A*, (2) (*out*, *T*) and *T*, and (3) (*out*, $\frac{1}{3}$) and $\frac{1}{2}$ (where the numbers are the probabilities with which *T* is selected by the two players).

It is not too difficult to see that subgame perfect Nash equilibrium is, in fact, a generalization of the backward induction solution, that, in other words, we have the following proposition:

Proposition. In a game of perfect information, the subgame perfect equilibria are precisely the backward induction solutions. Hence, whenever the backward induction solution is unique, there is a single subgame perfect equilibrium.

Sketch of a Proof

In a game of perfect information, a subgame starts at every node.[5] Consider, therefore, any node that is a final decision node. For a subgame perfect equilibrium, the decision maker at that node must pick the action that gives him the highest payoff, that is, must pick a best response. For backward induction, that constitutes a stage-one folding of the game tree.

At a penultimate decision node starts a game with two players: the penultimate and ultimate decision makers. A Nash equilibrium of this subgame is, by definition, both players playing best responses. We know what the best response of the ultimate decision maker is. A best response for the penultimate player is to find the best choice against the (already inferred) ultimate decision. And that is exactly the same thing as a stage-two folding of the tree in the backward induction procedure.

It should not be too difficult to see that finding Nash equilibria within every subgame is therefore equivalent to folding the tree within that subgame. It should, likewise, not be too difficult to see that if there is a unique way to fold the tree, there is also a unique Nash equilibrium in every subgame. ◇

[5] *The subgame that starts at a node, say α, is made up of all the nodes that follow α.*

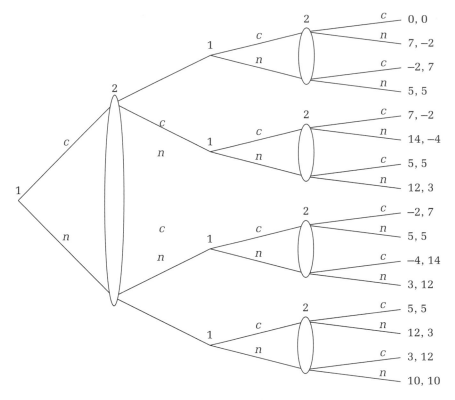

Figures, payoffs listed right to left:
c — 0, 0
n — 7, −2
c — −2, 7
n — 5, 5
c — 7, −2
n — 14, −4
c — 5, 5
n — 12, 3
c — −2, 7
n — 5, 5
c — −4, 14
n — 3, 12
c — 5, 5
n — 12, 3
c — 3, 12
n — 10, 10

FIGURE 13.5

13.4   TWO MORE EXAMPLES

To further develop these ideas we will analyze two more examples.

Example 2: Once-Repeated Prisoners' Dilemma

Suppose that the game of Prisoners' Dilemma is played twice. The first time around, the two players have a choice of (*confess* [c], *not confess* [n]). Then these choices are revealed and the two players again get to choose between c and n. The payoff to these two rounds of interaction is the sum of the payoffs in each round. The extensive form of the game is presented in Figure 13.5. Note, first of all, that there are five subgames; four of these are round-two interactions that follow the respective play of (c, c), (c, n), (n, c), and (n, n) in round one. The fifth is the whole game.

Let us start with the (final) subgame that follows (c, c) in round one. Subgame perfect equilibrium strategies must specify a pair of actions that form a Nash equilibrium within this subgame. That statement implies that each player's strategy must specify the play of c at this second round. (Why?) Indeed, more is true:

CONCEPT CHECK
CONTINUATIONS

Show that regardless of whether round-one play was (c, c), (c, n), (n, c), or (n, n), in a subgame perfect equilibrium round-two play has to be (c, c).

Hence, *regardless of what the players do in round one*, their round-two payoff is going to be the payoff to (c, c), that is, 0. Hence, the only two strategies to check in round one are the two that play, respectively, c or n in that round (and follow with c no matter what, in round two). In comparing the two strategies we clearly need only compare their first-round payoffs. An equivalent way of stating this point is that, in choosing between the two strategies, a player may as well treat his choice as if he is playing the Prisoners' Dilemma once. In that game, of course, the only Nash equilibrium is (c, c).

To summarize, the unique subgame perfect equilibrium is as follows: Each player confesses no matter what; each confesses the very first time and again in the second round (even if his opponent had not confessed in round one and even if he, mistakenly, did not confess the first time around).

In the next example, we return to the voting game of Chapter 1.

Example 3: Voting
Three legislators have the following preferences among three bills: A, B, and the status quo—or *neither* (N):

Voter 1: $A \succ N \succ B$

Voter 2: $B \succ A \succ N$

Voter 3: $N \succ A \succ B$

[6] *Figure 13.6 is only part of the extensive form, since it shows the round 2 contamination only after a B, B, A vote in round 1.*

[7] *And A can be the first-round victor in four possible ways: all three voters voted for that bill, only 1 and 2 did, only 1 and 3 did, or, finally, only 2 and 3 did.*

Voting proceeds in two rounds, and in each round voting is simultaneous. Bills A and B face off in the first round; the winner then goes up against the status quo (see Figure 13.6).[6]

From the extensive form it is clear that there are nine subgames: eight second-round—or final—subgames and the whole game itself. One set of final subgames is the second round of voting if A is the first-round victor,[7] and the other set of four subgames is the second round of voting if B wins the first round.

Evidently, the four subgames in which A is the first-round victor have identical second-round equilibrium possibilities. In fact, there are three Nash equilib-

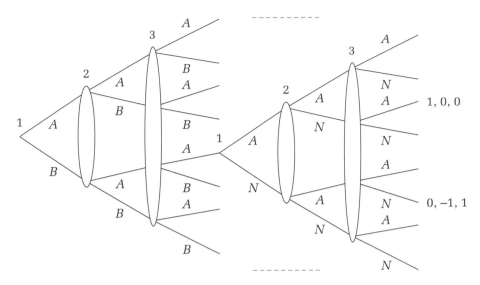

FIGURE 13.6

ria in each of those subgames, and one of those is a (weakly) dominant strategy solution:

CONCEPT CHECK
DOMINANT STRATEGY

Show that voting truthfully is a dominant strategy in the second round for every voter.

In the truthful-voting Nash equilibrium, A wins over N. There are, however, two other (trivial) Nash equilibria in this subgame: everybody votes for A or everybody votes for N. (Why are these Nash equilibria of the subgame?).[8] Since these last two equilibria involve the play of dominated strategies, I will exclude them in what follows (but see footnote 9). Likewise, in the round-two B-versus-N vote, there are three Nash equilibria: (1) everybody votes truthfully and N gets elected; (2) everybody votes N; and (3) everybody votes B (we will ignore the last two).

Let us now consider the penultimate subgame—the whole game. Since A will defeat N in the second round but B will not, in the first round each legislator really chooses between candidates A and N. Again, voting one's true preferences between A and N is a dominant strategy for each player. (Why?) Hence, there is one Nash equilibrium in which voters 1 and 2 vote for A while 3 votes for B; A gets elected. Put differently, the

[8] This is a more general, and annoying, phenomenon about voting games. It is worth voting one's preference only if there is (some) chance that the vote will make a difference. If I am convinced that my vote will make no difference to the outcome, I may as well vote any which way. This phenomenon can also affect real-world voting; voters who think that they will have no effect on the outcome simply stay away from the polling booth.

only subgame perfect (Nash) equilibrium in which no player ever plays a dominated strategy is the following set of strategies:

Voter 1:   *AAN*

Voter 2:   *AAB*

Voter 3:   *BNN*

where *AAN*, for example, is the strategy in which the first-round vote is for *A*, the second-round vote is also for *A* (against *N*) but is *N* (against *B*). There are two other Nash equilibria that involve the play of dominated strategies in the first round:

CONCEPT CHECK
FIRST ROUND WITH DOMINATED STRATEGIES

Show that everybody voting for *A* (followed by truthful voting in the second round) is a subgame perfect equilibrium. What about everybody voting for *B* in the first round?

To summarize, there is a single subgame perfect equilibrium in which no player plays a dominated strategy in either round: voter *i* votes for *A* in the first round if *A* is preferred to *N* (and in the second round votes truthfully). There are two other subgame perfect equilibria in which no dominated strategies are played in round two (where everyone votes truthfully), but they are in round one. In the first of these equilibria, everyone votes for *A* in the first round, whereas in the second, everyone votes for *B*.[9]

13.5   SOME REMARKS

The first thing to note about the concept of subgame perfect equilibrium is that it enshrines the notion that "bygones are bygones." It requires that no matter which subgame we start from, players must play a Nash equilibrium from that point on. This choice is required even if we got to that subgame by the play of something other than a Nash equilibrium strategy. On the one hand, the argument is really a rationality argument; rational players will recognize a profit opportunity when they see it. Hence, if they are asked not to play a best response, they will profitably deviate from such a prescription for play.

On the other hand, this is a very strong rationality postulate; no matter how irrational other players may have been in the past, a player still believes that they will be rational in the future. In other words, they will play Nash in the future although, for some reason that the player cannot explain, they have not played Nash in the past. Some people find this strong a dose of rationality disquieting!

[9] *There are also equilibria in which dominated strategies are played in both rounds. For example, everybody votes for A in each round. (Why is this a subgame perfect equilibrium? Are there others like it?)*

Second, to repeat a point made earlier, the way we solve for subgame perfect equilibria in a game that has an end—that is, a game with a finite number of nodes—is by backward induction. We look for Nash equilibria in the last subgame, then use them to solve for play in the penultimate subgame, and so on. In games that have an infinite number of decision nodes—that is, in infinite games—the subgame perfect equilibrium concept is still valid. We cannot, however, use backward induction anymore because there are no last subgames. In the next few chapters you will see how we can nevertheless proceed in this case.

13.6   CASE STUDY: PEACE IN THE WORLD WAR I TRENCHES

World War I was one of the bloodiest wars in human history.[10] Part of the reason was that this was the first war when new technologies, such as machine guns, with much greater destructive capabilities were available but the generals were still fighting a 19th-century war heavily dependent on infantry movements. It was also one of the slowest wars; for a couple of years the two sides were dug into trenches constantly fighting but gaining little territory.[11] The same regiments faced each other across the barbed wire month after dreary month. In a sense, the troops on either side got to know each other better through the months of stalemate than their respective high commands knew them or their ground conditions.[12]

One of the most unusual phenomena reported from the trenches was the implicit peace that broke out spontaneously among the soldiers doing the actual fighting. Observers reported that every day for a few hours the guns would fall silent in the trenches of Verdun, Somme, and Massines. These pauses would give the tired men a chance to rest and recuperate and cleanse themselves. What is more interesting is that the hours of peace were very regular; one report says that every day like clockwork the Germans would fire a lone shell into the same spot in no-man's-land, and that shot would signal the beginning of the temporary peace.

Here is a simple extensive form rendering of this phenomenon. Suppose that there can be two levels of preparedness: *high* (*H*) and *Low* (*L*).[13] Regardless of the level of preparedness each side has available two options on what it can do, *fight* (*f*) or *accommodate* (*a*). For example, if the level of preparedness is *high* then the strategic form (sub)game is as follows:

Central \ Allied	*f*	*a*
f	$-\frac{1}{2}, -\frac{1}{2}$	$1, -1$
a	$-1, 1$	$0, 0$

[10] *On the Allied Powers side ranged Britain, France, the United States, and Russia, while on the Central Powers side there was Germany, Austria-Hungary, and the Ottoman Empire.*

[11] *One of the bloodiest and slowest locales was along the French-German border, the so-called Western Front. In perhaps the most infamous battle in those trenches, the Battle of the Somme in 1916, in over four months of fighting the Allies gained only 125 square miles of ground along the Somme River. In order to do so they sacrificed 600,000 lives (400,000 British and 200,000 French) while the Germans lost 450,000 lives. For much fascinating information about this war you can visit a World Wide Web site called* Trenches on the Web *at worldwar1.com.*

[12] *One reason why casualties were as heavy as they were in the Battle of the Somme is that on the first day the British commander, Sir Henry Rawlinson, ordered his troops to march in formation* toward *the German machine guns.*

[13] *Think of* high *as having some of the soldiers always on alert while* low *is having them all "at ease."*

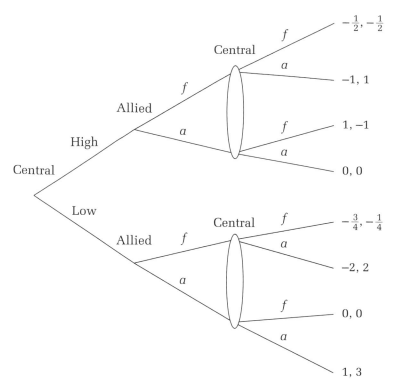

FIGURE 13.7

However, if the level of preparedness is *low* for the Germans, but remains *high* for the British-French, then the strategic form (sub)game looks like this:

Central \ Allied	f	a
f	$-\frac{3}{4}, -\frac{1}{4}$	$0, 0$
a	$-2, 2$	$1, 3$

Finally, suppose that the German (Central Powers) forces can determine unilaterally their level of preparedness (and that is what they signal to the Allied forces by the early evening lone shell; firing it indicates that they are descaling from *high* to *low*, while not firing indicates that they are maintaining the level of escalation at *high*).[14]

The extensive form game is displayed in Figure 13.7. Note that when the level of preparedness is *high*, f is a dominant strategy for both sides. So the only Nash equilibrium in that subgame is (f, f) with associated payoffs of $(-\frac{1}{2}, -\frac{1}{2})$. If the Germans choose to deescalate, then that subgame has a unique pure-strategy Nash equilibrium (a, a)—and the payoff for that is $(1, 3)$. Backing to the root of the tree, the German forces will choose to fire that signaling shell; that is, they will choose *low*.[15]

---

14 *In this analysis we are assuming that the Germans cannot lie about the implication of their signal; put differently, they can commit to deescalate. In Chapter 24 we will analyze conditions under which this signal will in fact be truthful.*

15 *Needless to add, this is a very simple analysis of a complex situation. In particular, we would have to add further elements to the game to explain why the two forces ever go back to fighting (later in the night). A practical reason during WWI was that the generals, far from the killing fields, were upset at reports that their men were making peace with the enemy.*

This case also illustrates the power of commitment, a topic we first encountered with games of perfect information. Since the Central Powers are able to commit to *low*— and they suffer disproportionately if there is fighting at that level of preparedness—(a, a) is a credible future play for the two adversaries. Consequently, in this example, both players are better off.

SUMMARY

1. A subgame is a part of the whole game that is a game in and of itself; it contains all the future consequences, and it includes all the information that is necessary to play this part of the game.

2. A strategy vector within a subgame is credible if it forms a Nash equilibrium within the subgame; no player has an incentive then to renege.

3. A strategy vector for the whole game is a subgame perfect (Nash) equilibrium if every containment within every subgame is a Nash equilibrium (of that subgame).

4. Subgame perfection can be used to select reasonable equilibria among the entire set of Nash equilibria in a game. For example, in the game of entry it says that the only circumstance in which Coke will enter is if it expects Pepsi (and itself) to accommodate entry.

EXERCISES

SECTION 13.1

Let us modify the timing structure of the game of entry. Suppose that Coke's entry decision is made at the same time that Pepsi decides between *tough* and *accommodate*. Then, if Coke chooses to enter, it has a further decision between *tough* and *accommodate*. Suppose that the payoffs at every terminal node that follow *enter* are exactly as before. If Coke stays *out*, then the payoffs are $(0, -1)$ if Pepsi plays T and $(0, 0)$ if it plays A.

13.1
Write down the extensive form of this game. How many subgames are there in this game?

13.2
Solve the game by backward induction. Be sure to detail every step.

13.3

Suppose the payoffs when Coke stays *out* are (0, 1) and (0, 0) instead when, respectively, Pepsi plays T and A. Solve this game by backward induction.

Let us yet again modify the game of entry. Suppose—as before—that Coke's entry decision and Pepsi's T/A decisions are simultaneous. Suppose, furthermore, that when Coke makes its subsequent choice between T and A it is unaware of Pepsi's choice.

13.4

Write down the extensive form. How many subgames are there in this game? How many strategies does Coke have? (Use the payoffs of exercise 13.1.)

13.5

Explain why this timing structure is equivalent to Coke and Pepsi making a single simultaneous decision. What are the strategies involved?

13.6

Find the Nash equilibria of the game.

SECTION 13.2

Consider the extensive form of exercises 13.1 through 13.3.

13.7

Identify a part of the game tree that is not a subgame because it does not start at a single decision node.

13.8

Identify a part of the tree that is not a subgame because it does not contain every successor to the node that starts this part of the tree.

13.9

Finally, identify a part of the tree that is not a subgame because it does not contain all the nodes in some information set although it contains some.

SECTION 13.4

Consider the following (idealized) model of voting in a Senate committee. The committee is made up of three members: Al (A), Bob (B), and Christopher (C), two Republicans and a Democrat, respectively. They are confronted with two versions of a bill (to end welfare as we know it). Version 1 proposes a radical restructuring of the current system, while Version 2 proposes a more modest overhaul. The committee members vote simultaneously, and they recommend the version that gets a majority of votes. At that point, the full Senate votes simultaneously and along party lines between that version and the current system. If a majority of the Senate votes in favor of the bill it passes; otherwise, it fails and the welfare system remains unchanged. Democrat and Republican preferences on the two versions and the current system are as follows:

Democrat: Version 2 ≻ Current system ≻ Version 1
Republican: Version 1 ≻ Version 2 ≻ Current system

13.10
Represent this setup as an extensive form game. (Within the committee distinguish between the members, but at the Senate level distinguish only between the two parties.)

13.11
Identify the subgames in the game.

13.12
Write down the strategies for each player in the game. Define a subgame perfect equilibrium.

13.13
What must be the votes cast in the Senate by (a) a Democrat and (b) a Republican if neither plays a dominated strategy?

13.14
Suppose that there is a Republican majority in the Senate. What is the subgame perfect equilibrium of this voting game (with no dominated strategies played)? Explain your answer in detail.

13.15
Suppose, however, that there is a Democratic majority in the Senate. What is the subgame perfect equilibrium of this voting game (with no dominated strategies played)? Again, explain your answer in detail.

The next few questions return to the model of *price competition*. To recall, we have two firms that set prices in a market with this demand curve:

$$Q = 6 - p$$

where p is the lower of the two prices. If the prices are different, the lower priced firm sells all the output. If the two firms post the same price, then each gets half the market. Suppose that prices can only be quoted in dollar units and costs of production are zero for both firms. Suppose, unlike in past versions of this problem, that prior to this price competition phase firm 2 has to make an entry decision. If firm 2 stays out, firm 1 remains a monopoly (and gets the maximum profits that can be generated with the given demand curve). If firm 2 enters, price competition ensues.

13.16
Write down the extensive form of the game. Identify the subgames.

13.17
Write down the strategies for each firm in the game. Define a subgame perfect equilibrium.

13.18
In a subgame perfect equilibrium, what must be the market price if firm 2 enters the market?

13.19
What is the subgame perfect equilibrium of this model? Does firm 2 enter the market?

13.20
Suppose that there is an entry cost of size c for entering this market (for example, the cost of advertising or promotional discounts). At what value of c does it not make sense for firm 2 to enter this market? Explain your answer. What is the subgame perfect equilibrium above this cost level?

SECTION 13.6

Consider the case study. Suppose that the payoff matrix, if the Germans have deescalated, is given by

Central \ Allied	f	a
f	$-\frac{3}{4}, -\frac{1}{4}$	$0, 0$
a	$-2, 2$	$1, 1$

13.21
Compute the Nash equilibrium within this subgame.

13.22
Draw the extensive form of the entire game. Be careful in filling in the payoffs to each of the terminal nodes.

13.23
Find the subgame perfect equilibrium of this game. Does peace break out in this example?

CHAPTER 14

FINITELY REPEATED GAMES

In the next two chapters we will discuss a special class of extensive form games, called *repeated games,* whose principal feature is that players interact not just once but many times. These games have helped explain why ongoing economic phenomena produce behavior very different from those observed in a one-time interaction.

The basic intuition for this difference is straightforward. If players believe that future behavior will be affected by the nature of current interaction, then they may behave in ways that they would not otherwise. In particular, *if* a player believes that "no good deed today will go unrewarded tomorrow," she will have a greater reason to do a good deed today. Equivalently, if she believes that "no bad deed today will go unpunished tomorrow," she may be less inclined to do a bad deed today. The prospect of *reciprocity* then, either by way of rewards or punishments, is what separates a repeated game from a one-time interaction. Of course these punishments and rewards have to be credible in the precise sense of the previous chapter; that is, players will only believe them if they are part of a subgame perfect equilibrium.

In section 14.1 we will give a definition of repeated games and then discuss several examples, including some real-world examples. In section 14.2 we will turn to a particular subclass of repeated games called *finitely repeated games*, analyze several examples of such games, and from them draw some general conclusions. Finally, in section 14.3 we will discuss a case study of Treasury bill auctions.

14.1   EXAMPLES AND ECONOMIC APPLICATIONS

14.1.1   THREE REPEATED GAMES AND A DEFINITION

In every repeated game there is a component game—sometimes called a *stage game*—that is played many times.

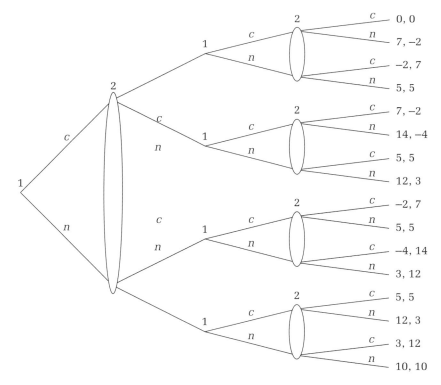

FIGURE 14.1

Example 1: Once-Repeated Prisoners' Dilemma

This is a repeat of example 2 from the previous chapter: the game of Prisoners' Dilemma once repeated. Two prisoners make a simultaneous choice between *confess* (*c*) and *not confess* (*n*). Their choices are revealed to them, and then they are allowed to make the same choices, that is, play the same game again. The payoffs in the game are the sum of the payoffs in each stage. The extensive form of this game is displayed in Figure 14.1.

Example 2: Finitely Repeated Modified Prisoners' Dilemma

The second example has a stage game that is a slight modification of the Prisoners' Dilemma—and we will therefore call it the Modified Prisoners' Dilemma. We add one strategy to the standard Prisoners' Dilemma; in addition to *c* and *n*, each player has a third strategy, say, *p* for "partly confess." Consider the following as a stage game:

1 \ 2	c	n	p
c	0, 0	7, −2	3, −1
n	−2, 7	5, 5	0, 6
p	−1, 3	6, 0	3, 3

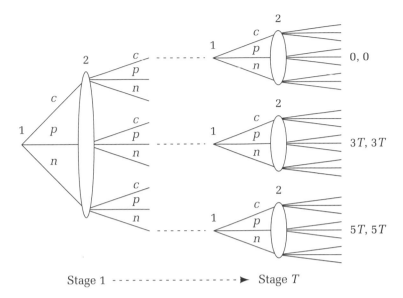

FIGURE 14.2

Suppose now that this stage game is played T times. At each of these stages, the two players get to choose from the three strategies, n, c, and p. At the end of each stage, they are told the choices made by both players, and then they get to make the same choices again. Again, the total payoffs in the repeated game are simply the sum of payoffs to the T stage games. The extensive form for this game is shown in Figure 14.2.

Example 3: Infinitely Repeated Prisoners' Dilemma

This example is again a modification of example 1. Suppose, as before, that at every stage the two players play the Prisoners' Dilemma. However, there is no fixed number of repetitions. Every time that they play the stage game, there is a probability δ that the same players will play the stage game again. Conversely, there is a probability $1 - \delta$ that the current interaction is the last one.[1] The extensive form of this game is therefore as presented in Figure 14.3.

This game is called the Infinitely Repeated Prisoners' Dilemma; the terminology refers to the fact that the game has no fixed end. The payoffs to the Infinitely Repeated Prisoners' Dilemma are computed as follows. Suppose that at the tth stage, player i gets a payoff of π_{it}. The likelihood that the tth stage will even get played is δ^t. Hence the expected payoff to the tth stage is $\delta^t \pi_{it}$. The total expected payoff is the sum of these stage-game expected payoffs; that is, it equals

$$\pi_{i0} + \delta \pi_{i1} + \delta^2 \pi_{i2} + \ldots + \delta^t \pi_{it} + \ldots \tag{14.1}$$

From these examples it is possible to see the general structure of a repeated game.

[1] *There is an alternative interpretation of δ. A player may prefer to get a payoff in stage t rather than wait to get exactly the same payoff in stage $t + 1$; (a unit of utility in) stage $t + 1$ may be only worth a fraction δ in stage t. This bias toward earlier payments is called time preference, and the associated fraction δ is called the discount factor (for a more extensive treatment of this issue, see section 15.1).*

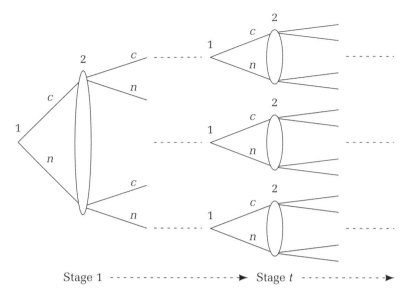

Stage 1 - - - - - - - - - - - - - - - - - - ➤ Stage t - - - - - - - - - - - ➤

FIGURE 14.3

Definition. A repeated game is defined by a stage game G and the number of its repetitions, say T. The stage game G is a game in strategic form: $G = \{S_i, \pi_i; i = 1, \ldots, N\}$ where S_i is player i's set of strategies and π_i is his payoff function [and it depends on $(s_1, s_2, \ldots, s_N)$].

If T is finite, we call the game a *finitely repeated game,* whereas if the repeated game has no fixed end we call it an *infinitely repeated game.* It is customary to compute the payoffs of a finitely repeated game as the sum of the payoffs in each stage. For the infinitely repeated game, a common way to compute payoffs is to add the (discounted) expected payoffs in the manner shown in equation 14.1. In the remainder of this chapter we will discuss finitely repeated games, and in the next one we will turn to infinitely repeated games.

14.1.2   FOUR ECONOMIC APPLICATIONS

Finitely Repeated Games

1.   **Treasury Bill Auction.**   The U.S. Treasury Department periodically sells securities to raise the cash needed to finance the federal government's expenditures and to repay maturing debt.[2] These securities are sold by auction, and the principal buyers at these auctions are the government bond departments of large financial institutions such as Salomon Brothers, Merrill Lynch, and Morgan Stanley.[3] The auctions are held on a very regular basis; on certain kinds of securities the auctions are weekly, and some others are monthly.[4]

The auctions work as follows: The Department of Treasury issues a press release about one week before each auction announcing the auction date, the amount, and the type of securities that are to be sold. A prospective buyer submits a "tender" that specifies

[2] *The securities that are sold vary by maturity—when a lump-sum payment will be made—and coupon—how much interest will be paid in the interim. The maturities vary from 13-week Treasury bills to 30-year Treasury bonds.*

[3] *In turn, the investment banks sell these securities to institutional investors such as pension funds as well as to individual investors.*

[4] *Thirteen- and 26-week Treasury bills are offered each week, and two- and five-year Treasury notes are issued once a month. For details about Treasury auctions, visit the Department of Treasury's web site at ustreas.gov.*

the price and amount that he would like. After all the tenders have arrived, the Treasury Department determines either a fixed price that they will charge on that lot of securities or a range for the price. The former system is called a *single-price auction* (since every buyer gets the same rate); this single price is the one at which the quantity demanded is equal to the amount being sold. The latter is called a *multiprice auction*; those willing to pay the highest price are allocated their demand first, then the next highest, and so on.[5]

This is clearly a repeated game. The players are the major financial institutions, and they remain unchanged from auction to auction. The stage game is the auction (for a particular kind of security, say, 26-week Treasury bills); it is a game with simultaneous moves because the tenders are submitted simultaneously. The payoffs are the subsequent profits that each institution makes from selling the securities to individual investors and pension funds. It becomes a finitely repeated game if we consider the 52 such auctions in a calender year as a group (and separate them from the auctions in previous and following years).[6] Treasury auctions will be studied in greater detail in section 14.3.

2. Competition in a Patented Drug's Market. When a new drug is successfully patented, no competing drug can be introduced that violates the patent's coverage as long as the patent is in force. Competing drugs therefore have to use a different chemical composition than the patented drug.[7] The competition among the patented drug and any follower drug *during* the patent period is an example of a finitely repeated game. It is clearly a game because there are only a few drug companies involved (and their payoffs are the profits that they make). It is a finitely repeated game because the patent period is finite.[8]

Infinitely Repeated Games

1. NASDAQ Market Making. The NASDAQ market is the second-largest stock market in the United States, after the New York Stock Exchange (NYSE). On this market, there are, on average, about ten dealers who "make the market" for every stock; each of these ten dealers quotes a buy and a sell price—the bid and the ask price—and stands ready to transact at those prices when orders come in. Orders are filled at the lowest ask price and at the highest bid price. Market makers make profits from the difference between the ask and the bid price, that is, from the difference between the price at which they sell to customers and the price at which they buy from (other) customers.

The stage game *G* is therefore a price competition model—like the Bertrand model that you have seen in previous chapters. The market makers strategically interact; each one knows that he can capture order flow by undercutting the rival market makers. This is a market—or game—in which there is no end date to the ongoing interaction; every time that dealers make a market they believe that there is a (high) probability that the same group of dealers will make the market again the next hour, or the next day. In other words, this is an infinitely repeated game. There is, of course, always the possibility that some dealer may leave or a new dealer may join the market; this is captured by the idea that the probability δ of continuing as an unchanged group is less than one. Market making in NASDAQ is the subject of Chapter 16.

[5] *Thirteen- and 26-week Treasury bills as well as three- and 10-year Treasury notes are sold in multiprice auctions, whereas two- and five-year Treasury notes are sold by way of single-price auctions.*

[6] *One reason for this approach is that the managers who oversee the financial institutions' strategies are typically paid on the basis of yearly performance.*

[7] *And competing drugs are getting introduced very rapidly these days. The drug AZT, which was introduced in 1987, had a competitor in Pravachol by 1991. The same length of time separated Prozac, introduced in 1988, from Zoloft. Also note that after the patent runs out, the field is wide open because the original drug's chemistry can be utilized by any competing drug.*

[8] *After the patent runs out, competition drives down profits for each firm. Since the bulk of the profits are made during the patent period, we can concentrate on that period for analytical purposes.*

2.   **The International Oil Market—or OPEC.**   The Organization of Petroleum Export-ing Countries is a group of oil producers who coordinate on the price at which they sell their output. You have seen some discussion of OPEC already in Chapter 6, and it will be discussed in even greater detail in Chapter 17, and so we will give only a brief overview here.

The stage game for this application is the international oil market. Producing countries or companies sell to various customers, who might themselves be companies or countries. The competition is over quantity; each producer determines how much crude it is going to pump over, say, the next month. The total amount produced—and the world demand for oil—then determines the price. Producers make profits on the basis of how much they sell and what the difference is between the (average) price at which they sell and their (average) cost of production.

The interaction is ongoing; Saudi Arabia and Venezuela fully expect to compete in the oil market a month, a year, a decade, and possibly even a century from now.[9] Indeed the issue for OPEC is precisely whether, given this ongoing nature of their competition, the producers can refrain from undercutting each other.

14.2   FINITELY REPEATED GAMES

The analysis of subgame perfect equilibria in finitely repeated games proceeds by way of backward induction. Recall, from the previous chapter, that this corresponds to folding the repeated game, one subgame at a time, from the end.

Analysis of Example 1

In example 1 the last subgames are those in the second stage (see Figure 14.1). As we saw in the previous chapter, no matter what gets played in the first stage, subgame perfect equilibrium second-stage play must be (c, c). Folding back to the first round, we see that the players face the game shown in Figure 14.4. Evidently, the only Nash equilibrium of this game is, again, (c, c). Hence, the players play each of the two stages as if they were playing each stage by itself. And they play the stage game Nash equilibrium regardless.

Indeed this observation can be confirmed more generally. Suppose the Prisoners' Dilemma is played $T + 1$ times, where T is any positive integer.

[9] *Of course, this game is not strictly infinitely repeated, since there is a zero probability that it will last, say, a million years or more. However, there is no certainty either about when the oil reserves will actually run out. Therefore, we can study this application, at first pass, as a game with no fixed end—that is, as an infinitely repeated game—possibly with a lot of discounting of the very distant future.*

CONCEPT CHECK
STEP 1

Argue that in the last two rounds of the T-times repeated Prisoners' Dilemma, the preceding analysis applies; each player plays c in each of those two stages.

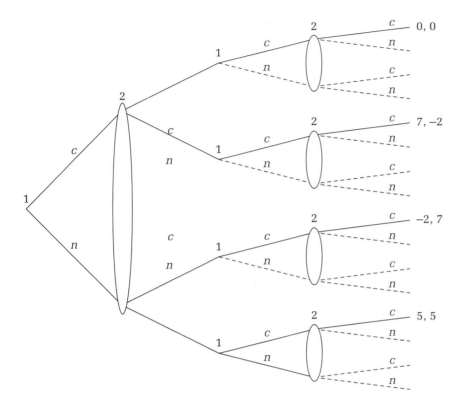

FIGURE 14.4

What happens when there are three rounds left? It is not too difficult to see that the effective game that remains after the first round is the same as Figure 14.4. Hence, we have the following:

CONCEPT CHECK
STEP 2

Show that, since play in the last two rounds will be independent of what happens in the current stage, players must treat the game as if there is exactly one stage left. Hence both players will confess.

So the three-round Prisoners' Dilemma, again, has only one subgame perfect equilibrium—and both players always confess in every subgame. But then we can use the observation for the three-stage Prisoners' Dilemma game to show that the thrice-repeated Prisoners' Dilemma also has a unique equilibrium, (*confess*, *confess*), all the time. And indeed we can extend the argument all the way back to the initial node of the T-times-repeated Prisoners' Dilemma:

CONCEPT CHECK
ALWAYS CONFESS

Show that the unique subgame perfect equilibrium of the T-times-repeated Prisoners' Dilemma is for each player to confess in every contingency.

Analysis of Example 2

Let us develop the argument for example 2 in steps. Consider, first, the case where the Modified Prisoners' Dilemma is played just once. You should be able to convince yourself from looking at the structure of payoffs that there are two Nash equilibria of this stage game—(c, c) and (p, p).

If the Modified Prisoners' Dilemma is repeated once, then in the second stage one of these two Nash equilibria has to be played. Since there are two Nash equilibria to choose from, there is now the possibility of reciprocal behavior; which of the two equilibria gets played may depend on what behavior is observed in the first stage. In particular, "good" behavior in the first stage may be rewarded by the better Nash equilibrium (p, p), whereas "bad" behavior may be punished by (c, c). Put differently, good behavior in the first stage may generate a belief among the players that there will be continuation of such cooperative behavior in the second stage, but if the first-stage behavior is itself bad, there is little reason to believe that the second stage will see cooperative behavior.

Consider the following strategy: At Stage 1, each player plays n, the "good" strategy. If they both do so, in the second stage each plays p. On the other hand, if either of them plays c or p in the first stage, then in the second stage they both play c. Put differently, the strategy specifies that in every second-stage subgame, except that which follows (n, n), the players play (c, c); only in the subgame that follows (n, n) do they reward themselves by playing (p, p).

CONCEPT CHECK

Argue that the preceding strategy is a subgame perfect equilibrium if player 1's payoff to (n, n) followed by (p, p) is greater than his payoff under (c, n) followed by (c, c). Show that it is.

Note that by playing n, neither player gets the highest payoff that he could achieve in that stage. By playing c a player would get himself a payoff of 7 rather than 5 in the first stage. [However, by doing so he would also jeopardize a future play of (p, p) and hence a future payoff of 3.] In other words, players do not necessarily play the first round according to stage-game Nash equilibrium strategies. This is precisely the lesson of repeated games; a player will be willing to sacrifice short-term gains from "doing bad" if he is convinced that by doing so he will get a reciprocal reward in the future.

Suppose the Modified Prisoners' Dilemma is played T times. Consider the following strategy pair: start with (n, n) and continue in that way at all stages except the last one [and at that stage, play (p, p)]. Follow this procedure provided neither player deviates from it (and plays something other than n at any of the first T stages). In the event of a deviation, play (c, c) from the subsequent stage onward.

CONCEPT CHECK
EQUILIBRIA

Show that the preceding strategy is a subgame perfect equilibrium.

Notice that we have not asserted that this strategy is the *only* subgame perfect equilibrium of this game. Indeed it is not. For instance, here is another one (in the once-repeated game): Start with (n, c). If that is in fact played, then play (p, p) in the second stage. Otherwise, play (c, c).

CONCEPT CHECK
ANOTHER EQUILIBRIUM

Show that the preceding strategy is a subgame perfect equilibrium.

Consider the following two strategies as yet other equilibria: (1) play (p, p) in the first round and in every one of the second round subgames or (2) play (c, c) in the first round and in every one of the subgames in the second round. These strategies are simply repeats of one-stage Nash equilibria. It should be clear that these continue to be subgame perfect equilibria of the finitely repeated Modified Prisoners' Dilemma. More generally, the following is true:

CONCEPT CHECK
REPEATING OUR MISTAKES

Consider any finitely repeated game. Show that one subgame perfect equilibrium of the repeated game is for players to play (myopically) a one-stage Nash equilibrium over and over again.

14.2.1   SOME GENERAL CONCLUSIONS ⚠

The two examples that we have analyzed contain some general conclusions. There is a fundamental difference between the finite repetition of stage games in which there is a unique Nash equilibrium and those in which there is more than one Nash equilibrium. When there is a single Nash equilibrium—as in the Prisoners' Dilemma—no matter how many times the game is repeated, there is still only one subgame perfect equilibrium. That equilibrium is to play the stage game Nash equilibrium repeatedly. In other words, the prospect of future interaction does not change players' behavior in any way; we can assert the following proposition:

Proposition.   Consider a finitely repeated game (G, T) with $G = \{S_i, \pi_i; i = 1, \ldots, N\}$. Suppose the stage game G has exactly one Nash equilibrium, say $(s_1^*, s_2^*, \ldots, s_N^*)$. Then the repeated game has a unique subgame perfect equilibrium. In this equilibrium, player i plays s_i^* at every one of the T stages, regardless of what might have been played, by him or any of the others, in any previous stage.

Sketch of Proof

The proof of this proposition is exactly the same as that which we have already seen for the T-repeated Prisoners' Dilemma. In the very last stage, every subgame perfect equilibrium must specify the play of the unique stage-game Nash equilibrium, $(s_1^*, s_2^*, \ldots, s_N^*)$. Consequently, play in the penultimate stage cannot be conditioned on future rewards because $(s_1^*, s_2^*, \ldots, s_N^*)$ will be played in the last stage no matter what is played in the penultimate stage. Hence, the penultimate stage will be treated as if it is a stage game by itself—and within that game the only possible equilibrium is, of course, $(s_1^*, s_2^*, \ldots, s_N^*)$.

Hence no matter how play proceeds in the first $T - 1$ stages, in the last two stages it must necessarily involve the play of the stage-game Nash equilibrium in each of those stages. This fact then implies that in the third-last stage no future rewards are expected by the players. Hence they treat this stage as a one-time interaction; its only outcome is therefore $(s_1^*, s_2^*, \ldots, s_N^*)$. And so on.   ◇

However, if there is more than one Nash equilibrium, there is always the possibility of sustaining good behavior in early stages of repeated interaction. This good behavior is sustained by the prospect of better future play than that which follows short-term opportunistic behavior. Again, the general argument is the same as the one that we saw in the context of the repeated Modified Prisoners' Dilemma. Good behavior in early interactions can be rewarded by the play of better Nash equilibria in future subgames, while any deviations from this behavior can be punished by the play of bad Nash equilibria in future subgames.[10]

14.3   CASE STUDY: TREASURY BILL AUCTIONS

The institutional structure of Treasury bill auctions was explained earlier in this chapter. We will therefore focus on one key aspect of these auctions, the pricing issue. Recall that for some securities, there is a single-price auction in which all buyers pay the same price. For some others, there is a multiprice auction in which different buyers pay different prices. The question that we will now investigate is the following: *If the Treasury wants to maximize the amount that it collects, which of the two auction forms should it use*?

In order to keep the analysis tractable, we will make several simplifying assumptions. First, we will assume that there are two financial institutions, or players, at this auction. Second, the quantity that the Treasury sells remains fixed from auction to auction; let this amount be 100.[11] Third, we will assume that there are two prices and two quantities that each buyer can offer; call the prices *high* (h) and *low* (l) and the amounts 50 and 75. Fourth, buyers care only about profits; denote the profit per security if the price is h as π_h and likewise the profit if the price is l as π_l. Suppose that both profit levels are positive (and, of course, $\pi_l > \pi_h$).

If each buyer wants to buy at a *high* price, then the total demand at that price is at least 100 and all of the Treasuries sell at that price. Likewise, if both buyers want to buy at the *low* price, then the market price is *low*. If, however, one of the buyers wants to buy at h while the other wants to buy at l, then the price outcome depends on the type of auction. In a single-price auction, the market price will be *low,* while in a multiprice auction one buyer will pay h and the other will pay l. In either case, the high bidder gets all of the quantity he asks for and the remaining quantity is allocated to the low bidder. Finally, if the price bids are the same, then the quantity is allocated in proportion to the quantity demands. For example, if one buyer wants 75 units and the other wants 50, then the former gets 60 of the available 100 units.[12]

With these assumptions, the strategic form of a *single-price auction* is as follows:

Buyer 1 \ Buyer 2	50, h	75, h	50, l	75, l
50, h	$50\pi_h, 50\pi_h$	$40\pi_h, 60\pi_h$	$50\pi_l, 50\pi_l$	$50\pi_l, 50\pi_l$
75, h	$60\pi_h, 40\pi_h$	$50\pi_h, 50\pi_h$	$75\pi_l, 25\pi_l$	$75\pi_l, 25\pi_l$
50, l	$50\pi_l, 50\pi_l$	$25\pi_l, 75\pi_l$	$50\pi_l, 50\pi_l$	$40\pi_l, 60\pi_l$
75, l	$50\pi_l, 50\pi_l$	$25\pi_l, 75\pi_l$	$60\pi_l, 40\pi_l$	$50\pi_l, 50\pi_l$

For example, if buyer 1 bids a high price against 50, l, then he gets all of his quantity at a low price; the price is low because there is no demand for all 100 units at price h. If he bids 75, l (against 50, l), then he gets 60 units allocated at the low price. Note furthermore

[10] *In the Modified Prisoners' Dilemma there are two Nash equilibria in the stage game, one of which is preferred by both players to the other equilibrium. In general there may not exist such unanimity in opinion; that is, there may be two Nash equilibria in the stage game, the first of which is preferred by player 1 while the second is preferred by player 2. Nevertheless it is still possible to sustain good behavior in early stages by an appropriate modification of the arguments discussed in the text. For details, consult Drew Fudenberg and Jean Tirole,* Game Theory *(Cambridge, MA: MIT Press, 1991).*

[11] *Note that we are looking at the repeated auction of any one kind of security, say, 26-week Treasury bills. The assumption that the same number of such bills are sold every week makes it a repeated game. If the quantity were to vary from week to week, each week's stage game would be a little different from every other week's. The current analysis can be generalized in that direction. In Chapter 17 we will look at repeated games with random variations in the stage game (for instance, because the federal government's financing needs vary randomly from time to time).*

[12] *The assumed quantity allocation rules are essentially the same as the Treasury Department's actual rules.*

that, at any price, it is always better to ask for a larger quantity—75, l dominates 50, l, and 75, h dominates 50, h. The reason is simple: 75, l dominates 50, l because at the consequent low price a higher quantity demand means a higher (and more profitable) allocation. Also, 75, h dominates 50, h; it has the same effect on price, and its quantity allocation is at least as high.

Similarly, the strategic form of a *multiprice auction* looks like this:

Buyer 1 \ Buyer 2	50, h	75, h	50, l	75, l
50, h	$50\pi_h, 50\pi_h$	$40\pi_h, 60\pi_h$	$50\pi_h, 50\pi_l$	$50\pi_h, 50\pi_l$
75, h	$60\pi_h, 40\pi_h$	$50\pi_h, 50\pi_h$	$75\pi_h, 25\pi_l$	$75\pi_h, 25\pi_l$
50, l	$50\pi_l, 50\pi_h$	$25\pi_l, 75\pi_h$	$50\pi_l, 50\pi_l$	$40\pi_l, 60\pi_l$
75, l	$50\pi_l, 50\pi_h$	$25\pi_l, 75\pi_h$	$60\pi_l, 40\pi_l$	$50\pi_l, 50\pi_l$

For precisely the same reason as before, again 75, l dominates 50, l, and 75, h dominates 50, h. From the point of view of stage-game Nash equilibrium analysis we can therefore look at the *reduced single-price auction*:

Buyer 1 \ Buyer 2	75, h	75, l
75, h	$50\pi_h, 50\pi_h$	$75\pi_l, 25\pi_l$
75, l	$25\pi_l, 75\pi_l$	$50\pi_l, 50\pi_l$

And this is the *reduced multiprice auction:*

Buyer 1 \ Buyer 2	75, h	75, l
75, h	$50\pi_h, 50\pi_h$	$75\pi_h, 25\pi_l$
75, l	$25\pi_l, 75\pi_h$	$50\pi_l, 50\pi_l$

(Note that the profits are different in the two cases when one bidder bids h and the other bids l.) On one hand, the Treasury would like the price to be high because a high price produces a larger revenue. On the other hand, the financial institutions would like the price to be low because a low price enables them to make a larger profit. Which is it going to be? And does it make a difference whether the auction is single price or multiprice? There are two cases to consider.

Case I: The Competitive Case

Suppose that it is less profitable to buy half the quantity even if it is at a low price; that is, suppose that $50\pi_h > 25\pi_l$. Then h is a dominant strategy in the *reduced single-price* auction. Hence the unique Nash equilibrium in the stage game is (h, h). The Treasury is especially happy because (h, h) in every stage is then the unique subgame perfect equilibrium as well. (Why?) Repeating the auction, as the Treasury does, makes no difference to the intensity of competition in the market and does not allow the participants to make credible deals to keep prices low.

Consider now the *reduced multiprice* auction. Now there might be a second Nash equilibrium if the best response to a low price is to also to bid low, that is, if $50\pi_l > 75\pi_h$.[13] In that case, (l, l) is also a Nash equilibrium; that is, the buyers have the incentive to implicitly collude and keep the price low. Hence one subgame perfect equilibrium is for both buyers to bid l all the time.[14]

Case II: The Collusive Case

Suppose instead that $50\pi_h < 25\pi_l$. It is straightforward to see the following:

CONCEPT CHECK
LOWBALLING

Show that in the *multiprice* auction, l is a dominant strategy (and hence, the buyers stiff the Treasury by offering low bids).

In the *single-price* auction there is still a unique Nash equilibrium, but it is now a mixed-strategy equilibrium.

CONCEPT CHECK
MIXED STRATEGY

Show that in the *single-price* auction, there is a unique mixed-strategy Nash equilibrium in the stage game. Compute this equilibrium (as a function of the parameters π_h and π_l).

By the proposition of section 14.2.1, the unique stage game play is also the unique subgame perfect equilibrium play. Hence, in multiprice auctions, (l, l) is played repeatedly, while in the single-price auction, the same (Nash equilibrium) mixture of l and h is played repeatedly. Since in the latter equilibrium the Treasury sees high prices at least some of the time, it clearly prefers it.

To summarize, the single-price auction is always preferred by the Treasury. In the competitive case, it guarantees high prices all the time, while in the collusive case it guarantees high prices some of the time. With the multi-price auction, the Treasury is either guaranteed a low price (in the collusive case) or can see any number of behaviors including periodic shifts in prices (in the competitive case).

At first sight this result seems counterintuitive; after all, when there is one high and one low bidder, in a multiprice auction the Treasury collects a high price from the high bidder, but in a single-price auction it gets a low price from both. The point, though, is that

[13] *If $50\pi_l < 75\pi_h$, however, then h is again a dominant strategy in this reduced form and hence (h, h) is the unique stage game Nash equilibrium.*

[14] *There are other equilibria as well. For instance, an alternating sequence of high and low prices is also a subgame perfect equilibrium. In the Exercises we will develop this point in greater detail.*

precisely because of that fact, no one wants to be a high bidder in the multiprice auction! Put differently, in a single-price auction, (l, l) is difficult to sustain as an equilibrium because each buyer has an incentive to raise his bid (after all, he does not pay a higher price by raising his bid but does get a larger quantity). In a multiprice auction, in contrast, a buyer may be gun-shy about raising his low bid—if the other bidder bids low—since he gets a larger quantity but at a higher price.

SUMMARY

1. A repeated game is a special kind of extensive form game in which the same component ("stage") game is played over and over again.

2. If the stage game is played a fixed number of times, it is called a finitely repeated game and the payoffs to this repeated game are taken to be the sum of payoffs to each of the stage games.

3. If the stage game has a unique Nash equilibrium, then there is a unique subgame perfect equilibrium of the finitely repeated game as well. This equilibrium involves simply repeating the stage game equilibrium over and over again.

4. If the stage game has multiple Nash equilibria, then there are many subgame perfect equilibria of the finitely repeated game. Some of them involve the play of strategies that are collectively more profitable for the players than the stage game Nash equilibria.

5. Such nonmyopic behavior is sustained by the expectation of reciprocity; a player may be willing to sacrifice short-term gains within any particular stage game if she anticipates that she will be rewarded in the future for having made such a sacrifice.

6. Treasury Bill auctions can be analyzed as finitely repeated games. Single-price auctions net the Treasury a higher revenue than multiprice auctions.

EXERCISES

SECTION 14.1

14.1
Provide one real-world example each of a finitely repeated game and an infinitely repeated game.

14.2

a. Write down the extensive form of the once-repeated Battle of the Sexes.

b. Sketch the extensive form of the infinitely repeated Battle of the Sexes.

14.3

a. Repeat exercise 14.2a for the Odd Couple stage game (of Chapter 4).

b. Sketch the T-times-repeated game for the Odd Couple stage game.

SECTION 14.2

14.4

Verify, with complete details, that a subgame perfect equilibrium in the once-repeated modified Prisoners' Dilemma is as follows: play (n, c) in the first stage followed by (p, p) [provided (n, c) is played in the first stage], but otherwise play (c, c) in the second stage.

14.5

Verify, with complete details, that a subgame perfect equilibrium in the once-repeated Modified Prisoners' Dilemma is as follows: play (c, c) in the first stage followed by (p, p). What can you conclude about the reverse—play (p, p) in the first stage followed by (c, c)? Explain your answer.

14.6

a. Show that in the T-times-repeated Battle of the Sexes game, a subgame perfect equilibrium is to play (*football*, *opera*) in every stage—regardless of what got played in the previous stages.

b. Show that in the T-times-repeated Battle of the Sexes game, a subgame perfect equilibrium is to play (*opera*, *football*) in every stage—regardless of what got played in the previous stages.

14.7

a. Based on your answers to the previous questions, can you show that one subgame perfect equilibrium, in every finitely repeated game, is to play a stage-game Nash equilibrium repeatedly.

b. And—if there is more than one stage-game Nash equilibrium—to alternate between these equilibria. Provide full details of the arguments in each part.

The next few questions return to the analysis of the model of (Bertrand) *price competition*. We have two (duopoly) stores that set prices in a market whose demand curve is given by

$$Q = 6 - p$$

where p is the lower of the two prices (and the lower priced store meets all the demand). If the two stores post the same price p, then each gets half the market; that is, each gets $\frac{6-p}{2}$. Suppose that prices can only be quoted in dollars and that costs of production are zero. Suppose, finally, that the two stores compete repeatedly, say, every week over a period of two years.

14.8
Sketch the extensive form of this game.

14.9
Write down the strategies for each store in the game. Define a subgame perfect equilibrium.

14.10
What is the subgame perfect equilibrium of this model? Explain your answer.

Consider the following three-player stage game:

1 \ 2	*Left*	*Right*		1 \ 2	*Left*	*Right*
Up	1, 1, 1	2, 0, 2		*Up*	0, 0, −1	−1, 0, 0
Down	0, 2, 2	0, 0, 0		*Down*	0, −1, 0	0, 0, 0
	Player 3 East				Player 3 West	

14.11
Find the (pure-strategy) Nash equilibria of this stage game.

Suppose that the game is repeated once. Consider the following strategy: play (*up*, *left*, *west*) followed by (*up*, *left*, *east*); but if anything other than (*up*, *left*, *west*) is played in the first stage, then follow with (*down*, *right*, *west*).

14.12
Is the preceding strategy a subgame perfect equilibrium? Explain.

14.13
What are the pure-strategy subgame perfect equilibria of the game?

14.14
Explain, in detail, which of the equilibria that you found in the previous question involve reciprocal promises (or threats).

SECTION 14.3

Let us turn to multiprice Treasury auctions.

14.15

Show that in the competitive case, *any* time pattern of high and low prices—such as *l* for two auctions followed by *h* for the next three—is also a subgame perfect equilibrium.[15] Be careful to spell out the arguments for every subgame.

Actually even more is true. *Within the same auction*, one bidder might bid *l* and the other might bid *h* (thereby completely throwing the Treasury off!). Let us study that phenomenon in the next few questions. Consider the following strategies: for the last T^* auctions (T^* to be specified later) each bidder bids low. Earlier, in even-numbered auctions the bids are (l, h), and in odd-numbered auctions the bids are (h, l), provided this behavior has been seen in the past. If not—that is, if a buyer bids *h* when it is his turn to bid *l* or vice versa—then the bids are (h, h) from that point on.

14.16

Show that in the last T^* auctions neither buyer has an incentive to bid other than *l*.

14.17

Show that in the auction phase prior to the last T^*, each buyer makes an average profit of $\frac{25\pi_l + 75\pi_h}{2}$ per auction. (Bear in mind that they alternate their bids.)

14.18

Show that after departing from this strategy, each gets a profit of $50\pi_h$ per auction.

14.19

Prove that alternating is more profitable, that is, $\frac{25\pi_l + 75\pi_h}{2} > 50\pi_h$. In other words, show that by departing from the bidding behavior in the current auction, a buyer expects a *future loss* of $(T - T^*)\left(\frac{25\pi_l + 75\pi_h}{2} - 50\pi_h\right) + T^*\left(50\pi_l - 50\pi_h\right)$ if there are T auctions remaining ($T > T^*$).

14.20

What about the *present gain*? Show that a buyer makes an additional profit of $50\pi_l - 75\pi_h$ by switching his bid from *h* to *l*, and by switching from *l* to *h* he makes an additional $50\pi_h - 25\pi_l$.

14.21

Finally, show that the future loss outweighs the present gain if T^* is large enough. Hence no buyer deviates from the strategy.

14.22

Finally establish that what the Treasury sees is pairs of *high* and *low bids* all year except toward the end when the bids are all *low*.

---

[15] *Provided that the best response to a low price is also to bid low, that is, if $50\pi_l > 75\pi_h$.*

CHAPTER 15

INFINITELY REPEATED GAMES

In this chapter we continue the discussion of ongoing strategic interaction by talking about infinitely repeated games, and especially the infinitely repeated Prisoners' Dilemma. In section 15.1, we make a technical detour to discuss how one can add up stage-game payoffs when there are an infinite number of stages. Section 15.2 then talks about the infinitely repeated Prisoners' Dilemma and answers the question, Can the players stop each other from always confessing (the finitely repeated Prisoners' Dilemma's unique outcome)? Section 15.3 shows that the idea of reciprocal threats and promises, introduced in section 15.2, is valid much more generally, and it finds expression in an influential result called the *folk theorem*. Finally, in section 15.4, we present an analysis of the Prisoners' Dilemma when one player's action choices are not observable to the other player.

15.1   DETOUR THROUGH DISCOUNTING

When a game has no identifiable end—that is, when T is infinite—we cannot simply add up payoffs because we run into problems if we do. First, the payoff numbers may add to infinity. Consider the play "(n, n) at every stage." Its total payoff after (a finite number of) T stages is $5T$. Similarly, the play "alternate between (c, n) and (n, c)" has a total payoff that is (essentially) $\frac{5}{2}T$.[1] It seems intuitive that the first play is better than the second, but how can we compare two infinities (when T is infinite)?

    A second problem is that the numbers may not add up the same way (for every T). Consider the following play: a repeated cycle comprising (n, c) five times followed by (n, n) twice. For player 1, the total payoff over any one cycle is $5 \times (-2) + (2 \times 5) = 0$; hence every seven stages the total payoff comes back to 0. However, the total payoff after 8, or 15, or 22 . . . stages is always -2.

[1] *Recall the strategic form of the Prisoners' Dilemma (page 36) and the convention that play starts at stage 0. For T even, the total payoff for player 1 is therefore $\frac{5}{2}T + 7$ when play starts with 1 playing c (against n), and it is $\frac{5}{2}T - 2$ if it starts with 1 playing n (against c). (As an exercise, compute player 2's payoffs for any T.)*

One way to resolve this seeming impasse is to treat future periods a little differently from the present—and it may be sensible to do so anyway. Suppose for a moment that payoffs are monetary. In that case, should we treat $100 today the same way that we treat $100 a month from now? The answer is no. After all, we can place today's $100 in the stock market and it would yield some return, say 1 percent. Hence in a month's time, we would have not $100 but rather $101 in hand. Another way of saying the same thing is that a future payment of $100 is worth less than $100 today. It is worth the amount of money today that would grow into $100 by next month. Since every dollar grows into 1.01 dollars, a payment of $100 next month is only worth $\frac{1}{1.01} \times 100$ today.

The multiplying factor $\frac{1}{1.01}$—which is approximately 0.99—is called a *discount factor*; it is the amount by which future payments are discounted to get their present-day equivalent. In our example, $1 a month from now is equivalent to 99 cents today. The discount factor is often denoted by the symbol δ.

A player may discount a future payoff even when payoffs are nonmonetary. For example, he may be impatient and simply prefer to have a utility payoff in hand rather than wait for it.[2] Or a player may be uncertain about the future.[3] He may believe that there is some positive probability $1 - \delta$ that the current interaction is the very last one. For example, if this is market interaction and the player is a firm's manager, then there is some probability that he may get fired, or a new product may be introduced by a rival, or the government may introduce new regulations, and so on. Hence the payoff a month from now should be assessed in expected terms by multiplying it by its probability δ.

For any of these explanations, the amount by which a payoff two stages from today is discounted is δ^2, three stages in the future is discounted by δ^3, and so on. Consequently, the *total discounted payoffs* for player i are

$$\pi_{i0} + \pi_{i1}\delta + \pi_{i2}\delta^2 + \cdots + \pi_{it}\delta^t + \cdots \qquad (15.1)$$

where π_{it} is the tth-stage payoff. This total cannot run off to infinity (or negative infinity).[4] Furthermore, it always adds up; that is, after we have added a sufficient number of stages, the total remains virtually the same no matter how many more stages get added on subsequently.

One fact about the discounted total is very useful to know:

Fact 1.   When the stage-game payoffs are 1 in every stage, the total $1 + \delta + \delta^2 + \cdots + \delta^t + \cdots$ is equal to $\frac{1}{1-\delta}$. Hence, when the stage-game payoffs are a constant, say π, then the total is equal to $\frac{\pi}{1-\delta}$.

This formula is actually easy to derive.[5] Applying the formula we see that when δ equals 0.8, the discounted total over the infinite horizon is $\frac{1}{0.2}$ or 5. The total is 2.5 when $\delta = 0.5$. Finally, when δ equals 0.8 and π equals 10, then the discounted total is 50.

[2] *This justification for discounting the future is called pure time preference.*

[3] *This is the explanation we gave in our brief discussion of this issue in the previous chapter.*

[4] *We assume that the stage payoffs, π_{it}, cannot be arbitrarily large.*

[5] *Denote the total $1 + \delta + \delta^2 + \cdots + \delta^t + \cdots$ by the symbol S. In particular, the total from the second term onward, that is, $\delta + \delta^2 + \cdots + \delta^t + \cdots$, is nothing but δS. The difference between the two totals is 1; that is, $S(1 - \delta) = 1$. It follows that $S = \frac{1}{1-\delta}$.*

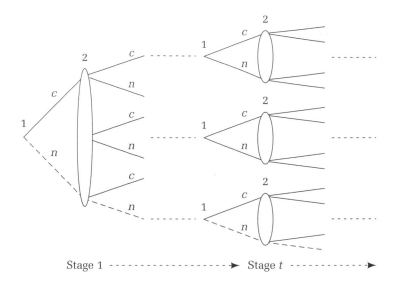

Stage 1 - - - - - - - - - - - - - - - -▶ Stage t - - - - - - - - - -▶

FIGURE 15.1

15.2 ANALYSIS OF EXAMPLE 3: TRIGGER STRATEGIES AND GOOD BEHAVIOR

Let us start with example 3 from Chapter 14. The Prisoners' Dilemma stage game is played period after period with no clearly defined last stage. The payoff to player i in the infinitely repeated game is the total discounted payoff given by equation 15.1.

Consider the following pair of strategies, one for each player: start by playing (n, n). Continue playing (n, n) if neither player confesses at any stage. However, if either player confesses at some stage, then play (c, c) from the subsequent stage onward. A strategy such as this is called a *grim trigger* strategy: a deviation from the desired behavior, (n, n), triggers a switch to a "punishment phase," (c, c). The trigger is grim in the sense that once the punishment phase is initiated, it is never revoked.

Let us check whether this pair of grim trigger strategies constitute a subgame perfect equilibrium. Note that in the infinitely repeated Prisoners' Dilemma there are an infinite number of subgames; indeed after every t stages of play, no matter how those stages were played, a new subgame starts. In principle, therefore, in order to check whether the exhibited strategies are subgame perfect equilibria, we have to check every one of these subgames. Of course we cannot and will not do that!

For the grim trigger strategy, there are really only two kinds of subgames—(1) the subgame that follows the repeated play of (n, n) in the first t stages and (2) every other subgame. This is pictured in Figure 15.1. Along the bottom (dashed) branch start subgames of type 1; everywhere else are subgames of the second type.

For type 2, the strategy specifies the play of (c, c) forever thereafter. Within this subgame, this is indeed a Nash equilibrium. No player can increase his payoff in any stage by playing n against c; furthermore, he does not change the expected pattern of play thereafter.

For subgames of type 1, let us check whether a player has an incentive to confess at any stage—while the other player plays n in that stage. Doing so would give the player who confesses an immediate payoff of 7 but would result in a payoff of 0 in every subsequent stage. (Why?) Staying with the strategy would yield this player a payoff of 5 in the current stage and a stream of 5 in every future period. Hence the total payoff to staying with the strategy is

$$5 + 5\delta + 5\delta^2 + \cdots + 5\delta^t + \cdots = \frac{5}{1-\delta}$$

It is clear that staying with the proposed grim trigger strategy is better, provided $\frac{5}{1-\delta} > 7$, that is, provided δ is greater than $\frac{2}{7}$. In particular, the "nice guy" behavior—both players *always play* (n, n), and neither ever succumbs to the temptation of confessing— turns out to be equilibrium play provided there is not too much discounting, that is, provided $\delta > \frac{2}{7}$. Note that this is exactly the opposite of the "nasty guy" behavior—both players *always play* (c, c)—that was found to be the *only* possible outcome in the finitely repeated Prisoners' Dilemma.

The intuition for this stark difference in conclusion is worth emphasizing. Niceness is sustainable in the infinitely repeated game because at every stage it is possible to make a conditional nice guy promise—if you are nice today, I will be nice tomorrow as well. (The accompanying threat is that if you are nasty today, I will be nasty forever after.) The promise guarantees a continuation of the payoff 5; the threat darkly suggests a drop down to 0 forever. Between them, they constitute a future loss of $\frac{5\delta}{1-\delta}$ worth of payoffs if a player unilaterally decides to be nasty today. This "stick-carrot" is a sufficient deterrent if the future matters, that is, if δ is large.[6]

To summarize, a grim trigger strategy has two components: first, there is the *grim* punishment, (c, c) forever. Second, there is the desired *nice guy* behavior, (n, n) forever. Any departure from the desired behavior *triggers* the punishment. We have seen that if δ is high enough, then the *grim* punishment is a sufficient deterrent and the *nice guy* behavior is achievable.

Let us now demonstrate two other things:

- The threat of the *grim* punishment might help achieve other behaviors as well.

- The *nice guy* behavior might be achievable with a different (and less severe) punishment.

There are, in fact, many *achievable behaviors* in the infinitely repeated Prisoners' Dilemma. Here is one: start with (n, c) and alternate between that pair and (c, n) provided both players stick to this plan (and otherwise, play $[c, c]$ forever).

[6] *This analysis also explains why niceness is lost in the finitely repeated game. Close to the end there is no future to promise; hence niceness unravels. But since the players know that it will unravel, there is no real future even in the middle. And so on.*

CONCEPT CHECK
GRIM EQUILIBRIUM

Show that if anything other than (n, c) is played at an even-numbered stage, or anything other than (c, n) at an odd-numbered stage, then playing (c, c) forever after is a Nash equilibrium.

What remains to check is whether either player will initiate the punishment phase, that is, whether or not the grim trigger is a sufficient deterrent. Suppose we are in an even-numbered stage. If player 1 deviates and plays c instead of n, she gets 0 in that period rather than -2. However, from the next stage onward, she will get 0 forever. By staying with n she gets, from the next stage onward, an infinite stream of alternating (c, n) and (n, c) payoffs; that is, she gets the infinite payoff stream

$$7\delta - 2\delta^2 + 7\delta^3 - 2\delta^4 + \cdots = \frac{7\delta - 2\delta^2}{1 - \delta^2}$$

CONCEPT CHECK
DETERRENCE

Show that player 1 will not deviate in an even-numbered stage if $\delta > \frac{2}{7}$. Also show that she will not deviate in an odd-numbered stage either. Finally, show that the grim trigger is a sufficient deterrent for player 2 as well if $\delta > \frac{2}{7}$.[7]

Now let us turn to *other punishments*. Consider the following: Start by playing (n, n) and continue playing (n, n) if neither player confesses; however, if either player confesses at some stage, then play (c, c) for the next T stages. Thereafter, revert to (n, n), bearing in mind, though, that every subsequent departure from (n, n) will also be met by the T stages of (c, c). A strategy such as this is called a *forgiving trigger:* a deviation from the desired behavior, (n, n), triggers a switch to a punishment phase, (c, c), but all is forgiven after T stages of punishment.

Is the forgiving trigger a sufficient deterrent? By playing c when he is supposed to play n, a player gets a payoff of 7. Then T stages of 0 follow, and then—once play reverts to (n, n)—an infinite stream of 5. So the total payoff from this "deviant" behavior is

$$7 + \delta^{T+1}[5 + 5\delta + 5\delta^2 + \cdots] = 7 + \frac{5\delta^{T+1}}{1 - \delta}$$

However, staying with the proposed *not confess* behavior yields an infinite stream of 5, that is, a lifetime payoff of $\frac{5}{1-\delta}$. The trigger is credible if $\frac{5}{1-\delta} > 7 + \frac{5\delta^{T+1}}{1-\delta}$, or equivalently

$$\frac{5(1 - \delta^{T+1})}{1 - \delta} > 7 \tag{15.2}$$

When the discount factor δ is close to 1, the left-hand side of equation 15.2 is approximately $5(T + 1)$.[8] Hence, when the future matters—that is, when δ is close to 1—even one period of punishment—that is, even $T = 1$—is sufficient.

In conclusion, it is worth reemphasizing that the unifying theme in each of the three equilibria is the power of future reciprocity. Threats and promises, if made in a subgame perfect credible way, are believable. If the stick is stern enough or the carrot sweet enough, then they can discourage opportunistic behavior today and get the players to play in a collectively optimal way. Actually they can do more; if the future punishments and rewards are sufficiently large, then they can induce the players to play today in a variety of ways that they would not otherwise. Both good behavior—(n, n) always—and more whimsical behavior—alternating between (n, c) and (c, n)—can be sustained by a significant future.

15.3   THE FOLK THEOREM ⚠

There is a more general result that we can derive about subgame perfect equilibria in the infinitely repeated Prisoners' Dilemma; this result is called the folk theorem of repeated games.[9]

The general result answers the question, What are *all possible behaviors* that can arise in equilibrium? The answer, it will turn out, is virtually anything! While this is not entirely satisfactory from the point of view of predictions, the result does highlight the absolute power of reciprocity. After you have seen the result, we will discuss its implications, richness, and shortcomings in greater detail.

Before we can present the result we need to define something called a *behavior cycle*.

Definition.   A behavior cycle is a repeated cycle of actions; play (n, n) for T_1 stages, then (c, c) for T_2 stages, followed by (n, c) for T_3 stages, and then (c, n) for T_4 stages. At the end of these $T_1 + T_2 + T_3 + T_4$ stages, start the cycle again, then yet again, and so on.

Some of the subcomponents of the cycle can be zero; that is, T_1 or T_2 or T_3 or T_4 can be zero. Indeed the nice guy behavior, (n, n) always, is one where $T_2 = T_3 = T_4 = 0$, whereas in the nasty guy behavior, (c, c) always, $T_1 = T_3 = T_4 = 0$. The alternating behavior—(n, c) in even periods and (c, n) in odd periods—is a behavior cycle where $T_1 = T_2 = 0$ and $T_3 = T_4 = 1$.

Let us call a behavior cycle *individually rational* if each player gets strictly positive payoffs within a cycle; that is, for each player the sum of stage payoffs over the $T_1 + T_2 + T_3 + T_4$ stages is positive. So the nice guy behavior cycle is individually rational, as is the alternating behavior. If the behavior cycle is $T_1 = 10$, $T_2 = 55$, $T_3 = 100$, and $T_4 = 15$, then it is not individually rational because player 1's payoff over the cycle equals $(10 \times 5) + (55 \times 0) + [100 \times (-2)] + (15 \times 7) = -45$.

[8] *We are using a result from calculus called L'Hospital's rule, which says that $\frac{1-\delta^{T+1}}{1-\delta}$ is approximately equal to $T + 1$ when δ is close to 1.*

[9] *This more general result is called the folk theorem because a simple version of it has been known for a long time and known to many "folks" in game theory. A modern, less simple, version of the result was proved in 1986 by Drew Fudenberg and Eric Maskin. You can find their result in the journal Econometrica, vol. 54, pp. 533–554, under the title "The Folk Theorem in Repeated Games under Discounting and with Incomplete Information."*

Denote the total length of a cycle T—that is, $T = T_1 + T_2 + T_3 + T_4$—and denote the total payoff of player i over the T stages, $P_i(T)$.[10]

The next two results constitute the *folk theorem* for the infinitely repeated Prisoners' Dilemma.

Folk Theorem

- **Equilibrium Behavior.** Consider any individually rational behavior cycle. Then this cycle is achievable as the play of a subgame perfect equilibrium whenever the discount factor δ is close to 1.

- **Equilibrium Strategy.** One strategy that constitutes an equilibrium is the grim trigger; start with the desired behavior cycle and continue with it if the two players do nothing else. If either player deviates to do something else, then play (c, c) forever after.

Sketch of a Proof

As before, if the grim trigger punishment is ever initiated, it gets carried out. So the only issue is, Would it ever get initiated? That is, is it a sufficient deterrent so that no player would want to have it initiated? A player initiates the punishment by failing, at some stage, to play the appropriate action in the behavior cycle. That play gives him a stage payoff—call it $\widetilde{\pi}_i$—in the current stage and thereafter a payoff of zero, on account of the grim trigger punishment.

Staying with the behavior cycle, however, yields a lifetime payoff that is essentially equal to $\frac{P_i(T)}{1-\delta^T}$.[11] Staying is better than initiating if $\frac{P_i(T)}{1-\delta^T} > \widetilde{\pi}_i$. Notice that the denominator of the left-hand side of the inequality vanishes as δ gets close to 1; in other words, the left-hand side becomes infinitely large. The right-hand side is a fixed constant. Eventually, for δ close to 1, not deviating has to be better. ◇

The proof is intuitive. It says that by deviating a player will lose out on $P_i(T) + P_i(T) + P_i(T) + \cdots$ for an infinite number of cycles. Clearly, that consideration has to be stronger than any immediate payoff of $\widetilde{\pi}_i$ no matter how large it is, as long as the future matters sufficiently.

Some general remarks follow:

All Potential Behaviors Are Equilibrium Behaviors

In any equilibrium, every player's payoff over a cycle must be at least zero. This statement is true because each player can guarantee himself a payoff that high by simply confessing at every stage. The folk theorem result says that not only are positive payoffs *necessary* for equilibrium but they are *sufficient* as well; every behavior cycle with positive payoffs *is* an equilibrium for high values of δ.

All Payoffs Are Accounted For

You might think that by looking only at cycles we are excluding certain kinds of behaviors. Although that is true, the restriction involves no loss because we are *not* excluding any possible payoffs. To explain, one way to think about the payoff to a behavior cycle is in terms of its *per-stage* payoff, $\frac{P_i(T)}{T}$. As we look at different behavior cycles we get

[10] Hence, $P_i(T) = T_1 \times \pi_i(n, n) + T_2 \times \pi_i(c, c) + T_3 \times \pi_i(n, c) + T_4 \times \pi_i(c, n)$. An individually rational behavior cycle is therefore a cycle for which $P_1(T) > 0$—and likewise $P_2(T) > 0$.

[11] We say "essentially" because the exact payoffs in every cycle are actually
$\left[1 + \delta + \cdots + \delta^{T_1-1}\right]\pi_i(n, n) + \delta^{T_1}\left[1 + \delta + \cdots + \delta^{T_2-1}\right]\pi_i(c, c) + \delta^{T_1+T_2}\left[1 + \delta + \cdots + \delta^{T_3-1}\right]\pi_i(n, c) + \delta^{T_1+T_2+T_3}\left[1 + \delta + \cdots + \delta^{T_4-1}\right]\pi_i(c, n)$.
When δ is close to 1, that sum is essentially $T_1 \times \pi_i(n, n) + T_2 \times \pi_i(c, c) + T_3 \times \pi_i(n, c) + T_4 \times \pi_i(c, n)$, that is, $P_i(T)$. Since every T periods this payoff is received, by Fact 1, the lifetime payoff is equal to $\frac{P_i(T)}{1-\delta^T}$.

different payoffs per stage. Suppose we look at a behavior that is *not* cyclical. This pattern will have a per-stage payoff as well.[12] It turns out that no matter what this per-stage payoff is, there is a behavior cycle that has exactly the same payoff per stage.

Future Needs to Matter

The result only works for high values of δ because that is exactly what is needed to make promises and threats have deterrent value. As we have seen before, a high δ means that future payoffs matter. In turn, that fact means future promises—or threats—can affect current behavior.

Infinitely Many Equilibria

An implication of the result is that there are an infinite number of subgame perfect equilibria in the infinitely repeated Prisoners' Dilemma. This is discouraging from the point of view of predictions. All that we can conclude is that the prospect of threats and rewards is so potent that players may be willing to do virtually anything.

A More General Conclusion

There is a more general result, called the folk theorem for infinitely repeated games, which asserts that by repeating any stage game—not just the Prisoners' Dilemma—we can get all individually rational behavior cycles as part of a subgame perfect equilibrium.[13]

Observable Actions

One shortcoming of the analysis so far is that it requires deviations to be perfectly observable—and hence immediately punishable. In many contexts this assumption is unrealistic because other players may not have precise information on what a rival has done in the past. In the next section you will see a generalization of the trigger strategy idea that takes account of this complication.

15.4 REPEATED GAMES WITH IMPERFECT DETECTION ⚠

Up until now we have assumed that each player sees the other player's action perfectly. In some contexts this is not a good assumption. For instance we can interpret the stage game of the Prisoners' Dilemma as a price competition model (with *confess* representing low price and *not confess* representing high price). In that case, actions may not be perfectly observable; for example, each firm might offer special discounts to certain customers or for bulk orders, and these discounts will typically not be observed by the competing firm.

It is quite likely, however, that a firm's profits will be observable. For the Prisoners' Dilemma that statement is equivalent to saying that, although the action chosen is not observable, the payoff is. You might wonder whether observable payoffs are equivalent to the actions themselves being observable. After all, if a payoff of 7 can only arise from

---

[12] *In general, for any behavior pattern, a per-stage payoff is defined as $\frac{\text{Total payoffs over T stages}}{T}$ whenever the number of stages T is large.*

[13] *This is subject to one further assumption when a game has more than two players.*

confessing (against *not confessing*), then can't we infer actions from payoffs? In general we can. To make the analysis meaningful, we therefore need to be a little careful with the interpretation of payoffs. Consider again the Prisoners' Dilemma stage game:

Calvin \ Klein	c	n
c	$0, 0$	$7, -2$
n	$-2, 7$	$5, 5$

Suppose that we interpret the payoffs in the matrix as expected, or average, payoffs. In other words, if (c, c) actually gets played, then the payoffs to the two players are uncertain and can take on any value (x, y). However, the average value of x is 0, as is the average value of y. Suppose also that any particular value of (x, y), say $(2, -1)$, can arise from the play of (c, c) but can also arise from the play of (c, n) or (n, c) or (n, n). Put differently, if (x, y) is the observed payoff, then neither player can be sure about what the opponent played. Of course, the likelihood that (x, y) will arise if (c, c) is actually played is different from the likelihood if (c, n) is played, and so on. Hence, having observed the payoffs, a player will typically assign different probabilities to the possibility that (c, c) was played versus the possibility that (c, n) was played.

If deviations cannot be perfectly detected, are we back to perpetual confessions? The answer, thankfully, is no. In order for players to not confess, however, it must be the case that their opponents view very low payoffs as evidence of *confession*. If that is not the case, then a player would have the incentive to drive his (nice guy) opponent's payment down by continually confessing against the other player's nonconfessions. This observation motivates the following definition:

Definition. A threshold trigger strategy is defined by a number, say m. Players start by playing (n, n) and continue to do so if both players' payoffs remain above m in every stage. The first time either payoff drops below m players play (c, c) for T stages; and then restart the strategy.

Hence a threshold strategy is defined by two parameters, the quickness of the trigger m and the severity of the trigger T. Let us now investigate when a threshold trigger strategy is an equilibrium and how good an equilibrium it is.

There will be two general conclusions:

- The more severe is the trigger, that is, the higher is T, the more likely it is that the strategy will be an equilibrium.

- The more severe or more quick (higher m) is the trigger, the less profitable is the strategy.

Put differently, there will be a tension: the more severe the trigger, the greater its deterrence value but, from excessive usage, the smaller its profits.

Suppose that a threshold trigger strategy is being played. Let us first compute its payoffs. Denote this payoff v. The payoff is given by

$$v = 5 + \delta \left[(1 - p_n)v + p_n \delta^T v \right] \tag{15.3}$$

where p_n is the probability that one of the two stage payoffs is less than m—that is, the trigger gets activated—even though the actions chosen were (n, n) as suggested. The first term, 5, in the right-hand side of equation 15.3 is the current stage's expected profit if both players play (n, n). The second term, $\delta(1 - p_n)v$ refers to the following: with probability $(1 - p_n)$ the trigger is not activated, and in that case we are back in the current situation with lifetime expected payoffs of v. Since all this happens one stage hence, it is discounted by δ. The last term, $p_n \delta^{T+1} v$, refers to the fact that with probability p_n the trigger *is* activated, T stages of zero profits follow, and then we return to the current situation with lifetime expected payoffs of v. That return will start $T + 1$ stages from the current one and hence is discounted by δ^{T+1}. Collecting terms, equation 15.3 yields

$$v = \frac{5}{1 - \delta[(1 - p_n) + p_n \delta^T]}$$

The quicker is the trigger (i.e., the higher is m), the higher is its likely use (the higher is p_n). In turn, that implies a lower value of $[(1 - p_n) + p_n \delta^T]$ and therefore a lower value of v. Similarly, the more severe is the trigger—that is, the longer is T—the lower is $[(1 - p_n) + p_n \delta^T]$ and hence the lower is v. To summarize, higher values of m or T make a trigger strategy, if followed, less attractive. Hence, the players would like to make the trigger milder by lowering the values of m and T. Therein lies the rub; that might simultaneously destroy a trigger's efficacy.

The trigger strategy is an equilibrium in the T stage punishment phase. A player cannot make positive average profits by choosing *not confess* in this phase, nor does he change the future profile of actions. So consider instead a stage when the players are supposed to be playing (n, n). By deviating, a player would get a discounted total payoff of

$$7 + \delta \left[(1 - p_c)v + p_c \delta^T v \right] \tag{15.4}$$

where p_c is the probability that the trigger will be activated by the play of (c, n); presumably, $p_c > p_n$.

CONCEPT CHECK
PAYOFF

Show that the lifetime payoff, after a deviation, is in fact given by equation 15.4.

Comparing equations 15.3 and 15.4 makes the incentives clear. On one hand, confession is immediately more gratifying because its payoff of 7 is higher than the 5 from not confessing. On the other hand, the future benefits are lower because there is a greater chance of triggering the punishment phase. The play (n, n) is sustainable provided

$$7 + \delta v[(1 - p_c) + p_c \delta^T] < 5 + \delta v[(1 - p_n) + p_n \delta^T]$$

that is, provided

$$2 < \delta v(1 - \delta^T)(p_c - p_n) \qquad \qquad \textbf{(15.5)}$$

From the definition of v it is straightforward to show that the more severe is the trigger—that is, the longer is T—the greater is its deterrent value. Put differently, long punishment phases get players to behave well.

CONCEPT CHECK
INCENTIVE (CALCULUS QUESTION)

Show that the higher is T, the more likely it is that equation 15.5 will be satisfied.

The deterrent effect of m is a little ambiguous. A higher value of m lowers v as we have seen. It may, however, increase $p_c - p_n$; that is, it may make confession comparatively easier to detect. The net effect will then depend on $v \times (p_c - p_n)$.

To summarize, a cousin of the trigger strategies that we encountered in the previous sections, called a threshold trigger strategy, can work to enforce (n, n) even when actions are unobservable. One key difference, though, is that every so often the punishment phase will be triggered whenever actions are unobservable; that is, along the equilibrium play path there will be periods of (c, c) interspersed among the (n, n)'s. These phases are wasteful in that they lower total payoffs. They are, however, necessary because without them each player would confess all the time. Hence, how long to spend in the punishment phase, and how frequently, needs to be carefully chosen in order to balance the two conflicting forces of waste and deterrence.

SUMMARY

1. In an infinitely repeated game, lifetime payoffs are computed by adding up the discounted payoffs at every stage of the game.

2. The grim trigger strategy comprises two parts: a desired behavior on the part of the players and a punishment regime—always *confess*—that is triggered whenever either player violates the desired behavior.

3. The grim trigger punishment can sustain the nice guy behavior—*never confess*—as the desired behavior provided players have a high discount factor.

4. The same punishment can sustain any behavior cycle that gives each player a strictly positive payoff over each cycle. This result is called the folk theorem for the infinitely repeated Prisoners' Dilemma.

5. Reciprocity (in threats and punishments) can sustain periodic bouts of nice guy behavior even if the actions chosen by a player are not observable to his opponent.

EXERCISES

SECTION 15.1

15.1

a. What is the discounted lifetime payoff of the following stage payoff sequence:

1, 3, 1, 3, 1, 3, . . .

b. What of

1, 1, . . . , 1, 3, 3, . . . , 3, 1, 1, 1, . . .

where each sequence of 1s and 3s lasts 10 stages? (You need only give the formula.)

15.2

a. What if the sequence of 1s lasts 10 stages but the 3s last 20?

b. What if the sequence of 1s lasts T_1 stages but the 3s last T_2?

15.3

a. Compute the payoff over the cycle $P(T)$ for exercise 15.1.

b. Repeat for exercise 15.2.

15.4

Consider the sum of discounted payoffs over the cycle. What is it equal to for the scenarios in exercises 15.1 and 15.2 when $\delta = 0.8$?

15.5

What if $\delta = 0.95$? Which one is closer to $P(T)$?

SECTION 15.2

15.6

Consider the infinitely repeated Prisoners' Dilemma. Show that the strategy that plays (c, c) in every subgame—regardless of past behavior—is a subgame perfect equilibrium

15.7

Suppose that a pair of strategies, say s_1^*, s_2^*, form a subgame perfect equilibrium of the infinitely repeated Prisoners' Dilemma. Suppose, furthermore, that these strategies prescribe play at every stage t that is independent of past behavior. Show that s_*^1, s_*^2 must be the same as the pair of strategies that play (c, c) in every subgame.

15.8

Explain briefly why a high value of δ is conducive to sustaining good behavior in the play of the infinitely repeated Prisoners' Dilemma.

15.9

Consider the forgiving trigger punishment. How high does the value of δ need to be in order for the *nice guy* behavior—(n, n) forever—to be achievable (as part of a subgame perfect equilibrium)? (Your answer will depend on the length of the punishment phase T.) How does your answer compare with what we found about the grim trigger punishment?

15.10

Can you show that the grim trigger is always a more efficient punishment in the sense that, no matter what behavior cycle we are trying to achieve, if the forgiving trigger is a sufficient deterrent, then so is the grim trigger?

15.11

Construct an example of a behavior cycle that is achievable by using the grim trigger punishment if $\delta = 0.9$? (Do not use any of the patterns that were discussed within the chapter.)

15.12

Is the behavior cycle of the previous question also achievable by using a forgiving trigger with trigger length 10? Explain your answer. If the answer is no, at what discount factor does the forgiving trigger become a sufficient deterrent?

SECTION 15.3

The next few questions return to the analysis of the model of *price competition* with a market whose demand curve is

$$Q = 6 - p$$

where p is the lower of the two prices. The lower priced firm gets the entire market, and if the two firms post the same price, then each gets half the market. Suppose that prices can only be quoted in dollar units and costs of production are zero. Suppose, finally, that price competition continues indefinitely; that is, every time the two firms compete they think that there is a probability δ that they will compete again.

15.13
Write down the extensive form of the game. Identify the subgames.

15.14
Write down the strategies for each firm in the game. Define a subgame perfect equilibrium.

15.15
Consider the following strategy: Price at 2 dollars each and continue with that price if it has been maintained by both firms in the past. Otherwise, switch to a price of a dollar. For what values of δ is this strategy a subgame perfect equilibrium? Explain.

15.16
Show that there is also a subgame perfect equilibrium in which the price is always 2 dollars but which is sustained by a forgiving trigger. Be explicit about the nature of the forgiving trigger.

15.17
Suppose that $\delta = 0.9$. What is the maximum price that can arise in a subgame perfect equilibrium of this model? Explain.

15.18
State a version of the folk theorem that is applicable for this price competition model.

15.19
Provide an argument in support of your stated result in exercise 15.18.

SECTION 15.5

Let us return to the infinitely repeated Prisoners' Dilemma but with unobservable actions. Suppose that there is a 50 percent chance that at least one player's stage payoff is less than 0 if the action that is played is (c, n)—or (n, c)—but there is only a 10 percent chance of that outcome if (n, n) is played. Suppose that the threshold trigger gets activated whenever a payoff less than 0 is observed.

15.20
Is a forgiving trigger of length 10 a sufficient deterrent if $\delta = 0.9$? What is the minimum value of δ at which it becomes a sufficient deterrent?

15.21

Compute the lifetime payoff to this strategy at the cutoff value of the discount factor that you computed in exercise 15.20.

15.22

Consider a punishment of length 20 instead. Show that this too is a sufficient deterrent. Show furthermore that its lifetime payoff is actually worse.

15.23

What can you infer about the length of the punishment phase from your previous answers? Explain.

15.24

Suppose that at $\delta = 0.9$ both of the following triggers are sufficient deterrents: (a) cutoff = 0 and length of punishment = 10 and (b) cutoff = −1 and length of punishment = 5. Suppose furthermore that there is a 5 percent chance that either player's payoff will be less than −1 if (n, n) is played. Which strategy will the players prefer?

15.25

Would your answer be any different if there were a 8 percent chance that either player's payoff will be less than −1 if (n, n) is played? Explain.

CHAPTER 16

AN APPLICATION: COMPETITION AND COLLUSION IN THE NASDAQ STOCK MARKET

In this chapter we will discuss an application of infinitely repeated games to a recent controversy: have investors been systematically overcharged on the NASDAQ stock market? Section 16.1 will explain the background to the question, section 16.2 will present a simple model to analyze it, and section 16.3 will discuss some further variations of that model. Finally, section 16.4 will contain the denouement to the plot line: were they or weren't they overcharged?

16.1   THE BACKGROUND

The NASDAQ stock market is the second-largest stock market in the United States after the New York Stock Exchange, the NYSE (and ahead of the American Stock Exchange, the AMEX, and all of the regional exchanges such as the stock markets in Philadelphia, Chicago, and San Francisco).[1] Furthermore, it is the fastest growing exchange. Its slogan is "The Stock Market for the *Next* 100 Years."

The NASDAQ market is unlike the NYSE[2] in at least a couple of ways. First, it has no physical location; rather, it trades online.[3] Second, unlike the NYSE, where there is a single "market maker" per stock, the NASDAQ has multiple market makers. (The average number ranges between 10 and 20 with up to 50 for more popular stocks such as Microsoft, MCI, Intel, and Amgen.)[4]

The roles of the market makers are also quite different at the two exchanges. At the NYSE, the market maker acts like a clearinghouse or auctioneer; he collects buy and sell orders and tries to find a price at which the quantity being bought matches the quantity being sold. In a sense, therefore, each potential buyer competes against every other buyer because he can be outbid by the latter; likewise sellers compete against each other.

[1] *Strictly speaking, the NASDAQ market is the largest in terms of share volume—the number of shares that get traded on a typical day. Its 1997 average of 647.8 million shares per day was 132 percent of the corresponding figure for the NYSE. It is second, after the NYSE, in terms of the dollar value of traded shares.*

[2] *The stock market for the last 100 years, if NASDAQ's publicists are to be believed.*

[3] *The NYSE, on the other hand, is located at the corner of Wall and Broad streets in downtown New York.*

[4] *Dealers is another name for market makers.*

At the NASDAQ, each market maker posts two quotes—an "ask" price at which he will sell the stock and a "bid" price at which he will buy. These quotes can only be in increments of an eighth of a dollar, and, typically, the ask price is higher than the bid. The lowest ask and the highest bid constitute the market prices (and are called the inside prices or inside quotes). On this market, dealers compete among themselves, and because there are multiple dealers per stock, the NASDAQ market has been claimed by its supporters to be more competitive than the NYSE. The key difference, though, and this will be crucial for our subsequent story, is that on the NASDAQ market, dealers do not compete against buyers and sellers because the relevant quotes are their own asks and bids. In particular, the asks or bids of non-market makers cannot set the market price.

At least this is the way things worked on NASDAQ till 1996. Why, you may ask, have things changed? Therein lies our tale!

In December 1994, two academics, William Christie and Paul Schultz, published a study that showed that an unusually high percentage of asks and bids on the NASDAQ were clustered around the "even eighths" of a dollar, that is, were clustered around, say, \$10, \$10$\frac{1}{4}$, \$10$\frac{1}{2}$, and \$10$\frac{3}{4}$.[5] Very few prices were at \$10$\frac{1}{8}$, \$10$\frac{3}{8}$, \$10$\frac{5}{8}$, and \$10$\frac{7}{8}$. Consequently, the difference between the ask and the bid—also called the *spread*—for all of these stocks was at least 25 cents and in many instances was as much as 50 cents.[6] This finding seemed puzzling because there could potentially be many investors who would be willing to buy or sell inside the spread, that is, pay more than the bid and sell at less than the ask. Such competition should, in principle, narrow the spread, especially on stocks that are heavily traded and hence have many interested buyers and sellers.[7]

All of this matters because larger spreads hurt potential investors and help market makers make greater profits than they would otherwise. On 10,000 shares, an extra spread of $\frac{1}{8}$ translates to an extra payment of \$1,250 by investors (and a similar-sized extra profit for market makers). It is instructive to recall that the *daily* volume on NASDAQ is about 650 million shares; an extra spread of $\frac{1}{8}$ translates for that volume to an extra payment by investors of about \$80 million dollars *daily*. There is also a further cost; in the long run investors could stay away from a market if they perceived that they were being overcharged.

Christie and Schultz offered no ironclad explanation for the missing-odd-eighth phenomenon. Instead they made the following conjecture: "Market makers interact frequently and over long periods of time with the same population of other market makers. Thus, in setting quotes, NASDAQ dealers are essentially engaged in an infinitely repeated game. Furthermore current and historical quotes of all market makers are available to all dealers. . . . The well-known folk theorem states that . . . collusion is a possible equilibrium" (p. 1834). Put more succinctly, they claimed that market makers are ripping off the public and that they are able to do so because they are in a repeated game.

Christie and Schultz go on to point out that the screen-based NASDAQ trading system allows immediate detection of dealers who undercut the "accepted" spread. Finally, the authors emphasize the importance in all this of a NASDAQ practice called *order preferencing;* this is a practice by which brokers—the middlemen who direct

[5] See "Why do NASDAQ Market Makers Avoid Odd-Eighth Quotes?" in the Journal of Finance, 1994, vol. 49, pp. 1813–1840. After their findings became public, the two authors noticed another phenomenon, which was the subject of a companion piece, "Why Did NASDAQ Market Makers Stop Avoiding Odd-Eighth Quotes?" This was coauthored with Jeffrey Harris, and it also appeared in the Journal of Finance, 1994, vol. 49, pp. 1841–1860.

[6] Based on 1991 quotes, Christie and Schultz found only 10 percent of the stocks had a spread of $\frac{1}{8}$, 39 percent had a spread of $\frac{1}{4}$, 5 percent had a spread of $\frac{3}{8}$, and 33 percent had a spread of $\frac{1}{2}$. The corresponding figures for the NYSE and AMEX were 25, 46, 22, and 5 percent. Hence, an investor would pay a spread of 50 cents on a third of NASDAQ stocks but only on 5 percent of NYSE stocks. To keep the comparisons meaningful, the authors tried to compare apples with apples; that is, they tried to compare companies with similar capitalizations.

[7] About half the time spreads were 50 cents for each of the following three heavily traded stocks: Apple, MCI, and Lotus. (Remember that in 1991 Apple was still in its glory days and Lotus had not yet been bought out by IBM.)

customer orders to the dealers—can choose to send an order to a dealer who does not have the best quote provided he matches that quote.

The Christie-Schultz finding—and their conjecture—unleashed a veritable firestorm. NASDAQ reacted with understandable outrage. They lined up an impressive collection of academics who argued that collusion was impossible because (a) there were too many market makers, and (b) even if there were not, there would be. In other words, they argued that with 10 or more dealers competing per stock, somebody would always have the incentive to undercut a collusive price and lure customers away. Furthermore, it is relatively easy to set up as a dealer in the NASDAQ market.[8] Hence, if there were collusive profits being made, many more people would want to become dealers. The fact that there is not such a clamor is evidence that dealers do not make large profits.

Everybody agrees, of course, that dealers need to make *some* profits in order to stay in business; they carry the risk of making losses on shares that they buy, they have costs of doing business, and so on. The question is, Are they making too much profit? Let us now turn to a repeated-game analysis of the Christie-Schultz argument and that of their detractors.[9]

16.2 THE ANALYSIS

16.2.1 A MODEL OF THE NASDAQ MARKET

The stage game of this model is the simultaneous submission of an ask and a bid quote by each market maker; in the course of a single trading day, there may be six such trading stages.[10] Suppose that there are N dealers for the stock in question. Let dealer i's ask be denoted a_i and his bid b_i. The best ask is the lowest; that is, it is the quote of the dealer who is asking for the smallest amount of money in order to sell the stock to a customer. Let a denote the best or inside ask, that is, $a = \min_i a_i$. Similarly, let b denote the inside bid, that is, $b = \max_i b_i$, the highest that any dealer is willing to pay for a share. The inside spread therefore is $a - b$.

In the current period, when these quotes are binding, all buy orders are executed at a price equal to a. The profit to a dealer from participating in this transaction depends on what the real value of this share is. If that value is v, then the dealer makes $a - v$ dollars worth of profit from each share.[11] Similarly a dealer who buys at the inside bid, stands to make $v - b$ dollars worth of profits from every share. Hence, if a total volume of $D(a)$ shares is demanded by the public at the price of a dollars, then market makers stand to make $(a - v)D(a)$ dollars worth of profits from selling the share. Likewise, if $S(b)$ is the volume of shares sold by the public at a bid price of b, market makers as a group make $(v - b)S(b)$ profit from that transaction. The profit that each dealer makes depends on the fraction of the aggregate order flow that he receives. If he does not post the best price, he makes nothing. To keep matters simple, let us suppose, to begin with, that every dealer with the inside quote gets an equal fraction of the orders.

[8] *For example, there is only a modest $10,000 fee that needs to be paid to become a market maker. By contrast the right to become a market maker on the NYSE trades for amounts between $250,000 and $300,000. The waiting period, before a dealer can start posting quotes on NASDAQ, is only a day.*

[9] *The analysis that follows is a simplified version of "Competition and Collusion in Dealer Markets" by Prajit K. Dutta and Ananth Madhavan, Journal of Finance, 1997, vol. 52, pp. 245–276. We should also mention that based on the Christie-Schultz paper and independent evidence, the Justice Department and the Securities and Exchange Commision (SEC) started separate investigations of the NASDAQ market. We will report their findings in section 16.4.*

[10] *This number is based on hourly quote revisions. A dealer may, of course, choose not to change his bid every hour.*

[11] *The real value of a share can be thought of as the discounted total of all payments that a shareholder will receive. These payments can include dividend payments as well as the proceeds from selling the share in the future.*

Let us also make matters simple by considering specific demand and supply functions for the stock. Suppose that these functions are given by

$$D(a) = 120 - 5a$$
$$S(b) = -80 + 5b$$

where the prices are in eighths of a dollar and the quantities are in units of 10,000 shares. By setting demand equal to supply, you can check that this is a stock whose market clears at a price of 20, or 2.5 dollars; at this price both demand and supply equal 200,000 shares.

Furthermore, it makes sense to assume that 20 is also the value of the stock, that is, $v = 20$. The reason why this is a sensible assumption is that, as the real value of the share, v can be interpreted as the average forecast among potential investors about the payback from this stock. If optimistic forecasts are just as likely as pessimistic forecasts, then the average is also the cutoff above which there are exactly as many optimists as there are pessimists below it; that is, it is the market-clearing price.[12]

Let us now turn to Nash equilibrium. It is straightforward to see that $a_i = b_i = v = 20$ is a Nash equilibrium of the stage game. If every other dealer is posting a competitive quote, a single dealer can do no better than go along with it. Of course every dealer makes zero profits from this equilibrium; consequently, this will constitute the benchmark punishment regime when we get to repeated trading.

16.2.2 COLLUSION

Before doing the repeated game analysis let us look at purely collusive pricing in the stage game. If the dealers set prices in order to maximize their collective profits, they would set an ask and a bid to solve the following maximization problem:

$$\text{Max}_{a \geq 20} (120 - 5a)(a - 20) + \text{Max}_{20 \geq b} (-80 + 5b)(20 - b) \tag{16.1}$$

Consider the profit-maximizing ask. The slope of the profit function is $220 - 10a$, and at a maximum-profit ask that slope must be equal to zero.[13] Hence, the collusive ask $a^* = 22$; that is, it equals 2.75 dollars. A similar exercise for the bid gives us the profit function's slope to be $180 - 10b$ and hence the collusive bid $b^* = 18$, or 2.25 dollars. Note that the collusive spread is therefore 50 cents (whereas the competitive spread is 0). The quantity that is sold by dealers at a price of 22, is 10, that is, 100,000 shares; that is also the quantity that is bought by them at a price of 18. Hence, at the end of the trading round, dealers have cleared all inventory off their books, and they take home a collective profit of $(22 - 18) \times 10$, or 40.[14]

If the stage game is played only once, that is, if dealers post quotes once and never again, then they will in fact find it impossible to sustain the collusive spread. To see this point, note that each dealer's profit from posting the collusive quote is $\frac{40}{N}$. On the other hand, by dropping the ask down to 21 and raising the bid to 19, any one dealer can draw away all the potential volume. At these quotes, the buy orders from the public will equal $120 - (5 \times 21)$, or 15 ($\times 10,000$), shares, and the sell orders will also be 15 shares at a bid of 19. Hence, this one dealer will clear his books and make a profit equal to (15×1)

[12] *The median of a distribution (of potential investors, say) is that value above which there is 50 percent of the (investor) population. The market clears at the median value because then there are just as many buyers as sellers. The dealers are interested in the average value of the share because they care about profits they make on average. When optimists and pessimists are equally likely in a distribution, its median and average coincide; that is, v is both the market-clearing price and the real value of the share.*

[13] *Recall that the slope of $ax - bx^2$ (with respect to a variable x) is $a - 2bx$, where a and b are constants. Also consult Chapter 25, where we discuss maximization problems such as this one, if any of this seems mysterious to you. Finally, in the maximization exercise we pretend that any number a can be chosen as an ask. In actuality, only integers can be chosen because prices have to be in units of eighths of a dollar. This pretense is harmless, since the profit-maximizing ask turns out to be an integer.*

[14] *Since prices are in eighths of a dollar and quantity is in units of 10,000 shares, a profit of 40 is equivalent to a dollar profit of $40 \times \frac{1}{8} \times 10,000$, or 50,000 dollars.*

$+ (15 \times 1) = 30$. As you can see, this profit of 30 is always greater than the shared profit of $\frac{40}{N}$ (since $N > 1$).

CONCEPT CHECK
ANOTHER STAGE GAME NASH EQUILIBRIUM

Show that asks and bids of 21 and 19, respectively, also constitute a Nash equilibrium of the stage game (with a spread of 25 cents).

We are now ready for the repeated game analysis. Consider the following grim trigger strategy: Each dealer begins with the collusive quotes and maintains them as long as the others have done so in the past. If any dealer undercuts, from the next trading round onward all dealers go to pricing at value v forever thereafter. As always, once the punishment regime has been initiated, no dealer can do any better by pricing at any price other than $v = 20$. Hence, in any subgame that has already seen a noncollusive price, pricing always at value is a Nash equilibrium.

Consider instead a situation where up until now the asks and bids have been collusive. By sticking with the strategy, a market maker expects a continued payoff of $\frac{40}{N}$, that is, a discounted total profit of $\frac{40}{N(1-\delta)}$, where δ, as always, denotes the discount factor. By undercutting the other dealers, a single market maker makes a profit of 30 in the current round but thereafter looks down the barrel of the threat of 0 profits. Sustaining collusion is the better option if

$$\frac{40}{N(1-\delta)} > 30$$

Clearly, the last condition translates to $N(1 - \delta) < \frac{4}{3}$. Note two immediate implications: First, the greater is the number of dealers, that is, the larger is N, the more difficult it is to meet the condition (and sustain collusion). In that sense, NASDAQ's backers were quite right in saying that the existence of many dealers on NASDAQ makes collusion harder. Second, the higher is the discount factor, that is, the larger is δ, the easier it is to meet the condition (and sustain collusion). This second implication we have already encountered (in the previous chapter).

The interesting question in the current context is, What is a realistic value for δ? Consider two of the interpretations of δ that you have seen. If it represents the probability that the dealers will interact with each other at least one more time, then δ is virtually 1. After all, between now and an hour from now (or even a day from now) how high can the likelihood be that someone in Merrill Lynch who makes the market for Apple will have quit his job or be fired or that Merrill Lynch would have decided to discontinue making the market in Apple's stock? If δ represents a preference for earlier payments because a current dollar can grow into more than a dollar in the future, again δ has to be virtually 1. How much interest, after all, can you collect between now and an hour from now (or even a day from today)?

To put that discussion into perspective, let us look at some numbers. If $N = 11$,[15] then collusion is sustainable provided that $\delta > \frac{29}{33} = 0.8788$, that is, provided that a dollar an hour from now is worth at least 88 cents. If $N = 50$, then collusion is sustainable provided that $\delta > \frac{73}{75} = 0.973$, that is, provided that a dollar an hour from now is worth at least 97 cents. It seems quite likely that the discount factor will be this high for trading rounds that are hourly. Put differently, it seems likely that collusion is sustainable even in heavily traded NASDAQ stocks as conjectured by Christie and Schultze.

This conclusion still leaves open the question, Why don't more dealer (or member firms) set up in this market? After all, each market maker (or each member firm) makes a discounted total profit of $\frac{40}{N(1-\delta)}$. When $N = 20$ and $\delta = 0.999$, this translates to yearly profits of almost $2.5 million.[16] In the next section we will turn to the question, Why aren't there more dealers?

16.2.3   More on Collusion

There are two more-benign—and more-plausible—punishment possibilities that might also sustain collusive pricing. One punishment, in the event of a departure from collusive pricing by some market maker, is to price forever thereafter at the alternative stage game Nash equilibrium:

Concept Check
Benign Punishment 1

Show that repeatedly pricing at an ask equal to 21 and bid equal to 19 constitutes an equilibrium in the repeated game.

The next question is, Is this punishment a sufficient deterrent? That is, would the threat of such a punishment prevent undercutting from the collusive asks and bids? Recall that the collective profit for this stage game Nash pricing structure is 30. Hence, by deviating against the collusive price, a market maker can grab all the customer orders and single-handedly make the collective profit. However, he then faces the threat of $\frac{30}{N}$ thereafter.

Concept Check
A Sufficient Deterrent

Show that collusion is sustainable if

$$\frac{40}{N(1-\delta)} > 30 + \frac{30\delta}{N(1-\delta)}$$

---

[15] *The NASDAQ web site (at nasd.com) cites that, on average, there are 11 market makers for every NASDAQ stock.*

[16] *Recall from the earlier discussion that 40 translates to $50,000 worth of profits. The discounted total is $\frac{50,000}{20 \times 0.001} = 2.5$ million (and with 1,500 hourly trading rounds a year, that is also effectively the annual total). In this context, remember that it costs $10,000 to become a market maker on NASDAQ.*

A little algebra rearranges that condition to be $N(1 - \delta) < \frac{4}{3} - \delta$. A sufficient condition is therefore $N(1 - \delta) < \frac{4}{3} - 1 = \frac{1}{3}$. Clearly, collusion is now harder to sustain;[17] put differently, the number of traders has to be smaller or the discount factor higher than was the case with the more severe zero-profit threat. That result should not be surprising; if the punishment is milder, there is a greater temptation to cheat! Again, for illustrative purposes, if $N = 11$, δ needs to be at least $\frac{32}{33}$, or 0.97, for the sufficient condition to be met.

A second benign punishment is a forgiving trigger in which spreads narrow for some number of trading rounds to punish deviation but then go back to the collusive spread. We will leave it to you to work out the details of this case in the Exercises.

Two things about the analysis are worth pointing out. First, when some market maker undercuts, everybody suffers in the subsequent punishment regime, the sinner as well as the good guys. This result might appear unrealistic—and it is. It is also inessential. If the punishment can be targeted, then we can achieve the same end by singling out the dealer who undercut and subjecting him to punishment. For instance, if a deviant market maker can be subsequently shut out of the market (while the others continue to price collusively), then it is as if he alone faces a grim trigger punishment. Hence all of our conclusions about the grim trigger apply here without any change. In the next section, we will discuss some institutional arrangements of the NASDAQ market that make it easier to shut out individual dealers.

Second, collusion is either sustainable or it is not; there is no possibility in the analysis that collusion may be sustainable in some markets—or on some days—but not in others. Furthermore, since the demand and supply functions remain the same from trading round to trading round, the size of the collusive spread also remains unchanged. In particular, if collusion is sustainable, then the observed spread is always 50 cents. In reality, the spread on the same stock changes from day to day—and often hour to hour. One can, however, do a more general analysis of collusion on the NASDAQ market that allows demand and supply functions to change. One conclusion that emerges from such an analysis is that collusion may be sustainable only some of the time. Another consequence is that the size of the collusive spread itself can vary from day to day or hour to hour.[18]

16.3 THE BROKER-DEALER RELATIONSHIP

Brokers are the ones who direct customer orders to dealers. Some of these brokers have been in the business for a long time as well. Consequently, over time, brokers typically build up relationships with particular dealers. These relationships—along with an associated institutional feature of the NASDAQ market—have a direct relevance to the collusive pricing question.

16.3.1 ORDER PREFERENCING

NASDAQ permits a broker to direct an order to a dealer even if that dealer's quote is not the best available quote. This practice is called order preferencing; a broker "preferences"

[17] *Recall that collusion is sustainable of $N(1 - \delta) < \frac{4}{3}$ under the stronger punishment of the previous section.*

[18] *The Dutta and Madhavan paper cited in footnote 9 does just such an analysis. Something similar in spirit will also be done in Chapter 17 when we study the oil cartel, OPEC.*

an order to a market maker who has agreed in advance to meet the inside price. In other words, if the inside ask is, say, \$10 and dealer i has posted an ask equal to $10\frac{1}{4}$, a broker could nevertheless send the order to i for execution. Of course dealer i would have to sell the stock at \$10, but as long as she is willing to do so, nothing improper would occur.

This practice has a simple consequence: a broker is indifferent about which dealers he directs orders to and does not have an incentive to seek out the best price. Put differently, a dealer who posts the best price will not necessarily attract all the volume at that price. Indeed if each broker has his own favorite market maker that he goes to all the time, then a dealer who undercuts gets *no* extra volume by undercutting; each broker will simply have his order filled at the undercut price by his favorite dealer.[19]

The implication of all this should be clear. Consider the following simple strategy: in every trading round, no matter what, each dealer prices collusively and arranges with her brokers to match the best price if it is better than the collusive ask and bid. By pricing collusively at 22 and 18, each market maker makes profits of $\frac{40}{N}$. By undercutting that price, to 21 and 19, each market maker lowers the collective profits down to 30. She does not, however, get any larger a fraction of that total; her profits from deviation are $\frac{30}{N}$. Clearly, no dealer has an incentive to undercut the collusive price.[20]

With order preferencing one does not even need trigger strategies—or any repeated game analysis—to sustain collusion. Actually that statement is not quite true. The relationship between a broker and his preferred dealer only makes sense from a repeated game viewpoint. We will not pursue that point here.

16.3.2 DEALERS BIG AND SMALL

In this subsection we will answer two questions. The second one will be, Why don't more people set up business as (profitable) NASDAQ market makers? The key again is the broker-dealer relationship. On account of that relationsip, not all dealers are created equal. Some market makers handle a larger fraction of the aggregate transactions than other market makers. So, the preliminary question will be, Is the market more or less competitive when there are dealers both big and small?

To simplify matters, suppose that there are two categories of market makers: *big* and *small*. Suppose that a big dealer handles twice as much volume as a small dealer (provided they both have the inside quote). Nevertheless, if a dealer is the only one with the inside quote, then he gets all the volume regardless of whether he started off big or small.[21] In other words if there are N big dealers and M small ones and they all have the inside quote, then each big dealer gets $\frac{2}{2N+M}$ of the aggregate volume and a small dealer gets $\frac{1}{2N+M}$.

Consider the following grim trigger strategy: price collusively until somebody undercuts and thereafter price at value. Let us consider the incentives of big and small dealers separately. Clearly in the punishment phase every dealer is making zero profits, and nobody can do much about it. So suppose instead that we are in a situation where the collusive arrangement has held up so far. A big dealer by deviating gets an immediate profit of 30—and thereafter nothing. By staying with the current arrangement he expects to get $\frac{2}{2N+M} \times 40$ in every trading round. So a big dealer will hold the line if

[19] *One reason for a broker to stick with a single dealer is that she gets a better price by doing so. During the course of a trading day, the price of a stock moves around, and a dealer has some discretion about when she executes an order. By going back repeatedly to the same dealer, a broker gives that dealer an incentive to execute buys at low ebbs and sells at high tides.*

[20] *"Match the best price" is a practice that is widely prevalent in other industries as well. In the New York metropolitan area, the largest discount electronics store is called Nobody Beats the Wiz; their boast is that their prices are so good, and they are so confident about those prices, that they will give a 10 percent discount on any published competitors' prices. Customers do not shop around because they think no one else can beat the Wiz's low price. What they don't realize is that actually no one else has any reason to beat the Wiz's high price!*

[21] *In this subsection we are therefore ignoring the order preferencing arrangements that we discussed earlier.*

$$\frac{80}{(2N+M)(1-\delta)} > 30$$

By the same argument a small dealer will price collusively if

$$\frac{40}{(2N+M)(1-\delta)} > 30$$

Clearly the small dealer is the weak link! Compared to a big market maker he has less at stake in collusive pricing and just as much to gain by abandoning it.

Which brings us to new market makers. Consider a market with N big dealers who are able to price collusively, that is, $N(1-\delta) < \frac{4}{3}$. Consequently, they make profits, $\frac{40}{N(1-\delta)}$, far in excess of the costs of setting up in business as a market maker. In comes a new entrant (who receives, say, half as much business as long-standing market makers with well-established broker relationships). Does he expect to make similar profits? The answer is no for two reasons.

First, collusion may no longer be sustainable; the entrant may be precisely what breaks collusion. This result would occur if $(2N+1)(1-\delta) > \frac{8}{3}$. Second, in any case, whether or not collusion is sustainable, the entrant is going to make half as much profit as the existing dealers. For instance, if collusion breaks down and instead the second-best Nash equilibrium with a spread of 25 cents is played, then the entrant makes $\frac{30}{(2N+1)(1-\delta)}$. Put differently, what tempts him to enter this business is the existing profit levels of $\frac{40}{N(1-\delta)}$; what discourages him from coming in is the realization that he will only make $\frac{30}{(2N+1)(1-\delta)}$, that is, about $\frac{3}{8}$ of that amount.[22]

16.4   THE EPILOGUE

Here is what has happened since the NASDAQ controversy started: The Justice Department wound up its investigation by concluding that they had indeed found evidence of collusive pricing by NASDAQ dealers. Indeed, they made their case not on the basis of implicit collusion of the sort that we have discussed in this chapter—in which no dealer need actually talk to another dealer—but rather on the basis of explicit collusion. In particular, they had tapes of phone conversations between market makers in which they arranged collusive pricing!

The SEC pushed NASDAQ to take steps that would make collusion in the future more difficult to sustain. In response NASDAQ has implemented a set of changes that have been approved by the SEC. The most important change in order-handling protocol is something that NASDAQ calls the *limit order display rule*. Put simply, this rule allows investors to compete with dealers in making the market (as they are able to do on the NYSE). A limit order is an order that specifies a quantity as well as a price; for example, buy 1,000 shares of Apple at $15. The limit order display rule requires market makers to display all customer limit orders that are priced better than the dealers' inside quotes. For instance, if the inside quotes are currently an ask of $15\frac{1}{8}$ and a bid of $14\frac{3}{4}$, and the

[22] *The ratio of* $\frac{30}{(2N+1)(1-\delta)}$ *to* $\frac{40}{N(1-\delta)}$ *is equal to* $\frac{3N}{4(2N+1)}$. *When N is large that last number is approximately* $\frac{3}{8}$.

limit order described comes in, then the dealers have to immediately revise their inside quotes to a bid of $15.[23]

All this has to make everyone *but* the dealers happy.

SUMMARY

1. The NASDAQ market is the largest stock market in the United States in terms of the number of shares traded and the second-largest in terms of the dollar value of those shares.

2. The NASDAQ market was rocked, in the early 1990s, by allegations of price fixing by market makers. The evidence that was offered was that many actively traded stocks had spreads of 25 and 50 cents.

3. A simple repeated game analysis shows that collusive pricing is possible even when there are multiple dealers for every stock. Collusion is more likely with fewer dealers and higher discount factors.

4. The possibility of collusion was increased by NASDAQ institutional features such as order preferencing and by long-standing broker-dealer relationships.

5. NASDAQ has recently instituted a number of rule changes that will make it harder for dealers to maintain collusive prices in the future.

EXERCISES

SECTION 16.1

16.1

Locate some information on the relative size of the NYSE, the NASDAQ market, and the AMEX. What measures of size do you think are relevant—number of shares that were traded, the dollar value of those shares, or something else? Explain your answer.

16.2

Do the same for the relative size of the three American exchanges vis-à-vis international stock markets such as the Tokyo Stock Exchange, the London Stock Exchange, and the Frankfurt Stock market.

[23] *This new rule was introduced for 50 stocks on January 20, 1997, and subsequently expanded to cover all NASDAQ stocks.*

SECTION 16.2

(Calculus Problem)   Consider the following specification of demand and supply functions:

$$D(a) = 140 - 5a$$
$$S(b) = -60 + 5b$$

16.3

a. Compute the market-clearing price.

b. What is the quantity that is transacted at that price?

c. If prices are in eighths of a dollar and quantities are in 10,000 shares, what is the dollar price and quantity traded in this equilibrium?

16.4

For the specification of demand and supply given by the previous question, what is the collusive ask price? What about the collusive bid price? Hence, what is the collusive spread? Do collusive market makers sell as much as they buy? (Continue to assume that the market-clearing price is the value of the share.)

16.5

What are the profit levels—in dollars—associated with the collusive prices?

16.6

Suppose that there are six trading rounds in a day. What is the total profit that market makers make daily? And yearly, assuming that there are 250 trading days in the year? What is the yearly profit per dealer if there are 20 dealers for this stock?

16.7

Could you compute the discounted total annual profits, if the discount factor is 0.99? For your computations, use the following formula:

$$1 + \delta + \delta^2 + \cdots + \delta^T = \frac{1 - \delta^T}{1 - \delta}$$

Note that exercises 16.8–16.19 refer to the same data as in exercises 16.3–16.7.

SECTION 16.3

16.8

Show that an ask and a bid of 20 is a stage game Nash equilibrium.

16.9

Consider the following grim trigger strategy: trade at the collusive quote unless some dealer undercuts; thereafter trade at the market-clearing price of 20. When is this an equilibrium? (Assume unless otherwise noted that the dealers with the inside quotes share the market equally.)

16.10
Show that an ask of 21 and a bid of 19 is also a stage game Nash equilibrium. What are the profits in that equilibrium?

16.11
Consider the following benign trigger strategy: trade at the collusive quote unless some dealer undercuts; thereafter trade at the Nash equilibrium. When is this strategy an equilibrium?

16.12
Consider, finally, the following forgiving trigger strategy: trade at the collusive quote unless some dealer undercuts; thereafter trade at the market-clearing price for T stages; then revert to the collusive quotes. When is this strategy an equilibrium?

16.13
Compare and explain the answers that you got in the previous three questions.

SECTION 16.4

16.14
Suppose there is perfect order preferencing—each broker has a favorite dealer to whom he directs order flow. Show that regardless of δ, collusive quotes are a subgame perfect equilibrium.

16.15
Can you show that the same conclusion is true regardless of what demand and supply function we consider?

Suppose that half of the twenty dealers are big dealers and get twice as much order flow as the remaining ten dealers.

16.16
Write down the condition that determines whether or not big dealers will undercut the collusive quotes (in a grim trigger strategy)? Do the same for the smaller dealers. At what δ will collusion be a sustainable strategy?

16.17
Suppose that the actual δ is less than the cutoff that you computed in exercise 16.16. Can you find an ask and a bid price, respectively, greater than 21 and smaller than 19 that can be sustained as an equilibrium? What are the profits in such an equilibrium?

16.18

Suppose that the big dealers shared some of their order flow with the small dealers. Explain why this practice might make collusion easier to sustain.

16.19

By sharing order flow, however, big dealers give up some of their own volume and hence potential profits associated with that volume. In your computations can you figure out whether it is ever worth the while of the big dealers to direct some order flow to the small dealers? Explain.

CHAPTER 17

AN APPLICATION: OPEC

In this chapter we will examine the oil-producing cartel, the Organization of Petroleum Exporting Countries (OPEC), and argue that a repeated-game perspective is useful to understand the working of this organization. We will start in section 17.1 with a brief review of OPEC and, in the course of that discussion, identify four key phases in the recent history of the oil industry. In section 17.2 we will outline a very simple model of the industry. In sections 17.3 and 17.4 we will employ the ideas of repeated-game theory to understand the four historical phases; in order to do so we will have to make a digression and discuss repeated games with demand uncertainty. Finally, section 17.5 will offer some further remarks on OPEC and the model used in this chapter.

17.1 OIL: A HISTORICAL REVIEW

OPEC is an organization of oil producers; it was formed in September 1960 at the primary urging of the bigger producers—Saudi Arabia, Iran, and Venezuela. OPEC has 13 member states; it does not include the Western producers and the former Soviet Union, but it does include virtually all the others—the Gulf States of Kuwait, Qatar, and the United Arab Emirates; the African nations of Libya and Nigeria; and Asian nations such as Indonesia. OPEC was the culmination of roughly a decade's worth of negotiations and the writing of bilateral agreements among member nations. To understand how OPEC came to be at the time that it did, we have to understand both the economics and the politics of oil.[1]

Oil production involves at least three key stages: drilling, refining, and shipping. Historically, oil companies from Europe and the United States have been the major players in all three areas of the industry. The influence of at least some of these companies goes back to "national concessions" that were granted by host governments in the first

[1] *Producer organizations exist— or have existed—for many other commodities as well. International organizations exist for coffee and diamonds. In the United States such producer groups were very popular in the 19th century. In sugar, railroads, steel, cement, and the like, groups or "trusts" controlled an overwhelming percentage of production. Public outrage over price-fixing by these trusts led to sweeping legislation in the 1880s that goes by the general name of "antitrust" legislation. The most famous of these laws is the Sherman Antitrust Act, which was passed in 1890 and continues to be a major tool for government industrial policy today.*

half of the 20th century. The archetype of these concessions—and indeed the very first one—was a concession that the shah of Persia (now Iran) granted to an Englishman called William Knox D'Arcy in 1901. This concession allowed D'Arcy's company, the Anglo-Persian Oil Company, formed for this express purpose, the right to prospect and drill for oil anywhere in Iran. In return, the shah was to be given a fraction of the profits.[2]

Similar agreements followed between the governments of Indonesia, Iraq, Saudi Arabia,[3] and Libya and companies such as Royal Dutch, Standard Oil, and Compagnie Française. These concessions lasted until about the 1940s and 1950s when one after the other the governments of these countries—some of them newly independent—terminated these arrangements.[4]

17.1.1 Production and Price History

In the first half of the 20th century the primary producers and exporters of oil were not in the Middle East; rather they were in the United States and Venezuela—and in later years in the Soviet Union.[5] Indeed oil was not discovered in Kuwait and Qatar until the 1950s. This overwhelming presence of Western oil lessened somewhat in the years between the two world wars, but even in 1945 almost half of the world's oil came from Western sources.

Two dramatic changes occurred during and after World War II. First, new sources of oil were discovered in the Middle East, and production capacity was greatly increased in Iran and Iraq (for the Allied war effort). Second, the postwar industrial boom in the United States increased demand severalfold. Indeed the United States went from being a net exporter to an importer of oil (by 1970, 60% of U.S. oil demand was being met by imports). By the mid-1960s, then, the Middle East had in fact emerged as the dominant oil-producing region in a world in which demand was increasing rapidly.

The price history of oil can be broken down roughly into four phases (these numbers are rounded off):[6]

- *Phase 1, Before 1960:* Prices were both *low* and *stable*. For example, the price of a barrel of oil only rose from $1.25 in 1950 to $1.75 in 1960.

- *Phase 2, 1960 to October 1973:* Prices remained *low* but began to *creep up*. Through the 1960s they remained in a one-dollar band—between $1.50 and $2.50—and by the middle of 1973 they were up to $5.

- *Phase 3, October 1973 to 1979:* Prices were both *high* and *stable*. The most dramatic phase was undoubtedly the mid-1970s; the price of a barrel of oil went from $5 to $17 in the last two months of 1973. It remained in the twenties throughout the decade.[7]

- *Phase 4, 1980 Onwards:* Prices have been *lower* and *unstable;* that is, there has been a lot of volatility. For example, prices were as high as $30 a barrel around 1982 and as low as $10 a barrel in the early 1990s. Through the first six months of 1996 prices were in the range of $15–$17 a barrel, and they had climbed up to $23 a barrel by the end of the year.[8]

In the next two sections we will try to understand these four phases in terms of a simple model of repeated games that emphasizes the role of demand conditions in the market for oil.

17.2   A SIMPLE MODEL OF THE OIL MARKET

Oil-producing nations, whether they are members of OPEC or not, compete with each other as Cournot-style competitors in the world oil market. Producers make decisions about the quantity that each of them is going to pump over, say, the next month. They have some flexibility in making this decision because they can choose to run their wells at less than full capacity.

The aggregate supply of world oil together with current demand determines the price for a barrel of crude oil. There is a very active worldwide *spot* market as well as a market in *oil futures*.[9] The main markets are the International Petroleum Exchange (IPE) based in London and the New York Mercantile Exchange (NYME). Oil producers such as Saudi Arabia also quote prices for their products, but these prices have to fall in line with prices on the IPE or NYME (or else some traders can make arbitrage profits by buying on the cheaper market and selling on the expensive market).

OPEC tries to ensure that this competition nevertheless generates high profits for the producers. It does so by specifying production quotas for its members. These quotas are set in such a way as to generate a target price for oil—with an associated desirable profit level for OPEC's members. Periodically, the oil ministers of the OPEC member countries meet to discuss the efficacy of the current quotas and whether or not to set fresh quota levels.

Let us reduce these observations to the following simple stage game. There are two oil producers—say, Saudi Arabia (SA) and Venezuela (VA).[10] Each of these producers can produce either a *high* output or a *low* output. SA and VA are different-sized producers; let us suppose, therefore, that the two output levels for SA are $Q_H = 10$ mbd and $Q_L = 8$ mbd; for VA these output levels are $q_H = 7$ mbd and $q_L = 5$ mbd. Aggregate output can therefore be any one of three levels; when both producers withhold output the total is 13 mbd, when only one withholds it is 15 mbd and when both overproduce it is 17 mbd.

On the demand side, let us suppose that demand conditions can be either *good* or *bad*. When conditions are *good*—that is, when demand is robust—suppose that a total output of 13 mbd fetches a price of $25 per barrel, whereas the price is only $22 per barrel for an aggregate output of 15 mbd and $19 for the highest output level. Finally, suppose that the marginal cost of production is $5 a barrel.[11] All this leads to the profit matrix for *good* demand periods shown in Table 17.1.

[8] *Note that none of these prices are adjusted for inflation. In other words, a $30 price in 1982 is much higher in real terms than a $23 price in late 1996.*

[9] *A spot market is a market in which a buyer can buy (different grades of) crude oil for immediate delivery. Oil futures are contracts that promise the buyer delivery at a specified date in the future, for example, the delivery of a hundred thousand barrels two months from the contract date.*

[10] *The two biggest producers of OPEC are Saudi Arabia, which accounts for a third of OPEC's total output of about 25 million barrels per day (mbd), and Iran, which accounts for about a sixth. Venezuela accounts for about a ninth. Venezuela, however, is the leading dissident within OPEC on what price the organization should aim for. That is the reason we have included them as the second player along with Saudi Arabia.*

[11] *These numbers have a rough congruence with actual production and price numbers in the current market. It will also become clear from the analysis that many of these assumptions on market structure and costs can be generalized without doing too much violence to either the arguments or the conclusions.*

TABLE 17.1

SA \ VA	q_L	q_H
Q_L	160, 100	136, 119
Q_H	170, 85	140, 98

TABLE 17.2

SA \ VA	q_L	q_H
Q_L	88, 55	80, 70
Q_H	100, 50	90, 63

CONCEPT CHECK

Derive each of the profit numbers in Table 17.1 from the information given to you about quantities and prices.

In contrast, when times are *bad*—that is, when demand is weak[12]—suppose the three prices are respectively $16, $15, and $14 per barrel for high, medium, and low total output. Suppose also that the costs of production are no different. This leads to the payoff matrix for low demand periods shown in Table 17.2. With these numbers we are finally ready to turn to our main plot line.

[12] *A natural way to think about demand conditions for oil is that they depend quite critically on world economic performance. In years that Western economies are growing robustly, demand for oil is robust as well, while periods of worldwide recession are accompanied by an anemic demand for oil. The other determinant is weather conditions; harsh winters produce an increase in the demand for (heating) oil. Given all this, it is natural to think about the actual demand condition as being uncertain and subject to change.*

17.3   OIL PRICES AND THE ROLE OF OPEC

- *Phase 1, Before 1960:*   The 1950s was the first decade of significant growth in oil demand. Yet the rates of growth were still far below what was to come in the 1960s and 1970s. The 1950s was also a period of low prices.

One explanation of the 1950s, then, is that demand at that time can be characterized as a bad or weak demand situation with associated profits like those in Table 17.2. In the stage game of Table 17.2 there is exactly one (dominant strategy) equilibrium; that is, each producer produces a high output. Saudi Arabia produces 10 mbd, Venezuela produces 7 mbd, and consequently the price is the low price of $14 per barrel. The associated profits are (90, 63).

Notice that when demand is weak, the dominant strategy equilibrium of overproduction and low prices also generates the highest collective profits for OPEC. The total profit of 153 cannot be improved upon by any other combination of production levels. Hence, it is individually as well as collectively rational for the group to produce at capacity and keep prices low.[13]

Things change, however, when demand increases.

- *Phase 2, 1960–October 1973:* The 1960s witnessed a continuing increase in demand; demand was significantly higher in this decade than in the 1950s, although per capita consumption was still below the levels that would be witnessed in the 1970s.

We will model these two observations in the following way: Suppose that in each period there is a chance that demand is robust, with payoffs given by Table 17.1. The probability that demand is robust in any given period will be denoted p; with the remaining probability, $(1 - p)$, profits are given by Table 17.2.[14]

When demand is robust we are in a true Prisoners' Dilemma situation. Although joint profits are maximized at (Q_L, q_L), the dominant strategy in the stage game is (Q_H, q_H). The stepped-up pace of deliberations among the producers who comprise OPEC can be seen as testament to their realizing that with increased demand they would really stand to benefit from higher prices.

The question is, Can OPEC maintain high prices in good years while continuing to target a low price in bad demand years? Well, the facts are that they were not able to hold up prices even in good years during the 1960s. We will see an explanation in the next section, but here is the punchline: there need to be enough good demand years— the probability p needs to be sufficiently high—for OPEC members not to undercut each other by overproducing in good years. And p was arguably not high enough in the 1960s.

- *Phase 3, October 1973–1979:* Things change in the early 1970s. Demand peaks around this time. A shorthand modeling of this condition is to imagine that demand is almost never anemic during this phase, that is, that p is (virtually) equal to 1.

The implication of this heightened demand for OPEC's pricing policies is familiar from Chapter 15. Let us analyze cartel sustainability using the familiar grim trigger strategy: production is low to begin with and remains low provided that honoring the quota remains the observed pumping pattern; if either producer starts to exceed its quota, this cooperation breaks down and each starts producing at capacity forever thereafter.

With the profit numbers given earlier, cooperating on withholding output yields Saudi Arabia a profit stream of

$$160 + 160\delta + 160\delta^2 + \cdots$$

(where δ represents the discount factor), whereas overproduction in any period yields an immediate increase of profits to 170 but is followed thereafter by the punishment of

[13] *Notice that the Saudis would do better if Venezuela withheld production while they continued to produce Q_H. In that case their profits would rise to 100 (from 90). The problem is that VA's profits would dip down to 50 (from 63) and SA has no way to compensate Venezuela for this loss.*

[14] *Notice that the 1950s were a period when demand was never robust, that is, a period when p was always equal to 0.*

a grim trigger, which yields a profit stream of

$$170 + 140\delta + 140\delta^2 + \cdots$$

Evidently it pays not to cheat against OPEC's high-price policy, provided that $\frac{160}{1-\delta} \geq 170 + \frac{140\delta}{1-\delta}$, that is, provided that the discount factor $\delta \geq \frac{1}{3}$. In contrast, cooperation yields Venezuela a profit stream of

$$100 + 100\delta + 100\delta^2 + \cdots$$

while overproduction in any one period yields

$$119 + 98\delta + 98\delta^2 + \cdots$$

Venezuela will refrain from overproducing only if $\frac{100}{1-\delta} \geq 119 + \frac{98\delta}{1-\delta}$, that is, if $\delta \geq \frac{19}{21}$. Notice that the smaller producer, VA, is the more fragile member of the coalition. They have more to gain from cheating against the cartel (an extra immediate boost of 19—rather than 10 for SA) and less to lose in the future (a drop of profits per stage by 2 rather than the 20 for SA). Hence they need to care more about the future—that is, their discount factor needs to be higher—in order for them to refrain from stabbing the cartel in the back.[15]

- *Phase 4, 1980 Onward:* This has been a period of unstable prices driven by demand uncertainty. Demand fluctuates in part because of conservation efforts in industrialized countries and increasing reliance on alternative energy sources. There have also been discoveries of non-OPEC oil supplies, such as from the North Sea. In other words, the probability of robust demand, p, is again less than 1.

This probability is, however, not as low as it was in the 1960s. Consequently, OPEC has been successful in maintaining high prices in good demand years. There is price volatility, though, on account of the fact that there were a number of bad years and in those years prices were lower.

In order to understand phases 2 and 4 in greater detail, however, we have to take a short detour through the theory of repeated games with varying stage games.

[15] *Note that we did not explicitly check subgames after one of the producers has already defected. It should be clear that in such a subgame "overproduction always" is a Nash equilibrium, for the same reason that "confessing always" was an equilibrium in the corresponding subgame of the infinitely repeated Prisoners' Dilemma.*

17.4 REPEATED GAMES WITH DEMAND UNCERTAINTY

In Chapters 14 and 15 we studied *repeated* games, that is, interactions in which exactly the *same game* is played time and time again. In many economic applications, such as competition within OPEC, the game that is played in any one year is typically a little different from the one played in the previous year. For instance, demand conditions in

TABLE 17.3

SA \ VA	q_L, q_L	q_L, q_H
Q_L, Q_L	$160p + 88(1-p), 100p + 55(1-p)$	$160p + 80(1-p), 100p + 70(1-p)$
Q_L, Q_H	$160p + 100(1-p), 100p + 50(1-p)$	$160p + 90(1-p), 100p + 63(1-p)$
Q_H, Q_L	$170p + 88(1-p), 85p + 55(1-p)$	$170p + 80(1-p), 85p + 70(1-p)$
Q_H, Q_H	$170p + 100(1-p), 85p + 50(1-p)$	$170p + 90(1-p), 85p + 63(1-p)$

the oil market may change from year to year. The question that we will discuss now is how to modify the analysis to take account of such variations in market conditions.[16]

Let us first modify the stage-game payoff matrix in an appropriate way. In any stage, each producer can now make any one of *four* decisions: withhold production regardless of demand conditions, withhold production only if demand conditions are good, withhold only if they are bad, and, finally, overproduce no matter what. In other words, SA has four strategies *within a stage game*: (Q_L, Q_L), (Q_L, Q_H), (Q_H, Q_L), and (Q_H, Q_H). In each case, interpret the first component as SA's choice if demand is good, while the second component is the choice if demand is bad. Likewise, VA has four analogous strategies within a stage game.

Denoting by p the probability that demand is going to be robust, and restricting attention to the two cases where VA chooses either (q_L, q_L) or (q_L, q_H), the expected profit to each producer in any given period is given by the payoff matrix of Table 17.3.

CONCEPT CHECK

Write down the analogue of Table 17.3 if VA chooses either (q_H, q_L) or (q_H, q_H).

Consider any pair of stage-game strategies; say, Q_L, Q_L for SA and q_L, q_H for VA, that is, the top-right combination. The total expected profits then are $160p + 80(1-p) + 100p + 70(1-p)$, that is, $260p + 150(1-p)$. We can similarly compute the total expected profits for every pair of strategies.

CONCEPT CHECK
PROFIT MAXIMIZATION

Show that the total expected profits are maximized if the two producers both produce *low* in good demand periods and *high* in bad demand periods.

[16] *The discussion in this section is related to an analysis of price competition with demand uncertainty by Julio Rotemberg and Garth Saloner; see "A Supergame Theoretic Model of Price Wars during Booms,"* American Economic Review, *1985, vol. 76, pp. 390–407.*

The question of interest then is, Can OPEC sustain this profit maximizing production policy? Again suppose that the "punishment" for cheating on OPEC is the following grim trigger: overproduction no matter what the market demand conditions are like, forever after. Note that by following the cartel's best policy—L output in good years, H in bad—SA gets a *future* profit stream, starting a period from today, of

$$[160p + (1-p)90]\delta + [160p + (1-p)90]\delta^2 + \cdots \qquad (17.1)$$

where, again, δ is the discount factor. Suppose that we are in a year when demand is good and SA has to decide whether or not to withhold production. By doing so it will get an immediate profit of 160 plus the expected profit from next period onward given by equation 17.1. On the other hand, SA could overproduce in that good year. Consequently, it would generate a profit of 170 in the current period. However, it would anticipate too that its future profits are going to be lower from retaliatory overproduction in the future. Hence, by producing an amount Q_H in the current period, SA gets lifetime expected profits of

$$170 + [140p + 90(1-p)]\delta + [140p + 90(1-p)]\delta^2 + \cdots$$

It is not profitable to overproduce if

$$160 + \frac{[160p + (1-p)90]\delta}{1-\delta} \geq 170 + \frac{[140p + 90(1-p)]\delta}{1-\delta}$$

Since $\frac{90(1-p)\delta}{1-\delta}$ is a common term on both sides, this expression simplifies. We can conclude that it does not pay for SA to undercut OPEC if

$$20p\frac{\delta}{1-\delta} \geq 10$$

from which emerges the following simple condition:

$$\delta \geq \frac{1}{1+2p} \qquad (17.2)$$

Note that when $p = 1$, that is, when demand is always good, this equation corresponds precisely to the previous section's condition: SA will not undercut OPEC if $\delta \geq \frac{1}{3}$. In general, the lower is p, that is, the less likely it is that world demand for oil will be good, the harder it is for OPEC to deter SA from cheating.

Let us do a parallel analysis of Venezuela's incentives.

CONCEPT CHECK
VENEZUELA'S PROFITS

Show that if current conditions are good, by producing at q_L, VA would get a lifetime expected profit equal to

$$100 + [100p + 63(1 - p)]\delta + [100p + 63(1 - p)]\delta^2 + \cdots$$

By producing q_H, VA can increase its immediate profits to 119, but thereafter it would get the lower expected profit stream of $98p + 63(1 - p)$ every period. Hence we have the following:

CONCEPT CHECK
VENEZUELA'S INCENTIVES

Show that VA will not cheat against OPEC quotas if

$$\delta \geq \frac{19}{19 + 2p} \qquad \qquad \text{(17.3)}$$

If demand is always good, that is, $p = 1$, then again we have the last section's condition. Again, cooperation is harder to sustain when p is lower. Equations 17.2 and 17.3 also prove the general point that the smaller producer VA is the weak link in OPEC.

If the current demand conditions are bad, OPEC desires a higher output from its two members. Clearly neither member has an incentive to act otherwise and withhold production. If they did so, they would simply lower immediate profits, and the grim trigger would also lower profits in the future.

An illustrative table is the following; the term "critical δ for SA" refers to the value of the discount factor above which the country will not cheat on the OPEC quota; that is, it is the solution of equation 17.2. Similarly, for VA it refers to the solution of equation 17.3.

Value of p	Critical δ for SA	Critical δ for VA
$\frac{1}{4}$	0.667	0.974
$\frac{1}{2}$	0.5	0.95
$\frac{3}{4}$	0.4	0.927
1	0.333	0.905

Note the two patterns: First, the *higher is p, the more effective is OPEC* (the bigger is the range of δ over which neither producer cheats). This conclusion should be intuitive; when demand conditions are bad, OPEC quotas are completely unnecessary, and ineffective anyway, because withholding output actually *lowers* total profits. It is only when demand is good that it is more attractive for each producer to cheat on his quota and increase his own profits at the expense of the cartel. Hence, cheating needs to be deterred by the threat of "flooding the market" in the future. If the future holds very few good demand periods, this is almost an empty threat because high production is a desirable outcome anyway in bad demand years.

Second, VA, the *smaller producer, is more likely to cheat on OPEC* (the critical δ is always higher for VA). This conclusion is also intuitive; the smaller producer has *more to gain today* by overproducing. After all, the only thing to worry about is that overproduction will depress the price in the current market, and that is less of a worry if current production is small.[17] They also have less to lose; after all if y dollars over all is what OPEC loses in the future from overproducing, VA cares less about this loss if it collects a smaller fraction of y than does SA.

The role of the discount factor is much as it was in the analysis of the previous chapter. A high δ denotes producers who care about future profits—and hence about future retaliatory production. A high δ therefore lowers the incentives to cheat against the cartel. Put differently, the higher the discount factor, the lower the critical probability p above which the cartel is sustainable.

The thesis of phases 2 and 4 can now be stated. In the 1960s, phase 2, demand was growing but not sufficiently quickly; that is, p was low. In particular, not all members of OPEC had an incentive to sustain a cartel.[18] Hence, OPEC was unable to maintain high prices even in good demand years. However, starting in the early 1980s, although demand dropped off from the early 1970s peak, it nevertheless has been sufficiently high. What we see, therefore, is high prices in good demand years and low prices in bad demand years.[19]

17.5 UNOBSERVED QUOTA VIOLATIONS ⚠

In the analysis thus far we have assumed that any quota violation is observable to the cartel partners. For example, if Venezuela pumps 2 million more barrels a day than they are supposed to, then the Saudis know it—and can take appropriate action. You might wonder how realistic this assumption is; cannot VA cheat on its quota without being found out? Cannot Petroleos de Venezuela load an extra few hundred thousand barrels on every tanker that sails away from its ports without OPEC noticing?

The answer, basically, is no. A lot of information about world oil production, refining, and transit is widely available. For example, weekly updates are available on the amount of oil *in transit* from all areas, from the Middle East to all areas, from the Middle East to the West, from the Middle East to the East, and so on.[20] Similarly, monthly updates are available on *production*; you can acquire information on total output, total OPEC output, output from individual producers, non-OPEC output, and the like. You can also get information on the quantities that have already been *committed to*; weekly updates are available on how much crude or gasoline or heating oil has been sold but not delivered yet by traders on the main markets of the NYME and IPE. And, of course, information is available on the recent prices of every conceivable grade of oil.

---

[17] *This argument can be formalized; the extra 2 mbd depresses the market price by three dollars, from P dollars a barrel to P – 3 dollars a barrel. The benefit to overproduction is therefore the additional profit, 2(P – 8) dollars (remember the costs of production are 5 dollars a barrel)—and this benefit is the same for all producers. The cost to overproduction is that all units are now sold at the lower price; if x mbd is the quota amount, then at a lower price there is a reduction of x × 3 of profits. Clearly that cost is higher if x is higher; SA will therefore be less likely to bust the quota. It should be clear that the argument works regardless of how much price falls on account of overproduction.*

[18] *This statement is historically true; the bigger producers such as Saudi Arabia and Iran were more eager than the smaller producers to reach an agreement on production quotas.*

[19] *That fact by itself can explain some price movements. Note too that a corollary of these arguments is that in phase 1 (p = 0) OPEC is not sustainable, and in phase 3 (p = 1) OPEC is sustainable (as long as VA is sufficiently patient).*

[20] *These figures, as well as the ones referred to in the next few sentences, can be readily accessed on the World Wide Web; for instance, you can find them on the home pages of the oil broker Norwegian Energy (UK), Ltd., at noenergy.com.*

However, partly to show that the conclusions of our previous analysis apply even when secret quota busting is possible, let us apply the lessons of section 15.4, "Repeated Games with Imperfect Detection," to OPEC. So the question is, Is OPEC sustainable if its members can cheat on quotas without getting directly caught? The hope for OPEC is indirect apprehension: overproduction will lower average oil prices (although here again, we will assume that it is never completely obvious from seeing a low price that in fact somebody overproduced).

So suppose that VA and SA can overproduce without getting directly caught. Overproduction does increase the likelihood of a low price. The distribution of prices, in good demand years, from a total output of 13 mbd and 15 mbd, respectively, is[21]

Output \ Probability	Price = $25	Price = $22	Price = $19
13 mbd	70%	20%	10%
15 mbd	20%	60%	20%

If nobody cheated and production was *13 mbd,* then the most likely price would be $25. Note that even when the price is $19 we cannot tell for sure that there has been overproduction; a *$19* price, however, is twice as likely if there was overproduction than if there was not. OPEC's hope then is to use some cutoff price from which to conclude that somebody overproduced. There are two possible cutoffs:

The Stern Trigger. Any price other than *$25* is taken as a signal of overproduction. In that case, cartel arrangements are abandoned, and (Q_H, q_H) is produced for T periods, after which the cartel is given a "second shot."

The Lenient Trigger. Only a price of *$19* is seen as evidence of cheating. In that case, cartel arrangements are abandoned, and (Q_H, q_H) is produced for T periods, followed by a resumption of cartel arrangements.

The questions are, Which trigger strategy is more profitable, stern or lenient, and can either of them deter cheating? And the answers are . . .

Profitability. If both strategies have sufficient deterrence, then it is more profitable to be lenient than to be stern.

By sufficient deterrence we mean that no matter which of the two strategies is played, neither SA nor VA will overproduce and total production will be *13 mbd.* The intuition for the profitability conclusion is then straightforward. Any observed price other than $25 is a "mistake" in the sense that it happened because of price uncertainty and not because of overproduction. Triggering retaliatory overproduction because of a mistake unnecessarily reduces profits, and so the less stern the trigger, the smaller the potential profits forgone.

[21] *There is a 20 percent chance that the price will be the next closest to the price that should have resulted and a 10 percent chance that the price will be two levels removed. We will also assume, in order to keep the discussion simple, that OPEC faces good demand conditions all the time. Those, after all, are the times when a member state would want to cheat in any case.*

Let us make all this precise. Suppose the stern trigger strategy is being played. Denote its lifetime expected profits to Venezuela by S.[22] This payoff can be computed as follows:

$$S = 100 + \delta \left[.7S + .3 \left(P + \delta^T S \right) \right] \tag{17.4}$$

where P is the profits realized during the punishment phase, that is, $P = \frac{1-\delta^T}{1-\delta} \times 98$. Equation 17.4 is derived as follows: the immediate profit is 100. In the next period, there is a 70 percent chance that punishment will be avoided, and in that case we are back to the current situation (with a lifetime payoff of S). There is also a 30 percent chance that retaliatory production will commence and last for T periods, and thereafter we will be back to the current situation. The expression can be simplified by collecting terms:

$$S = \frac{100 + .3P\delta}{1 - .7\delta - .3\delta^{T+1}}$$

CONCEPT CHECK
LIFETIME LENIENT PAYOFFS

By logic similar to that of equation 17.4, show that the payoffs from the lenient trigger are

$$L = \frac{100 + .1P\delta}{1 - .9\delta - .1\delta^{T+1}}$$

LENIENT IS MORE PROFITABLE

Show that $L > S$.

Looking at the two expressions for profits, L and S, it should also be clear that the longer the punishment period T, the lower the expected profits. Again this observation is intuitive; the deterrent is working, and hence every period of punishment is a period of lost profits. The fewer such periods the better.

At this point, you might be wondering, Why would one ever use the stern trigger? Similarly, why ever drag out the punishment phase? The common answer to these questions is that they may be better deterrents. Here is a result on deterrence:

Deterrence. A stern trigger may be a better deterrent than a lenient trigger. It is a better deterrent if

$$\frac{1}{2} \left[S(1 - \delta) - 98 \right] > \frac{1}{10} \left[L(1 - \delta) - 98 \right] \tag{17.5}$$

The relative deterrence condition, equation 17.5, has a natural interpretation. The two trigger strategies are possible deterrents because overproduction makes it more likely

[22] As in the last section, the critical partner will be VA, and so we will carry out all the computations for VA alone; in the Exercises you will verify that the parallel computations work for SA as well.

that the punishment phase will commence. Consider the stern trigger; since there is an 80 percent chance that punishment will be triggered if there is overproduction and only a 30 percent chance if the quota is adhered to, there is consequently a 50 percent *greater* likelihood of punishment if VA cheats. When the punishment phase commences, each period the profit forgone is $S(1-\delta) - 98$. This explains the left-hand side of equation 17.5. With the lenient trigger, however, there is a 10 percent increased likelihood of punishment if there is cheating, and each period the profit loss is $L(1-\delta) - 98$, thus explaining the right-hand side.[23]

On one hand, since a lenient trigger is more profitable, a stern trigger will never be employed if the lenient trigger also has a bigger deterrent. On the other hand, if the stern trigger is a bigger deterrent, that is, if equation 17.5 holds, then we have the following conclusion:

Choice. If the lenient trigger is a sufficient deterrent, it is always chosen. If the lenient trigger is not sufficient to deter cheating, but the stern trigger is, then the latter is chosen.

From the formulas it is not difficult to show that at least one of the triggers becomes a sufficient deterrent provided δ is high enough. To summarize, OPEC needs to initiate occasional periods of overproduction after having observed low prices in order to deter cheating against its quotas. However, it may be the case that these retaliatory phases are only instigated by extremely low prices and not by moderately low prices.

17.6   SOME FURTHER COMMENTS

The model of OPEC that we studied in this chapter is deliberately simplified on several dimensions. Some of these simplifications can be dispensed with only at the further cost of additional notation. For example, it should be easy enough to see that it is not essential that there be only two members of OPEC, nor is it essential that there be only two possible production levels. Likewise, the costs of production need not be the same.

One simplification that this story ignores—and which is somewhat important— is that OPEC's oil reserves are shrinking over time. This shrinkage will eventually have an impact on the profitability of any production policy.[24] It is unclear, however, how important an issue this is. New oil fields are constantly being discovered, expanding the size of available reserves.[25] Furthermore, known reserves are expected to last another 50 to 100 years at current levels of demand, and that horizon may be long enough for practical purposes.

A simplification that is very important (and that we ignored altogether) is the role of non-OPEC production. Production has been rapidly expanding in the North Sea oil fields, and this increased supply is putting pressure on oil prices—and consequently on the future of OPEC. OPEC has responded to this threat by trying to draw the non-OPEC producers into an implicit cartel and has urged them to restrain output expansion.[26]

[23] *Equation 17.5 can be derived as follows. The lifetime payoff to overproduction by VA is $119 + \delta \left[.2S + .8 \left(P + \delta^T S \right) \right]$; denote this sum D. From equation 17.4 the size of the deterrence, $S - D$, is seen to be $-19 + \delta \frac{1-\delta^T}{1-\delta} \frac{1}{2} [S(1-\delta) - 98]$. A similar computation reveals the size of the deterrence for the lenient trigger to be $-19 + \delta \frac{1-\delta^T}{1-\delta} \frac{1}{10} [L(1-\delta) - 98]$. The stern trigger is therefore a better deterrent if $\frac{1}{2} [S(1-\delta) - 98] > \frac{1}{10} [L(1-\delta) - 98]$.*

[24] *Issues such as these are addressed in a model that generalizes the repeated game structure; such games, called dynamic games, are studied in Chapter 18.*

[25] *The most extensive recent discovery is offshore oil reserves in the North Sea; Great Britain and Norway have been the main beneficiaries of this discovery. Even Saudi Arabia, in the early 1990s, discovered major deposits in a hitherto untapped region (central Saudi Arabia).*

[26] *After the June 1996 meeting of OPEC oil ministers, a press release issued by the OPEC News Agency said, "The conference also served notice on non-OPEC producers that it is in the common interest of both sides to work towards improving the price. . . . The ministers urged non-OPEC producers to exercise production restraint." A threat was also sounded: "Once again OPEC has reminded these countries of its willingness to cooperate while there is still room for dialogue."*

It remains to be seen whether non-OPEC producers will fall in line. As we have seen, the smaller producers have the least to gain from cartelization; hence the non-OPEC producers might need to expand substantially more before they find it in their interest to cooperate with OPEC.

Finally, in practice, OPEC does put up with some amount of overproduction (unlike the equilibria we studied where there is no overproduction). For instance, it is widely believed that Venezuela is producing a half million barrels a day more than its allotted quota. One way to rationalize such behavior is that our game is a little too simple, that pulling a trigger on retaliatory production has political costs that we have not modeled. Modeling these costs could lead to a conclusion that some—but not all—cheating is an acceptable part of equilibrium behavior.

SUMMARY

1. The oil cartel OPEC seeks to maintain high prices by restraining its members' production levels through explicit quotas. In recent years it has had mixed success.

2. The recent price history of world oil can be broken into four phases: pre-1960 when prices were low and stable, 1960s–1973 when prices were low but creeping up, 1973–1979 when prices were high and stable, and subsequent years when prices have been high and unstable.

3. This price history can be rationalized by way of two critical ideas—demand uncertainty and a repeated-game perspective. OPEC exists because its members realize that they are in a repeated game; OPEC can unravel if there is not sufficient persistence in high demand for oil.

4. The second phase in OPEC's price history can be understood as a period when there were not enough good demand years, and the fourth phase is one in which there were. OPEC was also sustainable in its second phase because of high demand (and in that phase demand was both high and stable).

5. In any market it is the smaller producers who have the most to gain from cheating on OPEC. Hence they are the most likely quota violators.

6. A similar analysis can be carried out even if quota violations are unobservable. In that case there will be strategic price uncertainty (in addition to that caused by demand uncertainty) as OPEC triggers occasional price wars on account of low prices.

EXERCISES

SECTION 17.2

Suppose that the production capabilities of Saudi Arabia and Venezuela and production costs are as in the text, but suppose that the price consequences are different. In particular, suppose that when the aggregate production is 13 mbd, 15 mbd, and 17 mbd, and demand is *good*, the respective prices are $24, $21, and $18 per barrel.

17.1
Write down the payoff matrix for *good* demand periods.

17.2
Identify the output combination that maximizes OPEC's joint profits. What is the stage-game Nash equilibrium?

17.3
Suppose that *good* demand is expected to persist forever. For what values of discount factors does a low production level become an equilibrium?

17.4
What conclusions, if any, can you draw from your answer about the link between higher prices and cartel sustainability? Explain your answer.

17.5
Suppose that, in addition to setting production quotas, OPEC can also redistribute profits. For example, SA can pay VA if the latter agrees to withhold production. If $\delta = \frac{3}{4}$ for both SA and VA, how much would SA have to pay VA for the latter not to overproduce? Explain any assumptions that you make in computing your answer.

Suppose now that *VA* not only has lower production capacity but also has higher costs of production. Suppose its costs of production are $6 per barrel.

17.6
Redo the payoff matrix. What is OPEC's profit-maximizing production target?

17.7
Redo exercise 17.3 for this new cost configuration.

17.8
What conclusions can you draw from your previous question about sustainability of OPEC when its members have different production costs?

SECTION 17.3

Let us revert to the setting of exercises 17.1 through 17.4. Suppose that OPEC *is* subject to demand uncertainty, and let p denote the probability of *good* demand.

17.9

Establish the two discount factor conditions that need to be satisfied in order for OPEC to be able to sustain the profit-maximizing output pattern of *low* output in *good* demand periods but *high* output in *bad* demand periods when the punishment used is the grim trigger punishment.

17.10

How would your answer be any different if OPEC used the forgiving trigger instead—and chose to overproduce for T periods only? Explain.

17.11

If the punishment used is the forgiving trigger, is there any reason to punish SA's transgressions any differently than VA's—for example, by having punishment lengths be different in the two cases? Explain your answer carefully and be sure to do some computations.

17.12

Establish the exact requirements for collusion sustainability if $p = \frac{1}{2}$.

17.13

In the last case and if $\delta = \frac{3}{4}$ for both SA and VA, how much would SA have to pay VA for the latter not to overproduce? Explain any assumptions that you make in computing your answer.

17.14

Based upon a comparison of your answers to exercises 17.5 and 17.13, what general conclusions can you draw about the effect of p on the "bribes" that SA would need to pay VA in order for the latter not to bust the cartel? Explain your answer carefully.

SECTION 17.4

In the next few questions we will consider SA's incentives to cheat on the cartel if cheating cannot be directly seen. In other words, we will complete the analysis begun in the chapter (where VA's incentives alone were considered).

17.15

Redo the computations of equation 17.4 to derive the lifetime payoffs for SA associated with the stern and the lenient triggers.

17.16

From the previous answer show that the lenient trigger is the more profitable strategy. Explain the answer.

17.17

Redo the computations of equation 17.5 to derive the relative deterrence capabilities of the stern and the lenient triggers.

17.18

Under what conditions will OPEC be forced to use the stern trigger (even if the lenient trigger works for one of its members)? Give a precise condition, and explain your answer.

CHAPTER 18

DYNAMIC GAMES WITH AN APPLICATION TO THE COMMONS PROBLEM

In this chapter we turn to a more general class of games, called *dynamic games*, in order to analyze ongoing interaction. Dynamic games are informally explained and motivated in section 18.1. Sections 18.2 through 18.4 will focus on a particular dynamic game, a dynamic version of the tragedy of the commons (first discussed in Chapter 7). Section 18.2 will lay out the basic model, and section 18.3 will discuss the socially desirable pattern of sustainable resource use. In section 18.4 we will examine the game equilibrium and contrast it with the socially desirable solution. Finally, in section 18.5, we will discuss which of the commons conclusions apply more generally to the whole class of dynamic games.

18.1 DYNAMIC GAMES: A PROLOGUE

Repeated games have proved to be real workhorses in the analysis of strategic situations that are ongoing and dynamic. Our analyses of Treasury auctions, pricing on the NAS-DAQ market, and oil production by OPEC have hopefully convinced you of that fact. One drawback of the repeated-game framework is that it presumes that literally the same stage game is played in every interaction. In other words, it assumes that the underlying *problem is static* (and unchanging) although players' *strategies could be dynamic* (and ever changing).

Dynamic games address this shortcoming: this is a class of games in which *both* the underlying problem *and* players' strategies are dynamic. A simple way to make a repeated game dynamic is to presume that there is something called a game *environment*. This environment can change from period to period, and it affects the payoffs within the stage game of any period. The environment can change for reasons beyond the players' control, or it may change because of what the players do.

To better explain dynamic games, let us discuss the three repeated game applications—OPEC, Treasury auctions, and NASDAQ—and demonstrate that in each case there are interesting generalizations of the problem that require us to step outside the purely repeated model. The generalizations can, however, be modeled as dynamic games, and we will point out the relevant game environment in each case.

Consider OPEC. In order to explain demand-driven world oil prices, in Chapter 17 we already had to step outside the pure repeated-game framework and allow stage games in good years to be different from those in bad years. In that example, the environment was the state of world oil demand—*good* or *bad*—and it was beyond OPEC's control. Additionally, production costs may depend on the size of remaining reserves.[1] In that case, the sizes of remaining deposits will also be part of the game environment (and they will determine current as well as future profitability). This part of the environment will be controlled by the players.

Consider Treasury auctions instead. To retain a repeated-game framework, we assumed in Chapter 14 that the Treasury sells the same amount of securities at every auction, and that assumption is clearly untrue. The Treasury decides on the amount based on the federal government's financial needs, and hence that amount varies from auction to auction. Potential profits to bidders are clearly higher when bigger lots are sold. Put differently, the environment for a stage game is the volume of T-bills on the auction block—and it is not controlled by the players.

Consider NASDAQ now. In order to apply a repeated game model we assumed that exactly the same number of buyers and sellers are in the market all the time. That assumption is again untrue. Demand depends on profit announcements by the company whose shares are being traded, on information about potential mergers and takeovers, on the likelihood of an economy-wide recession, on existing inventory with the market makers, and so on. These factors constitute the game environment in this case. Some of these factors are within the control of the dealers, but others are not.

Consider, finally, the commons problem of Chapter 7. (Recall that in this problem a resource is jointly utilized by a number of players who all have access to it; one example is fishing on the high seas, and another is surfing the Internet.) In the earlier discussion we had restricted attention to a one-time interaction. However, the heart of the commons problem (will open access lead to persistent overuse of the resource?) involves ongoing interaction. Here the game environment is the size of the resource, which evolves through time according to the pattern of past usage and affects payoffs in every stage game.

18.2   THE COMMONS PROBLEM: A MODEL

[1] *If reserves are plentiful, then it might be possible to extract oil from deposits that are closer to the surface or that contain a lower percentage of impurities.*

The game environment at period t is the size of the *resource stock* in that period, y_t; $y_t \geq 0$. The resource can be accessed by any player, and let us continue to assume that there are two players. Denote player i's *consumption*—or extraction—of the resource in

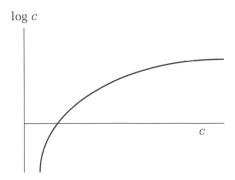

log c

c

FIGURE 18.1

period t by c_{it}. Again, it will be natural to only consider $c_{it} \geq 0$. Consumption gives player i a payoff or *utility*.

The exact value of y_t constrains the total amount that can be consumed; that is, at every period t it must be the case that

$$c_{1t} + c_{2t} \leq y_t \tag{18.1}$$

The amount of the resource not extracted, therefore, is $y_t - (c_{1t} + c_{2t})$. This is the *investment* that can generate future growth; call it x_t. From the preceding equation it follows that $x_t \geq 0$. Investment produces next period's stock y_{t+1} through a *production function*. In Chapter 7 we examined the case of an exhaustible resource (with no growth possibility); that is, we assumed $y_{t+1} = x_t$. By way of contrast, let us now consider a *renewable resource*, that is, a resource for which $y_{t+1} > x_t$ (at least for some investment levels).

In fact, in order to do some actual computations, we will specify particular forms for the utility and production functions.[2] Suppose that player i's utility from consuming amount c_i is given by log c_i; utility increases with the amount consumed, although the utility increase is smaller, the larger is the base from which consumption is further increased. The utility function is pictured in Figure 18.1.

We are also going to assume that investment x_t results in a period $t+1$ stock y_{t+1} of size $y_{t+1} = 10 \times \sqrt{x_t}$. Again higher investments produce higher stocks, although additional investment becomes less and less productive, as the base investment grows larger. The production function is pictured in Figure 18.2.[3]

Note that if investment x_t is equal to 0 in any period, then so is the stock y_{t+1} in the next period. This fact suggests a natural horizon for the game—it continues as long as there is a positive resource level and hence can potentially go on forever.

The questions of interest are these: How does the resource stock y_t evolve over time, and is there an eventual size that can be sustained? What is the socially optimal sustainable resource stock? Does strategic interaction lead to overextraction of the resource? In the next two sections we turn to these questions.

[2] *The specific example that we will discuss was first worked out by David Levhari and Leonard Mirman; see "The Great Fish War: A Solution Using Cournot-Nash Equilibrium," Bell Journal of Economics, vol. 11, pp. 322–334, 1980.*

[3] *Note that tomorrow's stock is larger than today's investment provided $x_t < 100$ but not otherwise. Also for future reference, recall that an alternative notation for $\sqrt{x}$ is $x^{0.5}$.*

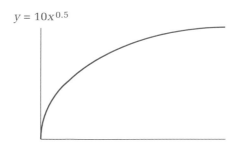

$y = 10x^{0.5}$

FIGURE 18.2

18.3 SUSTAINABLE DEVELOPMENT AND SOCIAL OPTIMUM ⚠

Let us start with social optimality: if one wants to make this society of two individuals as happy as they can be, how should one extract the resource?

18.3.1 A COMPUTATION OF THE SOCIAL OPTIMUM

To derive the socially optimal solution we need to consider the *sum* of the two players' utilities—and maximize it. We will proceed by way of backward induction. Suppose, to begin with, that there are exactly two periods. The extensive form can then be pictured as in Figure 18.3.[4]

If we are in the last period, with stock y, then we need to solve

$$\underset{c_1+c_2 \leq y}{\text{Max}} \quad \log c_1 + \log c_2$$

[4] *Note that an arc connecting two branches means that all intermediate choices, between the two branches, are also available. For instance if consumption c leads to a future stock of y (and c' leads to y') then the arc signifies that all consumptions between c and c' are also possible—and will lead to a stock between y and y'.*

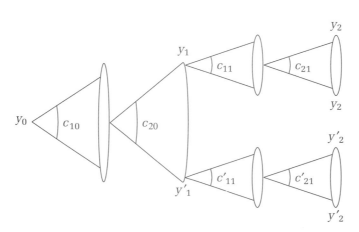

FIGURE 18.3

Since utility increases with consumption, there should never be any unused stock; that is, it must be that $c_1 + c_2 = y$. Hence the maximization problem can be rewritten as[5]

$$\max_{c_1} \log c_1 + \log(y - c_1)$$

The first-order condition for this maximization is $\frac{1}{c_1} = \frac{1}{y - c_1}$; that is, consumption should be equal, $c_1 = c_2$ (and equal to $\frac{y}{2}$).[6] Consequently, each player's socially optimal utility when there is one stage left and the available stock is y is given by $V^1(y) = \log \frac{y}{2} = \log y - \log 2$.[7] It will be useful to write this socially optimal utility as $\log y + A(1)$, where $A(1)$ is a shorthand for the constant, $- \log 2$.

Let us now fold the tree of Figure 18.3 back. When there are two periods left, the socially optimal extraction is found from solving the following problem:

$$\max_{c_1 + c_2 \leq y} \log c_1 + \log c_2 + 2\delta \, V^1[10(y - c_1 - c_2)^{0.5}]$$

where δ is the discount factor and $c_1 + c_2 \leq y$. Since $V^1[10(y - c_1 - c_2)^{0.5}] = \log[10(y - c_1 - c_2)^{0.5}] + A(1)$, which is equal to $\log 10 + \frac{1}{2} \log(y - c_1 - c_2) + A(1)$, we can rewrite the problem a little more simply as

$$\max_{c_1 + c_2 \leq y} \log c_1 + \log c_2 + \delta \log(y - c_1 - c_2)$$

where we have suppressed the additive constants $\log 10$ and $A(1)$ because they do not affect the optimal choice. (Why?) The first-order conditions are $\frac{1}{c_1} = \delta \, [y - c_1 - c_2]^{-1}$ and $\frac{1}{c_2} = \delta[y - c_1 - c_2]^{-1}$. Since the expressions are identical, it follows that the two consumptions must be equal, that is, $c_1 = c_2$. It further follows that this common consumption equals $\frac{y}{2+\delta}$. Notice that consumption is less than it is when there is only one period left; in particular, some investment is made toward period 2's stock.

After collecting terms, the socially optimal per capita utility V^2 can be written as $(1 + \frac{\delta}{2}) \log y + A(2)$, where $A(2)$ is a compilation of constants.[8]

What if there are more than two extraction periods? Instead of solving the general case right away, let us do just one more step of induction in order to spot a solution pattern. Suppose that there are three periods of resource usage. In the first period we have the following problem to solve:

$$\max_{c_1 + c_2 \leq y} \log c_1 + \log c_2 + 2\delta V^2\left[10(y - c_1 - c_2)^{0.5}\right]$$

CONCEPT CHECK

MAXIMAND

Show that, after substituting for V^2 and suppressing all irrelevant constants, we can rewrite the last expression as

$$\max_{c_1 + c_2 \leq y} \log c_1 + \log c_2 + \delta \left(1 + \frac{\delta}{2}\right) \log(y - c_1 - c_2)$$

[5] Throughout, we continue to assume $c_{it} \geq 0$.

[6] As always, for a more detailed discussion of first-order conditions see Chapter 25.

[7] We will repeatedly use two facts about the log function: (1) for any two positive numbers a and b, $\log ab = \log a + \log b$; (2) for any two numbers a and b, with a positive, $\log a^b = b \log a$. A third fact follows from these two: $\log \frac{a}{b} = \log a - \log b$. (Why?)

[8] And, if you must know and verify for yourself, $A(2) = - \log(2 + \delta) + \frac{\delta}{2} \log \frac{\delta}{(2+\delta)} + \delta \log 10 + \delta A(1)$. This expression is derived by substituting the optimal consumption policy into the preceding equation and adding back the suppressed constants $\log 10$ and $A(1)$.

The first-order conditions for this problem are $\frac{1}{c_1} = \delta(1 + \frac{\delta}{2})[y - c_1 - c_2]^{-1}$ and an identical expression for c_2; since the expressions are identical, it follows that $c_1 = c_2$.

CONCEPT CHECK

OPTIMAL SOLUTION

Show that the socially optimal consumption equals $\frac{y}{2}\left(1 + \frac{\delta}{2} + \frac{\delta^2}{4}\right)^{-1}$. Show also that the socially optimal utility for each player is of the form $(1 + \frac{\delta}{2} + \frac{\delta^2}{4}) \log y + A(3)$, where $A(3)$ is a compilation of constants.

At this stage we can see a pattern. We have the following results (and a conjecture):

Number of Periods Remaining	Consumption (Fraction of y)
1	$\frac{1}{2}$
2	$\frac{1}{2(1+\frac{\delta}{2})}$
3	$\frac{1}{2(1+\frac{\delta}{2}+\frac{\delta^2}{4})}$
T (conjecture)	$\frac{1}{2\left[1+\frac{\delta}{2}+\cdots+\left(\frac{\delta}{2}\right)^{T-1}\right]}$

In fact, we can take the conjecture a step further; in the infinite-period model every periods's consumption fraction will be identical, since there are exactly the same number of periods remaining in each case. This identical *consumption function*, call it $c(y)$, will be given by the limit of the optimal consumption as T tends to infinity. Since $1 + \frac{\delta}{2} + \cdots + \left(\frac{\delta}{2}\right)^{T-1} + \cdots = \frac{1}{1-\frac{\delta}{2}}$ we can in turn assert that

$$c(y) = \frac{1 - \frac{\delta}{2}}{2}y \qquad (18.2)$$

CONCEPT CHECK

INVESTMENT

Show that the associated optimal investment fraction is $\frac{\delta}{2}$; that is, the *investment function* is

$$x(y) = \frac{\delta}{2}y$$

Some Numbers

If $\delta = 0.8$, then each player consumes 30 percent of the available stock in every period while the remaining 40 percent forms the investment base. Hence, next period's resource stock is given by the formula $y_{t+1} = 10\sqrt{0.4y_t}$.

CONCEPT CHECK
RESOURCE DYNAMICS

Show that if $y_t = 90$, then y_{t+1} shrinks further down to 60. What is y_{t+1} if $y_t = 10$? Finally, show that if period t's stock is 40, then it neither shrinks nor grows.

In other words, the socially optimal *sustainable resource stock* is equal to 40.

Returning to the general case socially optimal lifetime utility, by extrapolation, is given by

$$V(y) = \frac{1}{1 - \frac{\delta}{2}} \log y + A$$

where A is a constant.[9]

18.3.2   AN EXPLANATION OF THE SOCIAL OPTIMUM

The determination of the social optimum requires a balance between society's desire for immediate versus future consumption. Increasing immediate consumption lowers the resource stock in the next period, and it lowers consumption then (and possibly also in subsequent periods). Suppose an additional unit of investment grows to $1 + k$ units of additional resource stock. An extraction policy achieves the right balance if society would neither want to cut current consumption by a unit (and have $1 + k$ additional consumption units in the next period) nor want to cut tomorrow's consumption by $1 + k$ units (and have an additional unit of consumption today).

Consider the second option, increasing today's consumption—equivalently, decreasing today's investment—by a unit. In our commons model, with production equal to $10\sqrt{x}$, a unit decline of investment produces a decrease in future stock equal to $\frac{5}{\sqrt{x}}$.[10]

Since the utility function is equal to $\log c$, a unit increase in per capita consumption today adds utility equal to approximately $\frac{1}{c}$.[11] A unit decrease in consumption in the next period similarly decreases that utility by $\frac{1}{c'}$ units, where c' is next period's per capita consumption. Since next period's consumption is discounted, next period's utility loss for every unit of consumption is actually equal to $\frac{\delta}{c'}$. This per-unit utility loss next period should then be multiplied by the number of lost units, that is, should be multiplied by $\frac{5}{\sqrt{x}}$.

[9] *And using this formula, verify that the consumption function is indeed given by equation 18.2.*

[10] *In other words, the slope of the production function, or marginal productivity, is $\frac{5}{\sqrt{x}}$.*

[11] *In other words, the slope of the utility function, or marginal utility, is $\frac{1}{c}$.*

Some Numbers

Consider three possible extraction rates, 40 percent, 60 percent, and 80 percent. In doing the comparisons below, we will consider values of $\delta = 0.8$ and current size of resource equal to 30. Note that current consumption (C) at a 40 percent extraction rate is 0.4×30, that is, 12, while current investment (x) is 0.6×30, that is, 18. This investment produces a stock tomorrow equal to $10\sqrt{18}$ and hence, at a 40 percent extraction rate, consumption tomorrow (c') equal to $4\sqrt{18}$. The consumption and investment numbers for extraction rates of 60 percent and 80 percent are computed similarly.

Extraction Rate	c	x	c' (Rate $\times 10\sqrt{x}$)	Gain $(\frac{1}{c})$	Loss $(\frac{\delta}{c'} \times \frac{5}{\sqrt{x}})$
40%	12	18	$4\sqrt{18}$	$\frac{1}{12}$	$\frac{1}{18}$
60%	18	12	$6\sqrt{12}$	$\frac{1}{18}$	$\frac{1}{18}$
80%	24	6	$8\sqrt{6}$	$\frac{1}{24}$	$\frac{1}{12}$

As you can see from the table, there is nothing to be gained from increasing current consumption if 60 percent of the resource is consumed every period. Consumption should be increased if only 40 percent is being currently extracted, and it should be curtailed if 80 percent is currently being consumed. Of course, 60 percent is the socially optimal extraction that we computed a few paragraphs back.

18.4   ACHIEVABLE DEVELOPMENT AND GAME EQUILIBRIUM ⚠

Let us now turn to the parallel analysis in a strategic, rather than social, setting. Suppose that the two players are extracting the resource unilaterally. Each player will then only consider her own utility and seek to pick extraction rates that maximize this utility.

18.4.1   A COMPUTATION OF THE GAME EQUILIBRIUM

Like the social optimum, the game equilibrium can also be solved by backward induction. Suppose, to begin with, that there are exactly two periods. The extensive form is that of Figure 18.3.[12]

Suppose we are in the last period with stock y. Since utility increases in the amount of consumption and there are no more periods afterward, each player will attempt to consume everything. Hence, the stage-game equilibrium is one where each player's actual consumption is $\frac{y}{2}$. Consequently, each player's equilibrium utility is given by $W^1(y) = \log \frac{y}{2} = \log y + B(1)$, where $B(1)$ equals the constant, $-\log 2$.

Let us now fold the tree of Figure 18.3 back. When there are two periods left, player 1 faces the following best-response problem:

[12] *For the game we also have to specify what happens when the desired consumptions add up to an amount greater than the available stock. We will assume, as in Chapter 7, that in this case the stock is divided equally between the two players.*

$$\underset{c_1 \leq (1-\theta)y}{\text{Max}} \log c_1 + \delta W^1 \left[10(y - c_1 - \theta y)^{0.5} \right]$$

where θ is the fraction of the resource that player 2 is expected to consume in the first period.[13] Since $W^1\left\{10[(1-\theta)y - c_1]^{0.5}\right\} = \log 10 + \frac{1}{2}\log[(1-\theta)y - c_1] + B(1)$ we can rewrite the problem as

$$\underset{c_1 \leq (1-\theta)y}{\text{Max}} \log c_1 + \frac{\delta}{2} \log[(1-\theta)y - c_1]$$

where we have suppressed the constants $\log 10$ and $B(1)$. The first-order condition is $\frac{1}{c_1} = \frac{\frac{\delta}{2}}{(1-\theta)y - c_1}$. Hence, the best-response consumption is given by $(1 + \frac{\delta}{2})c_1 = (1-\theta)y$. If we write consumption as a fraction of resource stock—that is, if we write it as $b(\theta)y$—then it follows that

$$b(\theta) = \frac{1 - \theta}{1 + \frac{\delta}{2}}$$

Since the game is symmetric, it is natural to first look for a symmetric equilibrium. In a symmetric equilibrium, each player chooses the same extraction rate, and the rate is such that it is a best response (to itself), that is, $b(\theta) = \theta$. Put differently, the extraction rate $\frac{1}{2 + \frac{\delta}{2}}$ is a symmetric equilibrium. After collecting terms, the equilibrium utility when there are two remaining periods, W^2, can be written as $(1 + \frac{\delta}{2}) \log y + B(2)$, where, as always, $B(2)$ denotes a constant.

Now suppose that there are three periods of resource usage.

CONCEPT CHECK
BEST-RESPONSE PROBLEM

After substituting for the formula for W^2, show that the first-period best-response problem of player 1 is

$$\underset{c_1 \leq (1-\theta)y}{\text{Max}} \log c_1 + \frac{\delta}{2}\left(1 + \frac{\delta}{2}\right) \log[(1-\theta)y - c_1]$$

The first-order condition for this problem is $\frac{1}{c_1} = \frac{\frac{\delta}{2}(1+\frac{\delta}{2})}{(1-\theta)y - c_1}$.

EQUILIBRIUM

Show that a symmetric equilibrium is for each player to extract a fraction equal to $\dfrac{1}{2 + \frac{\delta}{2} + \frac{\delta^2}{4}}$ (in the first period).

[13] *Note that we have assumed that player 1 will consume within his means, that is, that $c_1 \leq (1-\theta)y$. Otherwise, we know that there will be no consumption for either player in the last period. When utility is specified by the log function, a player will always avoid zero consumption in any period; that is, he will in fact consume within his means in the first period.*

As with the social optimality problem, we can now see a pattern.

Number of Periods	Consumption (Fraction of y)
1	$\frac{1}{2}$
2	$\frac{1}{2+\frac{\delta}{2}}$
3	$\frac{1}{2+\frac{\delta}{2}+\frac{\delta^2}{4}}$
T (conjecture)	$\frac{1}{2+\frac{\delta}{2}+\cdots+\left(\frac{\delta}{2}\right)^{T-1}}$

In the infinite-period model, the equilibrium *consumption function*, call it $c^*(y)$, will be given by the limit of the equilibrium consumption as T tends to infinity. Since $2 + \frac{\delta}{2} + \frac{\delta^2}{4} + \cdots + \left(\frac{\delta}{2}\right)^T + \cdots = 1 + \frac{1}{1-\frac{\delta}{2}}$ we can in turn assert that

$$c^*(y) = \frac{1 - \frac{\delta}{2}}{2 - \frac{\delta}{2}} y$$

Some Numbers

If $\delta = 0.8$, in equilibrium, each player consumes 37.5 percent of the available stock in every period while the remaining 25 percent forms the investment base. In this case, next period's resource stock is given by the formula, $y_{t+1} = 10\sqrt{0.25 \times y_t}$.

CONCEPT CHECK
RESOURCE DYNAMICS

Show that if $y_t = 100$, then y_{t+1} shrinks down to 50. Show that the stock grows if $y_t = 20$, and that if period t's stock is 25, then it neither shrinks nor grows.

In other words, the equilibrium *achievable resource stock* is equal to 25.

18.4.2   AN EXPLANATION OF THE EQUILIBRIUM

The determination of a game equilibrium, like the determination of the social optimum, requires a balance between immediate and future consumption. There is, however, one key difference between the two situations; in the game a player reaps only a part of the future consequences of his actions. Let us explain.

Suppose an additional unit of investment grows to $1 + k$ units of additional resource stock. A part of this increase is appropriated as future consumption by the other player; suppose this fraction is θ. In that case, from the perspective of the player who makes the common investment higher by withholding his own immediate consumption, the effective increase in the stock is not $1 + k$ but rather it is $(1 - \theta) \times (1 + k)$. An extraction policy for a player achieves the right balance if he would want neither to cut current consumption by a unit [and instead have $(1 - \theta) \times (1 + k)$ additional consumption units in the next period] nor to cut tomorrow's consumption by $(1 - \theta) \times (1 + k)$ units (and have an additional unit of consumption today).

Suppose, therefore, that a player increases today's consumption—equivalently, decreases today's investment—by a unit. As we have seen, a unit decline of investment produces a decrease in tomorrow's stock equal to $\frac{5}{\sqrt{x}}$, where x is the current investment. Suppose further that the other player's extraction rate is (the equilibrium rate of) 37.5 percent, or $\frac{3}{8}$. Then the effective decrease in stock is $\frac{5}{\sqrt{x}} \times \frac{5}{8}$.

Exactly as in the social optimality case, a unit increase in consumption today adds utility equal to approximately $\frac{1}{c}$ and a unit decrease in consumption in the next period decreases utility by $\frac{1}{c'}$ units, where c' is next periods's consumption. Since next period's consumption is discounted, next period's utility loss is actually $\frac{\delta}{c}$. This per unit utility loss should then be multiplied by the number of lost units, $\frac{5}{\sqrt{2}} \times \frac{5}{8}$.

Let us see which of the two—current gain or future loss—is higher, for three possible extraction rates for player 1, 30 percent, 37.5 percent, and 50 percent.[14] We will consider values of $\delta = 0.8$ and current size of resource equal to 40 and presume that the other player extracts at the equilibrium rate equal to 37.5 percent. Note that current consumption at a 30 percent extraction rate is 0.3×40, that is, 12. Together with the other player's consumption—equal to 15 at an extraction rate of 37.5 percent—that yields a current consumption total $(c_1 + c_2)$ of $12 + 15$, or 27. Hence, current investment (x) is 13. This investment produces a stock tomorrow equal to $10\sqrt{13}$ and hence, at the 30 percent extraction rate, consumption (c_1') equal to $3\sqrt{13}$. The consumption and investment numbers for extraction rates of 37.5 and 50 percent are similarly computed.

Extraction Rate	$c_1 + c_2$	x	c_1' (Rate $\times 10\sqrt{x}$)	Gain ($\frac{1}{c_1}$)	Loss ($\frac{\delta}{c_1'} \times \frac{5}{\sqrt{x}} \times \frac{5}{8}$)
30%	27	13	$3\sqrt{13}$	$\frac{1}{12}$	$\frac{5}{78}$
37.5%	30	10	$3.75\sqrt{10}$	$\frac{1}{15}$	$\frac{1}{15}$
50%	35	5	$5\sqrt{5}$	$\frac{1}{20}$	$\frac{1}{10}$

As you can see from the table, there is nothing to be gained from increasing current consumption if 37.5 percent of the resource is being consumed every period. Consumption should be increased if player 1 is only consuming 30 percent currently, and it should be curtailed if she is consuming 50 percent instead.

18.4.3   A COMPARISON OF THE SOCIALLY OPTIMAL AND THE EQUILIBRIUM OUTCOMES

The general lesson is that unilateral extraction leads to overextraction; *consumption in the equilibrium solution is higher than in the socially optimal solution.* Compare the two consumption functions: the socially optimal function $c(y)$ and the equilibrium function $c^*(y)$. Note the following:

[14] *Recall that 30 percent is the socially optimal rate and 37.5 percent is the equilibrium rate.*

$$c(y) = \frac{1 - \frac{\delta}{2}}{2} y < \frac{1 - \frac{\delta}{2}}{2 - \frac{\delta}{2}} y = c^*(y) \tag{18.3}$$

The equation holds simply because $2 - \frac{\delta}{2}$ is smaller than 2. The intuition for this conclusion is precisely that in the equilibrium solution a player only collects a part of his action's consequences. Hence, he is more likely to overextract because part of the burden of that overconsumption is borne by a lowering of the other player's future consumption.

Consider two different societies, one in which consumption is socially managed and another in which it is unilaterally determined. Imagine that both societies start with the same resource stock. By period 2, the first society would have a larger resource stock because it invested more in the first period. This incease implies in turn that this society would again have a larger investment level in period 2. This result would occur for two reasons; first, society 1 in any case invests a larger fraction of any resource stock. Second, it has a larger resource stock available. Now, hopefully, the continuation of this logic is also clear. In each period the socially managed society would have a larger resource stock, would invest more, and hence would continue to have a larger resource stock in the future. If y_t denotes the resource stock in the socially managed situation and y_t' denotes the equilibrium stock, then $y_t > y_t'$ for all periods $t > 1$ even though $y_1 = y_1'$.

Another consequence of this argument is that the sustainable socially optimal stock is higher than the achievable equilibrium stock. We have already seen this outcome with some numbers, but here is the general argument: A sustainable stock is one that keeps getting regenerated; that is, it is a level at which $y_t = y_{t+1}$ in all periods. Put differently, at the sustainable socially optimal stock, call it $\widehat{y}$, socially optimal investment $x(\widehat{y})$ exactly regenerates that stock, that is, $\widehat{y} = 10\sqrt{x(\widehat{y})}$. This stock is not achievable in equilibrium because the equilibrium investment at $\widehat{y}$ is less than $x(\widehat{y})$. In fact, the achievable equilibrium stock must be lower.

18.5 DYNAMIC GAMES: AN EPILOGUE

Two natural questions arise at this point: First, how general are the conclusions of the commons model; that is, do broadly similar conclusions arise in *any* dynamic game? Second, what have we learned that is different from the conclusion of the simpler repeated-games structure?

There are three conclusions that we have seen in the commons model. First, there is an equilibrium in which each player looks only at the size of the current resource stock, or game environment, to decide how much to consume.[15] Such strategies have a technical name; they are called Markovian strategies, and an equilibrium in these strategies is called a Markov perfect equilibrium (MPE). Markovian strategies are attractive because of their simplicity; they do not require a player to keep track of either what his opponent did in the past or how the resource has evolved in previous periods.

For general dynamic games, MPE always exists if the number of game environments is finite. When the environment can be any one of an infinite number, tricky mathematical

[15] *In the finite-horizon game, each player also looks at how many periods of extraction remain in order to make this choice.*

issues arise, and we do not know whether there is always an MPE.[16] In a repeated game, there is only one environment; hence a Markovian strategy is the same thing as choosing the same action over and over again. An MPE, therefore, is the same thing as playing a stage-game Nash equilibrium repeatedly. (Why?) Unlike a dynamic game, therefore, MPEs in repeated games do not lead to any interesting time patterns of behavior.

The second conclusion of our model is that there is a unique equilibrium (that looks similar to the socially optimal solution). This conclusion is not at all robust. In general dynamic games, there are many MPEs. When we additionally consider strategies that look like the trigger strategies of repeated games, we generate yet more equilibria.

The final conclusion was that equilibrium is socially suboptimal; too much of the resource is extracted and hence equilibrium utilities are lower than socially optimal utilities. This conclusion is very robust and shows up in a variety of dynamic games. And, of course, it also shows up with repeated games—unless the threat of punishment is imposed, equilibria are suboptimal. Using logic similar to that of repeated games, it is also possible to show that triggerlike strategies can sometimes remedy this problem in a dynamic game. If players believe that good behavior will be rewarded and bad behavior punished in the future, they might be inclined to behave themselves.

SUMMARY

1. Dynamic games generalize the framework of repeated games by allowing the game environment to change from period to period. They are needed to study problems that are fundamentally dynamic.

2. An example of a dynamic game is the commons problem in which players have access to a common property resource. The size of the resource constitutes the game's environment, and it evolves over time depending on the pattern of resource usage.

3. A socially optimal resource usage balances the competing social desires for immediate and future consumption. The optimal balance typically lies between the two extremes of no usage and complete exhaustion of the resource.

4. If the resource is used in a decentralized fashion, then each player's usage balances the competing desires for immediate individual consumption and future consumption. However, each player realizes that he will only get a fraction of any additional (common) future resource stock.

5. Typically, equilibrium usage leads to overextraction, relative to the social optimum. This phenomenon is called the tragedy of the commons.

[16] *Of course some games, such as our commons model, do have MPE even when there are an infinite number of possible environments.*

EXERCISES

SECTION 18.1

18.1

Give two examples of dynamic strategic interaction that should be studied as a dynamic game. Be sure to describe carefully what the game environment is, how it affects payoffs, and how it evolves.

18.2

Write down a simple dynamic game model of the Treasury auctions (section 14.3) when the quantity sold can vary from auction to auction. State explicitly any assumptions that you make.

18.3

Can you write down a simple dynamic game model for OPEC in which the costs of extraction depend on existing reserves in every period? For the purposes of this example you can utilize the numbers on extraction levels that we discussed in Chapter 17.

SECTION 18.2

18.4

For the production function used in the chapter, what is the stock that arises from investment level 50? What of investment level 20? level 90?

18.5

If the current size of the resource is 60, how much investment would there need to be to regenerate this stock level? What if the current resource stock is 90?

18.6

From the picture of the production function (Figure 18.2), and your answer to exercise 18.5, what can you conclude about sustainability of higher and higher stocks? Explain your answer.

18.7

The marginal productivity of investment is the additional stock that would result from a small increase in investment (for example, a unit increase). Graph the marginal productivity function $5/\sqrt{x}$, where x is the investment level. Can you explain its shape?

18.8

Explain the answers that you got in exercise 18.6 in light of what you concluded in exercise 18.7. Is it correct to say, "It becomes increasingly difficult to sustain larger resource levels"?

18.9

The marginal utility of consumption is the additional utility that would result from a small increase in consumption (for example, a unit increase). Graph the marginal utility function $\frac{1}{c}$, where c is the consumption level. Can you explain its shape?

SECTION 18.3

(Calculus problem)   Suppose that the production function is given by $20\sqrt{x}$ but the utility functions are the same as those in the text; that is, player i's utility is $\log c_i$. The next several questions will compute the social optimum and the game equilibrium for this case.

18.10

Formulate the social optimality problem when there is just one more period of extraction left. What is the socially optimal utility level?

18.11

Formulate the social optimality problem when there are two more periods of extraction left. What is the socially optimal consumption rule? What is the socially optimal utility level? (You do not have to write down all of the constants in the optimal utility.)

18.12

Repeat the previous question for three remaining periods of extraction.

18.13

What can you infer about the general case of T remaining extraction periods? What if there are an infinite number of periods? Explain your answers carefully.

18.14

How do your answers compare with those found in the chapter? Explain your finding.

18.15

For the special case of $\delta = 0.8$, compute the consumption and investment functions. What is the socially optimal sustainable resource level? How does your answer compare with that in the text?

SECTION 18.4

18.16

Now formulate the equilibrium problem when there is just one more period of extraction left. What is the equilibrium utility level?

18.17

Formulate the best-response problem of player 1 when there are two more periods of extraction left and player 2 is expected to consume a fraction θ of the current stock level. What is the best-response consumption fraction?

18.18

What is the symmetric equilibrium to this game? What is the equilibrium utility level? (You do not have to write down all of the constants in the equilibrium utility.)

18.19

Repeat exercises 18.17 and 18.18 for the case in which there are three remaining periods of extraction.

18.20

What can you infer about the general case of T remaining extraction periods? What if there are an infinite number of periods? Explain your answers carefully. How do your answers compare with those found in the chapter? Explain your finding.

18.21

For the special case of $\delta = 0.8$, compute the consumption and investment functions. What is the socially optimal sustainable resource level? How does your answer compare with that in the text?

PART FOUR

ASYMMETRIC INFORMATION GAMES: THEORY AND APPLICATIONS

CHAPTER **19**

MORAL HAZARD AND INCENTIVES THEORY

This chapter is the first in a series that brings players' information—what they know, and equally importantly, what they do not know—to center stage. It discusses a phenomenon called *moral hazard* that is important for the theory of incentives. In section 19.1 we give a definition and present several real-world examples of moral hazard. Section 19.2 presents a simple model and discusses a number of alternative incentive schemes. Section 19.3 analyzes the model and derives the optimal incentive scheme, and section 19.4 contains some general conclusions. Finally, in section 19.5, we discuss a case study on compensating primary care physicians in an HMO.

19.1   MORAL HAZARD: EXAMPLES AND A DEFINITION

The term **moral hazard** arises in insurance and refers to the fact that a person who has insurance coverage will have less incentive to take proper care of an insured object than a person who does not. For instance, if your expensive stereo equipment is fully insured against theft, you might be less careful about locking your door every time you step out of your dorm room; after all, even if the amplifier was stolen you would be able to replace it at no additional cost. Conversely, if you do not have comprehensive insurance on your car you may think twice about parking right in front of the rowdiest downtown bar on a Friday night.

 In each of these cases there is something that you as the insured *agent* prefer to do that the insurance company would rather you not do. In the first case, it is more convenient for you not to have to carry around a heavy set of keys. In the second, you prefer to get to your destination sooner rather than drive around for another 15 minutes looking for a safer parking spot. However, your actions expose the insurance company—

Moral hazard

A principal-agent problem arises when one economic agent—the agent—takes an action that affects another economic agent—the principal. A principal-agent problem has a moral-hazard component when the principal is unable to simply force the agent to act according to his interests.

in legalese, the *principal*—to unnecessary risk. In each of these cases it is also true that it is difficult for the insurance company to prove that you did not take adequate precaution.

This then is the heart of the moral-hazard problem: what is good for the agent is not (necessarily) good for the principal, and the principal cannot always be on hand to monitor what the agent does.

There are at least two reasons why a principal may be unable to enforce his will by simply asking the agent to act according to his (the principal's) interests. First, the agent's actions might not be observed by the principal. Second, the principal might be able to observe the agent's action all right but might be unable to prove breach of contract in a court of law. For instance, leaving your dorm room door unlocked is an action that is unobservable to the insurance company. Parking in front of the rowdiest bar is an observable action, but it might be impossible to prove to a court that you were fully aware of the risks of that action.

Whenever there is moral hazard, the principal has to devise schemes that will induce the agent to act in ways that the principal prefers. For example, insurance policies routinely have a deductible; this is a dollar amount on your claim that the insurance company will *not* pay. If your automobile insurance policy has a $500 deductible, then the first $500 worth of damage has to be paid out of pocket by you. In this case, you might think twice about parking in front of a rowdy bar! This chapter will study various schemes that a principal might come up with to give his agent appropriate incentives.

Let us turn now to some further examples of moral hazard from outside the insurance business. In each example, the first character in a pair is the principal, and the second, the agent.

Owner-Manager

The managers of a company take a number of actions that affect profitability but are largely unobserved by the owners (or shareholders, if it is a publicly held company); these include how hard the managers work, whether or not they make every effort to contain costs, whether they account for all possibilities before deciding on a new project, and so on. The preferences of owners and managers are in conflict if owners care only about the firm's profits whereas managers care additionally about such things as the number of hours that they work and the number of people under their direct control.

Client–Service Provider (For Example, Client-Lawyer, Patient-Doctor, Car Owner–Car Mechanic)

A doctor runs tests, makes diagnoses, and prescribes care for her patient. The appropriateness and quality of these actions are essentially unobservable to the patient, who does not have the expertise to judge these issues. And that statement is also true of the other examples. In each case, the preferences of the principal and agent are different; the doctor, for example, cares about her fees, the likelihood of being sued, and the like in addition to treating the patient. The patient is primarily interested in getting better.

Firm-Salesman

A salesman collects orders for her firm. Sometimes she may do so on the phone, and, more traditionally, she may do so by calling on her clients. Typically, the firm would like salesmen to maximize sales, but doing so may require the salesman to work incredibly long hours, travel miles away from home, be away from home days on end, and so on. You can see the divergence in preferences now; what is good for the principal may be too onerous for the agent. Furthermore, the firm typically cannot ensure that the salesman puts in hours that the latter might not want to.

There will be two essential questions in the principal-agent moral hazard problem:

- *What kind of incentives* should the principal give his agent to make her choose a prespecified action?

- *What action* should the principal specify? Should it be the action the principal most desires, the one that the agent prefers, or something in between?

19.2   A PRINCIPAL-AGENT MODEL

In this section we will present a simple model of moral hazard involving a principal and an agent and discuss some examples of incentive schemes that the principal might use to combat moral hazard.

The principal-agent game can be represented by the game tree of Figure 19.1. In drawing the tree we restrict attention to a simple case in which the agent can only choose among two actions and there are three consequences for each action of the agent.

At the root of the tree, the principal makes a decision about the kinds of incentives to offer his agent. For instance, the owner of a firm has to decide on the compensation package he will offer his manager.[1] After seeing the incentive scheme, the agent chooses her action among the two choices e_H and e_L, and these denote *high* and *low* effort respectively; the term *effort* includes decisions on how hard to work, what projects to select for the company (and, possibly, whether or not to look for another job).[2] The agent's action is unobservable to the principal. Since the agent chooses *after* the principal, the agent's decision nodes form the second stage of the tree.

The agent's action determines the firm's profitability; the three possible profit levels are denoted *good*, *medium*, and *bad*, and $g > m > b$. The profit determination is uncertain; that is, every action of the agent leads to a *probability distribution* over profits.[3] It is important that there not be a one-to-one relationship between the agent's action and the firm's profits; otherwise, the action would be exactly inferred from the

[1] *In the discussion that follows we will often refer to the principal as owner and to the agent as manager. The owner-manager story will provide a concrete context for the analysis although the conclusions will apply more generally to any principal-agent problem.*

[2] *In some of the examples the terminology—effort—needs to be interpreted in a very broad sense. For instance, an insured agent exerts care, a doctor chooses appropriate treatment, and a car mechanic fixes a car.*

[3] *As in earlier chapters, uncertainty is modeled via a fictional player— "nature." For instance, when the agent chooses action e_H, nature "chooses" among profit levels g, m, and b with probabilities 0.6, 0.3, and 0.1, respectively. Similarly, when the agent chooses e_L, nature assigns probabilities 0.1, 0.3, and 0.6 to the three profit levels.*

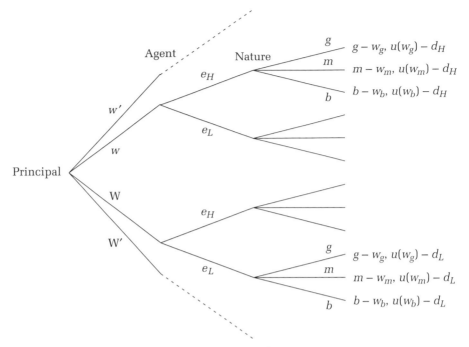

For e_H Prob.(g) = 0.6, Prob.(m) = 0.3 and Prob.(b) = 0.1

For e_L Prob.(g) = 0.1, Prob.(m) = 0.3 and Prob.(b) = 0.6

Figure 19.1

resultant profit. Uncertainty allows for such incompleteness in inference; upon seeing a profit level g, the principal is not sure whether the agent took action e_H or e_L.

Consider now the principal's payoffs. The principal pays the agent w_g if he observes profits of size g, w_m for profits equal to m, and w_b if profits are only equal to b. The principal can only reward on the basis of what he sees, that is, profits.[4] Consequently, the net profit for the principal is $g - w_g$ whenever gross profits are g, $m - w_m$ in the medium case, and $b - w_b$ in the bad profit scenario. We will assume that the principal only cares about net profits.

The agent gets a payoff, or utility, from her compensation as well as from the effort that she exerts. For example, if she is paid w_m and she has taken action e_H, then her total payoff is $u(w_m) - d_H$, where $u(w_m)$ is the utility from compensation w_m and d_H is the disutility of e_H. We will assume that the utility of compensation, $u(.)$, is an increasing, concave function, that is, that the agent prefers more money to less and is risk averse.[5] Finally, e_H stands for high effort in the sense that its disutility is greater, that is, $d_H > d_L$.

At various points in the discussion we will want to compute solutions to various incentive schemes explicitly. At those points, we will make the following special assumption:

[4] It will also be natural to presume that the principal cannot charge the agent for (the pleasure of) working for him; that is, we will only consider $w_g \geq 0$, $w_m \geq 0$, and $w_b \geq 0$.

[5] Risk aversion means that the agent prefers to avoid risky situations; in particular, she prefers to have a dollar for sure to a gamble in which she has an equal chance of losing that dollar and of winning an additional dollar. See Chapter 27 for further elaboration. For expositional ease, we shall also assume that $u(.)$ also has a slope.

Special Assumption (SA). $u(w) = 2\sqrt{w}$; $d_H = 10$; $d_L = 0$; and profit levels are $g = 200$, $m = 100$, and $b = 50$.

19.2.1 SOME EXAMPLES OF INCENTIVE SCHEMES

A Pure Wage Scheme

One possible compensation scheme is to treat the agent as a salaried employee who gets a fixed salary regardless of the firm's profits. Hence, $w_g = w_m = w_b = w$, for some salary level w.

In this case the agent's payoff, if she takes action e_H, is $u(w) - d_H$ (no matter what the profit level is) while the payoff from e_L is $u(w) - d_L$. Since the disutility d_H is higher, the agent would prefer to take action e_L, that is, would prefer not to exert high effort. This result should not cause any surprise; if her compensation does not depend on results, then the agent would prefer to take the action that she most prefers rather than that which is good for the principal (and the firm).[6]

A Pure Franchise Scheme

The opposite extreme is a pure franchise scheme in which the agent pays the principal a fixed sum of money—the franchise fee—regardless of profits. In this case, the agent bears all the risks and is like a "residual" owner.[7] Denote the franchise fee f. Therefore w_g is equal to $g - f$, w_m is the same thing as $m - f$, and w_b is equal to $b - f$.

If the agent takes the action e_H, her payoff is uncertain; with probability 0.6 it is $u(g - f) - d_H$, with probability 0.3 it is $u(m - f) - d_H$, and with probability 0.1 it is $u(b - f) - d_H$. Her expected payoff is therefore

$$\left[0.6 \times u(g - f)\right] + \left[0.3 \times u(m - f)\right] + \left[0.1 \times u(b - f)\right] - d_H$$

By similar reasoning her expected payoff from taking action e_L is

$$\left[0.1 \times u(g - f)\right] + \left[0.3 \times u(m - f)\right] + \left[0.6 \times u(b - f)\right] - d_L$$

It is no longer immediately obvious which of her two actions the agent prefers. Although e_H is more onerous, it has a higher probability that the agent's take will be $g - f$ rather than $b - f$. To fix some ideas, consider the numbers given in the special assumption (SA).

CONCEPT CHECK

FRANCHISE (SA)

Show that the agent will take action e_H if and only if

$$\sqrt{200 - f} - \sqrt{50 - f} \geq 10$$

---

[6] *Even at this preliminary stage of our discussion on incentives we seem to have gained some understanding of why there are never more than two counters open at the local post office, why so many postal workers feel the need to talk endlessly to each other, and why the only thing that is prompt at that office is the closing of the doors at the stroke of 5 P.M.*

[7] *Your local McDonald's is most likely a franchise.*

The highest fee that the principal can possibly charge is 50. (Why?) For that fee, the agent would take action e_H because $\sqrt{150} \geq 10$.

An Intermediate Scheme: Wage Plus Bonus

In the first two schemes, either the principal or the agent bears all the risks. In a pure wage scheme, the agent gets the same salary regardless of profit, while in a pure franchise scheme, the principal gets the same franchise fee (again regardless of profit level). In an intermediate scheme, the risks are shared; the agent is given a base wage w_b regardless of profit level. A bonus is paid to her only if a higher profit level m or g is observed; in the first case, the size of the bonus is $w_m - w_b$, while in the second case it is $w_g - w_b$. The agent bears some risk because at least one of the two bonuses is positive (and not zero), while the principal bears some risk because the bonus is less than the increase in profit.

If the agent takes the action e_H, her payoff is uncertain: with probability 0.6 it is $u(w_g) - d_H$; with probability 0.3 it is $u(w_m) - d_H$; and with probability 0.1 it is $u(w_b) - d_H$. Her expected payoff is therefore

$$\left[0.6 \times u(w_g)\right] + \left[0.3 \times u(w_m)\right] + \left[0.1 \times u(w_b)\right] - d_H \tag{19.1}$$

By the same reasoning, the agent's expected payoff from taking action e_L is

$$\left[0.1 \times u(w_g)\right] + \left[0.3 \times u(w_m)\right] + \left[0.6 \times u(w_b)\right] - d_L$$

It follows that the agent will take action e_H if and only if

$$0.5 \times \left[u(w_g) - u(w_b)\right] \geq d_H - d_L \tag{19.2}$$

An Infeasible Scheme: Effort-Based Wage

If moral hazard were not present, that is, if the principal could observe the agent's effort, he could pay the agent directly on that basis. As a benchmark comparison, let us see what happens in that instance. Denote the two wage levels w_H and w_L.

The agent will take action e_H if and only if

$$u(w_H) - d_H \geq u(w_L) - d_L \tag{19.3}$$

CONCEPT CHECK
BONUSES IN THE SA CASE

Consider the intermediate incentives case. Use equation 19.2 to write down the bonus that would induce the agent to pick e_H. Knowing that the lowest base wage w_b is 0, can you show that the bonus is 100? Repeat, using equation 19.3, for the infeasible case. Is the bonus in this case, $w_H - w_L$, bigger or smaller than 100?

19.3   THE OPTIMAL INCENTIVE SCHEME

In this section we will answer the question, Which incentive scheme should the principal offer his agent? Although we are particularly interested in the answer when there *is* moral hazard, it will be useful to first answer the question when there is not.

19.3.1   NO MORAL HAZARD

Just for this subsection let us imagine that the principal observes the agent's action and can therefore reward that effort directly. As we saw in the previous *effort-based wage* segment, the agent will choose e_H only if she is given an appropriate bonus $w_H - w_L$. If the agent chooses e_H, the principal's net expected profit equals

$$(0.6 \times g) + (0.3 \times m) + (0.1 \times b) - w_H$$

whereas if she chooses e_L, those profits equal

$$(0.1 \times g) + (0.3 \times m) + (0.6 \times b) - w_L$$

A straightforward calculation shows that the principal would rather offer the bonus—and have the agent work e_H—if and only if

$$0.5 \times (g - b) \geq w_H - w_L \tag{19.4}$$

The last condition has an easy interpretation: there is a 50 percent greater likelihood of the profit level g, rather than b, if effort e_H is exerted by the agent. In other words, there are increased expected profits of size $0.5 \times (g - b)$ if e_H is chosen, and the question is, Do those profits exceed the wage bonus $w_H - w_L$?

For SA, the increased expected profits equal 75 and the wage bonus required (as we hope you showed) is 25. So in this case the principal would indeed offer an incentive scheme $w_H = 25$, $w_L = 0$, and the agent would pick e_H.[8] Consequently, the principal's net expected profits would be 130 and the agent's payoff would be 0.

To summarize, the principal has one of two options: pay the wage bonus required to get the agent to pick e_H or, alternatively, pay no bonus and set $w_H = w_L(= 0)$, and count on the agent to pick e_L.[9] Two considerations determine the principal's choice: First, how large is the required bonus? That depends on how averse the agent is to hard work; that is, it depends on $d_H - d_L$. Second, how large is the consequent increase in profits; that is, how large is $g - b$? As equation 19.4 makes clear, the smaller the required bonus and the larger the increased profits, the more likely that the optimal is a wage-plus-bonus scheme.

19.3.2   MORAL HAZARD

Let us revert to the case of moral hazard (in which the agent's compensation can only depend on the observed profit level). Again, one option for the principal is to offer a pure wage scheme. Since the agent is definitely going to respond by picking e_L, the principal

---

[8] *Note that at these wages, the agent is exactly indifferent between e_H and e_L. The principal could make her strictly prefer e_H by setting w_H equal to 25.01.*

[9] *From the pure wage scheme discussion of the previous section we know that the agent will always pick e_L if she is a salaried employee.*

might as well offer a salary of 0. The principal's expected profits in that case will be $(0.1 \times g) + (0.3 \times m) + (0.6 \times b)$. For the SA case, the expected profit equals 80.

A second option is to offer a pure franchise scheme. In this case, the principal's net profit is exactly the franchise fee. In the SA case, as we saw earlier, the highest franchise fee that he can collect is 50. Hence, a pure wage scheme is better for the principal than a pure franchise scheme. The question is, Is an intermediate scheme even better than these two extremes?

If the agent picks action e_H, the principal's net expected profit equals

$$\left[0.6 \times (g - w_g)\right] + \left[0.3 \times (m - w_m)\right] + \left[0.1 \times (b - w_b)\right] \tag{19.5}$$

whereas if the agent chooses e_L those profits equal

$$\left[0.1 \times (g - w_g)\right] + \left[0.3 \times (m - w_m)\right] + \left[0.6 \times (b - w_b)\right] \tag{19.6}$$

CONCEPT CHECK
BONUS?

Use equations 19.5 and 19.6 to show that the principal would be willing to pay the appropriate wage bonus, $w_g - w_b$, if and only if

$$g - b \geq w_g - w_b \tag{19.7}$$

[10] *You might wonder why the medium profit level m and its associated compensation w_m have not played any role in the discussion so far. The reason is that m has the same probability, 0.3, for both actions. Its occurrence, therefore, does not give the principal any information about the agent's effort, nor does it affect the agent's incentives. Hence, $w_m = w_b$. (Why?) In the next subsection we will drop the equal-probability restriction, and we will see then that the medium outcome does play a role in determining the optimal incentive scheme.*

This last equation has the following interpretation: If the agent picks e_H there is a 50 percent greater likelihood that the profits will be g rather than b. Consequently, there is also a 50 percent greater likelihood that the principal will have to pay the bonus $w_g - w_b$. The principal finds the bonus worth paying if the increase in profits is larger than the required bonus. From the *wage plus bonus* segment of the previous section, and in particular equation 19.2, we know that this bonus is given implicitly by the requirement, $0.5 \times [u(w_g) - u(w_b)] = d_H - d_L$.

Hence, we have a qualitatively similar conclusion to the no-moral-hazard case: the principal will more likely pay the bonus if the work aversion $d_H - d_L$ is small or the increase in profits $g - b$ is large.[10] When he does pay the bonus, that is, when the pure wage scheme is inoptimal, he pays exactly that amount at which the agent is indifferent between actions e_H and e_L. The pure franchise scheme is inoptimal because the franchise bonuses, $m - b$ and $g - b$, are too large.

CONCEPT CHECK
OPTIMAL SCHEME IN THE SA CASE

First, show that it is worth the principal's while to pay the bonus, that is, equation 19.7 is satisfied. Then compute the optimal incentive scheme and show that the principal's expected profit is 95. What is the agent's expected payoff?

In comparing the SA numbers for the no-moral-hazard and the moral-hazard cases, note that the principal is worse off in the latter (expected net profits of 95 versus 130). The reason is that he has to pay the agent a larger bonus (100 versus 25) to get the agent to pick e_H.

19.4 SOME GENERAL CONCLUSIONS

There are two conclusions from the previous section that hold more generally:

- **Result 1:** To elicit hard work, you need to give bonuses for good results.

- **Result 2:** The higher the profits, the larger the bonus.

Result 1 follows straightforwardly from the discussion of the *pure wage scheme* in section 19.2. Suppose that no bonuses are offered; that is, we have a pure wage scheme. No matter how complex the model, we immediately know that the agent will always pick her most preferred action in that case, that is, will avoid hard work.[11]

Result 1 has an interesting and not so obvious consequence:

- **Corollary 1′:** The principal is always strictly worse off if there is moral hazard versus when there is not, unless he wants the agent to pick e_L.

When there is no moral hazard, the principal can condition the agent's payment directly on the effort level. So no matter what the profit outcome, the agent gets the same wage; that is, she faces a pure wage scheme. For the principal to be no worse off with moral hazard, he has to be able to offer a pure wage scheme *and* get the agent to pick the desired action. But we know that when there is moral hazard the only action that the agent will find it in her self-interest to pick is e_L.[12]

Result 2 holds in the model studied so far.[13] It seems a natural conjecture that it will always hold, that is, that we should always have $w_g \geq w_m \geq w_b$. Somewhat surprisingly

[11] *And Result 1 is pervasive. At the time a draft of this chapter was being written, the "story of the week" in New York tabloids was the Donald Trump—Marla Maples divorce. Perhaps the most interesting part of the divorce was its timing. Apparently, it took place in 1997 rather than a year later because the prenuptial agreement had a bonus scheme for Marla. It specified that if the marriage broke down within five years, she would get a payment between $1 million and $5 million (her baseline wage), but if it lasted more than five years then she would get a share of Trump's net worth (valued between $450 million and $2.5 billion). The Donald got out of the bonus payment by divorcing early! In a similar vein, Yankee third baseman Charlie Hayes got a bonus for keeping his weight under a cutoff, and Miami Heat point guard Tim Hardaway, brilliant but prone to inconsistency, got a bonus if his assists-to-turnovers ratio during the season was over 4.*

[12] *Note that it does not pay the principal to condition compensation on both effort and profits when there is no moral hazard. The reason is that the agent is risk averse and so does not like any unnecessary result-dependent uncertainty in her compensation. Since effort is observable, the principal cannot apply any additional incentive pressure by having the wage depend on results. So it is mutually beneficial not to make wages contingent on profit level.*

[13] *Note that in order to have the agent pick e_H the principal offers a positive bonus, that is, $w_g > w_b$. There is, however, no such bonus offered for the medium outcome; that is, $w_m = w_b$.*

it turns out that such monotonicity only holds under an additional condition called *monotone likelihood ratios*.

To get some feeling for what follows, let us modify the model a little bit. Suppose that e_L implies that there is (as before) a 0.1 probability of profit g, but now there is a probability p that the profit will be m (so far $p = 0.3$), and a remaining probability $0.9 - p$ that the profit level will be b. When effort e_H is exerted, the probabilities are (as before) 0.6, 0.3, and 0.1 for profits g, m, and b, respectively.

Whenever the probability p is less than 0.3, we are in a situation in which *both m and g* are more likely with hard work. When the principal sees m or g, he should therefore reward the agent in either case. The question is, which reward should be higher? The answer will be, whichever profit level is *relatively more likely* with e_H than with e_L.

Definition. The likelihood ration for profit level g is $\frac{\text{Probability of } g \text{ if } e_H \text{ is exerted}}{\text{Probability of } g \text{ if } e_L \text{ is exerted}}$. The likelihood ratio for profit level m is similarly defined.

Since the likelihoods of the profit level g are 0.6 and 0.1 (for e_H and e_L, respectively) the likelihood ratio is 6. In contrast, for profit level m, the likelihood ratio is $\frac{0.3}{p}$.

- **Result 2′:** The wage bonus for profit level g is higher than the bonus for m if and only if its likelihood ratio is greater than that for m, that is, if $6 > \frac{0.3}{p}$.

The intuition for the condition is this: Whenever a particular profit level is observed, the principal estimates the chance that this profit was realized because the agent exerted effort e_H and not e_L. The higher his estimate, the more he would like to reward the agent. The likelihood ratio is precisely that estimate. To further see why this conclusion makes sense, imagine that $p = 0$; that is, if the principal saw m he would be sure that the agent had in fact picked e_H. In that case the principal would want to induce the agent to do the right thing by offering a large sum of money if m were observed, but not very much if g were observed instead, since in the latter scenario the principal is still unsure of what the agent actually did.

Sketch of Proof

To formalize the intuition, consider the following thought exercise. Suppose that the agent does pick action e_H. In that case the principal's expected wage bill is

$$0.6w_g + 0.3w_m \tag{19.8}$$

[14] *The reason is that the profit level g is twice as likely as m, so that there is twice as much chance that the principal will have to make good on any promise about w_g.*

(since he will always pay base wage $w_b = 0$ to minimize on costs). From equation 19.8 it follows that starting from any pair of wages w_g and w_m, if the principal cuts w_m by \$2 while increasing w_g by \$1, his costs will remain unchanged. (Why?)[14] More generally, the principal's costs remain unchanged if he cuts w_m and increases w_g as long as the amount of the cut is twice the amount of the increase.

Suppose now that we start with equal-sized bonuses, that is, $w_g = w_m = w$ say, but at a level that prompts the agent to pick e_H. In other words,[15]

$$0.5u(w) + (0.3 - p)u(w) \geq d_H - d_L \qquad (19.9)$$

How would these incentives change if the principal in fact increased w_g by a small amount θ (while decreasing w_m by 2θ). The first term in the left-hand side of equation 19.9 would consequently increase by $0.5u'(w) \times \theta$, and the second term would decrease by $(0.3 - p)u'(w) \times 2\theta$ [where $u'(w)$ is the slope of the utility function at wage w].[16] The net effect on the agent's expected utility would therefore be

$$u'(w) \times \theta \times 0.6 \times \left(\frac{p}{0.3} - \frac{1}{6} \right)$$

where we have used the fact that $0.5 = 0.6 \times (1 - \frac{1}{6})$ and $2(0.3 - p) = 0.6 \times (1 - \frac{p}{0.3})$. Clearly the expression is positive if and only if $6 > \frac{0.3}{p}$, that is, if the likelihood ratio for g is higher than that for m. But if the expression is positive, then the agent prefers that her principal offer her this wage adjustment, that is, offer her a bigger bonus for g. In turn, the principal can therefore offer a θ increase in w_g, cut w_m by more than 2θ, yet be sure that the agent would continue to pick the high effort level e_H (why?) and save himself some money. So we have (almost) proved Result 2'.[17] ◇

19.4.1 EXTENSIONS AND GENERALIZATIONS

So far the agent's action has had three possible consequences. In general, there may be several more possibilities associated with every action. One can easily extend the model to allow for these; all it adds is notation. If there are n possible outcomes, there will be one base wage and $n - 1$ bonuses in an optimal scheme. The main conclusions—about the need for a bonus and the conditions under which the bonus should increase with profit level—will remain unchanged.

A second generalization would be to allow for any number of actions by the agent. Again for any action other than the one the agent most prefers, the principal will have to pay appropriate bonuses. It is not always true that the principal will want the agent to take the action that involves the most effort because that might require very sizable bonuses. He might settle for an intermediate action that has less expected profit but also a lower expected wage bill. Monotonicity in the bonuses—when such an intermediate action is being implemented—requires one more condition, in addition to increasing likelihood ratios.

We also assumed that the principal is risk neutral and the agent is risk averse. In general for the results to go through all one needs is for the principal to be more risk averse than the agent.

[15] *Check that equation 19.9 ensures that the agent prefers to take action e_H.*

[16] *We have used here the fact that $u(w + \theta) - u(w)$ is approximately equal to $u'(w) \times \theta$ whenever θ is a small number. Also note that, in deriving equation 19.9, we have set $u(0) = 0$, and we can do this without loss of generality.*

[17] *Strictly speaking we have shown that a higher bonus for g is better than an equal-sized bonus. We need to further show that it is also better than a lower bonus; the argument is very similar for that case.*

19.5   CASE STUDY: COMPENSATING PRIMARY CARE PHYSICIANS IN AN HMO

Managed care, through the institution of health maintenance organizations (HMOs), has transformed the health-care landscape in the United States. In an economy that has seen health-care costs rise precipitously[18] under more traditional health insurance arrangements, HMOs are viewed as the best hope for cost containment. In this section we will briefly discuss the institution of HMOs and the financial arrangements that they have with doctors on their panels.[19] At their core, these arrangements address moral-hazard problems and are structured in ways that have more than a passing resemblance to our salary-bonus incentive schemes.

Traditionally, doctors and hospitals billed insurance companies (and patients) for services provided. Since the patients paid only a small fraction of the fee, they had little incentive to shop around for the cheapest provider, nor did they have any incentive to buy a less complex procedure if that was available. Not surprisingly doctors and hospitals, who were paid only for procedures performed and hence had every incentive to do so, ended up overmedicating (and in some cases, overbilling) the patients.[20] Insurance companies, though aware of the problem, were unable to address it partly because of its moral-hazard aspect. After all, whether or not a procedure is truly necessary is known only to the physician.

Enter HMOs—the principals in this story. The first thing an HMO does is contract with a list of physicians; the physicians have their income risk reduced by having a regular customer base, and the HMO is able to write incentive schemes to directly address moral hazard issues and contain costs.

An HMO's costs arise from treating sick members, that is, from the fees that it has to pay the physicians (and hospitals) to cure the sick. Costs arise from two sources—first, routine visits (and routine procedures), including lab tests and immunizations, and second, specialty referrals and hospitalizations. Primary care physicians handle routine visits—and we will restrict ourselves to a discussion of their incentives (although parallel arguments apply to specialists and hospitals). The HMO's costs are minimized if members who fall ill are cured at least expense.[21] Meeting this goal means not providing two tests when one will suffice and yet making sure that an illness is treated before it flares up and has to be cured at much greater expense.

The agents—the primary care physicians—are the ones who make the actual calls on treatment and decide how many tests are necessary to make a diagnosis or determine what procedure is necessary to cure an illness. There is an obvious moral hazard in that "necessity of treatment" is unobservable; furthermore, there is always some uncertainty, so that it is not always possible to conclude from the fact that the patient got well that the doctor's procedure was unnecessary. (Conversely, the patient taking a turn for the worse does not necessarily imply that the doctor did not perform the necessary procedures.) Finally, the doctor is also concerned about additional factors, such as peer esteem,

[18] *The health-care sector accounts today for 15 percent of the U.S. GNP, a figure that is much higher than the corresponding figures (8 to 12%) for the rest of the industrialized world.*

[19] *For more detailed discussions see* The Managed Care Handbook, *edited by Peter Kongstvedt (Rockville, MD: Aspen, 1989) and* HMO—Rate Setting and Financial Strategy, *by Charles Wrightson (Ann Arbor, MI: Health Administration Press, 1990).*

[20] *Legal considerations—the threat of being sued if procedures were not performed—clearly added to these incentives.*

[21] *Additionally, costs are lowered if few members fall ill. This explains why HMOs—unlike traditional insurance companies—give their members positive incentives to stay healthy.*

malpractice, and the physician-patient relationship, that the HMO is less concerned with; these are the factors that determine her "disutility of effort."

In short we have a principal-agent relationship that looks a lot like our previous model. So what kind of incentive contracts do we see between HMOs and primary care physicians?

The most popular contracts have two elements—*capitation* and *withholds/bonus*. Capitation refers to a fixed (monthly) fee that an HMO pays to a physician for every member. This fee is paid regardless of any treatment during that period and is meant to cover the costs of any office visit and routine procedures such as immunizations. Obviously, a healthy member who never shows up to the doctor's offices is the doctor's best friend, and the worst is a very sick patient who requires many visitations. In summary, the capitation is much like a salary, or base wage, for the physician in that it is independent of performance indices.[22]

The withholds/bonus works as follows. For every member in a physician's care, the HMO sets aside a sum of money—withholds—for specialist expenses (specialist capitation fund) and hospital expenses (hospital capitation fund). The expenses incurred on specialists or hospitals on account of referrals from the primary care physician[23] are charged to the respective funds. If the total expenses are in excess of the withholds in the two funds, the primary care physician has the overflow subtracted from his capitation payment. Conversely, if the expenses are less than the withholds, the doctor gets a bonus based on the difference. The withholds discourage primary care physicians from making too many referrals and yet encourage them to treat an illness before it blows up and requires hospitalization and specialist attention. And this part of the incentive scheme looks a lot like a bonus!

SUMMARY

1. A principal-agent problem arises when one economic agent—the agent—takes an action that affects another economic agent—the principal. The problem involves moral hazard when the principal is not able to stipulate the agent's action.

2. Moral-hazard problems originally arose in insurance contexts, but they are actually quite pervasive.

3. To combat moral hazard, a principal can offer a variety of incentive schemes—wage-based, franchise-based, and wage-plus-bonus schemes.

4. Typically the principal will need to offer a bonus to get the agent to take any action other than the one that gives the latter least disutility. This statement also implies that a principal is strictly worse off with moral hazard (than without it).

[22] *The only way that capitation is different from a salary is that it is payment per member—and hence varies with the number of members who sign up with the physician. Some HMOs actually pay base salaries that are independent of the number of members in the physician's practice.*

[23] *Each member of an HMO has to have a referral from his primary care physician before he can see a specialist or be admitted to a hospital. This so-called gatekeeper role of a doctor allows the HMO to monitor the expenses associated with that doctor's patients.*

5. The size of the bonus will increase with the profit level provided a condition called monotone likelihood ratio is satisfied.

6. HMOs offer a capitation-withholds scheme to primary care physicians on their contracted list that looks a lot like a wage-bonus scheme.

EXERCISES

SECTION 19.1

19.1
Give two examples from the real world of moral-hazard problems (other than the examples given in the text). Clearly identify the principal, the agent, and the actions available to each player.

19.2
Consider the firm and salesperson problem. Lay out in detail the options available to each party as well as their likely objectives. Identify explicitly the source of moral hazard.

19.3
It has been argued that monitoring can solve the moral hazard problem. Discuss this statement. Be sure to give examples of moral-hazard contexts where monitoring is used.

19.4
Can you cite any moral hazard situation that you have been personally involved in either as a principal or as an agent? Explain.

SECTION 19.2

19.5
Draw the game tree for the special assumptions (SA) case. Be sure to fill in the exact payoffs at the terminal nodes.

Consider the SA case with the following modification: when the effort level e_L is taken, the probability of the three outcomes is respectively, 0.1, p, and 0.9 $-p$.

19.6
Suppose the principal offers a pure wage scheme. Discuss the agent's incentives. What are the principal's expected payoffs from such a scheme?

19.7

Suppose instead that the principal offers a pure franchise scheme with fee f. For what values of the fee (and probability p) would the agent take action e_H?

19.8

What is the principal's highest expected payoff from a franchise scheme? (Your answer will depend on the probability p.)

19.9

Consider finally an intermediate wage-plus-bonus scheme. Give a condition on the two bonuses that would induce the agent to take action e_H. Interpret the condition.

SECTION 19.3

19.10

(Calculus problem) What is the principal's highest expected payoff from a wage-plus-bonus scheme? (Compute your answer for the probability $p = 0.2$.) Is the worker's compensation increasing in the size of profits? Explain.

For the next two questions we are going to continue with the probabilities used in exercises 19.6 through 19.10. However, we will now use general notation (as in the text): utility function u, profit levels g, m, and b, and effort disutilities d_L and d_H.

19.11

Give a condition on the two bonuses that would induce the agent to take action e_H. Interpret the condition.

19.12

(Calculus problem) For $p = 0.2$, give a condition for the least costly compensation scheme—from the principal's point of view—that gets the agent to pick effort level e_H. Does you answer conform to Result 2'? Explain.

Consider a generalization of the model in which there are many possible effort levels. Let the minimum disutility of effort be normalized to zero.

19.13

"A bonus needs to be paid whenever we want the agent to pick an action that has a positive disutility." Prove the statement. (Recall $d_L = 0$.)

19.14

"That is also the only time that a bonus needs to be paid." Prove this statement as well.

SECTION 19.4

(Calculus problem)   In the next few questions we turn to worker monitoring in the presence of moral hazard. Work effort is measured by an index, e, that ranges between 0 and 1: 0 indicates complete idleness, and a value of 1 indicates fully effective work. The worker's utility function takes the form $U(w, e) = \frac{w}{e+1}$ where w is wage. On one hand, if the employee is checked by the supervisor, then the amount of effort, e, is revealed and the employee is paid ew. On the other hand, if the employee is not checked, then she is paid the full wage w. The probability of being checked is p, and this probability is independent of the worker's own behavior.

19.15
Set up the worker's maximization problem and determine the optimal effort level. (Hint: The slope of $\frac{pe+1-p}{e+1}$ is $\frac{2p-1}{(e+1)^2}$.)

19.16
Show that the worker either works the full amount possible ($e = 1$) or not at all ($e = 0$) depending on whether p is greater than or less than $\frac{1}{2}$.

(Calculus problem) Suppose now that an effort level e produces an expected (gross) profit of $\pi(e)$ for the firm. Suppose further that installing a monitoring technology involves a cost of $\theta(p)$; $\theta(.)$ increases in p, and it is costless if there is no monitoring, that is, $\theta(0) = 0$.

19.17
Set up the firm's choice problem. Give a condition under which it is better for the firm to install the technology. Interpret the condition.

19.18
Redo exercise 19.15 for the case in which $U(w, e) = \frac{\sqrt{w}}{e+1}$ and $p = \frac{1}{2}$. (Hint: the slope of $\frac{\sqrt{e}+1}{2(e+1)}$ is $\frac{1-e-2\sqrt{e}}{4\sqrt{e}(e+1)^2}$.)

19.19
Redo exercise 19.17 for the case in which the only two options for the firm are $p = 0$ and $p = \frac{1}{2}$.

19.20
In the previous exercises the firm chooses p prior to the worker choosing e. How would your answers change if instead the firm chose p after the worker decided on her effort level? Explain.

CHAPTER 20

GAMES WITH INCOMPLETE INFORMATION

This is the first in a series of chapters in which we will discuss incomplete information games. In Parts II and III, and again in Chapter 19, we analyzed imperfect information games in which a player is unaware of actions taken by other players, either in the past or contemporaneously. However, a player always knows the answers to such questions as, Who are the other players? What are their strategies? What are their preferences? And so on. *Incomplete information games* include situations where a player is unsure about the answer to some or all of those questions.

In section 20.1 we will discuss several games whose complete information versions were introduced in earlier chapters. In section 20.2 we will analyze one of those examples at length and introduce the concept of *Bayes-Nash equilibrium*. Section 20.3 will generalize the example and also present a structure, first proposed by John Harsanyi, for studying the whole class of incomplete information games. Section 20.4 will discuss dominance-based solution concepts, and section 20.5 will be devoted to a case study of final jeopardy.

20.1 SOME EXAMPLES

Example 1: Prisoners' Dilemma I

Suppose that player 1 has the usual preferences of the Prisoners' Dilemma game: he always prefers to confess regardless of whether player 2 confesses or not. Player 2's preferences are, however, unknown (to player 1); he can be either a *tough* or an *accommodating* player. A *tough* player has the Prisoners' Dilemma preferences, but an *accommodating* player prefers not confessing (to confessing). Hence the game can be represented by two payoff matrices, one for each type of player 2 (Tables 20.1a and 20.1b); player 1 does not know which is the relevant matrix, but player 2 does.

TABLE 20.1

1 \ 2	c	n		1 \ 2	c	n
c	0, 0	7, −2		c	0, −2	7, 0
n	−2, 7	5, 5		n	−2, 5	5, 7

(a) Tough   (b) Accommodating

TABLE 20.2

1 \ 2	c	n		1 \ 2	c	n
c	0, 0	7, −2		c	−2, −2	5, 0
n	−2, 7	5, 5		n	0, 5	7, 7

(a) Tough   (b) Accommodating

You can think of this as a stylized model of trade negotiations between two countries ("confess" = "no concessions" and "not confess" = "make concessions"). One country, say China, prefers never to concede to the other;[1] the second country, say the United States, could be represented by a *tough* negotiator as well—with Prisoners' Dilemma preferences—or she might be a more *accommodating* negotiator who most prefers mutual concessions and least prefers no concessions by either party. Another scenario that the game of Table 20.1 represents is negotiations between a labor union (such as the United Auto Workers, or UAW) and a firm (such as General Motors, or GM); the incompleteness of information may arise from not knowing how long GM can afford to keep its factories closed in the event of a strike.

Example 2: Prisoners' Dilemma II
One variant to the game arises if player 1's preferences themselves depend on whether he plays a tough or an accommodating player 2. For example, suppose that China has Prisoners' Dilemma preferences when confronted with a tough United States but has the opposite—accommodating preferences—if the United States happens to have those preferences as well. This is also the relevant scenario in a union-firm negotiation if an accommodating firm not only prefers to settle but also gives the union a better deal when it settles. Again, the real game is given by one of the matrices presented in Tables 20.2a and 20.2b; player 1 does not know which one it is, although player 2 does.

Example 3: Bertrand (Price) Competition
Recall the Bertrand price competition example. There are two competing firms producing identical goods; the lower priced firm gets the entire market, and if prices are equal the

TABLE 20.3

Firm 1 \ Firm 2	High	Medium	Low	Firm 1 \ Firm 2	High	Medium	Low
High	5, 5	0, 8	0, 6	High	5, 5	6, 3	10, 1
Medium	8, 0	4, 4	0, 6	Medium	3, 6	4, 4	5, 2
Low	6, 0	6, 3	3, 3	Low	1, 10	2, 5	3, 3
(a) Substitutes				(b) Complements			

TABLE 20.4

H \ W	F	O	H \ W	F	O
F	3, 1	0, 0	F	3, 0	0, 1
O	0, 0	1, 3	O	0, 3	1, 0
(a) Loving			(b) Leaving		

firms share the market equally . Finally, collective profits are highest for *high* prices and lowest for *low* prices.

Imagine now that there is a chance that firm 2's good, instead of being a substitute for 1's product, is actually a complement; that is, if firm 2 lowers its price, then firm 1's sales increase as well (at any given price for firm 1's good). Furthermore, suppose that, for any given rival's price, a firm's profit increases in its own price. All this leads to the payoff matrices of Tables 20.3a and 20.3b.

Again, the firm that has incomplete information—in this case firm 1—does not know which is the correct payoff matrix, but the other firm does. Note too that this is another instance where both players' payoffs depend on the incompleteness of information, that is, on whether the goods are substitutes or complements.

Example 4: Battle of the Sexes

Recall the Battle of the Sexes game. Husband (*H*) and wife (*W*) have to decide whether to go to a football game (*F*) or to the opera (*O*). They would rather be together than apart, but the husband prefers that they go to *F* together while his wife prefers they go to *O* together.

Suppose now that the husband is not sure of his wife's preferences. In particular, he does not know if his wife likes to be with him (*loving*) or if she prefers to go to either event by herself (*leaving*). In other words, he is unaware whether her preferences are the standard preferences, given by Table 20.4a, or whether they are given by Table 20.4b.

TABLE 20.5

1 \ 2	c	n		1 \ 2	c	n
c	$-2, 0$	$5, -2$		c	$-2, -2$	$5, 0$
n	$0, 7$	$7, 5$		n	$0, 5$	$7, 7$

(a) Player 1 Accommodating,   (b) Both Accommodating
Player 2 Tough

As a real-world scenario, consider voting in committees (such as a Senate subcommittee); two committee members' votes determine the fate of two rival bills, F and O. The rules require unanimity; if both members vote for a bill, it passes—and player H would really rather have bill F pass. If the votes are split, then neither bill makes it past the committee. The first type of player W prefers that one of the bills pass rather than neither, but the second type prefers that neither passes. In addition, she gets greatest pleasure in a vote split where she votes for H's preferred issue (since it makes her look accommodating).

In each of these examples, the incompleteness has been about player 2's preferences, and there were just two possible preferences in each case. In general, there may be incompleteness about player 1's preferences as well, and there may be many possible preferences. As you might suspect, all that happens is that the number of payoff matrices increases with the types of incompleteness. To give you an idea, let us present a version of example 1 in which either player can be tough or accommodating. The whole game is then described by Tables 20.1a and 20.1b (for *both "tough"* and *"1 tough, 2 accommodating,"* respectively) *plus* Tables 20.5a and 20.5b.

These examples suggest a definition: a **game of incomplete information** is one in which players do not know some relevant characteristics of their opponents, which may include their payoffs, their available options, and even their beliefs.

20.1.1 SOME ANALYSIS OF THE EXAMPLES

As the song goes, let us start at the very beginning (with example 1). Player 1 has Prisoners' Dilemma preferences quite independently of whether player 2 is tough or accommodating; put differently, for player 1, in either case c dominates n. It should not be a surprise then that player 1 will definitely play c. A tough player 2 has a dominant strategy as well—c—while an accommodating player 2 has a dominant strategy n. So the incomplete information game's *dominant strategy solution* is: c for player 1, c for tough player 2, and n for accommodating player 2.[2]

In Example 2 matters are a little more complicated. Player 2's behavior is unchanged: a tough player 2 has c as a dominant strategy, while an accommodating player 2 has n as a dominant strategy. The complication is player 1. She does not know whether she is playing Table 20.2a or 20.2b, that is, whether she is going to confront c or n. If she is relatively confident that it is the former, she would like to play c, but if she thinks it is much more likely that it is the latter, then she would do better with n.

Game of incomplete information

A game in which players lack some relevant information about their opponents.

[2] Be careful to note that the dominance criterion means slightly different things for the two players: for player 1, c dominates n in the sense that no matter whether the payoff matrix is Table 20.1a or 20.1b and no matter what either incarnation of player 2 does, the payoff to c is higher than the payoff to n. For player 2, the criterion is applied more modestly: On one hand, c dominates n for a tough player 2 in that it has a higher payoff no matter what player 1 does within the payoff matrix Table 20.1a. On the other hand, n dominates c for an accommodating player 2 in that it has a higher payoff irrespective of what player 1 does within payoff matrix 20.1b.

Suppose that she thinks there is a 0.9 probability that she is up against a *tough* player 2, that is, there is a 0.9 probability that she will confront c and a 0.1 probability that she will confront n. Playing c would therefore yield an expected payoff of $(0.9 \times 0) + (0.1 \times 5) = 0.5$, and playing n would yield $[0.9 \times (-2)] + (0.1 \times 7) = -1.1$; evidently it is better to play c in this case.

CONCEPT CHECK
LIKELY ACCOMMODATING

Check that if the probability of *tough* is 0.3, then n is a better choice for player 1. Can you show that if ρ denotes the probability that player 1 faces a tough player 2, then n is the preferred option for her if and only if $\rho < \frac{1}{2}$?

Example 3 is even a little more complicated! Let us start with player 2 because he knows whether the goods are substitutes or complements. In the latter case, he will definitely price *high*, since that is a dominant strategy for him. In the former case, he will definitely not price *high*, since that is a dominated strategy. Unlike example 2, however, player 2 does not have a dominant strategy in one of the possible cases, that is, that of substitutes. Consequently, even if player 1 has an assessment of how likely is it that the goods are substitutes, he cannot compute his expected payoffs from that fact alone. He will also have to make a guess about how likely is it that player 2 will play *medium* or *low* in the substitutes case. But in turn that likelihood will depend on player 2's guess about player 1's price choice . . . [3]

Finally, example 4 is the most complicated of the lot. Here player 2—the informed player—does not have a dominant strategy in either incarnation. So the uninformed player has a harder time predicting what player 2 will do, in part because that depends on what player 1 himself does. The next section will discuss this example in gory detail.

20.2   A COMPLETE ANALYSIS OF EXAMPLE 4

20.2.1   BAYES-NASH EQUILIBRIUM
Three assumptions underlie Example 4:

- *Assumption 1:* The wife knows her preferences; that is, she knows whether the "right" game is given by Table 20.4a or 20.4b.

- *Assumption 2:* The husband does not know his wife's real preferences; he attaches a probability ρ to the fact that her true preferences are given by Table 20.4a (and therefore a probability $1 - \rho$ to Table 20.4b).

[3] *Example 3 will reappear in section 20.4 when we illustrate dominance solvability (and also in the Exercises to illustrate the concept of Bayes-Nash equilibrium).*

• *Assumption 3:* The wife knows her husband's estimate of her preferences; that is, she knows the value of ρ.

Of the three assumptions surely the most controversial is the last one. It goes by the name of the *assumption of a common prior*. What this means precisely is that there is a common estimate that both players have about what is known to be unknown. One interpretation is that in the larger population of players—who could be cast in the role of a "wife"—a fraction ρ like to be with their husbands, and this fact is commonly known. The further information that any specific wife has is knowing which part of the population she herself belongs to.

Let us turn to equilibrium analysis. In three papers written in 1967 and 1968,[4] John Harsanyi proposed a generalization of Nash equilibrium that is appropriate for an incomplete information game. *Harsanyi's proposal* was in two parts.

• First, turn the game of *incomplete information* into a game of *imperfect information*.

To do so, reinterpret the game as follows: an artificial player—"nature"—picks from the two possible player preferences—or "types"—the true preference or type of player 2 (and informs the wife but not the husband of this choice). The corresponding extensive form is therefore as displayed in Figure 20.1.[5]

Now all players have the same *ex ante* knowledge, that is, that it is a game of complete information; *ex post*, the husband does not know nature's move although the wife does. In any game of imperfect information, an appropriate equilibrium concept is Nash equilibrium. So,

• Second, use *Nash equilibrium* (of this imperfect information version) as the solution concept.

In incomplete information games, Nash equilibrium is given a special name; it is called a *Bayes-Nash equilibrium*. We will now compute Bayes-Nash equilibria in example 4. Note that a pure strategy for the husband is a choice of F or O; a mixed strategy is the choice of a probability on F (and denote this probability λ). A strategy for the wife is a pair; its first component is the choice that a wife with the first set of preferences—call her a type 1 wife—will make and the second component is a type 2 wife's choice. Hence a pure strategy for the wife is one of the four pairs (F, F), (F, O), (O, F), and (O, O), and a mixed strategy is a pair (μ_1, μ_2), where μ_i is the probability that the type i wife will play F.

Definition. A Bayes-Nash equilibrium of the game is a triple (λ, μ_1, μ_2) in which each player (and each type of player) plays a best response, as follows: (1) The probability μ_i maximizes a type i wife's payoffs if the husband selects F with probability λ. This holds for both $i = 1$ and 2. (2) The probability λ maximizes the husband's expected payoffs if

[4] *The papers have a common title, "Games with Incomplete Information Played by Bayesian Players," and they appeared over three issues in the journal* Management Science, *vol. 14, pp. 159–182, 320–334, and 486–502.*

[5] *Two stories can be told to explain this interpretation. In the first, the player is known, but his preferences are not. For instance, in the trade negotiation example the identity of the United States' chief negotiator may be known (to China) but not her toughness. Hence it is as if nature whispers her type in the ear of the (known) player. A second interpretation is that nature selects from a "population" of potential players; each player's preferences are known, but what is not known is nature's player choice. What is unknown to the Chinese trade representative, for example, is who is going to be chief U.S. negotiator. Also note that the first payoff in any pair is the wife's payoff.*

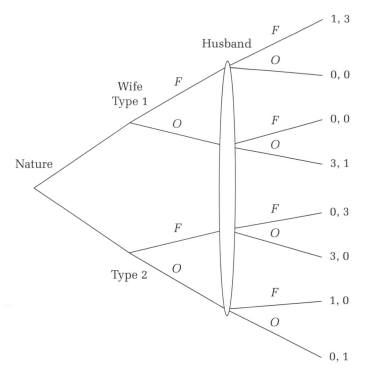

FIGURE 20.1

he believes that with probability ρ he will encounter a type 1 wife who will play F with probability μ_1 (while with probability $1 - \rho$ he will encounter a type 2 wife who will play F with probability μ_2).

20.2.2 PURE-STRATEGY BAYES-NASH EQUILIBRIA

Suppose that the husband plays F for sure, that is, that $\lambda = 1$. In a best response, a type 1 wife must play F, and conversely, a type 2 wife must play O (i.e., $\mu_1 = 1$, $\mu_2 = 0$). The only remaining question is whether or not the husband maximizes his expected payoffs by playing F [against (F, O)]. By playing F, he gets an expected payoff of 3ρ (since he gets 3 by playing against the type 1 wife and 0 against the type 2 wife and the former has probability ρ). By the same logic, by playing O, the husband gets an expected payoff of $1 - \rho$. Evidently, F is a best response if $3\rho \geq 1 - \rho$, or equivalently if $\rho \geq \frac{1}{4}$. Hence, if the likelihood of the wife being of type 1 is at least 25 percent, then it is a Bayes-Nash equilibrium for the husband to play F while the wives play (F, O).

The only other candidate for a pure-strategy equilibrium is the one in which the husband picks O instead. In a best response to this strategy a type 1 wife must also pick O, while a type 2 wife must pick F.

CONCEPT CHECK
BEST RESPONSE FOR HUSBAND

Show that O is a best response for the husband against (O, F) if $3(1 - \rho) \leq \rho$, that is, if $\rho \geq \frac{3}{4}$.

To summarize, we have the following proposition:

Proposition 1. There are two pure-strategy Bayes-Nash equilibria whenever $\rho \geq \frac{3}{4}$. In the first, the husband plays F while the wives play (F, O), and in the second, the husband plays O and the wives play (O, F). If $\frac{1}{4} \leq \rho < \frac{3}{4}$, there is only one pure-strategy Bayes-Nash equilibrium, namely, the first. Finally, if $\rho < \frac{1}{4}$, there is no pure-strategy Bayes-Nash equilibrium.

20.2.3 MIXED-STRATEGY BAYES-NASH EQUILIBRIA

The proposition leaves us with the following two (related) questions. First, what are the mixed-strategy Bayes-Nash equilibria of this game? Second, what happens for $\rho < \frac{1}{4}$? To develop some intuition, consider the limit case $\rho = 0$ (this is equivalent to saying that the husband knows for sure that his wife is of type 2, i.e., that we are in the complete information game of Table 20.4b).

In that game there is no pure-strategy Nash equilibrium. Notice that this is essentially the matching pennies game—the husband wants to match and go to the same event, but his wife wants to mismatch and go to different events. Clearly they cannot both be satisfied in their desires. There is, however, a mixed-strategy Nash equilibrium.

CONCEPT CHECK
MIXED EQUILIBRIUM ($\rho = 0$)

Show that if $\lambda = \frac{3}{4}$, then the wife is indifferent between F and O; likewise, when $\mu_2 = \frac{1}{4}$, the husband is indifferent. Hence the (unique) mixed-strategy Nash equilibrium is $\lambda = \frac{3}{4}$, $\mu_2 = \frac{1}{4}$.

One guess, then, about what happens in the incomplete information game with low—but positive—ρ is that the Bayes-Nash equilibrium must also be a mixed-strategy equilibrium. Let us now verify this. Suppose that the husband plays F with probability λ. A type 1 wife's expected payoff from playing F is therefore λ (why?), while that from playing O is $3(1 - \lambda)$. The wife would play a mixed strategy only if she were indifferent between F and O, that is, if $\lambda = 3(1 - \lambda)$ or $\lambda = \frac{3}{4}$.

Note that a type 2 wife gets the same payoffs from playing F as a type 1 wife gets from playing O, and, conversely, she gets the same payoffs from playing O as a type 1 wife gets from playing F. That result proves the following claim:

CONCEPT CHECK
TYPE 2 IS THE OPPOSITE OF TYPE 1

Show that a type 2 wife will also be indifferent between playing F and O at $\lambda = \frac{3}{4}$.

Now consider the husband's best response. If the wives play (μ_1, μ_2), then the husband's expected payoff from playing F is given by

$$3\mu_1\rho + 3\mu_2(1 - \rho) \tag{20.1}$$

With probability ρ, the husband will meet a type 1 wife who plays F with probability μ_1—in which case, the husband's payoff is 3—and plays O with probability $1 - \mu_1$—and then the husband's payoff is 0. Add to this payoff the fact that, with probability $1 - \rho$, the husband will meet a type 2 wife who plays F with probability μ_2—yielding the husband a payoff of 3—and plays O with probability $1 - \mu_2$—yielding the husband a payoff of 0.

By the same logic, the husband's expected payoff from playing O is given by

$$(1 - \mu_1)\rho + (1 - \mu_2)(1 - \rho) \tag{20.2}$$

If the expression in equation 20.1 exceeds the expression in equation 20.2, the husband strictly prefers F to O (and vice versa if equation 20.1 is less than equation 20.2). The husband is indifferent only if the two expressions are equal; in this case, both F and O are best responses and any mixture between them—in particular, $\lambda = \frac{3}{4}$—is a best response. After collecting terms, the two expected payoffs are seen to be equal if

$$\rho(4\mu_1 - 1) = (1 - \rho)(1 - 4\mu_2) \tag{20.3}$$

Provided the mixed strategies (μ_1, μ_2) satisfy equation 20.3, the husband has a mixed-strategy best response—and in particular a best response $\lambda = \frac{3}{4}$. When the husband plays $\lambda = \frac{3}{4}$, in turn, any mixed strategy pair (μ_1, μ_2) is a best response for the wives—in particular, the (μ_1, μ_2) given by equation 20.3. Summarizing all this, we have proved the following proposition:

Proposition 2. Regardless of the value of ρ, there is always a mixed-strategy Bayes-Nash equilibrium; in particular, $\lambda = \frac{3}{4}, \mu_1, \mu_2) = (\frac{1}{4}, \frac{1}{4})$. There may be additional mixed-strategy Bayes-Nash equilibria, and these are characterized by $\lambda = \frac{3}{4}$, and (μ_1, μ_2) that satisfy equation 20.3.

What we learned in this section is that in a Bayes-Nash equilibrium, the informed player chooses a strategy based on her information, and consequently this choice can be different for different types of this player. The uninformed player realizes that different types will play different strategies; that is, he realizes that he is in effect facing a mixed strategy with the probability weights in the mixture given by the odds on the different types. He therefore has to choose the best response to this mixed strategy. An equilibrium occurs when no type of informed player—or the uninformed player—wishes to alter her strategy choice.

20.3   MORE GENERAL CONSIDERATIONS ⚠

The first thing that we will do in this section is generalize example 4 to show you that the Harsanyi approach—reducing incompleteness to imperfection of information—works for sources of incompleteness more general than payoff ignorance. Then we will introduce a very general framework that will accommodate example 4, and every other example, as special cases.

20.3.1   A MODIFIED EXAMPLE

As before, the wife can have preferences of type 1 or 2. Additionally, the husband is one of two types: he is either a "pessimist" (type 1) who thinks that there is only a low probability $\underline{\rho}$ that his wife would like to be with him. Or he is an "optimist" (type 2) who thinks that there is a high probability $\overline{\rho}$ that his wife is of Type 1; $\overline{\rho} > \underline{\rho}$. Finally, and here is the common prior assumption again, husband and wife believe that there is a probability q that the husband is a pessimist.

The analysis proceeds in a manner similar to that of the earlier example. Note first that this incomplete information game can be reduced to the imperfect information game displayed in Figure 20.2.

A strategy for the type i wife is the choice of μ_i, the probability with which she picks F. The "pair" of wives is characterized, as before, by the strategy pair (μ_1, μ_2). By the same logic, the strategy for the husband of type i is λ_i—the probability with which he picks F—and the pair of husbands is characterized by the strategy pair (λ_1, λ_2).

Definition.   A Bayes-Nash equilibrium of the modified example is a quadruple (λ_1, λ_2) and (μ_1, μ_2) such that each type of each player plays a best response: (1) For each type of wife, μ_i maximizes expected payoffs if a type j husband selects F with probability λ_j, $j = 1, 2$, and there is a probability q of encountering a type 1 husband.[6] (2) For each type of husband, the choice λ_j maximizes expected payoffs if a type i wife selects F with probability μ_i, $i = 1, 2$. The type 1 husband believes that with probability $\underline{\rho}$ he will encounter a type 1 wife, while a type 2 husband believes that probability is actually $\overline{\rho}$.

[6] *The probability q_i is defined in section 20.3.2.*

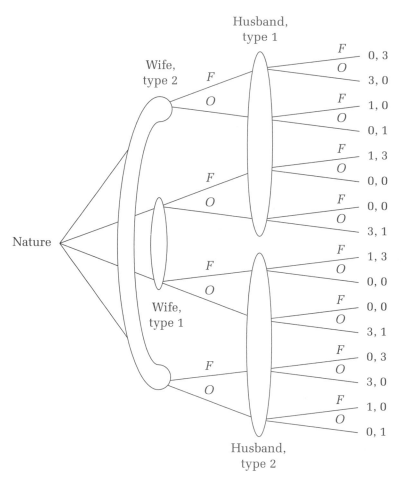

FIGURE 20.2

We will not try to look for all the Bayes-Nash equilibria but will only look for some of the pure-strategy ones. In fact, let us check for equilibria in which both types of husbands play the same strategy, say F. Since a type 1 wife wants to be with her husband, she has a unique best response (and she selects F as well). By the same logic, the type 2 wife selects O.

The question then is, Is it a best response for husbands of either type to play F against (F, O)? In the previous section we have seen that the answer is yes provided $\rho \geq \frac{1}{4}$. (Why?)

This is not the only pure-strategy Bayes-Nash equilibrium of this game. It can be easily shown that there is another.

CONCEPT CHECK
ANOTHER EQUILIBRIUM

Show that if $\underline{\rho} \geq \frac{3}{4}$, then a pure-strategy Bayes-Nash equilibrium, regardless of the value of q, is for the husbands to play O while the wives play (O, F).

20.3.2 A GENERAL FRAMEWORK

The general framework that Harsanyi proposed for studying games of incomplete information follows up on the ideas of the previous examples. Take a game with, say, two players. Suppose that player 1 does not have some relevant information about player 2, such as player 2's preferences. Let the possible values of this unknown variable be denoted $\theta_1, \theta_2, \ldots, \theta_L$. (In each of the examples, there have been two possible values to this variable.) Player 2 may not, similarly, have some relevant information about player 1, and let the possible values of this unknown variable be denoted $\psi_1, \psi_2, \ldots, \psi_M$.

This game of incomplete information is now reduced to a game of imperfect information by imagining that nature moves first and "chooses" a pair ψ_j, θ_i. Player 2 is made aware of θ_i; then this player picks a strategy to maximize her expected payoffs given what she believes is the distribution over player 1's types. Symmetrically, player 1 is made aware of ψ_j and as type j picks a strategy to maximize his expected payoffs given what he believes is the distribution over player 2's types. If we can find strategies, for every type of each player, that are best responses to each other, then we have a Bayes-Nash equilibrium.

The only thing that remains to specify is what distributions the two players use in computing their expected payoffs. And this is where we make the common prior assumption: before knowing anything else, the players share a common prior estimation of how likely is any pair ψ_j, θ_i. For instance, in examples 1 through 4, the only incompleteness was about player 2's information, and that information could be of two possible types, θ_1 and θ_2. The common prior was that probability of type θ_1 equals ρ.

In the modified Battle of the Sexes example, there is incompleteness about both players' information described by the pairs θ_1, θ_2 (respectively, loving and leaving wives) and ψ_1, ψ_2 (respectively, pessimistic and optimistic husbands). The prior distribution is given by the following table:

$H \setminus W$	Loving (Type 1)	Leaving (Type 2)
Pessimist (Type 1)	$q \times \underline{\rho}$	$q \times (1 - \underline{\rho})$
Optimist (Type 2)	$(1 - q) \times \overline{\rho}$	$(1 - q) \times (1 - \overline{\rho})$

[7] *For a discussion of conditional probability, see section 26.1.1.*

Note that the (common) prior distribution can be used to determine the conditional probability of the other player's types.[7] For example, a *loving* wife assigns a conditional probability $\frac{q\rho}{q\rho+(1-q)\bar{\rho}}$ to the possibility that her husband is a pessimist. Call that conditional probability q_1. Similarly, the conditional probability of drawing a pessimist is $\frac{q(1-\rho)}{q(1-\rho)+(1-q)(1-\bar{\rho})}$ for a *leaving* wife. Call that q_2.

20.4 DOMINANCE-BASED SOLUTION CONCEPTS ⚠

In the previous two sections we discussed a generalization of Nash equilibrium to incomplete information games. In this section we will discuss solution concepts based on the idea of dominance. The general motivation is exactly the same as in complete information games; if there is a dominant strategy, then it is the only rational strategy to play, and if a strategy is dominated, then no rational player should use it. And so on.

The definition of "domination" is a little subtle. In a complete information game a strategy a is dominated by an alternative strategy b if it yields a lower payoff than b for every strategy that a rival player can choose. In an incomplete information game, a player does not know the rival's type. So a strategy a is dominated by b if it yields a lower *expected payoff* than b for every *list* of strategies; a list contains one strategy for every type of the rival, and expectations are computed according to the prior distribution.

Let us start with *dominant strategy solution*. A game has a dominant strategy solution if each player has a dominant strategy. It is easy to see that Prisoners' Dilemma I (Table 20.1) is a game with a dominant strategy solution—the dominant strategies are c for player 1 and (c, n) for player 2. It is a little less easy to see that Prisoners' Dilemma II (Table 20.2) is also a game with a dominant strategy solution provided $\rho > \frac{1}{2}$. Consider player 1; c dominates n if it has a higher expected payoff against every strategy pair for the (informed) player 2. Against (c, n) for example, the expected payoffs of c are

$$0 \times \rho + 5 \times (1 - \rho)$$

while the expected payoffs of n are

$$-2 \times \rho + 7 \times (1 - \rho)$$

The first payoff is higher if $\rho > \frac{1}{2}$. And that is true even if we consider any of the other strategy pairs. Indeed we can show that a dominant strategy solution always exists.

CONCEPT CHECK
EXAMPLE 2

Show that a dominant strategy solution always exists. If $\rho > \frac{1}{2}$, the dominant strategies are c for player 1 and (c, n) for 2. If $\rho < \frac{1}{2}$, player 1's dominant strategy changes to n.

Even if the game does not have a dominant strategy solution, it may be dominance-solvable; that is, there may be an outcome to iterated elimination of dominated strategies (IEDS). As with complete information games, this will involve eliminating strategies that successively become dominated, once players rule out strategic options for themselves and their rivals. To illustrate we will use the Bertrand price competition example, example 3 (with a prior probability $\frac{1}{2}$ that player 2 is type 1). For easy reference we reproduce it:

Type 1

1 \ 2	High	Medium	Low
High	5, 5	0, 8	0, 6
Medium	8, 0	4, 4	0, 6
Low	6, 0	6, 3	3, 3

Type 2

1 \ 2	High	Medium	Low
High	5, 5	6, 3	10, 1
Medium	3, 6	4, 4	5, 2
Low	1, 10	2, 5	3, 3

Firm 2 is the informed firm and so for this player the dominance criterion is the same as in any complete information game. For a type 1 player *high* is dominated by both *medium* and *low* (and those two strategies are noncomparable). For a type 2 player, *high* dominates both *medium* and *low*.

Firm 1 can face either type of player 2 and hence confronts a pair (or list) of possibilities—such as *high, medium*. A price choice such as *high*—against *high, medium*—yields an expected payoff of 5.5. For *high* to be dominated by, say, *low*, it would have to yield a lower expected payoff against every one of the possible pairs of player 2 strategies. It is straightforward to show that *high* neither dominates *low* nor is dominated by it.[8] In fact you should check for yourself that there is no dominated strategy for player 1.

Eliminating the only dominated strategies—*high* for type 1 of player 2 and both *medium* and *low* for type 2—we have the following part of the payoff matrices remaining:

Type 1

Firm 1 \ Firm 2	Medium	Low
High	0, 8	0, 6
Medium	4, 4	0, 6
Low	6, 3	3, 3

Type 2

Firm 1 \ Firm 2	High
High	5, 5
Medium	3, 6
Low	1, 10

[8] *Against* high, medium, *a choice of* low *only yields an expected payoff of 4. However, against* medium, medium, *a choice of* high *yields an expected payoff of 3, whereas* low *yields 4.*

Now we can ask, Can there be a second round of elimination of strategies? The answer is yes.

CONCEPT CHECK
DOMINATION ROUND II

Show that for player 1 the strategy *medium* is now dominated by *low*.

Eliminating *medium* we have the following payoff matrices:

Type 1

Firm 1 \ Firm 2	*Medium*	*Low*
High	0, 8	0, 6
Low	6, 3	3, 3

Type 2

Firm 1 \ Firm 2	*High*
High	5, 5
Low	1, 10

CONCEPT CHECK
DOMINATION ROUND III

Show that *low* is now a dominated strategy for type 1 player 2.

Eliminating that strategy we have

Type 1

Firm 1 \ Firm 2	*Medium*
High	0, 8
Low	6, 3

Type 2

Firm 1 \ Firm 2	*High*
High	5, 5
Low	1, 10

Against *medium*, *high* player 1 gets an expected payoff of 2.5 by playing *high* and 3.5 by playing *low*. Hence *high* is eliminated; the outcome to IEDS in this incomplete information game is *low* for player 1 and *medium*, *high* for player 2.

The procedure can be generalized in a natural way to games with more than two players and more than two types for each player. At each stage we check for dominated strategies for every player, and we do so by considering lists of strategies for all rival players. Every list has to contain a strategy choice for each type of that player.

20.5   CASE STUDY: FINAL JEOPARDY

Suppose that you are a contestant on the popular quiz show "Jeopardy!" The last segment of the half-hour contest is called Final Jeopardy and consists of just one question. Before you know what the question is, but after you know the category that the question comes from, you have to make a wager (and you are allowed to bet any amount up to your winnings till that point). If subsequently you answer the final question correctly, your wager gets added to your winnings but otherwise it is subtracted from that total. The other two contestants also make wagers, and their final totals are computed in an identical fashion. The contestant with the maximum amount at the very end takes home her winnings while the other two get (essentially) nothing.

The question is, how much should you wager? Suppose the category is "American Civil War." Presumably your wager will depend on your knowledge of this category. Let us denote the probability that you will correctly answer a question in this category θ.[9] It is likely that the more confident you are in your knowledge, that is, the higher is θ, the more you should bet. The difficult part is deciding how much is enough to beat out your rivals? That clearly depends on how much they wager. That is, what is their strategy? It also depends on how knowledgable you think they are (after all, like you, they will bet more if they are more knowledgable, and they are also more likely to add to their total in that case). The right wager may also depend on how much money you have already won—and how much they have.

For instance, suppose you currently have $10,000 and they have $7,500 each. Then a medium-sized wager of $5,001—and a correct answer—guarantees you victory. But that wager also guarantees you a loss—if you answer incorrectly—against an opponent who only wagers small, say, $2,500. You could have bet nothing and guaranteed victory against the $2,500 opponent (since the rules of "Jeopardy!" allow all contestants to keep their winnings in the event of a tie). On the other hand, the zero bet might be too little against an opponent who bets everything—and answers correctly. And then there is a third possibility for you—betting everything.

Note that this is a game of incomplete information. Each player is knowledgable about certain categories, and only he know what these categories are. After the category is announced, a player knows the likelihood that he will answer correctly; that is, he knows his type. At the same time, he does not know the others' types. (And, of course, he does not know their strategies.)

To help you see the benefits and costs of different-sized wagers we provide an illustrative table. In each cell is a list of the circumstances under which you will win with those bets and (in parentheses) how much you will take home if you do win. Note that we continue to assume that you currently have $10,000 and the others have $7,500 each.[10]

[9] *This probability θ could be an objective probability. For example, after answering hundreds of practice questions in this category you know exactly the likelihood of being correct on the American Civil War. Or it can be a subjective probability; that is, it can simply be a "gut reaction" that you have about your chances of answering correctly.*

[10] *Recall the rule that in case of a tie each player gets to keep his winnings.*

1's Wager \ 2's Wager	Small (= 2,500)	Large (= 7,500)
Small (= 0)	Always (10,000)	Opponents incorrect (10,000)
Medium (= 5,001)	You correct (15,001)	You correct (15,001); everybody incorrect (4,999)
Large (= 10,000)	You correct (20,000)	You correct (20,000)

Note that which of your wagers is best seems to depend on θ, your opponents' strategies, their θs, and so on; for instance, against small bettors, 10,000 definitely does better than 5,001. Similarly 5,001 does worse than 0 against a small bettor if the likelihood θ that you will be correct is low. Against large bettors, whether or not 5,001 does better than 0 depends on the others' θ; the more likely it is that at least one of them will answer correctly, the less attractive is a bet of 0. And if 0 is better against a small-bettor opponent but worse against a large-bettor opponent, then there is the further question, What strategies are the opponents going to play? And then there are the additional complications if the wealth levels are 10,000 and 5,000—or 10,000 and 15,000 . . . !

Despite this seeming complexity, the winning strategy is surprisingly simple if a player believes that he has at least a 50 percent chance of answering correctly, that is, $\theta \geq 0.5$ (and if he is interested in maximizing his expected winnings):

Proposition 3. Suppose that $\theta \geq 0.5$ and that the objective is to maximize expected winnings. Then the dominant strategy in Final Jeopardy is to bet everything.

Sketch of a Proof[11]

Suppose that you do in fact bet everything. Then your expected winning is

$$20,000 \times \theta \times P(20,000)$$

where $P(20,000)$ is the probability that 20,000 is enough to win; that is, it is the maximum among all three totals. This probability will typically depend on the others' wagers, their likelihood of answering correctly, and the three wealth levels heading into Final Jeopardy.[12]

Suppose instead that you bet an amount equal to b. Then your expected winning is

$$[(10,000 + b) \times \theta \times P(10,000 + b)] + [(10,000 - b) \times (1 - \theta) \times P(10,000 - b)] \quad \textbf{(20.4)}$$

A moment's reflection produces the following observation:

CONCEPT CHECK
MORE IS MORE LIKELY THE MAXIMUM

Show that $P(20,000)$ is bigger than $P(10,000 + b)$ and $P(10,000 - b)$ (no matter what the others' strategies, types, and wealth levels).

In that case, equation 20.4 says that the expected winning from betting b is smaller than

$$[(10,000 + b) \times \theta + (10,000 - b) \times (1 - \theta)] \times P(20,000)$$

[11] For a more complete description, see my paper "Final Jeopardy," 1998, mimeo, Columbia University.

[12] For example, if the other two wealth levels are 7,500 each, then $P(20,000) = 1$. (Why?) But if they are 12,500 each—and the other players' wagers are 10,000—then 20,000 is enough only if both your opponents answer incorrectly. Or if one of them wagers 10,000 and the other wagers 5,000, then 20,000 suffices if the high bettor answers incorrectly.

and that is equal to

$$[10,000 + (2\theta - 1)b] \times P(20,000)$$

Since $\theta \geq 0.5$, the last expression is clearly maximized at $b = 10,000$; that is, the best option is to bet everything![13]   ◇

SUMMARY

1.   A game of incomplete information is one in which players do not know some relevant characteristics of their opponents. This may include the others' payoffs, their available options, and even their beliefs.

2.   A way to represent such a situation is to imagine that a player can be one of several types, and each type has a different payoff function. Furthermore, every player knows his own type but not that of the others. All players share a common probability distribution, called a prior, over the possible types.

3.   A Bayes-Nash equilibrium is one in which each type of player plays a best response against a type-dependent strategy vector of his opponent.

4.   For a given prior, a strategy s dominates another strategy s' if the former yields a higher expected payoff than the latter against all possible type-dependent strategy vectors of the opponents. A dominant strategy solution and dominance solvability are defined in the same way as in complete information games.

5.   In Final Jeopardy a player has a dominant strategy if he thinks that his likelihood of answering a question correctly is at least 50 percent.

[13] *In the discussion above we kept things simple by ignoring a "Jeopardy!" rule: the player who wins not only gets to keep his winning total, but also gets to come back the next day. Hence a player should not only maximize current expected winnings but also future expected winnings. For a full treatment, see the paper cited in footnote 11.*

EXERCISES

SECTION 20.1

20.1
Give an example of a real-world problem in which the players do not know each other's payoffs.

20.2

Give yet another example of a real-world problem in which the players do not know something else about each other—something other than payoffs.

20.3

Show that, regardless of the value of ρ, the likelihood of a tough player 2, there is only one best response for each player in example 1.

20.4

In the modification of example 1 that is presented at the end of the section, does either player have a dominant strategy? Do both players have dominant strategies? Explain your answer.

We now turn to a variant of example 2. In this variant, only a tough player 2 has a dominant strategy:

1 \ 2	c	n
c	$0, 0$	$7, -2$
n	$-2, 7$	$5, 5$

1 \ 2	c	n
c	$-2, 0$	$5, -2$
n	$0, 5$	$7, 7$

20.5

Argue that a tough player 2 will always play c but an accommodating player 2 might play either c or n.

20.6

Suppose that player 1 is expected to play c. What is an accommodating player 2's best response?

20.7

For what values of ρ will player 1 want to play c, in response to c by both kinds of player 2? Explain.

20.8

Discuss what might happen for values of ρ other than the ones you computed in exercise 20.7.

SECTION 20.2

Let us analyze Bayes-Nash equilibria in the Bertrand pricing problem. The payoff matrices are given in Tables 20.3a and 20.3b.

20.9
Argue that firm 2 will always price *high* in the complements case but never price *high* in the substitutes case.

20.10
Suppose that firm 2 prices *medium* in the substitutes case. What is the best response of firm 1? (You can make any assumptions that seem fit for the prior probability, but be careful to detail the assumptions explicitly.)

20.11
Find a Bayes-Nash equilibrium in which firm 2 plays *medium* and *high* in the two cases of substitutes and complements.

20.12
Fully characterize all Bayes-Nash equilibria in which firm 2 plays *medium* and *high*.

20.13
Consider instead Bayes-Nash equilibria in which firm 2 plays *low* and *high*. Can you give a complete characterization of all such equilibria?

20.14
Find at least one mixed-strategy Bayes-Nash equilibrium in the Bertrand pricing game.

20.15
Is there a general condition, like equation 20.3, that needs to be satisfied by all mixed-strategy Bayes-Nash equilibria of this game? Explain your answer.

20.16
Give a complete argument to establish the Bayes-Nash equilibria in the Battle of the Sexes game in which the husband plays O.

20.17
Prove that there are no pure strategy Bayes-Nash equilibria if $\rho < \frac{1}{4}$.

20.18
Prove that a type 2 wife gets the same payoffs from playing F as a type 1 wife gets from playing O (and vice versa).

We now turn to the Battle of the Sexes game.

20.19
Verify the following claims for the case $\rho = 0$:

a. If $\lambda = \frac{3}{4}$, then the wife is indifferent between F and O.

b. Likewise, when $\mu_2 = \frac{1}{4}$, the husband is indifferent between F and O .

20.20
For any ρ, verify the following claim:

A type 2 wife will be indifferent between playing F and O at $\lambda = \frac{3}{4}$. So will a type 1 wife.

20.21
Compute the mixed-strategy Nash equilibrium when $\rho = 1$, that is, for the standard Battle of the Sexes game. What relation does this equilibrium have to the mixed-strategy Bayes-Nash equilibrium for all ρ, $\lambda = \frac{3}{4}$, $\mu_1 = \mu_2 = \frac{1}{4}$ that is computed in the text? Can you give an intuition as to why this equilibrium works for all ρ?

SECTION 20.3

We now turn to the modified Battle of the Sexes example.

20.22
Show that if $\underline{\rho} \geq \frac{3}{4}$, then a pure-strategy Bayes-Nash equilibrium, regardless of the value of q, is for the husbands to play O while the wives of type 1 and 2 play, respectively, O and F.

20.23
Show that if $q = \frac{1}{2}$, $\overline{\rho} = \frac{3}{4}$, and $\underline{\rho} = \frac{1}{4}$, then there is a pure-strategy equilibrium in which the two types of husband play F and O, respectively, and conversely the two types of wives play O and F. (Be sure to use the conditional probability priors q_1 and q_2.)

20.24
Are there any other pure-strategy Bayes-Nash equilibria that exist in this game? Explain.

20.25
Take a game in which there are M types of player 1 and L types of player 2. Draw the extensive-form imperfect-information game tree that corresponds to this game.

SECTION 20.4

The next two questions concern the Bertrand pricing game.

20.26
Check that there is no dominated strategy for player 1 in step 1 of the IEDS procedure.

20.27

Show that neither *low* nor *high* is dominated for player 1 in step 2 of the procedure.

Consider the following incomplete information game in which only player 2 knows the correct payoff matrix and $\rho > \frac{1}{2}$:

1 \ 2	c	n
c	0, 0	5, −2
n	−2, 7	7, 5

1 \ 2	c	n
c	−2, 0	5, −2
n	0, 5	7, 7

20.28

Solve the game by the IEDS criterion.

20.29

Provide one modification to the game after which it no longer has an IEDS solution.

SECTION 20.5

20.30

Argue in detail why Final Jeopardy is a game of incomplete information.

For questions 20.31 and 20.32 use the data in Section 20.5

20.31

Compute $P(15,000)$ if the others bet small. Repeat when the others bet large.

20.32

Show that $P(10,000)$ is smaller than $P(20,000)$ no matter whether the others bet small or large.

20.33

Prove proposition 3 when wealth levels are, respectively, 10,000, 9,000, and 13,000. Be careful to detail your arguments.

CHAPTER 21

AN APPLICATION: INCOMPLETE INFORMATION IN A COURNOT DUOPOLY

In this chapter we return to the Cournot model (of quantity competition) in an oligopolistic market. In Chapter 6 we analyzed the model under a complete information assumption; each firm was assumed to know all payoff-relevant characteristics about its competitor (and itself) including data on production costs, market demand, and so on. In this chapter, we will drop that patently unrealistic assumption and ask, How do production, prices, and profits change if there is incomplete information?

In section 21.1 we will outline the basic Cournot model with one-sided incompleteness and determine the Bayes-Nash equilibrium of that model. In section 21.2, we will see how the outcome differs from the complete information solution, and in section 21.3 we will analyze the types of informed firms that have an incentive to share their information. In section 21.4 we will turn to two-sided incompleteness of information. Finally, section 21.5 will be devoted to generalizations and extensions.

21.1   A MODEL AND ITS EQUILIBRIUM

21.1.1   THE BASIC MODEL

In the Cournot model, two firms compete in the market for a homogeneous product, that is, a market in which consumers have no brand loyalty. The firms are hence faced with a common (inverse) demand curve given, say, by

$P = a - bQ$

where $a > 0$, $b > 0$, $Q = Q_1 + Q_2$ is the aggregate quantity produced by firms 1 and 2, and P is the price. As illustration, we will refer occasionally to a special case:

Special Case (SC). $a = 10$ and $b = 1$; that is, the inverse demand curve is $P = 10 - Q$.

So far everything is as in Chapter 6. Now comes the difference. Suppose that firm 2's costs are unknown to firm 1, although the latter's costs are known to both parties.[1] In fact, suppose that firm 1 has a constant marginal cost function; the cost of producing quantity Q_1 is, say, cQ_1 (where $c > 0$ is the constant marginal cost).

Firm 2 also has constant marginal costs except the actual value of the marginal cost is known only to firm 2's owners (or managers). Specifically, the marginal cost is $c + \epsilon$, where ϵ is a random variable that ranges between, say, $-\Xi$ and Ξ with mean zero (and distribution function F).[2] Hence, on average, firm 2's marginal costs are the same as firm 1's, that is, c, but more technologically adept firm 2s have a marginal cost less than c (and this outcome occurs when $\epsilon < 0$). Conversely, inefficient firm 2s have a marginal cost greater than c (that is, have $\epsilon > 0$). The deviation from the cost norm, ϵ, is known to firm 2 but not to firm 1. The distribution F is known to both firms; that is, there is a common prior.

The question that we are interested in is, How much quantity would each firm produce (in a Bayes-Nash equilibrium)? For firm 1 the answer will be given by a single number Q_1. For firm 2 the answer will be given by a whole list of numbers, $Q_2(\epsilon)$, one number for each possible cost level $c + \epsilon$. The reason that different cost producers will want to produce different amounts is intuitive; after all, if marginal revenue is $15, it will be profitable to produce another unit if marginal costs are $10 but not if they are $20.

In computing a Bayes-Nash equilibrium, each firm first has to conjecture how much the other firm (or every type of the other firm) might produce; these conjectures will give the firm an idea about market price. Second, the firm has to determine how much to produce after weighing the benefits from increasing production—that is, that it will sell more units—against the costs of doing so—that is, that these extra units will sell at a lower price (and will need to be produced at a higher cost). An incomplete-information Bayes-Nash equilibrium will obtain when every type of each firm satisfactorily resolves these two issues.

21.1.2 BAYES-NASH EQUILIBRIUM

Let us start with firm 2, the informed firm. Suppose its costs are $c + \epsilon$ and its conjecture is that firm 1 will produce $\widetilde{Q}_1$; it has to decide how much to produce. The market price will be $a - b(\widetilde{Q}_1 + Q_2)$ and hence revenues will be $[a - b(\widetilde{Q}_1 + Q_2)]Q_2$. Since total costs are $(c + \epsilon)Q_2$, the profit-maximizing quantity can be determined from the following exercise:

$$\underset{Q_2 \geq 0}{\text{Max}} \quad [a - b(\widetilde{Q}_1 + Q_2)]Q_2 - (c + \epsilon)Q_2 \tag{21.1}$$

The maximum-profit quantity can be computed from the first-order condition to the problem:[3]

$$a - c - \epsilon - b\widetilde{Q}_1 = 2bQ_2$$

or the maximum profit quantity is $\frac{a-c-\epsilon-b\widetilde{Q}_1}{2b}$.[4] What we have computed is the *best response* of firm 2 to a quantity choice $\widetilde{Q}_1$ of firm 1. Note that this best response depends

[1] For instance, imagine that firm 1 is a long-established firm and firm 2 is a more recent entrant in the market.

[2] And the marginal cost is always nonnegative, that is, $c - \Xi \geq 0$.

[3] As always, by the first-order condition we refer to the fact that at the profit-maximizing quantity the slope, or derivative, of the profit function must be zero. The derivative is $(a - b\widetilde{Q}_1 - c - \epsilon) - 2bQ_2$. Also note that profit maximization is done subject to the constraint that the quantity chosen be zero or positive. See also Chapter 25.

[4] If $Q_1 > \frac{a-c-\epsilon}{b}$, then the formula yields a negative value for the profit-maximizing quantity; put differently, firm 1's profits are then maximized at quantity 0.

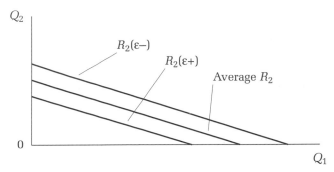

Q_2

$R_2(\varepsilon-)$

$R_2(\varepsilon+)$

Average R_2

0

Q_1

Best-response functions: $\varepsilon- < \varepsilon+$

FIGURE 21.1

on the cost parameter ϵ much as we had thought it would; the higher it is, that is, the higher firm 2's costs are, the less it produces in a best response.

Indeed it is useful to earmark as a baseline the production of the *average* firm 2 type (whose $\epsilon = 0$). A (nonaverage) ϵ type produces $\frac{\epsilon}{2b}$ less than the baseline if $\epsilon > 0$, whereas if it has lower costs than the average, that is, if $\epsilon < 0$, then it produces more than the average.

CONCEPT CHECK
SC CASE

Show that in the SC case, with $c = 1$, if $\widetilde{Q}_1 = 5$, then the baseline is to produce 2 units, but if $\epsilon = -2$, then firm 2 should produce 3 units. What is the best response if $\epsilon = 1$?

The preceding formula gives us the best response of any type of firm 2 for any quantity that it conjectures firm 1 might produce. Denote this best response function $R_2^\epsilon(.)$. We have shown that

$$R_2^\epsilon(Q_1) = \begin{cases} \frac{a-c-\epsilon-bQ_1}{2b}, & \text{if } Q_1 \le \frac{a-c-\epsilon}{b} \\ 0, & \text{if } Q_1 > \frac{a-c-\epsilon}{b} \end{cases} \qquad (21.2)$$

Let us graph the best-response functions (Figure 21.1). Note that as the cost parameter ϵ decreases we move toward the right to find the corresponding best-response function.

Let us now turn to firm 1, the uninformed firm. It realizes that different types of firm 2 will produce different amounts. Hence, it conjectures a type-dependent quantity function $Q_2(\epsilon)$. Since it does not know what firm 2's actual costs are—and hence what quantity level it will produce—the uninformed firm necessarily faces uncertainty in

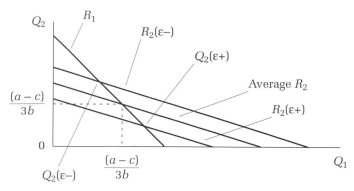

Bayes-Nash equilibrium

FIGURE 21.2

profits. The maximization of this firm's *expected* profit is given by the following exercise:

$$\underset{Q \geq 0}{\text{Max}}\{a - b[Q_1 + EQ_2(\epsilon)]\}Q_1 - cQ_1 \qquad \textbf{(21.3)}$$

where $EQ_2(\epsilon)$ is the expected quantity that firm 2 might produce—and the expectation is taken with respect to the distribution function F over the cost parameter ϵ. Somewhat more compactly, let us refer to this expected quantity as simply Q_2.

CONCEPT CHECK
BEST RESPONSE FOR FIRM 1

By a reasoning similar to the one for firm 2, show that firm 1's best response function is

$$R_1(Q_2) = \begin{cases} \frac{a-c-bQ_2}{2b}, & \text{if } Q_2 \leq \frac{a-c}{b} \\ 0, & \text{if } Q_2 > \frac{a-c}{b} \end{cases} \qquad \textbf{(21.4)}$$

A figure that incorporates the best-response function of firm 1 as well as the family of best-response functions for firm 2 can now be given, in Figure 21.2.[5]

At any Bayes-Nash equilibrium, Q_1^*, $Q_2^*(\epsilon)$, the conjectures coincide with the best responses. In other words, the amount $Q_2^*(\epsilon)$ that firm 1 conjectures an ϵ-type of firm 2 will produce is equal to that types's production, that is, is equal to $R_2^\epsilon(Q_1^*)$; in particular, firm 1's average conjecture, Q_2^*, equals the average firm 2 production $ER_2^\epsilon(Q_1^*)$. Likewise, the amount Q_1^* that the different types conjecture about firm 1's production also turns out to be correct; that is, it is equal to $R_1(Q_2^*)$:

$$ER_2^\epsilon(Q_1^*) = Q_2^*$$
$$R_1(Q_2^*) = Q_1^*$$

[5] *Be a little careful in reading Figure 21.2. On the vertical axis are plotted both the actual quantities that the different types of firm 2 produce in best response and the average firm 2 quantity that firm 1 best responds to.*

Explicit computation now yields the *equilibrium quantities* (actual for firm 1, average for firm 2):

$$Q_1^* = Q_2^* = \frac{a-c}{3b}$$

It then follows from our earlier discussion that the quantity produced by an ϵ type is given by

$$Q_2^*(\epsilon) = \frac{a-c}{3b} - \frac{\epsilon}{2b}$$

Note that in equilibrium the low-cost producers produce more than the high-cost ones.[6]

The distribution of *prices* can be easily computed. Since $P^*(\epsilon) = a - b[Q_1^* + Q_2^*(\epsilon)]$ we can write $P^*(\epsilon) = a - b(Q_1^* + Q_2^*) + \frac{\epsilon}{2}$. The first component can be interpreted as an average price; denote it P^*. Hence the actual price is the average price P^* plus an adjustment equal to $\frac{\epsilon}{2}$. On one hand, whenever firm 2 is a low-cost producer, it produces more than average and hence drives down the price. On the other hand, whenever the actual costs are higher than average—that is, ϵ is bigger than zero—firm 2 produces less than the average and therefore the price increases.

What about *profits*? Again they will depend on firm 2's costs. Intuitively you would expect that firm 1 would prefer an inefficient rival (who would not drive down the price as much). On the other hand, firm 2's profits should be negatively related to its costs. After all, a more efficient firm can always produce the same amount as a less efficient type and generate greater profit. We leave you to formalize these intuitions with a bit of algebra:

CONCEPT CHECK
EQUILIBRIUM PROFITS

Show that the equilibrium profit functions are

$$\pi_1^*(\epsilon) = (P^* + \frac{\epsilon}{2} - c)Q_1^*$$

$$\pi_2^*(\epsilon) = (P^* - c - \frac{\epsilon}{2})(Q_2^* - \frac{\epsilon}{2b})$$

(21.5)

Note that the equilibrium profit for firm 1 is highest when firm 2's costs are highest. Similarly, profits are highest for firm 2s with the least costs, that is, for firms with $\epsilon = -\Xi$, and they decrease all the way to the highest costs, that is, to $\epsilon = \Xi$. Hence a more efficient firm 2 implies lower profits for firm 1 and higher profits for firm 2.

To have a concrete handle available, you should plug the formulas for quantities, price, and profits into the illustrative example:

[6] *From this point on we will reserve the notation Q_1^* and Q_2^* for the (average) quantity level $\frac{a-c}{3b}$.*

CONCEPT CHECK
SC CASE

Show that $Q_1^* = Q_2^* = 3$ and $Q_2^*(\epsilon) = 3 - \frac{\epsilon}{2}$ while $P^*(\epsilon) = 4 + \frac{\epsilon}{2}$. Finally, the equilibrium profit for firm 1 is $9 + \frac{3\epsilon}{2}$ (highest when firm 2's costs are highest), and the profit level for firm 2 is given by $(3 - \frac{\epsilon}{2})^2$.

21.2   THE COMPLETE INFORMATION SOLUTION

In this section we will analyze the complete information Cournot-Nash solution when firm 2's costs are *known* to be $c + \epsilon$. The motivation for studying this issue is the following question: Which type of firm 2 has the most to gain from its cost information being made public? Answering that question will, in turn, allow us to look at ways in which such firms can make their information public.

Let us start with the best-response problem of firm 2 (for any conjectured production level of firm 1). A little thought makes it clear that this is identical to the same problem under incomplete information; that is, it is precisely the maximization of equation 21.1. After all, firm 2 knows exactly what it knew before, its costs, and is trying to achieve the same goal, to maximize profits! Hence, firm 2's best response function is given by equation 21.2.

The difference is that firm 1 now knows the type of firm 2. This fact has two implications. First, firm 1's conjecture will be about one quantity level—rather than a type-dependent quantity function. Second, and consequently, its profits are no longer uncertain. The profit maximization problem is therefore

$$\underset{Q_1 \geq 0}{\text{Max}} \ [a - b(Q_1 + Q_2)]Q_1 - cQ_1$$

Because this problem is qualitatively similar, you should be able to show the following:

CONCEPT CHECK
BEST RESPONSE OF FIRM 1

Show that the best-response function is

$$R_1(Q_2) = \frac{a - c - bQ_2}{2b}$$

The intersection of the two best-response functions[7] gives us the Cournot-Nash equilibrium of this game. This *equilibrium*, denoted $\widehat{Q}_1(\epsilon), \widehat{Q}_2(\epsilon)$, is easily computed to be

$$\widehat{Q}_1(\epsilon) = \frac{a-c}{3b} + \frac{\epsilon}{3b}$$

$$\widehat{Q}_2(\epsilon) = \frac{a-c}{3b} - \frac{2\epsilon}{3b}$$

Note two key *differences* with the incomplete information solution. First, firm 1 takes firm 2's costs into account in deciding how much to produce. It lowers output below the baseline level $\frac{a-c}{3b}$ for an efficient rival and increases output against an inefficient rival. This difference is purely driven by strategic considerations; after all, firm 1's costs are no different than in the previous section, but the mere fact of knowing that a low-cost rival will find it profitable to expand production beyond the baseline level induces firm 1 to cut back its own output (in an attempt to hold up the price).

The second difference is that firm 2 itself adjusts output around the base level $\frac{a-c}{3b}$ more aggressively than in the incomplete information case. More specifically, $\widehat{Q}_2(\epsilon)$ is strictly larger than $Q_2^*(\epsilon)$ if $\epsilon < 0$ and strictly smaller if $\epsilon > 0$. The reason is straightforward: knowing that firm 1 will hold its output, a low-cost firm 2 will find it profitable to push past the point where it would have stopped otherwise. Conversely, a high-cost firm 2 will have to withhold more output below the base level because it knows that firm 1 is going to produce more than $\frac{a-c}{3b}$.

This discussion suggests that all efficient types of firm 2, that is, those with $\epsilon < 0$, would like to have their costs publicly revealed, while inefficient types with $\epsilon > 0$ would like to hide in the crowd of unknowns. Let us confirm that conjecture by looking at equilibrium profits.

Substituting the equilibrium quantities into the demand function yields the equilibrium *price* $P^* + \frac{\epsilon}{3}$ (where P^* is again the price corresponding to the baseline production of $\frac{a-c}{3b}$ by each firm). Consequently, the profits are given by

$$\widehat{\pi}_1(\epsilon) = (P^* + \frac{\epsilon}{3} - c)(Q_1^* + \frac{\epsilon}{3b})$$

$$\widehat{\pi}_2(\epsilon) = (P^* - c - \frac{2\epsilon}{3})(Q_2^* - \frac{2\epsilon}{3b})$$

(21.6)

A comparison of equations 21.5 and 21.6 confirms the conjecture: a low-cost firm 2 benefits from having its costs made public because the consequent price is higher and it produces more in equilibrium. Conversely, a high-cost firm 2 suffers because it sells a smaller quantity at a lower price.

Let us put together these observations for the special case:

[7] Note that the best response of firm 1 is to produce nothing if $Q_2 > \frac{a-c}{b}$. Likewise, the best response of firm 2 is to produce nothing if $Q_1 > \frac{a-c-\epsilon}{b}$.

	Incomplete Information	Complete Information
Q_1	3	$3 + \frac{\epsilon}{3}$
Q_2	$3 - \frac{\epsilon}{2}$	$3 - \frac{2\epsilon}{3}$
P	$4 + \frac{\epsilon}{2}$	$4 + \frac{\epsilon}{3}$
π_1	$(3 + \frac{\epsilon}{2}) \times 3$	$(3 + \frac{\epsilon}{3}) \times (3 + \frac{\epsilon}{3})$
π_2	$(3 - \frac{\epsilon}{2}) \times (3 - \frac{\epsilon}{2})$	$(3 - \frac{2\epsilon}{3}) \times (3 - \frac{2\epsilon}{3})$

CONCEPT CHECK
COMPARISONS

Verify that in the SC case low-cost firm 2s produce more, sell at a higher price, and—consequently—make higher profits in the complete (versus the incomplete) information solution. Verify also that exactly the opposite is true for high-cost firm 2s. What can you say about firm 1?

21.3   REVEALING COSTS TO A RIVAL ⚠

The next question therefore is, Will an efficient firm 2 make the information about its low costs public? This section will treat the simplest case in which a firm is able to reveal its costs to its rival credibly and costlessly if it desires to do so.[8] The punch line of this section is going to be that in fact *every* type of firm 2—and not just the more efficient ones—will find it in its best interests to reveal information about its costs.

The reasoning is as follows: Suppose that only firms with $\epsilon < 0$ revealed their costs. In that case, nonrevelation is also informative; it tells firm 1 that it is definitely facing an inefficient rival with a cost parameter $\epsilon > 0$. Since firm 1 now presumes that its average rival has a cost, say $\bar{\epsilon}(> 0)$, this presumption creates incentives for those rivals who are relatively more efficient than this average—that is, those who have a cost parameter between 0 and $\bar{\epsilon}$—to reveal that information. However, in that case nonrevelation indicates that costs must actually be higher than $\bar{\epsilon}$. And so on.

Let us make all of this precise. Suppose that after learning its costs and before producing, firm 2 can reveal this cost figure to firm 1—or it can choose not to do so. Assume that revelation is credible in the sense that firm 2 cannot lie (and it is costless). After revelation—or lack thereof—the two firms compete on quantities. Hence a strategy for firm 2 is a type-dependent choice of whether or not to reveal and how much to produce thereafter. A strategy for firm 1 is how much to produce depending on what it has learned in the revelation phase (and it learns even if nothing is revealed). We will restrict attention to strategies in which firm 1 concludes from nonrevelation that firm 2's costs must be higher than some level $\tilde{\epsilon}$.[9]

[8] For instance, a firm might include cost figures in its annual report (and be able to get an independent auditor to certify the authenticity of the figures relatively inexpensively).

[9] Some more sophisticated arguments can be used to show that those are the only kind of beliefs that "make sense"; that is, it is not sensible for firm 1 to conclude from nonrevelation that costs must be higher than $\tilde{\epsilon}$ or lower than ϵ' or . . .

The post-revelation-phase solution is the complete-information Cournot-Nash equilibrium if costs have been revealed—or the incomplete-information Bayes-Nash equilibrium if they have not. A full equilibrium of the game is given by an $\tilde{\epsilon}$ such that firm 2s with costs at or below $\tilde{\epsilon}$ will reveal those costs—and prefer the corresponding Cournot-Nash profits to the Bayes-Nash profits of a game with costs presumed to lie between $\tilde{\epsilon}$ and Ξ. At the same time, firm 2s with costs above $\tilde{\epsilon}$ will prefer the Bayes-Nash profits to the Cournot-Nash profits (once they reveal costs).

The result that we will demonstrate is as follows:

Proposition. In equilibrium, $\tilde{\epsilon} = \Xi$. Put differently, every type of firm 2 will reveal its costs.

Sketch of a Proof

Fix any $\tilde{\epsilon} < \Xi$. Consider any firm 2. Equation 21.2 gives us this firm's best-response function (regardless of whether it made its cost information public).[10]

If costs have not been revealed, firm 1 picks a best response to the average quantity it expects will be produced by types between $\tilde{\epsilon}$ and Ξ; denote this average $\overline{\tilde{Q}}_2$. From the discussion in section 21.1 the best response is

$$R_1(\overline{\tilde{Q}}_2) = \frac{a - c - b\overline{\tilde{Q}}_2}{2b}$$

In equilibrium, the average quantity produced in best response by firm 2, keeping in mind that the only ones who do not reveal costs are those firms with $\epsilon > \tilde{\epsilon}$, $E\left[R_2^\epsilon(Q_1) \mid \epsilon > \tilde{\epsilon}\right]$, must equal the average quantity conjectured, that is, $\overline{\tilde{Q}}_2$. Writing $\bar{\epsilon}$ for the average parameter between $\tilde{\epsilon}$ and Ξ, and invoking equation 21.2, all this implies Bayes-Nash equilibrium quantities, $\tilde{Q}_1$, $\tilde{Q}_2(\epsilon)$, equal to

$$\tilde{Q}_1 = Q_1^* + \frac{\bar{\epsilon}}{3b}$$

$$\tilde{Q}_2(\epsilon) = Q_2^* - \left(\frac{\bar{\epsilon}}{6b} + \frac{\epsilon}{2b}\right)$$

where, as always, $Q_1^* = Q_2^* = \frac{a-c}{3b}$, the baseline production level. Compare the quantity produced by firm 2 with the complete information quantity $\hat{Q}_2(\epsilon)$. Notice that all types that are more efficient than the average type $\bar{\epsilon}$ produce a smaller amount in this Bayes-Nash equilibrium.[11]

The price in equilibrium is $P^* + \frac{\epsilon}{2} - \frac{\bar{\epsilon}}{6}$ (where P^* is again the price corresponding to the baseline production of $\frac{a-c}{3b}$ by each firm). Again notice that this price is lower than the complete information price if $\epsilon < \bar{\epsilon}$.

The consequent profits are given by

$$\tilde{\pi}_1(\epsilon) = (P^* + \frac{\epsilon}{2} - \frac{\bar{\epsilon}}{6} - c)(Q_1^* + \frac{\bar{\epsilon}}{3b})$$

$$\tilde{\pi}_2(\epsilon) = (P^* - c - \frac{\epsilon}{2} - \frac{\bar{\epsilon}}{6})(Q_2^* - \frac{\bar{\epsilon}}{6b} - \frac{\epsilon}{2b})$$

[10] Again note that whether or not it makes its information public, firm 2 itself has exactly the same information and seeks to achieve the same goal in either case; hence its best-response function is identical after revelation and nonrevelation.

[11] The reasoning is exactly the same as in the previous section. Firm 1 will pretend that it is facing a firm of type $\bar{\epsilon}$ and will choose output accordingly. Those types of firm 2 that are lower cost than this average will therefore have to withhold some of the output that they would have liked to produce.

Verify that for a firm with $\epsilon < \bar{\epsilon}$, quantity and price are lower than in the complete-information Cournot-Nash equilibrium, equation 21.6. Hence it generates lower profits.

Put differently, all of these firms would prefer to reveal their costs in the first stage. In particular, firms that have a cost parameter between $\tilde{\epsilon}$ and $\bar{\epsilon}$ prefer to reveal their costs rather than not reveal (as they are supposed to in this candidate equilibrium). Put still differently, the only possible equilibrium is $\tilde{\epsilon} = \bar{\epsilon} = \Xi$; that is, all types reveal their costs. (Why?)[12] ◇

21.4 TWO-SIDED INCOMPLETENESS OF INFORMATION

So far we have restricted attention to one-sided incompleteness of information in which only firm 2's costs are unknown to its rival. The techniques of analysis extend straightforwardly, however, to the case where neither firm knows its rival's costs (but does, of course, know its own). Suppose then that firm 1's costs are $c + \theta$ where θ is a parameter that is only known to firm 1's owners (or managers). Furthermore, the random variable θ has mean zero.

Each firm makes a conjecture about the type-dependent quantity choice of the other firm. The maximization of expected profits by firm 1 is given by the following problem:

$$\underset{Q_1 \geq 0}{\text{Max}}\{a - b[Q_1 + E_F Q_2(\epsilon)]\}Q_1 - (c+\theta)Q_1$$

That expression yields as a best-response function the following:

$$R_1^\theta(Q_1) = \frac{a - c - \theta - bQ_2}{2b} \tag{21.7}$$

where Q_2 is shorthand for the average quantity $EQ_2(\epsilon)$.[13] Analogous expressions hold for firm 2. Collecting all of the preceding, we can derive the *Bayes-Nash equilibria* to be

$$Q_1^*(\theta) = Q_1^* - \frac{\theta}{2b}$$

$$Q_2^*(\epsilon) = Q_2^* - \frac{\epsilon}{2b}$$

The corresponding *price* can be found to be $P^* + \frac{\theta+\epsilon}{2}$, where P^* is, of course, the price that corresponds to each firm producing the baseline amount $\frac{a-c}{3b}$. Consequently, the *profits* in equilibrium are

[12] *In Chapter 24 we will examine a class of games called signaling games. At that point you should return to this section. You will see that what we have just discussed is a signaling game with a "separating equilibrium" in which each firm truthfully reveals its type.*

[13] *As before, the best response is to produce nothing if $Q_2 > \frac{a-c-\theta}{b}$.*

$$\pi_1^*(\theta, \epsilon) = \left(P^* + \frac{\epsilon - \theta}{2} - c\right)\left(Q_1^* - \frac{\theta}{2b}\right)$$

$$\pi_2^*(\theta, \epsilon) = \left(P^* + \frac{\theta - \epsilon}{2} - c\right)\left(Q_2^* - \frac{\epsilon}{2b}\right)$$

(21.8)

To summarize our conclusions, whenever there is incompleteness of information, the firm that has information acts on its information by adjusting up or down on an average type's behavior (producing more than the average if costs are low and less than the average if costs are high). The firm that does not have information behaves as if it is confronted with the average type of its rival.[14] Consequently, low-cost firms lose out when information is incomplete, but inefficient firms do better by hiding in the crowd.

The expressions in equation 21.8 for profits (and the associated price and quantity) are the most general for this model; the price, quantity, and profits for the complete information model of Chapter 6 follow by setting $\theta = \epsilon = 0$, and the expressions for one-sided incompleteness follow from setting either $\theta = 0$ or $\epsilon = 0$.

21.5 GENERALIZATIONS AND EXTENSIONS

21.5.1 OLIGOPOLY

It is straightforward to allow for more than two firms, that is, to consider an oligopolistic market. If there are N firms producing identical products, the inverse demand function can be written as before as $P = a - bQ$, the only difference being that the aggregate quantity is $Q = Q_1 + Q_2 + \cdots + Q_N$. Suppose that each of these firms has a marginal cost known only to itself. Let us write the ith firm's marginal cost as $c + \epsilon_i$ where ϵ_i is a random variable with mean zero (and the cost parameter is independently drawn for each firm).[15]

Reasoning identical to the two-firm case yields the following:

CONCEPT CHECK

BEST RESPONSE

Show that if firm 1 conjectures that each of the other firms will produce an average amount Q_i, then its profit-maximizing quantity is

$$R_1(Q_i) = \frac{a - c - \epsilon_1 - (N-1)bQ_i}{2b}$$

In a Bayes-Nash equilibrium, the average best response has to be equal to the conjectured average, so it must be the case that $ER_1(Q_i) = Q_i$. (Why?) That equation yields the following:

[14] *This last statement is a special property of the Cournot model. In general games, the uninformed player reacts to the entire list of type-dependent choices of its rival and not just to the average.*

[15] *Put differently, knowing its own cost does not give firm i a sharper prediction about firm j's costs (than not knowing its own cost). This is a reasonable assumption if the sources for cost variability are different for different firms. The case where firm i's costs are related to firm j's costs can be analyzed in a similar way; the formulas will look a little different.*

CONCEPT CHECK
BAYES-NASH EQUILIBRIUM

Show that the average quantity in an oligopolistic market is[16]

$$Q_i^* = \frac{a - c}{(N + 1)b}$$

Total quantity produced in the market, on average, is therefore $\frac{N(a-c)}{(N+1)b}$ and hence the average price is $\frac{a}{N+1} + \frac{Nc}{N+1}$. As the number of firms becomes very large, that is, as N approaches infinity, the average price approaches the (marginal) cost c. In other words, an oligopoly with many firms looks, on average, a lot like a perfectly competitive industry (in which competition drives price down to marginal cost).

We could further work out the complete information solution under oligopoly by following the same reasoning as in a duopoly. Again it is the case that low-cost firms stand to gain from having information about their costs revealed, whereas high-cost firms lose.

21.5.2   DEMAND UNCERTAINTY

So far we have only discussed uncertainty about costs. The other likely source of uncertainty in this market is demand, and a very similar analysis can be carried out for that case.

Suppose that the actual inverse demand function is $P = (a - \theta - \epsilon) - b(Q_1 + Q_2)$, where θ and ϵ are random variables (with, need we say, mean zero). The value of θ is known to firm 1 but not to firm 2 (and vice versa for ϵ).[17] A strategy for firm 1 is a type- (or θ-) dependent quantity choice, $Q_1(\theta)$. Likewise a strategy for firm 2 is a list of choices $Q_2(\epsilon)$, a choice for every ϵ. Each firm maximizes expected profits given a conjecture about the other firm's strategy choice.

Arguments identical to the preceding will yield the following:

CONCEPT CHECK
UNKNOWN DEMAND

Show that the best-response function for firm 1 is

$$R_1^\theta(Q_2) = \frac{a - c - \theta - bQ_2}{2b}$$

and an identical best-response function for firm 2 (and Q_2 is the conjectured average production of firm 2).

[16] *In the preceding analysis, we have restricted ourselves to symmetric Bayes-Nash equilibria.*

[17] *You could imagine that both firms do market research that gives them some idea about demand. If only they were able to pool their survey findings, they would learn the real state of demand.*

Note that this is exactly the same as the reaction function, given by equation 21.7, when there is cost uncertainty. Put differently, from firm 1's point of view, knowing that its costs are θ away from the norm c induces exactly the same behavior as knowing that market demand is θ away from its norm of a. This relationship is intuitive; in either case every extra unit of production changes profits per unit of production by θ; for cost uncertainty, marginal costs change by θ dollars, and for demand uncertainty, marginal revenues change by the same θ dollars. Hence, the equilibrium quantities, and profits are exactly the same as in section 21.4.

SUMMARY

1. In real-world oligopolistic markets there is likely to be a lot of incompleteness of information; a firm is unlikely to know its rivals' costs, aspects of market demand, and so on.

2. In a Cournot duopoly with one-sided incompleteness, the informed firm chooses quantity based on its actual costs, while the uninformed firm chooses it on the basis of its conjecture about the cost of the average informed firm.

3. In a Bayes-Nash equilibrium, profits of firm 2 decrease with the level of its marginal cost—the lower the cost, the higher the equilibrium profit. Profits of firm 1 increase with firm 2's cost.

4. If firm 2's costs were made public, then the resultant Cournot-Nash equilibrium would be more profitable than the Bayes-Nash equilibrium for firm 2s with costs lower than the average—and vice versa for those firms with costs higher than the average.

5. Hence, lower cost firm 2s have an incentive to make that information public. That leads to a result that actually all types of firm 2s make their cost information public.

6. With two-sided incompleteness, the analysis and conclusions are very similar to the one-sided case. Similarly the analysis can be extended to oligopolies, and to demand uncertainty.

EXERCISES

SECTION 21.1

21.1
Give two examples of markets in which firms compete over quantities and two where they compete over prices.

Suppose that market demand in a duopoly is subject to uncertainty so that the actual demand is

$$10 - \epsilon - (Q_1 + Q_2) \tag{21.9}$$

where ϵ is a random variable.

21.2
Give an interpretation of ϵ; that is, discuss possible sources of demand uncertainty. Which ones can lead to one-sided incompleteness of information (with firm 2 aware of the value of ϵ, but not firm 1)? Explain.

Suppose that there is one-sided incompleteness, ϵ is a random variable with mean zero, costs of production are zero, and the firms are Cournot competitors.

21.3
Write down the expected profit function of the uninformed firm (firm 1) as well as the profit functions of the different types of the informed firm (firm 2).

21.4
Formulate and solve the best-response problem for a firm 2 that knows the demand parameter ϵ to be 2.

21.5
In general show that the best response is given by

$$R_2^{\epsilon}(Q_1) = \frac{10 - \epsilon - Q_1}{2}, \text{ if } Q_1 \leq 10 - \epsilon$$

$$= 0, \text{ if } Q_1 > 10 - \epsilon \tag{21.10}$$

21.6
Give an interpretation for why the best-response production level is decreasing in ϵ and in the other firm's (conjectured) quantity.

21.7
Derive the general form of the best-response function for firm 1 if the conjectured average production by firm 2 is Q_2.

21.8
Solve for the Bayes-Nash equilibrium quantities of this model. Determine the distribution of prices and profits in equilibrium. Interpret the effect of ϵ on each of these objects, quantities, prices, and profits.

21.9
Comment on any similarities that you may have uncovered between this analysis of demand uncertainty and the analysis in the text of cost uncertainty. Explain your answer.

SECTION 21.2

Let us turn to complete information; that is, for the next few questions assume that ϵ is known to both firms.

21.10

Formulate the best-response problem for firm 2 when it knows the value of ϵ to be 1. Find the best response.

21.11

Repeat exerise 21.10 for firm 1.

21.12

What is the general form of the best-response function for firm 2 for any value of ϵ? What about firm 1? Explain your answers.

21.13

What is the Cournot-Nash equilibrium of this complete information game? Compute quantities, price, and profits.

21.14

How do the complete-information quantities and profits compare with those in the incomplete-information Bayes-Nash equilibrium? (Compare these objects at a fixed value for ϵ.)

SECTION 21.3

Let us revert to one-sided incompleteness, but now suppose that the informed firm could make its information public to the uninformed firm.

21.15

Based on your answers to the previous exercises, can you tell which types of firm 2 would like to have their information revealed?

21.16

If firm 2 had the option to reveal its information before quantities were chosen, conduct an analysis similar to that in the text to determine what information would be revealed in the equilibrium of this game.

21.17

How does your answer compare with that obtained in the text for the cost uncertainty case? Provide intuition for any differences that you may notice.

SECTION 21.4

Let us now proceed to cost uncertainty. Consider the two-sided incompleteness case in which firm 1's cost parameter is θ and firm 2's is ϵ, and both random variables have mean zero.

21.18

Verify in detail that the best-response function of firm 1 is given by

$$R_1^\theta(Q_1) = \frac{a - c - \theta - bQ_2}{2b} \tag{21.11}$$

where Q_2 is shorthand for the average quantity $EQ_2(\epsilon)$.

21.19

Verify in detail again that the Bayes-Nash equilibrium of this game is

$$Q_1^*(\theta) = Q_1^* - \frac{\theta}{2b}$$

$$Q_2^*(\epsilon) = Q_2^* - \frac{\epsilon}{2b}$$

21.20

Consider instead the complete information version of this problem in which θ and ϵ are known. Find the Cournot-Nash equilibrium. Compute quantities, prices, and profits as functions of the parameters θ and ϵ.

21.21

How does the complete information solution compare with the Bayes-Nash equilibrium? Which firms have higher profits in the former case? Provide an interpretation for your results.

SECTION 21.5

21.22

Show that if firm 1 conjectures that each of the other firms is going to produce an average amount Q_i, then the profit-maximizing quantity that firm 1 should produce is

$$R_1(Q_i) = \frac{a - c - \epsilon_1 - (N - 1)bQ_i}{2b}$$

21.23

Argue in details that in a Bayes-Nash equilibrium, the average best response has to be equal to the conjectured average, so it must be the case that $ER_1(Q_i) = Q_i$.

21.24

Prove consequently that the following is the average quantity in a Bayes-Nash equilibrium

$$Q_i^* = \frac{a - c}{(N + 1)b}$$

CHAPTER 22

MECHANISM DESIGN, THE REVELATION PRINCIPLE, AND SALES TO AN UNKNOWN BUYER

This chapter and the next will study an entirely new topic called *mechanism design* (and its applications). We will informally motivate the topic by providing economic contexts in section 22.1. In section 22.2 we will study an example with a single player with an unknown valuation for the good being sold. Section 22.3 will discuss the general framework of mechanism design and state a fundamental result called the *revelation principle*. Finally, in section 22.4, we will discuss a more extended version of the example studied two sections earlier.

22.1 MECHANISM DESIGN: THE ECONOMIC CONTEXT

So far in this text we have taken the game played to be a given (and simply tried to infer what the players in the given game might do). Mechanism design goes back a step and asks, What would happen if the rules of a game (or "mechanism") are "designed" so as to achieve some desirable objective? In doing the mechanism design, of course, one has to bear in mind that the players who will eventually play the game will act in their self-interest (and find their way to an equilibrium). Yet some games—or mechanisms—may have more desirable equilibria than others; the point of mechanism design is therefore to find the game that has the "best" equilibrium.[1]

What is taken as given in a typical mechanism-design problem is the group of players. What the mechanism designer is free to choose is the game; she can specify what choices are available to the players and what the consequences of their actions are. There are two constraints on the designer. First, there cannot be any coercion; she cannot design a mechanism that the players will refuse to play. Second, she has to have reasonable expectations; she can only expect that players will play an equilibrium within the game that she designs. The designer herself is typically an economic agent whose

[1] *All terms in quotation marks will be defined more precisely later on in this chapter.*

fortunes are tied to the actions of the players; an optimal design is a mechanism whose equilibrium has the best outcome from the designer's point of view.[2]

To make all this more transparent, let us discuss some examples and applications of mechanism design.

Example 1: The Commons Problem

Consider the following two mechanisms or games involving the commons.

- **Game 1:** The government—the mechanism designer in this case—auctions off the rights to the common resource to the highest bidder every year. The bids are made after the government decides how much the winning bidder will be allowed to extract that year.

- **Game 2:** The government auctions off the rights to extract from the common once and for all. The winning bidder is then allowed to extract over time in any manner that he prefers.

The second mechanism is typically called privatization! The first mechanism is akin to restricted privatization, with periodically reviewed limits on the amount of extraction. In a similar fashion you can probably think of some other mechanisms. For example, yet another one is not to control the potential extraction amount but to impose a tax on the actual extraction. Each one of these mechanisms will have a different equilibrium extraction pattern and government revenues, and the optimal one is that combination most preferred by the government.

Example 2: Selling the da Vinci Diaries (Selling to a Single Buyer with Unknown Valuation)

Suppose that Sotheby's Parke-Bernet Galleries has been entrusted with the sale of the diaries of Leonardo da Vinci and its most promising buyer is Bill Gates, the chairman of Microsoft. Sotheby's would like to get the highest price for the diaries, but the problem is that it does not know how much they are worth to Mr. Gates—and therefore how much he is willing to pay to have them. For the purposes of simplicity let us imagine that Gates may either be a real aficionado, or he may be a less passionate fan (who derives a lower level of utility from possessing the diaries).

Here are two different ways that Sotheby's might proceed:

- **Game 1:** Post a really high price that will only be acceptable to an aficionado (and risk losing a less passionate fan in order to make a very profitable sale).

- **Game 2:** Post two prices. A buyer willing to pay the higher price is told that he will get the diaries for sure, while a buyer only willing to pay the lower price is told that there is some chance that the sellers (on whose behalf Sotheby's acts) may withdraw the diaries.

[2] *In a sense, mechanism design is therefore a marriage of the principal-agent framework of Chapter 19 and the concept of Bayes-Nash equilibrium that was discussed in Chapter 20. The mechanism designer is the principal, the players are the agents, and the equilibrium concept is Bayes-Nash.*

There may be yet other mechanisms even better than these two; an optimal mechanism (for Sotheby's and the sellers) is the one for which the expected sale price is the highest.

Example 3: Auctions (Selling to One of Many Buyers with Unknown Valuations)

Suppose instead that Sotheby's puts the da Vinci diaries up for auction, thereby making them available to any bidder (who registers ahead of time with Sotheby's—recall the discussion of Chapter 3) and let us suppose that the diaries will be granted to the highest bidder. Since now there are multiple bidders, it is even more likely that Sotheby's does not know the exact valuation that each of the bidders attaches to the diaries.

What Sotheby's would ideally like to do is identify which of the bidders has the highest valuation and then sell the diaries to him (at the valuation). But therein lies the rub. A bidder with a high valuation has no reason to let Sotheby's know that fact for fear of having to pay a high price. How should Sotheby's conduct the auction so as to extract the highest expected price? Can Sotheby's get the bidder with the highest valuation to acknowledge that fact if it promises not to charge him a price as high as his valuation?

There are many different ways in which Sotheby's can proceed. Here are two:

- **Game 1:** The highest bidder gets the diaries and pays the amount of his bid ("first-price auction").

- **Game 2:** The highest bidder gets the diaries but only has to pay the amount of the next highest bid ("second-price auction")

22.2   A SIMPLE EXAMPLE: SELLING TO A BUYER WITH AN UNKNOWN VALUATION

We will now analyze example 2 in some detail. Suppose that, as an aficionado, Mr. Gates receives utility θ from having the diaries but as a mere fan he only gets utility equal to μ (and $\theta > \mu > 0$). In particular, an aficionado who pays a price p gets a net utility—or surplus—equal to $\theta - p$ from the transaction (while a fan gets a surplus equal to $\mu - p$). Suppose further that while Bill Gates knows whether or not he is an aficionado, Sotheby's does not; it attaches a probability ρ to that possibility.

To answer the question, "How should Sotheby's sell to Bill Gates," we will first step outside the current setup and imagine that Sotheby's somehow finds out what Mr. Gates' real passion is. Then we will revert to the current (incomplete information) setup in which Sotheby's does not know.

22.2.1   KNOWN PASSION

A buyer with valuation θ is willing to pay up to θ for the diaries. Similarly, a mere fan is willing to pay up to μ. Given that information, Sotheby's price policy is clear: it sets two prices, θ and μ. On one hand, if Mr. Gates is known to be an aficionado, then Sotheby's makes a take-it-or-leave-it offer to sell the diaries to him at a price equal to θ. On the other hand, if he is known to be a mere fan, then they make a take-it-or-leave-it offer at price μ. In each case, the buyer is indifferent between taking the offer and rejecting it. (Or Sotheby's could sweeten the deal by making the offer a dollar—or a hundred thousand dollars—below θ and μ, respectively, thereby making Bill Gates strictly prefer the deal to passing up on it.)[3]

Before it is known whether Mr. Gates is an aficionado or not, Sotheby's anticipates an expected sale price equal to $\rho\theta + (1 - \rho)\mu$. A special case that we will return to periodically is this:

Special Numbers Case (SN). $\theta = \$40$ million, $\mu = \$10$ million, and $\rho = \frac{1}{2}$.

Hence the expected sale price—or expected revenue—for Sotheby's is $25 million. (And Bill Gates' expected surplus is zero.) This is the benchmark against which Sotheby's success will be measured in the real model in which Sotheby's does not know the true passion of its buyer.

Let us turn now to that model.

22.2.2 UNKNOWN PASSION

- **Option 1:** *Ask the buyer*—and then charge a price based on the buyer's report; say $p(\theta)$ if the buyer says he is an aficionado and $p(\mu)$ otherwise.

As long as $p(\theta) > p(\mu)$, no buyer will ever own up to being an aficionado. Hence, all transactions will be made at the price $p(\mu)$. However, if $p(\theta) = p(\mu)$, then a buyer will truthfully report his valuation, but again all transactions are made at a flat fee (which applies to buyers of both passions). So this option is equivalent to the following:

- **Option 2:** *Set a flat price p* (that either kind of buyer has to pay).

For either of these two options, the highest flat price that Sotheby's can charge is μ, the mere fan's valuation.[4] At that price, buyers of both passions will buy and the aficionado will retain part of his utility, $(\theta - \mu)$, from possessing the da Vinci diaries. In the SN case, either of these options nets Sotheby's $10 million dollars and the aficionado a surplus of $30 million.

The question is, Can Sotheby's do any better than a flat price offer? Note that the best flat price that attracts both kinds of buyers is equal to μ. If Sotheby's is going to get the aficionado to pay a price higher than μ, it can only do so by making the lower price alternative a little less attractive; one way of doing so is to make the purchase at that price not a sure thing:

[3] For the da Vinci diaries we are talking about a price of $30 million—and so a hundred thousand is mere change!

[4] We are making an implicit assumption that the low-valuation buyer must be offered a price that he will find acceptable. Otherwise, if a fan anticipates a price offer in excess of μ, he will not bother dealing with Sotheby's. This is called the individual-rationality assumption; we will make it explicit and discuss it in detail shortly.

- **Option 3:** *Guarantee purchase at a higher price.* A buyer can guarantee purchase at a higher price of, say, $\frac{\theta}{2}$. At the lower price of μ there is a 50 percent probability that Sotheby's will withdraw the diaries from sale.[5]

Note that an aficionado gets a surplus of $\frac{\theta}{2}$ from picking the guaranteed higher price purchase. If he chooses the uncertain lower price alternative, then there is a 50 percent chance that his surplus will be $\theta - \mu$ but an equal likelihood that it will be 0; hence the expected surplus is $\frac{\theta - \mu}{2}$. The aficionado clearly prefers the guarantee.

CONCEPT CHECK
MERE FAN'S CHOICE

Show that a mere fan gets 0 surplus from the lower price option and $\mu - \frac{\theta}{2}$ from the guaranteed higher price. As long as $\mu < \frac{\theta}{2}$, the mere fan prefers the uncertain alternative.

With probability ρ Sotheby's will sell (to the aficionado) at a price equal to $\frac{\theta}{2}$; with probability $\frac{1-\rho}{2}$ they will sell (to the mere fan) at a price equal to μ; (and with remaining probability $\frac{1-\rho}{2}$ they will not make a sale. Hence their expected sales revenues are $\rho\frac{\theta}{2} + (1 - \rho)\frac{\mu}{2}$, and this is greater than μ (the revenue from the flat fee) provided $\rho \geq \frac{\mu}{\theta - \mu}$.

CONCEPT CHECK
SN CASE

Show that the expected sales revenues are $12.5 million. How does this amount compare with the flat fee?

In turn, the guaranteed fee that we have used as illustration is a special case of a more general class of guaranteed fees:

- **Option 4:** *Guarantee sale at a higher price and offer a probabilistic sale at a lower price.* At a price p a buyer can have the diaries for sure, but at a price q ($< p$) there is a probability $1 - Q$ that Sotheby's will take the diaries off the market.[6]

An aficionado will prefer the sure sale if

$$\theta - p \geq Q(\theta - q)$$

that is, if $\theta \geq \frac{p - Qq}{1 - Q}$. Conversely, a fan will prefer the uncertain lower priced sale if

[5] *This pricing scheme is actually used in practice. In New York City there are telephone reservation systems for cinema tickets that will guarantee you a ticket at a $2 premium over the standard sale price. By not reserving early you run the risk that, by the time you show up at the theater, the film will have sold out. Ticketing agencies for plays, musicals, and concerts also work on this principle.*

[6] *In option 3 we looked at the special case in which $p = \frac{\theta}{2}$, $q = \mu$, and $Q = \frac{1}{2}$.*

$$Q(\mu - q) \geq \mu - p$$

that is, if $\mu \leq \frac{p-Qq}{1-Q}$. Collecting all this together, the aficionado will prefer the sure sale *and* the fan will prefer uncertainty if

$$\theta \geq \frac{p - Qq}{1 - Q} \geq \mu \qquad\qquad (22.1)$$

Equation 22.1 is called the *incentive-compatibility constraint;* it is in each buyer's interests to pick the price intended for him. Note that if Sotheby's sets the price p—that which is intended for the aficionado—too close to his valuation θ, it would simply encourage him to take a chance on the lower priced offer. It will also not do to set the probability $1 - Q$, the uncertainty intended for the mere fan, too low because again the aficionado might then be encouraged to take a chance on the lower price.

There is one more constraint on Sotheby's behavior: there cannot be any coercion; that is, the prices cannot be any higher than the corresponding utilities to the buyers:[7]

$$\theta \geq p, \mu \geq q \qquad\qquad (22.2)$$

The no-coercion constraint is also called the *individual-rationality constraint.* Sotheby's *expected sales revenues* from this mechanism are equal to

$$\rho p + (1 - \rho)Qq \qquad\qquad (22.3)$$

as long as equation 22.1 holds. (Why?) The full problem can now be stated: Find p, q, and Q so as to maximize the expected sales revenues subject to the individual-rationality and the incentive-compatibility constraints.

The incentive-compatibility constraint for the aficionado, $\theta \geq \frac{p-Qq}{1-Q}$ implies that the sure price p must be less than θ. (Why?) Hence the individual-rationality constraint for this buyer will be automatically met. As a consequence, the incentive-compatibility constraint must be met with no room to spare, that is, $\theta = \frac{p-Qq}{1-Q}$. The reason is that if $\theta > \frac{p-Qq}{1-Q}$, Sotheby's can raise the price p, continue to satisfy *all* the constraints, *and* make more money.

An immediate consequence of the preceding argument is that the incentive-compatibility constraint for the mere fan must have room to spare, that is, that $\frac{p-Qq}{1-Q} > \mu$. (Why?) Finally, that conclusion in turn implies that $\mu = q$; again, if $\mu > q$, the price q can be raised without violating the incentive-compatibility constraints (why?) and Sotheby's would make more money.

Collecting all these conclusions together we have,

$$q = \mu \quad \text{and} \quad \theta = \frac{p - Qq}{1 - Q}$$

After substitution that implies

$$p = Q\mu + (1 - Q)\theta$$

This expression implies, by substituting into equation 22.3, that Sotheby's expected revenues are

$$Q\mu + (1 - Q)\rho\theta \qquad (22.4)$$

Since all the constraints are satisfied, what remains is to choose the probability of sale Q to maximize the expected revenues (given by equation 22.4). There are two cases to consider:

- **Case 1:** $\mu < \rho\theta$. *Only sell to the aficionado*
  The optimal choice in this case is $Q = 0$; that is, Sotheby's refuses to sell to the mere fan (and $p = \theta$). So Sotheby's passes up on sales to low-valuation buyers just so as to extract all of the surplus from the aficionado.

- **Case 2:** $\mu > \rho\theta$. *Maximize sales*
  The optimal choice in this case is $Q = 1$, and hence $p = \mu$. So in this case the best Sotheby's can do is in fact to use a flat fee system, sell to both kinds of buyers, and give up part of the aficionado's surplus.

CONCEPT CHECK
SN CASE

Check that the optimal scheme is to restrict participation to the aficionado. What is Sotheby's expected revenue?

There is an alternative way in which this guaranteed sale mechanism can be specified. Paradoxically, this way will look a little bit like the very first option we examined (and rejected as being not sensible!).

- **Option 5:** *Tell me who you are.* Mr. Gates is asked by Sotheby's how strongly he feels about the diaries. If he says θ, he is guaranteed a sale at price p. If he says μ, he can, with probability Q, have the diaries at price q.

Clearly this last option produces exactly the same effect as the previous two options. It gives an aficionado the incentive to own up to being one and convinces a fan that he too should reveal himself truthfully. Since it involves the buyer *revealing* his true passion, this mechanism is called a *direct-revelation mechanism*.[8]

[8] *It is called direct because it involves a buyer reporting his passion directly, rather than having it inferred from something else that he might do.*

22.3   MECHANISM DESIGN AND THE REVELATION PRINCIPLE ⚠

The procedure used in the previous section is more general than the example might suggest, and so is the result. In this section we will outline the general procedure and present a fundamental result called the *revelation principle*.

22.3.1   SINGLE PLAYER

Suppose we have a single player who can be one of two types, θ and μ. As in Chapters 20 and 21, we can think of a player's type as a characteristic that affects his payoff; for the same action, a type θ player will typically get a different payoff than a type μ player. In the da Vinci diaries problem, a type is the maximum amount a buyer is willing to pay. In the Cournot model of Chapter 21, a type is a description of a firm's costs.

Mechanism

A game, or set of rules, that specifies the strategies a player can choose from, and the outcome for every choice.

A **mechanism** is a game (or a set of rules) that specifies the strategies that the player can choose from and the outcome for every choice. Denote a representative strategy, as always, by s, and the outcome by t. What is a given is the payoff function (and that depends on the strategy chosen, the outcome, and the type); denote the payoff of a type θ player, $\pi(s, t, \theta)$ (and similarly for a type μ player). Put differently, the player types θ and μ, as well as the payoff function π, are outside the designer's control, but the specification of available (s,t) pairs is not.

For instance in the guaranteed sale mechanism of option 3, the strategies made available to a buyer are "accept the high-priced sure offer" or "accept the lower priced uncertain offer." If the former strategy is chosen, then the outcome is that the buyer pays $\frac{\theta}{2}$ and gets the diaries. If the latter is chosen, then the outcome is that the buyer has a 50 percent chance of getting the diaries at a price μ and a 50% chance of coming up empty-handed.[9] The payoff is the type-dependent value of the diaries minus the price.

Within any mechanism, consider a possible assignment s^*, t^* for the type θ player and s', t' for the type μ player. This assignment is said to be *incentive compatible* if each type prefers its own assignment to any other strategy (and its consequent outcome), that is, if

$$\pi(s^*, t^*, \theta) \geq \pi(s, t, \theta) \quad \text{for all } s, t \tag{22.5}$$
$$\pi(s', t', \mu) \geq \pi(s, t, \mu) \quad \text{for all } s, t$$

(and, in particular, the θ type prefers s^*, t^* to s', t' while the μ type prefers the reverse). No player can be coerced into playing a mechanism. This constraint is captured by the idea that there is always an outside option, with payoff denoted π_0, and each player type has to be offered an assignment that guarantees that payoff:

[9] *Note that in this mechanism the outcomes are random. Whenever that is the case we will interpret the payoff $\pi(s, t, \theta)$ as an expected payoff.*

$$\pi(s^*, t^*, \theta) \geq \pi_0 \tag{22.6}$$
$$\pi(s', t', \mu) \geq \pi_0$$

These last two inequalities are called *individual-rationality* constraints because no rational player would willingly participate in a mechanism that yields a payoff worse than his outside option.

The *mechanism-design* problem is for the designer—also known as the principal—to find a mechanism and an associated incentive-compatible, individually rational assignment that gives her the highest payoff. The principal's payoff typically depends on the strategy chosen by the player and its outcome.

In general there are many mechanisms available to the principal, and some of them can be quite complex. It turns out, however, that we can restrict attention to a simple class of mechanisms called **direct-revelation mechanisms**. These are mechanisms in which the strategy set of a player is simply a report of his type.

Each type of player is free to lie about his real type. A θ type can claim that he is really really a μ type, and a μ type can always pretend to be a θ type. Suppose, however, that the direct-revelation mechanism is one in which a report of θ leads to an assignment equal to (s^*, t^*) while a report of μ leads to (s', t'). In that case, the incentive-compatibility constraints, equation 22.5, imply that each type will tell the truth. The individual rationality constraints, equation 22.6, imply that each type will agree to play this mechanism. In short, this direct-revelation mechanism [with assignments (s^*, t^*) and (s', t')] will induce truth telling and voluntary participation by the player with unknown type.

Hence we have shown that direct-revelation mechanisms—and truth-inducing assignments—suffice:

> **Direct-revelation mechanism**
> A direct-revelation mechanism is one in which the strategy set of the player is simply a report about his type. Every report leads to an assignment.

Proposition 1 (Revelation Principle I). For any mechanism and an incentive-compatible, individually rational assignment, there is a direct-revelation mechanism in which truth telling is incentive compatible, individually rational, and which produces an identical assignment. Hence a principal can restrict attention to direct-revelation mechanisms and truth-telling assignments within those mechanisms.

22.3.2 MANY PLAYERS

Suppose instead that there are many players. Since the argument is the same whether the number is two or 20, we will only discuss the two-player case. Player 1 can be one of two types, θ or μ, and so can player 2. There is a common prior probability that type θ has a likelihood equal to ρ.

Consider any mechanism with assignment (s_1^*, t_1^*) and (s_1', t_1') for the two types of player 1 and assignment (s_2^*, t_2^*) and (s_2', t_2') for the two types of player 2. Each player derives a payoff from both his assignment and that of the other player. As in the single-player case, the payoff function is integral to a player but not the available strategies and their outcomes.

Let $E\pi_i(s_i^*, t_i^*, \theta)$ denote the expected payoff of player i, $i = 1$ or 2. For instance, when $i = 1$,

$$E\pi_1(s_1^*, t_1^*, \theta) = \rho\pi_1(s_1^*, t_1^*, s_2^*, t_2^*, \theta) + (1 - \rho)\pi_1(s_1^*, t_1^*, s_2', t_2', \theta)$$

since there is a probability ρ that player 1 will be confronted with a type θ player 2, who is expected to play s_2^*, t_2^*, and a probability $1 - \rho$ that he will play a type μ player, who is expected to play s_2', t_2'. In a similar fashion we can define the expected payoff of a μ type of player 1 who plans on playing s_1', t_1' himself; call this $E\pi_1(s_1', t_1', \mu)$. Analogous concepts can be defined also for player 2 of either type. Within the mechanism, a player is free to choose whatever strategies he wants; $E\pi_1(s, t, \mu)$ will denote the expected payoff of a type μ player 1, for instance, who picks some arbitrary strategy s with an associated outcome t.

These assignments form a Bayes-Nash equilibrium if they are best responses for each type of each player, that is, for $i = 1, 2$:

$$E\pi_i(s_i^*, t_i^*, \theta) \geq E\pi_i(s, t, \theta) \text{ for all } s, t \tag{22.7}$$

$$E\pi_i(s_i', t_i', \mu) \geq E\pi_i(s, t, \mu) \text{ for all } s, t$$

Now consider the following direct-revelation mechanism in which each player directly reports his type. If the reports are both θ, then each player gets the star (*) assignment; that is, player i gets (s_i^*, t_i^*). Similarly, if the reports are both μ, then each player gets the prime (') assignment. If player 1 reports θ while player 2 reports μ, then player 1 gets the star assignment (s_1^*, t_1^*) while player 2 gets the prime assignment s_2', t_2', and vice versa if player 2 reports θ while 1 reports μ.

It is not difficult to see that in this direct-revelation mechanism, truth telling is a Bayes-Nash equilibrium. After all, an implication of equation 22.7 is that a type θ player prefers the star assignment to the prime and a μ player prefers the converse. This analysis leads to the following version of the revelation principle for many-player games:

Proposition 2 (Revelation Principle II). For any mechanism and any Bayes-Nash equilibrium of that mechanism, there is a direct-revelation mechanism with truth telling as a Bayes-Nash equilibrium that has an identical assignment. Hence a principal can restrict attention to direct-revelation mechanisms and truth-telling equilibria within those mechanisms.

We are going to illustrate this many-player version of the revelation principle when we turn to auctions in the next chapter.

22.4   A MORE GENERAL EXAMPLE: SELLING VARIABLE AMOUNTS ⚠

We will now analyze a more general version of the example studied in section 22.2. The setting will be more general in that the seller can sell any positive quantity of the good to the potential buyer, and higher production levels are costlier for the seller. Suppose that a quantity Q produces utility equal to $\theta U(Q)$ for the θ type buyer but only $\mu U(Q)$ for the

μ type buyer, $\theta > \mu$. If the θ buyer has to pay $b(Q)$ dollars, his net surplus is $\theta U(Q) - b(Q)$ (and similarly for the μ type).

To keep the exposition simple we will assume that costs of production are $2Q$, $\theta = 2$, and $\mu = 1$; the utility function U is equal to $10Q - Q^2$; and the outside option has zero utility.

22.4.1 KNOWN TYPE

If the seller can uncover the type of the buyer, then she should charge an amount equal to the buyer's utility. For instance, a θ type should be charged $2(10Q - Q^2)$ for quantity Q. The only decision then for the seller is how much to sell. That is solved from the following problem:

$$\underset{Q \geq 0}{\text{Max}} \; 2(10Q - Q^2) - 2Q$$

Setting marginal profit equal to zero implies $18 - 4Q = 0$; in other words, 4.5 units should be sold to the θ type buyer and he should be charged $2[(10 \times 4.5) - 4.5^2]$, that is, $49.50.

Similar arguments apply to the μ type buyer:

CONCEPT CHECK
THE μ TYPE

Show that the type μ buyer should be sold 4 units and charged $24 dollars.

These transactions will be the benchmark against which we will judge the seller's performance when she does not know the buyer's type.

22.4.2 UNKNOWN TYPE

By virtue of the revelation principle we know that we can restrict ourselves to direct-revelation mechanisms in which the buyer is asked to report his type. If he reports himself to be a θ type, he gets a quantity equal to Q and has to pay M dollars, but if he says that he is a μ type, he is asked to pay m dollars for q units of the good. The seller gets to choose the two quantities Q and q and the two payments M and m.[10] The question of interest is, What choice would yield the seller the highest expected profits?

Note first that if the two quantities are the same, that is, if $Q = q$, then the two payments have to be the same as well. Otherwise, both types of buyers will report themselves as the type that has the lower payment. For example, if the quantity 4 units is offered for both reports, then the equal payment must be 24 dollars (given individual-rationality considerations for the μ type buyer). Since the cost of production is 8 dollars, the seller will net a 16-dollar profit from this option. Can she do better?

[10] *In principle we can also allow for random outcomes. Based on his report, the buyer gets a distribution over price-payment pairs. In this problem we can restrict attention to nonrandom outcomes without any loss of generality.*

A second option is to sell only to the aficionado. For example, sell 4.5 units to the θ reporter and nothing to a buyer who says his type is μ, and charge the former $49.50.

CONCEPT CHECK
SELLING ONLY TO THE AFICIONADO

Show that the preceding scheme will induce each type of buyer to report his type truthfully and will net the seller an expected profit of $\rho \times 40.5$ dollars.

Is there a middle option that does even better than the two extremes? To answer the question let us now be a little more precise. The incentive-compatibility constraints are

$$2(10Q - Q^2) - M \geq 2(10q - q^2) - m \tag{22.8}$$
$$(10q - q^2) - m \geq (10Q - Q^2) - M$$

The individual rationality constraints are

$$2(10Q - Q^2) - M \geq 0 \tag{22.9}$$
$$(10q - q^2) - m \geq 0$$

The seller's expected profits are

$$\rho(M - 2Q) + (1 - \rho)(m - 2q)$$

It is clear that the seller would like to make the two payments M and m as high as possible without violating either the incentive-compatibility or the individual-rationality constraint. In turn, we can conclude that in an optimal solution at least one of the two constraints in equation 22.9 has to hold with an equality. Otherwise, the seller can increase both M and m by appropriate equal amounts (thereby leaving the incentive constraints of equation 22.8 unchanged), continue to satisfy the individual rationality constraints, *and* increase revenues. In fact, it is the μ type's utility that must be exactly equal to zero, that is,

$$(10q - q^2) - m = 0$$

This relation holds because the θ type can always report himself to be a μ type and thereby get a utility equal to $2(10q - q^2) - m$, and of course this is greater than $(10q - q^2) - m$. Put differently, the utility to the truthful report, $2(10Q - Q^2) - M$, must be even larger, and hence greater than zero.

It can be shown, however, that the incentive-compatibility constraint must exactly hold for the θ type, that is, that in the profit-maximizing solution

$$2(10Q - Q^2) - M = 2(10q - q^2) - m$$

If this were not the case, that is, if the θ type strictly prefers his assignment to that of the μ type, then the seller could increase his payment M a little bit. The θ type would still prefer his own assignment and would still get a net utility above zero, the μ type would have even greater reason to prefer his own assignment, *and* the seller would have increased her expected revenues.

Substituting these last two conclusions into the seller's expected profits and collecting terms we get

$$\max\nolimits_{Q,q} \; \rho(18Q - 2Q^2) + (1 - 2\rho)(10q - q^2) - (1 - \rho)2q$$

In fact, as you can see from this above expression, the choice of Q can be made independently from the choice of q and vice versa, since there are no terms that involve both the quantities simultaneously.[11] Put differently, we can pick Q by simply maximizing $18Q - 2Q^2$. Amazingly enough, the optimal choice is $Q = 4.5$, exactly the same answer as we obtained in the previous subsection! However, the payment is lower than the $49.50 that was determined in the previous subsection; the aficionado gets a positive surplus from his transaction. (Why?)

Similarly we can pick q by maximizing $(1 - 2\rho)(10q - q^2) - (1 - \rho)2q$. The marginal profit for that expression is equal to zero if $4 - 9\rho - (1 - 2\rho)q = 0$, that is, if $q = \frac{4 - 9\rho}{1 - 2\rho}$. This is the profit-maximizing quantity. For example, if $\rho = \frac{1}{4}$, then $q = 3.5$. Note that this quantity is less than the seller would have chosen to sell had she known the buyers' types. It is possible to show, in fact, that the quantity q is always less than the 4 units the seller would have sold if she could infer the buyer's real passion to be μ. Indeed for $\rho \geq \frac{4}{9}$, $q = 0$; that is, the buyer concentrates on selling only to the aficionado.

Collecting all this together we have the following:

Proposition 3. In the optimal mechanism there are two cases:

- **Case 1** $(\rho \geq \frac{4}{9})$. Sell only to the aficionado, and charge him a price equal to his utility, that is, $49.50.

- **Case 2** $(\rho < \frac{4}{9})$. Sell to both types of buyers. To the μ type she sells an amount $\frac{4 - 9\rho}{1 - 2\rho}$, (less than she would have sold had she known that buyer's type for sure). However, she charges him a payment equal to his utility for that quantity. To the θ type she sells 4.5 units (exactly the same amount that she would have sold him if she knew his type). However, she charges an amount less than his utility.

Remark

The intuition for the result is straightforward. *If* the θ buyer is to be sold 4.5 units, he has to be charged a payment less than $49.50 because that price gives him zero net surplus and he always has the option of buying the quantity meant for the μ type. The only time he can be charged that amount is when nothing is being sold to the μ type. In addition, in order to further discourage the θ buyer from lying, there has to be a cutback in the quantity

[11] *Strictly speaking, this last statement is true subject to one subtle qualification. It must always be true that the μ type prefer his own assignment to that of the θ type. That statement, combined with the fact that the θ type is indifferent between the two assignments, implies that it must always be the case that the quantity Q is at least as large as the quantity q.*

sold to the μ buyer. The smaller is q, the closer is the payment to \$49.50. Finally, it *is* optimal to sell the θ buyer a quantity equal to 4.5 units because the μ player never covets the θ player's quantity and a value of 4.5 units for that latter quantity maximizes the seller's revenues.

SUMMARY

1.   Mechanism design by a principal involves the choice of a game—or mechanism—whose equilibrium has properties desirable to the principal. In designing a mechanism, the principal takes the players and their payoffs as given, but not the available strategies and outcomes.

2.   Although any mechanism can be specified by a principal, she can—without any loss of her payoffs—restrict attention to direct-revelation mechanisms and truth-inducing equilibria of those mechanisms. This result is called the revelation principle.

3.   In selling an object to a buyer with two possible payoff types, a seller will pick one of two options: either set a price that is just acceptable to the low-payoff type (which gives the high-payoff type a positive surplus) or shut out the former by setting a price that is just acceptable to the high-payoff type.

4.   In selling multiple units to a buyer with two possible payoff types, a seller will again pick one of two options: either specify a quantity and payment that is just acceptable to the low-payoff type (which gives the high-payoff type a positive surplus) or shut out the former by selling a quantity (at high payment) that is just acceptable to the high-payoff type.

EXERCISES

SECTION 22.1

22.1
"The single player mechanism design setup can be used when there are many players but they do not interact in any fashion." Explain why this statement is true.

22.2
Give two examples of a mechanism-design problem from the real world in which there is a single player and two in which there are many noninteracting players.

22.3

Consider the NASDAQ market-making problem that was studied in Chapter 16. Argue that the NASDAQ market's governing body, the group that decides the rules according to which investors buy and sell in that market, is really a principal solving a mechanism-design problem. Can you identify the players and their payoffs (including those of the governing body)?

22.4

Describe the current NASDAQ mechanism carefully and suggest one set of rule changes that can make the market even more competitive.

22.5

It has been argued by some people that mechanism design is only relevant for domestic problems and that it is inapplicable for international problems (such as global warming) because there is no well-defined principal for the latter problem. Comment on this position.

SECTION 22.2

22.6

In addition to the options listed in the text, can you think of any other ways by which Sotheby's can sell the da Vinci diaries? Explain.

22.7

How would you describe a mechanism in which Bill Gates makes a take-it-or-leave-it offer to Sotheby's? Are mechanisms like these allowable in the current setup in which Sotheby's comes up with the rules of the game? Explain.

22.8

Show that the incentive-compatibility constraint for the aficionado, $\theta \geq \frac{p-Qq}{1-Q}$, implies that the sure price p must be strictly less than θ (as long as $Q > 0$).

22.9

Show also that the incentive compatibility constraint will consequently be met with no room to spare, that is, that $\theta = \frac{p-Qq}{1-Q}$.

22.10

Can you prove that then the incentive compatibility constraint for the mere fan must have room to spare, that is, that $\frac{p-Qq}{1-Q} > \mu$?

22.11

Finally, prove that $\mu = q$.

22.12

Demonstrate that Sotheby's expected revenues can be rewritten as

$$Q\mu + (1 - Q)\rho\theta$$

Suppose that Sotheby's is interested in not only the expected sales revenue but also the buyer's surplus. However, they are more interested in the revenues than the surplus (and they put twice as much weight on the former).

22.13
Write out Sotheby's payoff function.

22.14
Write out the incentive-compatibility and individual-rationality constraints for the buyer. Argue that exactly the same constraints hold with equality as in the text.

22.15
Characterize the optimal solution for Sotheby's. Is it still the case that there are no probabilistic sales in the optimal mechanism? Explain your answer.

SECTION 22.3

22.16
Formally outline the steps involved in proving the revelation principle for the single-player case.

22.17
When the principal is the government, the individual rationality constraints are irrelevant (since a nation's citizens cannot disobey the laws of the land). Show that this fact would allow a government agency to do even better in its mechanism-design problem than if it also had to worry about individual rationality constraints.

22.18
Consider a single-player problem in which the number of types of the player is L. Formally prove that the revelation principle holds in this case as well.

22.19
Prove the revelation principle for the many-player case when there are N players, although each player can be of two types.

22.20
Repeat exercise 22.19 for the case in which each player can be one of L types.

The next few exercises will explore a mechanism-design problem for a firm—called the principal contractor—that can either build a good in-house or can subcontract to another firm. The costs of production are either θ or μ, $\theta < \mu$. Suppose too that the principal knows that its own costs are μ but does not know the other firm's costs.

22.21

Formulate the mechanism-design problem facing the principal contractor, assume that it seeks to minimize expected costs.

22.22

Identify the optimal direct-revelation mechanism. Can this optimal mechanism be implemented with a simple pricing scheme? Explain.

22.23

Suppose that there is a third possible cost level $\lambda > \mu$. Redo the analysis of the previous two questions taking account of this additional cost level.

SECTION 22.4

(Calculus problem)   The next few questions concern the variable quantity model. Suppose that $U(Q)$ is given by $\sqrt{Q}$. The other data are those given in the text.

22.24

Solve the problem when player types are known to the mechanism designer.

22.25

Rewrite the incentive-compatibility and individual-rationality constraints for the case in which player types are unknown.

22.26

Argue that even with this utility function it is the θ type's incentive-compatibility constraint and the μ type's individual-rationality constraint that will be met with equality.

22.27

Can you make a general argument for that last conclusion? What conditions would need to be satisfied by the utility function? Explain your answer.

22.28

Solve the mechanism-design problem for the given utility function.

CHAPTER **23**

AN APPLICATION: AUCTIONS

This chapter will discuss a market mechanism that is used to sell all manner of goods, the mechanism of auctions. In section 23.1 we will discuss the kinds of goods sold by auction and the rules of the most commonly used auctions. Sections 23.2 and 23.3 will contain analyses of two of these auctions, second- and first-price auctions. In section 23.4 we will apply the revelation principle to characterize the optimal—or revenue-maximizing— auction and compare the performance of the second- and first-price auctions against this yardstick. Section 23.5 will conclude.

23.1 BACKGROUND AND EXAMPLES

Auctions are used to sell all kinds of things. If you are interested in buying a Rembrandt drawing, you could bid for one at an auction run by Sotheby's Parke-Bernet Galleries or Christie's. Or you could bid for a used Chevrolet Caprice at a General Services Administration (GSA) auction of government equipment. If you are buying a house in a new development, you could bid for it at the developer's auction. Or again, you could bid for the rights to be one of two providers of wireless service in New York City at an auction run by the Federal Communication Commission (FCC). If you are interested in a round-trip plane ticket between Baltimore and Paris you could bid for it online at the web site of Travel.Com.[1] Or maybe you want to have the exclusive rights to develop oil in Kazakhstan. If you are lucky enough to be a majority owner of a major league ball club, you could bid for a free-agent player at an auction run by the player's agent. And, if you are in charge of the Treasuries desk for Salomon Brothers, you could bid for federal government bonds at U.S. Treasury auctions.

A typical auction is characterized by one seller and a number of potential buyers. Often the seller is unsure about how much each buyer is willing to pay to have each

[1] *Indeed you can bid for an astonishing variety of things online. A simple search of the topic "Auctions Online" brought up over 200,000 entries. Included were auctions for sports cards (Allen Iverson GoldTop anyone?), automobiles (how about a 1927 Bentley with gold fixtures?), computer equipment, travel packages, stereo equipment, coins, stamps, land for development, vacation homes, . . .*

good. Indeed if he had that information, he would not need to auction the merchandise; instead he could simply negotiate to sell each item to the buyer with the highest valuation. The seller might be selling just one unit of a good, such as a one-of-a-kind Rembrandt drawing or exclusive oil development rights or a free-agent player; or he might be selling multiple units, such as a fleet of government cars or wireless rights to various cities in the United States or a number of round-trip tickets; or maybe he is selling a number of different goods all at once, such as government cars and office equipment or Rembrandt and Dürer drawings.

There are many different kinds of auctions. In virtually every auction the highest bidder gets the good. What varies between different types of auctions is two things: first, how the highest bidder is determined and, second, how much the highest bidder has to pay.

A common auction is the *ascending-bid auction*: it starts at some low bid, each bidder can raise the bid at any time,[2] and bidding continues till such time as there is exactly one bidder left. The increments by which the bids are raised are typically small percentages of the bids.[3] Art auctions at Sotheby's, real estate auctions, the FCC auction, the free-agent auction, and the Travel.Com auctions are all run as ascending-bid auctions. Ascending-bid auctions are also called *English auctions.*

A second kind of auction, called a *descending-bid auction,* starts at a high price, and the auctioneer keeps lowering the price till the point at which somebody is willing to buy the good. This mechanism is used to sell flowers in the world's largest wholesale flower market in Amsterdam. Accordingly, such auctions are also called *Dutch auctions.*[4]

In these two kinds of auctions there are multiple chances for each player to bid. An alternative is an auction in which the seller solicits a (single) sealed bid from each potential buyer. The highest bidder is given the object, but the amount that he has to pay can vary. In a *first-price auction* he has to pay his bid, but in a *second-price auction* he only has to pay the amount bid by the next highest bidder. The GSA auction, the Treasury auction, and the oil rights auction are examples of sealed-bid first-price auctions.

There is a certain similarity between ascending-bid and sealed-bid second-price auctions. In the former, bidding stops when there is exactly one bidder left. Imagine that bidding at that point has reached $100, and that the previous bid—at which there was at least one more bidder around—was $99. Then, the winner pays $100, and the last bidder to drop out bid $99 (and was not willing to bid $100). In an analogous bidding situation in a sealed-bid second-price auction the price that the winner would pay would be exactly the second-highest bid, that is, $99. In other words, when the increments in an ascending-bid auction are small, the winner pays an amount very close to the second-highest bid.

Similarly, there is a close relationship between descending-bid and first-price auctions. Suppose that $100 is the price at which there is a first bidder in a descending-bid auction. She pays $100, and there is no other bidder willing to bid that amount (for example, the next bidder might only have come in at $90). If this were a sealed-bid first-price auction, the results would have been identical; the good would have gone to the

[2] Or there is an auctioneer who raises the bid and ascertains that there are in fact bidders who are willing to go with the higher bid.

[3] The increments are sometimes specified in percentages; for instance, a bidder has to raise a bid by 5 percent or more. At other times, the bidder or auctioneer is left the discretion to choose increments of any size.

[4] An alternative theory is that the name is a pejorative (for this "kookier" auction)—in much the same way that the English language has unflattering phrases such as Dutch courage and Dutch treat (for drink-induced bravado and a supposed treat at which the guests end up paying their share)!

$100 bidder at that price.[5] You should keep these similarities in mind as we work our way through second- and first-price auctions.

23.1.1   BASIC MODEL

In each of the three sections that follow we will use the same basic assumptions for buyers and the seller (the assumptions are discussed in detail in section 23.5):

1. There is a single unit of a good that has to be sold.

2. There are two buyers, 1 and 2. Each buyer values the good at either θ or μ, $\theta > \mu$, both types are equally likely, and the valuations are independent.[6] A type θ buyer's payoff is $\theta - price$ if he gets the object, and 0 otherwise. (Similarly a type μ buyer's payoff is either $\mu - price$ or 0.)

3. The seller is interested in maximizing the (expected) sale price.

23.2   SECOND-PRICE AUCTIONS

To briefly recall the rules, the higher bidder gets the object and pays the lower bid as price. If the bids are identical, then there is an equal chance that either bidder gets the object. Depending on his type, the winner gets a payoff equal to the difference between θ (or μ) and the lower bid, and the loser gets a payoff equal to 0.

A remarkable result about the second-price auction states that it is a *dominant strategy* for each bidder—regardless of type—to bid *exactly the value* of the object. In other words, it is a dominant strategy for a θ type to bid exactly θ dollars and for a μ type to bid μ dollars. In particular, it does not pay either type to "save a little" and "shave" their bids by bidding, say, 90 percent of what the object is really worth (nor is it worth overbidding to have a "better chance" of winning). Moreover, bidding in this fashion gives a player the highest expected payoff *regardless* of his opponent's bidding strategy, whether that is to bid truthfully or to do something completely different.[7]

Proposition 1. In a second-price auction, it is a dominant strategy for (each type of) each player to bid exactly his valuation of the object.

Proof
Since the two players are identical, it suffices to consider any one of them, say, player 1. Suppose that his valuation is θ. Let us compare a truthful bid of θ against an alternative bid, say, p.

If p is greater than θ, there are some bids of player 2 against which player 1 gets the object having bid p (but would not have got it by bidding truthfully; these are bids

[5] *Of course, the set of strategies open to a bidder in an English or Dutch auction is much richer than those available in a sealed-bid auction. For instance, in the latter case there is no possibility of watching the other bids as the auction proceeds to form conjectures about the other bidders' types.*

[6] *Meaning that buyer 1 cannot infer anything about buyer 2's valuation from knowing his own.*

[7] *Second-price auctions were first promoted in 1963 by the Columbia University economist William Vickrey on the basis of precisely this amazing result (which he proved). The result is all the more amazing because Vickrey proved it at a time when the study of incomplete-information games was still in its infancy, indeed, was barely out of its crib. (Harsanyi had yet to propose the very concept of Bayes-Nash equilibrium, for example.) For this and other work, Vickrey was awarded the Nobel Prize in 1996. Unfortunately, Bill died of a heart attack a mere two days after hearing of his award and hence was deprived of a wider audience for his many new and unorthodox ideas.*

greater than θ but less than p). However, in all of these cases, player 1's payoff from winning is negative because he pays a price (equal to player 2's bid) that is greater than his valuation. On the other hand, if player 1 wins because player 2's bid is less than θ, then he would have also won with a truthful bid, and he would have paid the same price regardless.

If p is less than θ then there are some bids of player 2 against which player 1 gets the object having bid θ (but would not have got it by bidding p; these are bids of player 2 smaller than θ but greater than p). In all of these cases, player 1's payoff—if he wins—is positive, since he pays a price that is smaller than his valuation. Of course, he loses this opportunity to win if he shaves his bid down to p. On the other hand, if player 2's bid is greater than θ, then player 1 would not get the object regardless of whether his own bid is θ or p. Finally, if player 2's bid is less than p, then player 1 wins in either case and pays the same price regardless.

Combining all these arguments, we have shown that it is a dominant strategy for the θ type to bid exactly that amount and no more nor no less. A very similar set of arguments shows that it is a dominant strategy for the μ type to bid truthfully as well.

◇

Remark

It should be easy to see that the proof does not depend on the fact that there are only two bidders or that there are only two types to each bidder. Nor indeed that each type of buyer has a prior probability of $\frac{1}{2}$. Indeed the result is true no matter how many bidders there are, how many types each bidder might have, and how likely the different types are.

For easy reference, let us compute equilibrium price and payoff in this auction. Suppose that a player is of type θ. He gets the object under two circumstances; the other player is of type μ (and in that case he is the sole winner) or the other player is of type θ as well (and in that case he has a 50% chance of being the winner). Since the two types of the opponent are equally likely, a θ type player's probability of winning, denoted $P(\theta)$, equals $\frac{1}{2}(1 + \frac{1}{2}) = \frac{3}{4}$.

The μ type buyer gets the object only if his opponent is also a μ type buyer, and then he has a 50 percent chance of winning. Hence he has a probability of winning, denoted $P(\mu)$, that equals $\frac{1}{2} \times \frac{1}{2} = \frac{1}{4}$.

A type θ buyer gets the object at price μ (if the other player is of type μ) and at price θ (when the other player is of type θ as well, and he has a 50% chance of being the eventual winner in that case). Since the two types of the opponent are equally likely, his *expected payment,* denoted $M(\theta)$, is given by

$$M(\theta) = \frac{1}{2}\left(\mu + \frac{\theta}{2}\right) \tag{23.1}$$

Put differently, his *expected surplus,* $\theta P(\theta) - M(\theta)$ is equal to $\frac{\theta - \mu}{2}$. For instance, if $\theta = \$50$ (million) and $\mu = \$10$ (million), then the expected surplus is 20 million.

CONCEPT CHECK
THE μ TYPE BUYER

Show that his expected payment is $M(\mu) = \frac{1}{2} \times \frac{\mu}{2}$ and his expected surplus, $\mu P(\mu) - M(\mu)$, is zero.

23.3   FIRST-PRICE AUCTIONS ⚠

Let us now turn to first-price auctions. The difference in rules is that now the higher bidder (who is still the winner of the auction) has to pay his own bid.

Unlike the second-price auction, there is no dominant strategy.[8] Hence, the solution concept that we will need to use is Bayes-Nash equilibrium. Since this is a symmetric game, let us restrict attention to symmetric equilibria, that is, equilibria in which each buyer plays the same overall strategy and the only determinant of the actual bid is a buyer's type. So we will look for one bid for the θ type bidder, call it p, and another one for the μ type, call it q, such that p is a best response for the θ type against (p, q) (and likewise, q is a best response for the μ type).

The first thing to verify is that truthful bidding, $p = \theta$ and $q = \mu$, is not a Bayes-Nash equilibrium. In particular, the θ type has zero net surplus from bidding this way, whereas he can get positive net surplus by bidding, say, a dollar less than θ. In that instance, he would get a surplus of one dollar whenever he confronts a μ type bidder.[9] In other words, in equilibrium, $p < \theta$.

The second thing to note is that, in equilibrium, the θ type buyer has to play a *continuous mixed strategy*.[10] To see why this statement must be true, note that if his opponent bids p for certain, and since $p < \theta$, a θ type buyer can always bid a cent more, get the object for sure, and—since his price is only marginally more than p—enjoy greater net surplus than he would have got from a 50 percent share at a bid of p.

In contrast, the μ type buyer must bid nonrandomly and, in fact, must pay full price, that is, $q = \mu$. We will show you later why this statement is true. For now, note that if it is not, and if the opponent's bid $q < \mu$, then by bidding a cent more than q, a μ type buyer can guarantee himself a win against another μ type buyer (and be virtually unchanged in his prospects versus a θ type opponent). Again, this tactic is preferable to having only a 50 percent chance of winning by bidding q (like the opponent).

All this can be collected together in the following proposition:

Proposition 2.   There is a symmetric Bayes-Nash equilibrium of the first-price auction in which the μ type buyer bids his valuation while the θ type buyer plays a mixed strategy that assigns probability to all bids between μ and $\frac{\theta+\mu}{2}$. For any bid b between those extremes the probability that the bid will be less than b is given by $\frac{b-\mu}{\theta-b}$.

[8] *After all, in comparing any two bids, the higher one is better if the opponent bids high, because it could win the object (whereas the lower bid might lose). The higher bid is worse if the opponent bids low, because now a lower bid might have won the object as well and the higher bid is simply wasteful of money.*

[9] *We are presuming here that μ is more than a dollar below θ. In general, the argument works for any bid strictly between μ and θ.*

[10] *By a continuous mixed strategy over an interval of bids, say between $0 and $10, we mean a strategy with the following properties: the probability that the bid will be less than $0 is 0, that it will be less than $10 is 1, that it will be less than any number between $0 and $10 is positive (and increasing with the number), and, finally, that it will be any one number, such as $5.71, is zero. An example is a mixed strategy in which the probability that the bid will be less than b is $\frac{b}{10}$ (whenever b is between 0 and 10). A mixed strategy that is not continuous is one that places probability $\frac{1}{2}$ each on the two bids $0 and $10.*

Proof

The μ type buyer will never bid above his valuation, and any bid less than μ will lose for sure. (Why?) Hence, a bid of μ is a best response to the proposed type-dependent strategy.

Now consider a θ type buyer. If he bids b, between the two extremes of μ and $\frac{\theta+\mu}{2}$, he has a probability equal to $\frac{b-\mu}{\theta-b}$ that he will beat out a θ opponent's bid and a probability 1 that he will win against a μ opponent. In either case he will pay the amount of his bid. In other words, his net surplus will be

$$\frac{1}{2}\left(\frac{b-\mu}{\theta-b}+1\right)(\theta-b)=\frac{\theta-\mu}{2}$$

Note that this net surplus is independent of the bid b! Put differently, regardless of what bid between μ and $\frac{\theta+\mu}{2}$ he makes, he gets the same (positive) amount of expected payoff. It is pointless to bid less than μ—and get zero payoff—or above $\frac{\theta+\mu}{2}$, since a bid exactly at $\frac{\theta+\mu}{2}$ also wins the object for sure and minimizes on the price paid. Combining all this, the mixed strategy given is a best response for the type θ buyer. The proposition is proved. ◇

Remark

In fact, it can be shown that there is *no other Bayes-Nash equilibrium* in this game. The arguments preceding the proposition essentially establish the following: for either type of buyer, an equilibrium strategy has to be either a nonrandom bid (equal to that type's valuation), or it has to be a continuous mixed strategy. For example, a μ type's strategy can be either to bid μ or to bid continuously between, say, a low bid of $\underline{b}$ and a high bid of $\overline{b}$.

In the Exercises you will show that a mixed strategy cannot be a best response for the μ type buyer. The basic argument is in two steps: For a mixed strategy to be a best response, each bid in its support has to be a best response itself—including the lowest possible bid $\underline{b}$. But the net expected surplus from this bid has to be zero (since it has a zero probability of winning). That result can only mean that $\underline{b} = \overline{b} = \mu$. (Hint: If $\underline{b} < \mu$, can you show that bids in between have a positive expected surplus?)

Let us now turn to the θ type buyer. Since he will never bid his valuation, the only possibility for him is a mixed strategy with support, say, between a low bid of $\underline{b}$ and a high bid of $\overline{b}$. In fact it can be shown that $\underline{b} = \mu$. The expected surplus for that bid is $\frac{\theta-\mu}{2}$. Since every bid that is a best response has to have this same surplus, it must be the case that for every such bid b

$$\frac{1}{2}\left[1+\text{Prob}(bids \le b)\right](\theta-b)=\frac{\theta-\mu}{2}$$

It follows from simple algebra that $\text{Prob}(bids \le b) = \frac{b-\mu}{\theta-b}$. And so we have shown not only that the exhibited strategy was a Bayes-Nash equilibrium but also that it is the only possible equilibrium!

In conclusion, we note that the net surplus for the μ type buyer is zero, and for the θ type it is $\frac{\theta-\mu}{2}$. These are exactly the same surpluses that we computed for the second-price auction! So although the θ type buyers bid very differently in the two auctions—truthfully in one and shaving their bid in the other—they end up with the same surplus. Note too that the probabilities of winning are also the same: the μ type only wins against another μ type and then he has a 50 percent chance of winning. Hence $P(\mu)$ is again $\frac{1}{4}$ and $P(\theta)$ is $\frac{3}{4}$.

Note that the expected revenue from a θ type is the same in both auctions. After all, the net surplus to the buyer, $\theta P(\theta) - M(\theta)$, is the same in the two auctions ($= \frac{\theta-\mu}{2}$) and so is the win probability $P(\theta)$. It follows that the expected revenue, $M(\theta)$, must also be the same.

CONCEPT CHECK
THE μ TYPE BUYER

Show that his expected payment equals $\frac{\mu}{4}$, as in the second-price auction.

This result—that the seller's expected revenue is the same for first- and second-price auctions—is sometimes referred to as *revenue equivalence* between the two auctions.

23.4   OPTIMAL AUCTIONS ⚠

We turn now to optimal auctions, that is, auctions that maximize the seller's expected revenues. We have so far seen two kinds of auctions in gory detail—second- and first-price auctions (and discussed how English and Dutch auctions are their close cousins). Somewhat surprisingly we saw that the seller has the same expected revenue in these two auctions. The optimality question is, If there are no limits placed on the auction rules—except that buyers cannot be forced to participate and that they will act in their self-interest—can the seller do any better than in a first- or second-price auction?

We will now answer that question by using the revelation principle. Thanks to that result we can restrict attention to direct-revelation mechanisms (in which each buyer is asked to report his type, and based on the two reports, the seller decides whether or not to sell the object, and if he does, the probability that he sells it to buyer 1). The reports also determine the payment that the buyers have to make to the seller. The object will be to find the probabilities of sale and the payments in such a way as to maximize the expected revenue of the seller.[11]

Unfortunately, in order to proceed further, we have to introduce some more notation. Let $P(\theta, \mu)$ denote the probability that buyer 1 is given the object if he reports his

[11] *We will also restrict attention to symmetric mechanisms in which the two reports (rather than the identities of the two players) are the sole determinants of the payments and sale probabilities.*

type to be θ while buyer 2 claims to be of type μ. Hence, the probability that buyer 2 gets the object is $1 - P(\theta, \mu)$; by symmetry, this is also the probability that buyer 1 will get the object if the reports are reversed, that is, if buyer 1 reports μ and buyer 2 reports θ. If both buyers report θ, then each has a probability $\frac{1}{2}$ of getting the object, while if they both report μ, each has a probability $P(\mu, \mu)$. Note that the seller may choose not to sell the object if he gets a report of μ from both buyers; that is, it is possible that $P(\mu, \mu) < \frac{1}{2}$.[12]

If buyer 1 reports his type to be θ, and expects his opponents to report his type truthfully, then buyer 1 expects to win with probability $\frac{1}{2}$ (if the other buyer is of θ type) and with probability $P(\theta, \mu)$ (if buyer 2 is a μ type buyer). In other words, his expected win probability from that report, call it $P(\theta)$, is

$$P(\theta) = \frac{1}{2}\left[\frac{1}{2} + P(\theta, \mu)\right] \tag{23.2}$$

For a μ type report, the expected win probability $P(\mu)$ is

$$P(\mu) = \frac{1}{2}\left[1 - P(\theta, \mu) + P(\mu, \mu)\right] \tag{23.3}$$

Denote the expected payment from reporting a θ type as $M(\theta)$ and that from reporting a μ type as $M(\mu)$. Therefore, a θ type buyer will report his own type truthfully if

$$\theta P(\theta) - M(\theta) \geq \theta P(\mu) - M(\mu)$$

Similarly, the incentive-compatibility constraint of the μ type buyer is given by

$$\mu P(\mu) - M(\mu) \geq \mu P(\theta) - M(\theta)$$

Finally, the two individual rationality constraints are

$$\theta P(\theta) - M(\theta) \geq 0$$
$$\mu P(\mu) - M(\mu) \geq 0$$

The expected revenue of the seller is given by $\frac{M(\theta) + M(\mu)}{2}$, since each type of buyer is equally likely. If you go back and compare the incentive-compatibility and individual-rationality constraints for this problem with those for the single-buyer problem discussed in Chapter 22, you will find that they are identical. Indeed, identical arguments also establish that in an optimal solution, the incentive constraint for the θ type and the individual-rationality constraint for the μ type must hold with equality:[13]

$$\theta P(\theta) - M(\theta) = \theta P(\mu) - M(\mu)$$
$$\mu P(\mu) - M(\mu) = 0 \tag{23.4}$$

Substituting these conclusions into the seller's expected revenues and collecting terms gives us the following expression for expected revenues:

$$\frac{\theta}{2}\left[P(\theta) - P(\mu)\right] + \mu P(\mu)$$

---

[12] *We have implicitly assumed that the seller will sell the object if at least one of the reports is θ. In general, he can choose not to sell in these good circumstances (even though all he needs is one high-valuation buyer). Allowing for this counterintuitive "no-sale" possibility only adds more notation. Since it will be the case that the seller will always sell under these circumstances, we avoid introducing unnecessary notation.*

[13] *This rule is proved in detail in the Exercises.*

Substituting from equations 23.2 and 23.3 and collecting terms one more time gives us the following expected seller revenue:

$$\frac{\theta - \mu}{2} P(\theta, \mu) + \frac{2\mu - \theta}{4} P(\mu, \mu) + c \tag{23.5}$$

where c is a constant equal to $\frac{\mu}{2} - \frac{\theta}{8}$. It is clear that the seller's expected revenues are maximized if $P(\theta, \mu) = 1$, that is, if he sells to the buyer who reports the higher valuation. Furthermore, $P(\mu, \mu)$ is either 0 or $\frac{1}{2}$ (the most it can be) depending on which of two cases prevails:

Proposition 3, Case 1 ($\mu > \frac{\theta}{2}$). In this case, $P(\mu, \mu) = \frac{1}{2}$: the optimal auction is to sell to the higher report if there are two distinct reports, and, if the reports are identical, to sell to either buyer with 50 percent probability each.

Proposition 3, Case 2 ($\mu < \frac{\theta}{2}$). In this case $P(\mu, \mu) = 0$ [and hence $P(\mu) = 0$]: the optimal auction is never to sell to a μ report (and to sell with 50 percent probability each to either buyer if both reports are θ).

In Case 1 the probabilities of sale are

$$P(\theta) = \frac{3}{4} \quad \text{and} \quad P(\mu) = \frac{1}{4}$$

From equation 23.2 it follows that the expected sale price in Case 1 is

$$M(\theta) = \frac{2\theta + \mu}{4} \quad \text{and} \quad M(\mu) = \frac{\mu}{4}$$

Since the two types are equally likely, the per buyer *expected revenue* for the seller is therefore $\frac{\theta + \mu}{4}$.

In Case 2, since $P(\mu) = 0$, therefore $M(\mu)$ is also 0. It is easy to check that, as a consequence, $M(\theta) = \frac{3\theta}{4}$. Since there is a 50 percent chance that any buyer is of θ type, the overall per buyer *expected revenue* for the seller is $\frac{3\theta}{8}$.

23.4.1   HOW WELL DO THE FIRST- AND SECOND-PRICE AUCTIONS DO?

First- and second-price auctions are pervasive.[14] How well do they match up against the optimal auction? For each of these auctions, we have derived the formula for the seller's expected revenue (and shown them to be equal). Recall that from a θ type buyer the expected collection is $M(\theta) = \frac{1}{2}(\mu + \frac{\theta}{2})$ and from a μ type buyer it is $M(\mu) = \frac{\mu}{4}$. Since the two types are equally likely, the per buyer overall expected revenue for the seller is

$$\frac{3\mu + \theta}{8}$$

Recall now the two cases for the optimal auction:

[14] *Actually, the sealed-bid second-price auction is rare, but its close cousin, the English auction, is pervasive.*

- **Case 1** ($\mu > \frac{\theta}{2}$). In this case, the probabilities of sale are $P(\theta) = \frac{3}{4}$ and $P(\mu) = \frac{1}{4}$, exactly the same probabilities as in both first- and second-price auctions (check!). So at least those two auctions are getting the good into the right hands. But are they charging the right amounts?

  The expected revenue for the optimal auction is $\frac{\theta+\mu}{4}$. It is easy to see that this is higher than the first- and second-price auctions' revenue (by an amount equal to $\frac{\theta-\mu}{8}$). By way of explanation, note first that the expected payment of the μ type is exactly the same in all three auctions ($= \frac{\mu}{4}$). Hence, the first- and second-price auctions must be collecting less from the high-valuation buyer. Indeed $M(\theta)$ is $\frac{2\theta+\mu}{4}$ in the optimal auction but only $\frac{\theta+2\mu}{4}$ for the standard ones.

  The reason that the standard auctions do not bring the seller as much revenue as they could is that they do not sufficiently charge the type θ buyer when he is the sole effective competitor, that is, when the other buyer's type is μ. For example, the second-price auction charges him only μ when that is the lower bid—and lets him enjoy the surplus $\theta - \mu$. In the same auction, a way to correct for this shortfall is for the buyer to charge the winner an additional amount $\frac{\theta-\mu}{2}$ (above the lower bid) whenever the two bids are different. It can be shown that truthful reporting continues to be a Bayes-Nash equilibrium[15] (although it is no longer a dominant strategy). The seller gets this additional revenue from each buyer with probability $\frac{1}{4}$ (the probability that he is a θ type and the other buyer is a μ type). Hence the seller's additional expected revenue is $\frac{\theta-\mu}{2} \times \frac{1}{4} = \frac{\theta-\mu}{8}$. Put differently, this modified second-price auction is optimal.

- **Case 2** ($\mu < \frac{\theta}{2}$). In this case, the optimal auction sells to the θ type buyer alone; that is, there is no sale when both buyers report their type to be μ. In both first- and second-price auctions, there is always a sale; hence they are inoptimal. Put differently, the optimal auction forces a high price out of the high-valuation buyer by not selling to low-valuation buyers. The standard auctions are "too democratic."

CONCEPT CHECK
SPECIAL CASE

When $\theta = 50$ (million) and $\mu = 10$ (million), show that the relevant case is Case 2. What is the expected revenue for the optimal auction? The first- and second-price auctions? How would your answers change if $\theta = 15$?

23.5   FINAL REMARKS

Some of the results of the previous auctions can be derived much more generally (how-ever, some other more slightly general auctions cannot be analyzed at all with the current techniques).

---

[15] *The details for the argument are in the Exercises.*

Let us start with Assumption 1—that a single unit of a single good is being auctioned. This assumption is fairly critical. Without it, the analysis is much more complicated and the conclusions are incomplete. For example, if multiple units of a single good are auctioned, then a bid can no longer be a number but rather has to be a whole schedule that indicates the bid for different quantity levels. In that case, it is unclear what one means by a high bidder and how much that bidder should pay in either the first- or second-price auction. A similar problem arises when single units of a whole package of goods are auctioned.[16]

Part of Assumption 2—that there are two equally likely types, and each type derives utility equal to the net surplus—can be generalized in various ways. For example, in the Exercises, we will walk you through the details of the case where the two types are not equally likely. A summary of the result there is that nothing changes. The assumption that there are two players and two types can also be generalized quite easily. Again the results do not change very much.[17] What is more difficult to generalize is the assumption that the two players are identical (and independent) in terms of information and preferences.

SUMMARY

1. Auctions are used to sell a wide variety of goods and services. Two popular types of auctions are the first- and second-price sealed-bid auctions (and their close cousins, descending- and ascending-bid auctions, respectively).

2. Quite a lot is known about auctioning a single unit of a good to players who have independent private valuations (and maximize their expected surplus in the auction).

3. In a second-price auction it is a dominant strategy for a player to truthfully bid her valuation. This is the best strategy for her regardless of her beliefs about the others' valuations and their bidding strategies.

4. In a first-price auction—with two types θ and μ—there is a symmetric Bayes-Nash equilibrium in which the lower valuation type bids truthfully and the higher one's bidding strategy is random and continuous.

5. In order to determine the auction that maximizes his expected revenue, the seller can use a direct-revelation mechanism. He can have each buyer report her valuation and charge them on the basis of the reports.

6. There are two cases for the optimal auction: if $\frac{\theta}{2} > \mu$, then the seller should never sell to a low (μ) report (and he should charge θ if there is a high report). In the alternative case, the seller should sell to the high report if there is only one such report (and sell with 50% probability to either buyer if the reports are identical).

[16] *For some research on these kinds of generalizations, see Lawrence Ausubel's 1997 article "An Efficient Ascending Bid Auction for Multiple Objects," mimeo, University of Maryland, College Park.*

[17] *Should you decide to read about these generalizations, consult Chapter 7 of Fudenberg and Tirole's Game Theory (MIT Press, 1991).*

EXERCISES

SECTION 23.1

23.1
Give an example of an ascending-bid auction and a descending-bid auction (not from the text). In each case be careful to detail the buyers and sellers, their likely preferences, and the incompleteness of information.

23.2
Repeat exercise 23.1 with sealed-bid first- and second-price auctions.

23.3
Give two examples of auctions not discussed in the text (these can include variants on the auctions that *are* discussed).

SECTION 23.2

The next few questions consider a general second-price auction with an arbitrary number of bidders and bidder types.

23.4
Suppose that there are N bidders; each bidder is one of two types, θ and μ, and each type is equally likely. Show that truthful bidding is a dominant strategy for the θ type. Repeat for the μ type. Be sure to detail your arguments.

23.5
What is the probability of winning for a θ type bidder? (You do not have to solve the formula fully, but you have to have the correct formula!) What is the formula for the expected payoff?

23.6
Repeat question 23.5 for a μ type bidder.

23.7
Suppose instead that although there are only two bidders, each bidder can be any one of L types, $\theta_1, \theta_2, \ldots, \theta_L$. Show that for any one of these types it is a dominant strategy to bid truthfully.

SECTION 23.3

23.8

Show formally that no matter how many bidders there are and how many bidder types, there is no dominant strategy for a representative bidder type in a first-price auction.

In the next few questions we will formally prove that there can be no other Bayes-Nash equilibrium in the first-price auction other than the one studied in the text.

23.9

Show the following: for either type of buyer, an equilibrium strategy has to be one of two sorts; it has to be either a nonrandom bid equal to that type's valuation, or it has to be a continuous mixed strategy.

23.10

Hence a μ type buyer's strategy can be either to bid μ or to bid continuously between, say, a low bid of $\underline{b}$ and a high bid of $\overline{b}$. Show that the net surplus from a bid of $\underline{b}$ must be zero.

23.11

Show that this fact in turn implies that $\underline{b} = \overline{b} = \mu$. (Hint: What happens if the opponent's low bid $\underline{b}$ is less than μ?)

Let us now turn to the θ type buyer.

23.12

Prove formally that he will never bid his valuation and so the only possibility for him is a mixed strategy, with support, say, between a low bid of $\underline{b}$ and a high bid of $\overline{b}$.

23.13

Show that $\underline{b}$ will never be greater than μ. (Hint: Note that the lowest bidder wins only against a μ type opponent.)

23.14

In fact, show that $\underline{b} = \mu$. Show that the net surplus of such a bidder is $\frac{\theta - \mu}{2}$.

23.15

Show that it then follows that Prob. (bids $\leq b$) $= \frac{b - \mu}{\theta - b}$.

SECTION 23.4

In the next few questions you will formally show that the incentive constraint for the θ type and the rationality constraint for the μ type must hold with equality in the optimal auction.

23.16

Show that at least one of the individual rationality constraints has to hold—or else the seller can increase his expected revenues.

23.17

Show that if the individual rationality constraint holds for the μ type then it also has to hold for the θ type. Conclude that the individual rationality constraint of the μ type always has to hold with equality.

23.18

Prove that if the individual-rationality constraint of the θ type is an inequality, then the incentive constraint for the same type must hold with equality (or else the seller would increase revenues).

23.19

Formally derive the expression for expected seller revenue, equation 23.5.

In the next few questions we consider a modification of the second-price auction that raises the same revenue as the optimal auction. Recall that this modification charges the winner an amount equal to $\frac{\theta - \mu}{2}$ (in addition to the lower bid) whenever the two bids are different.

23.20

Suppose that a player anticipates that his opponent will bid truthfully, that is, that the bids will equal θ and μ from the two types of his opponent. Show that a θ buyer will only get a positive surplus if he bids at or above μ (and competes against a low-valuation opponent).

23.21

Prove that a bid of θ is therefore a best response for the high-valuation buyer.

23.22

Show that it continues to be a best response for the low-valuation buyer to bid her valuation. What have you concluded about the Bayes-Nash equilibria of this auction?

SECTION 23.5

The next set of exercises work through the analyses when the prior probability of the θ type can be any number between 0 and 1 (and is not necessarily $\frac{1}{2}$). Suppose in fact that the prior probability of a type θ is ρ (and hence there is a probability $1 - \rho$ that a player can be a type μ). Let us start with the second-price auction.

23.23

Show that truthful bidding continues to be a dominant strategy in the second-price auction.

23.24

Show that the consequent probabilities of winning become

$$P(\theta) = \left(\rho \times \frac{1}{2}\right) + (1 - \rho) \times 1 = 1 - \frac{\rho}{2}$$

$$P(\mu) = (1 - \rho) \times \frac{1}{2} = \frac{1 - \rho}{2}$$

23.25

Show similarly that the expected payments become

$$M(\theta) = (1 - \rho)\mu + \frac{\rho\theta}{2}$$

$$M(\mu) = (1 - \rho)\frac{\mu}{2}$$

23.26

Establish that the θ type buyer's expected surplus is $(1 - \rho) \times (\theta - \mu)$ and the μ type has zero surplus.

Let us now turn to the first-price auction.

23.27

Show that the following strategies constitute a Bayes-Nash equilibrium. The μ type buyer bids her valuation. The θ type buyer uses a continuous mixed strategy on the interval of bids μ to $\rho\theta + (1 - \rho)\mu$. The probability that the bid is less than b is given by $\frac{1-\rho}{\rho} \times \frac{b-\mu}{\theta-b}$.

23.28

Show that the θ type buyer now has an expected surplus of $(1 - \rho)(\theta - \mu)$.

23.29

Establish that the probabilities of winning, $P(\theta)$ and $P(\mu)$, are the same as in the second-price auction.

23.30

a. Argue that the expected payment of the μ type buyer is unchanged at $(1 - \rho)\frac{\mu}{2}$.

b. Using the same argument as for the case $\rho = \frac{1}{2}$, show that the expected payment of the θ type bidder is also the same as in the second-price auction; that is, revenue equivalence holds.

Finally, let us consider optimal auctions with arbitrary priors. The probabilities of winning, $P(\theta)$ and $P(\mu)$, are now given by

$$P(\theta) = \frac{\rho}{2} + (1 - \rho)P(\theta, \mu)$$

$$P(\mu) = \rho[1 - P(\theta, \mu)] + (1 - \rho)P(\mu, \mu)$$

(23.6)

23.31

Show that the individual-rationality constraints and the incentive-compatibility constraints are unchanged. Argue that the individual-rationality constraint for the μ type buyer and the incentive-compatibility constraint for type θ buyer must still hold with equality (for exactly the same reasons as before).

23.32

Consequently, derive the seller's expected revenues to be $\rho\theta P(\theta) + (\mu - \rho\theta)P(\mu)$.

23.33

After substituting from equation 23.6, show that in any optimal auction $P(\theta, \mu) = 1$.

23.34

Show that whether or not the object is sold when there are two low-valuation reports depends on $\mu - \rho\theta$. State and prove a result, with two cases, relating to this fact.

CHAPTER 24

SIGNALING GAMES AND THE LEMONS PROBLEM

In this chapter we turn to a class of incomplete information games called *signaling games*. Section 24.1 contains a motivation for these games and two examples. In section 24.2 we formally define a signaling game as well as an appropriate solution concept called *perfect Bayesian equilibrium* (which will turn out to be a refinement of Bayes-Nash equilibrium). Signaling games have been used quite extensively in applications; their economic motivation was provided by George Akerlof in a seminal analysis of markets where buyers are uncertain about product quality.[1] Hence, in section 24.3 we turn to precisely that application. Section 24.4 contains a case study, Used Cars—A Market Full of Lemons? Section 24.5 concludes.

24.1 MOTIVATION AND TWO EXAMPLES

Suppose, as in Chapters 20 through 22, that we have a game with two players and that one of them knows something that affects both payoffs. For example, in Chapter 20's Battle of the Sexes, the wife knows whether or not she is a loving spouse; in the Cournot model of Chapter 21, a firm knows its production costs; and, in Chapter 22, Bill Gates knows his willingness to pay for the da Vinci diaries. In each case, the informed player will want to reveal certain kinds of information. For instance, in the Cournot model a low-cost firm would like to make its costs public (and thereby discourage its rival from producing very much). Bill Gates, if he is a mere fan (with a low valuation), would like to let Sotheby's know it (and thereby draw a lower priced offer). In other words, these types of players will want to *signal* their type to the uninformed player.

    Of course, the remaining type—a higher cost duopolist in the Cournot model, or a real aficionado of the da Vinci diaries—has precisely the opposite incentives; they would like it if the uninformed player did *not* find out their information. Put differently, if the

---

[1] *We would very much recommend that you read the 1970 Akerlof paper, "The Market for Lemons: Quality Uncertainty and the Market Mechanism,"* Quarterly Journal of Economics, *vol. 89, pp. 488-500. It contains important ideas but no difficult mathematics.*

TABLE 24.1

1 \ 2	c	n		1 \ 2	c	n
c	0, 0	7, −2		c	−2, −2	5, 0
n	−2, 7	5, 5		n	0, 5	7, 7

(a) Tough   (b) Accommodating

signal were merely talk, then these types too would claim to be a lower cost firm and a mere fan, respectively. And the uninformed player would typically be smart enough to realize this fact and discount his opponent's talk.

He will believe certain signals; for example, he will believe a signal that is profitable for a particular type of sender but unprofitable for an alternative type. For instance, in the Cournot duopoly, if he finds his rival investing in a factory that would break even only if the rival's costs are low, then he is likely to believe the signal conveyed by the building of the factory.

Two points ought to stand out from this discussion:

1. It is in the self-interest of certain types of informed players to signal their information. The uninformed player should always process the signal to learn something she did not know about her opponent.

2. The signal has to be credible in the sense that it must not be in the self-interest of other types to send the very same signal (or if it is, then the uninformed player will account for that fact).

Signaling games and their equilibria incorporate these two features. Before going to the general analysis, however, let us discuss two examples.

Example 1: Prisoners' Dilemma

This is an incomplete information variant of the Prisoners' Dilemma (introduced as example 2 in Chapter 20). Both players' payoffs depend on whether player 2 is *tough* or *accommodating;* player 1 does not know which one it is although player 2 does; see Tables 24.1a and 24.1b.

Note that whether or not the uninformed player (player 1) should play *confess* or *not confess* depends critically on which type his opponent happens to be. Hence, player 1 would greatly benefit from getting a signal about player 2's type. A number of different things can serve as signals. For starters, let us suppose that player 2 can "make his actions speak louder than words"; that is, he can pick his action—c or n—ahead of player 1, and that choice is a signal of his type. The extensive form for this signaling game is therefore as displayed in Figure 24.1.[2]

[2] *Note that because player 2 appears before player 1 in the extensive form, we have written player 2's payoff as the first component of each part of payoffs.*

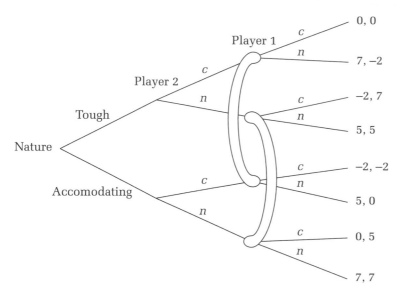

FIGURE 24.1

Example 2: The da Vinci Diaries

A whole class of signaling games is given by the direct-revelation games of Chapter 22. For example, consider the da Vinci diary direct-revelation game between Sotheby's and Bill Gates. Mr. Gates files a report about his type (he may choose to lie), and this report is the signal. After receiving the signal, Sotheby's has to implement a preannounced price and likelihood of sale. Suppose that Sotheby's has only two options available: sell for sure at price $\frac{\theta}{2}$ or sell with probability 50 percent at a price of μ.[3] Suppose as before, that the buyer cannot be coerced into buying at a price above his valuation for the object.

The signaling game is therefore as shown in Figure 24.2.

24.1.1   A FIRST ANALYSIS OF THE EXAMPLES

In everything that follows keep in mind the two main questions: First, does an informed player have a reason to signal his type? Second, can he do so credibly? That is, can he choose a signal that the other type will not also choose?

Example 1

Both types of the informed player, player 2, would like to get a high payoff. For a type 1 player, the payoffs are higher if his opponent plays n (rather than c). Hence he would like to send a signal that would cause player 1 to play n. Consider a type 2 player instead. Her payoffs are also higher if player 1 plays n. So each type has a reason to signal; can they do so credibly?

Suppose that after receiving the two signals, player 1 is able to tell whether he is playing a type 1 or a type 2 player. (This can only happen if the two signals are different.)[4]

---

[3] And suppose that $\frac{\theta}{2} > \mu$.

[4] For instance, type 1 might signal by picking c and type 2 by picking n. In that case, when player 1 sees c, he knows that the correct payoff matrix is Table 24.1a. However, if he sees n he infers that it is Table 24.1b. The two types can also be distinguished if they pick n and c, respectively.

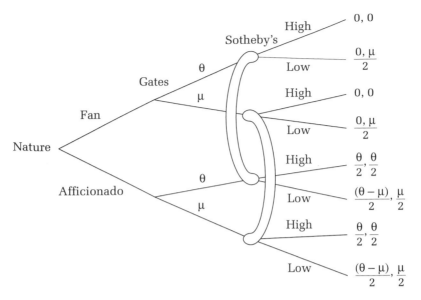

FIGURE 24.2

Note that now player 1 is fully informed; that is, we have either a game of complete information given by Table 24.1a or one given by Table 24.1b. Consequently, player 1 will either pick c (his dominant strategy in Table 24.1a) or n (his dominant strategy in Table 24.1b) depending on what he learns from the signal.

But now we have a credibility problem; type 1—who would like to have the initially uninformed player 1 pick n—will want to send the same signal as his type 2 counterpart just so he can fool player 1 into picking n. Knowing this, player 1—no fool himself!—will look at the signal that he receives and infer that he should infer nothing.

Example 2

Unlike the previous example, here it is possible for the two types to credibly signal their valuations. We will show you why.

Note that if the types can be distinguished by the seller, then she would charge the μ type buyer the lower priced uncertain outcome and charge the higher valuation buyer $\frac{\theta}{2}$.[5] Knowing this, a high-valuation buyer has two choices: confirm that he is a high-valuation buyer and get charged $\frac{\theta}{2}$ or lie about his valuation and get charged μ with a 50 percent likelihood (and be unable to buy with a remaining probability of 50%). The former option nets a utility surplus equal to $\frac{\theta}{2}$, whereas the latter yields a net surplus of $\frac{\theta-\mu}{2}$. Clearly, the high-valuation buyer will truthfully report his type. The low-valuation buyer gains a zero surplus from either price, and so a truthful signal is a best choice for him as well.

[5] *The low-valuation buyer will refuse to buy at a price of $\frac{\theta}{2}$, so it makes little sense to offer him that option. The high-valuation buyer will accept both prices; the higher price yields the seller a profit of $\frac{\theta}{2}$, whereas the lower price yields an expected profit of $\frac{\mu}{2}$. Hence the seller prefers the higher price.*

To summarize here are the two conclusions from the examples:

1. If the uninformed player can tell the types apart, then he will play a best response in the consequent complete-information game.

2. Each informed type understands conclusion 1. This fact determines whether some type will want to hide behind the veil of another type (by sending the same signal).

In the next section, we will do a more complete analysis of both examples.

24.2 A DEFINITION, AN EQUILIBRIUM CONCEPT, AND EXAMPLES ⚠

24.2.1 DEFINITION

In a signaling game there are two players. Player 2 has some private information that affects the payoff of both players. As always, we will describe this information as being part of a player's type, and to keep things simple, we will assume that there are two types—θ and μ (with a prior probability ρ that the type is θ).

The informed player sends a signal, denoted s, to player 1 and after receiving the signal, the latter takes an action, denoted t. Player 2's type, her signal, and the action of player 1 together determine each player's payoff. Denote player 2's payoff as $\pi(s, t, \theta)$, if she is a θ type, and as $\pi(s, t, \mu)$ if she is a μ type player. Denote player 1's payoff similarly as $\Pi(s, t, \theta)$ and $\Pi(s, t, \mu)$.

The extensive form of the signaling game is therefore given by the diagram in Figure 24.3.

In example 1, the signal is player 2's choice of n or c (similarly player 1's action is a choice of n or c). In example 2, the signal is the buyer's report on his type, and the principal's (or seller's) action is the choice of a price and a sale probability.[6]

24.2.2 PERFECT BAYESIAN EQUILIBRIUM

A type-dependent strategy for the informed player 2 is a pair of signals, say, s^* for type θ and s' for type μ. A strategy for player 1 is a signal-dependent choice; let us denote the action chosen after receiving a representative signal s as $t(s)$. Since this action is chosen after seeing player 2's signal, player 1 at that point may have a revised estimate of the prior probability ρ on the two types; call this estimate $\rho(s)$.

A *perfect Bayesian equilibrium* (PBE) is given by

• *Best response of each type of player 2*

$$\pi[s^*, t(s^*), \theta] \geq \pi[s, t(s), \theta] \quad \text{for all } s$$
$$\pi[s', t(s'), \mu] \geq \pi[s, t(s), \mu] \quad \text{for all } s$$

(24.1)

[6] *There is a more general point that example 2 illustrates. Any direct-revelation game can be thought of as a signaling game; the informed agent's report about his type is his signal. The outcome to every report is the principal's action. Put differently, one of the mechanisms that a principal can choose in a mechanism-design problem is a signaling game to be played by the agent and himself. For more on this issue, see section 24.5.*

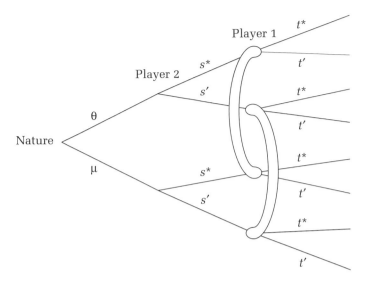

Figure 24.3

- *Best response of player 1*, for every s,

$$\rho(s)\,\Pi[s, t(s), \theta] + [1 - \rho(s)]\,\Pi[s, t(s), \mu] \geq \rho(s)\,\Pi(s, t, \theta)$$
$$+ [1 - \rho(s)]\,\Pi(s, t, \mu) \quad \text{for all } t \tag{24.2}$$

- *Correct estimate revision*, in either of two cases:

Case 1: $s^* \neq s'$

$$\rho(s) = \begin{cases} 1 & \text{if } s = s^* \\ 0 & \text{if } s = s' \\ \text{any fraction} & \text{if } s \text{ is neither } s^* \text{ nor } s' \end{cases} \tag{24.3}$$

Case 2: $s^* = s'$

$$\rho(s) = \begin{cases} \rho & \text{if } s = s^* \text{ or } s' \\ \text{any fraction} & \text{if } s \text{ is neither } s^* \text{ nor } s' \end{cases}$$

Let us work our way backward through the three equations. In words, equation 24.3 says the following: if player 1 expects to receive different signals, that is, if $s^* \neq s'$, then upon receipt of s^* he knows he is facing a type 1 player; that is, $\rho(s) = 1$ [and conversely upon receiving a signal of s' he knows he is faced with a type 2 player, that is, $\rho(s) = 0$]. If he expects to receive the same signal, that is, if $s^* = s'$, then he concludes nothing from getting that signal; that is, $\rho(s) = \rho$. What is he to do when he receives a signal that he did not expect, that is, if the signal is *neither s^* nor s'*? Well, he might think it was a mistake (and that player 2 really meant to send either s^* or s'). Or he might think that player 2 changed her mind. Since there are multiple explanations, we can be agnostic—

the last part of equation 24.3 says any rationalization is acceptable; that is, any revision is correct.

Equation 24.2 says that—based on the correct estimate of the two types—player 1 must pick each one of his actions $t(s)$ in order to maximize his expected payoffs. In particular it requires that he play best responses within the consequent complete-information games if he learns his opponent's type. Notice that the arbitrariness in specifying the estimate, when player 1 receives an unexpected signal, spills over to equation 24.2 because different specifications of $\rho(s)$ will engender quite different best responses.

Finally, equation 24.1 is a standard best-response condition for the informed player of every type. Note that although player 1's choices $t(s)$, for signals other than s^* or s', are essentially arbitrary, the exact assignment does matter to player 2; after all, if a θ type were to switch the signal from s^* to s, how the payoffs change would depend on $t(s)$.[7]

A perfect Bayesian equilibrium adds one further restriction to a plain old Bayes-Nash equilibrium and that is equation 24.3—that is, that the uninformed player is now allowed to (correctly) process information that becomes available to him in the course of the game. On one hand, a PBE in which the two types send distinct signals, and therefore can be distinguished from each other, is called a *separating equilibrium*. On the other hand, an equilibrium in which the two types send identical signals, and therefore cannot be distinguished from each other, is called a *pooling equilibrium*.[8]

24.2.3   A FURTHER ANALYSIS OF THE EXAMPLES

Example 1

We have already shown that there is no separating equilibrium. The only candidate therefore is a pooling equilibrium, that is, one in which the two types both pick n or c.

Suppose, for the purposes of this discussion, that the prior probability on type θ is less than 50 percent, that is, $\rho < \frac{1}{2}$. (In the Exercises you will analyze the case where $\rho \geq \frac{1}{2}$.)

CONCEPT CHECK
PLAYER 1

If both types pick c, show that it is better for player 1 to play n.

What remains to check is player 2's best responses. Note that a type 1 player gets a payoff of 7 in this candidate equilibrium while a type 2 gets 5. Clearly the first type can do no better. (Why?) Whether or not the second type can do better depends on how player 1 treats an unexpected signal of n. If he stays with an action choice of n, then player 2 would do better—and get a payoff of 7. Hence in this case type 2 would not signal by playing c but rather would signal by playing n. But if upon receipt of signal n, player 1 in

[7] *There are further—and more complicated—generalizations of the equilibrium concept in which this arbitrariness is somewhat reduced. One such concept is called* sequential equilibrium.

[8] *The definition that we have given is for pure-strategy PBE. The definition can be extended to mixed-strategy PBE in the usual way.*

fact switches to c, then player 2's payoff would drop down to 0. In turn, player 1 would want to play c upon receiving a signal of n if he believes that the likelihood of type 1 is at least $\frac{1}{2}$, that is, $\rho(n) \geq \frac{1}{2}$.

To summarize, one perfect Bayesian pooling equilibrium is for both types of the agent to signal c, that is, $s^* = s' = c$, thereby eliciting a play of n by the principal, that is, $t(c) = n$. Neither type of player 2 wants to change his signal if $t(n) = c$. The pair of actions $t(c) = n$ and $t(n) = c$ is a best response for player 1 if $\rho(n) \geq \frac{1}{2}$.

CONCEPT CHECK
ANOTHER EQUILIBRIUM

Show that $s^* = s' = n$ leads to a play of $t(n) = n$ (recall that $\rho < \frac{1}{2}$) and that neither type wants to switch his signal if $t(c) = c$. In turn, show that this choice of action is a best response for player 1 if the signal c leads to $\rho(c) \geq \frac{1}{2}$.

Example 2

We have already shown you one separating PBE in this game. Let us now look at pooling equilibria instead.

Suppose that the two types of buyers send the same signal; either they both report θ, or they both report μ. Since the signal does not convey any information, the seller still presumes that there is a probability ρ that the buyer is of type θ. By charging the higher price he can expect a sale only to the higher valuation buyer, and hence the expected profit from this strategy is $\rho\frac{\theta}{2}$. If he charges the probabilistic lower price, however, then both types of buyers will buy, although there will be an actual transaction only 50 percent of the time. Consequently, the expected profit from this strategy is $\frac{\mu}{2}$. The higher price is the better choice if and only if $\rho\theta \geq \mu$.

Will either buyer want to switch his signal? The μ type buyer receives zero net surplus regardless of the price and hence has no reason to want to switch. The θ type buyer gets a net surplus equal to $\frac{\theta}{2}$ from the higher priced alternative and a net surplus of $\frac{\theta - \mu}{2}$ if he is charged the probabilistic lower price. Hence he does not want to switch either.

CONCEPT CHECK
ANOTHER CASE ($\rho\theta < \mu$)

[9] *Indeed any belief in which the seller thinks the prior probability of the θ type is less than $\frac{\mu}{\theta}$ would lead him to charge the lower probabilistic price.*

Show that there are two pooling equilibria (with signals θ, θ and μ, μ). Upon receiving the expected signal, the seller charges μ (with a 50% sale probability). Upon receiving an unexpected signal, the seller presumes that the buyer is of the μ type and (again) charges the lower probabilistic price.[9]

24.3   SIGNALING PRODUCT QUALITY

The initial motivation for analyzing signaling games—and indeed a major motivation for an entire subject called *information economics*—came from Akerlof's discussion of markets with uncertain product quality (see note 1). Akerlof modeled the following scenario: buyers in a market are uncertain about the exact quality of the good they are buying, but sellers, who have greater experience with it are more certain about quality. He asked, How are market price and availability affected by buyer uncertainty? Would buyers only be willing to pay for average quality? Would that fact prompt sellers with goods of better than average quality to withhold their merchandise? Would such decisions lead to a situation in which bad-quality goods drive out better quality ones?

   Akerlof showed that the answer to each of these questions can be a resounding yes. We will first demonstrate the logic behind such a breakdown of the market, and then we will analyze the role of signaling in ameliorating the problem.

24.3.1   THE BAD CAN DRIVE OUT THE GOOD

Imagine that there are only two product possibilities—good-quality merchandise and lemons (or bad-quality merchandise). Suppose that a buyer cannot tell one from the other but a seller can. Suppose also that what distinguishes bad from good is that they have different costs of upkeep and repairs. For example, suppose that expected repair costs are $200 on a good-quality product and $1,700 on a lemon.

   Suppose that a potential *buyer* values the object—before accounting for repair costs—at $3,200; hence his net valuation is $3,000 for a good product and $1,500 for a lemon. Suppose also that a *seller* has an intrinsic valuation of $2,700; that is, a seller of good quality if he held on to the product would have a valuation of $2,500 while a seller of a lemon would have a valuation of $1,000.

   To help you remember all the numbers here is a table of the relevant ones:

	Good Quality	Lemon
Net valuation of buyer	3,000	1,500
Net valuation of seller	2,500	1,000

   If a lemon is known to be a lemon, then its owner would negotiate solely with buyers looking for lemons. Consequently, the price of a lemon would be somewhere between the $1,000 that sellers are willing to take and the $1,500 that buyers are willing to pay. Likewise, the buyers of good quality would negotiate with similarly endowed sellers and settle on a price somewhere between $2,500 and $3,000. And both qualities of goods would get sold in this market.

   Now suppose that a buyer cannot tell a lemon from good quality. The maximum that he would be willing to bid would depend on how likely it is that he is buying a lemon. Suppose, for illustration's sake, that there are an equal number of lemons and good-quality items in the market. In that case the average valuation for a buyer is $\frac{1,500+3,000}{2}$, or $2,250.

The buyer in any transaction will not want to go beyond $2,250, and the seller of a lemon will accept such an offer (since he values the good at $1,000), but the seller of good-quality merchandise will refuse (and keep his good valued at $2,500). Consequently, the only goods that will get sold will be lemons—the bad will have driven the good out of this market. Note too that the buyer who recognizes this fact will only make offers between $1,000 and $1,500, since he will clearly be overpaying if he pays $2,250 for a lemon that is only worth $1,500 to him.[10]

Notice that there is no quick fix for this problem. For instance, it does not do for a buyer, if he sees his first offer refused, to say to himself, "Ah, I have found a good product," and raise his offer to $2,500. If the seller of a lemon anticipated such behavior, he too would refuse the first offer! Nor does it do for the seller to give a verbal guarantee, because lemon owners will have every incentive to give the most sincere guarantees.

The problem does not go away, either, if there are more than two quality levels. Indeed in many ways it can get worse. Suppose that there is a third quality level—intermediate quality. A buyer who is unable to distinguish between the three levels will pay for average quality, thereby losing the good-quality sellers. If the buyer is cognizant of that fact, he will only be willing to pay for average quality after taking an average over only lemons and intermediates. In turn intermediates' sellers, whose merchandise is now better than the average, will sit out the market. Their withdrawal will lead buyers essentially to bid for lemons, and those will be the only goods sold.

And you can extend this logic to four or five (or more) quality levels. To the extent that lemons constitute a smaller and smaller fraction of available goods when there are more and more quality levels, the market breakdown becomes even more stark.

24.3.2 GOOD CAN SIGNAL QUALITY?

Sellers of good-quality merchandise might want to signal the superior quality of their product. As we have seen, it does not suffice merely to offer verbal assurances, since lemon owners are just as capable of providing those very same assurances. One way to put one's money where one's mouth is, so to speak, is for sellers to offer a *warranty* (against possible repairs after purchase). Warranties can be offered for any fraction of repair costs between 0 and 100 percent; we will keep matters simple by considering only the two extreme cases—complete warranty (100% coverage) and no warranty (0% coverage). Sellers decide whether or not to include a warranty before buyers decide how much to offer for the merchandise.

Payoffs under Warranty

When a seller offers a complete warranty on a good, he will accept a price p for the good only if that price is at least his intrinsic valuation 2,700. After all, if the price were any lower, the seller might as well hold onto his good. (Why?) If $p \geq 2,700$, then the payoff to a lemon seller is $p - 1,700$, and that to a good-quality seller is $p - 200$. The buyer's

[10] *For alternative parameter values it is possible that quality levels other than lemons may get sold as well. Although a buyer will only pay for average quality, this payment may still be enough to compensate the better-than-average-quality sellers because their intrinsic valuation is less than that of buyers. For instance, when lemons have a probability of $\frac{1}{4}$, the maximum that a buyer will pay is $\frac{1,500 + (3 \times 3,000)}{4} = \$2,625$, and good-quality sellers would be willing to sell their merchandise.*

TABLE 24.2

Price	Warranty	No Warranty	Price	Warranty	No Warranty
1,000	0, 1,000	500, 1,000	1,000	0, 2,500	0, 2,500
1,500	0, 1,000	0, 1,500	1,500	0, 2,500	0, 2,500
⋮	⋮	⋮	⋮	⋮	⋮
2,500	0, 1,000	−1,000, 2,500	2,500	0, 2,500	500, 2,500
2,700	500, 1,000	−1,200, 2,700	2,700	500, 2,500	300, 2,700
2,900	300, 1,200	−1,400, 2,900	2,900	300, 2,700	100, 2,900
(a) Lemon			(b) Good Quality		

payoff in either case is $3,200 - p$. If $p < 2,700$, since there is no sale, a buyer gets zero payoff while the two types of sellers get payoffs of 1,000 and 2,500, respectively.

Payoffs with No Warranty

A lemon seller will accept any price p that is at least 1,000; the buyer's payoff will be $1,500 - p$ and the seller's p. However, a good quality seller will only accept $p \geq 2,500$; the buyer's payoff will be $3,000 - p$ and the seller's p.

This analysis gives us the payoff matrices of Tables 24.2a and 24.2b (in each pair, the first payoff is the buyer's and the second is the seller's).

Consider the following strategies: *A lemon seller offers no warranty, but a good quality seller does. The buyer bids $2,700 if there is a warranty and $1,000 if there is not.*

PBE Analysis

Since the signals are distinct, a buyer can tell whether or not he is bidding on a lemon, and given the seller's strategies, the absence of a warranty implies a lemon. The buyer's best response is to bid the lowest acceptable price; hence, once he spots a lemon (and knows that he is in Table 24.2a), he should bid $1,000, and otherwise he should bid $2,700—exactly as in the candidate strategies.

What about the two types of sellers? If a lemon owner offers a warranty, he would get an offer of $2,700, but he would expect to pay $1,700 in warranty costs; so he would be no better off by switching his signal. A good-quality owner could switch to not offering a warranty and get a $1,000 offer. This possibility is strictly worse than getting a $2,700 offer with a $200 warranty cost tag attached. So he never wants to switch. Put differently, we have a separating perfect Bayesian equilibrium.

24.4   CASE STUDY: USED CARS—A MARKET FOR LEMONS?

A market with uncertain product quality is that for used cars—and Akerlof borrowed from that market the terminology of "lemons."[11] In this section we ask, Are there signs of breakdown in this market? And is there evidence of signaling by sellers? Here are some facts about this market:

1.   The average 1994 car depreciated 37 percent in its first year. By the end of the second year it had depreciated 50 percent (if you tried to sell your 1994 car in 1996, you would get only half the price that you had paid for it a mere two years before.)

2.   Of all used cars purchased, 20 percent are sold through new car dealerships, and another 15 percent are sold through independent used car dealerships. Dealerships typically offer warranties on the used cars that they sell.

3.   The average price of a used car in 1994 was about $11,500. The average private-party sale price on a used car was about $2,000 less than the average sale price at dealers.[12]

The first fact is a striking illustration of the lemons problem. There are some people who sell their cars within the first couple of years because their circumstances change—they move out of town, they cannot afford to make car payments, they get married and the spouse already has a car, and so on. These are people whose cars are good-quality cars. If you as a buyer were convinced of their reason for selling, you would be willing to pay 80 to 90 percent of the purchase price (for a car that has been driven only about a year or so).

Then there are people who sell because their cars are lemons—the car developed serious mechanical problems, it is at the mechanic's all the time, and the like. These are cars that you as a buyer are willing to pay a lot less than the purchase price for.

Among new cars, the fraction of lemons is very very small, maybe 1 percent. So in principle most of the people selling a new used car are those whose circumstances have changed. Hence, if you are willing to pay them 80 to 90 percent of their purchase price, you should be willing to purchase an "average" new used car for, say, 75 percent of its original price. Right? Well, not quite because now the lemon logic kicks in. Sellers who value their car at more than 75 percent don't sell, you as a buyer know that, and hence your average is between lemons and cars worth less than 75 percent. You offer 65 percent. Now even more people with changed circumstances decide to hold onto their cars. (Maybe the kids need a car, or they take the old car to their new home, or . . . .) So now you figure that very likely the cars remaining in the market are lemons and you only offer 55%. And so on.

[11] *The principles of game theory and economics are largely context-free; you do need to know details about an economy to judge whether or not a certain principle is true. Unfortunately, the same cannot be said for the jargon of economics. I remember reading Akerlof's paper as a student in India and being totally mystified as to what certain citric fruits and used cars have in common!*

[12] *These and other facts, along with much helpful advice about how to go about buying a used car, can be found at the web site of a company called Edmunds (at edmunds.com).*

The second and third facts are good illustrations of the role of signaling in this market. The only reason to pay more to a dealer is that the dealer offers a warranty. You say to yourself, "No seller of a lemon can offer a warranty, and so I should be willing to pay more to the dealer." Indeed if there were not this signaling element, then there would really be no good reason for dealers to be involved in this market. After all, whatever profits a dealer makes could have been split between the original seller and the eventual buyer.[13]

Indeed there is yet another "fact" about this market, and that is that private sellers often provide other kinds of quality signals. For example, some sellers have the car inspected by a mechanic of the buyer's choice, some turn over past service records, some make relatively expensive repairs before selling, and so on.

24.5 CONCLUDING REMARKS

In this section we will comment on the link between signaling games and mechanism design. The difference between these two topics is in who gets to go first: the informed (agent) or the uninformed (principal).

In a mechanism-design problem, the principal moves first and offers a set of options to the agent. Different types of agents might choose among the options differently. Note two things: (a) agents select after knowing the full consequences of each choice, and (b) *after the fact* the principal knows her agent's type, but because she moves first she cannot use that information in taking her own action.

In a signaling game the agent moves first by signaling. Different types of agents might pick different signals—or strategies—in anticipation of what the principal is going to do after she sees the signal. In this setup, however, (a) the agent can only guess as to how the principal is going to react to an out-of-equilibrium signal. Furthermore, (b) the principal can use information about her agent that she has learned from the signal before taking her own action.

The general setting, in which some players have better information, is known as the problem of *adverse selection*. Both approaches, mechanism design and signaling, have been employed for this problem. When a health or life insurance company offers a whole menu of policies and lets its clients decide what they want, the company is solving a mechanism-design problem. Similarly, an airline or a phone company may offer a variety of price options. In each of these cases it is the uninformed party that offers the options to the informed party.

In contrast, when used car sellers offer warranties or manufacturers offer money-back guarantees if customers are not fully satisfied, then they are offering a signal.[14] In these cases it is the informed party that creates options for the uninformed party. One of the first applications of signaling models in economics was to education.[15] The thought here is that by going to school an individual can signal superior intellect and greater competence—qualities that an employer would value highly.

[13] *There is the further question, Why don't private sellers offer warranties? They could then convince buyers to buy from them directly and avoid paying the dealers' markup. Part of the answer clearly is that it is inconvenient and costly for private individuals to do so.*

[14] *One of the more interesting offers recently was made by British Airways. They guaranteed that if you traveled business class between New York and London and were not fully satisfied with the service (you would simply have to say so) they would give you a free round-trip coach-class ticket anywhere in the United States. Unfortunately, it is then a dominant strategy for every passenger to claim that the service was terrible! I am not sure what results it produced for British Airways, but the program was shut down after a little while.*

[15] *See "Market Signaling" by A. M. Spence. Cambridge, MA: Harvard University Press, 1973.*

SUMMARY

1. In a game of one-sided incomplete information, the informed player will have an incentive to convey his information to the uninformed player if doing so will change the latter's action to the former's advantage.

2. A signaling game is one in which an informed player can take actions that can convey such information. The signal will, however, be noninformative if multiple types of informed players have incentives to send identical signals.

3. A perfect Bayesian equilibrium (PBE) is a signal choice by every informed type and an action choice by the uninformed player in which (a) the signals are correctly processed, (b) the uninformed player maximizes her expected payoff after correctly processing the signal, and (c) informed types send the most profitable signals.

4. A separating PBE is one in which different types send different signals and hence the initially uninformed player is fully informed by the time she takes her action. A pooling PBE is one in which the signals are noninformative.

5. In a market with uncertain product quality, bad-quality merchandise can drive out better quality goods. This phenomenon is called the lemons problem. By offering warranties—that is, by sending signals—good-quality sellers might be able to ameliorate the problem.

EXERCISES

SECTION 24.1

24.1
Give two examples, other than the ones discussed in the text, of market signaling. Identify clearly what each player's actions are.

24.2
Informally describe the market outcome in your two examples. What factors are important in determining whether the outcome is a separating or a pooling one?

SECTION 24.2

The first few questions concern example 1 in the chapter.

24.3

Explain why the argument that there are no perfect Bayesian separating equilibria is valid no matter what the value of the prior probability ρ.

Suppose that ρ is actually greater than 50 percent. Given exercise 24.3, we need only look for pooling equilibria.

24.4

Consider a signal of c by each of the informed agent types. Show that the best response for player 1 is to play c. Show that the payoff is 0 for the θ type and -2 for the μ type of player 2.

24.5

Argue that the μ type player can always do better by sending n as signal. Can you conclude that there is no pure-strategy pooling equilibrium in which the two types send the signal c?

24.6

Consider a signal of n by each of the informed agent types. Show that the best response for player 1 is to play c. Argue that the θ type can then do better by sending c as signal. What can you conclude about pure-strategy pooling equilibria in this game?

In the next few questions, therefore, we will look for a mixed-strategy PBE.

24.7

Consider the following strategy for player 1: $t(c) = c$ and $t(n) = c$ with probability $\frac{5}{7}$ (and with remaining probability $\frac{2}{7}$, she picks n after signal n). Show that the θ type is consequently indifferent between his two signals while the μ type strictly prefers to send the signal n.

24.8

Consider therefore the following signal strategy for player 2: the θ type sends the signal c with probability p while the μ type sends the signal n. If the principal receives a signal c, what can he conclude about the types of player 2? What is his best-response action $t(c)$?

24.9

For what value of p is the principal indifferent between picking actions c and n? Is a strategy of picking $t(n) = c$ with probability $\frac{5}{7}$ a best response? Explain. Summarize your findings about a PBE for this case ($\rho > \frac{1}{2}$).

The next few questions are about the incomplete information Bertrand (price) competition example of Chapter 20; firm 2 knows which is the correct payoff matrix (Table 24.3a

TABLE 24.3

1 \ 2	High	Medium	Low	1 \ 2	High	Medium	Low
High	5, 5	0, 8	0, 6	High	5, 5	6, 3	10, 1
Medium	8, 0	4, 4	0, 6	Medium	3, 6	4, 4	5, 2
Low	6, 0	6, 3	3, 3	Low	1, 10	2, 5	3, 3
(a)				(b)			

or 24.3b), but firm 1 does not. Suppose that the informed player can make his price choice before the uninformed player.

24.10

We will first investigate separating equilibria; suppose that player 1 can figure out player 2's type. Show from Table 24.3a that he will never play h. Show that a type 1 player 2's payoff—if his signal is correctly inferred and best responded to—can never be more than 3.

24.11

However, if player 1 recognizes that he is really playing Table 24.3b, show that it is a dominant strategy for him to play h. What are the possible payoffs for player 2 in this case?

24.12

Demonstrate that a type 1 player will want to send the same signal that a type 2 player is supposed to send. What can you conclude about separating equilibria in this game?

24.13

Suppose that $\rho \leq \frac{2}{5}$. Show that there is a pooling equilibrium in which both types signal by picking h. (Be careful to lay out every detail on the strategies.)

SECTION 24.3

In the next few questions we will explore the lemons problem with a third quality level, intermediate, whose repair costs are $500. Hence a buyer values this quality at $2,700 and a seller at $2,200.

24.14

If each quality level is just as prevalent in the population, show that a buyer will not be willing to pay any more than $2,400 for the merchandise. What kind of goods get sold at that price?

24.15

If only intermediates and lemons are sold in the market, how much will a buyer be willing to pay for a good? Would both of these kinds of buyers sell at this price? What is the market outcome?

24.16

Redo the exercises 24.14 and 24.15 for the case where the probabilities of lemons, intermediates, and good quality are $\frac{1}{4}$, $\frac{1}{2}$, and $\frac{1}{4}$, respectively.

24.17

Redo exercises 24.14 and 24.15 again for the case where lemons are only half as likely as either intermediates or good-quality merchandise. What have you learned about market breakdown from this exercise and the previous one?

24.18

If the probabilities of the three quality levels are, respectively, p, q, and $1 - p - q$, can you give general conditions for each of the following outcomes?

a. Only lemons are sold.

b. Lemons and intermediate-quality goods are sold but not good-quality merchandise.

c. All three quality levels are sold.

24.19

If the repair costs of the three quality levels are, respectively, p, q, and r and each quality is just as likely, can you give general conditions for each of the following outcomes?

a. Only lemons are sold.

b. Lemons and intermediate-quality goods are sold but not good-quality merchandise.

c. All three quality levels are sold.

The next few questions are concerned with the signaling game version of the lemons problem.

24.20

Show that there is no separating equilibrium other than the one analyzed in the text.

24.21

Consider a candidate pooling equilibrium in which both types offer warranties. What would the buyer bid for the good? Specify a belief that the buyer has when he gets an unexpected "no warranty" signal such that the buyer's bid and warranties by both sellers constitute a PBE.

24.22

Repeat exercise 24.21 for a pooling equilibrium in which neither seller offers a warranty.

SECTION 24.4

24.23

Some people have argued that the lemons problem can be ameliorated by way of government regulation. Suppose that the government passes a law that states that the owner of a lemon is entitled to trade in his car for another new car ("lemon laws" exist in many states, such as New Jersey). Argue in some detail that if the only kinds of cars were lemons and good cars (which are being sold because their owners' circumstances changed), the problem would indeed be solved.

24.24

How would your analysis change if there are more than two quality levels—lemons, intermediates, and good-quality cars? Explain your answer in detail.

24.25

What kind of regulation would be required to solve the problem that you uncovered in the previous question? Comment on the feasibility of such regulation.

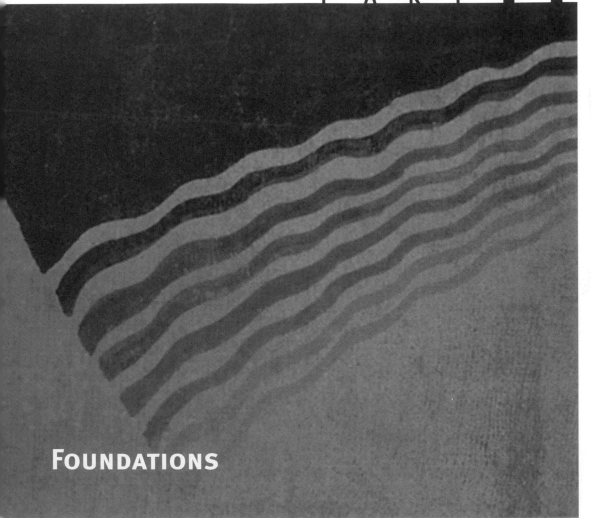

PART **FIVE**

FOUNDATIONS

CHAPTER 25

CALCULUS AND OPTIMIZATION

This is the first of three chapters that will develop the mathematics used in the text. In this chapter we will discuss calculus and optimization theory. The next chapter will discuss probability and expectation, and in Chapter 27 we will turn to decision theory. Each chapter will be a quick romp through a vast subject that can easily constitute a semester-long course by itself. Hence the chapters are meant only as refreshers and appetizers: refreshers that recall concepts and results that you have already seen or appetizers that send you to the main course.[1]

In section 25.1 we will discuss three subtopics: variables, functions, and slopes of functions. In this section we will also define a special category of functions called concave functions. Finally, in section 25.2, we will discuss necessary and sufficient conditions for optimization and give several examples to illustrate the results.

25.1   A CALCULUS PRIMER

The most basic entity in mathematics is called a *variable*. A variable is an object that can take on any number of possible values. For instance, the number of stars that are visible to the naked eye is a variable. This number can change with location—northern versus southern hemisphere, other light sources, Times Square versus rural Georgia—or with time of year. Likewise, the value of the Dow-Jones index is a variable. This number can change as factors affecting firm profitability change—interest rates, unemployment levels, or the trade deficit. Yet other variables include market price, the world's forest cover, the percentage of firms that declare bankruptcy, the size of the world's oil reserves, bids made in Final Jeopardy, and the depreciation of new cars within a year of purchase.

[1] *For calculus and optimization the main course can be found, for example, in A. C. Chiang's* Fundamental Methods of Mathematical Economics, *2nd ed. (New York: McGraw-Hill, 1984). If you wish to consult a book for a further treatment of probability and expectation, look at P. Newbold's* Statistics for Business and Economics, *4th ed. (Englewood Cliffs, NJ: Prentice Hall, 1995). Finally, a somewhat advanced treatment of decision theory can be found in* Mathematics for Economists *by L. Blume and C. Simon (New York: W. W. Norton, 1994).*

What is not a variable is an entity that cannot change in value; such an entity is called a *constant*. Physical constants such as the speed of light or π are not variables. Neither is the location of Central Park or the face value of a one-dollar bill.[2]

There are two kinds of variables: *independent* and *dependent* variables. Dependent variables take their value from the values of independent variables. For example, the price of bagels is an independent variable that determines the number of bagels bought at Columbia Bagels (on any weekday morning). That number also depends on the price of muffins at nearby University Food Market, the number of people who live in the Morningside Heights neighborhood (where the store is located), their income level, the price of cream cheese, and so on. Similarly, the amount of fuel consumption in the world depends on the price of oil, the price of substitute energy sources, time of year, available technologies, world GNPs, and other factors.[3]

It is standard to denote an independent variable by the symbol x and a dependent one by the symbol y.

25.1.1   FUNCTIONS

A *function* is a mathematical description that tells us the value of the dependent variable y for every value of the independent variable x. The notation for a function is f; that is, we write $y = f(x)$, and interpret the notation as "f takes every value of x and transforms it into a value $f(x)$."

The simplest example of a function is

$$f(x) = a + bx \tag{25.1}$$

[2] *The face value is a constant—at one dollar—although what that dollar buys is a variable that changes with the price index.*

where a and b are constants. For instance, when $a = 10$ and $b = -1$, then this is the function $f(x) = 10 - x$. Hence, when $x = 5$, $y = f(x) = 10 - 5 = 5$. Likewise, when $x = 37$, $y = -27$. Indeed a compact way of representing this particular function is by means of a graph, as seen in Figure 25.1. Note that the relationship between x and y is given by a straight line. Indeed this is true for the more general equation, equation 25.1. Its graph is pictured in Figure 25.2.[4] On account of the linear relationship, equations such as the ones given by equation 25.1 are called *linear functions*.

[3] *As you might guess, what is independent and what is dependent will depend on the context. For instance, if we analyze equilibrium conditions in the world oil market, then the price of oil is a dependent variable that is determined by the quantities demanded and supplied.*

By way of contrast, consider a graph such as the one given by Figure 25.3. Evidently the relationship between x and y is not linear; a function that generates such a graph is called a *nonlinear function*. In this particular instance, the function whose graph has been represented by Figure 25.3 is given by the general form

$$y = a + bx + cx^2 \tag{25.2}$$

[4] *In the graph we have taken the value of b to be a positive number, and so there is a positive relation between the independent and dependent variables; y is seen to increase as x increases.*

where a, b, and c are constants. The class of functions that are given by equation 25.2 are called *quadratic functions*. Once we specify values for the constants a, b, and c we get a specific quadratic function. For instance, the figure has been drawn for $y = 10 + x - 2x^2$, that is, for $a = 10$, $b = 1$, and $c = -2$.

[5] *For this function, b and c are positive constants and the variable x only takes on positive values.*

Another category of nonlinear functions is given by $y = a \log \frac{bx}{c}$, where, again, a, b, and c are constants.[5] This class is called the *log function*. Since $\log \frac{bx}{c}$ is equal

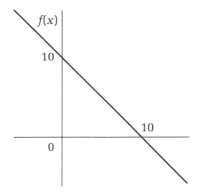

FIGURE 25.1

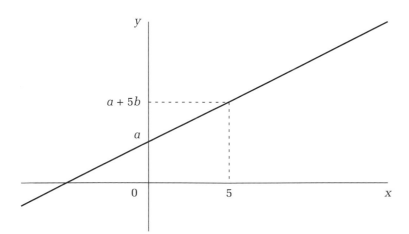

FIGURE 25.2

to $\log bx - \log c$ and, in turn, $\log bx$ is equal to $\log b + \log x$, we can rewrite the log function as

$$y = a \log x + d \tag{25.3}$$

where $d = a(\log b - \log c)$, a constant. For values of $a = 1$ and $d = 2$, we have drawn the graph of the log function in Figure 25.4.

25.1.2 SLOPES

For our purposes the most important concept related to a function is the *slope* of the function; it is a measure of the change in the dependent variable y when the independent variable x changes.

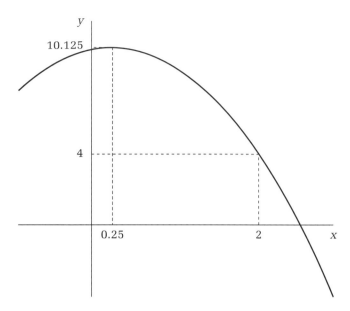

FIGURE 25.3

Consider the *linear function*, $y = 10 - x$ graphed in Figure 25.1. If x increases by one unit, say, from $x = 5$ to $x = 6$, y decreases from 5 to 4. Indeed, whenever x increases to $x + 1$ the change in y is $[10 - (x + 1)] - [10 - x]$, that is, -1. Hence, for every unit increase in x there is always a unit decrease in y, and this statement is true no matter what value of x we start from.

Indeed something more is true. If we consider an increase of x by 13 units, it is easy to verify that it leads to a decrease of y by 13 units. Or if we consider a change of x by Δ units, then y changes by $-\Delta$ units; this statement is true whether Δ equals 1, or 13, or -245. Put differently, the ratio

$$\frac{\text{Change in } y}{\text{Change in } x} \qquad\qquad (25.4)$$

is always equal to -1, and this is true no matter what size change in x we consider, and no matter which initial value of x we consider the change from. Equation 25.4 gives the rate of change (in y as x changes)—and it is the precise definition of slope for a linear function.

For the general linear function, $y = a + bx$, the rate of change—or slope—when x changes from x' to x^* is

$$\frac{a + bx^* - (a + bx')}{x^* - x'} = b$$

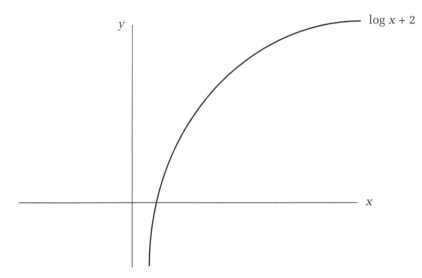

$\log x + 2$

FIGURE 25.4

In other words, *for any linear function, the slope is given by the constant b*. When b is positive, the linear function slopes upward; when it is negative, the function slopes downward.

Let us turn now to *nonlinear functions*. Here matters are a little more complicated. Consider $y = 10 + x - 2x^2$. When x increases from 5 to 6, the dependent variable changes from -35 to -56. And when x further increases from 6 to 7, then y changes to -81. Notice, therefore, that the size of the effect of a unit change in x depends on the initial value of x. Similarly, the ratio $\frac{\text{Change in } y}{\text{Change in } x}$ depends on how big the change in x is; a unit change from $x = 5$ leads to a ratio equal to $\frac{-21}{1} = -21$, and a two-unit change leads to a ratio value equal to $\frac{-46}{2} = -23$.

So we cannot always use equation 25.4 as the definition of slope for a nonlinear function. It turns out, however, that if we consider changes in x that are very close to 0 in size—such as a change by 0.0001 units or a change of 0.0002 units—then the ratio is essentially the same. Furthermore, for such small changes the ratio is essentially the same as the slope of the straight line that forms the tangent to the function.

And this is the definition: *The slope of a nonlinear function at some value of x, say at $x = 5$, is the slope of the (linear) tangent to the function at $x = 5$.*[6] It is clear from looking at the graph that the slope therefore varies with x (unlike in the case of a linear function).

25.1.3 SOME FORMULAS

There are well-known formulas for the slope of the quadratic and the log function. The *slope of the quadratic function*, $y = a + bx + cx^2$ is given by

---

[6] *A function need not have a well-defined tangent at every x, that is, it need not have a slope everywhere.*

$b + 2cx$

If we consider the function $y = 10 + x - 2x^2$, then its slope is $1 - 4x$. As you can verify from Figure 25.3, the slope is positive up to $x = \frac{1}{4}$ and negative thereafter.

On the other hand, the *log function*, $y = a \log x + d$, has *slope* equal to

$$\frac{a}{x}$$

Hence for the function $y = \log x + 2$, the slope is $\frac{1}{x}$. Another log function is $y = a \log (bx + c)$. The slope of this function is $\frac{ab}{bx+c}$.

Two other formulas about slopes are very useful to know. First, the slope of the function $a \times f(x)$ where a is a constant, is nothing but a times the slope of f. Second, if we have a sum of two functions, f and g, that is, $y = f(x) + g(x)$, then the slope of the sum function is nothing but the sum of the slopes of the two functions.

Sum of Two Linear Functions: The slope of the sum function $y = a + bx + c + dx = a + c + (b + d)x$ is $b + d$. Hence, the slope of $y = (10 - x) + 227 + 6x$ is $-1 + 6$, or 5.

Sum of a Linear and a Quadratic Function: Similarly, the slope of $y = (a + bx) + (c + dx + ex^2)$ is $b + d + 2ex$. So the slope of $y = 10 - x + 10 + x - 2x^2$ is $-1 + 1 - 4x = -4x$.

Sum of a Quadratic and a Log Function: And the slope of $y = a + bx + cx^2 + d \log x + e$ is $b + 2cx + \frac{d}{x}$. Hence, the slope of $10 + x - 2x^2 - \log x$ is equal to $1 - 4x - \frac{1}{x}$.

25.1.4   Concave Functions

If a function has the property that the higher the value of x the lower its slope, then the function is said to be *concave*. For instance, consider the function $y = 10 + x - 2x^2$. We just showed that its slope is $1 - 4x$. Hence the slope decreases with x; that is, the function is concave. You can also see that fact by looking at Figure 25.3; up to $x = \frac{1}{4}$, where the function is rising, it rises more and more slowly; that is, it becomes flatter and flatter. Beyond that value the function falls, and as you can see it falls faster and faster as x increases.

Since the slope of a general quadratic function is $b + 2cx$, the slope decreases with x if and only if the constant c is negative. Hence all quadratic functions for which c is negative are concave, and those with c positive are not concave.

As another example, consider the log function, $\log x + 2$. We have told you that its slope is $\frac{1}{x}$ (the function is only defined for $x > 0$). Again, as x increases, $\frac{1}{x}$ decreases, and hence the function is concave. You can also see that relationship by looking at the graph of the function, Figure 25.4; the function becomes flatter and flatter as x increases. For a general log function, $a \log x + d$, the slope is equal to $\frac{a}{x}$; as long as a is positive, the slope decreases with x. Hence such a function is concave.

For a linear function, the slope is unchanged (and equal to b) no matter what value of x we consider. In other words, although the slope does not actually decrease with x, it does not increase either. Hence we can think of this as a borderline case and also call it a concave function. Sometimes to distinguish functions such as $10 + x - 2x^2$ or the log function $\log x + 2$, whose slope actually decreases in x, we call those functions *strictly concave* functions.

From the previous subsection you know that the slope of the sum of two functions is the sum of the slopes. Hence if each of the functions is concave, and therefore each has a slope that decreases with x, then so must the sum of the slopes decrease with x. Put differently, the sum of two concave functions is also concave. By exactly the same reasoning, $af(x)$ is also a concave function whenever f is a concave function and a is a positive constant.

In Chapter 27 you will see that there is a surprising connection between concave functions and risk attitudes in the presence of uncertainty.

25.2 AN OPTIMIZATION THEORY PRIMER

In this book, the function that we are interested in is the payoff (or utility) function of a player. The independent variable in such a function is the player's strategy. Often we look for the best such strategy; that is, we look for the strategy choice that makes the value of the payoff function greatest. To equip us to carry out that optimization exercise we need to know how to find, for any function f, that value of x at which the function attains its greatest value.

Here is a more precise statement of our quest: find conditions that characterize any x^* such that $f(x^*) \geq f(x)$ for all x. The last statement leaves open the possibility that there may be more than one such x^*. We will therefore additionally give conditions that characterize a unique maximum, that is, an x^* for which $f(x^*) > f(x)$ for all $x \neq x^*$.[7]

25.2.1 NECESSARY CONDITIONS

Suppose, to begin with, that the independent variable x can take on any real-numbered value. For illustration's sake refer to Figure 25.3, the graph of the function $y = 10 + x - 2x^2$.

Consider any x at which the slope of the function is positive, that is, $x < \frac{1}{4}$. Since the slope is positive—y increases as we increase x—we are able to increase y further; we must, therefore, not have yet hit the optimum value x^*.

Consider instead any x at which the slope is negative, that is, $x > \frac{1}{4}$. Now things are exactly the opposite. Since the slope is negative, y can be increased by decreasing the value of x—and so we must not yet be at x^*. And that step brings us to our last candidate for x^*, $x = \frac{1}{4}$. As you can see from the graph, the function does in fact attain its highest value at $\frac{1}{4}$, that is, at an x where the slope is 0.

There is a more general finding from this analysis:

Proposition 1 (Necessary Condition for a Maximum). If a function f attains its maximum at x^*, then the slope of the function at x^* must be zero.

[7] *We will consider only functions that have a slope at all values of x.*

Put differently, you can immediately discard as inoptimal all x at which the slope is not equal to zero. This necessary condition also has a physical analogy. Imagine that you are climbing up a hill. As long as the hill slopes upward, you are yet to get to the summit. Conversely, if the hill slopes downward at your feet, then you have already been to the summit.

Proposition 1's conclusion—at the optimum the slope must be zero—is sometimes called the *first-order condition for an optimum*. The reason for that terminology is that the slope is sometimes referred to as a first-order concept and the condition that it has to obey at a maximum is that it must be equal to zero.

The function $y = 10 - x$ (Figure 25.1) always slopes downward; hence it has no maximum. On the other hand, the function $y = \log x + 2$ (Figure 25.4) always slopes upward; again it has no maximum because the further along with x that you go, the higher is the value of y that you generate. These two examples illustrate one reason why Proposition 1 is called a *necessary* condition—*if* x^* is a maximum, *then* its slope must be zero. In particular, the condition does not guarantee that a maximum will always exist.

25.2.2   SUFFICIENT CONDITIONS

There is also no guarantee that merely because the slope is zero, the function must be at a peak. If you think about it, when you reach the lowest point in the Grand Canyon, then too the slope is zero. Put differently, the *minimum* of a function is also characterized by zero slope. Let us illustrate this case with a different quadratic function, $y = 10 - x + 2x^2$, Figure 25.5. For this function, the slope is zero at $\frac{1}{4}$, but now that value corresponds to a minimum rather than a maximum of the function.

So how can we distinguish a maximum from a minimum? When do we know that if the slope is zero it is so because we have reached a maximum? When do we have *sufficient* cause for celebration? It turns out that this will be the case if the function is concave. Recall that a function is strictly concave if its slope decreases with x. Well, if the slope is 0 at x^*, then it must be positive prior to x^*; that is, the function must still be climbing at those points and hence must be below $f(x^*)$. Likewise the slope must be negative beyond x^*; that is, the function must be decreasing in that region and at those points must be below $f(x^*)$.

Things are pretty much the same if the function is concave but not necessarily strictly concave. The additional possibility here is that the slope may be zero at x^*—and also at points close to x^*. In that case, these other points are also points of maximum for the function. Collecting all this together we can state:

Proposition 2 (Sufficient Condition for a Maximum).   If the slope of a concave function is zero at x^*, then the function attains a maximum at that point. If the function is strictly concave then there can be at most one such point at which the slope is zero; that is, there is a unique maximum.

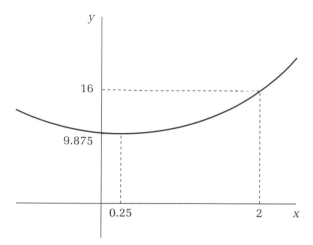

FIGURE 25.5

25.2.3 FEASIBILITY CONSTRAINTS

In many economic contexts, there are constraints that have to be satisfied by the independent variable x. A common one is that it cannot take on negative values. For instance, neither price nor quantity can be negative. Another common constraint is that we can only pick those values of x for which yet another function, say g, takes on nonnegative values. For example, in an investment problem we can only consider strategies that generate a rate of return that is at least as high as the market rate.

Consider nonnegativity constraints first. When there are such constraints, the necessary condition for an optimum needs to be modified somewhat. To see why this must be the case, consider the quadratic function, $y = 10 - x - 2x^2$, Figure 25.6.

Note that we have drawn the graph only for nonnegative values of x, that is, for $x \geq 0$. (The negative values of x are graphed by a broken line.) As you can see, the highest value of the function (in nonnegative territory) is achieved at $x = 0$, and at this point the slope of the function is not zero but rather it is negative. What that observation tells us is that if we could, we would want to reduce the value of x even further [and doing so would increase $f(x)$]. But of course we cannot. Put differently, the necessary condition for an optimum now divides into two cases: If $x^* = 0$, then the slope of the function at the optimum has to be less than or equal to zero. All that we can say for sure is that if we increase x we will lower y. On the other hand, if $x^* > 0$, then the slope at that point has to be zero because if it is positive we will want to go forward and if it is negative we will want to decrease x.

Indeed this idea can be generalized. Consider any set of feasibility constraints that puts limits on the values of the independent variable; for example, suppose that $30 \geq x \geq 0$. It should be clear that if the optimum x^* is strictly between 0 and 30, then

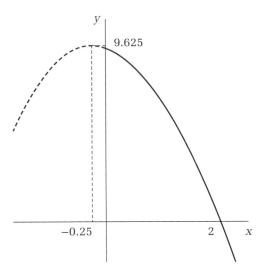

FIGURE 25.6

the slope of the function f has to be zero at that point. After all, we do have the room to either increase or decrease x, and if the slope were not zero we would want to do one or the other in order to increase the value of f. However, if the optimum is reached at either of the two corners, then the slope could be negative (if $x^* = 0$) or positive (if $x^* = 30$). We call any x that is strictly in between the two corners, where neither constraint is binding, an *interior* value of the variable.

And this statement is true even more generally: Suppose that x needs to satisfy another constraint such as $g(x) \geq 0$. Call a value of x interior if there is room to spare under this constraint as well, that is, if $g(x) > 0$. We have the following condition:

Proposition 3 (Necessary Condition for a Maximum Subject to Feasibility Constraints).
Suppose that x^* is an optimum that is interior relative to the constraints $g(x) \geq 0$ and $a \geq x \geq 0$, where a is some constant. Then the slope at x^* must be zero.

What about sufficient conditions? Suppose that f and g are both concave functions. Then one sufficient condition is identical to that of the last subsection: if there is an x^* that is feasible and at which the slope of f is zero, then that x^* is a maximum. Actually, for this problem there is even a slightly weaker requirement that signals an optimum:

Proposition 4 (Sufficient Condition for a Maximum Subject to Feasibility Constraints).
Suppose that f and g are concave functions. Suppose too that we can find a feasible x^* and a nonnegative constant λ for which two conditions are satisfied: $\lambda g(x^*) = 0$ and the

slope of the sum function $f(x) + \lambda g(x)$ is zero. Then x^* is a maximum. In particular, if the slope of f is zero at x^*, then we have a maximum.

The special case in the last sentence follows because we can always set $\lambda = 0$ if we already have the slope of f to be zero at some x^*; thereby we will have satisfied the sufficient condition for a maximum.

25.2.4   QUADRATIC AND LOG FUNCTIONS

Example 1

The quadratic function $y = 10 + 8x - x^2$ has a slope function equal to $8 - 2x$. Since the slope decreases in x, this is a strictly concave function. There is a unique value of $x^*(= 4)$ at which the function has slope zero (and this then is the unique maximum).

Example 2

Consider a sum function such as $y = \left(10 + x - 2x^2\right) + (7x - 17)$.

CONCEPT CHECK

CONCAVITY AND OPTIMUM

Show that each component of the sum is concave and hence so is the sum function. Show that the slope equals $8 - 4x$. Show finally that $x^* = 2$. Why is this a unique maximum for the function?

Example 3

Consider instead a sum function such as $y = \left(10 + x - 2x^2\right) - (7x - 17)$. Suppose we want to maximize this function subject to the constraint that $x \geq 0$.

CONCEPT CHECK

CONSTRAINED OPTIMUM

Show that the slope of this function equals $-4x - 6$. Show that its unique maximum is attained at $x = 0$? Is the slope 0 at that point?

Example 4: General Quadratic Example

Consider $y = a + bx + cx^2$ (and $c < 0$).

CONCEPT CHECK
OPTIMUM

Show that the first-order condition is $b + 2cx^* = 0$. How would your answer change if x is required to be nonnegative?

Example 5
Consider the function $2 \log x - 8x$.

CONCEPT CHECK
CONCAVITY AND OPTIMUM

Show that the function is strictly concave and the slope equals $\frac{2}{x} - 8$. Show finally that $x^* = \frac{1}{4}$. Why is this a unique maximum for the function?

Example 6
Consider $y = \log(30 - x)$.[8] The slope of the function, applying the formula from the previous section, is $-\frac{1}{30-x}$. As x increases, the denominator becomes smaller and hence the slope becomes more and more negative. Put differently, the function is also concave. It attains a maximum at $x = 0$.

SUMMARY

1. A dependent variable y takes its value from the values of an independent variable x. A function is a mathematical representation of the relationship between an independent and a dependent variable.

2. A common example of a function is a linear function, $y = a + bx$, where a and b are constants. Examples of nonlinear functions include quadratic and log functions.

3. The slope of a linear function is the ratio $\frac{\text{Change in } y}{\text{Change in } x}$; it equals the constant b. The slope of a nonlinear function at x is the slope of the linear tangent to the function at that point.

4. A concave function is one whose slope decreases with the value of x.

[8] *As we have said before, the log function is only defined for positive values of the independent variable. In particular $30 - x$ therefore needs to be positive; that is, for this example we need to restrict attention to x between 0 and 30.*

5. When there are no restrictions on x, if a function attains a maximum at x^*, its slope must be zero at that point. Conversely, if a concave function has slope zero at a point x^*, then it must attain a maximum at that point.

6. When x is constrained to be nonnegative, at a maximum $x^* > 0$, the slope of the function must be zero. Again if a concave function has slope zero at a point x^*, then it must attain a maximum at that point.

EXERCISES

SECTION 25.1

25.1
Give three examples of variables. Indicate in each case why the value of the object is not constant.

25.2
Give three examples of constants. Indicate in each case why the value of the object is constant.

25.3
Give three examples of pairs of an independent and a dependent variable.

25.4
Graph the following linear functions:

a. $y = 2 + 3x$

b. $y = 2 - 3x$

c. $y = 20 + 3x$

25.5
Graph the following quadratic functions:

a. $y = 2 + 3x - x^2$

b. $y = 2 - 3x + \frac{1}{2}x^2$

c. $y = 20 + 3x - 2x^2$

For the exercises that follow, whenever you see the function log x, assume that $x > 0$.

25.6

Graph the following log functions:

a. $y = 2 + 3 \log x$

b. $y = 2 - 3 \log x$

c. $y = 20 + 3 \log x$

25.7

Compute the slope of the functions in the three examples of exercise 25.4. (Do not apply the formula; instead use the definition of the slope of a linear function, $\frac{\text{Change in } y}{\text{Change in } x}$.)

25.8

Compute the slope of the functions in the three examples of exercise 25.5 at $x = -3$, $x = 0$, and $x = 10$. (In these cases, do apply the formula for the slope of a quadratic function.)

25.9

For the three examples of exercise 25.5, graph the general formula for the slope as a function of x.

25.10

Compute the slope of the functions in the three examples of exercise 25.6 at $x = 1$, $x = 5$, and $x = 100$. (Apply the formula for the slope of a log function.)

25.11

Compute the general formula for the slope for each of the following sum functions:

a. $y = 2 + 3x - x^2 + (2 - 3 \log x)$

b. $y = 20 + 3x + (2 - 3x + \frac{1}{2}x^2)$

In each case also compute the specific value for the slope at $x = 6$ and $x = 15$.

25.12

Repeat exercise 25.11 for the following sum functions. (In each case, a through d refer to constants.)

a. $y = a + bx - x^2 + (d - \log x)$

b. $y = a + x + (2 - cx + dx^2)$

25.13

Consider the following functions:

a. $y = 2 - 3 \log(2 + 3x)$

b. $y = 14 - 9x + 3x^2$

Find the slopes for the specific values $x = 1$, $x = 5$, and $x = 100$.

25.14

Find the general formula of the slope of these functions:

a. $2 \log x + \log(100 - x)$, for x between 0 and 100

b. $2 \log 5x + \log(100 - x)$, again for x between 0 and 100

c. $\log x + \log(2 + 3x - x^2)$, for x between 0 and 3

In each case, also compute the specific values of the slope at $x = 2$.

25.15

Show that $af(x)$ is also a concave function whenever f is a concave function and a is a positive constant.

25.16

Show that $af(x) + bg(x)$ is also a concave function whenever f and g are concave functions and a and b are positive constants.

25.17

Verify that the following functions are concave:

a. $2 - 5x - x^2$

b. $\log(100 - x)$, with x defined between 0 and 100

c. $2 + 3 \log x$

25.18

Verify that the following functions are concave:

a. $15x - 3x^2$

b. $\log(80 - 16x)$ for x between 0 and 5

c. $51 \log x$

SECTION 25.2

25.19

By examining the general formula of the slope of the following functions, determine which values of x are *not* points at which the function is at a maximum:

a. $2 \log x + \log(100 - x)$, for x between 0 and 100

b. $2 \log 5x + \log(100 - x)$, again for x between 0 and 100

c. $\log x + \log(2 + 3x - x^2)$, for x between 0 and 3

25.20

Find x at which the slope is equal to zero, for the following:

a. $y = 2 + 3x - x^2 + (2 - 3 \log x)$

b. $y = 20 + 3x + (2 - 3x + \frac{1}{2}x^2)$

25.21
Has your search in exercise 25.19 generated points of maxima? (Hint: Check for the concavity of the functions concerned.)

25.22
Repeat exercise 25.21 for the functions in exercise 25.20.

25.23
Find the point(s) of maximum value for the following functions:

a. $15x - 3x^2$

b. $\log(80 - 16x)$ for x between 0 and 5

c. $51 \log x - \frac{1}{2}x^2$

25.24
Find the point(s) of maximum value for the following functions:

a. $2x + \log(100 - x)$, for x between 0 and 100

b. $-5x^2 + \log(100 - x)$, again for x between 0 and 100

c. $3x + \log(2 + 3x - x^2)$, for x between 0 and 3

25.25
Find the point(s) of maximum value for the following functions:

a. $2 - 5x - x^2$

b. $\log(100 - x)$, with x defined between 0 and 100

c. $2 + 3 \log x - \frac{1}{2}x^2$

25.26
Find the general formulas for the point(s) of maximum value for the following functions:

a. $y = a + bx - x^2 + (d - \log x)$

b. $y = a + x + (2 - cx + dx^2)$

State precisely any restrictions that you need to place on the value of the constants.

25.27
In exercise 25.19, did you identify points of maxima that are interior? Explain.

25.28
Repeat exercise 25.27 for the functions in exercise 25.24.

25.29

Find the points of maxima of f subject to the constraints that $x \geq 0$ and $g(x) \geq 0$.

a. $f = 2 + 3 \log x$ and $g = 2 + 3x - x^2$

b. $f = 20 - 3x$ and $g = 2 + 3x - x^2$

25.30

Repeat exercise 25.29 for the following functions:

a. $f = 10 + \log x + \log(10 - x)$ and $g = 10x - x^2$

b. $f = 1 + x - x^2$ and $g = 1 - x^2$

CHAPTER 26

PROBABILITY AND EXPECTATION

Uncertainty plays a role in game theory for several reasons: players may be uncertain about whom they are playing against or how the game is going to proceed, or they may be uncertain about what their opponents are going to do, or they may wish to be uncertain about the exact action that they themselves might take (so as to keep their opponents guessing).

In section 26.1 we will discuss the principal way in which uncertainty can be mathematically described. Within this section we will also discuss a subtopic called independence and conditional probability. In section 26.2 we will turn to a discussion of averages over uncertain events.

26.1   PROBABILITY

There is a common framework within which we can represent any uncertain situation, be it a lottery, a coin toss, a course grade, the performance of a stock, the strategy of a rival, the outcome of a game, and so on. There are three components to this common description: a sample space, an event space, and a probability function.

A *sample space* contains a list of all possible outcomes to the uncertainty. For example in a *coin toss* the sample space is {heads (H), tails (T)}; in a *roll of a die*, it is {1, 2, . . . , 6}; in a *lottery*, the sample space is {win (W), lose (L)}; in the *price of a stock*—when the price can only move by a sixteenth of a dollar—it is $\{\frac{1}{16} \times n;\ n = 0, 1, 2, \ldots\}$; and so on. The sample space may have a finite or an infinite number of elements.

The *event space* is the set of subsets of the sample space; that is, each element of the event space is a set of outcomes. In other words, an outcome is *one* possible way, and an event is one of *several* possible ways, in which uncertainty may get resolved.

To fix ideas, consider the four sample spaces described previously. For the *coin toss*, the associated event space is (H, T, {H, T}, Φ).[1] In the *die roll*, it is (1, . . . , 6, {1, 2}, {1, 3}, . . . , {5, 6}, {1, 2, 3}, {1, 2, 4}, . . . , {4, 5, 6}, {1, 2, 3, 4}, . . . , Φ); the event {1, 2, 4}, for instance, should be interpreted as "either 1 or 2 or 4 will come up when the die is rolled." Similarly, {4, 5, 6} describes the event that the outcome of the die roll is at least as high as 4. For the *lottery*, the event space is (W, L, {W,L}, Φ). In each of these examples, the event space is finite.

In contrast, the event space is infinite in the *stock price* example; it is, in fact, equal to an infinite number of categories of possible outcomes—all possible prices, all possible pairs of prices, all possible price triples, and so on.[2]

$$\frac{1}{16} \times n; \quad n = 0, 1, 2, \ldots ;$$

$$\left\{ \frac{1}{16} \times n_1, \frac{1}{16} \times n_2 \right\}; \quad n_1, n_2 = 0, 1, 2, \ldots ;$$

$$\left\{ \frac{1}{16} \times n_1, \frac{1}{16} \times n_2, \frac{1}{16} \times n_3 \right\}; \quad n_1, n_2, n_3 = 0, 1, 2, \ldots$$

$$\vdots$$

Finally, a *probability function*, $p(.)$, is an assignment of a fractional number to each event. This fraction should be interpreted as the *likelihood* that the event in question will actually happen. This likelihood could be an objective assignment, arising out of a description of the physical phenomenon; or it could be a subjective likelihood, arising out of a player's beliefs about the way in which uncertainty might resolve itself.

For instance, in the first two examples, we could use the physical description of a coin toss or a die roll to assign the appropriate probabilities.[3] In the first example, for a fair coin, we will assign $p(H) = p(T) = \frac{1}{2}$, $p(H$ or $T) = 1$, $p(\Phi) = 0$. Exactly the same objective approach would give us the following probability function for the second example; p(any one number) $= \frac{1}{6}$, p(either of any two numbers) $= \frac{1}{3}, \ldots, p$(any number at all) $= 1$, p(no number) $= 0$.

The assignment of probabilities in the third example would depend on the nature of the lottery. In a lottery in which exactly one of, say, 1 million ticket holders wins, the probability of winning for the holder of a single ticket is $p(W) = \frac{1}{1 \text{ million}}$. The probability would have to be subjectively assigned if you did not know how many other people also bought tickets to the lottery. In a slot machine, however, the chances of winning depend only on the configuration of the machine and not on how many other people have played that machine. Hence, the probability of winning is an objective probability.

The daily New York State lotto is an example of a lottery in which the likelihood of winning depends both on objective factors and on how many other people are playing the lottery. The way this lottery works is the following: In sequence, six balls are drawn from an urn full of numbered balls. The numbers associated with these six balls constitutes the winning combination for the day. Each holder of a lottery ticket chooses six numbers at the time he purchases his ticket. The winner of the lottery is the individual (if any)

[1] Φ *is notation for the empty set, that is, a set that has no elements. By convention, all event spaces include the empty set. Think of this as the possibility that "nothing will happen," in a coin toss, that "neither H nor T will happen."*

[2] *You may have noticed that the event space is finite whenever the sample space is finite. Indeed the converse is true as well; the event space is finite only if the sample space is finite.*

[3] *Another popular way to assign probabilities—and this works for events that have been going on for a long time like a series of coin tosses—is to assign to each event the relative frequency of the observed occurrence. In that case, the probability of getting a head on the next toss of the coin is taken to be the fraction of the previous coin tosses that resulted in a head.*

whose picks match the numbers drawn later that day. If there are multiple matches, then the prize is shared.[4]

Subjective beliefs would be the appropriate way of assigning probabilities in the stock price example.

The probability function is required to satisfy two properties:[5]

1. The probability of the sample space is 1.

2. For any two disjoint sets E and F in the event space,

$$p(E \text{ or } F) = p(E) + p(F)$$

The first requirement is really a consistency condition. It says that all of the possible outcomes must be included in the sample space. Since two events are disjoint if and only if they are mutually exclusive, the second requirement says that the likelihood of one of two mutually exclusive events happening is the sum of the likelihoods of each one individually happening.

To see these two properties at work, consider an event, say E, and its complement, say F (i.e., consider the set F made up of all possible outcomes that are not in E). By definition, these two sets, E and F, are disjoint and therefore, by property 2, $p(E \text{ or } F) = p(E) + p(F)$. However, it is also the case that between them, E and F cover all possible outcomes; that is, they cover the sample space. (Why?) Hence, by property 1, $p(E) + p(F) = 1$. Therefore, the probability of the complement of an event E—that is, the probability of "not E"—is $1 - p(E)$.

As another application, consider two events E and F that are not disjoint. What should be the probability that either of these events will happen; that is, what should $p(E \text{ or } F)$ be? This probability is not $p(E) + p(F)$ because that would double-count the outcomes that are in both the events E and F. The natural thing to do would be to count these outcomes once; either within E or F. To that end, denote F/E as the set of outcomes in F that do not belong to E as well. Evidently, E and F/E are disjoint sets. Hence, by property 2, $p(E \text{ or } F/E) = p(E) + p(F/E)$. Note, furthermore, that the event E or F/E is really the same event as E or F. (Why?) Collecting all this together, we have $p(E \text{ or } F) = p(E) + p(F/E)$.

Finally, let us apply all of the ideas of this section to a *game*. Consider the following simultaneous-move game:

1 \ 2	L	C	R
U	0, 0	0, 1	1, 2
M	1, 0	1, 1	1, 1
D	2, 0	2, 2	2, 2

Suppose that there is uncertainty about exactly which strategies will be played by the two players. Consider player 1. The *sample space* of his strategic uncertainty is,

[4] *The drawing of numbers for the state lotto is conducted on television. For those of you in the New York metropolitan area who wish to tune in, it is conducted every night during the 11 P.M. news broadcast on the ABC affiliate, Channel 7. Prizes can range up to 14 million dollars.*

[5] *Two sets are said to be disjoint if they have no intersection. Two sets in the event space are disjoint if there is no shared outcome between them. For instance the events {1,2,3} and {4,5} are disjoint.*

therefore, $\{U, M, D\}$; the *event space* is $(U, M, D; \{U, M\}, \{U, D\}, \{M, D\}; \{U, M, D\})$. The event D means "D will get played," whereas the event $\{U, D\}$ means "either U or D will get played," and the event $\{U, M, D\}$ means "any one of the three strategies will get played."

The *probability function* is an assignment of likelihoods to each of the seven possible events. Given property 2, one way to accomplish this purpose is to assign probabilities to the three outcomes and then "build up" the probability of an event as the sum of the probabilities of all the outcomes contained in that event. For instance, say player 1 is half as likely to play U as either M or D. In that case, $p(U) := \frac{1}{5}$, $p(M) = p(D) = \frac{2}{5}$; $p(\{U, M\}) = p(\{U, D\}) = \frac{3}{5}$, $p(\{M, D\}) = \frac{4}{5}$, and $p(\{U, M, D\}) = 1$.

CONCEPT CHECK
PLAYER 2

Write down player 2's *sample* and *event spaces*. If player 2 is equally likely to play her three strategies, write down the *probability function*.

Note that these two assignments satisfy the two requirements on the probability function. If we take the two disjoint sets $\{U, M\}$ and $\{D\}$ for example, the probability that either of these events will happen—$\{U, M\}$ *or* $\{D\}$, that is, $\{U, M, D\}$—is exactly the sum of $p(\{U, M\})$ and $p(D)$.[6]

So far almost all of the examples that we have considered are those with a finite number of outcomes. It is instructive sometimes to look instead at examples that involves an infinite number of outcomes.

To motivate such an example imagine that you draw a line 10 inches long on a piece of paper. Then you close your eyes and place a pin at some random point on the line.[7] Now the pin could be anywhere on that line—at an inch from the beginning, 3.5 inches, 2.789 inches, or, as your measuring scale becomes more and more accurate, at 7.9998 inches, 5.006748904 inches, and so on. In other words, any point on that line—and there are an infinite number of them—is a possibility. Furthermore, any point is just as likely as any other, or, if you wish, any half-inch segment is just as likely to contain your pinpoint as any other half-inch segment.

This discussion can be formalized by the following probability assignment: Consider any segment between the beginning and x inches from the beginning. It gets a probability assignment of $\frac{x}{10}$. Hence the half line between 0 and 5 inches has a probability assignment of $\frac{5}{10}$, or 50 percent. The segment between 0 and 7.6 inches has an assignment of $\frac{7.6}{10}$, or 76 percent; again this is exactly the fraction that it represents of the entire line, and hence this is a natural assignment if you choose to place the pin with your eyes closed.

This probability assignment is called a *uniform distribution*; "uniform" refers to the fact that the uncertainty is uniformly spread over all possible outcomes. More formally,

[6] *The method by which we picked a probability function for the players' strategies can be applied to any uncertain situation with a finite number of outcomes. To illustrate, suppose the sample space is $\{s_1, s_2, \ldots, s_M\}$. Pick an assignment of probabilities to the M outcomes, say, $p_1, p_2, \ldots, p_M$. Then given any event, say $\{s_3, s_8, s_{27}\}$, the probability to be assigned to this event is $p_3 + p_8 + p_{27}$.*

[7] *Okay, so it might take you a few tries before you actually land the pin on the line!*

if the outcomes to an uncertain occurrence can be given numerical values, and if these values lie between two constants a and b, the assignment is said to be uniform if for any x between a and b, the probability of the segment between a and x is $\frac{x-a}{b-a}$.

26.1.1   INDEPENDENCE AND CONDITIONAL PROBABILITY

Often we are asked to evaluate the likelihood that two specific events will occur in two resolutions of uncertainty. For example, we may evaluate the likelihood that on two throws of a coin we will get an H followed by a T, or that on two rolls of a die an even and then an odd number will turn up, or the stock price will go up and then come down by $\frac{1}{16}$. Let the two events be denoted E and F. The events are said to be *independent* if and only if

$$p(E \text{ and } F) = p(E) \times p(F)$$

If two events are not independent, they are said to be *dependent*. The first two examples in the preceding paragraph are independent events. The third example may or may not be, and whether it is or is not will depend on the underlying reason why the stock went up in the first place. If it went up because of a good earnings report, then the events may not be independent; the likelihood that the stock will then go down is not the same as the likelihood would have been without the earnings report.

In the game of the previous subsection, if the two players choose their strategies unilaterally, then the pair of strategies are independent choices. For instance, suppose that player 1 chooses U, M, and D according to the probabilities $\frac{1}{2}$, $\frac{1}{6}$, and $\frac{1}{3}$ and player 2 chooses between L, C, and R according to the probabilities $\frac{1}{4}$, $\frac{1}{6}$, and $\frac{7}{12}$ (and they choose unilaterally). In that case the probability that the pair U and C gets chosen is $\frac{1}{2} \times \frac{1}{6}$, while the probability that M and R get chosen is $\frac{1}{6} \times \frac{7}{12}$.

An example of dependent events comes from the nightly drawing for the New York State lottery. Recall that from an urn full of balls, each of which carries an identifying number, balls are drawn in sequence and without replacement. Suppose that there are a hundred balls in the urn. The likelihood that any one of them will be drawn is therefore $\frac{1}{100}$. However, the likelihood that any pair of them will be drawn is not $\frac{1}{100} \times \frac{1}{100}$ but rather $\frac{1}{100} \times \frac{1}{99}$. (Why? See the discussion that follows if you are in doubt.) Another example is the likelihood of reinjuring an already twisted ankle.

To deal with dependent events, we use the notion of a *conditional probability*. The conditional probability that an event F will happen given that we know an event E has already happened is denoted $p(F \mid E)$. For example, if the urn has six differently numbered balls in it, the conditional probability of drawing ball number 6 if some other ball has already been drawn is $\frac{1}{5}$, whereas if number 6 has already been drawn, the conditional probability is 0. The likelihood that two dependent events E and F will both happen is then

$$p(E \text{ and } F) = p(E) \times p(F \mid E)$$

CONCEPT CHECK
COORDINATED DECISIONS

Suppose that in the simultaneous-move game of the preceding subsection the two players coordinate their decisions: they toss a coin and if the coin comes out heads, player 1 picks U and player 2 chooses C. If the coin comes out tails, they respectively choose M and R. Compute $p(C \mid U)$, $p(L \mid U)$, and $p(R \mid U)$. Also compute $p(M \mid R)$, $p(U \mid R)$, and $p(D \mid R)$.

26.2 RANDOM VARIABLES AND EXPECTATION

In many instances it is convenient to think of the outcomes to uncertainty in a quantitative form. If we take the outcomes and assign to each outcome a real number, we get what is called a *random variable*. For example, outcomes to the roll of a die or the stock's price are (already numbered and therefore are) random variables; they take on the values $\{1, 2, \ldots, 6\}$ and $\{\frac{1}{16} \times n; n = 0, 1, 2, \ldots\}$, respectively. In some instances, a random variable may be the monetary reward associated with the uncertain outcomes. For example, if the lottery costs a dollar to enter and the winnings total $14 million, then the monetary random variable that describes the uncertainty of the lottery is $+14$ million and -1.

The *expectation* of a random variable is its average value. The formula for the average of a set of n numbers is $\frac{Total}{n}$. Notice that if a particular number, say 51, shows up twice in the set of numbers, then it gets added twice in the total; that is, the average is $\frac{51 + 51 + Total\ of\ numbers\ other\ than\ 51}{n}$. Alternatively, the average equals $\left(\frac{2}{n} \times 51\right) + \frac{Total\ of\ numbers\ other\ than\ 51}{n}$. We can follow this procedure for every number that shows up in the total, that is, weight it by the number of times it is included in the set of n numbers. Put another way, the expectation—or average—is a weighted sum of the (numbered) realizations, the weights being the associated probabilities.

For instance, the expected value of the die roll is $[(\frac{1}{6} \times 1) + (\frac{1}{6} \times 2) + \cdots + (\frac{1}{6} \times 6)] = \frac{1}{6} \times (1 + 2 + \cdots + 6) = 3.5$. If the probability of winning the lottery is $\frac{1}{14\ million}$ then the expected value of the lottery is $\frac{1}{14\ million} \times 14$ million $+ \left(1 - \frac{1}{14\ million}\right) \times (-1) = -\frac{1}{14\ million}$.

Let us denote, in general, an outcome by the symbol ω and the associated random variable by $X(\omega)$. The expectation of the random variable can then be formally written as[8]

$$EX = \sum_{\omega} p(\omega)X(\omega)$$

To fix ideas, examine the game-theory example that was discussed earlier. Consider the two strategies: for player 1, $p(U) = \frac{1}{5}$, $p(M) = p(D) = \frac{2}{5}$, and for player 2, $p(L) = p(C) = p(R) = \frac{1}{3}$. Let us compute the expected payoffs for player 1. Note first that,

[8] *The notation $\sum_{\omega}$ means add up $p(\omega) \times (\omega)$ over all possible ω.*

since the two players are choosing their strategies unilaterally, pairs of strategies are in fact independent events. It follows, therefore, that $p(U \text{ and } C) = p(U) \times p(C)$. Hence, $p(U) \times p(C) = \frac{1}{15}$. By extension, we have

$$Expected\ payoff\ of\ player\ 1 = \left(\frac{1}{15} \times 1\right) + \left[\frac{2}{15} \times (1+1+1)\right] + \left[\frac{2}{15} \times (2+2+2)\right]$$

$$= \frac{1}{15} + \frac{6}{15} + \frac{12}{15} = \frac{19}{15}$$

Concept Check
Player 2

Compute the expected payoff of player 2 (for the same pair of strategies).

26.2.1 Conditional Expectation

When two random variables are independent, knowing how one has occurred does not tell us much about the likelihood of occurrence of the other. In particular, therefore, knowing what value the first random variable took does not tell us anything about the expectation of the second random variable.

To illustrate this point consider two tosses of a coin. If we know that the first toss produced a head, we would still expect that there is a 50 percent chance of a head on the second toss. And similarly, if we are told instead that the first toss produced a tail. In other words, assigning, say, a numerical value of -1 to heads and 1 to tails, the expectation of the second toss is $(\frac{1}{2} \times -1) + (\frac{1}{2} \times 1) = 0$, and this expectation is the same regardless of whether the first toss produced heads or tails.

In contrast, consider drawing two balls, without replacement, from an urn containing five balls marked with the numbers 1, 2, 3, 4, and 5. If the first ball that is drawn is marked 4, then the expected number from the second drawing is

$$\left(\frac{1}{4} \times 1\right) + \left(\frac{1}{4} \times 2\right) + \left(\frac{1}{4} \times 3\right) + \left(\frac{1}{4} \times 5\right) = \frac{1}{4} \times (1+2+3+5) = \frac{11}{4}$$

However, if the first ball drawn is 2, then the expectation of the second draw is

$$\left(\frac{1}{4} \times 1\right) + \left(\frac{1}{4} \times 3\right) + \left(\frac{1}{4} \times 4\right) + \left(\frac{1}{4} \times 5\right) = \frac{1}{4} \times (1+3+4+5) = \frac{13}{4}$$

The reason why the two expectations were different is the fact that the two drawings are not independent events but rather are dependent. Put differently, the conditional probabilities of the second draw are different depending on whether the first draw yielded number 2 or 4.

Consider two random variables $X(\omega)$ and $Y(\omega)$ that are dependent, and denote the conditional probability of Y given a particular value $\bar{x}$ as $p(Y(\omega) \mid x = \bar{x})$. Then the *conditional expectation* of the random variable Y is denoted as

$$E(Y \mid x = \overline{x}) = \sum_{\omega} p[Y(\omega) \mid x = \overline{x}] \, Y(\omega)$$

Remark

To suggest the broadness of the framework described in this chapter—and also to shorten verbal descriptions—we often refer to *any* uncertain situation as a *lottery*. In other words, we refer to coin tosses, die rolls, stock price movements, and strategy choices in a game by the common moniker *lottery*.

SUMMARY

1. Any uncertainty can be represented by a triple—a sample space, an event space, and a probability function.

2. The sample space is the set of all possible outcomes, whereas the event space is the set of all possible groups of outcomes. The probability function assigns a likelihood—or probability—to each event.

3. Two realizations of uncertainty are independent if the probability of the pair of events is the product of their individual probabilities.

4. The expectation of a random variable—or its average—is the weighted sum of the numbered outcomes, the weights being the probabilities attached to each outcome.

EXERCISES

SECTION 26.1

26.1
Give three examples of uncertain situations with a finite number of outcomes.

26.2
Give two examples of uncertain situations with an infinite number of outcomes.

26.3
For exercise 26.1, in each case carefully list the outcomes and the consequent possible events.

26.4

Repeat exercise 26.3 for exercise 26.2 (although you will obviously not be able to list *all* the possible outcomes and events!).

26.5

For exercise 26.1, assign a probability function to each example. Explain whether the assignment is being made objectively or subjectively.

26.6

Repeat exercise 26.5 for the examples in exercise 26.2.

26.7

Suppose that the set F is the complement of E. Why must it be true that between them, E and F cover all possible outcomes, that is, they cover the sample space?

26.8

Explain why the event E *or* F/E is really the same event as E *or* F. Does your answer depend on the fact of E and F being nondisjoint? Explain.

26.9

Detail the arguments that establish the following property:

$$p(E \text{ or } F) = p(E) + p(F/E)$$

In the following exercises consider the game that was considered in the chapter.

26.10

Find the probability assignment in which player 1 is just as likely to play each of his three strategies. (Be sure to assign probabilities to every event.)

26.11

Find the probability assignment in which player 1 is three times as likely to play U as each of his other two strategies. (Be sure to assign probabilities to every event.)

26.12

Find the probability assignment in which player 2 is three times as likely to play C as each of his other two strategies. (Be sure to assign probabilities to every event.)

26.13

Consider the uncertainty associated with the hair color that the basketball player Dennis Rodman will exhibit on any given night. List the sample and event spaces (okay, color combinations are also allowed). How would you assign a probability function to this uncertainty? How would Dennis Rodman?

26.14

Consider the uncertainty associated with drawing a card from a deck of cards. List the sample and event spaces (you do not have to list all possibilities but list the categories). How would you assign a probability function to this uncertainty?

26.15

Consider a uniform distribution between the two values 0 and 1. What is the probability that x lies between 0 and $\frac{1}{3}$? What then is the probability that x lies between $\frac{1}{3}$ and 1? What is the probability that x lies between any two fractions, a and b?

26.16

Draw a graph with the value of x on the horizontal axis and the probability assignment to numbers between 0 and x, under the uniform distribution of exercise 26.15, on the vertical axis.

26.17

Repeat exercise 26.16 for a uniform distribution between the two values 0 and 10.

26.18

Explain why the likelihood that any pair of balls will be drawn out of an urn full of 100 balls is not $\frac{1}{100} \times \frac{1}{100}$ but rather is $\frac{1}{100} \times \frac{1}{99}$.

26.19

Suppose the balls are drawn with replacement; that is, after a ball has been drawn it is thrown back into the urn before the next number is drawn. Explain why the likelihood that any pair of balls will be drawn out of an urn full of 100 balls is now $\frac{1}{100} \times \frac{1}{100}$.

26.20

Give an example of a pair of events that is independent. And one of a pair that is not.

Consider again the game in the chapter. Let us write its table with probabilities instead of payoffs; that is, the probability in the cell (U, C) represents the probability that player 1 will play U *and* player 2 will play C:

1 \ 2	L	C	R
U	0	$\frac{1}{12}$	$\frac{2}{7}$
M	$\frac{1}{12}$	$\frac{1}{6}$	0
D	$\frac{1}{6}$	0	$\frac{3}{14}$

26.21

What is the probability that U will get played? (Hint: What are the possible combinations of strategies that include U?)

26.22

Find the conditional probability of L given U. Repeat with the conditional probability of C given U.

26.23

Find the conditional probability of U given C. Repeat with the conditional probability of M given C.

SECTION 26.2

Consider the game yet again, but now with the payoffs restored to the matrix:

1 \ 2	L	C	R
U	0, 0	0, 1	1, 2
M	1, 0	1, 1	2, 1
D	2, 0	1, 2	2, 2

26.24

Consider the two strategies: for player 1, $p(U) = \frac{1}{5}$, $p(M) = p(D) = \frac{2}{5}$, and for player 2, $p(L) = p(C) = p(R) = \frac{1}{3}$. Compute the expected payoff of player 2.

26.25

Consider instead the following two strategies: for player 2, $p(L) = \frac{1}{5}$, $p(C) = p(R) = \frac{2}{5}$, and for player 1, $p(U) = p(M) = p(D) = \frac{1}{3}$. Compute the expected payoffs of both players.

26.26

Suppose that player 1 plays U while 2 plays L, C, and R with probabilities p, q, and $1 - p - q$. Compute player 1's expected payoff (your answer will involve the two variables p and q).

26.27

What is player 2's expected payoff from the strategies of the previous question? At what values of p and q does player 2 derive the greatest expected payoff? Explain.

26.28

Repeat exercises 26.6 and 26.27 for the case in which player 1 plays M instead.

26.29

Suppose that a random variable can take on one of three values, 0, $\frac{1}{2}$, and 1, and suppose that all three values are just as likely. What is the expectation of this random variable?

26.30

Repeat exercise 26.29 for the case in which the random variable can take on any one of seven values, 0, $\frac{1}{6}$, $\frac{2}{6}$, ..., 1.

26.31

Can you use your answer in exercises 26.29 and 26.30 to conjecture the expected value of a random variable that is uniformly distributed between 0 and 1? Explain your answer.

26.32

What about the expectation of a random variable that is uniformly distributed between 10 and 20?

26.33

Consider drawing two balls, without replacement, from an urn containing five balls marked with the numbers 1, 2, 3, 4, and 5. If the first ball drawn is marked 3, compute the expected number from the second drawing.

26.34

Repeat exercise 26.33 for a first draw that produces the number 5 ball.

26.35

Consider drawing two balls, without replacement, from an urn containing five balls marked with the numbers 2, 2, 3, 4, and 4. If the first ball drawn is marked 3, compute the expected number from the second drawing.

26.36

Repeat exercise 26.35 for a first draw that produces a number 2 ball.

CHAPTER 27

UTILITY AND EXPECTED UTILITY

In this chapter we will discuss how a player faced with a multiplicity of choices might go about assigning payoff or utility numbers to each choice. The task of finding the best choice can then be reduced to the task of locating the highest utility number. We will proceed in three steps: first, in section 27.1, we will review the theory of utility assignments under *certainty*. Then, in section 27.2, we will use the conclusions of the certainty model to build a theory of utility assignments under *uncertainty*, that is, a theory of decision making over lotteries. In section 27.3 we will demonstrate how to apply the conclusions of the uncertainty model to analyze a player's attitudes toward *risk*.

27.1 DECISION MAKING UNDER CERTAINTY

In this section we will ask, If there are a number of possible options—or outcomes—and they are exactly known, how should a player choose between them?

Let the outcomes be denoted a, b, c, and so on. The starting point is the idea of a *preference relation* over outcomes. A preference relation, denoted $\succeq$, is a comparison between any two outcomes: "$a \succeq b$" should be read as "the outcome a is at least as good as the outcome b." We impose the following rationality postulates on the preference relation:

1. $\succeq$ satisfies *completeness*; for all outcome pairs a and b, either $a \succeq b$, or $b \succeq a$, or both.

2. $\succeq$ satisfies *transitivity*; for all outcome triples, a, b, and c, $a \succeq b$ and $b \succeq c$ implies $a \succeq c$.

Completeness says we cannot reply "I do not know" when confronted with a comparison between two outcomes. Transitivity is a little more demanding because it rules out cycles of the form: "I like doctor a because of his politeness (over doctor b); I like b more than c because she is more knowledgeable; and actually between a and c, I prefer c since his clinic is closer to my home."[1]

From the at-least-as-good-as relation we can derive the "strictly better than" relation: outcome a is *strictly better* than b (denoted $a \succ b$) if and only if $a \succeq b$ *but not $b \succeq a$*. One can also define an "indifference" relation: the decision maker is *indifferent* between outcomes a and b (denoted $a \sim b$) if $a \succeq b$ and $b \succeq a$.

When there are an infinite number of possible outcomes, some of the alternatives may be very close to each other. In such a case preferences need to satisfy one other requirement, called *continuity*:[2]

3.   If all of the outcomes $a_1, a_2, a_3, \ldots$ are at least as good as b and the chain collapses onto a, then a must be as good as b.

How then can we make decisions? Let us start with the choice between a finite number of outcomes. One procedure is simply to work through pairs of choices: compare a and b, then compare the winner to alternative c, then compare the winner of the second contest against alternative d, and so on. Since preferences are complete, each of these comparisons yields a winner.[3] Since preferences are transitive, we will never be caught in a cycle, and eventually we will have an overall winner. This is a somewhat cumbersome procedure, especially when the number of outcomes is large. What we would like to do more simply is assign a number (called utility) to each possible outcome and choose the outcome that has the largest number.

Under the three restrictions there is, in fact, a way to assign utility numbers and (when there are an infinite number of outcomes) to do so in a continuous fashion. It is easy enough to see why this must be the case, under restrictions 1 and 2 by themselves, when there are only a finite number of outcomes. Suppose there are five outcomes, (a, b, c, d, e), and let us suppose that

$$b \sim d \succ a \succ c \succ e$$

One way to assign utilities is to decide on an origin and a scale of assignment, for example, $u(e) = 1$, and each strictly better outcome gets one point more (whereas indifferent outcomes get the same number). So one possible assignment is $(3, 4, 2, 4, 1)$.

A utility assignment $u(.)$ is *consistent* with the preferences if for any two outcomes a and b, $a \succeq b$ if and only if $u(a) \geq u(b)$. It is clear that there are multiple consistent utility assignments to the same preferences. For the preceding preferences, for example, we could change the origin to 10 and the scale to 5 and get another consistent assignment: $(20, 25, 15, 25, 10)$. Actually even more is true: we need not even have the same scale; another consistent assignment is $(30, 55, 2, 55, 1)$. In other words any *monotone* function of the original assignment is also a consistent utility assignment.[4]

[1] *Put another way, all of these factors—politeness, knowledge-ability, distance, and so on—are already incorporated in the preference relation. They play a role in determining whether or not a is at least as good as b, but they cannot lead to ranking reversals. Also note that preferences can change over time; a may be preferred to b today but may not have been a year ago. Completeness and transitivity are only required of preferences at any one point in time.*

[2] *Note that a chain $a_1, a_2, a_3, \ldots$ is said to collapse onto a if for large values of n the outcomes a_n are very close to a. More precisely, the difference between a_n and a approaches zero as n approaches infinity.*

[3] *In the case of a tie—or indifference—pick either alternative.*

[4] *A function f is said to be monotone if f assigns a higher value $f(x_j)$, greater than $f(x_i)$, if and only if x_j itself is bigger than x_i.*

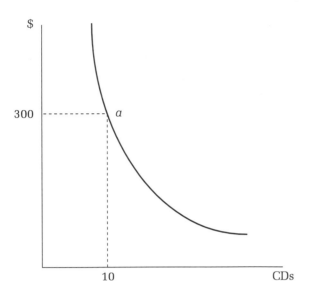

FIGURE 27.1

When there are an infinite number of outcomes, the approach to utility assignment is qualitatively similar. As a first step we can bracket with alternative a all choices that are just as good as a. Such a set of alternatives is called an indifference set or *indifference curve*. Consider Figure 27.1. On the horizontal axis is the quantity of some object, say, the number of CDs. On the vertical axis is the money left over to buy other things. For instance, the alternative a corresponds to monthly purchases of 10 CDs with a remaining budget of $300 (to spend on clothes, and movies, and . . .). The indifference curve through a includes all options that are just as good as a.

Then we can rank various indifference curves. Since there are an infinite number of alternatives, each indifference curve—like the one in Figure 27.1—may have an infinite number of choices within it. Furthermore, there may be an infinite number of indifference curves. For instance, the whole picture for the CDs-money indifference curves might look something like Figure 27.2.

Each level of indifference curve gets a utility number; higher indifference curves get higher numbers. Hence the utility assignment will be a function (like the ones we saw in Chapter 25). Given the continuity restriction, 3, we will in fact be able to assign nearby indifference curves utility numbers that are themselves close to each other.

Hence the decision-making problem can be restated as, For any consistent assignment of utilities, find the outcome that has the largest utility number; that is, solve the following optimization problem:[5]

[5] *Recall that we introduced the notation ω in the previous chapter to denote outcomes.*

$$\max_\omega u(\omega)$$

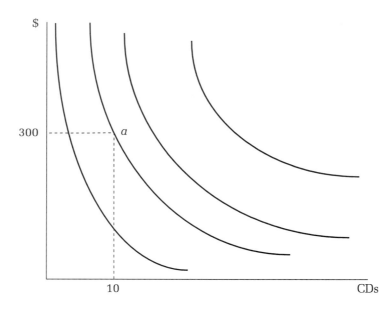

FIGURE 27.2

When the set of outcomes is finite we can search by hand—or use some algorithm—to find the outcome that corresponds to the highest utility. When the number of outcomes is infinite, then we can use the techniques of optimization theory that we outlined in Chapter 25 to isolate the best choice.

27.2   DECISION MAKING UNDER UNCERTAINTY

We now turn to decision making under uncertainty. The alternatives are now uncertain; that is, they are lotteries. Here is an example:

Lottery A: Buying (scalper's) tickets for a New York Knicks game that could cost 20, 25, 30, or 35 dollars with equal probabilities

Lottery B: Staying in and studying for the game theory midterm exam, which could raise your score by 5, 10, or 15 points with probabilities .5, .4, and .1

Lottery C: Going to the West End Gate bar, watching the Knicks on television, and drinking beer (which is going to cost you a sum of $10).[6]

The question for this section is, How should a decision maker analyze the relevant uncertainty and choose between the various lotteries? In the next subsection we will state

[6] *Notice that there is no uncertainty in this third alternative. However, we can think of it as a lottery that assigns probability 1 to the outcome going to the bar, and assigns probability 0 to all other outcomes.*

a first version of the answer, called the expected utility theorem, and in the following subsection we will sketch a proof of that result.

27.2.1 THE EXPECTED UTILITY THEOREM AND THE EXPECTED RETURN PUZZLE

One possible way to proceed is to assume that the decision maker has a preference relation directly over lotteries so that she is able to assert something like "I prefer lottery A to lottery C, but between lotteries A and B, I am indifferent." If that relation is complete, transitive, and continuous, then we know from the previous section that there is a continuous utility representation for it. In other words, there is a utility function, say U, defined over lotteries such that lottery A $\succeq$ lottery C if and only if $U(A) \geq U(C)$. We could then simply pick the lottery with the highest utility number.

A utility function over lotteries is conceptually cumbersome, and many people have trouble articulating such preferences in a consistent way. For example, the way alternatives are framed can become very important for such an articulation.[7] Furthermore, a lottery does have a special structure—it is a probability distribution over possible outcomes. So the question is, Can the utility function over lotteries be deduced from a utility function over the outcomes (under some additional restrictions)? In the present example, there is a utility function, say u, that attaches a utility number to the outcome "seeing the Knicks game at $25 a ticket" as also to the outcome "5 more points in the midterm exam."[8] The question is, Can preferences over the different *lotteries* be deduced from u?

Von Neumann and Morgenstern proved the following remarkable result:

Expected Utility Theorem I. A utility function over any lottery can be written as the expected utility of the outcomes that make up this lottery (under some reasonable additional restrictions).

Suppose we have a lottery with n possible outcomes $x_1, x_2, \ldots, x_n$, and an associated list of probabilities for each outcome. Denote this list $p_1, p_2, \ldots, p_n$. The theorem says that the utility of this lottery is equal to the *expected utility*[9]

$$p_1 \times u(x_1) + p_2 \times u(x_2) + \cdots + p_n \times u(x_n) \tag{27.1}$$

This is a remarkable result because it greatly simplifies the comparison of different lotteries. Although each lottery is characterized by the whole list of probability numbers, the utility of this long list can be reduced to just one number, namely, the expected utility. For instance, suppose we want to compare the lottery $p_1, p_2, \ldots, p_n$ with another one that has probabilities $q_1, q_2, \ldots, q_n$, then all we really need to compare are the two numbers, $p_1 u(x_1) + p_2 u(x_2) + \cdots + p_n u(x_n)$ versus $q_1 u(x_1) + q_2 u(x_2) + \cdots + q_n u(x_n)$.

For instance, the expected utility assignment to lottery A—tickets for a Knicks game that could cost 20, 25, 30, or 35 dollars with equal probabilities—can be written as

$$\tfrac{1}{4} u(20, K) + \tfrac{1}{4} u(25, K) + \tfrac{1}{4} u(30, K) + \tfrac{1}{4} u(35, K)$$

[7] *Two psychologists, Daniel Kahneman and Amos Tversky, have made this point in many contexts. An example is the following two pairs of lotteries:*

Pair 1: 600 people are struck with a disease that could kill. Vaccine 1 will save 400 for sure, while the second will either save no one (with probability $\tfrac{1}{3}$) or will save everyone (with probability $\tfrac{2}{3}$).

Pair 2: Again 600 people are struck with a disease that could kill. Vaccine 1 will kill 200 people for sure, while 2 implies a $\tfrac{2}{3}$ chance no one will die and a $\tfrac{1}{3}$ chance that everyone will.

Note that the two pairs of alternatives are identical decision situations (since "save" is equivalent to "not kill"). In experiments most people chose vaccine 1 in the first pair but vaccine 2 in the second!

[8] *For future use, denote the utility number to seeing the Knicks at ticket prices 20, 25, 30, and 35 dollars, respectively, $u(20, K)$, $u(25, K)$, $u(30, K)$, and $u(35, K)$. Denote the utility numbers to staying in, studying for the midterm, and increasing the score by 5, 10, and 15 points, respectively, $u(5, S)$, $u(10, S)$, and $u(15, S)$. Finally, denote the utility number to watching the Knicks at West End Bar for 10 dollars by $u(10, W)$.*

[9] *Strictly speaking, the result says that there exists a utility function u, defined over the possible outcomes, such that equation 27.1 holds. This more correct version is stated as Expected Utility Theorem II on page 440.*

Similarly, the expected utility assignment to lottery B—stay in and study for the game theory exam—is

$$0.5u(5, S) + 0.4u(10, S) + 0.1u(15, S)$$

Finally, the utility assignment to the lottery C—go to the West End Gate bar—is simply $u(10, W)$.

Let us illustrate with yet another example. Suppose that the outcomes are monetary; so x is a dollar figure. Suppose furthermore that the utility function over outcomes is given by $u(x) = \log(10 + x)$. Then a lottery such as "Win \$5 if heads, lose \$5 if tails" has expected utility equal to

$$0.5 \log 15 + 0.5 \log 5 \qquad \textbf{(27.2)}$$

CONCEPT CHECK
EXPECTED UTILITY

Show that the lottery "Win \$25 with probability 0.3, win \$18 with probability 0.1, lose \$8 with probability 0.4, and lose \$2 with probability 0.2" has expected utility equal to

$$0.3 \log 35 + 0.1 \log 28 + 0.4 \log 2 + 0.2 \log 8 \qquad \textbf{(27.3)}$$

The utility function u is called the Von Neumann–Morgenstern utility function.

Before getting to a detailed discussion of the Von Neumann–Morgenstern theorem, let us discuss why we cannot simply define the utility of a lottery as the expectation of the random variable associated with the lottery. For instance, for lottery A, why does it not suffice to set $u(20, K) = 20$, $u(25, K) = 25$, and so on, and hence compute the utility of the lottery itself as $\frac{1}{4} \times (20 + 25 + 30 + 35) = \frac{110}{4}$? Similarly in the case of monetary lotteries, why not simply compute the *expected monetary return*?

The reason is that if we only evaluated lotteries according to their expected returns, we would run into some apparent inconsistencies in behavior. Perhaps the most famous instance of such an inconsistency is the *St. Petersburg paradox* (due to Nicholas Bernoulli).[10] Consider the following lottery: a coin is tossed repeatedly. The first time H comes up, a payment is made; if the first H is at the kth toss, the payment is 2^k dollars. How much would you be willing to pay for this lottery? The same question, put differently, is, What is the utility value of this lottery? Note that the expected monetary return of this lottery can be written as $\sum_{k=1}^{\infty} \left(2^k \times \frac{1}{2^k}\right) = 1 + 1 + 1 + 1 \ldots$. So the expectation is infinite. Does that fact mean we would pay an infinite sum to play this lottery? Most people would not do so. Put another way, expected return is not a good utility representation for many preferences. (More on this topic in the next section.)

[10] *There is some controversy about who exactly was the first one to propose the St. Petersburg paradox. It might have been the brother of Nicholas Bernoulli, the equally brilliant Daniel Bernoulli, or it could have been the mathematician Leonhard Euler. The reason for the place name in the paradox is that around 1725 these three Swiss scientists were all invited to work at Catherine the Great's newly established St. Petersburg Academy of the Sciences. Daniel Bernoulli was the first one to propose a solution to the paradox; we will see this solution in the next section.*

27.2.2 DETAILS ON THE VON NEUMANN–MORGENSTERN THEOREM ⚠

To explain what follows,[11] it is important to distinguish between *simple* and *compound* lotteries. A *simple lottery* is what we have so far called a lottery: uncertainty over a set of outcomes. A *compound lottery* is one whose outcomes are lotteries themselves. For example, a coin is tossed, and if it comes out H you get the simple lottery A whereas if it comes out T you get the lottery B; this compound lottery is denoted $\frac{1}{2}A + \frac{1}{2}B$. More generally, a compound lottery (denoted $\alpha A + (1-\alpha)B$) has probability α that the outcome will be a simple lottery A and probability $1 - \alpha$ that it will be B instead.

An example of a compound lottery is the following: You go to a Knicks game, and the ticket will cost you either 20, 25, or 30 dollars (with equal probabilities) if you arrive early, whereas if you arrive late, the ticket will cost you 25, 30, or 35 dollars with probabilities $\frac{1}{4}$, $\frac{1}{4}$, and $\frac{1}{2}$. There is a $\frac{1}{3}$ probability that the number 1 or number 9 subway that you take to Madison Square Garden will be late.

Every compound lottery can be reduced to a simple lottery. In this example, the "real" probability distribution is over the outcomes, ticket prices of 20, 25, 30, and 35 dollars. In particular, the probability that you will in fact pay $25 can be decomposed into two events: you get to the game early, and then there is a $\frac{1}{3}$ probability that you pay $25 for your ticket, or you get to the game late, and then there is $\frac{1}{4}$ probability that this is the ticket price. Furthermore, there is a $\frac{2}{3}$ probability that you will get to the game early. Hence, the probability of buying your ticket at $25 is $\left(\frac{2}{3} \times \frac{1}{3}\right) + \left(\frac{1}{3} \times \frac{1}{4}\right) = \frac{11}{36}$.

CONCEPT CHECK
PROBABILITIES

Show that the probabilities of buying the ticket for 20, 30, and 35 dollars are, respectively, $\frac{2}{9}$, $\frac{11}{36}$, and $\frac{1}{6}$.

One restriction on preferences that we will soon discuss is that a decision maker is always indifferent between a compound lottery and the associated simple lottery. That is, the basketball fan in the example is indifferent between the compound lottery and a simple lottery with probabilities $\frac{2}{9}$, $\frac{11}{36}$, $\frac{11}{36}$, and $\frac{1}{6}$ of buying the ticket for 20, 25, 30, and 35 dollars, respectively.

For simplicity, we will also make the following assumption: there is a best and worst outcome, denoted respectively b and w; it is preferable to have b for sure rather than any lottery. Likewise, any lottery is preferable to having w for sure; that is, $b \succeq$ any lottery $\succeq w$. As we saw earlier in this chapter, a sure event—the outcome x will happen with probability 1—can be thought of as a lottery as well: denote it $\delta(x)$. Finally, a simple lottery with outcomes x and y, with probabilities α and $1 - \alpha$, respectively, will be written as $\alpha\delta(x) + (1-\alpha)\delta(y)$.

[11] *This subsection is a little complicated, and hence you may wish to skip it on first reading. Make sure, though, to understand the conclusion—the Von Neumann–Morgenstern expected utility theorem—and be sure to read the section itself sometime during the semester.*

Von Neumann–Morgenstern Restrictions

Von Neumann and Morgenstern require preferences over lotteries to satisfy the following restrictions (in addition to completeness and transitivity):

3. *Monotonicity:* Consider lotteries with outcomes b and w only. The preference between them is based solely on the likelihood of b:

$$\alpha\delta(b) + (1 - \alpha)\delta(w) \succeq \beta\delta(b) + (1 - \beta)\delta(w) \quad \text{if and only if } \alpha \geq \beta$$

4. *Archimedean:* For any intermediate outcome a there must be a lottery over b and w that is just as *good* as a; there is α such that

$$\delta(a) \sim \alpha\delta(b) + (1 - \alpha)\delta(w)$$

5. *Substitution:* If two lotteries are equally good $A \sim B$, then for all lotteries C,

$$\alpha A + (1 - \alpha)C \sim \alpha B + (1 - \alpha)C$$

6. Compound lotteries are equivalent to a simple lottery with the same *distribution* over final outcomes.

The complete statement of the theorem is as follows:

Expected Utility Theorem II. Under these restrictions there is a utility representation u over sure outcomes such that lottery A is at least as good as lottery B if and only if the expected utility to lottery A is at least as high as the expected utility to lottery B.

Sketch of the Proof

Consider any outcome x. By virtue of the Archimedean axiom there is a lottery over the best and worst outcomes, $u(x)\delta(b) + [1 - u(x)]\delta(w)$ that is just as good as the sure outcome ($u(x)$ is therefore a probability). We can repeat this exercise for an alternative outcome, say y, and find the corresponding number $u(y)$ (such that y is just as good as the lottery $u(y)\delta(b) + [1 - u(y)]\delta(w)$).

By virtue of the monotonicity axiom, the two lotteries $u(x)\delta(b) + [1 - u(x)]\delta(w)$ and $u(y)\delta(b) + [1 - u(y)]\delta(w)$ can be compared by looking at the two numbers $u(x)$ and $u(y)$ alone. Indeed the first is better than the second if and only if $u(x) > u(y)$. In turn, this fact says that the outcome x is better than y if and only if $u(x) > u(y)$. (Why?) Put differently, the numbers $u(x)$, $u(y)$, and so on are exactly like utilities over the sure outcomes x and y. (Why?)

Now take a lottery A and suppose for simplicity that it is made up of the two outcomes x and y (with probabilities p and $1 - p$, respectively). By virtue of the substitution axiom, A is just as good as the compound lottery that yields the simple lottery $u(x)\delta(b) + [1 - u(x)]\delta(w)$ with probability p and $u(y)\delta(b) + [1 - u(y)]\delta(w)$ with remaining probability $1 - p$. (Why?) By the compound lottery restriction, this compound lottery—and hence the original lottery A—is equivalent to the simple lottery

$$[pu(x) + (1 - p)u(y)] \, \delta(b) + [p[1 - u(x)] + (1 - p)[1 - u(y)]] \, \delta(w) \qquad \textbf{(27.4)}$$

Notice that the weight attached to the outcome b is the "expected utility" $pu(x) + (1 - p)u(y)$. Consider an alternative lottery B and suppose that it is also made up of the two outcomes x and y (with probabilities q and $1 - q$, respectively). A repetition of all these steps will yield that B is equivalent to the simple lottery

$$[qu(x) + (1 - q)u(y)] \, \delta(b) + [q[1 - u(x)] + (1 - q)[1 - u(y)]] \, \delta(w) \qquad \textbf{(27.5)}$$

Equations 27.4 and 27.5 essentially prove the theorem. These are two simple lotteries over the best and worst outcomes. By virtue of monotonicity they can be ranked by looking at the weight attached to the outcome b, that is, by comparing $pu(x) + (1 - p)u(y)$ and $qu(x) + (1 - q)u(y)$. But that is the same thing as saying that lottery A is better than B if and only if $pu(x) + (1 - p)u(y) > qu(x) + (1 - q)u(y)$. (Why?)
◇

27.2.3 PAYOFFS IN A GAME

In any game that we study in this text, the payoffs are Von Neumann–Morgenstern utilities. The payoff to a game that has uncertain outcomes, then, is the Von Neumann–Morgenstern expected utility. The Von Neumann–Morgenstern utilities are the entries in the matrix representation of a two-person game in strategic form or the entries at the terminal nodes of a tree in the extensive form.

27.3   RISK AVERSION

Whenever there is uncertainty, a decision maker is exposed to risk. A natural question to ask is, (When) Does the decision maker prefer not to be so exposed? It will turn out that whenever the Von Neumann–Morgenstern utility function u is concave the decision maker will be averse to risk. Hence, risk attitudes will be seen to be already embedded in the utility function u.

In this section we will only consider lotteries whose outcomes are dollar figures. Consider the following pair of lotteries:

Lottery A: Win $1 if heads, lose $1 if tails

Lottery B: Win $5 if heads, lose $5 if tails

The two lotteries have the same win (and loss) probabilities, that is, $\frac{1}{2}$. What distinguishes them is that the amount that can be won (or lost) is smaller for lottery A than B. This is a special case of more general conditions under which we can say that lottery A is *less risky* than lottery B.

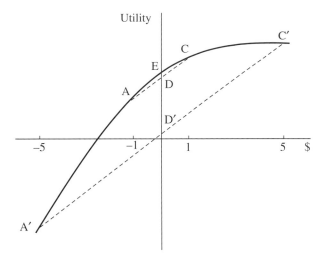

FIGURE 27.3

The first lottery will be preferred to the second if and only if its expected utility is greater, that is, if $\frac{1}{2}[u(1) + u(-1)] > \frac{1}{2}[u(5) + u(-5)]$. In turn this inequality can be written as

$$u(5) - u(1) < u(-1) - u(-5)$$

Whether or not that inequality is valid depends on the *slope* of the utility function u; the inequality holds if the rate of change in utility between -5 and -1, $u(-1) - u(-5)$, is greater than the rate of change between 1 and 5, $u(5) - u(1)$. Hence if the decision maker's preferences are such that an additional \$4 is worth less—in utility terms—if he already has \$1, than an additional \$4 is worth when he only has $-\$5$, then he should go with the first, less risky, lottery. Put differently still, if additional money yields less and less utility as he grows richer, then he would prefer the less risky alternative. This is equivalent to saying, *If u is concave, go with less risk*.

Another way of seeing the same thing is by means of a graph. We will first demonstrate how to represent expected utility graphically. Consider Figure 27.3. Point A corresponds to the utility level $u(-1)$, that is, corresponds to losing \$1. Similarly, point C corresponds to the utility level $u(1)$, that is, corresponds to winning \$1. *After* the uncertainty of the first lottery has resolved itself, the decision maker will find himself either at A or at C. *Before* the uncertainty is resolved, however, he does not know which of these points he might end up at. He does believe, though, that he is just as likely to be at A as at C; hence his expected, or average, utility should be halfway between A and C, namely, halfway on the line segment between A and C, that is, at D.

By the same logic the expected utility of the second lottery is given by D'. The graph now tells you that D is higher than D'; that is, the first lottery is the preferred one. The reason is precisely that the amount of utility loss, A down to A', is bigger than the amount of utility gain, C up to C', exactly as we saw algebraically before.

Indeed we can go further and ask how the lotteries compare to a situation in which there is no uncertainty. Note that for both of these lotteries the decision maker expects to break even. After all, he wins the same amount that he loses, and winning and losing are equally likely. So the certainty situation is that in which he gets \$0 for sure, that is, does not gamble. It should be straightforward to see from Figure 27.3 that this option (point E) is even better (than either lottery).

This example can be generalized. Recall that for a lottery A in which the outcomes are $x_1, x_2, \ldots, x_n$ with probabilities, respectively, of $p_1, p_2, \ldots, p_n$, the expected return of this lottery, denoted EA, is

$$EA = p_1 x_1 + p_2 x_2 + \cdots + p_n x_n$$

Suppose that this decision maker's Von Neumann–Morgenstern utility function u is strictly concave. A consequence is that no matter how complicated a lottery you consider, *having the expected return EA for sure is always strictly preferred to the lottery A*. In fact, one can show that the converse is true as well. If the expected return EA for sure *is strictly preferred* to the lottery A—and this is true for all lotteries—then the underlying function u must be strictly concave.

Hence here is a definition of risk avoidance—or **risk aversion**: if a decision maker prefers the expected return of every lottery to the lottery, he is said to be risk averse. Equivalently, he is said to be risk averse if his Von Neumann–Morgenstern utility function is concave.

One example of a concave utility function, is $u(x) = \log x$. With these preferences, the St. Petersburg paradox can be resolved. Notice that in this case the expected utility is given by

$$\sum_{k=1}^{\infty} \frac{\log 2^k}{2^k}$$

It can be shown that this sum is finite. In particular, therefore, a person with these preferences would not be willing to pay an infinite sum of money to participate in the St. Petersburg gamble. The intuition for this result is straightforward. A risk-averse person gets less and less utility from additional winnings at high wealth levels. In particular, the expected utility of the kth payout, $\frac{\log 2^k}{2^k}$, becomes smaller as k increases.[12] Hence, the cumulative prospect of large winnings does not add up to infinite utility.[13]

We should note that there are two other alternatives to risk aversion. A player is *risk neutral* if the expected utility of a lottery is nothing but its expected return. Alternatively, such a decision maker must have a utility function $u(x) = x$.

Risk aversion
A preference for the sure outcome—the expected return of a lottery—over the lottery itself.

[12] *In fact the sum is finite because the ratio of the $(k+1)$th term to the kth is roughly $\frac{2^k}{2^{k+1}}$, that is, $\frac{1}{2}$, when k is large. Hence the sum behaves much like the geometric series $1 + \frac{1}{2} + \frac{1}{2^2} + \frac{1}{2^3} + \cdots$ (which is known to be finite).*

[13] *Daniel Bernoulli was the first person to offer a resolution to his brother's paradox; he suggested that a better representation of preferences toward large sums of money is the log utility function.*

If an additional $1 gives a greater increase in utility as the current level of wealth increases, then we have *risk-loving* preferences. Whereas risk aversion implies that a lottery whose expected return is zero is never accepted (over the alternative of not playing the lottery), the converse is true for risk-loving preferences. In particular, a risk-loving decision maker would pick lottery B in the choice scenario.

SUMMARY

1. The basic building block of decision making is a preference relation $\succeq$; if outcome a is at least as good as outcome b, we write $a \succeq b$.

2. If the preference relation is complete, transitive, and continuous, then it can represented by a continuous utility function u that has the property that $a \succeq b$ if and only if $u(a) \geq u(b)$.

3. An uncertain situation—or lottery—is a probability distribution over a set of outcomes. In making choices between lotteries, a decision maker in principle has to take account of the entire distribution as well as the outcomes themselves.

4. Under some reasonable restrictions, Von Neumann and Morgenstern showed that the utility of a lottery can be written as the expected utility to the outcomes that make up the lottery.

5. A risk-averse decision maker always prefers to have the expected return (of a monetary lottery) to the lottery itself. Risk aversion is equivalent to having a concave utility function over the lottery's outcomes.

EXERCISES

SECTION 27.1

27.1
Give two examples of a decision problem under certainty.

27.2
Transform the same examples into problems under uncertainty. In each case carefully detail the space of outcomes—and the lotteries over these outcomes.

27.3

Take the sample space of this chapter's various evening entertainments—Knicks at alternative prices, staying in and studying, and drinking at the West End Bar—and write your preference relation over that space. Are your preferences complete and transitive?

27.4

Repeat the previous question for one of the two examples that you gave in exercise 27.1.

27.5

Explain carefully why any monotone function of a utility assignment is also a utility assignment (which is consistent with the underlying preferences). Consequently, provide two utility assignments for your preferences over the entertainment outcomes.

27.6

Repeat exercise 27.5 for the examples you gave in exercise 27.10.

27.7

Suppose sports teams in a league like the NBA are ranked by their winning percentage (i.e., the fraction of games that each team has played that it actually won). Is this ranking complete and transitive? Explain.

27.8

Suppose instead that team a is ranked above team b if and only if a has won more than half of its games against b (and they are said to be indifferent if they have split their games). Is this ranking complete and transitive? Explain.

We now move to infinite numbers of choices. Suppose the choices are to be made over pairs of CDs and sums of money.

27.9

Let alternative a correspond to 10 CDs and $300. Draw the indifference curve that includes a if this person is always willing to trade a CD for $10.

27.10

Draw the whole set of indifference curves for these preferences, assuming the same willingness to trade.

27.11

Denote CDs by the symbol c and money by the symbol m. Show that one possible utility function for these preferences is

$$u(c, m) = 10c + m \qquad\qquad (27.6)$$

27.12

Find a monotone function of the preceding utility assignment that is consistent with the preferences.

27.13

Suppose instead that the utility function is given by

$$u(c, m) = 120 \log(1 + c) + m \qquad\qquad \textbf{(27.7)}$$

Draw a representative indifference curve.

27.14

Suppose that the decision maker has \$500 to spend and CDs cost \$12. Show that the available CD-money options can be written in terms of the following budget equation:

$$12c + m = 500$$

27.15

Use the previous equation to substitute into the utility function of equation 27.6. Consequently derive a utility function that depends on c alone.

27.16

Solve for the utility-maximizing choice of CDs.

27.17

Repeat exercises 27.15 and 27.16 for the utility function given by equation 27.7.

27.18

Repeat exercises 27.16 and 27.17 for a price of CDs equal to \$8.

SECTION 27.3

Consider a utility function over dollars x defined as $u(x) = \log(10 + x)$.

27.19

Compute the exact value of the expected utility of the two lotteries, lottery A and lottery B, discussed in the text.

27.20

Suppose that we compare the two lotteries with a third lottery—win either \$13 or \$16 with probability $\frac{1}{4}$ each and lose \$4 with the remaining probability. How do the three lotteries rank?

27.21

What is the sure outcome that is just as good as the lottery introduced in exercise 27.20?

27.22

Repeat exercises 27.20 and 27.21 for the case in which the utility over outcomes is instead given by $10 + x$.

Consider the following simultaneous-move game (where the payoffs in each cell are the Von Neumann–Morgenstern utilities for that pair of strategies):

1 \ 2	L	C	R
U	0, 0	0, 1	1, 2
M	1, 0	1, 1	2, 1
D	2, 0	1, 2	2, 2

27.23

Suppose that player 2 plays the strategy L. Compute player 1's expected payoff from playing a strategy that picks each of her strategies with equal probability.

27.24

Repeat exercise 27.23 for player 2 playing R instead.

27.25

Repeat exercises 27.23 and 27.24 with player 1 playing U or M with equal probabilities and D with half that probability.

27.26

Find player 2's expected payoffs in exercises 27.24 and 27.25.

27.27

Suppose that each player is equally likely to play each one of her strategies. Compute their expected payoffs.

The next few questions fill in the details of the proof of the expected utility theorem.

27.28

Explain why the two lotteries $u(x)\delta(b) + [1 - u(x)]\delta(w)$ and $u(y)\delta(b) + [1 - u(y)]\delta(w)$ can be compared by looking at the two numbers $u(x)$ and $u(y)$ alone [and furthermore that the first lottery is better than the second if and only if $u(x) > u(y)$].

27.29

Show that the outcome x is better than y if and only if $u(x) > u(y)$. Establish that the numbers $u(x)$, $u(y)$, and so on are exactly like utilities over the certain outcomes.

Now take a lottery A made up of the two outcomes x and y (with probabilities p and $1 - p$, respectively).

27.30
Show that A is just as good as the compound lottery that yields the simple lottery $u(x)\delta(b) + [1 - u(x)]\delta(w)$ with probability p and $u(y)\delta(b) + [1 - u(y)]\delta(w)$ with remaining probability $1 - p$.

27.31
Show that two lotteries can be ranked by looking at the weight attached to the outcome b, that is, by comparing $pu(x) + (1 - p)u(y)$ and $qu(x) + (1 - q)u(y)$.

SECTION 27.4

Consider the pair of lotteries analyzed in section 27.3.

27.32
Redo Figure 27.3. Carefully show why the expected utility of the second lottery is at D'.

27.33
Show that the expected return to both lotteries is $0.

27.34
What is the utility of the sure option $0 on your figure? Can you explain algebraically why this sure option is better than the first lottery?

27.35
Graph the expected utility of the lottery "Win $10 and lose $10 with equal probabilities."

27.36
Repeat exercise 27.35 for the lottery "Win $10 with probability $\frac{3}{4}$ and lose $30 with probability $\frac{1}{4}$." Can you tell from your graph which of these two lotteries, this one or the one in exercise 27.35, would be preferred? Explain.

Consider the following pair of lotteries:

Lottery A: $1,000 if die rolls 6 or 1, $0 otherwise

Lottery B: $0 if die rolls 6, $400 otherwise

27.37
Compute the expected monetary return for each lottery. Show that they are equal.

27.38

Under what conditions is the expected utility to the second lottery higher (than that to the first)?

27.39

Can you show that a risk-neutral decision maker must have a utility function $u(x) = x$?

CHAPTER 28

EXISTENCE OF NASH EQUILIBRIA

The most widely used solution concept in game theory (and this book) is Nash equilibrium. We used it extensively in Part II when we analyzed strategic form games and their applications. A refinement of Nash equilibrium, subgame perfect (Nash) equilibrium, was the main solution concept in Part III's extensive form game analysis. Another refinement, Bayes-Nash equilibrium, was the principal solution tool for the games of incomplete information in Part IV. Since Nash equilibrium turns out to be such an important idea, it is worth asking whether we always know that one exists. The answer to that question is the content of this chapter.

Section 28.1 reviews definitions and examples and emphasizes the role of mixed strategies for the existence question. We will introduce a relevant piece of mathematics called fixed-point theorems in section 28.2 and apply it to Nash equilibrium existence in section 28.3. Throughout this chapter we will try to convey mathematical ideas and results in a comprehensible way even at the risk of occasionally being somewhat imprecise.

28.1   DEFINITION AND EXAMPLES

Let us recall the definition of a Nash equilibrium (NE), and allow explicitly for mixed strategies; as usual, a pure strategy is thought of as a special case of a mixed strategy.

Consider a game with N players, $i = 1, \ldots, N$. A mixed strategy for player i is a probability distribution p_i on his pure strategies, and a representative pure strategy is s_i. In principle, the number of pure strategies could be infinite.[1]

[1] *An example of a game where there are an infinite number of pure strategies is the Cournot duopoly game. Similarly, there are an infinite number of pure strategies in the commons problem.*

Definition. A vector of mixed strategies $p^* = p_1^*, p_2^*, \ldots, p_N^*$ constitutes a Nash equilibrium if each player's strategy is a best response to the array of other players' strategies; that is, if for all players i,

$$\pi_i(p^*) \geq \pi_i(p_i, p_{-i}^*) \qquad \text{for all } p_i \tag{28.1}$$

where $\pi_i(p_i, p_{-i}^*)$ is the notation for the expected payoff to the mixed strategy vector (p_i, p_{-i}^*).[2]

Before proceeding any further, let us recall two games and directly compute the Nash equilibria in each.

Example 1: Squash

Player 1 \ Player 2	*Forward* (F)	*Backward* (B)
Front (f)	20, 80	70, 30
Back (b)	90, 10	30, 70

The first conclusion is about pure-strategy equilibria:

CONCEPT CHECK
NO PURE NE

Verify that there are no pure-strategy Nash equilibria in the game of squash.

A mixed-strategy equilibrium is given by player 1 playing f with probability $\frac{6}{11}$ while player 2 plays F with probability $\frac{4}{11}$. When player 2 plays this mixed strategy, the expected payoff to player 1 from either of her pure strategies is $\frac{570}{11}$. Hence playing f with probability $\frac{6}{11}$ is a best response for player 1.

CONCEPT CHECK
MIXED NE

Verify that the exhibited strategy is a best response for player 2. Also show that this is the unique mixed-strategy Nash equilibrium of the game.

---

[2] *Hence,* $\pi_i(p_i, p_{-i}^*) = \sum_{s_1}$ $\ldots \sum_{s_N} [p_1^*(s_1) \times \ldots$ $p_{i-1}^*(s_{i-1}) \times p_i(s_i) \times$ $p_{i+1}^*(s_{i+1}) \times \ldots$ $p_N^*(s_N)] \pi_i(s_1, \ldots, s_N).$

A second example is the following modification to Battle of the Sexes:

Example 2: Modified Battle of the Sexes

Husband \ Wife	*Football*	*Opera*	*Home*
Football	3, 1	0, 0	0, 0
Opera	0, 0	1, 3	0, 0
Home	0, 0	0, 0	2, 2

In this game there are three pure-strategy Nash equilibria: (F, F), (O, O), (H, H). There are also four mixed-strategy Nash equilibria; three of these involve each player mixing over pairs of pure strategies, and a fourth involves mixing over all three pure strategies. In this example, therefore, there is an embarrassment of riches in that there are many Nash equilibria to choose from.

To summarize, the two examples tell us that there is always at least one Nash equilibrium in a game—possibly only in mixed strategies. There may, however, be more than one such equilibrium. In the next two sections we will see that the conclusions of these examples are actually very general.

28.2 MATHEMATICAL BACKGROUND: FIXED POINTS

In this section two ideas are discussed: first, it is shown that Nash equilibria are mathematically equivalent to something called fixed points of the best-response functions, and second, it is argued that fixed points exist for certain kinds of functions.

In order to understand the first idea, we need some notation. Let $R_i(p_1, p_2, \ldots, p_N)$ denote player i's best response to the strategy choice of the other players, $p_{-i} = p_1, p_2, \ldots, p_{i-1}, p_{i+1}, \ldots, p_N$.[3] An alternative definition of a Nash equilibrium is the following: $p_1^*, p_2^*, \ldots, p_N^*$ *is a Nash equilibrium if for every player* $i = 1, \ldots, N$,

$$p_i^* = R_i(p_1^*, p_2^*, \ldots, p_N^*) \tag{28.2}$$

Equation 28.2 simply says that a Nash equilibrium is an array of strategies that no player would like to change. (The converse is also true; if no player wants to change his strategy then we have a Nash equilibrium.) Take any candidate for a Nash equilibrium, say $\widetilde{p} = \widetilde{p}_1, \widetilde{p}_2, \ldots, \widetilde{p}_N$, apply to it the *best-response function*, and produce the strategy array $R_1(\widetilde{p}), R_2(\widetilde{p}), \ldots, R_N(\widetilde{p})$. As equation 28.2 makes clear, a Nash equilibrium is a *fixed point* of the best-response function; if we start with a Nash equilibrium strategy array and apply the best-response mapping, then we remain fixed at that point.

The search for a Nash equilibrium can therefore be reformulated as the search for a fixed point of the best-response functions. This formulation is useful because there is a very well developed theory in mathematics that deals with the question "When does a function, say f, that maps a set X into X, have a fixed point?" In other words, under what conditions on the function f and the set X, is there always an x^* such that $x^* = f(x^*)$?

[3] *If there is more than one best response for player i, then R_i should be thought of as a set of strategies, each of which is a best response. We will first discuss the case where there is a unique best response [and $R_i(p_1, p_2, \ldots, p_N)$ is that best-response strategy].*

We will not discuss the most general version of these fixed-point results because they involve mathematics beyond the scope of this book. However, what we will do is very informally discuss two results for the special case where the set X is a subset of the real line. In order to have a fixed point, two conditions need to be satisfied:

1.   The set X has to be *compact* and *convex*.

2.   The function f has to be *continuous*.

A set is *compact* if (a) it is not unboundedly large and (b) there is no element outside the set that is arbitrarily close to elements within it.[4] Let us see, by way of some examples, what these conditions mean. A set that has unboundedly large elements is the set of all real numbers at least as large as 0; this set is denoted $[0, \infty)$. Conversely, a set that has no unbounded element is the set of all real numbers that are at least as large as 0 but no larger than 1; this set is denoted $[0, 1]$.

An example that has an element outside the set arbitrarily close to elements within it is the set of all real numbers between 0 and 1 not including either of the end points; this set is denoted $(0, 1)$. Neither of the end points is in the set, and yet each of them is arbitrarily close to elements of the set; 0, for example, is arbitrarily close to $\frac{1}{n}$, $n = 2, 3, \ldots$ (for sufficiently large values of the integer n). In contrast, $[0, 1]$ is a set where condition b holds. No matter which element outside this set we pick, say 1.1, there is nothing in the set that is less than a distance of 0.1 from this point.

So, $[0, 1]$ is a compact set while neither $[0, \infty)$ nor $(0, 1)$ is compact.

A set X is *convex* if it does not have any holes in it. For example, the set $\left[0, \frac{1}{3}\right] \cup \left[\frac{2}{3}, 1\right]$ is not convex because it does not contain $\left(\frac{1}{3}, \frac{2}{3}\right)$ which is therefore a hole in the set. On the other hand, the set $[0, 1]$ is a convex set.[5] In fact, the only sets in the real line that are convex are sets of the form $[a, b]$, that is, sets that contain all numbers between a and b.[6]

A function f is said to be *continuous* if it has no jumps in it; you can draw the function without taking your pencil off the page. So the function, $f(x) = \frac{1}{2}x + \frac{1}{3}$ and the function $f(x) = \sqrt{x}$ are continuous functions. However, the function $f(x) = \frac{1}{2}x + \frac{1}{3}$ for x in $\left[0, \frac{1}{3}\right]$ but $f(x) = \frac{1}{3}x$ for x in $\left[\frac{1}{3}, 1\right]$ is not continuous.

A fixed-point result that is widely used is the following:

Theorem (Brouwer). Suppose that X is a compact, convex subset of the real line. Suppose further that f takes values in X and is a continuous function. Then there is a fixed point of f; that is, there is x^* such that $x^* = f(x^*)$.

Consider $X = [0, 1]$ and the two continuous functions $f(x) = \frac{1}{2}x + \frac{1}{3}$ and $f(x) = \sqrt{x}$. In the first case, the fixed point is $x^* = \frac{2}{3}$, whereas in the second case there are two fixed points, $x^* = 0$ and $x^* = 1$. (Show these results algebraically, and also see Figures 28.1 and 28.2.)

[4] *For those with some background in real analysis, all we are saying is that a set is compact if it is bounded and closed. For those who do not have this background but are frustrated by the (lack of) detail that we can provide here, hunt down a real-analysis or advanced-calculus text such as W. Rudin's* Principles of Mathematical Analysis *(New York: McGraw-Hill, 1983).*

[5] *Again, for further discussion look at a real-analysis or a convex-analysis text.*

[6] *It is not important whether the end points are in the set or not. In other words, the set* (a, b)— *which does not include either end point—is also a convex set.*

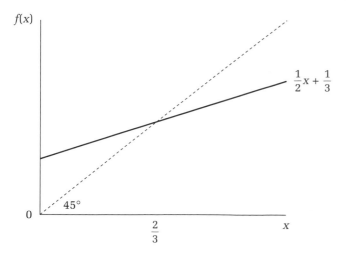

FIGURE 28.1

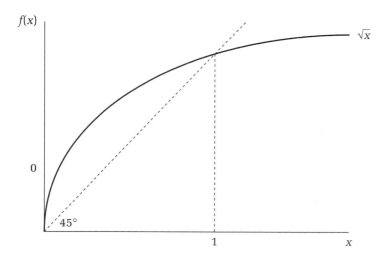

FIGURE 28.2

The reason why these conditions play an important role in the theorem can be seen by asking why there might not be a fixed point if any of the conditions are violated. For example, consider the discontinuous function $f(x) = \frac{1}{2}x + \frac{1}{3}$ for x in $\left[0, \frac{1}{3}\right]$ but $f(x) = \frac{1}{3}x$ for x in $\left[\frac{1}{3}, 1\right]$. This function does not have a fixed point. Similarly, we can find examples of noncompact and nonconvex sets, including the ones given here, on which continuous functions do not have fixed points. (In the Exercises you will be producing a number of these examples.)

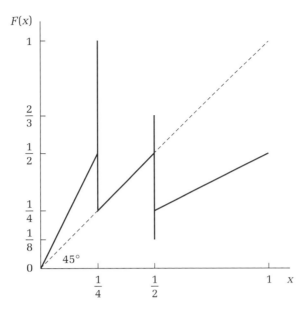

FIGURE 28.3

In most games, there are certain strategies of the other players against which player i has not one but multiple best responses. When that is the case the best-response function will no longer be a (single-valued) function but rather will be multivalued. Hence we will need a fixed-point result that applies to multivalued functions. There is a very close cousin of the Brouwer fixed-point theorem that then becomes relevant. This result is called the Kakutani fixed-point theorem. We present this result next.

In order to explain the result, we have to formally define a multi-convex-valued function. Thankfully this object is exactly what it says it is: F is a multi-convex-valued function if at every x we get as the dependent variable not a single number but rather a *convex set* of numbers $F(x)$. The fact that an independent variable produces a *set* of dependent values is the multivalued part of the terminology. The fact that this set is convex is the convex-valued part. Since a single point is also trivially a convex set, it means that at many values of x, $F(x)$ can be akin to an ordinary function, that is, may be single-valued.

As an example of a multi-convex-valued function, consider Figure 28.3. F is defined on $[0, 1]$. At all values of x other than $x = \frac{1}{4}$ and $\frac{1}{2}$, $F(x)$ is a single point:

$$F(x) = \begin{cases} 2x, & \text{for } x \text{ in } \left[0, \frac{1}{4}\right) \\ x, & \text{for } x \text{ in } \left(\frac{1}{4}, \frac{1}{2}\right) \\ \frac{1}{2}x, & \text{for } x \text{ in } \left(\frac{1}{2}, 1\right] \end{cases}$$

At $x = \frac{1}{4}$ and $\frac{1}{2}$, $F(x)$ is multivalued; $F\left(\frac{1}{4}\right)$ is equal to $\left[\frac{1}{4}, 1\right]$, while $F\left(\frac{1}{2}\right)$ is equal to $\left[\frac{1}{8}, \frac{2}{3}\right]$.

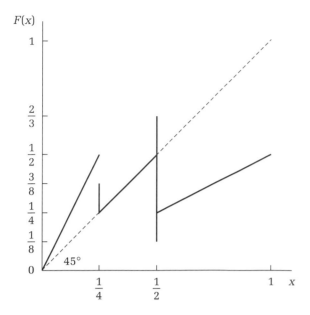

$F(x)$

$45°$

FIGURE 28.4

Although F is no longer single-valued, it is still possible to define a notion of continuity. Before we do so formally, though, let us motivate the idea by discussing Figure 28.3. Notice that as long as we stay away from the two values of x where the function is multivalued, $x = \frac{1}{4}$ and $\frac{1}{2}$, we can just use the notion of continuity that applies to an ordinary function; can we draw the graph without taking a pencil off the page? Since the answer is yes, we know that there are three continuous segments corresponding to x values in $\left[0, \frac{1}{4}\right)$, $\left(\frac{1}{4}, \frac{1}{2}\right)$, and $\left(\frac{1}{2}, 1\right]$.

The potential complications are at $x = \frac{1}{4}$ and $\frac{1}{2}$. However, we can ask, Is it possible to get from the continuous segment over $\left[0, \frac{1}{4}\right)$ to the continuous segment over $\left(\frac{1}{4}, \frac{1}{2}\right)$ without the pencil leaving the page? {And likewise can we move from x values in $\left(\frac{1}{4}, \frac{1}{2}\right)$ to x values in $\left(\frac{1}{2}, 1\right]$ without jumps?} If the answer to both questions is yes, then the multi-convex-valued function is (upper semi-) continuous. And of course our example is.

The same idea can be applied to any multi-convex-valued function. If the single-valued segments are continuous and if it is possible to travel the multivalued segments without taking a pencil off the page, then we say that a multi-convex-valued function is (upper semi-) continuous.

The modification of F in Figure 28.4 is not upper semicontinuous. Note that when you arrive at $x = \frac{1}{4}$ you need to leave the function because it jumps down to the set $\left[\frac{1}{4}, \frac{3}{8}\right]$.

We will say that F takes values in the set X if $F(x)$ is a subset of X for all x. The fixed-point theorem is as follows:

Theorem (Kakutani). Suppose that X is a compact, convex subset of the real line and that F is a multi-convex-valued function that takes values in X. Suppose further that F is an upper semicontinuous function. Then there is a fixed point of F; that is, there is x^* such that x^* is in the set $F(x^*)$.

28.3   EXISTENCE OF NASH EQUILIBRIA: RESULTS AND INTUITION

The existence theorem that John Nash proved in the early 1950s is the following:

Theorem (Nash). Suppose that a game has a finite number of strategies for each player. Then there is at least one Nash equilibrium (possibly in mixed strategies).

As with Brouwer's and Kakutani's theorems, we will not attempt to prove Nash's theorem. However, the logic is straightforward enough to convey, especially in light of our discussion in the previous section. The set of mixed strategies turns out to be both compact and convex. Note that when a player has only two pure strategies, his mixed strategies are completely described by the probability with which he plays the first of his pure strategies. Hence the set of mixed strategies is given by the set [0, 1]. And this set is, as we saw, compact and convex. The same logic carries over even when a player has more than two pure strategies.

The best-response function is a multi-convex-valued function. This is the case because either of two things must be true for a player's best response. Either there is a unique best response; that is, we have a single-valued function (and that is trivially also a multi-convex-valued function). Or, if a player has two best responses, then, as we saw in Chapter 8, any average of these best responses is also a best response; that is, any convex set that includes the two as the end points is also a best response. Finally, the best-response function also turns out to be an upper semicontinuous function. Hence, by Kakutani's fixed-point theorem, the best-response function has a fixed point; put differently, there is a Nash equilibrium.[7]

Recall that games such as matching pennies and squash have no Nash equilibria in pure strategies; they only have Nash equilibria in mixed strategies. The reason that we cannot assert that there is always a Nash equilibrium in pure strategies is that the set of pure strategies is not convex; hence, the fixed-point result does not guarantee an equilibrium in pure strategies.

Let us now turn to infinite number of strategies. We will give you some additional conditions under which a game with an infinite number of strategies will not only have an equilibrium but will have one in pure strategies.

[7] *The careful reader will have noted that the set of mixed strategies X (in our earlier notation) is not a subset of the real line. However, Kakutani's and Brouwer's fixed-point theorems can still be used, since they do in fact apply to sets more general than just those in the real line.*

Theorem. Suppose that each player's pure strategy set is $[a, b]$, where a and b are two constants, and that each player's payoff function is continuous and strictly concave in his own pure strategy. Then there is at least one pure-strategy Nash equilibrium of the game.

The fixed-point theorem that applies here is Brouwer's theorem. We restrict attention only to pure strategies now. The set of such strategies is convex and compact because they are of the form $[a, b]$. The best-response function turns out to be single-valued because the payoff function is strictly concave.[8] This function is also continuous. Hence there is a fixed point of the best response function; that is, there is a Nash equilibrium.

This last result is applicable to the Cournot model and the commons problem.

What we will do now is give you some further feel for Nash's theorem by working out in detail the best-response function and hence the Nash equilibrium in the following game:

1 \ 2	L	R
U	1, 0	2, 3
D	0, 2	4, 0

CONCEPT CHECK
NO PURE NE

Check that there is no Nash equilibrium in pure strategies in this game.

Now let us consider mixed strategies; for player 1, all mixed strategies can be described by the probability with which the strategy U is played; call this probability p. Likewise, for player 2, all mixed strategies can be described by the probability with which L is played; call that q.

Best Response Mappings

Since a player will play one of her pure strategies if either of them is a best response by itself (and will play a mixed strategy only if both of her pure strategies yield her the same payoff), it suffices to first check pure-strategy best responses.

Against q, U yields a payoff of $q + 2(1 - q)$ while D yields $4(1 - q)$. Evidently, U is a best response by itself—respectively, D is a best response by itself—if $q > \frac{2}{3}$—respectively, $q < \frac{2}{3}$. At $q = \frac{2}{3}$, player 1 is indifferent between her two pure strategies; any mixture, that is, any p in $[0, 1]$, is then a best response.

[8] *The argument for this result is identical to the reason why a risk-averse individual prefers a (for sure) average to a lottery over two outcomes. If we have two best responses, then the pure strategy that is an average of the two is strictly preferred to a mixed-strategy lottery over them. In turn, this fact means that the average is strictly preferred to each of the (purported) best responses because the mixed strategy is as good as each pure strategy.*

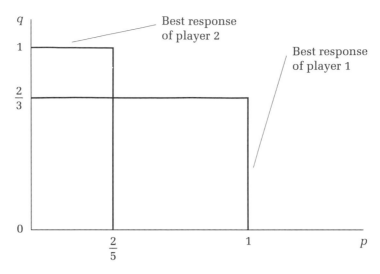

FIGURE 28.5

CONCEPT CHECK
BEST RESPONSE OF PLAYER 2

Show that for $p < \frac{2}{5}$, L is the unique best response, while for $p > \frac{2}{5}$, R is the unique best response. At $p = \frac{2}{5}$, any q in [0, 1] is a best response.

The best-response functions are graphed in Figure 28.5. Note that the strategy spaces—[0, 1] for each player—are compact and convex. From the graph it is clear that the best-response mapping is continuous. The theorem applies therefore. Of course, we can also see that conclusion by noting that the intersection of the two best responses, $p = \frac{2}{5}$ and $q = \frac{2}{3}$, is a Nash equilibrium.

In this chapter we have only discussed the existence of Nash equilibria. The discussion applies, however, to subgame perfect Nash and Bayes-Nash equilibria as well. The results carry over to those two cases in the sense that we can show the existence of those equilibria by appealing to the two results of this section. The formal details will have to wait for your next course in game theory!

SUMMARY

1. A Nash equilibrium is a fixed point of the best-response functions because no player has an incentive to change his strategy at such an equilibrium.

2. Brouwer's and Kakutani's fixed-point theorems give conditions under which a function (and a multi-convex-valued function, respectively) has at least one fixed point.

3. Kakutani's fixed-point theorem can be applied to prove Nash's existence result: every finite game has a Nash equilibrium (possibly in mixed strategies).

4. Brouwer's fixed-point theorem can be used to prove an existence theorem when there are an infinite number of pure strategies: under the convexity conditions of this result, there is always a Nash equilibrium in pure strategies.

EXERCISES

SECTION 28.1

28.1
Check that in matching pennies there are no pure-strategy Nash equilibria.

28.2
Check that a mixed-strategy equilibrium of the game is given by both players playing H with probability $\frac{1}{2}$.

28.3
Show that there are no other mixed-strategy Nash equilibria in this game.

28.4
Verify that the following game has no pure-strategy Nash equilibrium:

1 \ 2	L	R
U	2, 0	2, 6
D	0, 7	5, 0

28.5
Compute the mixed-strategy Nash equilibrium of the game.

28.6
Consider the modified Battle of the Sexes example. Show that, in addition to the pure-strategy equilibria, there are also four mixed-strategy Nash equilibria. Compute these equilibria.

SECTION 28.2

28.7

Show that the set $[0, \infty)$ contains arbitrarily large numbers.

28.8

Can you give two other examples of sets that have arbitrarily large numbers?

28.9

Show that the set $(0, 1)$ has numbers arbitrarily close to 1.

28.10

Can you give another example of a set that has elements in it that are arbitrarily close to a point outside the set?

Take any subset A of the real line, and let us say that it has a hole if we can find a number x that is not in A between two numbers y and z that are in A.

28.11

Show that $[0, 1]$ has no holes. Show likewise that $(0, 1)$ has no holes either.

28.12

Repeat exercise 28.11 for $[a, b]$ and (a, b) where a and b are constants.

28.13

How about $[a, b)$ and $(a, b]$ where the first set does not contain b (but does contain a), and vice versa for the second set? Are these sets convex? Explain.

28.14

Can you show that the sets of the previous two questions are the only convex sets in the real line, that is, the only possible sets that have no holes?

28.15

Give two examples of sets that are not convex.

28.16

Draw a graph of $f(x) = \frac{1}{2}x + \frac{1}{3}$.

28.17

Repeat for the function $f(x) = \sqrt{x}$. Do your drawings show any jumps in the two functions? Explain.

28.18

What about the function $f(x) = \frac{1}{2}x + \frac{1}{3}$ for x in $\left[0, \frac{1}{3}\right]$ but $f(x) = \frac{1}{3}x$ for x in $\left[\frac{1}{3}, 1\right]$? Show graphically that this function is not continuous.

28.19

Show that the function of exercise 28.18 does not have a fixed point (in $[0, 1]$).

28.20

Find a continuous function that is defined on $[0, \infty)$—and takes nonnegative values—that does not have a fixed point.

28.21

Repeat exercise 28.20 for the case in which the function is defined on the nonconvex set $\left[0, \frac{1}{3}\right] \cup \left[\frac{2}{3}, 1\right]$. [Make sure that $f(x)$ always takes values in the same nonconvex set.]

28.22

Using the definition of a convex set, can you show that a single point is itself a convex set?

28.23

Can you formally show that a function that is single-valued for every x is also a multi-convex-valued function?

28.24

Draw the following multi-convex-valued function: F is defined on $[0, 1]$. At all values of x other than $x = \frac{1}{2}$, $F(x)$ is a single point. Indeed on $\left[0, \frac{1}{2}\right]$, $F(x)$ is equal to $2x$. On $\left[\frac{1}{2}, 1\right]$ it is equal to $\frac{1}{2}x$. At $x = \frac{1}{2}$, $F(x)$ is multivalued; $F\left(\frac{1}{2}\right)$ is equal to $\left[\frac{1}{8}, 1\right]$. Is the function upper semicontinuous?

28.25

Give an example of a multi-convex-valued function that is (upper semi-) continuous and one that is not.

SECTION 28.3

28.26

Show that when a player has only two pure strategies, the set of mixed strategies is given by the set $[0, 1]$.

28.27

Show formally that any best-response function is a multi-convex-valued function. (You can restrict the formal argument to the case where there are only two pure strategies.)

28.28

For the infinite strategies case, show why we cannot have two pure-strategy best responses when payoffs are strictly concave.

28.29

Verify with detail that the conditions of the second theorem are satisfied by the Cournot model of Chapter 6.

28.30

Repeat exercise 28.29 for the commons problem of Chapter 7.

INDEX

2